Founders 108   Mu Doc

Strons 303   Sort " 9 / 10:00 on

Modern Advanced Accounting

first

canadian

edition

Modern Advanced Accounting

first canadian edition

A. N. Mosich, Ph.D., C.P.A.
Ernst & Whinney Professor of Accounting
University of Southern California

E. John Larsen, D.B.A., C.P.A.
Associate Professor of Accounting
University of Southern California

Murray W. Hilton, B. Comm., M.B.A., C.A.,
Professor of Accounting
University of Manitoba

McGraw-Hill Ryerson Limited

Toronto Montreal New York Auckland Bogotá
Cairo Caracas Hamburg Lisbon
London Madrid Mexico Milan New Delhi Panama Paris
San Juan São Paulo Singapore Sydney Tokyo

MODERN ADVANCED ACCOUNTING, FIRST CANADIAN EDITION

ISBN 0-07-548901-5

1 2 3 4 5 6 7 8 9   THB   6 5 4 3 2 1 0 9 8 7

Printed and bound in Canada

Care has been taken to trace ownership of copyright material contained in this text.
The publishers will gladly take any information that will enable them to rectify any
reference or credit in subsequent editions.

Canadian Cataloguing in Publication Data

Mosich, A. N.
  Modern advanced accounting

Includes index.
ISBN 0-07-548901-5
1. Accounting.   I. Larsen, E. John   II. Hilton,
Murray W.   III. Title.

HF5635.M67 1986   657′.046   C85-099829-8

CONTENTS

sale of land on the instalment plan. Retail sale of merchandise on the instalment plan. Alternative computation of gross profit percentage. Defaults and repossessions. Other accounting issues relating to instalment sales. Presentation of instalment sales data in financial statements.

The meaning of consignments. Distinguishing between a consignment and a sale. Rights and duties of the consignee. The account sales. Accounting for consignees. Accounting for consignors. Separate determination of gross profit. Accounting for consignor illustrated. Accounting for partial sale of consigned merchandise. Return of unsold merchandise by consignee. Advances from consignees. Nature of the Consignment Out account.

Handbook Section 1650. Transactions involving foreign currencies. Transaction gains and losses. Transaction gains and losses from noncurrent monetary items. Forward exchange contracts. Premiums and discounts on forward exchange contracts. Hedging an account receivable. Hedging an account payable. Hedging prior to a foreign currency transaction.

Alternative methods for translating foreign entities' financial statements prior to Section 1650. Standards for translation established by Section 1650. Exchange rates for translation process. Treatment of exchange gains and losses. Illustration of translation of a foreign entity's financial statements. Self-sustaining foreign operation. Integrated foreign operation.

PART FIVE ACCOUNTING FOR FIDUCIARIES

PREFACE

The main purpose of this First Canadian Edition is to present a complete coverage of topics traditionally included in advanced accounting courses in a manner that is clear and easy to comprehend. The emphasis throughout the book is on financial accounting concepts and an analysis of the problems that arise in the application of these underlying concepts to specialized accounting entities — partnerships, branches, affiliated companies, local government units, nonprofit organizations, and estates and trusts — and on special topics such as instalment sales, consignments, segment reporting, interim reporting, international operations and bankruptcy. Applicable **CICA pronouncements and research studies** have been fully incorporated. In those areas where there are no CICA pronouncements, the statements of other accounting rule-making bodies have been included. The NCGA's "Government Accounting and Financial Reporting Principles" and FASB statements are examples.

This book may be used in a one-semester or two-quarter course at either the undergraduate or the graduate level.

We have prepared the First Canadian Edition of *Modern Advanced Accounting* as a companion volume for the *Intermediate Accounting* text by Mosich, Larsen, Lam, and Johnston, thus creating a coordinated series for the important intermediate-advanced financial accounting sequence of courses as a foundation for a professional education for accountants.

Unique Features of This Edition

Business combinations and consolidated financial statements are thoroughly covered in seven chapters. In an eighth chapter, two related topics, the proportionate consolidation presentation of investments in joint ventures and segment reporting complete the discussion. The treatment of consolidations includes many schedules, checks and proofs that highlight the important interrelationships involved. The handling of unrealized asset profits and the related income tax allocation problems are discussed as a single topic. (Many textbooks either ignore the income tax issue or treat it separately.) While initial chapters focus on the financial statement approach of preparing consolidation working papers, the nonworking paper approach is subtly introduced later to reflect the emphasis that Canadian professional examinations place on it.

There are a variety of questions, short exercises and problems at the end of each chapter, many of which have been adapted from professional examinations. Probably no more than a third of the problems would be used in a given course; consequently ample opportunity exists to vary homework assignments from semester to semester. Many suggested solutions to consolidation problems are presented using a nonworking paper approach.

Organization of Subject Matter

We anticipate that the organization of chapters into five cohesive and meaningful parts will be useful to instructors and students. The arrangement should facilitate the planning and presentation of the subject matter and, we hope, make it easier for students to learn and retain the concepts and procedures presented. A brief description of the contents of each of the five parts follows.

Part One: Accounting for partnerships and branches
(Chapters 1 to 3)

The first part deals with the accounting principles and procedures for partnerships and branch operations. Partnerships are covered in the first two chapters, which carry the student from the basic concepts often presented in the introductory accounting course to the professional examination level, with its more complex problems of profit sharing, realignment of partners' equities, and liquidation. Chapter 3, which deals with home office–branch relationships and combined financial statements, provides a logical stepping-stone to the seven chapters dealing with business combinations and consolidated financial statements.

The Eliminations column in the working paper for combined financial statements of home office and branch is presented as a single column to parallel the form used in the working papers for consolidated financial statements in Chapters 5 to 10.

Part Two: Business combinations and
consolidated financial statements
(Chapters 4 to 11)

Chapter 4 covers the accounting for business combinations under the purchase and pooling of interest methods. Strengths and weaknesses of both methods are thoroughly evaluated.

Chapter 5 discusses the preparation of consolidated financial statements on acquisition date involving wholly owned and less than wholly owned subsidiaries. The calculation and allocation of the purchase discrepancy is introduced, as are the parent company and entity theories of consolidation. (The proprietary theory is illustrated in Chapter 11.)

The preparation of consolidation financial statement working papers subsequent to date of acquisition when the parent has adopted the equity method is the subject of Chapter 6. The use of the purchase discrepancy amortization schedule as a valuable aid to the student in organizing the calculations required in the consolidation process becomes evident.

In Chapter 7, the equity method illustrations used previously are repeated under the assumption that the parent has instead used the cost method. Proofs and checks involving the calculation of consolidated net income and retained earnings reinforce the student's understanding of consolidation concepts. The chapter concludes with a discussion of Sections 3050, 1580 and 1600 of the **CICA Handbook**.

The elimination of unrealized profits in nondepreciable assets with income tax allocation is discussed in a nonworking paper format in Chapter 8, while Chapter 9 covers unrealized profits in depreciable assets and gains and losses resulting from intercompany bondholdings. Instructors who wish to omit intercompany bonds can do so without disturbing continuity. The organization of the many calculations required prior to the preparation of the consolidated statements is illustrated.

Other consolidation issues such as ownership change, indirect ownership, subsidiary preferred shares and the consolidated statement of changes in financial position are the subject matter for Chapter 10.

Chapter 11 concludes Part Two by discussing the accounting for investments in joint ventures, segment reporting and interim financial statements.

Part Three: Accounting for nonbusiness organizations (Chapters 12 to 14)

Fund accounting at the local government level is discussed in two chapters. The general fund is covered in Chapter 12, and the other funds and account groups in Chapter 13. This part of the book is concluded with Chapter 14, "Accounting for Nonprofit Organizations."

The objectives of financial reporting by nonbusiness organizations, as included in FASB Statement of Financial Accounting Concepts No. 4, are discussed in Chapter 12 to set the stage for accounting principles illustrated in this section of the textbook. The discussion and illustrations relating to governmental units are based on Governmental Accounting and Financial Reporting Principles, issued in 1979 by the National Council on Governmental Accounting. Variations in Canadian practice are highlighted. The observations and recommendations of two recent **CICA research studies** on financial reporting for local governments and nonprofit organizations help to present a clearer picture of the state of flux currently existing in the nonbusiness area in Canada.

Part Four: Special topics in financial accounting
(Chapters 15 and 16)

Instalment sales and consignments are discussed in Chapter 15. In Chapter 16, the accounting for transactions involving foreign currencies and the translation of financial statements of foreign operations as required by **CICA Handbook** Section 1650 are thoroughly covered.

Part Five: Accounting for fiduciaries
(Chapters 17 and 18)

The final section of the book includes chapters entitled "Receivership and Bankruptcy: Liquidation and Reorganization" and "Accounting for Estates and Trusts." Although some instructors may not cover these two traditional topics in their courses, we feel that it is imperative to include them for those who wish to do so. Many accountants in today's practice environment must assist clients with problems of receivership and bankruptcy, liquidation, reorganization, and the accounting for estates and trusts.

We have incorporated the relevant provisions of the **Bankruptcy Act of Canada** in Chapter 17. However, in our discussion of estates and trust, we focus on financial accounting matters rather than on the complex estate provisions of various provincial statutes.

The pronouncements of the CICA and the FASB and other authoritative bodies are interwoven into the discussion and the problem material throughout the book. However, we believe that an accounting textbook should encourage students to participate in a critical evaluation of accounting principles and make them aware of the conflicts and shortcomings that exist within the traditional structure of accounting theory. Therefore, we have tried to provide students with a conceptual framework for making this evaluation.

Review Questions, Exercises, Cases, and Problems

An abundance of learning and assignment material is provided at the end of each chapter. This material is divided into four groups: review questions, exercises, cases, and problems. All end-of-chapter material has been tested in class by the authors.

The review questions are intended for use by students as a self-testing and review device to measure their comprehension of key points in each chapter. Many of the questions are provocative, which makes them suitable for class discussion and written assignments.

An exercise typically covers a specific point or topic and does not require extensive computations. Instructors may use the exercises to supplement problem assignments, for class discussion, and for examination purposes.

The cases require analytical reasoning but involve little or no quantitative data. Students are required to analyze business situations, to apply accounting principles, and to propose or evaluate a course of action. However, they are not required to prepare lengthy working papers or otherwise to manipulate accounting data on an extensive scale. The cases have proved to be an effective means of encouraging students to take positions in the argument of controversial accounting issues. Many of the cases have been adapted from actual business situations, court cases, or professional examinations. The review questions and cases are especially recommended if the instructor wishes to develop student skills in communicating accounting concepts and in evaluating the merits of opposing arguments.

Many of the problems are new, and those carried over from the American edition generally have been updated and revised. A feature of this edition is the inclusion of a large number of short problems closely correlated with the text material. The difficulty rating of problems is carefully tailored to help students achieve a smooth learning progression based on the "building-block approach."

A comprehensive solutions manual is available to adopters of the text. The solutions manual contains answers to all review questions, exercises, cases and problems in the text. In addition, at the beginning of each chapter, there are short descriptions, time estimates, and difficulty ratings for each of the problems, to help instructors choose problems that best fit the needs of their individual classes and courses in terms of scope, level, and emphasis. Please contact your local McGraw-Hill Ryerson representative to request your instructor copy.

Comments and suggestions from readers would be most appreciated, and should be directed to the Sponsoring Editor, College Division, McGraw-Hill Ryerson Limited, 330 Progress Avenue, Scarborough, Ontario, M1P 2Z5.

A.N. Mosich
E. John Larson
Murray W. Hilton

ACKNOWLEDGEMENTS

Many very helpful comments and suggestions came from the following individuals who reviewed portions of the manuscript: Dick Chesley, Joe Cheung, Nabil Elias, James Cutt, Avril Preston-Thomas, Wayne Hopkins, Keith Collins, Bill Buckwold, Mary Sealey and Jack Tepley. Three of my students, Craig Roskos, Bruce Rothney and Annette Raine spent countless hours helping me prepare the solutions manual. Bea Ryland, Karen Morrow, Jennifer Jones and Cathy Watt were particularly helpful in providing typing services at a moment's notice. To these people and those whom I have inadvertently omitted mentioning I am extremely grateful.

I am also grateful to the Canadian Institute of Chartered Accountants for permission to quote from the Handbook and research publications, and to the Society of Management Accountants for permission to adapt some of their examination questions. I acknowledge the permission received from the American Institute of Certified Public Accountants to quote from many of its pronouncements and to adapt material from the Uniform CPA Examinations, and the Financial Accounting Standards Board for permission to quote from its statements, discussion memoranda, interpretations and exposure drafts.

And finally I must express my deep appreciation to the editorial and production staff of McGraw-Hill Ryerson whose extreme patience and encouragement helped me through this project which many times appeared to be an endless one.

March 1987
Winnipeg, Manitoba   Murray W. Hilton

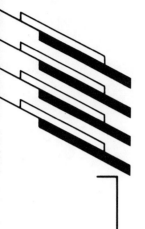

ACCOUNTING
FOR PARTNERSHIPS
AND BRANCHES

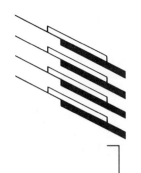

1 PARTNERSHIP ORGANIZATION AND OPERATION

Nature of partnerships

Much of our discussion of partnerships is based on the Partnership Act passed by the British Parliament in 1890. All of the common law provinces in Canada have passed partnership acts and while they are not all identical, they have adopted substantially all of the provisions of the British Act. Our future references to "the acts" will refer to provisions contained in most provincial acts. The acts define a partnership (often referred to as a firm) as "the relation which subsists between persons carrying on a business in common with a view to profit." In this definition, the term *persons* includes individuals and other partnerships, and in some provinces corporations may become partners. The creation of a partnership requires no approval by a province; in fact, a partnership may be formed without a written contract, although a carefully formulated written contract is highly desirable.

Partnerships traditionally are associated with the practice of law, medicine, public accounting, and other professions, and also with small business enterprises. In some provinces the licensed professional person such as the CA is forbidden to incorporate on grounds that the creation of a corporate entity might weaken the confidential relationship between the practitioner and the client. However, at least one province has approved legislation designed to permit *professional corporations*. A few large industrial and merchandising enterprises also operate as partnerships.

ORGANIZATION OF A PARTNERSHIP

Characteristics of a partnership

The basic characteristics of a partnership are summarized below.

Ease of Formation   In contrast to a corporation, a partnership may be created by an oral or written contract between two or more persons, or may be implied by their conduct. This advantage of convenience and minimum expense in the formation of a partnership in some cases may be offset by certain difficulties inherent in such an informal organizational structure.

Limited Life   A partnership may be ended by the death, retirement, bankruptcy, or incapacity of a partner. The admission of a new partner to the partnership legally ends the former partnership and establishes a new one.

Mutual Agency   Each partner has the authority to act for the partnership and to enter into contracts on its behalf. However, acts beyond the normal scope of business operations, such as the borrowing of funds by a partner, generally do not bind the partnership unless specific authority has been given to the partner to enter into such transactions.

Unlimited Liability   The term *general partnership* refers to a firm in which all the partners are personally responsible for debts of the firm and all have authority to act for the firm. Each partner in a general partnership is personally responsible for the liabilities of the firm. Creditors having difficulty in collecting from the partnership will be likely to turn to those individual members of the firm who have other financial resources. In a *limited partnership* one or more of the partners has no personal liability for debts of the partnership. The activities of limited partners are somewhat restricted, and they must maintain an agreed investment in the partnership. Statutes providing for limited partnerships require that at least one member of the firm be a general partner, and that the name of the limited partner(s) cannot be included in the partnership name.

Co-ownership of Partnership Assets and Earnings   When individuals invest assets in a partnership, they retain no claim to those specific assets but simply acquire an ownership *equity in all assets* of the partnership. Every member of a partnership also has an ownership equity in earnings; in fact, participation in earnings and losses is one of the tests of the existence of a partnership.

Deciding between a partnership and a corporation

One of the most important considerations in choosing between a partnership and the corporate form of business organization is the income tax status of the enterprise and of its owners. A partnership itself pays no income tax. Each partner pays tax on his share of the partnership income regardless of whether he received more or less than this amount of cash from the partnership during the year. A copy of the financial statements of the partnership is submitted with the personal tax returns filed by each partner.

The corporation is a separate legal entity subject to a corporate income tax. The net income, when and if distributed to shareholders in the form of dividends, is also taxable income to the shareholders, although there are provisions which provide relief from this potential double taxation of corporate net income. This is particularly true for shareholders who are taxed at the lowest marginal rates. Income tax rates and regulations are subject to frequent change, and new interpretations of the rules often arise. The tax status of the owners also is likely to change from year to year. For all these reasons, management should review the tax implications of the partnership and corporate forms of organization so that the business enterprise may adapt most successfully to the income tax environment.

The burden of taxation is not the only factor influencing a choice between the partnership and the corporate form of organization. Perhaps the factor that most often tips the scales in favour of incorporation is the opportunity for obtaining larger amounts of capital when ownership can be divided into shares of capital stock, readily transferable, and offering the advantages inherent in the separation of ownership and management.

Is the partnership a separate entity?

In accounting literature, the legal aspects of partnerships generally have received more emphasis than the managerial and financial issues. It has been common practice to distinguish a partnership from a corporation by saying that a partnership was an "association of persons" and a corporation was a separate entity. Such a distinction unfortunately stresses the legal form rather than the economic substance of the business organization. In terms of managerial policy and business objectives, many partnerships are as truly business and accounting entities as are corporations. Such partnerships typically are guided by long-range plans not likely to be affected by the admission or withdrawal of a single member. In these firms the accounting policies should reflect the fact that the partnership is an entity apart from its owners.

Viewing the partnership as a business and accounting entity often will aid in developing financial statements that provide the most meaningful picture of financial position and results of operations. Among the accounting policies to be stressed is continuity in asset valuation, despite changes in the income-sharing ratio and changes in personnel. Another helpful step may be recognition in expense accounts of the value of personal services rendered by partners who also hold managerial positions. In theoretical discussions, considerable support is found for viewing every business enterprise as an accounting entity, apart from its owners, regardless of the form of legal organization. A managing partner under this view is both an employee and an owner. The value of the personal services rendered by a partner is an expense of managing the partnership.

The inclusion of partners' salaries among expenses has been opposed by some accountants on grounds that partners' salaries may be set at unrealistic levels and that the partnership is an association of individuals who are owners and not employees of the partnership.

A partnership has the characteristics of a separate entity in that it may hold title to property in its own name, may enter into contracts, and may sue or be sued as an entity. In practice, many accountants are accustomed to viewing partnerships as separate entities with continuity of accounting policies and asset valuations not broken by changes in partnership personnel.

The partnership contract

Although a partnership may exist on the basis of an oral agreement or be implied by the actions of its members, good business practice demands that the partnership contract be clearly stated in writing. Among the more important points to be covered by the partnership contract are:

1 The date of formation of the partnership, the duration of the contract, the names of the partners, and the name and business activities of the partnership.

2 The assets to be invested by each partner, the procedure for valuing noncash investments, and the penalties for failure to invest and maintain the agreed amount of capital.

3 The authority to be vested in each partner and the rights and duties of each.

4 The accounting period to be used, the nature of accounting records, financial statements, and audits by professional accountants.

5 The plan for sharing net income or loss, including the frequency of income measurement and the distribution of the net income or loss to the partners.

6 The salaries and drawings allowed to partners and the penalties, if any, for excessive withdrawals.

7 Insurance on the lives of partners, with the partnership or surviving partners named as beneficiaries.

8 Provision for arbitration of disputes and liquidation of the partnership at the end of the specified term of the contract or at the death or withdrawal of a partner. Especially important in avoiding disputes is agreement on procedures for the valuation of the partnership and the method of settlement with the estate of a deceased partner.

One advantage of developing a partnership contract with the aid of attorneys and accountants is that the process of reaching agreement on specific issues will develop a better understanding among the partners on many issues that might be highly controversial if not settled at the outset. Of course, it is seldom possible to cover specifically in a partnership contract every issue that may later arise. Revision of the partnership contract generally requires the approval of all partners.

Disputes arising among partners that cannot be resolved by reference to the partnership contract may be settled by arbitration or in courts of law. The partner who is not satisfied with the handling of disputes always has the right to withdraw from the partnership.

Owners' equity accounts for partners

Accounting for a partnership differs from accounting for a single proprietorship or a corporation with respect to the sharing of net income and losses and the maintenance of the owners' equity accounts. Although it would be possible to maintain partnership accounting records with only one equity account for each partner, the usual practice is to maintain three types of accounts. These equity accounts consist of (1) *capital* accounts, (2) *drawing* or *personal* accounts, and (3) accounts for *loans* to and from partners.

The original investment by each partner is recorded by debiting the assets invested, crediting any liabilities assumed by the firm, and crediting the partner's capital account with the current fair value of net assets invested. Subsequent to the original investment, the partner's equity is *in-*

creased by additional investments and by a share of net income; the partner's equity is *decreased* by withdrawal of assets and by a share of net losses.

Another possible source of increase or decrease in partners' equity arises from changes in ownership, as described in subsequent sections of this chapter.

The original investment of assets by partners is recorded by credits to the capital accounts; drawings by partners in anticipation of net income or drawings that are considered salary allowances are recorded by debits to the drawing accounts. However, a large withdrawal that is viewed as a permanent reduction in the ownership equity of a partner is debited directly to the partner's capital account.

At the end of the accounting period, the net income or net loss in the Income Summary account is transferred to the partners' capital accounts in accordance with the partnership contract. The debit balances in the drawing accounts at the end of the year also are closed to the partners' capital accounts. Because the accounting procedures for partners' equity accounts are not subject to government regulations as in the case of capital stock and other shareholders' equity accounts of a corporation, many deviations from the procedures described here are possible.

Loans to and from partners

Occasionally, a partner may withdraw a substantial sum from the partnership with the intention of repaying this amount. Such a transaction may be debited to the Loans Receivable from Partners account rather than to the partner's drawing account.

On the other hand, a partner may make an advance to the partnership that is viewed as a loan rather than an increase in the capital account. This type of transaction is recorded by a credit to Loans Payable to Partners and generally is accompanied by the issuance of a note payable. Amounts due from partners may be reflected as assets in the balance sheet and amounts owing to partners shown as liabilities. The classification of these items as current or long-term generally depends on the maturity date, although these *related party transactions* may result in noncurrent classification of the partners' loans, regardless of maturity dates.

If a substantial unsecured loan has been made by a partnership to one of the partners and repayment appears doubtful, the better financial statement presentation may be to offset the receivable against the partner's capital account. If this is not done, assets and the partners' equity may be inflated to the point of being misleading. In any event, adequate disclosure calls for separate listing of any receivables from partners.

Valuation of investments by partners

The investment by a partner in the firm often includes assets other than cash. It is imperative that the partners agree on the current fair value of assets at the time of their investment and that the assets be recorded at current fair values. Any gains or losses resulting from the disposal of such assets during the operation of the partnership, or at the time of liquidation, are divided according to the plan for sharing net income or losses. Equitable treatment of the individual partners, therefore, requires a starting point of current fair values recorded for all assets invested in the firm. It then will follow that partnership gains or losses from disposal of noncash assets invested by the partners will be limited to the difference between the disposal price and the current fair value of the assets when invested by the partners, adjusted for any depreciation or amortization to the date of disposal.

INCOME-SHARING PLANS

Partners' equity in assets versus share in earnings

The equity of a partner in the net assets of the partnership should be distinguished from a partner's share in earnings. Thus, to say that David Jones is a one-third partner is not a clear statement. Jones may have a one-third equity in the net assets but have a larger or smaller share in the earnings of the firm. Such a statement might also be interpreted to mean that Jones was entitled to one-third of the earnings, although his capital account represented much more or much less than one-third of the total partners' capital. To state the matter concisely, partners may agree on any type of *income-sharing plan* (or *profit and loss ratio*), regardless of the amount of their respective capital accounts. The acts state that if partners fail to specify a plan for sharing net income and net loss, *it shall be assumed that they intended to share equally*. Because income sharing is of such great importance, it is extremely rare to find a situation in which the partnership contract is silent on this point.

Division of net income or loss

The many possible plans for sharing of net income or loss among partners may be summarized into the following four categories:

1 Equally, or in some other ratio
2 In the ratio of partners' capital account balances on a particular date, or in the ratio of average capital account balances during the year
3 Allowing salaries to partners and dividing the remaining net income or loss in a specified ratio
4 Allowing salaries to partners, allowing interest on capital account balances, and dividing the remaining net income or loss in a specified ratio

These variations in income-sharing plans emphasize that the value of personal services rendered by individual partners may vary widely, as may the amounts of capital invested by each partner. The amount and quality of managerial services rendered and the amount of capital invested often are important factors in the success or failure of a partnership. Therefore, provisions may be made for salaries to partners and interest on their respective capital account balances as a preliminary step in the division of net income or loss. Any remaining net income or loss then may be divided in a specified ratio.

Another factor affecting the success of a partnership may be that one of the partners has large personal financial resources, thus giving the partnership a high credit rating. Similarly, partners who are well known in a profession or industry may contribute importantly to the success of the partnership even though they may not participate actively in the operations of the partnership. These two factors may be taken into account in the income-sharing plan by judicious selection of the ratio in which any remaining net income or loss is divided.

We now shall illustrate how each of the methods of dividing net income or loss may be applied. This series of illustrations is based on data for A & B Partnership, which earned a net income of $30,000 in Year 1, the first year of operations. The partnership contract provides that each partner may withdraw $500 on the last day of each month. The drawings are recorded by debits to the partners' drawing accounts and are not a factor in the division of net income or loss. All other withdrawals, investments, and net income or loss are entered in the partners' capital accounts.

Partner A originally invested $40,000 on January 1, Year 1, and invested an additional $10,000 on April 1. Partner B invested $80,000 on January 1 and withdrew $5,000 on July 1. These transactions are illustrated in the following capital, drawing, and Income Summary accounts:

General ledger accounts for Year 1

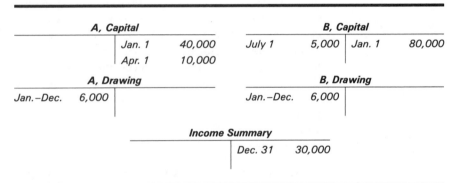

Division of Earnings Equally or in Some Other Ratio   Many partnership contracts provide that net income or loss is to be divided equally. Also, if the partners have made no specific agreement for sharing earnings, the acts provide that an intent of equal division will be assumed. The net income of $30,000 for the A & B Partnership is transferred at the end of Year 1 from the Income Summary account to the partners' capital accounts by the following journal entry:

Journal entry to close Income Summary account

Income Summary	30,000	
A, Capital		15,000
B, Capital		15,000

To record division of net income for Year 1 equally between A and B.

The drawing accounts are closed to the partners' capital accounts at the end of Year 1 as follows:

A, Capital	6,000	
B, Capital	6,000	
A, Drawing		6,000
B, Drawing		6,000
To close drawing accounts.		

After the drawing accounts are closed, the capital accounts show the ownership equity of each partner.

If the A & B Partnership had reported a net loss of, say, $20,000 during the first year, the Income Summary account would show a debit balance of $20,000. This loss would be transferred to the partners' capital accounts by a debit to each capital account for $10,000 and a credit to the Income Summary account for $20,000.

Assuming that A and B share earnings in the ratio of 60% to A and 40% to B, and that net income amounted to $30,000, the net income would be divided $18,000 to A and $12,000 to B. The agreement that A should receive 60% of the net income (perhaps because of greater experience and personal contacts) would cause Partner A to absorb a larger share of the net loss if the business operated unprofitably. Some partnership contracts provide that a net income is to be divided in a certain ratio, such as 60% to A and 40% to B, but that a net loss is divided equally or in some other ratio. Another variation intended to compensate for unequal contributions by the partners provides that agreed ratio (60% and 40% in our example) shall be applicable to a given amount of income but that additional income shall be shared in some other ratio.

Division of Earnings in Ratio of Partners' Capital Account Balances
Division of partnership earnings in proportion to the capital invested by each partner is most likely to be found in partnerships in which substantial investment is the principal ingredient for success. For example, a partnership engaged in the acquisition of land for investment might select this method of dividing net income. To avoid controversy, it is essential that the partnership contract specify whether the income-sharing ratio is based on the original capital investments, the capital account balances at the beginning of each year, the balances at the end of each year (before the distribution of net income or loss), or the average balances during each year.

Continuing our illustration for the A & B Partnership, assume that the partnership contract calls for division of net income in the ratio of *original capital investments*. The net income of $30,000 for Year 1 is divided as follows:

A: $30,000 × $40,000/$120,000 = $10,000

B: $30,000 × $80,000/$120,000 = $20,000

The journal entry to close the Income Summary account would be similar to the journal entry illustrated on page 9.

Assuming that the net income is divided in the ratio of capital account balances at the *end of the year* (before drawings and the distribution of net income), the net income of $30,000 for Year 1 is divided as follows:

A: $30,000 × $50,000/$125,000 = $12,000
B: $30,000 × $75,000/$125,000 = $18,000

Division of net income on the basis of (1) original capital investments, (2) yearly beginning capital account balances, or (3) yearly ending capital account balances may prove inequitable if there are material changes in capital accounts during the year. Use of average balances as a basis for sharing income is preferable because it reflects the capital actually available for use by the partnership during the year.

If the partnership contract provides for sharing net income in the ratio of average capital account balances during the year, it also should state the amount of drawings each partner may make without affecting the capital account. In our continuing example for the A & B Partnership, the partners are entitled to withdraw $500 monthly. Any additional withdrawals or investments are entered in the partners' capital accounts and therefore influence the computation of the average capital ratio. The partnership contract also should state whether capital account balances are to be computed to the nearest month or to the nearest day.

The computations of average capital account balances and the division of net income for the A & B Partnership for Year 1 follow:

A & B PARTNERSHIP
Computation of Average Capital Account Balances
For Year 1

Partner	Date	Increase (decrease) in capital	Capital account balance	Fraction of year unchanged	Average capital account balances
A	Jan. 1	$40,000	$40,000	1/4	$ 10,000
	Apr. 1	10,000	50,000	3/4	37,500
					$ 47,500
B	Jan. 1	80,000	80,000	1/2	$ 40,000
	July 1	(5,000)	75,000	1/2	37,500
					$ 77,500
Total average capitals for A and B					$125,000

Division of net income:

To A: $30,000 × $47,500/$125,000 . . . . $ 11,400
To B: $30,000 × $77,500/$125,000   18,600
Total net income . . . . $ 30,000

Interest on Partners' Capital Account Balances with Remaining Net Income or Loss Divided in Specified Ratio   In the preceding section, the plan for dividing the entire net income in the ratio of partners' capital account balances was based on the assumption that invested capital was the dominant factor in profitable operation of the partnership. However, in most cases the amount of invested capital is only one factor that contributes to the success of the partnership. Consequently, many partnerships choose to divide only a portion of net income in the capital ratio, and to divide the remainder equally or in some other ratio.

To allow interest on partners' capital account balances at 15%, for example, is the same as dividing a part of net income in the ratio of partners' capital balances. If the partners agree to allow interest on capital as a first step in the division of net income, they should specify the interest rate to be used and also state whether interest is to be computed on capital account balances on specific dates or on average balances during the year.

Let us again use our basic illustration for the A & B Partnership with a net income of $30,000 for Year 1, and capital account balances as shown on page 11. Assume that the partnership contract allows interest on partners' average capital account balances at 15%, with any remaining net income or loss to be divided equally. The net income of $30,000 for Year 1 is divided as follows:

<table>
<tr><td style="padding-right:2em">Division of net income
with interest allowed on
average capital
balances</td><td></td><td>A</td><td>B</td><td>Combined</td></tr>
<tr><td></td><td>Interest on average capital balances:</td><td></td><td></td><td></td></tr>
<tr><td></td><td>A: $47,500 × 0.15 . . . .</td><td>$ 7,125</td><td></td><td>$ 7,125</td></tr>
<tr><td></td><td>B: $77,500 × 0.15 . . . .</td><td></td><td>$11,625</td><td>11,625</td></tr>
<tr><td></td><td>Subtotal . . . .</td><td></td><td></td><td>$18,750</td></tr>
<tr><td></td><td>Balance ($30,000 − $18,750) divided equally</td><td>5,625</td><td>5,625</td><td>11,250</td></tr>
<tr><td></td><td>Totals . . . .</td><td>$12,750</td><td>$17,250</td><td>$30,000</td></tr>
</table>

The journal entry to close the Income Summary account at the end of Year 1 follows:

<table>
<tr><td style="padding-right:2em">Closing the Income
Summary account</td><td>Income Summary . . . .</td><td>30,000</td><td></td></tr>
<tr><td></td><td>A, Capital . . . .</td><td></td><td>12,750</td></tr>
<tr><td></td><td>B, Capital . . . .</td><td></td><td>17,250</td></tr>
<tr><td></td><td>To record division of net income for Year 1.</td><td></td><td></td></tr>
</table>

As a separate case, assume that the A & B Partnership was unsuccessful in Year 1 and incurred a net loss of $1,000. If the partnership contract provides for allowing interest on capital accounts, this provision *must be enforced, regardless of whether operations are profitable or un-*

profitable. The only justification for omitting the allowance of interest on partners' capital accounts during a loss year would be in the case of a partnership contract containing a specific provision requiring such omission. Note in the following analysis that the $1,000 debit balance in the Income Summary account resulting from the net loss is increased by the allowance of interest to $19,750 and is then divided equally between A and B:

Division of net loss

	A	B	Combined
Interest on average capital balances:			
A: $47,500 × 0.15	$7,125		$ 7,125
B: $77,500 × 0.15		$11,625	11,625
Subtotal			$18,750
Resulting deficiency ($1,000 + $18,750) divided equally	(9,875)	(9,875)	(19,750)
Totals	$(2,750)	$ 1,750	$ (1,000)

The journal entry to close the Income Summary account at the end of Year 1 is shown below:

Closing the Income Summary account with a debit balance

A, Capital	2,750	
Income Summary		1,000
B, Capital		1,750
To record division of net loss for Year 1.		

At first thought, the idea of a net loss of $1,000 causing one partner's capital to increase and the other partner's capital to decrease may appear unreasonable, but there is sound logic to support this result. Partner B invested substantially more capital than did Partner A; this capital was used to carry on operations, and the fact that a net loss was incurred in the first year is no reason to ignore B's larger capital investment.

A significant contrast between two of the income-sharing plans we have discussed (the capital-ratio plan and the interest-on-capital-accounts plan) is apparent if we consider the case of a partnership operating at a loss. Under the capital-ratio plan, the partner who invested more capital is required to bear a larger share of the net loss. This result may be considered unreasonable, because the investment of capital presumably is not the cause of a net loss. Under the interest-on-capital-accounts plan of sharing earnings, the partner who invested more capital receives credit for this factor and is charged with a lesser share of the net loss, or may even end up with a net credit.

We have considered interest allowances on partners' capital accounts as a technique for sharing partnership earnings equitably but as having no effect on the determination of the net income or loss of the partnership. Interest on partners' capital accounts *is not an expense of the partnership*, but interest on loans from partners is regarded as expense and a factor in the determination of net income or loss. Similarly, interest earned on loans to partners represents an element of revenue. This treatment is consistent with the point made earlier that loans to and from partners are assets and liabilities of the partnership.

Another item of expense arising from dealings between a partnership and one of its partners is commonly encountered when the partnership leases property from a lessor who is also a partner. Rent expense and a liability for rent are recognized in such situations. The lessor, although a partner, also is a creditor of the partnership.

Salary Allowances with Remaining Net Income or Loss Divided in Specified Ratio   In discussing salaries to partners, we must distinguish between salaries and drawings. Because the term *salaries* suggests weekly or monthly cash payments for personal services, accountants should be quite specific in suggesting and defining the terminology used in accounting for a partnership. We have used the term *drawings* in only one sense; a withdrawal of assets that reduces the partner's equity but plays no part in the division of net income. We shall limit the word *salaries* in partnership accounting to mean *a device for sharing net income*. When the term *salaries* is used with this meaning, the division of net income is the same, regardless of whether salaries have been paid.

A partnership contract that permits partners to make regular withdrawals of specific amounts should state whether such withdrawals are intended to be a factor in the division of net income or loss. Assume, for example, that the contract states that Partner A may make drawings of $300 monthly and Partner B $800. If the intent is not clearly stated to include or exclude these drawings as an element in the division of net income, controversy is probable, because one interpretation will favour Partner A and the opposing interpretation will favour Partner B.

Assuming that Partner A has more experience and ability than Partner B and also devotes more time to the partnership, it seems reasonable that the partners will want to recognize the more valuable contribution of personal services by A in choosing a plan for division of net income or loss. One approach to this objective would be to adopt an unequal ratio: for example, 70% of net income or loss to A and 30% to B. However, the use of such a ratio usually is not a satisfactory solution, for the same two reasons mentioned in criticizing the capital ratio as a profit-sharing plan. A ratio based only on personal services may not reflect the fact that other factors apart from personal services of partners are important in determining the profitability of the partnership. A second significant point is that if the partnership sustains a net loss, the partner rendering the most personal services will absorb a larger portion of the net loss.

A simple solution to the problem of recognizing unequal personal services by partners is to provide in the partnership contract for varying salary allowances to partners, with the remaining net income or loss divided equally or in some other ratio. Let us apply this reasoning to our continuing illustration for the A & B Partnership, and assume that the partnership contract provides for an annual salary of $10,000 to A and $6,000 to B, with any remaining net income or loss to be divided equally. The salaries are not actually paid during the year. The net income of $30,000 for Year 1 is divided as follows:

<table>
<tr><td>**Division of net income with salary allowances**</td><td></td><td>*A*</td><td>*B*</td><td>*Combined*</td></tr>
<tr><td></td><td>Salaries ....</td><td>*$10,000*</td><td>*$ 6,000*</td><td>*$16,000*</td></tr>
<tr><td></td><td>Balance ($30,000 − $16,000) divided equally . .</td><td>*7,000*</td><td>*7,000*</td><td>*14,000*</td></tr>
<tr><td></td><td>Totals ....</td><td>*$17,000*</td><td>*$13,000*</td><td>*$30,000*</td></tr>
</table>

If partners choose to take their monthly salaries in cash, these payments should be debited to the partners' drawing accounts.

Bonus to Managing Partner Based on Income   A partnership contract may provide for a bonus to the managing partner equal to a given percentage of income. The contract should state whether the basis of the bonus is income before deduction of the bonus or income after the bonus. For example, assume that the A & B Partnership provides for a bonus to Partner A of 25% of income **before** deduction of the bonus, and that the remaining income is divided equally. As in the preceding examples, the income before the bonus is assumed to be $30,000. After the bonus of $7,500 to A, the remaining $22,500 of income is divided $11,250 to A and $11,250 to B. Thus, A's share of income is $18,750 and B's share is $11,250.

If the partnership contract provided for a bonus of 25% of income **after** the bonus to Partner A, the bonus is computed as follows:

Bonus based on income after bonus

Bonus + income after bonus = $30,000

$\quad$ **Let X = income after bonus**

$\quad$ **$0.25X$ = bonus**

Then $1.25X$ = $30,000 income before bonus

$\qquad$ **X = $30,000 ÷ 1.25**

$\qquad$ **X = $24,000**

$\quad$ **$0.25X$ = $6,000 bonus to Partner A**[1]

Thus, the net income of $30,000 in this case is divided $18,000 to A and $12,000 to B.

1 An alternative computation consists of converting the bonus percentage to a fraction. The bonus then can be computed by adding the numerator to the denominator and applying the resulting fraction to the income before the bonus. In the preceding example, 25% is converted to ¼, and by adding the numerator to the denominator, the ¼ becomes ⅕ (4 + 1 = 5). One-fifth of $30,000 equals $6,000.

The concept of a bonus is not applicable to a net loss. When a partnership operates at a loss, the bonus provision is ignored. The partnership contract also may specify that extraordinary items or other unusual gains and losses are to be excluded from the basis for the computation of the bonus.

Salaries to Partners with Interest on Capital Accounts   Many partnerships divide net income or loss by allowing salaries to partners and also interest on their capital account balances. Any remaining net income or loss is divided equally or in some other ratio. Such plans have the merit of recognizing that the value of personal services rendered by different partners may vary, and that differences in amounts invested also warrant recognition in an equitable plan for sharing net income or loss. The procedures for carrying out this type of plan are the same as those illustrated in earlier sections.

Financial statements for a partnership

Income Statement   Explanations of the division of net income between partners may be included in the income statement or in a note to the financial statements. This information is sometimes referred to as the **distribution section** of the income statement. The following illustration for the A & B Partnership shows, in a highly condensed income statement for the year ended December 31, Year 1, the division of net income equally after a bonus to Partner A of 25% of income after the bonus.

A & B PARTNERSHIP
Income Statement
For Year Ended December 31, Year 1

Sales	$300,000
Cost of goods sold	180,000
Gross profit on sales	$120,000
Operating expenses	90,000
Net income	$ 30,000
Distribution of net income:	
Partner A (including bonus of $6,000)	$18,000
Partner B	12,000
Total	$30,000

If salaries paid to partners are included in operating expenses, the amount of such salaries should be disclosed. Internal reports used to appraise the performance of profit centres may call for different accounting concepts and classifications from those generally used for the financial statements prepared for outsiders. To develop meaningful cost data for internal use, accountants may treat partners' salaries as expenses rather than as a device for dividing net income. This approach is particularly appropriate if one profit centre (for example, a branch) has a partner as active manager and another profit centre is managed by a salaried employee. For external reporting purposes section 1800 of the *CICA Handbook* requires disclosure of the treatment of salaries and interest in the financial statements. The section does not specify a preferred method of reporting.

Statement of Partners' Capital   Partners generally want a complete explanation of the changes in their capital accounts each year. To meet this need, a *statement of partners' capital* generally is prepared. The following illustrative statement of partners' capital for the A & B Partnership is based on the capital accounts presented on page 9, and uses the division of net income for Year 1 illustrated in the income statement on page 16.

A & B PARTNERSHIP

Statement of Partners' Capital
For Year Ended December 31, Year 1

	A	B	Combined
Partners' capital, beginning of year	$40,000	$80,000	$120,000
Additional investment (or withdrawal) of			
capital	10,000	(5,000)	5,000
Balances before net income and drawings	$50,000	$75,000	$125,000
Add: Net income	18,000	12,000	30,000
Subtotal	$68,000	$87,000	$155,000
Less: Drawings	6,000	6,000	12,000
Partners' capital, end of year	$62,000	$81,000	$143,000

Partners' capital is reported as owners' equity in the balance sheet of the partnership, as illustrated on page 18.

Balance Sheet   A condensed balance sheet for the A & B Partnership on December 31, Year 1, is presented on page 18.

Adjustment of net income of prior years

Any business enterprise, whether it be organized as a single proprietorship, partnership, or corporation, will from time to time discover errors made in the measurement of net income in prior accounting periods. Examples include errors in the computation of depreciation, errors in inventory valuation, and omission of accruals of revenue and expenses. When such errors come to light, the question arises as to whether the corrections should be treated as part of the determination of net income for the current period or in the same manner as *prior period adjustments* and entered directly to partners' capital accounts.

A & B PARTNERSHIP
Balance Sheet
December 31, Year 1

Assets		Liabilities & Partners' Capital		
Current assets	$ 45,000	Current liabilities		$ 20,000
Other assets	155,000	Long-term debt		37,000
		Total liabilities		$ 57,000
		Partners' capital:		
		Partner A . .	$62,000	
		Partner B . . .	81,000	143,000
		Total liabilities &		
Total assets	$200,000	partners' capital		$200,000

The correction of prior years' net income becomes particularly important when the profit-sharing plan has been changed. For example, assume that in Year 1 the net income for A & B Partnership was $30,000 and that the partners shared the net income equally, but in Year 2 they changed the income-sharing ratio to 60% for A and 40% for B. During Year 2, it was discovered that the inventories at the end of Year 1 were overstated by $10,000 because of clerical errors. The $10,000 reduction in the net income for Year 1 should be divided $5,000 to each partner, in accordance with the income-sharing ratio in effect for Year 1, the *year in which the error occurred*.

Somewhat related to the correction of errors of prior periods is the treatment of nonoperating gains and losses. When the income-sharing ratio of a partnership is changed, the partners should consider the differences that exist between the carrying amounts of assets and their current fair values. For example, assume that the A & B Partnership owns marketable securities acquired for $20,000 that have appreciated to $50,000 on the date when the income-sharing ratio is changed from 50% for each partner to 60% for A and 40% for B. If the securities were sold for $50,000 just prior to the change in the income-sharing ratio, the $30,000 gain would be divided $15,000 to A and $15,000 to B; if the securities were sold immediately after establishment of the 60:40 income-sharing ratio, the gain would be divided $18,000 to A and only $12,000 to B.

A solution sometimes suggested for such partnership problems is to revalue the assets to current fair value when the income-sharing plan is changed or when a new partner is added or an old one retires. In most cases the revaluation of assets may be justified, but in general the continuity of historical cost valuations in a partnership is desirable, for the same reasons that support the use of the cost principle in a corporation. A secondary objection to revaluation of assets is that, with a few exceptions such as marketable securities, satisfactory evidence of current fair value is seldom available. The best solution to the problem of a change in the ratio of income sharing usually may be achieved by making appropriate adjustments among partners' capitals rather than by a restatement of carrying amounts.

When accountants act in the role of management consultants to a partnership, they should bring to the attention of the partners any significant differences between carrying amounts and current fair values of assets, and make the partners aware of the implications of a change in the income-sharing ratio.

CHANGES IN OWNERSHIP

Accounting for changes in partners

Most changes in the ownership of a partnership are accomplished without interruption of its operations. For example, when a large and well-established partnership promotes one of its employees to partner there is usually no significant change in the financial condition or the operating routines of the partnership. However, from a legal viewpoint a partnership is dissolved by the retirement or death of a partner or by the admission of a new partner.

Dissolution of a partnership also may result from the bankruptcy of the firm or of any partner, the expiration of a time period stated in the partnership contract, or the mutual agreement of the partners to end their association. Thus, the term *dissolution* may be used to describe events ranging from a minor change of ownership interest not affecting operations of the partnership to a decision by the partners to terminate their business relationship.

Accountants are concerned with the economic substance of a transaction rather than with its legal form. Therefore, they must evaluate all the circumstances of the individual case to determine how a change in partners should be recorded. In the remaining pages of this chapter, we describe and illustrate the principal kinds of changes in the ownership of a partnership.

Accounting and managerial issues

Although a partnership is ended in a legal sense when a partner withdraws or a new partner is added, the partnership often continues with little outward evidence of change. In current accounting practice, a partner's interest often is viewed as a share in a continuing business enterprise that may be transferred, much as shares of capital stock are transferred between shareholders, without disturbing the continuity of the enterprise. For example, if a partner of a CA firm wishes to retire or a new partner enters the firm, the contract for the change in ownership should be planned carefully to avoid disturbing client relationships. In a large CA firm with hundreds of partners, the decision to promote an employee to the rank of partner often may be made by a committee rather than by action of all partners.

Changes in the ownership of a partnership raise a number of accounting and managerial issues on which the professional accountant can serve as consultant. Among these issues are the setting of terms for admission of a new partner, the possible revaluation of assets, the development of a new plan for the division of net income or loss, and the determination of the amount to be paid to a retiring partner.

Admission of a new partner

When a new partner is admitted to a firm of perhaps two or three partners, it is particularly appropriate to consider the fairness and adequacy of past accounting policies and the need for correction of errors in prior years' accounting data. The terms of admission of a new partner often are influenced by the level and trend of past earnings, because they may be indicative of future earnings. Sometimes specific accounting policies, such as the use of the completed-contract method of accounting for long-term construction contracts, may cause the accounting records to convey a misleading impression of earnings in the years preceding the admission of a new partner.

Adjustments of the accounting records may be necessary to restate the carrying amounts of assets and liabilities to current fair values before a new partner is admitted.

As an alternative to revaluation of the assets, it may be preferable to evaluate any discrepancies between the carrying amounts and current fair values of assets and adjust the terms for admission of the new partner. In other words, the amounts invested by the incoming partner can be set at a level that reflects the current fair value of the partnership, even though the carrying amounts of assets remain unchanged in the accounting records. If assets have appreciated in value but such appreciation is ignored, the disposal of the assets after admission of a new partner will cause the new partner to share in net income that accrued before the new partner joined the firm.

The admission of a new partner to a partnership may be effected by an *acquisition* of all or part of the interest of one or more of the existing partners, or by an *investment* of assets by the new partner, with a resultant increase in the net assets of the partnership.

Acquisition of an interest by direct payment to one or more partners

If a new partner acquires an interest from one or more of the existing partners, the transaction is recorded by opening a capital account for the new partner and decreasing the capital accounts of the selling partners by the same amount. No assets are received by the partnership; the transfer of assets is a private transaction between two or more partners.

As an illustration of this situation, assume that L and M share earnings equally and that each has a capital account balance of $60,000. Partner N (with the consent of M) acquires one-half of L's interest in the partnership. The journal entry to record this change in ownership follows:

N acquires one-half of L's interest in partnership	*L, Capital*	*30,000*
	N, Capital	*30,000*
	To record transfer of one-half of L's capital to N.	

The price paid by N for half of L's interest may have been the carrying amount of $30,000 or it may have been more or less than the carrying amount. Possibly no price was established; L may have made a gift to N of the equity in the partnership, or perhaps N won it in a poker game. Regardless of the terms of the transaction between L and N, the journal entry illustrated above is all that is required in the partnership's accounting records. No change has occurred in the assets, liabilities, or total partners' capital of the partnership.

To explore further some of the implications involved in the acquisition of an interest by an incoming partner, assume that N paid $40,000 to L for one-half of L's $60,000 equity in the partnership. Some accountants have suggested that the willingness of the new partner to pay $10,000 in excess of carrying amount for a one-fourth interest in the total capital of the partnership indicates that the total capital is worth $40,000 ($10,000 ÷ 0.25 = $40,000) more than is shown in the accounting records. They reason that the assets should be written up by $40,000, or goodwill of $40,000 should be recorded with offsetting credits of $20,000 each to the capital accounts of the existing partners, L and M. However, most accountants take the position that the payment by N to L is a personal transaction between them and that the partnership, which has neither received nor distributed any assets, should make no journal entry, other than to transfer one-half of L's capital to N.

What are the arguments for these two opposing views? Those who advocate a write-up of assets stress the legal concept of dissolution of the former partnership and formation of a new partnership. This change in identity of owners, it is argued, justifies departure from the going-concern principle and the revaluation of assets to current fair values to achieve an accurate measurement of the capital invested by each member of the new partnership.

The opposing argument, that the acquisition of an interest by a new partner requires only a transfer from the capital account of the selling partner to the capital account of the new partner, is based on several points. First, the partnership did not participate in negotiating the price paid by N to L. Many factors other than the valuation of assets may have been involved in the negotiations between the two individuals. Perhaps N paid more than carrying amount because N was allowed very generous credit terms or received more than a one-fourth share in earnings. Perhaps the new partner was anxious to join the firm because of the personal abilities of L and M, or because of the anticipated growth in the particular industry. Based on these and other similar reasons, we may conclude that the price paid for a partnership interest by a new partner to an existing partner does not provide sufficient evidence to support extensive changes in the carrying amounts of the partnership's assets.

Investment in partnership by new partner

A new partner may gain admission by investing assets directly in the partnership, thus increasing the total assets and partners' capital of the partnership. For example, assume that X and Y share earnings equally and that each has a capital account balance of $60,000. Assume also that the carrying amounts of the partnership assets are approximately equal to current fair values and that Z owns a tract of land that could be used for expansion of operations. X and Y agree to admit Z to the partnership by investment of the land; earnings of the new firm are to be shared equally. The land had cost Z $50,000, but has a current fair value of $80,000. The admission of Z is recorded as follows:

Land	80,000	
Z, Capital		80,000
To record admission of Z to partnership.		

Z has a capital account $20,000 larger than the capital accounts of X and Y. In other words, Z owns a 40% ($80,000 ÷ $200,000 = 0.40) interest in the firm. The fact that the three partners share earnings equally does not require that their capital accounts be equal.

Bonus or goodwill allowed to existing partners

In a profitable, well-established firm, the partners may insist that a portion of the investment by a new partner be allowed to them as a bonus or that goodwill be recorded and credited to the existing partners. The new partner may agree to such terms because of the benefits to be gained by becoming a member of a firm with high earning power.

Bonus to Existing Partners Assume that, in the A & B Partnership, A and B share earnings equally and have capital account balances of $45,000 each. The carrying amounts of the partnership net assets are assumed to approximate current fair values. The partners agree to admit C to a one-third interest in capital and a one-third share in earnings for an investment of $60,000. The total assets of the new firm amount to $150,000 ($45,000 + $45,000 + $60,000 = $150,000). The following journal entry gives C a one-third interest in capital, and credits the $10,000 bonus equally between A and B in accordance with their prior contract to share earnings equally:

Cash	60,000	
A, Capital		5,000
B, Capital		5,000
C, Capital		50,000
To record investment by C for a one-third interest in capital,		
with bonus of $10,000 divided between A and B in their income-		
sharing ratio.		

Goodwill to Existing Partners   In the preceding illustration, C invested $60,000 but received a capital account of only $50,000, representing a one-third interest in the firm. C might prefer that the full amount invested, $60,000, be credited to C's capital account. This could be done while still allotting C a one-third interest if goodwill is recorded in the accounting records, with the offsetting credit divided equally between the two existing partners. If C is to be given a one-third interest represented by a capital account of $60,000, the total indicated capital of the partnership is $180,000, and the total capital of A and B must equal $120,000 ($180,000 × $^{2}/_{3}$ = $120,000). Because their present combined capital accounts amount to $90,000, a write-up of $30,000 in the net assets is recorded as follows:

Recording implied goodwill

Cash	60,000	
Goodwill	30,000	
A, Capital		15,000
B, Capital		15,000
C, Capital		60,000

To record investment by C for a one-third interest in capital, with goodwill of $30,000 divided between A and B in their income-sharing ratio.

Evaluation of Bonus and Goodwill Methods   When a new partner invests an amount larger than the carrying amount of the interest acquired, the transaction usually should be recorded by allowing a bonus to the existing partners. The bonus method has the advantage of adhering to the cost principle and views the partnership as a continuing accounting entity. The alternative method of recording the goodwill implied by the amount invested by the new partner is not considered acceptable by the authors. Use of the goodwill method signifies the substitution of estimated current fair value of an asset rather than valuation on a cost basis. The goodwill of $30,000 recorded in the preceding example was not paid for by the partnership. Its existence is implied by the amount invested by the new partner for a one-third interest in the firm. The amount invested by the new partner may have been influenced by many factors, some of which may be personal rather than economic in nature.

Apart from the questionable theoretical basis for such recognition of goodwill, there are other practical difficulties. The presence of goodwill created in this manner is likely to evoke criticism of the partnership's financial statements, and such criticism may lead the partnership to amortize or to write off the goodwill.[2] Also, if the partnership should be liquidated, the

2 According to *APB Opinion No. 17*, "Intangible Assets," only purchased goodwill should be recorded in the accounting records, and it must be amortized over a period of 40 years or less. The *CICA Handbook* Section 1580 states that goodwill arising from a business combination must be amortized in the same manner.

goodwill probably would have to be written off as a loss. Will the recording of goodwill and its subsequent write-off injure one partner and benefit another? The net results to the individual partners will be the same under the bonus and goodwill methods only if two specific conditions are met: (1) the new partner's share of earnings must be equal to the percentage equity in net assets the new partner receives at the time of admission, and (2) the existing partners must continue to share earnings between themselves in the same ratio as in the original partnership. Both these conditions were met in our example; that is, the new partner received a one-third interest in the net assets and earnings, and the existing partners shared earnings equally both before and after the admission of C to the partnership.

Assume, however, that A, B, and C agreed to share earnings 40%, 40%, and 20%, respectively. The goodwill method would benefit C and injure A and B as compared with the bonus method. This is illustrated below. The first of the two necessary conditions for equivalent results from the bonus method and goodwill method is no longer met. Partner C's share of earnings is not equal to C's share of assets. C is now assumed to have a 20% share of earnings, although as in the preceding example C has a one-third share of assets. The use of the goodwill method for the admission of C and the subsequent write-off of the goodwill would cause a $4,000 ($54,000 − $50,000 = $4,000) shift of capital from Partners A and B to Partner C. The preceding discussion may be summarized as follows: ***When the new partner's share of earnings exceeds the new partner's share of assets, the new partner will benefit from the use of the bonus method.***

Comparison of bonus and goodwill methods	A	B	C	Combined
Capital balances if bonus method is used	$50,000	$50,000	$50,000	$150,000
Capital balances if goodwill method is used	$60,000	$60,000	$60,000	$180,000
Write-off of goodwill (40%, 40%, 20%)	(12,000)	(12,000)	(6,000)	(30,000)
Capital balances after write-off of goodwill	48,000	$48,000	$54,000	$150,000

Fairness of Asset Valuation In the preceding examples of bonus or goodwill allowed to the existing partners, it was assumed that the carrying amounts of assets in the accounting records of the original partnership approximated current fair values. However, if land and buildings, for example, have been owned by the partnership for many years, their carrying amounts and current fair values may be quite far apart.

To bring this problem into focus, let us assume that the net assets of the A & B Partnership, carried at $90,000, were estimated to have a current fair value of $120,000 at the time of admission of C as a partner. Our previous example called for C to receive a one-third interest for an investment of $60,000. Why not write up the assets from $90,000 to $120,000, with a corresponding increase in the capital accounts of the existing partners? Neither a bonus nor the recognition of goodwill then would be necessary to record the admission of C to a one-third interest for an investment of $60,000 because this investment is equal to one-third of the total capital of $180,000 ($120,000 + $60,000 = $180,000).

Such restatement of asset values would not be acceptable practice in a corporation simply because the market price of the corporation's capital stock had risen. If we assume the existence of certain conditions in a partnership, adherence to cost as a basis for asset valuation is as appropriate a policy as for a corporation. These specific conditions are that the income-sharing ratio should correspond to the share of equity held by each partner, and that the income-sharing ratio should continue unchanged. When these conditions do not exist, a restatement of assets from carrying amount to current fair value may be the most convenient method of achieving equity among the partners.

Bonus or goodwill allowed to new partner

An existing partnership may be anxious to admit a new partner to the firm, because the partnership needs cash or because the new partner has valuable skills and business contacts. To ensure the admission of the new partner, the present firm may offer the new partner a larger capital account balance than the amount invested by the new partner.

Bonus to New Partner   Assume that F and G, who share earnings equally and have capital account balances of $35,000 each, offer H a one-third interest in assets and a one-third share of earnings for an investment of $20,000 cash. Their offer is based on a need for more cash and on the conviction that H's personal skills and business contacts will be of great value to the partnership. The investment of $20,000 by H, when added to the existing capital of $70,000, gives a total capital of $90,000, of which H is entitled to one-third, or $30,000. The excess of H's capital account balance over the amount invested represents a $10,000 bonus allowed to H by F and G. Because F and G share earnings equally, the $10,000 bonus is debited to their capital accounts in equal amounts, as shown by the following journal entry to record the admission of H to the partnership:

Recording bonus to new partner	Cash	20,000	
	F, Capital	5,000	
	G, Capital	5,000	
	H, Capital		30,000
	To record admission of H, with bonus of $10,000 from F and G.		

In outlining this method of accounting for the admission of H, we have assumed that the net assets of the partnership were valued properly. If the admission of the new partner to a one-third interest for an investment of $20,000 was based on recognition that the net assets of the partnership were worth only $40,000, consideration should be given to writing down net assets by $30,000. Such write-downs would be proper if, for example, accounts receivable included doubtful accounts or if inventories were obsolete.

Goodwill to New Partner   Assume that the new partner H is the owner of a successful business enterprise that H invests in the partnership rather than making an investment in cash. Using the same data as in the preceding example, assume that F and G with capital account balances of $35,000 each give H a one-third interest in assets and earnings. The identifiable tangible and intangible net assets comprising the enterprise owned by H are worth $20,000, but, because of its superior earnings record, a current fair value for this enterprise is agreed to be $35,000. The admission of H to the partnership is recorded as below.

<table>
<tr><td>**New partner invests goodwill**</td><td>Identifiable Tangible and Intangible Net Assets . . . .</td><td>20,000</td><td></td></tr>
<tr><td></td><td>Goodwill . . . .</td><td>15,000</td><td></td></tr>
<tr><td></td><td>   H, Capital . . . .</td><td></td><td>35,000</td></tr>
<tr><td></td><td colspan="3">To record admission of H; goodwill is assigned to business enterprise invested by H.</td></tr>
</table>

The point to be stressed here is that generally goodwill is recognized as part of the investment of a new partner *only when the new partner invests a going business enterprise of superior earning power*. If H is admitted by reason of a cash investment and is credited with a capital account larger than the cash invested, the difference should be recorded as a bonus to H from the existing partners, or undervalued tangible assets should be written up to current fair value. Goodwill should be recorded only when substantiated by objective evidence.

Retirement of a partner

A partner retiring from a partnership usually receives cash or other assets directly from the partnership. It is also possible that a retiring partner might arrange for the sale of a partnership interest to one or more of the continuing partners or to an outsider. Because we have already considered the accounting principles applicable to the latter situation, our discussion of the retirement of a partner is limited to the situation in which the partner receives settlement from the assets of the partnership.

An assumption underlying this discussion is that the partner has a right to withdraw under the terms of the partnership contract. A partner always has the *power* to withdraw, as distinguished from the *right* to withdraw. A partner who withdraws in violation of the terms of the partnership contract, and without the consent of the other partners, may be liable for damages.

Computation of the Settlement Price   What is a fair measurement of the equity of a retiring partner? A first indication is the amount of the retiring partner's capital account balance, but this amount may need to be adjusted before it represents an equitable settlement price. Adjustments may include the correction of errors in accounting data or the recognition of differences between carrying amounts of net assets and their current fair values. Before making any adjustments, the accountant should refer to the partnership contract, which may contain specific provisions for computing the amount to be paid a retiring partner. For example, these provisions might require an appraisal of assets, an audit by professional accountants, or a valuation of the partnership as a going concern according to a prescribed formula. If the partnership has not maintained accurate accounting records or has not been audited, it is possible that the capital account balances are misstated because of incorrect depreciation expense, failure to provide for doubtful accounts expense, and other accounting deficiencies.

If the partnership contract does not contain provisions for the computation of the retiring partner's equity, the accountant may be able to obtain authorization from the partners to follow a specific approach to determine an equitable settlement price.

In most cases, the equity of the retiring partner is computed on the basis of current fair values of partnership net assets. The gain or loss indicated by the difference between the carrying amounts of assets and their current fair values is divided in the income-sharing ratio. After the equity of the retiring partner has been computed in terms of current fair values for assets, the partners may agree to settle by payment of this amount, or they may agree on a different amount. The computation of an estimated current fair value for the partner's equity is a necessary step in reaching a settlement. An independent decision is made whether to record the current fair values and the related changes in partners' capital in the accounting records.

Payment of Bonus to Retiring Partner   The partnership contract may provide for recognition of goodwill at the time of a partner's retirement and may specify the methods for computing the goodwill. Usually the amount of the computed goodwill is allocated to the partners' capital accounts in the income-sharing ratio. For example, assume that C is to retire from the A, B & C Partnership. Each partner has a capital account balance of $60,000, and earnings are shared equally. The partnership contract states that a retiring partner is to receive the balance in the retiring partner's capital account plus a share of any goodwill. At the time of C's retirement, goodwill in the amount of $30,000 is computed to the mutual satisfaction of the partners. In the opinion of the authors, this goodwill should not be entered in the accounting records of the partnership.

Serious objections exist to recording goodwill as determined in this fashion. Because only $10,000 of the goodwill is included in the payment for C's equity, the remaining $20,000 of goodwill *has not* been paid for by the partnership. Its inclusion in the balance sheet of the partnership is not supported by either the cost principle or objective evidence. The fact that the partners "voted" for $30,000 of goodwill does not meet the need for objective evidence of asset values. As an alternative, it would be possible to record only $10,000 of goodwill and credit C's capital for the same amount, because this amount was paid for by the partnership as a condition of C's retirement. This method is perhaps more justifiable, but objective evidence that goodwill exists still is lacking. The most satisfactory method of accounting for the retirement of partner C is to treat the amount paid to C for goodwill as a $10,000 bonus. Because the settlement with C is for the balance of C's capital account of $60,000, plus estimated goodwill of $10,000, the journal entry below to record the amount paid to C is recommended.

Bonus paid to a retiring partner	C, Capital	60,000	
	A, Capital	5,000	
	B, Capital	5,000	
	Cash		70,000

To record payment to retiring partner C, including a bonus of $10,000.

The bonus method illustrated here is appropriate whenever the settlement with the retiring partner exceeds the carrying amount of that partner's capital. The agreement for settlement may or may not use the term **goodwill**; the essence of the matter is the determination of the amount to be paid to the retiring partner.

Settlement with Retiring Partner for Less than Carrying Amount   A partner anxious to escape from an unsatisfactory business situation may accept less than his or her equity on retirement. In other cases, willingness by a retiring partner to accept a settlement below carrying amount may reflect personal problems. Another possible explanation is that the retiring partner considers the net assets of the partnership to be overvalued, or anticipates lower earnings in future years.

In brief, there are many factors that may induce a partner to accept less than the carrying amount of his or her capital account balance on withdrawal from a partnership. Because a settlement below carrying amount seldom is supported by objective evidence of overvaluation of assets, the preferred accounting treatment is to leave net asset valuations undisturbed unless a large amount of goodwill is carried in the accounting records. The difference between the retiring partner's capital account balance and the amount paid in settlement should be credited as a bonus to the continuing partners.

For example, assume that A, B, and C share earnings equally and that each has a capital account balance of $60,000. B retires from the partnership and receives $50,000. The journal entry to record B's retirement follows:

B, Capital	60,000	
Cash		50,000
A, Capital		5,000
C, Capital		5,000

To record retirement of partner B for an amount less than
carrying amount of B's equity.

The final settlement with a retiring partner often is deferred for some time after the partner's withdrawal to permit the accumulation of cash, the determination of net income to date of withdrawal, the obtaining of bank loans, or other steps needed to complete the transaction. The retirement of a partner does not terminate the retiring partner's personal responsibility for partnership debts existing on the date of retirement.

Death of a Partner   A partnership contract often provides that partners shall acquire life insurance policies on each other's lives so that funds will be available for settlement with the estate of a deceased partner. A *buy-sell agreement* may be formed by the partners, whereby the partners commit their estates to sell their equities in the partnership and the surviving partners to acquire such equities. Another form of such an agreement gives the surviving partners an *option to buy*, or "right of first refusal," rather than imposing an obligation to buy.

REVIEW QUESTIONS

1 In the formation of a partnership, partners often invest such assets as land, buildings, and machinery as well as cash. Should these noncash assets be recorded by the partnership at current fair value, at cost to the partners, or at some other amount? Give reasons for your answer.

2 Some CA firms have thousands of staff members, and hundreds of partners, and operate on a national or international basis. Would the corporate form of organization be more appropriate than the partnership form for such large organizations? Explain.

3 Explain the proper presentation in the balance sheet of loans to and from partners, and the accounting treatment of interest on such loans.

4 Explain how partners' salaries should be shown in the income statement of a partnership, if at all.

5 List at least five items that should be included in a partnership contract.

6 List at least five methods by which earnings may be divided among partners.

7 Ainsley & Burton admitted Paul Craig to a one-third interest in the firm for his investment of $50,000. Does this offer mean that Craig would be entitled to one-third of the partnership earnings?

8 Duncan and Eastwick are negotiating a partnership contract, with Duncan investing $60,000 and Eastwick $20,000. Duncan suggests that interest be allowed on average capital account balances at 8% and that any remaining earnings

be divided in the ratio of average capital account balances. Eastwick prefers that the entire earnings be divided in the ratio of average capital account balances. Comment on these proposals.

9 The partnership contract of Peel and Quay is very brief on the subject of sharing earnings. It states: "Earnings are to be divided 80% to Peel and 20% to Quay, and each partner is entitled to draw $2,000 a month." What difficulties do you see in implementing this contract? Illustrate possible difficulties under the assumption that the partnership had net income of $100,000 in the first year.

10 Muir and Miller operated a partnership for several years, sharing net income and losses equally. On January 1, Year 6, they agreed to revise the income-sharing ratio to 70% for Muir and 30% for Miller, because of Miller's desire for semiretirement. On March 1 the partnership received $10,000 in settlement of a disputed error on a contract completed in Year 5. Because the outcome of the dispute had been considered highly uncertain, no receivable had been recognized. Explain the accounting treatment you would recommend for the $10,000 cash receipt.

11 Should the carrying amounts of partnership assets be restated to correspond with current fair values whenever a partner withdraws or a new partner is admitted to the firm? Explain fully and give specific examples.

12 A new partner admitted to an established firm often is required to invest an amount of cash larger than the carrying amount of the interest in net assets the new partner acquires. In what ways may such a transaction be recorded? What is the principal argument for each method?

13 Bono, Claire, and Drummond have operated a partnership for many years and have shared net income and losses equally. The partners now agree that Gray, a key employee of the firm who is an able manager but has limited financial resources, should become a partner with a one-sixth interest in capital. It is further agreed that the four partners will share net income and losses equally in the future. Bono suggests that the net assets in the accounting records of the partnership should be restated to current fair values at the time Gray is admitted, but Claire and Drummond advocate that the accounting records be left undisturbed. What is the argument for restating net assets at the time of Gray's admission? What alternative, if any, would you suggest for such restatement of net assets?

14 The partnership of Ed Loeser, Peter Wylie, and Herman Martin has operated successfully for many years, but Martin now plans to retire. In discussions of the settlement to be made with Martin, the point was made that inventories had been valued on a lifo basis for many years. Martin suggested that the current replacement cost of the inventories be determined and the excess of this amount over the carrying amount be regarded as a gain to be shared equally. Loeser objected to this suggestion on grounds that any method of inventory valuation would give reasonably accurate results provided it were followed consistently and that a departure from the long-established method of inventory valuation used by the partnership would produce an erroneous earnings picture over the life of the partnership. Evaluate the objections raised by Loeser.

15 George Lewis and Anna Marlin are partners who share net income and losses equally. They offer to admit Betty Naylor to a one-third interest in assets and in earnings for an investment of $50,000 cash. The total capital of the partnership prior to Naylor's admission was $110,000. Naylor makes a counteroffer of $40,000, explaining that her investigation of the partnership indicates that many receivables are past due and that a significant amount of obsolescence

exists in the inventories. Lewis and Marlin deny both these points. They contend that inventories are valued in accordance with generally accepted accounting principles and that the receivables are fully collectible. However, after prolonged negotiation, the admission price of $40,000 proposed by Naylor is agreed upon. Explain two ways in which the admission of Naylor could be recorded and indicate which method is preferable. Comment on the possibility of recording goodwill.

16 Two partners invested $200 each to form a partnership for the construction of a shopping centre. The partnership obtained a loan of $800,000 to finance construction, but no payment on this loan was due for two years. Each partner withdrew cash of $50,000 from the partnership from the proceeds of the loan. How should the investment of $400 and the withdrawal of $100,000 be presented in the balance sheet of the partnership?

17 An auditor was asked to give an opinion on the financial statements of a limited partnership in which a corporation is the general partner. Should the financial statements of the limited partnership and the auditor's report thereon include the financial statements of the general partner?

EXERCISES

Ex. 1-1 Select the best answer for each of the following multiple-choice questions:

1 On March 1, Year 1, Sally Smith and Diane Dale formed a partnership, each investing assets (at current fair values) as follows:

	Smith	Dale
Cash	$30,000	$ 70,000
Equipment	35,000	75,000
Building		225,000

The building is subject to a mortgage note payable of $180,000, which is to be assumed by the partnership. The partnership contract provides that Smith and Dale share net income and losses 30% and 70%, respectively. On March 1, Year 1, the balance in Dale's capital account should be:
a $190,000   **b** $205,000   **c** $214,000   **d** $270,000

2 The capital account balances of the partnership of Newton, Sharman, and Jackson on June 1, Year 1, are presented below, along with their respective income-sharing percentages:

Paul Newton (50%)	$139,200
Gene Sharman (33⅓%)	208,800
John Jackson (16⅔%)	96,000
Total	$444,000

On June 1, Year 1, Edward Sidney was admitted to the partnership when he acquired, for $132,000, a proportionate interest from Newton and Sharman in the net assets and income of the partnership. As a result of this transaction, Sidney acquired a one-fifth interest in the net assets and income of the partnership. Assuming that implied goodwill is not to be recorded, what is the combined gain realized by Newton and Sharman on the sale of a portion of their interests in the partnership to Sidney?
a $0   **b** $43,200   **c** $62,400   **d** $82,000

3 Adonis and Brutus share net income and losses in the ratio of 7:3, respectively. On November 5, Year 4, their capital account balances were as follows:

Adonis $70,000
Brutus 60,000

Adonis and Brutus agreed to admit Cato as a partner with a one-third interest in the partnership capital and net income or losses for an investment of $50,000. The new partnership will begin with total capital of $180,000. Immediately after Cato's admission to the partnership, what are the capital account balances of Adonis, Brutus, and Cato, respectively?

a $60,000, $60,000, $60,000
b $63,000, $57,000, $60,000
c $63,333, $56,667, $60,000
d $70,000, $60,000, $50,000

Questions **4** and **5** are based on the following information:
Presented below is the condensed balance sheet of the partnership of Kane, Clark, and Lane, who share income and losses in the ratio of 6:3:1, respectively.

Assets

Cash	$ 85,000
Other assets	415,000
Total assets	$500,000

Liabilities & Partners' Capital

Liabilities	$ 80,000
Kane, capital	252,000
Clark, capital	126,000
Lane, capital	42,000
Total liabilities & partners' capital	$500,000

4 The assets and liabilities in the above balance sheet are fairly valued, and the partnership wishes to admit Bayer with a 25% interest in the capital and income without recording goodwill or bonus. How much should Bayer invest in cash or other assets?

a $70,000 **b** $105,000 **c** $125,000 **d** $140,000

5 Assume that the partners agree instead to sell Bayer 20% of their respective interests in capital and income for a total payment of $90,000. The payment by Bayer is to be made directly to the individual partners. The partners agree that implied goodwill is to be recorded prior to the acquisition by Bayer. What are the capital account balances of Kane, Clark, and Lane, respectively, after the acquisition by Bayer?

a $198,000, $99,000, $33,000
b $201,600, $100,800, $33,600
c $216,000, $108,000, $36,000
d $255,600, $127,800, $42,600

Ex. 1-2 Monte Whipple, a partner in the Deep Venture Partnership, has a 30% participation in net income or losses. Whipple's capital account had a net decrease of $60,000 during Year 4. During Year 4, Whipple withdrew $130,000 (debited to his capital account) and invested assets with a current fair value of $25,000. Compute the net income of the Deep Venture Partnership for Year 4.

Ex. 1-3 The partnership contract of the Dunin, Lum & Beers Partnership provided that Dunin as managing partner should receive a bonus equal to 20% of earnings and that the remaining earnings should be divided 40% each to Dunin and Lum and 20% to Beers. Earnings for the first year (before the bonus) amounted to $63,600.

Explain two alternative ways in which the bonus provision could be interpreted. Compute the division of the year's earnings under each alternative.

Ex. 1-4 Emma Neal and Sally Drew are partners sharing net income or losses equally; each has a capital account balance of $100,000. Drew (with the consent of Neal) sold one-fifth of her interest to her daughter Paula for $25,000, with payment to be made in five annual instalments without any interest charge.

Prepare a journal entry to record the change in ownership, and explain why you would or would not recommend a change in the valuation of net assets in the accounting records of the partnership.

Ex. 1-5 L and M are partners with capital account balances of $70,000 each who share net income or losses equally. The partners agree to admit N to a one-third interest in net assets and a one-third share in net income or losses for N's investment of $100,000 in the firm. Assume that the net assets are fairly valued and that N's admission is recorded by allowing a bonus to L and M.

Prepare a journal entry to record the admission of N to the partnership.

Ex. 1-6 Assume that A and B share earnings and losses in a 60:40 ratio. Their capital account balances are A, $60,000 and B, $40,000. They agree to admit C to a 30% interest in net assets and a 20% interest in earnings for C's investment of $51,000. The new income-sharing ratio is to be 48:32:20 for A, B, and C, respectively. The partners are discussing whether to record the admission of C by a bonus to A and B or by recording goodwill.

What would be the amount of the bonus to A and B, respectively? What would be the total goodwill implied by C's investment? Would the goodwill method be more advantageous to C if the goodwill were written off in full two years later? What would be the dollar amount of the advantage or disadvantage to C from use of the goodwill method?

Ex. 1-7 The partnership of Timish and Hamilton was formed on March 1. The current fair values of the assets invested by each partner are as follows:

	Timish	Hamilton
Cash	$ 25,000	$35,000
Inventories		55,000
Land		25,000
Building		75,000
Equipment	115,000	

The building is subject to a mortgage loan of $30,000, which is to be assumed by the partnership. The partnership contract provides that Timish and Hamilton share net income and losses 40% and 60%, respectively.

a Compute the balance of Hamilton's capital account on March 1, assuming that each partner is credited for the full amount of net assets invested.

b If the partnership contract provides that the partners initially should have an equal interest in partnership capital with no recognition of intangible assets, what would be the balance in Timish's capital account on March 1?

Ex. 1-8 Lewis and Mason have capital account balances at the beginning of the year of $40,000 and $45,000, respectively. They share net income and losses as follows: (1)

8% interest on beginning capital balances, (2) salary allowance of $15,000 to Lewis and $7,500 to Mason, and (3) remainder in 3:2 ratio. The partnership reported net income of $10,000 for the current year, before interest and salary allowances to partners.

a Show how the net income of $10,000 should be divided between Lewis and Mason.

b Assuming that Lewis and Mason simply agree to share earnings in a 3:2 ratio with a minimum of $15,000 guaranteed to Mason, show how the net income of $10,000 should be divided between Lewis and Mason.

Ex. 1-9 Activity in the capital accounts for Hare and Ida for Year 10 follows:

	Hare	Ida
Balances, Jan. 1	$20,000	$40,000
Investment, July 1	10,000	
Withdrawal, Oct. 1		20,000

Net income for the year amounted to $24,000 before interest or salary allowances. Determine the division of the net income under each of the following assumptions:

a The partnership contract is silent as to sharing of net income and losses.

b Net income and losses are divided on the basis of average capital account balances (not including the net income or loss for the current year).

c Net income and losses are divided on the basis of beginning capital account balances.

d Net income and losses are divided on the basis of ending capital account balances (not including the net income for the current year).

Ex. 1-10 Floyd Austin and Samuel Bradford are partners who share net income and losses equally and have equal capital account balances. The net assets of the partnership have a carrying amount of $40,000. Jason Crade is admitted to the partnership with a one-third interest in earnings and net assets. To acquire this interest, Crade invests $17,000 cash in the partnership.

Prepare journal entries to show two methods of recording the admission of Crade in the accounting records of the partnership. State the conditions (if any) under which each method would be appropriate.

Ex. 1-11 A and B have capital account balances of $15,000 and $10,000, respectively. They share net income and losses in a 3:1 ratio. What journal entries would be made to record the admission of C to the partnership under each of the following conditions?

a C invests $15,000 for a one-fourth interest in net assets; the total partnership capital after C's admission is to be $40,000.

b C invests $15,000, of which $5,000 is considered a bonus to A and B. In conjunction with the admission of C, the carrying amount of the inventories is increased by $8,000. C's capital account is recorded at $10,000.

Ex. 1-12 Paul and Quinn formed a partnership on January 2, Year 4, and agreed to share net income and losses 90% and 10%, respectively. Paul invested cash of $25,000. Quinn invested no assets but had a specialized expertise and managed the firm full time. There were no withdrawals during the year. The partnership contract provided for the following:

(1) Partners' capital accounts are to be credited annually with interest at 5% of beginning capital account balances.

(2) Quinn is to be paid a salary of $1,000 a month.

(3) Quinn is to receive a bonus of 20% of income before deduction of salary, bonus, and interest on partners' capital account balances.

(4) Bonus, interest, and Quinn's salary are to be considered expenses.

The Year 4 income statement for the partnership includes the following:

Revenue	$96,450
Expenses (including salary, interest, and bonus to Quinn)	49,700
Net income	$46,750

Compute Quinn's bonus for Year 4.

Ex. 1-13 On June 30, Year 2, the balance sheet for the partnership of Tanabe, Usui, and Seashore and their respective income-sharing percentages were as follows:

Assets

Current assets	$185,000
Plant assets (net)	200,000
Total assets	$385,000

Liabilities & Partners' Capital

Accounts payable	$ 85,000
Tanabe, loan	15,000
Tanabe, capital (20%)	70,000
Usui, capital (20%)	65,000
Seashore, capital (60%)	150,000
Total liabilities & partners' capital	$385,000

Tanabe decided to retire from the partnership, and by mutual agreement the plant assets were adjusted to their current fair value of $260,000. The partnership paid $92,000 cash for Tanabe's equity in the partnership, exclusive of the loan, which was repaid in full. No goodwill was recorded in this transaction.

Prepare journal entries to record the adjustment of assets to current fair value and Tanabe's retirement from the partnership.

Ex. 1-14 The accountant for the Fox, Gee & Hay Partnership prepared the following journal entries during the year ended August 31, Year 10:

Year 9

Sept. 1	Cash	50,000	
	Goodwill	150,000	
	Fox, Capital ($150,000 × 0.25)		37,500
	Gee, Capital ($150,000 × 0.75)		112,500
	Hay, Capital		50,000

To record admission of Hay for a 20% interest in net assets, with goodwill credited to Fox and Gee in their former income-sharing ratio. Goodwill is computed as follows:

Implied total capital, based on Hay's investment	
($50,000 × 5)	$250,000
Less: Net assets prior to Hay's	
admission	100,000
Goodwill	$150,000

Aug. 31 Income Summary   30,000
             Fox, Capital ($30,000 × 0.20)   6,000
             Gee, Capital ($30,000 × 0.60)   18,000
             Hay, Capital ($30,000 × 0.20)   6,000
             To divide net income for the year in the residual income-
             sharing ratio of Fox, 20%; Gee, 60%; Hay, 20%. Pro-
             vision in partnership contract requiring $40,000 an-
             nual salary allowance to Hay is disregarded because
             net income is only $30,000.

Prepare journal entries on August 31, Year 10, to correct the accounting records, which have not been closed for the year ended August 31, Year 10. Assume that Hay's admission to the partnership should have been recorded by the bonus method.

CASES

Case 1-1 When asked how the organizers of a business enterprise might choose between a partnership and a corporation in order to minimize the burden of taxation, an accounting student replied as follows:

"The choice is very simple. Organization as a partnership will result in only one income tax, that is, the tax on individual income. If the enterprise is incorporated, it must pay income taxes, and in addition the shareholders must pay income taxes when the net income of the corporation is distributed to them. Consequently, the partnership form of organization always provides a lesser burden of taxation."

Instructions Do you agree with the student? Explain.

Case 1-2 X, Y, and Z, partners who share net income and losses equally, reported operating income of $30,000 for the first year of operations. However, near the end of the year, they learned of two unfavourable developments: (a) the bankruptcy of Sasha, maker of a two-year promissory note for $20,000 payable to Partner X that had been endorsed to the partnership by Partner X at the face amount as X's original investment; and (b) the appearance on the market of new competing patented devices that rendered worthless a patent transferred to the partnership by Partner Y at a value of $10,000 as part of Y's original investment.

The partnership had retained the promissory note with the expectation of discounting it when cash was needed. Quarterly interest payments had been received regularly prior to the bankruptcy of Sasha, but present prospects were for no further collections of interest or principal.

Partner Z states that the $30,000 operating income should be divided $10,000 to each partner, with the $20,000 loss on the note debited to the capital account of Partner X and the $10,000 loss on the patent debited to the capital account of Partner Y.

Instructions Do you agree with Partner Z? Explain.

Case 1-3 Sally Decker and Jane Evanson have been partners for many years and have shared net income and losses equally. They own and operate a resort hotel that includes a golf course and other recreational facilities. Decker has maintained a larger capital investment than Evanson, but Evanson has devoted much more time to the management of the hotel.

The hotel is located in one of the fastest-growing areas in the country and has been expanding rapidly. To help meet the problems of expansion, the partners admit

Laura Fane as a partner with a one-third interest in net assets and earnings. Fane is known as an excellent administrator and has ample cash to invest for her share in the partnership. You are retained by the partnership to give advice on any accounting issue created by the admission of Fane as a partner.

Instructions List the accounting issues that deserve consideration. Prepare a set of recommendations to guide the partners in dealing with them.

Case 1-4 Mark Granich and Mike Pickett formed a partnership on January 2. Granich invested cash of $50,000 and Pickett invested cash of $20,000 and marketable securities (short-term investments) with a current fair value of $80,000. A portion of the securities was sold at carrying amount in January to provide funds for operations.

   The partnership contract stated that net income and losses were to be divided in the capital ratio and that each partner was entitled to withdraw $1,000 monthly. Granich withdrew $1,000 on the last day of each month, but Pickett made no withdrawals until July 1, when he withdrew all the securities that had not been sold by the partnership. The securities that Pickett withdrew had a current fair value of $41,000 when invested in the partnership on January 2 and a current fair value of $62,000 on July 1 when withdrawn. Pickett instructed the accountant for the partnership to record the transaction by reducing his capital account by $41,000, which was done. Income from operations for the first year amounted to $24,000. Income tax issues may be ignored.

Instructions You are asked to determine the proper division of net income for the first year. If the income-sharing provision of the partnership contract is at all unsatisfactory, state the assumptions you would make to arrive at an equitable interpretation of the partners' intentions. What adjustments, if any, do you believe should be made in the accounting records of the partnership?

PROBLEMS

1-1 The Leeds & Mayes Partnership was organized and began operations on March 1, Year 1. On that date, Leeann Leeds invested $150,000, and Marilyn Mayes invested land and building with current fair values of $80,000 and $100,000, respectively. Mayes also invested $60,000 in the partnership on November 1, Year 1, because of a shortage of working capital. The partnership contract includes the following income-sharing plan:

	Leeds	Mayes
Annual salary	$18,000	$24,000
Annual interest on average capital account balances	10%	10%
Remainder	50%	50%

The annual salary may be withdrawn by each partner in 12 monthly instalments.

   During the year ended February 28, Year 2, the Leeds & Mayes Partnership had net sales of $500,000, cost of goods sold of $280,000, and operating expenses of $100,000 (excluding partners' salaries and interest on partners' average capital account balances). Each partner had monthly cash drawings in accordance with the partnership contract.

Instructions
a Prepare a condensed income statement for the Leeds & Mayes Partnership for the year ended February 28, Year 2. Show the division of net income in a supporting exhibit.
b Prepare a statement of partners' capital for the Leeds & Mayes Partnership for the year ended February 28, Year 2.

1-2 Grove and Hayes share net income or losses 40% and 60%, respectively. On January 2, Year 6, Lisa Ivan was admitted to the new Grove, Hayes & Ivan Partnership by the investment of the net assets of her highly profitable single proprietorship. The partners agreed to the following current fair values of the identifiable net assets of Ivan's single proprietorship:

Current assets	$ 70,000
Plant assets	230,000
Total assets	$300,000
Less: Liabilities	200,000
Net assets	$100,000

The balance sheet of the Grove & Hayes Partnership on December 31, Year 5, follows:

GROVE & HAYES PARTNERSHIP

Condensed Balance Sheet

December 31, Year 5

Assets		Liabilities & Partners' Capital	
Current assets	$100,000	Liabilities	$300,000
Plant assets (net)	500,000	Louis Grove, capital	200,000
		Ray Hayes, capital	100,000
Total	$600,000	Total	$600,000

Ivan's capital account was credited for $120,000. The partners agreed further that the carrying amounts of the net assets of the Grove & Hayes Partnership were equal to their current fair values, and that the accounting records of the old partnership should be used for the new partnership. The following income-sharing plan was adopted for the new partnership:

(1) A bonus of 10% of net income after deduction of the bonus to Ivan as managing partner
(2) Remaining net income or loss as follows: 30% to Grove, 40% to Hayes, and 30% to Ivan

For the year ended December 31, Year 6, the Grove, Hayes & Ivan Partnership had net income of $55,000 before the bonus to Ivan.

Instructions Prepare journal entries for the Grove, Hayes & Ivan Partnership to record the following (include supporting computations in the explanations for the entries):

a The admission of Ivan to the partnership on January 2, Year 6.
b The division of net income for the year ended December 31, Year 6.

1-3 Donald and Erika formed a partnership at the beginning of Year 1. Their capital accounts show the following changes during Year 1:

	Donald	Erika
Original investment, Jan. 3, Year 1	$120,000	$180,000
Investments: May 1	15,000	
July 1		15,000
Withdrawals: Nov. 1	(30,000)	(75,000)
Capital account balances, Dec. 31, Year 1	$105,000	$120,000

The net income for Year 1, before allowances for salaries or interest, was $69,600. The net income included an extraordinary gain of $12,000.

Instructions   Determine each partner's share of net income to the nearest dollar, assuming the following alternative income-sharing plans:

a The partnership contract is silent as to division of net income or loss.

b Income before extraordinary items is shared equally after allowance of 10% interest on average capital account balances (computed to the nearest month) and after allowance of $20,000 to Donald and $30,000 to Erika as salaries. Extraordinary items are shared in the ratio of original investments.

c Income before extraordinary items is shared on the basis of average capital account balances, and extraordinary items are shared on the basis of original investments.

d Income before extraordinary items is shared equally between Donald and Erika, after allowance of a 25% bonus to Erika based on income before extraordinary items after the bonus. Extraordinary items are shared on the basis of original investments.

1-4   The Alex, Baron & Crane Partnership was formed on January 2, Year 1. The original cash investments were as follows:

Alex	$ 96,000
Baron	144,000
Crane	216,000

According to the partnership contract, net income or loss is to be divided among the partners as follows:

(1) Salaries of $14,400 for Alex, $12,000 for Baron, and $13,600 for Crane
(2) Interest at 12% on the average capital account balances during the year
(3) Remainder divided equally

Net income for the year ended December 31, Year 1, was $92,080. Alex invested an additional $24,000 in the partnership on July 1; Crane withdrew $36,000 from the partnership on October 1; and Alex, Baron, and Crane withdrew $15,000 each against their shares of net income for the year.

Instructions

a Prepare a working paper to divide the net income among the partners. Show supporting computations.

b Prepare a statement of partners' capital for the year ended December 31, Year 1.

1-5   C and D wish to acquire the partnership interest of their partner E on July 10, Year 3. Partnership assets are to be used to acquire E's partnership interest. The balance sheet for the CDE Partnership on that date shows the following:

CDE PARTNERSHIP

Balance Sheet
July 10, Year 3

Assets		Liabilities & Partners' Capital	
Cash	$ 74,000	Liabilities	$ 45,000
Receivables (net)	36,000	C, capital	120,000
Equipment (net)	135,000	D, capital	60,000
Goodwill	30,000	E, capital	50,000
Total	$275,000	Total	$275,000

C, D, and E share earnings in the ratio of 3:2:1, respectively.

Instructions Record E's withdrawal under each of the following assumptions:

a E is paid $54,000, and the excess paid over the balance of E's capital account balance is recorded as a bonus to E from C and D.

b E is paid $45,000 and the difference is recorded as a bonus to C and D from E.

c E is paid $45,000, and goodwill currently in the accounting records of the partnership is reduced by the total amount implicit in the transaction.

d E accepts cash of $40,500 and equipment with a current fair value of $9,000. The equipment cost $30,000 and was 60% depreciated, with no residual value.

Record any gain or loss on the disposal of the equipment directly in the partners' capital accounts.

1-6 Linz and Ohno started a partnership in Year 1. Each partner invested $12,000 cash and was entitled to receive 50% of net income and losses. At the beginning of Year 3, Ruiz was admitted to the partnership for an investment of $14,500. Ruiz's admission to the partnership was recorded by a debit to Cash and a credit to Ruiz, Capital for $14,500. The income-sharing ratio for the new partnership was set at 3:2:1 for Linz, Ohno, and Ruiz, respectively.

Additional information is given below for each of the first four years ending on December 31:

	Year 1	Year 2	Year 3	Year 4	Total
Net income as reported . . .	$18,000	$27,500	$36,000	$44,700	$126,200
Drawings (equal amounts					
for each partner)	15,000	22,000	27,000	15,600	79,600
Accounts receivable not					
recorded at year-end . . .	5,000	8,000	15,000	18,000	46,000
Merchandise erroneously					
omitted from inventories					
at year-end	3,000	4,500	6,600	11,300	25,400
Accounts payable not					
recorded at year-end . . .	6,000	4,000	10,000	17,500	37,500
Capital account balances					
at end of year:					
Linz	13,500	16,250	25,250	42,400	
Ohno	13,500	16,250	19,250	28,950	
Ruiz			11,500	13,750	

Each year the income statement was prepared on the cash basis of accounting; that is, accounts receivable were not recorded and payments for merchandise were treated as cost of goods sold. All accounts receivable are considered collectible.

Instructions

a Prepare a statement of partners' capital covering the four-year period based on the accrual basis of accounting. Combine net income and drawings for Years 1 and 2 and for Years 3 and 4. Prepare an exhibit to restate net income from the cash to the accrual basis of accounting for the first two-year period (Years 1 and 2) and for the second two-year period (Years 3 and 4).

b Prepare a balance sheet for the partnership on December 31, Year 4. Prepare an exhibit to compute cash (assuming that the only assets and liabilities are cash, accounts receivable, inventories, and accounts payable).

c Using the information given in the problem and the partners' capital account balances on December 31, Year 4, determined in part **a**, prepare a journal entry to restate the accounting records of the partnership from the cash basis of accounting to the accrual basis of accounting.

1-7 Allen, Bates, and Cray share net income and losses in a 3:2:1 ratio, respectively. The partnership has been successful, as indicated by the data below concerning the partners' capital accounts.

At this time, Cray became ill and retired from the partnership, receiving $30,000 cash. Allen and Bates decided to continue the partnership and to share net income and losses equally. However, as a condition of this change in the income-sharing ratio, Bates agreed to invest an additional $12,000 cash in the firm. The investment was made, but the partners had difficulty in agreeing on the method to be used in recording Cray's withdrawal from the firm. Allen wanted to record the entire amount of goodwill of the partnership implied by the amount paid for Cray's interest. Bates argued that the amount of goodwill to be recorded should not be larger than the amount paid for Cray's share of the partnership goodwill. The accountant for the firm pointed out that the income-sharing ratio was being changed and suggested that this was a reason for recognizing the goodwill of the partnership prior to Cray's withdrawal. Cray suggested that the entire controversy over goodwill could be avoided by recording any amount paid to a withdrawing partner in excess of that partner's capital account balance as a bonus from the other partners.

	Original investments	Retained earnings	Present balances
Allen, capital	$38,000	$42,000	$ 80,000
Bates, capital	21,300	28,000	49,300
Cray, capital	11,500	12,500	24,000
Totals	$70,800	$82,500	$153,300

Instructions
a Prepare journal entries in the accounting records of the partnership required by the recommendation of each of the three partners (three independent sets of journal entries).
b Assume that the partnership is sold to Western Company for $171,300 cash shortly after the withdrawal of Cray, with Western assuming the partnership liabilities. Prepare analyses showing how the cash would be divided between Allen and Bates under each of the three alternative methods for handling the withdrawal of Cray as previously described.
c For this portion of the problem, assume the same data as to original investments and retained earnings by Allen, Bates, and Cray. However, rather than having Cray withdraw from the partnership, assume that the three partners agree to admit Dale as a fourth partner for an investment of $45,100 cash in the firm. Dale is given a 25% interest in the net assets and a 25% share in net income and losses. Allen, Bates, and Cray will share the remaining 75% of net income and losses in the same original ratio existing among them prior to admission of Dale to the firm. Allen, Bates, and Cray each withdraw $10,000 cash from the partnership. Prepare the journal entries needed to record the withdrawals of cash and the admission of Dale to the partnership under (1) the goodwill method, and (2) the bonus method.
d Assume the same facts presented in c above, and further that the partnership net assets are sold for $176,400 shortly after the admission of Dale to the firm. The purchaser assumes the partnership liabilities. Prepare an analysis showing how the cash would be distributed among the four partners if the admission of Dale had been recorded by use of (1) the goodwill method, and (2) the bonus method.

1-8 A paint store operated as a partnership by D, E, and F was completely destroyed by fire on December 31, Year 12. The only assets remaining were the bank account with a balance of $26,765 and a claim against an insurance company that was settled for $220,000 early in Year 13. All accounting records were destroyed in the fire. All creditors of the partnership have presented their claims, which amounted in total to $32,000 on December 31, Year 12.

The present partnership was formed on January 2, Year 11. Prior to that time D and E had been partners for several years and had shared net income and losses equally. No written partnership contract was prepared for the new firm, and a dispute has arisen as to the terms of the partners' oral contract for sharing net income and losses. The new firm has not used the services of professional accountants, except for assistance with the preparation of tax returns on December 31, Year 11.

You are retained by the partnership to determine the income-sharing plan that was followed for Year 11 and to apply this same plan to the events of Year 12, thus determining the present equity of each partner in the partnership. The partners agree in writing that the income-sharing plan used in Year 11 was correct and should be applied in an identical manner to the net income or loss for Year 12. The information available to you consists of a copy of the financial statements filed for tax purposes for Year 11, and a statement of the withdrawals made by the partners during Year 12. This latter statement has been agreed to in writing by the partners and appears as follows:

	D	E	F	Combined
Merchandise	$ 1,500	$850	$2,300	$ 4,650
Salaries	8,000		6,000	14,000
Other cash withdrawals	750			750
Total withdrawals	$10,250	$850	$8,300	$19,400

Partner D explained to you that the $750 in "other cash withdrawals" resulted from the partnership's accidental payment of a personal debt of D when the invoice was sent to the partnership address.

From the partnership tax return for Year 11, you obtain the following information:

	D	E	F	Combined
Capital balances, Jan 1, Year 11	$40,000	$50,000	$92,500	$182,500
Capital balances, Dec. 31, Year 11	$51,000	$61,000	$85,300	$197,300
Division of net income for Year 11:				
Salaries	$12,000	$15,000	$ 6,000	$ 33,000
Interest on capital balances . . .	2,000	2,500	4,625	9,125
Remainder (15:30:55 ratio) . . .	6,821	13,643	25,011	45,475
Totals	$20,821	$31,143	$35,636	$ 87,600

Instructions

a Prepare a statement of partners' capital for the D, E & F Partnership for Year 12, supported by a summary showing the computation of net income or loss for Year 12 and the division of the net income or loss among the partners in accordance with the income-sharing plan followed in Year 11. Round computations to the nearest dollar.

b How much cash will each partner receive if the D, E & F Partnership is terminated early in Year 13?

1-9 The Beran & Curb Partnership has maintained its accounting records on the accrual basis of accounting, except for the method of handling credit losses. Doubtful accounts expense has been recognized by a direct write-off to expense at the time specific accounts receivable were determined to be uncollectible.

The partners are anticipating the admission of a third member, Franco Meglio, to the firm, and they retain you to review the accounting records before this action is taken. You suggest that the firm change retroactively to the allowance method of accounting for doubtful accounts receivable so that the planning for admission of Meglio can be based on the accrual basis of accounting. The following information is available:

Year accounts receivable originated	Accounts receivable written off			Additional estimated uncollectible accounts
	Year 2	Year 3	Year 4	
1	$1,200	$ 200		
2	1,500	1,300	$ 600	$ 450
3		1,800	1,400	1,250
4			2,200	4,800
Totals . . .	$2,700	$3,300	$4,200	$6,500

The partners shared earnings equally until Year 4. In Year 4 the income-sharing plan was changed as follows: salaries of $8,000 and $6,000 to be allowed Beran and Curb, respectively; the remainder to be divided 60% to Beran and 40% to Curb. Net income of the partnership for Year 4 was $42,000.

Instructions

a Prepare a journal entry giving effect to the change in accounting method for doubtful accounts expense. Support the entry with a summary showing changes in net income for the year.

b Assume that after you prepared the journal entry in **a** above, Beran's capital is reported at $48,000 and Curb's capital is reported at $22,000. If Franco Meglio invested $30,000 for a 20% interest in net assets of the partnership and a 25% share in net income, illustrate by journal entries two methods that may be used to record Meglio's admission to the partnership. Any increase in the capital of Beran and Curb is to be divided 60% and 40%. What method would be more advantageous to Meglio if the goodwill is later substantiated through a sale of the partnership at a gain? What method would be more advantageous to Meglio if we assume that the goodwill is written off in the year following his admission to the firm?

1-10 The law firm of L, M, and N was organized on January 3, Year 1, when the three attorneys decided to combine their individual law practices. The partners reached agreement on the following matters:

(1) All partners would invest in the firm the assets and liabilities of their single proprietorships and would be credited with capital accounts equal to the carrying amounts of the net assets taken over by the partnership. The partners personally guaranteed that the accounts receivable invested were collectible. The assets and liabilities acquired by the partnership in this manner were as follows:

	L	M	N
Cash	$10,000	$10,000	$10,000
Accounts receivable	28,000	12,000	32,000
Law library and furniture	8,600	5,000	12,400
Accumulated depreciation	(4,800)	(3,000)	(9,400)
Total assets	$41,800	$24,000	$45,000
Less: Accounts payable	1,600	3,800	4,400
Net assets (capital invested)	$40,200	$20,200	$40,600

(2) The partners decided to occupy N's office space until the lease expired on June 30, Year 1. The monthly rental was $1,200, but the partners agreed that this was an excessive rate for the space provided and that $900 monthly would be reasonable. They agreed that the excess rent would be charged to N at the end of the year. When the lease expired on June 30, Year 1, the partners moved to a new office with a monthly rental of $1,000.

(3) The income-sharing agreement did not provide for salaries to the partners but specified that individual partners should receive 20% of the gross fees billed to their respective clients during the first year of the partnership. The balance of the fees after deduction of operating expenses was to be credited to the partners' capital accounts as follows: L, 40%; M, 40%; N, 20%.

A new partner, Z, was admitted to the partnership on April 1, Year 1; Z was to receive 20% of the fees from new clients after April 1 after deduction of expenses applicable to these fees. Expenses were to be apportioned to the new clients' fees in the same ratio that total expenses, other than doubtful accounts expense, bore to total gross fees.

(4) Fees were billed during Year 1 as follows:

L's clients	$ 44,000
M's clients	24,000
N's clients	22,000
New clients acquired after Jan. 3, Year 1:	
Prior to Apr. 1	6,000
After Apr. 1	24,000
Total revenue from fees	$120,000

(5) Total expenses for Year 1 were $38,700, excluding depreciation and doubtful accounts expense but including the total amount paid for rent. The partnership uses the direct write-off method for doubtful accounts expense. Depreciation was to be computed at the rate of 10% on original cost to individual partners of depreciable assets invested by them. Depreciable assets were acquired during Year 1 for $10,000, on which one-half year's depreciation was to be taken.

(6) Cash withdrawals debited to the partners' drawing accounts during Year 1 were as follows:

L	$10,400
M	8,800
N	11,600
Z	5,000
Total	$35,800

(7) Accounts receivable invested by L in the amount of $2,400 and by M in the amount of $900 proved to be uncollectible. Also, a new client billed in March

for $3,000 had received a discharge in bankruptcy, in which a settlement of 40 cents on the dollar was made.

Instructions Prepare a statement of partners' capital for the year ended December 31, Year 1. Show supporting computations and disregard income taxes.

1-11 The Ebony Partnership engaged you to adjust its accounting records and convert them to the accrual basis of accounting in anticipation of the admission of Orr as a new partner. Some ledger accounts were on the accrual basis and others were on the cash basis. The accounting records were closed on December 31, Year 5, by the accountant for the partnership, who prepared the following general ledger trial balance:

EBONY PARTNERSHIP

Trial Balance
December 31, Year 5

Cash	$ 18,250	
Accounts receivable	40,000	
Inventories	26,000	
Land	79,000	
Buildings	50,000	
Accumulated depreciation of buildings		$ 2,000
Equipment	56,000	
Accumulated depreciation of equipment		8,250
Goodwill	5,000	
Accounts payable		64,000
Reserve for future inventory losses		10,000
Lui, capital		60,000
Mason, capital		80,000
Neary, capital		50,000
Totals	$274,250	$274,250

Your inquiries disclosed the following:

(1) The partnership was organized on January 2, Year 4, with no provision in the partnership contract for the sharing of net income and losses. During Year 4, net income was distributed equally among the partners. The partnership contract was amended effective January 1, Year 5, to provide for the following income-sharing ratio: Lui, 50%; Mason, 30%; and Neary, 20%. The amended partnership contract also stated that the accounting records were to be maintained on the accrual basis of accounting and that any adjustments necessary for Year 5 should be allocated according to the Year 5 distribution of earnings.

(2) The following amounts were not recorded as prepayments or accruals:

	December 31,	
	Year 5	Year 4
Unexpired insurance	$1,450	$ 650
Advances from customers	200	1,100
Accrued interest payable		300

The advances from customers were recorded as sales in the year the cash was received.

(3) In Year 5, a provision of $10,000 was recorded (by a debit to expense) for anticipated declines in inventory prices. You convinced the partners that the provision was unnecessary and should be removed from the accounting records.

(4) Equipment acquired for $4,400 on January 3, Year 5, was debited to expense. This equipment has an estimated economic life of 10 years and an estimated residual value of $400. The partnership depreciates its equipment by the declining-balance method at twice the straight-line rate.

(5) The partners agreed to establish an allowance for doubtful accounts at 2% of current accounts receivable and 5% of past-due accounts. On December 31, Year 4, the partnership had $54,000 of accounts receivable, of which only $4,000 was past due. On December 31, Year 5, 15% of accounts receivable was past due, of which $4,000 represented sales made in Year 4, and was considered collectible. The partnership had written off uncollectible accounts receivable in the year the accounts became worthless as follows:

	Year 5	Year 4
Year 5 accounts receivable	$ 800	
Year 4 accounts receivable	1,000	$250

(6) Goodwill was recorded improperly in Year 5 and credited to the partners' capital accounts in the income-sharing ratio in recognition of an increase in the value of the partnership resulting from improved sales volume. The partners agreed to write off the goodwill before Orr was admitted to the partnership.

Instructions

a Prepare an adjusted trial balance for the partnership on December 31, Year 5, on the accrual basis of accounting. All adjustments affecting net income should be made directly to partners' capital accounts. Number and explain the adjustments in the working paper. Show supporting computations. (Do not prepare formal financial statements or formal journal entries. The working paper should have pairs of columns for Unadjusted Trial Balance, Adjustments, and Adjusted Trial Balance.)

b Without prejudice to your solution to part **a** above, assume that the net assets of the partnership were properly valued, that the adjusted total of the partners' capital on December 31, Year 5, was $196,000, and that Orr invested $75,000 in the partnership. Compute the amount of goodwill that might be recorded in the partnership accounting records under each of the following alternative assumptions, and allocate the goodwill to the partners:

(1) Orr is to be granted a one-fourth interest in the partnership. The other partners will retain their 50:30:20 income-sharing ratio for the remaining three-fourths interest in earnings.

(2) The partnership has been earning, and expects to continue to earn, an annual return of 22% on invested capital. The normal rate of return for comparable partnerships is 20%. The superior earnings (expected earnings of the new partnership in excess of the normal rate of return) are to be capitalized as goodwill at 25%. The partners are to share earnings (including any goodwill) in the following ratio: Lui, 40%; Mason, 30%; Neary, 10%; Orr, 20%.

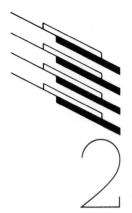

2 PARTNERSHIP LIQUIDATION

LIQUIDATION OF A PARTNERSHIP

The meaning of liquidation

The liquidation of a partnership means winding up its activities, usually by selling assets, paying liabilities, and distributing any remaining cash to the partners. In some cases, the partnership net assets may be sold as a unit; in other cases, the assets may be sold in instalments, and most or all of the cash received must be used to pay creditors. A business enterprise that has ended normal operations and is in the process of converting its assets to cash and making settlements with its creditors is said to be *in liquidation*, or in the process of being liquidated. This process of liquidation may be completed quickly, or it may require several months or even years.

The term *liquidation* also is used in a narrower sense to mean the payment of liabilities; however, in this chapter we use it only in the broader sense of bringing to a close the activities of a partnership. Another term commonly used in liquidation is *realization*, which means the conversion of assets to cash.

When the decision is made to liquidate a partnership, the accounting records should be adjusted and closed, and the net income or loss for the final period of operations entered in the capital accounts of the partners.

The liquidation process usually begins with the sale of noncash assets. The losses or gains from realization of assets should be divided among the partners in the income-sharing ratio and entered in their capital accounts. The amounts shown as their respective equities at this point are the basis for settlement. However, before any payment to partners, all outside creditors must be paid in full. If the cash obtained from the sale of assets is insufficient to pay liabilities in full, any unpaid creditor may act to enforce collection from the personal assets of any partner, regardless of whether that partner has a positive or negative capital account balance. As pointed out in

Chapter 1, a partnership is viewed as an entity for many purposes such as changes in partners, but it cannot use the shield of a separate entity to protect partners personally against the claims of partnership creditors.

Division of losses and gains during liquidation

The underlying theme in accounting for the liquidation of a partnership may be stated as follows: ***Distribute the loss or gain from the realization of assets before distributing the cash***. As assets are sold, any loss or gain is allocated to the partners' capital accounts in the income-sharing ratio. The income-sharing ratio used during the operation of the partnership also is applicable to the losses and gains during liquidation, unless the partners have a different agreement.

When the net loss or gain from liquidation is divided among the partners, the final balances in the partners' capital and loan accounts will be equal to the cash available for distribution to them. ***Payments are then made in the amounts of the partners' respective equities in the partnership.***

Distribution of cash or other assets to partners

The amount of cash, if any, that a partner is entitled to receive in a liquidation cannot be determined until partners' capital accounts have been adjusted for any loss or gain on the realization of the assets. Strictly interpreted, this reasoning might indicate that no cash can be distributed to a partner until after all the assets have been sold, because the net loss or gain will not be known until the sale of all assets has been completed. In this chapter we illustrate a series of liquidations in which the realization of assets is completed before any payments are made to partners. Also, we consider liquidation in instalments; that is, payments to partners after a portion of the assets has been sold and all liabilities paid, but with the final loss or gain from sale of the remaining assets not known. The instalment payments to partners are computed by a method that provides a safeguard against overpayment.

An important service by accountants to a partnership in liquidation is to determine proper distribution of cash or other assets to individual partners after the liabilities have been paid. The partners may choose to receive certain assets, such as automobiles or furniture, ***in kind*** rather than to convert such property to cash. Regardless of whether cash or other assets are distributed to partners, it is imperative to follow the basic rule that no distribution of assets may be made to partners until after all possible losses and liquidation expenses have been considered. Failure to follow this basic rule may result in overpayments to one or more partners and underpayments to others. If a partner who receives the overpayment is unable to return the excess payment, the person who authorized such payments may become personally liable for any losses sustained by the other partners.

The partnership acts list the order for distribution of cash by a liquidating partnership as (1) payment of creditors in full, (2) payment of partners' loan accounts, and (3) payment of partners' capital accounts. The indicated priority of parners' loans over partners' capital appears to be a legal fiction. This rule is nullified for all practical purposes by an established legal doctrine called the *right of offset*. If a partner's capital account has a debit balance (or even a potential debit balance depending on possible future losses), any credit balance in that partner's loan account must be offset against the deficiency (or potential deficiency) in the capital account. However, if a partner with a loan account receives any cash, the payment is recorded by a debit to the loan account.

Because of the right of offset, the total amount of cash received by a partner during liquidation always will be the same as if loans to the partnership had been recorded in the partner's capital account. Furthermore, the existence of a partner's loan account will not advance the time of payment to any partner during the liquidation. Consequently, in the preparation of a *statement of realization and liquidation* (see page 50) the number of columns may be reduced by combining the amount of a partner's loan with the amount shown in the partner's capital account. The statement of realization and liquidation then will include only one column for each partner; the first amount in the column will be the total equity (including any loans) of the partner at the beginning of liquidation.

Combining the capital and loan accounts of a partner in the statement of realization and liquidation does not imply combining these accounts in the ledger. Separate ledger accounts for capital and for loans should be maintained to provide a clear record of the terms under which assets were invested by the partners.

Final settlement with partners

The amount that each partner receives from the liquidation of a partnership will be equal to (1) the capital invested, whether recorded in a capital account or in a loan account; (2) a share of operating net income or loss minus drawings; and (3) a share of loss or gain from the realization of assets in the course of liquidation. In other words, each partner will receive in the settlement the amount of his or her equity in the partnership. The amount of a partner's equity is increased by the positive factors of investing capital and sharing in net income; it is decreased by the negative factors of drawings and sharing in net losses. If the negative factors are larger, the partner will have a capital deficiency (a debit balance in a capital account), and the partner must pay to the partnership the amount of such deficiency. Failure to make good a capital deficiency by payment to the partnership would mean that the partner had not lived up to the partnership contract for sharing net income or loss. This would cause the other partners to bear more than their contractual share of losses, and thus to receive less in settlement than their equities in the partnership.

Equity of each partner is sufficient to absorb loss from liquidation

Assume that A and B, who share net income and losses equally, decide to liquidate their partnership. A balance sheet on June 30, Year 5, just prior to liquidation, follows:

A & B PARTNERSHIP
Balance Sheet
June 30, Year 5

Assets		Liabilities & Partners' Capital	
Cash	$10,000	Liabilities	$20,000
Other assets	75,000	B, loan	20,000
		A, capital	40,000
		B, capital	5,000
Total	$85,000	Total	$85,000

As a first step in the liquidation, the noncash assets with a carrying amount of $75,000 are sold for cash of $35,000, with a resultant loss of $40,000 absorbed equally by A and B. Because B's capital account is only $5,000, it is necessary for the accountant to exercise the right of offset by transferring $15,000 from B's loan account to B's capital account. The statement of realization and liquidation below, covering the period July 1-15, Year 5, shows the division of the loss between the partners, the payment of creditors, and the distribution of the remaining cash to the partners. (The income-sharing ratio appears next to each partner's name.)

In the statement of realization and liquidation, B's loan account of $20,000 and capital account of $5,000 may be combined to obtain an equity of $25,000 for B. As stated earlier, such a procedure would be appropriate because the legal priority of a partner's loan account has no significance in determining either the total amount of cash paid to a partner or the timing of cash payments to partners during liquidation.

In the preceding illustration, partner A received cash of $20,000 and partner B received $5,000. Neither partner received payment until after creditors had been paid in full. Because assets consist entirely of $25,000 cash at this point, it is reasonable to assume that cheques to A and B for

A & B PARTNERSHIP
Statement of Realization and Liquidation
July 1–15, Year 5

	Assets				Partners' capital	
	Cash	Other	Liabilities	B, loan	A(50%)	B(50%)
Balances before liquidation	$10,000	$75,000	$20,000	$20,000	$40,000	$ 5,000
Sale of assets at a loss of $40,000	35,000	(75,000)			(20,000)	(20,000)
Balances	$45,000		$20,000	$20,000	$20,000	$(15,000)
Payment to creditors	(20,000)		(20,000)			
Balances	$25,000			$20,000	$20,000	$(15,000)
Offset B's capital deficit against loan account . .				(15,000)		15,000
Balances	$25,000			$ 5,000	$20,000	$ -0-
Payments to partners	(25,000)			(5,000)	(20,000)	-0-

$20,000 and $5,000, respectively, were written and delivered to the partners at the same time. It is apparent that a partner's loan account has no special significance in the liquidation process. Therefore, in succeeding illustrations we do not show a partner's loan account in a separate column of the statement of realization and liquidation. Whenever a partner's loan account is encountered, it may be combined with the partner's capital account balance in the statement of realization and liquidation.

Equity of one partner is not sufficient to absorb that partner's share of loss from liquidation

In this case, the loss on realization of assets when distributed in the income-sharing ratio results in a debit balance in the capital account of one of the partners. It may be assumed that the partner with a debit balance has no loan account, or that the total of the partner's capital account and loan account combined is less than the partner's share of the loss on realization. To fulfil an agreement to share a given percentage of partnership earnings, the partner must pay to the partnership sufficient cash to eliminate any capital deficiency. If the partner is unable to do so, the deficiency must be absorbed by the other partners as an additional loss to be shared in the same proportion as they have previously shared earnings among themselves. To illustrate, assume the balance sheet below for the D, E & F Partnership just prior to liquidation.

Balance sheet for partnership to be liquidated

D, E & F PARTNERSHIP
Balance Sheet
May 20, Year 10

Assets		Liabilities & Partners' Capital	
Cash	$ 20,000	Liabilities	$ 30,000
Other assets	80,000	D, capital	40,000
		E, capital	21,000
		F, capital	9,000
Total	$100,000	Total	$100,000

The income-sharing ratio is D, 20%; E, 40%; and F, 40%. The other assets with a carrying amount of $80,000 are sold for $50,000 cash, resulting in a loss of $30,000. Partner F is charged with 40% of this loss, or $12,000, which creates a deficiency of $3,000 in F's capital account. In the statement of realization and liquidation on page 52, it is assumed that F pays the $3,000 to the partnership.

Next, let us change one condition of the preceding illustration by assuming that partner F was not able to pay the $3,000 debt to the partnership. If the cash on hand after payment of creditors is to be distributed to D and E without a delay to determine the collectibility of the $3,000 claim against

F, the statement of realization and liquidation would appear as illustrated below.

The cash payments of $33,000 to D and $7,000 to E leave each of them with a sufficient credit balance to absorb their share of the additional loss if F is unable to pay the $3,000 debt to the partnership. The income-sharing ratio is 20% for D and 40% for E; consequently, the possible additional loss of $3,000 would be charged to them in the proportion of ²/₆ or $1,000 to D, and ⁴/₆ or $2,000 to E. The payment of the $40,000 cash available to partners is divided between them in a manner that reduces D's capital account balance to $1,000 and E's balance to $2,000.

Illustration of completed liquidation

D, E & F PARTNERSHIP

Statement of Realization and Liquidation

May 21–31, Year 10

	Assets			Partners' capital		
	Cash	Other	Liabilities	D(20%)	E(40%)	F(40%)
Balances before liquidation	$20,000	$80,000	$30,000	$40,000	$21,000	$ 9,000
Sale of assets at a loss of $30,000	50,000	(80,000)		(6,000)	(12,000)	(12,000)
Balances	$70,000		$30,000	$34,000	$ 9,000	$ (3,000)
Payment to creditors	(30,000)		(30,000)			
Balances	$40,000			$34,000	$ 9,000	$ (3,000)
Cash received from F	3,000					3,000
Balances	$43,000			$34,000	$ 9,000	$ -0-
Payments to partners	(43,000)			(34,000)	(9,000)	-0-

Illustration of incomplete liquidation

D, E & F PARTNERSHIP

Statement of Realization and Liquidation

May 21–31, Year 10

	Assets			Partners' capital		
	Cash	Other	Liabilities	D(20%)	E(40%)	F(40%)
Balances before liquidation	$20,000	$80,000	$30,000	$40,000	$21,000	$ 9,000
Sale of assets at a loss of $30,000	50,000	(80,000)		(6,000)	(12,000)	(12,000)
Balances	$70,000		$30,000	$34,000	$ 9,000	$ (3,000)
Payment to creditors	(30,000)		(30,000)			
Balances	$40,000			$34,000	$ 9,000	$ (3,000)
Payments to partners	(40,000)			(33,000)	(7,000)	
Balances				$ 1,000	$ 2,000	$ (3,000)

If the $3,000 is later collected from F, this amount will be divided $1,000 to D and $2,000 to E. The preceding statement of realization and liquidation then may be completed as follows:

Completion of
liquidation: deficiency
paid by Partner F

	Cash	D(20%)	E(40%)	F(40%)
Balance from page 52		$1,000	$2,000	$(3,000)
Cash received from F	$3,000			3,000
Payments to partners	(3,000)	(1,000)	(2,000)	

However, if the $3,000 due from F is determined to be uncollectible, the statement of realization and liquidation would be completed with the write-off of F's deficit shown as an additional loss absorbed by D and E as follows:

Completion of
liquidation: Partner F
unable to pay deficiency

	Cash	D(20%)	E(40%)	F(40%)
Balance from page 52		$1,000	$2,000	$(3,000)
Additional loss from inability to collect deficiency from F		(1,000)	(2,000)	3,000

Equities of two partners are not sufficient to absorb their shares of loss from liquidation

We already have observed that inability of a partner to make good a deficiency in a capital account causes an additional loss to the other partners. A partner may have sufficient capital, or combination of capital and loan accounts, to absorb any direct share of loss on the realization of assets, but not a sufficient equity to absorb additional actual or potential losses caused by inability of the partnership to collect the deficiency in another partner's capital account. In brief, one capital deficiency, if not collectible, may cause a second capital deficiency that may or may not be collectible.

Assume that J, K, L, and M, partners, share net income and losses 10%, 20%, 30%, and 40%, respectively. Their capital account balances for the period August 1–15, Year 4, are as shown in the statement of realization and liquidation on page 54. The assets are realized at a loss of $80,000, and creditors are paid in full. Cash of $20,000 is available for distribution to the partners. In this distribution, the guiding principle is to pay each partner an amount equal to the excess of a partner's capital account balance over any additional possible losses that may be charged to each partner. In other words, a partner's capital account balance is reduced to an amount necessary to absorb any additional losses that may be charged against that partner because of the uncollectibility of deficiencies owed by other partners.

Exhibit 1, page 55, prepared in support of the statement of realization and liquidation on page 54, shows that the $20,000 of available cash can be

J, K, L & M PARTNERSHIP
Statement of Realization and Liquidation
August 1–15, Year 4

	Assets			Partners' capital			
	Cash	Other	Liabilities	J(10%)	K(20%)	L(30%)	M(40%)
Balances before liquidation	$ 20,000	$200,000	$120,000	$30,000	$32,000	$30,000	$ 8,000
Sales of assets at a loss of $80,000	120,000	(200,000)		(8,000)	(16,000)	(24,000)	(32,000)
Balances	$140,000		$120,000	$22,000	$16,000	$ 6,000	$(24,000)
Payment to creditors	(120,000)		(120,000)				
Balances	$ 20,000			$22,000	$16,000	$ 6,000	$(24,000)
Payments to partners (**Exhibit 1** on page 55) . . .	(20,000)			(16,000)	(4,000)		
Balances				$ 6,000	$12,000	$ 6,000	$(24,000)

distributed $16,000 to J and $4,000 to K. If the $24,000 deficiency in M's capital proves uncollectible, the additional loss to be divided among the other three partners will cause L's capital account to change from a $6,000 credit balance to a $6,000 debit balance (deficiency). L, therefore, is not eligible to receive a cash payment. If this deficiency in L's capital account proves uncollectible, the balances remaining in the capital accounts of J and K, after the cash payment indicated above, will be equal to the amounts ($2,000 and $4,000, respectively) needed to absorb the additional loss shifted from L's capital account.

	J, K, L & M PARTNERSHIP				Exhibit 1
	Computation of Cash Payments to Partners				
	August 15, Year 4				
			Partners' capital		
		J(10%)	K(20%)	L(30%)	M(40%)
Capital account balances before distribution of cash to partners		$22,000	$16,000	$ 6,000	$(24,000)
Additional loss to J, K, and L if M's deficiency is uncollectible (ratio of 10:20:30) .		(4,000)	(8,000)	(12,000)	24,000
Balances		$18,000	$ 8,000	$ (6,000)	
Additional loss to J and K if L's deficiency is uncollectible (ratio of 10:20)		(2,000)	(4,000)	6,000	
Amounts that may be paid to partners		$16,000	$ 4,000		

The statement of realization and liquidation for the period August 1–15, Year 4, is illustrated on page 54.

Partnership is insolvent but partners are personally solvent

If a partnership is *insolvent*, at least one and perhaps all of the partners will have debit balances in their capital accounts. In any event, the total of the debit balances will exceed the total of the credit balances. If the partner or partners with a capital deficiency pay the required amount, the partnership will have cash to pay its liabilities in full. However, the creditors may demand payment from *any* partner individually, regardless of whether a partner's capital account shows a deficiency or a credit balance. In terms of relationships with creditors, the partnership is not a separate entity. A partner who makes payments to partnership creditors receives a credit to the capital account. As an illustration of an insolvent partnership whose partners are personally solvent (have assets in excess of liabilities) assume that N, O, and P, who share net income and losses equally, present the following balance sheet just prior to liquidation on May 10, Year 8:

N, O & P PARTNERSHIP
Balance Sheet
May 10, Year 8

Assets		Liabilities & Partners' Capital	
Cash	$ 15,000	Liabilities	$ 65,000
Other assets	85,000	N, capital	18,000
		O, capital	10,000
		P, capital	7,000
Total	$100,000	Total	$100,000

On May 12, Year 8, the other assets with a carrying amount of $85,000 are sold for $40,000 cash, which causes a loss of $45,000 to be divided equally among the partners. The total cash of $55,000 is paid to the creditors, which leaves unpaid liabilities of $10,000. Partner N has a credit balance of $3,000 after absorbing one-third of the loss. Partners O and P owe the partnership $5,000 and $8,000, respectively. Assuming that on May 30, Year 8, O and P pay in the amounts of their deficiencies, the partnership will use $10,000 of the $13,000 available cash to pay the remaining liabilities and will distribute $3,000 to N. These events are portrayed in the statement of realization and liquidation below:

Assume that there was some delay in collecting the $13,000 in deficiencies from O and P, and during this period the creditors demanded and received payment of their $10,000 in claims from partner N. This payment by N would cause N's equity to increase from $3,000 to $13,000. When the $13,000 is received from O and P by the partnership, it would be paid to N.

N, O & P PARTNERSHIP
Statement of Realization and Liquidation
May 10–30, Year 8

	Assets			Partners' capital		
	Cash	Other	Liabilities	N(⅓)	O(⅓)	P(⅓)
Balance before liquidation	$15,000	$85,000	$65,000	$18,000	$10,000	$ 7,000
Sale of assets at a loss of $45,000	40,000	(85,000)		(15,000)	(15,000)	(15,000)
Balances	$55,000		$65,000	$ 3,000	$ (5,000)	$ (8,000)
Partial payment to creditors	(55,000)		(55,000)			
Balances	$ -0-		$10,000	$ 3,000	$ (5,000)	$ (8,000)
Cash received from O and P	13,000				5,000	8,000
Balances	$13,000		$10,000	$ 3,000		
Final payment to creditors	(10,000)		(10,000)			
Balances	$ 3,000			$ 3,000		
Payment to N	(3,000)			(3,000)		

Another alternative is that creditors might collect the final $10,000 due them directly from O or P. Payments by these partners to creditors would be credited to their capital accounts and thus would eliminate or reduce their debts to the firm. As long as we assume that the partners with deficiencies make payment to the partnership or directly to partnership creditors, the results are the same. Creditors will be paid in full and partners will share losses on liquidation as provided in the partnership contract.

Partnership is insolvent and partners are personally insolvent

In the preceding illustration of an insolvent partnership, we assumed that the partners were personally solvent and therefore able to pay their capital deficiencies. We shall now consider an insolvent partnership in which one or more of the partners are personally insolvent. This situation raises a question as to the relative rights of two groups of creditors: (1) those persons who extended credit to the partnership, and (2) those persons who extended credit to the partners as individuals. The relative rights of these two groups of creditors are governed by the provisions of the partnership and bankruptcy laws relating to the *marshalling of assets*. These rules provide that assets of the partnership are first available to creditors of the partnership, and that assets owned individually by the partners are first available to their personal creditors. After the debts of the partnership have been paid in full, the creditors of an individual partner have a claim against the assets (if any) of the partnership to the extent of that partner's equity in the partnership.

After the personal creditors of a partner have been paid in full from the personal assets of the partner, any remaining personal assets are available to partnership creditors, regardless of whether the partner's capital account shows a credit or a debit balance. Such claims by creditors of the partnership are permitted only when these creditors are unable to obtain payment from the partnership.

To illustrate the relative rights of creditors of an insolvent partnership and personal creditors of an insolvent partner, assume that R, S, and T, who share net income and losses equally, have the following balance sheet just prior to liquidation on November 30, Year 10:

R, S & T PARTNERSHIP
Balance Sheet
November 30, Year 10

Assets		Liabilities & Partners' Capital	
Cash	$ 10,000	Liabilities	$ 60,000
Other assets	100,000	R, capital	5,000
		S, capital	15,000
		T, capital	30,000
Total	$110,000	Total	$110,000

Assume also that on November 30, Year 10, the partners have the following personal assets and liabilities apart from the equities they have in the partnership:

Partner	Personal assets	Personal liabilities
R	$100,000	$25,000
S	50,000	50,000
T	5,000	60,000

The realization of partnership assets results in a loss of $60,000, as shown in the statement of realization and liquidation below for the period December 1–12, Year 10:

R, S & T PARTNERSHIP
Statement of Realization and Liquidation
December 1–12, Year 10

| | Assets | | | Partners' capital | | |
	Cash	Other	Liabilities	R(⅓)	S(⅓)	T(⅓)
Balances before liquidation	$10,000	$100,000	$60,000	$ 5,000	$15,000	$30,000
Sale of assets at a loss of $60,000	40,000	(100,000)		(20,000)	(20,000)	(20,000)
Balances	$50,000		$60,000	$(15,000)	$ (5,000)	$10,000
Payment to creditors	(50,000)		(50,000)			
Balances			$10,000	$(15,000)	$ (5,000)	$10,000

The creditors of the partnership have received all the assets of the partnership and still have unpaid claims of $10,000. They cannot collect from S or T personally because the personal assets of these two partners are just sufficient or are insufficient to meet their personal liabilities. However, the partnership creditors can collect the $10,000 in full from R, who is personally solvent. By chance, R has a capital deficiency of $15,000, but this is of no concern to creditors of the partnership, who can collect in full from any partner who has sufficient personal assets, regardless of whether that partner's capital account has a debit or a credit balance. The statement of realization and liquidation is now continued (see page 59) to show the payment by R personally of the final $10,000 due to partnership creditors. Because our assumptions about R's personal finances showed that R had $100,000 of assets and only $25,000 in liabilities, R is able to invest the additional $5,000 needed to offset the capital deficiency. This $5,000 cash is paid to partner T, the only partner with a positive capital account balance.

	Cash	Liabilities	Partners' capital		
			R(⅓)	S(⅓)	T(⅓)
Balances carried forward		$10,000	$(15,000)	$(5,000)	$10,000
Payment by R to partnership creditors		(10,000)	10,000		
Balances			$ (5,000)	$(5,000)	$10,000
Additional investment by R	$5,000		5,000		
Balances	$5,000			$(5,000)	$10,000
Payment to T (or T's creditors)	(5,000)				(5,000)
Balances				$(5,000)	$ 5,000

The continued statement of realization and liquidation now shows that S owes $5,000 to the firm; however, S's personal assets of $50,000 are exactly equal to S's personal liabilities of $50,000. Under the rules of marshalling of assets, all the personal assets of S will go to personal creditors; therefore, the $5,000 deficiency in S's capital account represents an additional loss to be shared equally by R and T. To conclude the liquidation, R, who is personally solvent, will be required to pay $2,500 to the partnership, and the amount will go to T or to T's personal creditors, because T is insolvent. These payments are shown below to complete the statement of realization and liquidation for the R, S & T Partnership:

	Cash	Partners' capital		
		R(⅓)	S(⅓)	T(⅓)
Balances carried forward			$(5,000)	$5,000
Write off S's deficiency as uncollectible		$(2,500)	5,000	(2,500)
Balances		$(2,500)		$2,500
Cash invested by R	$2,500	2,500		
Balances	$2,500			$2,500
Payment to T (or T's creditors)	(2,500)			(2,500)

The final results of the liquidation show that the partnership creditors received payment in full because of the personal financial status of partner R. Because R was personally solvent, the personal creditors of R also were paid in full. The personal creditors of S were paid in full, thereby exhausting S's personal assets; however, because S failed to make good the $5,000 capital deficiency, an additional loss of $5,000 was shifted to R and T. The personal creditors of T received all of T's personal assets of $5,000 and also $7,500 from the partnership, representing T's equity in the firm. However, T's personal creditors were able to collect only $12,500 ($5,000 + $7,500 = $12,500) on their total claims of $60,000.

INSTALMENT PAYMENTS TO PARTNERS

In the illustrations of partnership liquidation in the preceding sections, all the assets were sold and the total loss from liquidation was divided among the partners before any payments were made to them. However, the liquidation of some partnerships may extend over many months or even years. In such extended liquidations the partners usually will want to receive cash as it becomes available rather than waiting until all assets have been converted to cash. Instalment payments to partners are proper if the necessary safeguards are used to ensure that all creditors are paid in full and that no partners are paid more than the amount to which they would be entitled after all losses on realization of assets have become known.

Liquidation in instalments may be regarded as a process of selling some assets, paying creditors, paying the remaining available cash to partners, selling additional assets, and making further payments to partners. The liquidation continues until all assets have been sold and all cash has been distributed to creditors and partners.

The circumstances of instalment liquidation are likely to vary; consequently, our approach is to emphasize the general principles guiding liquidation in instalments rather than to provide illustrative models of all possible liquidation situations. Among the variables that cause partnership liquidations to differ are the sufficiency of each partner's capital to absorb that partner's share of the possible losses remaining after each instalment, the shifting of losses from one partner to another because of inability to collect a capital deficiency, the offsetting of loan accounts against capital deficiencies, and the possible need for setting aside cash to meet future liquidation expenses or unpaid liabilities.

General principles guiding instalment payment procedures

The critical element in instalment liquidations is that the liquidator authorizes cash payments to partners before losses that may be incurred on the liquidation are known. If payments are made to partners and later losses cause deficiencies to develop in the capital accounts, the liquidator will have to ask for the return of the payments. If the payments cannot be recovered, the liquidator may be personally liable to the other partners for the loss caused them by the improper distribution of cash. Because of this danger, the only safe policy for determining instalment cash payments to partners is as follows:

1 Assume a total loss on all remaining assets and provide for all possible losses, including potential liquidation expenses.
2 Assume that any partner with a potential capital deficiency will be unable to pay anything to the firm; in other words, distribute each instalment of cash as if no more cash would be forthcoming, either from sale of assets or from collection of deficiencies from partners.

Under these assumptions the liquidator will authorize a payment to a partner only if that partner has a credit balance in the capital account (or in the capital and loan accounts combined) in excess of the amount required to absorb a portion of the maximum possible loss that may be incurred on liquidation. A partner's "share of the maximum possible loss" would include any loss that may result from the inability of partners to make good any potential capital deficiencies.

When instalment payments are made according to these rules, the effect will be to bring the equities of the partners to the income-sharing ratio as quickly as possible. *When instalment payments have proceeded to the point that the partners' capital account balances (equities) correspond to the income-sharing ratio, all subsequent payments may be made in that ratio,* because each partner's equity will be sufficient to absorb an appropriate share of the maximum possible remaining loss.

Advance planning for instalment payments to partners

The amounts of cash that could be distributed safely to the partners each month (or at any other point in time) may be determined by computing the impact on partners' equities (capital and loan balances) of the maximum possible remaining loss. Although this method is sound, it is somewhat cumbersome. Furthermore, it does not show at the beginning of the liquidation how cash will be divided among the partners as it becomes available. For these reasons, it is more efficient to prepare a complete *cash distribution program* in advance to show how cash will be divided during liquidation. If such a program is prepared, any amounts of cash received from the sale of partnership assets can be paid immediately to the partners as specified in this program.

Assume that X, Y, and Z, who share net income and losses in a 4:3:2 ratio, decide to liquidate and want a complete cash distribution program prepared in advance. The balance sheet for the X, Y & Z Partnership just prior to liquidation on July 5, Year 1, is as follows:

X, Y & Z PARTNERSHIP
Balance Sheet
July 5, Year 1

Assets		Liabilities & Partners' Capital	
Cash	$ 8,000	Liabilities	$ 61,000
Other assets	192,000	X, capital	40,000
		Y, capital	45,000
		Z, capital	54,000
Total	$200,000	Total	$200,000

The first $61,000 of available cash must, of course, be paid to creditors; any additional amount can be paid to partners. The amount of cash to be paid to partners during liquidation may be developed as illustrated below. The steps used to prepare this cash distribution program are explained on page 63.

X, Y & Z PARTNERSHIP
Cash Distributions to Partners during Liquidation
July 5, Year 1

	X	Y	Z
Capital account balances before liquidation	$40,000	$45,000	$54,000
Income-sharing ratio	4	3	2
Divide capital account balances before liquidation by income-sharing ratio to obtain capital per unit of income sharing for each partner	$10,000	$15,000	$27,000
Required reduction in capital per unit of income sharing for Z to bring Z's balance down to the next highest balance (for partner Y). This is the amount of the first cash distribution to a partner **per unit** of the partner's income sharing. Because Z has 2 units of income sharing, Z will receive the first $24,000 ($12,000 × 2 = $24,000)			(12,000)
Capital per unit of income sharing	$10,000	$15,000	$15,000
Required reduction in capital per unit of income sharing for Y and Z to bring their balances down to X's balance, which is the lowest capital per unit of income sharing. The required reduction is multiplied by each partner's income-sharing ratio to determine the amount of cash to be paid. Thus Y receives $15,000 ($5,000 × 3 = $15,000), and Z receives $10,000 ($5,000 × 2 = $10,000)		(5,000)	(5,000)
Capital per unit of income sharing after payment of $15,000 to Y and $34,000 to Z. **Remaining cash now may be distributed in the income-sharing ratio**	$10,000	$10,000	$10,000

Summary of cash distribution program:

To creditors before partners receive anything	$ 61,000		
To partners:			
(1) First distribution of $24,000 to Z:			
$12,000 × 2	24,000		$24,000
(2) Second distribution of $25,000 to Y and Z in 3:2 ratio:			
Y— $5,000 × 3 . . . . $15,000			
Z— $5,000 × 2 . . . . 10,000 25,000		$15,000	10,000
	$110,000		
(3) Any amount in excess of $110,000 to X, Y, and Z in income-sharing ratio	4/9	3/9	2/9

1 The "capital account balances before liquidation" represent the **equities** of the partners in the partnership, that is, the balance in a partner's capital account, plus or minus the balance (if any) of a loan made by a partner to the partnership or a loan made by the partnership to a partner.

2 The capital account balance before liquidation for each partner is divided by each partner's income-sharing ratio to determine the amount of capital per unit of income sharing for each partner. This step is critical because it (**a**) identifies the partner with the largest capital per unit of income sharing who, therefore, will be the first to receive cash, (**b**) facilitates the ranking of partners in the order in which they are entitled to receive cash, and (**c**) provides the basis for determining the amount of cash each partner receives at various stages of liquidation. Because Z's capital per unit of income sharing is largest ($27,000), Z will be the first to receive cash, followed by Y, and finally by X.

3 Z receives enough cash to bring Z's capital of $27,000 per unit of income sharing down to $15,000 so that it will be equal to the balance for Y, the second ranking partner. To accomplish this, Z's capital per unit of income sharing must be reduced by $12,000, and because Z has two units of income sharing, Z must receive $24,000 ($12,000 × 2 = $24,000) before Y receives any cash.

4 At this point, the capital per unit of income sharing for Y and for Z is $15,000, indicating that they are entitled to receive cash until their capital per unit of income sharing is reduced by $5,000 to bring them down to the $10,000 balance for X, the lowest ranking partner. Because Y has three units and Z has two units of income sharing, Y receives $15,000 ($5,000 × 3 = $15,000) and Z receives an additional $10,000 ($5,000 × 2 = $10,000) before X receives any cash. After Z receives $24,000, Y and Z would share any amount of cash available up to a maximum amount of $25,000 in a 3:2 ratio.

5 After Y has received $15,000 and Z has received $34,000 ($24,000 + $10,000 = $34,000), the capital per unit of income sharing is $10,000 for each partner, and any additional cash is paid to the partners in the income-sharing ratio (4:3:2), because their capital account balances have been reduced to the income-sharing ratio. This is illustrated below:

	X(4/9)	Y(3/9)	Z(2/9)
Capital account balances before liquidation	$40,000	$45,000	$54,000
First payment of cash to Z			(24,000)
Second payment of cash to Y and Z in 3:2 ratio		(15,000)	(10,000)
Capital account balances (in income-sharing ratio of 4:3:2) after payment of $49,000 to Y and Z	$40,000	$30,000	$20,000

Only when instalment payments reach the point at which partners' capital account balances correspond to the income-sharing ratio can subsequent payments be made in that ratio.[1]

We should point out that a cash distribution program, such as the one on page 62, also may be used to ascertain an equitable distribution of noncash assets to partners. The current fair value of noncash assets such as marketable securities, inventories, or equipment distributed to partners should be

1 The procedure for preparing a cash distribution program illustrated above can be used regardless of the number of partners involved and the complexity of the income-sharing ratio. For example, assume that partners share earnings as follows: A 41.2%, B 32.3%, C 26.5%. We may view the income-sharing ratio as 412 for A, 323 for B, and 265 for C and apply the same technique illustrated in this section.

treated as equivalent to cash payments. If a distribution of noncash assets departs from the cash distribution program by giving one of the partners a larger distribution than that partner is entitled to receive, subsequent distributions should be adjusted to allow the remaining partners to "make up" the distribution prematurely made to one of the partners. In such cases, a ***revised cash distribution program must be prepared***, because the original relationship among the partners' capital account balances has been disrupted.

Any losses or gains on the sale of assets during liquidation are allocated to the partners in the income-sharing ratio. Thus, the degree to which the capital account balances do not correspond with the income-sharing ratio is not altered by such losses or gains. Consequently, losses or gains from the realization of assets in the course of partnership liquidation do not affect the cash distribution program prepared prior to the start of liquidation.

To illustrate how the cash distribution program can be used, assume that the realization of assets by the X, Y & Z Partnership from July 5 to September 30, Year 1, is as follows:

X, Y & Z PARTNERSHIP

Realization of Assets

July 5–September 30, Year 1

Date	Carrying amount of assets sold	Loss on sale	Cash received by partnership
July 31	$ 62,000	$13,500	$ 48,500
August 31	66,000	36,000	30,000
September 30	64,000	31,500	32,500
Totals	$192,000	$81,000	$111,000

X, Y & Z PARTNERSHIP

Distributions of Cash to Creditors and Partners

July 5–September 30, Year 1

Date	Cash	Liabilities	Partners' capital		
			X(⁴⁄₉)	Y(³⁄₉)	Z(²⁄₉)
July 31 (includes $8,000 on hand July 5)	$ 56,500	$56,500			
August 31	30,000	4,500			$24,000 }
				$ 900	600 }
September 30	32,500			14,100	9,400 }
			$4,000	3,000	2,000 }
Totals	$119,000	$61,000	$4,000	$18,000	$36,000

X, Y & Z PARTNERSHIP
Statement of Realization and Liquidation
July 5–September 30, Year 1

	Assets			Partners' capital		
	Cash	Other	Liabilities	X(4⁄9)	Y(3⁄9)	Z(2⁄9)
Balances before liquidation	$ 8,000	$192,000	$61,000	$40,000	$45,000	$54,000
July 31 instalment:						
Sale of assets at a loss of $13,500	48,500	(62,000)		(6,000)	(4,500)	(3,000)
Balances	$56,500	$130,000	$61,000	$34,000	$40,500	$51,000
Payment to creditors	(56,500)		(56,500)			
Balances	$ -0-	$130,000	$ 4,500	$34,000	$40,500	$51,000
Aug. 31 instalment:						
Sale of assets at a loss of $36,000	30,000	(66,000)		(16,000)	(12,000)	(8,000)
Balances	$30,000	$ 64,000	$ 4,500	$18,000	$28,500	$43,000
Payment to creditors	(4,500)		(4,500)			
Balances before any payments to partners ...	$25,500	$ 64,000		$18,000	$28,500	$43,000
Payments to partners	(25,500)				(900)	(24,600)
Balances	$ -0-	$ 64,000		$18,000	$27,600	$18,400
Sept. 30 instalment:						
Sale of assets at a loss of $31,500	32,500	(64,000)		(14,000)	(10,500)	(7,000)
Balances	$32,500			$ 4,000	$17,100	$11,400
Payments to partners	(32,500)			(4,000)	(17,100)	(11,400)

The cash available each month should be paid to creditors and partners according to the summary of cash distribution program on page 62. The distributions of cash appear at the bottom of page 64.

The entire cash balance of $56,500 available on July 31 is paid to creditors, leaving $4,500 in unpaid liabilities. When $30,000 becomes available on August 31, $4,500 should be paid to creditors, leaving $25,500 to be paid to the partners according to the cash distribution program developed earlier. The program calls for Z to receive the first $24,000 available for distribution to partners, and for Y and Z to share the next $25,000 in a 3:2 ratio. On August 31 only $1,500 ($30,000 − $4,500 − $24,000 = $1,500) is available for payment to Y and Z; thus Y and Z receive $900 and $600, respectively. Of the $32,500 available on September 30, the first $23,500 is paid to Y and Z in a 3:2 ratio, or $14,100 and $9,400, respectively, in order to complete the distribution of $25,000 to Y and Z before X participates; this leaves $9,000 ($32,500 − $23,500 = $9,000) to be distributed to X, Y, and Z in the 4:3:2 income-sharing ratio.

A complete statement of realization and liquidation for X, Y & Z Partnership is presented above.

The summary journal entries required to record the realization of assets and to complete the liquidation of the X, Y & Z Partnership appear on page 66.

July 31	Cash	48,500	
	X, Capital	6,000	
	Y, Capital	4,500	
	Z, Capital	3,000	
	Other Assets		62,000

To record sale of assets and division of $13,500 loss
among partners in 4:3:2 ratio.

	Liabilities	56,500	
	Cash		56,500

To record partial payment to creditors.

Aug. 31	Cash	30,000	
	X, Capital	16,000	
	Y, Capital	12,000	
	Z, Capital	8,000	
	Other Assets		66,000

To record sale of assets and division of $36,000 loss
among partners in 4:3:2 ratio.

	Liabilities	4,500	
	Y, Capital	900	
	Z, Capital	24,600	
	Cash		30,000

To record payment of balance due to creditors and
first instalment to partners.

Sept. 30	Cash	32,500	
	X, Capital	14,000	
	Y, Capital	10,500	
	Z, Capital	7,000	
	Other Assets		64,000

To record sale of remaining assets and division of
$31,500 loss among partners in 4:3:2 ratio.

	X, Capital	4,000	
	Y, Capital	17,100	
	Z, Capital	11,400	
	Cash		32,500

To record final instalment to partners to complete
the liquidation of the partnership.

Withholding of cash for unpaid liabilities and liquidation expenses

As previously emphasized, creditors are entitled to payment in full before
anything is paid to partners. However, in some cases the liquidator may find
it more convenient to set aside in a separate fund the cash required to pay

certain liabilities, and to distribute the remaining cash to the partners. The withholding of cash for payment of recorded liabilities is appropriate when for any reason it is not practicable or advisable (as when the amount of the claim is in dispute) to pay an obligation before cash is distributed to partners. An amount of cash set aside, and equal to recorded unpaid liabilities, is not a factor in computing possible future losses; the possible future loss is measured by the amount of noncash assets, any *unrecorded* liabilities, and any potential liquidation expenses that may be incurred.

Any expenses incurred during the liquidation should be deducted to determine the cash available for distribution to partners. Expenses of liquidation thereby are treated as part of the total loss from liquidation. However, in some cases, the liquidator may wish to withhold cash in anticipation of future liquidation expenses. The amount of cash withheld or set aside for future liquidation expenses or for payment of liabilities not recorded in the accounting records should be combined with the noncash assets in the computation of the maximum possible loss that may be incurred to complete the liquidation of the partnership.

INCORPORATION OF A PARTNERSHIP

Most partnerships should evaluate the possible advantages to be gained by incorporating. Among such advantages are limited liability, ease of attracting outside capital, and possible income tax savings.

To assure that each partner receives an equitable portion of the capital stock issued by the new corporation, the assets of the partnership must be adjusted to current fair value before being transferred to the corporation. Any identifiable intangible asset or goodwill developed by the partnership is included among the assets transferred to the corporation.

To illustrate the incorporation of a partnership, assume that Blair and Benson, partners who share net income and losses in a 4:1 ratio, organize B & B Corporation to take over the net assets of the partnership. The balance sheet of the partnership on June 30, Year 10, the date of incorporation, is shown on page 68.

After an appraisal of the equipment and an audit of the financial statements, it is agreed that the following adjustments are required to restate the net assets of the partnership to current fair value:

(1) Increase the allowance for doubtful accounts to $1,000.
(2) Increase the inventories to current replacement cost of $30,000.
(3) Increase the equipment to reproduction cost new of $70,000, less accumulated depreciation on this basis of $30,500, that is, to a current fair value of $39,500.
(4) Record accrued liabilities of $1,100.
(5) Record goodwill of $10,000.

B & B Corporation is authorized to issue 10,000 shares of $10 par common stock. It issues 5,500 shares of common stock valued at $15 a share to

BLAIR & BENSON PARTNERSHIP
Balance Sheet
June 30, Year 10

Assets

Cash		$12,000
Accounts receivable	$28,100	
Less: Allowance for doubtful accounts	600	27,500
Inventories		25,500
Equipment	$60,000	
Less: Accumulated depreciation of equipment	26,000	34,000
Total assets		$99,000

Liabilities & Partners' Capital

Liabilities:		
Accounts payable		$35,000
Partners' capital:		
Blair, capital	$47,990	
Benson, capital	16,010	64,000
Total liabilities & partners' capital		$99,000

the partnership, in exchange for the net assets of the partnership. The 5,500 shares received by the partnership are divided between the partners on the basis of the adjusted balances in their capital accounts. Partners may withdraw small amounts of cash to round their capital account balances to even amounts, thus avoiding the issuance of fractional shares. This step completes the dissolution and liquidation of the partnership.

Although the accounting records of the partnership may be modified to serve as the records of the new corporation, it is customary to open a new set of records for the corporation. If this alternative is followed, the procedures required are:

In accounting records of partnership:

1 Prepare journal entries for revaluation of assets, including recognition of goodwill, if any.
2 Record any cash withdrawals necessary to adjust partners' capital account balances to round amounts. (In some instances the contract may call for transfer to the corporation of all assets except cash.)
3 Record the transfer of assets and liabilities to the corporation, the receipt of the common stock by the partnership, and the distribution of the common stock to the partners in settlement of the balances in their capital accounts.

The journal entries to adjust and eliminate the accounting records of the Blair & Benson Partnership are illustrated on page 69.

In accounting records of new corporation:

1 Record the acquisition of assets and liabilities (including obligation to pay for the net assets) from the partnership at current fair values.

Inventories ($30,000 − $25,500)	4,500	
Equipment ($70,000 − $60,000)	10,000	
Goodwill	10,000	
Allowance for Doubtful Accounts ($1,000 − $600)		400
Accumulated Depreciation of Equipment		
($30,500 − $26,000)		4,500
Accrued Liabilities		1,100
Blair, Capital ($18,500 × 0.80)		14,800
Benson, Capital ($18,500 × 0.20)		3,700

To adjust assets and liabilities to agreed amounts and to divide net gain
of $18,500 between partners in 4:1 ratio.

Receivable from B & B Corporation ($64,000 + $18,500)	82,500	
Accounts Payable	35,000	
Accrued Liabilities	1,100	
Allowance for Doubtful Accounts	1,000	
Accumulated Depreciation of Equipment	30,500	
Cash		12,000
Accounts Receivable		28,100
Inventories		30,000
Equipment		70,000
Goodwill		10,000

To record transfer of assets and liabilities to B & B Corporation.

Common Stock of B & B Corporation	82,500	
Receivable from B & B Corporation		82,500

To record receipt of 5,500 shares of $10 par common stock valued at
$15 a share in payment for net assets transferred to B & B Corporation.

Blair, Capital ($47,990 + $14,800)	62,790	
Benson, Capital ($16,010 + $3,700)	19,710	
Common Stock of B & B Corporation		82,500

To record distribution of common stock of B & B Corporation to partners:
4,186 shares to Blair and 1,314 shares to Benson.

2 Record the issuance of common stock at current fair value in payment of the
obligation to the partnership.

The journal entries to open the accounting records of B & B Corporation
on June 30, Year 10, are illustrated at the top of page 70.

Note that the allowance for doubtful accounts is recorded in the accounting records of B & B Corporation because the specific accounts receivable
that may not be collected are not known. In contrast, the depreciation
recorded by the Blair & Benson Partnership is ignored because the "cost" of
the equipment to the new corporation is $39,500. The opening balance
sheet for B & B Corporation appears in the middle of page 70.

Cash	12,000	
Accounts Receivable	28,100	
Inventories	30,000	
Equipment	39,500	
Goodwill	10,000	
Allowance for Doubtful Accounts		1,000
Accounts Payable		35,000
Accrued Liabilities		1,100
Payable to Blair & Benson Partnership		82,500

To record acquisition of assets and liabilities from Blair & Benson
Partnership.

Payable to Blair & Benson Partnership	82,500	
Common Stock, $10 par		55,000
Premium on common stock		27,500

To record issuance of 5,500 shares of common stock valued at $15 a
share in payment for net assets of Blair & Benson Partnership.

B & B CORPORATION
Balance Sheet
June 30, Year 10

Assets

Cash		$ 12,000
Accounts receivable	$28,100	
Less: Allowance for doubtful accounts	1,000	27,100
Inventories		30,000
Equipment		39,500
Goodwill		10,000
Total assets		$118,600

Liabilities & Shareholders' Equity

Liabilities:		
Accounts payable		$ 35,000
Accrued liabilities		1,100
Total liabilities		$ 36,100
Shareholders' equity:		
Common stock, $10 par, authorized 10,000 shares, issued and		
outstanding 5,500 shares	$55,000	
Contributed surplus	27,500	82,500
Total liabilities & shareholders' equity		$118,600

Income tax aspects concerning incorporation of a partnership

For income tax purposes, no gain or loss is recognized on the incorporation
of a partnership if the former partners hold control of the corporation

immediately after the transfer. As a result of this rule, the income tax basis of the assets transferred is the same for the corporation as it was for the partnership. The capital cost allowance is continued for income tax purposes on the basis of the original cost to the partnership.

Thus, a conflict exists between the action required for income tax purposes and that indicated by accounting theory. From the viewpoint of accounting theory, the assets appropriately are recorded in the accounting records of the corporation at the new cost basis established by the transfer of ownership and substantiated by the market (or current fair) value of the shares of capital stock issued for these assets. As a practical solution to this conflict between income tax requirements and theoretical considerations, the corporation maintains a separate set of supplementary records for depreciable assets to facilitate the computation of capital cost allowance for income tax purposes.

REVIEW QUESTIONS

1 Agasse and Bowman, partners, have capital accounts of $60,000 and $80,000, respectively. In addition, Agasse has made a noninterest-bearing loan of $20,000 to the firm. Agasse and Bowman now decide to liquidate their partnership. What priority or advantage, if any, will Agasse enjoy in the liquidation with respect to the loan account?

2 State briefly the procedure to be followed in a partnership liquidation when a debit balance arises in the capital account of one of the partners.

3 In the liquidation of the partnership of Camm, Dehn, and Ellerman, the sale of the assets resulted in a loss that produced the following balances in the capital accounts: Camm, $25,000 credit; Dehn, $12,500 credit; and Ellerman, $5,000 debit. The partners shared net income and losses in a 5:3:2 ratio. All liabilities have been paid, and $32,500 of cash is available for distribution to partners. However, it is not possible to determine at present whether Ellerman will be able to make good the $5,000 capital deficiency. May the cash on hand be distributed without a delay to determine the collectibility of the amount due from Ellerman? Explain.

4 After disposing of all assets and distributing all available cash to creditors, the A, B & C Partnership still had accounts payable of $12,000. The capital account of Partner A showed a credit balance of $16,000 and that of B a credit balance of $2,000. Creditors of the partnership demanded payment from A, who replied that the three partners shared earnings equally and had begun operations with equal capital investments. A, therefore, offered to pay the creditors one-third of their claims and no more. What is your opinion of the position taken by A? What is the balance in C's capital account? What journal entry, if any, should be made in the partnership accounting records for a payment by A personally to the partnership creditors?

5 In the Avery, Blum & Chee Partnership, Avery serves as managing partner. The partnership contract provides that Avery is entitled to an annual salary of $12,000, payable in 12 equal monthly instalments, and that remaining net income or loss shall be divided equally. On June 30, the partnership suspended operations and began liquidation. Because of a shortage of working capital, Avery had not drawn any salary for the last two months of operations. How should Avery's

claim for $2,000 of "unpaid wages" be handled in the liquidation of the partnership?

6 M and N are partners and have agreed to share earnings equally. State your reasons in support of dividing losses incurred in liquidation equally or in the ratio of capital account balances.

7 State briefly the basic principle to be observed in the distribution of cash to partners when the liquidation of a partnership extends over several months.

8 During the instalment liquidation of a partnership, it is necessary to determine the possible future loss from sale of the remaining assets. What journal entries, if any, should be made to reflect in the partners' capital accounts their respective shares of the maximum possible loss that may be incurred during the remaining stages of liquidation?

9 The X, Y & Z Partnership is liquidated over a period of 11 months, with several distributions of cash to the partners. Will the total amount of cash received by each partner under these circumstances be more, less, or the same amount as if the liquidator had retained all cash until all assets had been sold and had then made a single payment to the partners?

10 Under what circumstances, if any, is it sound practice for a partnership undergoing instalment liquidation to distribute cash to partners in the income-sharing ratio?

11 Judd, Klein, and Lund, partners who share earnings equally, have capital account balances of $30,000, $25,000, and $21,000, respectively, when the partnership begins liquidation. Among the assets is a note receivable from Klein in the amount of $7,000. All liabilities have been paid. The first assets sold during the liquidation are marketable securities with a carrying amount of $15,000, for which cash of $18,000 is received. How should this $18,000 be divided among the partners?

12 When the R, S & T Partnership began the process of liquidation, the capital account balances were R, $38,000; S, $35,000; and T, $32,000. When the liquidation was complete, R had received less cash than either of the other two partners. List several factors that might explain why the partner with the largest capital account balance might receive the smallest amount of cash in liquidation.

13 A partnership operated by Mann and Field decided to incorporate as Manfield Corporation. The entire capital stock of the new corporation was divided equally between Mann and Field because they had been equal partners. An appraisal report obtained on the date of incorporation indicated that the land and buildings had increased in value by 50% while owned by the partnership. Should the assets be increased to appraisal value or maintained at original cost to the partnership when transferred to the corporation's accounting records? If the assets are revalued, will the corporation be permitted to take depreciation on the increased valuations for income tax purposes? Explain.

EXERCISES

Ex. 2-1 Select the best answer for each of the following multiple-choice questions:

1 Which of the following will not result in a dissolution of a partnership?
  a The bankruptcy of a partner, as long as the partnership itself remains solvent
  b The death of a partner, as long as the deceased partner's will provides that the executor shall become a partner in the deceased partner's place
  c The wrongful withdrawal of a partner in contravention of the partnership contract

d The assignment by a partner of his or her entire partnership interest to another party

2 An insolvent partner's obligation to pay any deficiency in his or her capital account ranks:
  a Ahead of claims of unpaid creditors of the partnership
  b Second to claims of individual creditors of the insolvent partner
  c Before claims of the individual creditors of the partner and claims of unpaid creditors of the partnership
  d In some other order

3 During the liquidation of the Wayne, Forbes, Cable & Towne Partnership, Forbes paid a partnership account payable in the amount of $3,600. The appropriate journal entry in the partnership accounting records is:
  a No entry
  b Accounts Payable 3,600
      Forbes, Capital 3,600
  c Cash 3,600
      Forbes, Capital 3,600
  d Accounts Payable 3,600
      Forbes, Drawing 3,600

4 Q, R, S, and T are partners sharing net income and losses equally. The partnership is insolvent and is to be liquidated. The status of the partnership and each partner is as follows:

	Partnership capital account balance	Personal assets (exclusive of partnership interest)	Personal liabilities (exclusive of partnership interest)
Q	$15,000 cr	$100,000	$40,000
R	10,000 cr	30,000	60,000
S	20,000 dr	80,000	5,000
T	30,000 dr	1,000	28,000

In accordance with the rule of marshalling of assets, the creditors of the partnership:
  a Must first seek recovery against S, because S is solvent personally and has a negative capital balance
  b Will not be paid in full regardless of how they proceed legally, because the partnership assets are less than the partnership liabilities
  c Will have to share R's interest in the partnership on a pro rata basis with R's personal creditors
  d Have first claim to the partnership assets before any partner's personal creditors have rights to the partnership assets

5 Jenson, Smith, and Hart, partners, share net income and losses in the ratio of 5:3:2, respectively. The partners decided to liquidate the partnership when its assets consisted of cash, $40,000, and other assets, $210,000; the liabilities and partners' capital were as follows:

Liabilities	$60,000
Jenson, capital	48,000
Smith, capital	72,000
Hart, capital	70,000

The partnership will be liquidated over a prolonged period of time. As cash is available it will be distributed to the partners. The first sale of noncash assets with a carrying amount of $120,000 realized $90,000. How much cash should be distributed to each partner after this sale?

	Jenson	Smith	Hart
a	$45,000	$27,000	$18,000
b	$35,000	$21,000	$14,000
c	$ -0-	$30,000	$40,000
d	$ -0-	$28,800	$41,200

Ex. 2-2 Pullias and Mautner are partners who share net income and losses in a 60:40 ratio. They have decided to liquidate their partnership. A portion of the assets has been sold, but other assets with a carrying amount of $42,000 still must be realized. All liabilities have been paid, and cash of $20,000 is available for distribution to partners. The capital accounts show balances of $40,000 for Pullias and $22,000 for Mautner.

How should the cash be divided?

Ex. 2-3 Nicosia and Odmark started a partnership some years ago and managed to operate profitably for several years. Recently, however, they lost a substantial legal suit and incurred unexpected losses on accounts receivable and inventories. As a result, they decided to liquidate. They sold all assets, and only $18,000 was available to pay liabilities, which amounted to $33,000. Their capital account balances before the start of liquidation and their income-sharing ratios are shown below:

	Capital account balances	Income-sharing ratios
Nicosia	$23,000	60%
Odmark	13,500	40%

a Compute the total loss incurred on the liquidation of the partnership.

b Show how the final settlement should be made between the partners, after Nicosia pays $15,000 to creditors. Nicosia is personally insolvent after paying the creditors, but Odmark has personal net assets in excess of $100,000.

Ex. 2-4 After sale of a portion of the assets of the X, Y & Z Partnership, which is being liquidated, the capital accounts are X, $33,000; Y, $40,000; and Z, $42,000. Cash of $42,000 and other assets with a carrying amount of $78,000 are on hand. Creditors' claims total $5,000. X, Y, and Z share net income and losses equally.

Compute the cash payments that can be made to the partners at this time.

Ex. 2-5 When Kane and Lobo, partners who shared earnings equally, were incapacitated in an airplane accident, a liquidator was appointed to wind up their partnership. The accounting records showed cash, $35,000; other assets, $110,000; liabilities, $20,000; Kane's capital, $71,000; and Lobo's capital, $54,000. Because of the highly specialized nature of the noncash assets, the liquidator anticipated that considerable time would be required to dispose of them. The expenses of liquidating the partnership (advertising, rent, travel, etc.) are estimated at $10,000.

Compute the amount of cash that can be distributed safely to each partner at this time.

Ex. 2-6 The following balance sheet was prepared for the Pardee, Quon & Ramsey Partnership on March 31, Year 8. (Each partner's income-sharing ratio is given in parentheses):

Assets		Liabilities & Partners' Capital	
Cash	$ 25,000	Liabilities	$ 52,000
Other assets	180,000	Pardee, capital (40%) . . .	40,000
		Quon, capital (40%)	65,000
		Ramsey, capital (20%) . .	48,000
Total	$205,000	Total	$205,000

a The partnership is being liquidated by the sale of assets in instalments. The first sale of noncash assets having a carrying amount of $90,000 realizes $50,000, and all cash available after settlement with creditors is distributed to partners. Compute the amount of cash each partner should receive in the first instalment.

b If the facts are as in **a** above, except that $3,000 cash is withheld for possible liquidation expenses, how much cash should each partner receive?

c As a separate case, assume that each partner properly received some cash in the distribution after the second sale of assets. The cash to be distributed amounts to $14,000 from the third sale of assets, and unsold assets with a $6,000 carrying amount remain. How should the $14,000 be distributed to partners?

Ex. 2-7 On November 10, Year 3, D, E, and F, partners, have capital account balances of $20,000, $25,000, and $9,000, respectively, and share net income and losses in 4:2:1 ratio.

a Prepare a cash distribution program for liquidation of the partnership in instalments.

b How much will be paid to all partners if D receives only $4,000 on liquidation?

c If D received a $13,000 share of the cash paid pursuant to liquidation, how much did F receive?

d If E received only $11,000 as a result of the liquidation, what was the loss to the partnership on the sale of assets? (No partner invested any additional assets in the partnership.)

Ex. 2-8 The balance sheet for P & Q Partnership on June 1 of Year 10 follows:

Assets		*Liabilities & Partners' Capital*	
Cash	$ 5,000	Liabilities	$20,000
Other assets	55,000	P, capital	22,500
		Q, capital	17,500
Total	$60,000	Total	$60,000

Partners share net income and losses as follows: P, 60%; Q, 40%. In June, assets with a carrying amount of $22,000 are sold for $18,000, creditors are paid in full, and $2,000 is paid to partners in a manner to reduce their capital account balances closer to the income-sharing ratio. In July, assets with a carrying amount of $10,000 are sold for $12,000, liquidation expenses of $500 are paid, and cash of $12,500 is distributed to partners. In August, the remaining assets are sold for $22,500, and final settlement is made between the partners.

Compute the amount of cash each partner should receive in June, July, and August.

Ex. 2-9 The net equities and income-sharing ratios for E, F, G, and H, partners, before liquidation on May 5, Year 5, are as follows:

	E	*F*	*G*	*H*
Net equity in partnership	$36,000	$32,400	$8,000	$(100)
Income-sharing ratio	6	4	2	1

Assets will be sold for cash significantly in excess of carrying amounts.

Prepare a program showing how cash should be distributed to the partners as it becomes available in the course of liquidation.

Ex. 2-10 McKee and Nelson enter into a contract to speculate on the stock market, each using approximately $5,000 of personal cash. The net income and losses are to be divided equally, and settlement is to be made at the end of the year after all securities have been sold. A summary of the monthly brokerage statements for the year follows:

	McKee	Nelson
Total of all purchase confirmations	$45,000	$18,000
Total of all sales confirmations	48,700	16,800
Interest charged on margin accounts	80	50
Dividends credited to accounts	40	100

How should settlement be made between McKee and Nelson at the end of the year?

Ex. 2-11 The balance sheet for the Conner & Wayland Partnership, immediately before the partnership was incorporated as Conway Corporation, follows:

CONNER & WAYLAND PARTNERSHIP
Balance Sheet
September 30, Year 5

Assets			Liabilities & Partners' Capital		
Cash	$ 10,500		Accounts payable . . .	$ 16,400	
Accounts receivable	15,900				
Inventories	42,000		Conner, capital	60,000	
Equipment (net of $18,000			Wayland, capital	52,000	
accumulated depreciation) . . .	60,000				
Total	$128,400		Total	$128,400	

The following adjustments to the balance sheet of the partnership are recommended by a professional accountant before new accounting records for Conway Corporation are opened:

(1) An allowance for doubtful accounts is established in the amount of $1,200.
(2) Short-term prepayments of $800 are recorded.
(3) The current fair value of inventories is $48,000, and the current fair value of equipment is $72,000.
(4) Accrued liabilities are estimated at $750.

Prepare an opening balance sheet for Conway Corporation on October 1, Year 5, assuming that 10,000 shares of $5 par common stock are issued to the partners in exchange for their equities in the partnership. Equipment is recorded at current fair value; 50,000 shares of common stock are authorized to be issued.

CASES

Case 2-1 The Hodgkins, Olafson & Stevens Partnership is insolvent and is in the process of liquidation. After the assets were converted to cash and the resultant liquidation loss was distributed equally among the partners, their financial positions were as follows:

	Equity in partnership	Personal financial position other than equity in partnership	
		Assets	Liabilities
Scott Hodgkins	$30,000	$110,000	$45,000
Greg Olafson	(21,000)	20,000	40,000
Brent Stevens	(55,000)	55,000	45,000

Instructions Explain the prospects for collection by:

a The creditors of the partnership.

b The personal creditors of each partner.

c Hodgkins from the other partners. Compute the total loss that Hodgkins will absorb on the liquidation of the partnership.

Case 2-2 On November 15, Year 1, in beginning the liquidation of the X, Y & Z Partnership, the liquidator found that an 8% note payable for $100,000 issued by the partnership had six months remaining until maturity on May 15, Year 2. Interest had been paid to November 15. Terms of the note provided that interest at 8% to the maturity date must be paid in full in the event the note is paid prior to maturity. The liquidator had paid all other liabilities and had on hand cash of $150,000. The remaining noncash assets had a carrying amount of $200,000. The liquidator believed that six months would be required to dispose of them and that the realization of the noncash assets over this period would produce cash at least 25% in excess of the carrying amount of the assets.

Partner X made the following statement to the liquidator: "I realize you can't pay the partners until creditors have been paid in full, but I need cash for another venture. So I'd like for you to pay the note and interest to May 15, Year 2, immediately and to distribute the remaining cash to the partners." Partner Y objected to this proposal for immediate cash payments because it would entail a loss of $4,000. Y argued that if such action were taken, the total interest cost of $4,000 should be debited to X's capital account. Partner Z had no particular concern in the matter, but as a convenience agreed to assume the note liability in return for $102,000 cash payment from the liquidator. To protect the noteholder against loss, Z offered to deposit collateral of $104,000 in government bonds. The noteholder expressed willingness to accept this arrangement. Partner Z specified that the proposed payment of $102,000 would be in Z's new role as a creditor and that it would not affect Z's right to receive any cash distributions in the course of liquidation.

Instructions Evaluate the proposal by each partner. What action should be taken by the liquidator? Would your answer differ if the assumptions were changed to indicate a probable loss on the realization of the remaining noncash assets?

Case 2-3 Lois Allen and Barbara Brett formed a partnership and share net income and losses equally. Although the partners began business with equal capitals, Allen made more frequent withdrawals than Brett, with the result that her capital account became the smaller of the two. The partners have now decided to liquidate the partnership on June 30; on that date the accounting records were closed and financial statements were prepared. The balance sheet showed a capital account for Allen of $40,000 and Brett's capital as $60,000. In addition, the balance sheet showed that Brett had made a $10,000 loan to the partnership.

The liquidation of the partnership was managed by Allen, because Brett was hospitalized by an auto accident on July 1, the day after regular operations were suspended. The procedures followed by Allen were as follows: First, to sell all the assets at the best prices obtainable; second, to pay the creditors in full; third to pay Brett's loan account; and fourth, to divide all remaining cash between Brett and herself in the 40:60 ratio represented by their capital account balances.

When Brett was released from the hospital on July 5, Allen informed her that through good luck and hard work, she had been able to sell the assets and complete the liquidation during the five days of Brett's hospitalization. As the first step in the liquidation, Allen delivered two cashier's cheques to Brett. One cheque was for $10,000 in payment of the loan account; the other was in settlement of Brett's capital account balance.

Instructions

a Do you approve the procedures followed in the liquidation? Explain fully.

b Assume that the liquidation procedures followed resulted in the payment of $24,000 to Brett in addition to the payment of her loan account in full. What was the amount of gain or loss on the liquidation? If you believe that other methods should have been followed in the liquidation, explain how much more or less Brett would have received under the procedure you recommend.

Case 2-4 In reply to a question as to how settlement with partners should be made during liquidation of a partnership, Student J made the following statement:

"Accounting records usually are based on cost and reflect the going-concern principle. When a partnership is liquidated, it is often necessary to sell the assets for a fraction of their carrying amount. Consequently, a partner usually receives in liquidation a settlement far below the amount of his or her equity in the partnership."

Student K offered the following comment:

"I agree fully with what J has said, but she might have gone further and added that no payment should ever be made to any partner until all the assets of the partnership have been sold and all creditors have been paid in full. Until these steps have been completed, the residual amount available for distribution to partners is unknown, and therefore any earlier payment to a partner might have to be returned. If partners were unable to return such amount, the person who authorized the payments might be held personally responsible."

Student L made the following statement:

"In the liquidation of a partnership, each partner receives the amount of his or her equity — no more and no less. As to timing of payments, it is often helpful to a partner to receive a partial payment before the assets are sold and creditors are paid in full. If proper precautions are taken, such early partial payments are quite satisfactory."

Instructions Evaluate the statement made by each student.

PROBLEMS

2-1 Carson and Worden decided to dissolve and liquidate their partnership on September 23, Year 10. On that date, the balance sheet of the partnership was as shown below (partners' income-sharing percentages are indicated parenthetically).

On September 23, Year 10, other assets with a carrying amount of $70,000 were sold for $60,000, and $64,000 cash was distributed to creditors and partners. On October 1, Year 10, the remaining other assets were sold for $18,000 and all available cash was distributed to partners.

CARSON & WORDEN PARTNERSHIP
Balance Sheet
September 23, Year 10

Assets		Liabilities & Partners' Capital	
Cash	$ 5,000	Accounts payable	$ 15,000
Other assets	100,000	Loan payable to Worden . .	10,000
		Carson, capital (40%) . . .	60,000
		Worden, capital (60%) . .	20,000
Total	$105,000	Total	$105,000

Instructions

a Prepare a cash distribution program on September 23, Year 10, to determine the proper distribution of cash to partners as it becomes available.

b Prepare journal entries on September 23, Year 10, and October 1, Year 10, to record the sales of assets and distributions of cash to creditors and partners.

2-2 On December 31, Year 5, the accounting records of the X, Y & Z Partnership included the following information:

X, drawing (debit balance)	$ (24,000)
Z, drawing (debit balance)	(9,000)
Y, loan	30,000
X, capital	123,000
Y, capital	100,500
Z, capital	108,000

Total assets amounted to $478,500, including $52,500 cash, and liabilities totalled $150,000. The partnership was liquidated on December 31, Year 5, and Z received $83,250 cash pursuant to the liquidation. X, Y, and Z share net income and losses in a 5:3:2 ratio, respectively.

Instructions
a Compute the total loss from the liquidation of the partnership.
b Prepare a statement of realization and liquidation.
c Prepare journal entries for the accounting records of the partnership to complete the liquidation.

2-3 The following balance sheet was prepared for Cody's, a partnership, immediately prior to liquidation:

CODY'S

Balance Sheet
March 31, Year 5

Assets		Liabilities & Partners' Capital	
Cash	$ 10,000	Liabilities	$ 27,000
Investments in common		John Coe, capital	72,000
shares	20,000	Karen Dee, capital	31,000
Other assets	100,000		
Total	$130,000	Total	$130,000

Coe and Dee share operating income in a 2:1 ratio and capital gains and losses in a 3:1 ratio. The transactions to complete the liquidation are as follows:

Apr. 1   Coe takes over the portfolio of investments in common shares at an agreed current fair value of $44,000.

Apr. 3   Other assets and the trade name, Cody's, are sold to Wong Products for $200,000 face amount of 12% bonds with a current fair value of $180,000. The gain on this transaction is a capital gain.

Apr. 7   Wong Products 12% bonds with a face amount of $40,000 are sold for $35,600 cash. The loss on this transaction is a capital loss.

Apr. 8   Liabilities are paid.

Apr. 10   Coe withdraws $100,000 face amount and Dee withdraws $60,000 face amount of Wong Products 12% bonds at carrying amounts.

Apr. 15   Any available cash is paid to Coe and Dee.

Instructions   Prepare journal entries for Cody's to record the foregoing transactions.

2-4 Following is the balance sheet for the Adams, Barna & Coleman Partnership on June 4, Year 5:

ADAMS, BARNA & COLEMAN PARTNERSHIP

Balance Sheet
June 4, Year 5

Assets		Liabilities & Partners' Capital	
Cash	$ 6,000	Liabilities	$ 20,000
Other assets	94,000	Barna, loan	4,000
		Adams, capital	27,000
		Barna, capital	39,000
		Coleman, capital	10,000
Total	$100,000	Total	$100,000

The partners share net income and losses as follows: Adams, 40%; Barna, 40%; and Coleman, 20%. On June 4, Year 5, other assets were sold for $30,700, and $20,500 had to be paid to liquidate the liabilities because of unrecorded claims amounting to $500. Adams and Barna are personally solvent, but Coleman's personal liabilities exceed personal assets by $6,000.

Instructions
a Prepare a statement of realization and liquidation. Combine Barna's loan and capital account balances.
b Prepare journal entries to record the liquidation.
c How much cash would other assets have to realize on liquidation in order that Coleman would take enough cash out of the partnership to pay personal creditors in full? Assume that $20,500 is required to liquidate the partnership liabilities.

2-5 The accountant for the Horizon Partnership prepared the balance sheet below immediately prior to liquidation of the partnership.
During May, Year 3, assets with a carrying amount of $105,000 were sold for $75,000 cash, and all liabilities were paid. During June, assets with a carrying amount of $61,000 were sold for $25,000 cash, and in July the remaining assets with a carrying amount of $114,000 were sold for $81,000 cash. The cash available at the end of each month was distributed promptly. The partners shared net income and losses equally.

HORIZON PARTNERSHIP

Balance Sheet
April 30, Year 3

Assets		Liabilities & Partners' Capital	
Cash	$ 20,000	Liabilities	$ 80,000
Other assets	280,000	Holman, capital	60,000
		Rizzo, capital	70,000
		Onegin, capital	90,000
Total	$300,000	Total	$300,000

Instructions
a Prepare a statement of realization and liquidation covering the entire period of liquidation, and a supporting working paper showing the computation of instalment payments to partners as cash becomes available.
b At what point in liquidation did the partners' capital accounts have balances corresponding to the income-sharing ratio? Of what significance is this relationship with respect to subsequent cash distributions to partners?

2-6 Love, Mears, and Newman decided to form a partnership on January 10, Year 6. Their capital investments and income-sharing ratios are listed below:

Love: $45,000 — 50%

Mears: $30,000 — 30%, with a salary allowance of $18,000 a year, or a proportionate amount for a period less than a year

Newman: $24,000 — 20%

During the first six months of Year 6, the partners were not particularly concerned over the poor volume of business and the net loss of $42,000 reported by their accountant, because they had been told that it would take at least six months to establish their business and to achieve profitable operations. Business during the second half of the year did not improve, and the partners decided to go out of business before additional losses were incurred. The decision to liquidate was hastened when two major customers filed bankruptcy petitions.

The sale of assets was completed in October, Year 6, and all available cash was paid to creditors. Suppliers' invoices of $5,400 remained unpaid at this time. The personal financial status of each partner on October 31, Year 6, was as follows:

	Personal assets	Personal liabilities
Love	$30,000	$25,500
Mears	60,000	15,000
Newman	75,000	42,000

The partners had made no cash withdrawals during Year 6; however, in August Newman had withdrawn merchandise with a cost of $1,200 and Mears had taken title to equipment at a current fair value of $750, which was equal to the carrying amount of the equipment.

The partners have decided to end the partnership immediately and to arrive at a settlement in accordance with the provisions of the partnership acts.

Instructions Prepare a four-column statement of partners' capital (including liquidation) for the period January 10, Year 6, to October 31, Year 6. You need not show the changes in liabilities, cash, or noncash assets; however, the changes in the combined capital and individual capital accounts of the three partners should be shown.

2-7 Partners Denson, Eastin, and Feller share net income and losses in a 5:3:2 ratio, respectively. At the end of a very unprofitable year, they decided to liquidate the firm. The partners' capital account balances on this date were as follows: Denson, $22,000; Eastin, $24,900; Feller, $15,000. The liabilities in the balance sheet amounted to $30,000, including a loan of $10,000 from Denson. The cash balance was $6,000.

The partners plan to sell the noncash assets on a piecemeal basis and to distribute cash as rapidly as it becomes available. All three partners are personally solvent.

Instructions Answer each of the following questions and show how you reached your conclusions. (Each question is independent of the others. An advance program for cash distributions to partners would be helpful.)

a If Eastin received $2,000 from the first distribution of cash, how much did Denson and Feller each receive at that time?

b If Denson received a total of $20,000 as a result of the liquidation, what was the total amount realized by the partnership on the sale of the noncash assets?

c If Feller received $6,200 on the first distribution of cash, how much did Denson receive at that time?

2-8 Adderly and Boggs were attorneys who became acquainted because of their interest in auto racing. They decided to form a partnership, and persuaded a third attorney, Cobb, to join with them. The partnership had limited accounting records, but an employee maintained a careful daily record of cash receipts, which were almost entirely cheques received through the mail. The only other record was the chequebook used for all payments by the partnership. Some working papers were on file relating to income tax returns of prior years.

Early in Year 5, the partners quarrelled over the use of partnership funds; this quarrel led to a decision to liquidate the firm as of June 30, Year 5. You were retained to assemble the financial data needed for an equitable distribution of assets. You learn that the partnership was formed in Year 1, with equal capital investments and agreement to share net income and losses equally. By inspection of the income tax return for the year ended December 31, Year 4, you determine that the amounts of depreciable assets and accumulated depreciation on December 31, Year 4, were as follows:

	Depreciable assets (cost)	Accumulated depreciation, Dec. 31, Year 4
Office equipment	$ 7,500	$ 2,250
Library of reference books	4,500	900
Automobiles:		
Bentley — assigned to Adderly	20,000	6,000
Buick — assigned to Boggs	5,000	1,000
Cadillac — assigned to Cobb	15,000	3,000
Totals	$52,000	$13,150

By reference to the cash records, you find that fees received from clients for the first six months of Year 5 amounted to $310,000. Cash payments are summarized below.

The automobiles were depreciated on a straight-line basis over a five-year economic life with no residual value, and depreciation was treated as an expense of the partnership. A 10-year economic life was used for depreciation of office equipment and the library. As a step in the liquidation, the partners agreed that the automobiles acquired from partnership funds should be retained by the partners to whom assigned. They also agreed on equal distribution of the office equipment among them in kind. The entire library will be distributed to Adderly.

Automobile and miscellaneous expenses	$ 9,490
Entertainment expense	30,000
Wages and salaries expense	80,510
Rent expense	9,000
Drawings: Adderly	45,000
Drawings: Boggs	50,000
Drawings: Cobb	60,000
Total cash payments	$284,000

All assets distributed were assigned current fair values equal to carrying amounts.

Cash on hand and in bank on June 30, Year 5, amounted to $70,010. **The capital account balances of the partners were equal on December 31, Year 4.** Assume that the partnership had no other assets or liabilities, either at the beginning or at the end of the six-month period ended June 30, Year 5.

Instructions Prepare a statement of partners' capital for the period January 1 to June 30, Year 5, including the final distribution of cash and other assets to partners. To support this statement, prepare an income statement for the six months ended June 30, Year 5.

2-9 On August 10, Year 4, Alison Ho, Jodie Thompson, and George Cole agreed to acquire a speculative second mortgage note on undeveloped real estate. They invested

$110,800, $66,100 and $25,000, respectively, and agreed on an income-sharing ratio of 4:2:1, respectively.

On September 1, Year 4, the partnership acquired for $201,000 a second mortgage note with an unpaid principal balance of $245,000. The amount paid included interest accrued from June 30, Year 4, and legal fees of $1,000. The note principal matures at the rate of $5,000 each quarter. Interest at the annual rate of 12% on the unpaid principal balance also is due quarterly.

Regular interest and principal payments were received on September 30 and December 31, Year 4. A petty cash fund of $100 was established, and collection expenses of $260 were paid in December.

In addition to the regular payment on September 30, the mortgagor made an early payment of $20,000 principal plus a penalty of 2% (on $20,000) for early payment.

Because of the speculative nature of the second mortgage note, the partners agreed to defer recognition of the discount as revenue until their investment of $201,000 had been fully recovered.

Instructions

a Assuming that no cash distributions were made to the partners, prepare a working paper to compute the amount of cash available for distribution to the partners on December 31, Year 4.

b After payment of collection expenses, the partners wish to distribute the cash as soon as possible so that they individually can reinvest it. Prepare a working paper showing how any available cash should be distributed to the partners by instalments as it becomes available.

c Show how the cash on hand on December 31, Year 4, as computed in **a**, should be distributed to the partners.

2-10 After several years of successful operation of a partnership, Luis and Anna decided to incorporate and sell stock to public investors.

On January 2, Year 5, Luisanna, Inc., was organized with authorization to issue 150,000 shares of $10 par common stock. It issued 20,000 shares for cash to public investors at $16 a share. Luis and Anna agreed to accept shares at the same price in amounts equal to their respective capital account balances, after making the adjustments indicated below and after making cash withdrawals sufficient to avoid the need for issuing less than a multiple of 100 shares to either of the two partners. In payment for such shares, the partnership's net assets were transferred to the corporation and common share certificates were issued. A new set of accounting records was opened for the corporation.

The after-closing trial balance of the Luis & Anna Partnership on December 31, Year 4, follows:

LUIS & ANNA PARTNERSHIP

After-Closing Trial Balance
December 31, Year 4

Cash	$ 37,000	
Accounts receivable	30,000	
Inventories	56,000	
Land	28,000	
Buildings	50,000	
Accumulated depreciation of buildings		$ 17,000
Accounts payable		10,000
Luis, capital		63,000
Anna, capital		111,000
Totals	$201,000	$201,000

The partnership contract provided that Luis is to receive 40% of net income or loss and Anna 60%. The partners approved the following adjustments to the accounting records of the partnership on December 31, Year 4:

(1) Record short-term prepayments of $1,500 and accrued liabilities of $750.
(2) Provide an allowance for doubtful accounts of $12,000.
(3) Increase the carrying amount of land to a current fair value of $45,000.
(4) Increase inventories to present replacement cost of $75,000.

Instructions
a Prepare a single journal entry to adjust the accounting records of the Luis & Anna Partnership to current fair value. Also prepare all other entries needed to record the foregoing transactions.
b Prepare the journal entries necessary to record the foregoing transactions in the accounting records of Luisanna, Inc., on January 2, Year 5.
c Prepare the opening balance sheet for Luisanna, Inc., after the foregoing transactions have been recorded.

2-11 D, E & F Partnership has called on you to assist in winding up the affairs of the partnership. You are able to gather the following information:

(1) The trial balance of the partnership on March 1, Year 3, is as follows:

D, E & F PARTNERSHIP
Trial Balance
March 1, Year 3

Cash	$ 10,000	
Accounts receivable (net)	22,000	
Inventories	14,000	
Plant assets (net)	99,000	
D, loan receivable	12,000	
F, loan receivable	7,500	
Accounts payable		$ 21,000
D, capital		67,000
E, capital		45,000
F, capital		31,500
Totals	$164,500	$164,500

(2) The partners share net income and losses as follows: D, 40%; E, 40%; and F, 20%.
(3) The partners are considering an offer of $104,000 for the accounts receivable, inventories, and plant assets on March 1, Year 3.

Instructions
a Prepare a cash distribution program as of March 1, Year 3, and show how the total available cash of $114,000 ($10,000 + $104,000 = $114,000) would be distributed if the accounts receivable, inventories, and plant assets are sold for $104,000.
b Assume the same facts as in a, except that the partners have decided to liquidate the partnership instead of accepting the offer of $104,000. Cash is distributed to the partners at the end of each month. A summary of the liquidation transactions follows:

March: $16,500 collected on accounts receivable, balance is uncollectible.

$10,000 received for all inventories.

$1,000 liquidation expenses paid.

$8,000 cash retained for possible liquidation expenses.

April: $1,500 liquidation expenses paid. As part payment of F's capital account balance, F accepted equipment that had a carrying amount of $4,000. The partners agreed that a current fair value of $10,000 was appropriate for the equipment for liquidation purposes.

$3,500 cash retained for possible liquidation expenses.

May: $92,000 received on sale of remaining plant assets.

$1,000 liquidation expenses paid. No cash was retained.

Prepare a summary of cash distributions for the three months ended May 31, Year 3, that shows how the cash was distributed each month.

2-12 A, B, C, and D decided to liquidate their partnership. They plan to sell the assets gradually in order to minimize losses. They share net income and losses as follows: A 40%; B 35%; C 15%; and D 10%. Presented below is the partnership's trial balance on October 1, Year 8, the date on which liquidation began:

A, B, C & D PARTNERSHIP
Trial Balance
October 1, Year 8

Cash	$ 23,400	
Accounts receivable (net)	51,800	
Inventories, Oct. 1, Year 8	85,200	
Equipment (net)	39,600	
Accounts payable		$ 29,000
A, loan		12,000
B, loan		20,000
A, capital		40,000
B, capital		43,000
C, capital		36,000
D, capital		20,000
Totals	$200,000	$200,000

Instructions
a Prepare a working paper on October 1, Year 8, showing how cash will be distributed among partners in instalments as it becomes available. To simplify computations, restate the income-sharing ratio to 8:7:3:2.

b On October 31, Year 8, cash of $65,200 was available for creditors and partners. How should the $65,200 be distributed?

c If, instead of being liquidated, the partnership continued operations and earned $69,300 for the year ended September 30, Year 9, how should this income be divided if, in addition to the aforementioned income-sharing arrangement, it was provided that D receive a bonus of 5% of the income after treating the bonus as an expense? The income of $69,300 is before deduction of the bonus to D.

2-13 John Lee and Fred Moss started separate manufacturing enterprises and operated as single proprietorships for many years. In Year 8, they agreed to form a partnership, each transferring the assets and liabilities of his proprietorship to the new partnership.

Their income-sharing plan has been altered several times since Year 8, in order to recognize the changing contribution of each partner to the success of the partnership.

The current plan calls for the partnership net income (before interest on capital account balances and partners' salaries) to be distributed as follows:

(1) Interest of 10% a year on beginning capital account balances.
(2) Salary allowances: Lee, $25,000; Moss, $20,000.
(3) Balance of net income, 60% to Lee and 40% to Moss.
(4) Interest and salary allowances are to be allocated to partners, regardless of the amount of net income. Any excess of such allowances over the amount of net income available is to be absorbed by Lee and Moss in the residual income-sharing ratio.

On December 31, Year 16, the accountant for the partnership prepared the following preliminary balance sheet:

LEE & MOSS PARTNERSHIP
Preliminary Balance Sheet
December 31, Year 16

Assets			Liabilities & Partners' Capital		
Cash	$	180,000	Notes payable	$	154,500
Notes receivable		60,000	Accounts payable		135,000
Accounts receivable		250,000	Accrued liabilities		20,000
Less: Allowance for doubtful			Mortgage note payable		310,000
accounts		(15,000)	Lee, capital, Jan.		
Inventories		225,000	1, Year 16 ..... $521,900		
Land		150,000	Lee, drawings ... (40,000)		481,900
Buildings (net of accumulated			Moss, capital, Jan.		
depreciation of $200,000) ..		500,000	1, Year 16 ..... $428,600		
Machinery (net of accum-			Moss, drawings .. (30,000)		398,600
ulated depreciation of			Net income for Year 16		100,000
$120,000)		250,000			
Total		$1,600,000	Total		$1,600,000

Incorporation of partnership

The net income of $100,000 for Year 16 was distributed according to the partnership contract, and the partners decided to incorporate as the L & M Corporation, effective December 31, Year 16, as follows:

(1) Each partner is to receive 25,000 shares of 10% cumulative, $10 par preferred stock. A total of 100,000 shares of preferred stock is authorized to be issued. The current fair value of the preferred stock is equal to its par value.
(2) A total of 250,000 shares of common stock with a stated value of $0.10 a share will be issued to the partners in proportion to their adjusted capital account balances [item (3) below] after issuance of the preferred stock. A total of 500,000 shares of common stock is authorized to be issued.
(3) The accounting records of the partnership will be retained by the corporation; however, the following adjustments are required:

   (a) Short-term prepayments of $10,000 (consisting of rents, supplies, insurance, etc.) have been recorded as expenses by the partnership. The partners wish to report these assets in the opening balance sheet of the corporation.

(b) Costs of organizing the corporation, $12,500, have been inadvertently recorded as expenses by the partnership during Year 16.

(c) The accrued liabilities in the partnership's balance sheet on December 31, Year 16, do not include $3,000 of interest that has accrued on notes payable.

The activities of the L & M Corporation for the year ended December 31, Year 17, are summarized below:

(4) Net income (after income taxes) amounted to $120,000.

(5) Dividends of $1 a share were declared and paid on the preferred stock, and cash dividends of $0.12 a share were declared and paid on the common stock.

Instructions

a Allocate the net income of $100,000 for Year 16 to the partners pursuant to the income-sharing plan, and compute the capital account balance for each partner on December 31, Year 16.

b Starting with the capital account balances on December 31, Year 16, as determined in part **a**, prepare a working paper to adjust the partners' capital accounts in accordance with the incorporation plan and determine the number of shares of common stock to be issued to each partner. (Round shares to be issued to the nearest whole share.)

c Prepare journal entries on December 31, Year 16, to adjust the accounting records of the partnership, and to change the partnership to a corporation. Assume that the preferred shares and common shares are issued directly to Lee and Moss instead of first being transferred to the partnership.

d Prepare the shareholders' equity section of the balance sheet for the L & M Corporation on December 31, Year 17.

3

ACCOUNTING FOR BRANCHES; COMBINED FINANCIAL STATEMENTS

Branches and divisions

As a business enterprise grows it often establishes branches to market its products over a larger territory. The term **branch** has been used to describe a business unit located at some distance from the home office that carries merchandise, makes sales, approves customers' credit, and makes collections from its customers.

A branch may obtain merchandise solely from the home office, or a portion may be purchased from outside suppliers. The cash receipts of the branch often are deposited in a bank account belonging to the home office; the branch expenses then are paid from an imprest cash fund or a bank account provided by the home office. As the imprest fund is depleted, the branch submits a list of cash payments supported by vouchers and receives a cheque from the home office to replenish the fund.

The use of an imprest fund gives the home office strong control over the cash transactions of the branch. However, it is common practice for a large branch to maintain its own bank accounts; that is, to deposit its cash receipts and issue its own cheques. The extent of autonomy and responsibility given to a branch varies even among different branches of the same business enterprise.

A segment of a business enterprise also may be operated as a **division**. The accounting procedures for a division not organized as a separate corporation (**subsidiary company**) are similar to those used for branches. When a segment of a business enterprise is operated as a separate corporation, consolidated financial statements generally would be required. Consolidated financial statements are described in Chapters 5 through 10; accounting and reporting problems for segments of business enterprises are included in Chapter 11.

Accounting system for a sales agency

The term *sales agency* sometimes is applied to a business unit that performs only a small portion of the functions traditionally associated with a branch. For example, a sales agency usually carries samples of products but does not have an inventory of merchandise. Orders are taken from customers and transmitted to the home office, which approves the customers' credit and ships the merchandise directly to customers. The agency's accounts receivable are maintained at the home office, which also performs the collection function. An imprest cash fund generally is maintained at the sales agency for the payment of operating expenses.

A sales agency that does not carry an inventory of merchandise, maintain receivables, or make collections has no need for a complete set of accounting records. All that is needed is a record of sales to customers and a summary of cash payments supported by vouchers.

If the home office wants to measure the profitability of each sales agency separately, it will establish in the general ledger separate revenue and expense accounts in the name of the agency, for example, Sales: Lakeview Agency; Rent Expense: Lakeview Agency. The cost of goods sold by each agency also must be determined. When a perpetual inventory system is in use, shipments to customers of the Lakeview Agency are debited to Cost of Goods Sold: Lakeview Agency and credited to Inventories.

When a periodic inventory system is used, a shipment of goods sold by an agency may be recorded by a debit to Cost of Goods Sold: Lakeview Agency and a credit to Shipments to Agencies. This journal entry is recorded only at the end of the accounting period if a memorandum record is maintained during the period listing the cost of goods shipped to fill sales orders received from agencies. At the end of the period the Shipments to Agencies account is offset against the total of beginning inventories and purchases to determine the cost of goods available for sale for the home office in its own operations.

Office furniture or other assets located at a sales agency may be carried in a separate account in the general ledger of the home office, or control over such assets may be achieved by use of a subsidiary ledger with a detailed record for each item showing cost, location, and other data.

Illustrative Journal Entries for a Sales Agency   The journal entries required for the home office in connection with the operation of a sales agency are illustrated on page 90, assuming that the perpetual inventory system is used.

Accounting system for a branch

The extent of the accounting activity at a branch depends on company policy. The policies of one company may provide for a complete set of accounting records at each branch; policies of another company may concentrate all accounting records in the home office. In some of the drug and grocery chain stores, for example, the branches submit daily reports and documents to the home office, which enters all transactions by branches in

Journal entries for home
office to record agency
activities

HOME OFFICE

General Journal

Inventory of Samples: Lakeview Agency	1,500	
Inventories		1,500
To record merchandise shipped to agency for use as samples.		
Imprest Cash Fund: Lakeview Agency	1,000	
Cash		1,000
To establish agency imprest cash fund.		
Accounts Receivable	50,000	
Sales: Lakeview Agency		50,000
To record sales made through Lakeview Agency.		
Cost of Goods Sold: Lakeview Agency	35,000	
Inventories		35,000
To record cost of goods sold through Lakeview Agency.		
Various Expense Accounts: Lakeview Agency	10,000	
Cash		10,000
To replenish imprest cash fund. (This entry represents several cheques		
sent to the agency during the accounting period.)		
Sales: Lakeview Agency	50,000	
Cost of Goods Sold: Lakeview Agency		35,000
Various Expense Accounts: Lakeview Agency		10,000
Income Summary: Lakeview Agency		5,000
To close revenue and expense accounts to a separate Income Summary		
account for sales agency.		
Income Summary: Lakeview Agency	5,000	
Income Summary		5,000
To close agency net income to Income Summary account.		

computerized accounting records kept in a central location. The home office may not even conduct operations of its own but merely serve as an accounting and control centre for the branches.

In many fields of business, a branch maintains a complete set of accounting records consisting of journals, ledgers, and a chart of accounts similar to those of an independent business enterprise. Financial statements are prepared at regular intervals by the branch and forwarded to the home office. The number and types of accounts, the internal control system, the form and content of financial statements, and the accounting policies generally are prescribed by the home office.

In the remainder of this chapter we are concerned with a branch operation that maintains a complete set of accounting records. Transactions recorded by branches ordinarily should include all controllable expenses and revenue for which branch managers are responsible. If branch managers have responsibility over all branch assets and all expenditures, then the branch accounting records should reflect this responsibility. Expenses such as depreciation are not subject to control by branch managers; therefore, both the plant assets and the related depreciation accounts generally are maintained by the home office.

Reciprocal accounts

The accounting records maintained by a branch include a Home Office account that is credited for all merchandise, cash, or other resources provided by the home office; it is debited for all cash, merchandise, or other assets sent by the branch to the home office or to other branches. The Home Office account is an ownership equity account that shows the net investment by the home office in the branch. At the end of the accounting period when the branch closes its accounting records, the Income Summary account is closed to the Home Office account. A net income increases the credit balance in the Home Office account; a net loss decreases this balance.

In the home office accounting records, a *reciprocal account* with a title such as Investment in Branch is maintained. This asset account is debited for cash, merchandise, and services provided to the branch by the home office, and for net income reported by the branch. It is credited for the cash or other assets received from the branch, and for any net loss reported by the branch. Thus accounting for the Investment in Branch account is similar to the *equity method* of accounting. A separate investment account generally is maintained by the home office for each branch. If there is only one branch, the account title is likely to be Investment in Branch; if there are numerous branches, each account title includes a name or number to identify the individual branch.

Expenses incurred by home office and charged to branches

Some business enterprises follow a policy of notifying branches of expenses incurred by the home office on the branches' behalf. As previously mentioned, plant assets located at branches generally are carried in the home office accounting records. If a plant asset is acquired by the home office for the branch, the journal entry for the acquisition is a debit to an asset account and credit to Cash or Accounts Payable. If the branch acquires a plant asset, it debits the Home Office account and credits Cash or Accounts Payable. The home office debits an asset account, such as Equipment: Elba Branch, and credits the reciprocal account Investment in Elba Branch.

The home office also usually acquires insurance, pays property and other taxes, and arranges for advertising that benefits all branches. Clearly, such expenses as depreciation, property taxes, insurance, and advertising must be considered in determining the profitability of a branch. A policy decision must be made as to whether these expense data are to be retained at the home office or are to be reported to the branches so that the income statement prepared by each branch will give a complete picture of its operations.

If the home office does not make sales itself but functions only as an accounting and control centre, most or all of its expenses may be allocated to the branches. To facilitate comparison of the operating results of the various branches, the home office may charge each branch interest on the capital invested in that branch. Such interest expense recorded by the branches would be offset by interest revenue recorded by the home office and would not appear in the *combined* income statement of the business enterprise as a whole.

Alternative methods of billing merchandise shipments to branch

Three alternative methods are available to the home office for billing merchandise shipped to a branch. The shipments may be billed (1) at cost, (2) at cost plus an appropriate percentage, or (3) at retail selling price.[1] Of course, the shipment of merchandise to a branch does not constitute a sale, because ownership of the merchandise does not change.

Billing *at cost* is the simplest procedure and is widely used. It avoids the complication of unrealized gross profit in inventories and permits the financial statements of branches to give a meaningful picture of operations. However, billing merchandise to branches at cost attributes all gross profits of the enterprise to the branches, even though some of the merchandise may be manufactured by the home office. Under these circumstances, cost may not be the most realistic basis for billing shipments to branches.

Billing shipments to a branch *at a percentage above cost* (such as 110% of cost) may be intended to allocate a reasonable gross profit to home office operations. When merchandise is billed to a branch at a price above cost, the net income reported by the branch will be understated and the ending inventories will be overstated for the enterprise as a whole. Adjustments must be made by the home office to eliminate the excess of billed prices over cost in the preparation of combined financial statements for the home office and the branch.

Billing shipments to a branch *at retail selling price* may be based on a desire to strengthen internal control over inventories. The Inventories account of the branch shows the merchandise received and sold at retail selling prices. Consequently, the account will show the ending inventories that should be on hand priced at retail. The home office record of shipments to a branch, when considered along with sales reported by the branch, provides a perpetual inventory stated at selling price. If the physical inventories taken periodically at the branch do not agree with the amounts thus determined, an error or theft is indicated and should be investigated promptly.

1 Billing of merchandise to branches at a price above cost is illustrated on pages 99 to 102.

Separate financial statements for branch and home office

A separate income statement and balance sheet should be prepared for the branch so that management of the enterprise may review the operating results and financial position of the branch. The income statement has no unusual features if merchandise is billed to the branch at cost. However, if merchandise is billed to the branch at retail selling price, the income statement will show a net loss approximating the amount of operating expenses. The only unusual aspect of the balance sheet for a branch is the use of the Home Office account in lieu of the ownership equity accounts for a separate business enterprise. The separate financial statements prepared for a branch may be revised at the home office to include expenses incurred by the home office allocable to the branch, and to show branch operations after elimination of any intracompany profits on merchandise shipments.

Separate financial statements also may be prepared for the home office so that management will be able to appraise the results of its operations and its financial position. However, it is important to emphasize that separate financial statements of the home office and of the branch are prepared for internal use only; they do not meet the needs of investors, or other external users of financial statements.

Combined financial statements for home office and branch

A balance sheet for distribution to creditors, shareholders, and government agencies must show the financial position of the business enterprise as a *single entity*. A convenient starting point in the preparation of a combined balance sheet consists of the adjusted trial balances of the home office and of the branch. A working paper for the combination of these trial balances is illustrated on page 97.

The assets and liabilities of the branch are substituted for the Investment in Branch account included in the home office trial balance. Similar accounts are combined to produce one amount for the total cash, accounts receivable, and other assets and liabilities of the enterprise as a whole.

In the preparation of a combined balance sheet, reciprocal accounts are eliminated because they lose all significance when the branch and home office are viewed as a single entity. The Home Office account is offset against the Investment in Branch account; also any receivables and payables between branches or between the home office and a branch are eliminated.

The operating results of the enterprise (the home office and all branches) are shown by an income statement in which the revenue and expenses of the branches are combined with corresponding revenue and expenses for the home office. Any intracompany profits or losses must be eliminated.

Illustrative Journal Entries of Operation of a Branch   Assume that Smaldino Company bills merchandise to Branch X at cost, and that the branch maintains complete accounting records and prepares financial statements. *Both the home office and the branch use the perpetual* *inventory system*. Equipment used at the branch is carried in the home office accounting records. Certain expenses, such as advertising and insurance, are incurred by the home office on behalf of the branch and are billed to the branch. Transactions during the first year (Year 1) of operations of the branch are summarized below:

Transactions for Year 1:
(1) Cash of $1,000 was sent to the branch
(2) Merchandise with a cost of $60,000 was shipped to the branch

Typical home office and branch transactions (perpetual inventory system)

Home Office Accounting Records			Branch Accounting Records		
(1) Investment in			Cash	1,000	
Branch X	1,000		Home Office ..		1,000
Cash		1,000			
(2) Investment in			Inventories	60,000	
Branch X	60,000		Home Office ..		60,000
Inventories ...		60,000			
(3) Equipment:			Home Office	500	
Branch X	500		Cash		500
Investment in					
Branch X ...		500			
(4) None			Accounts		
			Receivable	80,000	
			Cost of Goods Sold ..	45,000	
			Sales		80,000
			Inventories ...		45,000
(5) None			Cash	62,000	
			Accounts		
			Receivable ..		62,000
(6) None			Operating Expenses .	20,000	
			Cash		20,000
(7) Cash	37,500		Home Office	37,500	
Investment in			Cash		37,500
Branch X ...		37,500			
(8) Investment in			Operating Expenses .	3,000	
Branch X	3,000		Home Office ..		3,000
Operating					
Expenses ..		3,000			

(3) Equipment was acquired by the branch for $500, to be carried in home office accounting records (Other assets for the branch normally are acquired by the home office)

(4) Credit sales by the branch amounted to $80,000; the cost of the merchandise sold was $45,000

(5) Collections of accounts receivable by the branch amounted to $62,000

(6) Payments for operating expenses by the branch totalled $20,000

(7) Cash of $37,500 was remitted by the branch to the home office

(8) Operating expenses incurred by the home office and charged to the branch totalled $3,000

These transactions are recorded by the home office and by the branch as illustrated on page 94.

When the branch obtains merchandise from outsiders as well as from the home office, the merchandise acquired from the home office should be recorded in a separate Inventories from Home Office account.

In the home office accounting records, the Investment in Branch X account has a debit balance of $26,000 (before the accounting records are closed and the branch net income of $12,000 is transferred to the Investment in Branch X account), as illustrated below.

Reciprocal account in home office general ledger

Investment in Branch X

Date	Explanation	Debit	Credit	Balance
	Cash sent to branch	1,000		1,000 dr
	Merchandise billed to branch at cost	60,000		61,000 dr
	Equipment acquired by branch, carried in home office accounting records		500	60,500 dr
	Cash received from branch		37,500	23,000 dr
	Operating expenses billed to branch	3,000		26,000 dr

In the branch accounting records, the Home Office account has a credit balance of $26,000 (before the accounting records are closed and the net income of $12,000 is transferred to the Home Office account), as shown below.

Reciprocal account in branch general ledger

Home Office

Date	Explanation	Debit	Credit	Balance
	Cash received from home office		1,000	1,000 cr
	Merchandise received from home office		60,000	61,000 cr
	Equipment acquired by branch	500		60,500 cr
	Cash sent to home office	37,500		23,000 cr
	Operating expenses billed by home office		3,000	26,000 cr

Assume that the perpetual inventories of $15,000 ($60,000 − $45,000 = $15,000) at the end of Year 1 for Branch X had been verified by a physical count. The adjusting and closing entries relating to the branch are given below.

<table>
<tr><td>Adjusting and closing entries (perpetual inventory system)</td><td colspan="2">Home Office Accounting Records</td><td colspan="2">Branch Accounting Records</td></tr>
<tr><td></td><td colspan="2">None</td><td>Sales ....80,000</td><td></td></tr>
<tr><td></td><td></td><td></td><td>Cost of Goods</td><td></td></tr>
<tr><td></td><td></td><td></td><td>Sold ......</td><td>45,000</td></tr>
<tr><td></td><td></td><td></td><td>Operating</td><td></td></tr>
<tr><td></td><td></td><td></td><td>Expenses ...</td><td>23,000</td></tr>
<tr><td></td><td></td><td></td><td>Income</td><td></td></tr>
<tr><td></td><td></td><td></td><td>Summary ...</td><td>12,000</td></tr>
<tr><td></td><td>Investment in</td><td></td><td>Income Summary ...12,000</td><td></td></tr>
<tr><td></td><td>Branch X ....12,000</td><td></td><td>Home Office ..</td><td>12,000</td></tr>
<tr><td></td><td>Income:</td><td></td><td></td><td></td></tr>
<tr><td></td><td>Branch X ...</td><td>12,000</td><td></td><td></td></tr>
<tr><td></td><td>Income: Branch X ...12,000</td><td></td><td>None</td><td></td></tr>
<tr><td></td><td>Income</td><td></td><td></td><td></td></tr>
<tr><td></td><td>Summary ...</td><td>12,000</td><td></td><td></td></tr>
</table>

Working paper for combined financial statements

A working paper for combined financial statements has three purposes: (1) to combine ledger account balances for like assets and liabilities, (2) to eliminate any intracompany profits or losses, and (3) to eliminate the reciprocal accounts. The working paper illustrated on page 97 for Smaldino Company is based on the branch transactions illustrated on pages 93 to 96 and additional assumed data for the home office trial balance. All the routine year-end adjusting entries are assumed to have been made, and the working paper is begun with the adjusted trial balances of the home office and the branch. Income taxes are ignored in this illustration.

Note that the $26,000 debit balance in the Investment in Branch X account and the $26,000 credit balance in the Home Office account are the balances before the respective accounting records are closed, that is, before the $12,000 net income of the branch is entered in these two reciprocal accounts. In the Elimination column, elimination (a) offsets the Investment in Branch X account against the Home Office account. *This elimination appears in the working paper only;* it is not recorded in the accounting records of either the home office or the branch, because its only purpose is to facilitate the preparation of combined financial statements.

SMALDINO COMPANY

Working Paper for Combined Financial Statements of Home Office and Branch X
For Year Ended December 31, Year 1
(Perpetual Inventory System: Billings at Cost)

| | Adjusted trial balances | | | | Elimination | Combined | |
| | Home office | | Branch | | Debit | | |
	Debit	Credit	Debit	Credit	(Credit)	Debit	Credit
Income statement							
Sales		400,000		80,000			480,000
Cost of goods							
sold	235,000		45,000			280,000	
Operating expenses	90,000		23,000			113,000	
Subtotals	325,000	400,000	68,000	80,000		393,000	480,000
Net income (to							
statement of re-							
tained earnings							
below)	75,000		12,000			87,000	
Totals	400,000	400,000	80,000	80,000		480,000	480,000
Statement of retained							
earnings							
Retained earnings,							
Jan. 1, Year 1 ..		70,000					70,000
Net income (from							
above)		75,000		12,000			87,000
Dividends	40,000					40,000	
Retained earnings,							
Dec. 31, Year 1							
(to balance sheet							
below)						117,000	
Totals						157,000	157,000
Balance Sheet							
Cash	24,000		5,000			29,000	
Accounts receivable							
(net)	40,000		18,000			58,000	
Inventories	45,000		15,000			60,000	
Investment in							
Branch X	26,000				(a) (26,000)		
Equipment	150,000					150,000	
Accumulated							
depreciation ...		10,000					10,000
Accounts							
payable		20,000					20,000
Home office				26,000	(a) 26,000		
Common stock,							
$10 par		150,000					150,000
Retained earnings							
(from above) ...							117,000
Totals	325,000	325,000	38,000	38,000	-0-	297,000	297,000

(a) To eliminate reciprocal accounts.

Combined Financial Statements Illustrated   The working paper on page 97 provides the information for the combined financial statements of Smaldino Company below.

SMALDINO COMPANY
Income Statement
For Year Ended December 31, Year 1

Sales	$480,000
Cost of goods sold	280,000
Gross profit on sales	$200,000
Operating expenses	113,000
Net income	87,000
Earnings per share	$ 5.80

SMALDINO COMPANY
Statement of Retained Earnings
For Year Ended December 31, Year 1

Retained earnings, beginning of year	$ 70,000
Add: Net income	87,000
Subtotal	$157,000
Less: Dividends	40,000
Retained earnings, end of year	$117,000

SMALDINO COMPANY
Balance Sheet
December 31, Year 1

Assets

Cash		$ 29,000
Accounts receivable (net)		58,000
Inventories		60,000
Equipment	$150,000	
Less: Accumulated depreciation	10,000	140,000
Total assets		$287,000

Liabilities & Shareholders' Equity

Liabilities:		
Accounts payable		$ 20,000
Shareholders' equity:		
Common stock, $10 par	$150,000	
Retained earnings	117,000	267,000
Total liabilities & shareholders' equity		$287,000

Billing of merchandise to branches at price above cost

As explained earlier, some business enterprises bill merchandise to branches at cost plus a markup percentage, or at retail selling price. Because both these methods involve similar modifications of accounting procedures, a single example illustrates the key points involved. We shall now repeat the illustration for Smaldino Company, with one changed assumption: the home office bills merchandise to the branch at 50% above cost.

Under this assumption the journal entries for the first year's transactions by the home office and the branch are the same as those previously presented on page 94, except for the journal entries showing shipments from the home office to the branch. These shipments ($60,000 + 50% markup = $90,000) are recorded under a perpetual inventory system as follows:

Shipment to branch at a price above cost (perpetual inventory system)

Home Office Accounting Records		Branch Accounting Records	
(2) Investment in		Inventories 90,000	
Branch X 90,000		Home Office	90,000
Inventories	60,000		
Allowance for			
Overvaluation			
of Inventories:			
Branch X	30,000		

In the home office accounting records the Investment in Branch X account now has a debit balance of $56,000 before the accounting records are closed and the branch net income or loss is entered in the Investment in Branch X account. This amount is $30,000 larger than the $26,000 balance in the prior illustration; the increase represents the 50% markup over cost of the merchandise shipped to Branch X. The Investment in Branch X account is illustrated below:

Reciprocal account in home office ledger

Investment in Branch X

Date	Explanation	Debit	Credit	Balance
	Cash sent to branch	1,000		1,000 dr
	Merchandise billed to branch at 50% above cost	90,000		91,000 dr
	Equipment acquired by branch, carried in home office accounting records		500	90,500 dr
	Cash received from branch		37,500	53,000 dr
	Operating expenses billed to branch	3,000		56,000 dr

In the branch accounting records the Home Office account now has a credit balance of $56,000, before the accounting records are closed and the branch net income or loss is entered in the Home Office account:

CHAPTER 3   ACCOUNTING FOR BRANCHES; COMBINED FINANCIAL STATEMENTS   **99**

	Home Office			
Date	Explanation	Debit	Credit	Balance
	Cash received from home office		1,000	1,000 cr
	Merchandise received from home office		90,000	91,000 cr
	Equipment acquired by branch	500		90,500 cr
	Cash sent to home office	37,500		53,000 cr
	Operating expenses billed by home office		3,000	56,000 cr

The branch recorded the merchandise received from the home office at the billed price of $90,000; the home office recorded the shipment by credits of $60,000 to Inventories and $30,000 to the Allowance for Overvaluation of Inventories: Branch X account. Use of the allowance account enables the home office to maintain a record of the cost of merchandise shipped to the branch, as well as the amount of the unrealized gross profit on the shipments.

At the end of the accounting period, the branch will report its inventories (based on billed prices) at $22,500. The cost of these inventories is $15,000 (computed as follows: $22,500 ÷ 1.50 = $15,000). In the home office accounting records, the required balance in the Allowance for Overvaluation of Inventories: Branch X account is $7,500; thus, this account must be reduced from its present balance of $30,000 to $7,500. The reason for this reduction is that the 50% markup of billed prices over cost has become realized gross profit with respect to the merchandise sold by the branch. Consequently, at the end of the year the home office should reduce its allowance for overvaluation of the branch inventories to the $7,500 excess valuation contained in the ending inventories. The adjustment of $22,500 in the allowance account is transferred as a credit to the Income: Branch X account, because it represents additional gross profit on branch operations

Home Office Accounting Records

Income: Branch X   10,500
    Investment in Branch X   10,500
To record net loss reported by branch.

Allowance for Overvaluation of Inventories: Branch X   22,500
    Income: Branch X   22,500
To reduce allowance to amount by which ending inventories of branch
exceed cost.

Income: Branch X   12,000
    Income Summary   12,000
To close branch net income (as adjusted) to Income Summary.

over that reported by the branch. Thus, the actual net income for the branch is $12,000, the same as in the prior illustration in which merchandise was billed to the branch at cost. Under the present assumption, however, the branch reports a net loss of $10,500. This amount is recorded by the home office and adjusted to a net income of $12,000, as shown by the journal entries at the end of Year 1 at the bottom of page 100.

After these journal entries have been posted, the accounts in the home office general ledger used to portray branch operations appear as shown below.

End-of-period balances in home office accounting records

Investment in Branch X

Date	Explanation	Debit	Credit	Balance
	Cash sent to branch	1,000		1,000 dr
	Merchandise billed to branch at 50% above cost	90,000		91,000 dr
	Equipment acquired by branch, carried in home office accounting records		500	90,500 dr
	Cash received from branch		37,500	53,000 dr
	Operating expenses billed to branch	3,000		56,000 dr
	Net loss for Year 1 reported by branch		10,500	45,500 dr

Allowance for Overvaluation of Inventories: Branch X

Date	Explanation	Debit	Credit	Balance
	Markup of merchandise shipped to branch during Year 1 (50% of cost)		30,000	30,000 cr
	Realization of 50% markup on merchandise sold by branch during Year 1	22,500		7,500 cr

Income: Branch X

Date	Explanation	Debit	Credit	Balance
	Net loss reported by branch for Year 1	10,500		10,500 dr
	Realization of 50% markup on merchandise sold by branch		22,500	12,000 cr
	Net income of branch (as adjusted) closed to Income Summary account	12,000		-0-

In a separate balance sheet for the home office, the $7,500 credit balance in the Allowance for Overvaluation of Inventories: Branch X account is deducted from the $45,500 debit balance in the Investment in Branch X account.

The closing entries for the branch at the end of Year 1 are on page 102. After these closing entries have been posted by the branch, the Home Office account in the branch accounting records (below) will have a credit balance of $45,500, the same as the debit balance in the Investment in Branch X account in the accounting records of the home office.

Closing entries for branch (perpetual inventory system)

Branch Accounting Records

Sales	80,000	
Income Summary	10,500	
Cost of Goods Sold		67,500
Operating Expenses		23,000
To close revenue and expense accounts.		
Home Office	10,500	
Income Summary		10,500
To close the net loss in the Income Summary account to the Home Office account.		

Compare this account with Investment in Branch X account on page 101

Home Office

Date	Explanation	Debit	Credit	Balance
	Cash received from home office		1,000	1,000 cr
	Merchandise received from home office		90,000	91,000 cr
	Equipment acquired by branch	500		90,500 cr
	Cash sent to home office	37,500		53,000 cr
	Operating expenses billed by home office		3,000	56,000 cr
	Net loss for Year 1	10,500		45,500 cr

Working paper when billings to branches are at prices above cost

The working paper for combined financial statements when billings to the branch are made at prices above cost is shown on page 103. It differs from the previously illustrated working paper by the inclusion of an elimination to restate the ending inventories of the branch to cost. Also, the net loss reported by the branch is adjusted by the $22,500 of merchandise markup that was realized as a result of sales by the branch. As stated earlier, the amounts in the Eliminations column appear only in the working paper. The amounts represent a mechanical step to aid in the preparation of combined financial statements and are not entered in the accounting records of either the home office or the branch.

Note that the amounts in the Combined columns of this working paper are exactly the same as in the working paper prepared when the merchandise shipments to the branch were billed at cost. Consequently, the combined financial statements would be identical with those presented on page 98.

SMALDINO COMPANY
Working Paper for Combined Financial Statements of Home Office and Branch X
For Year Ended December 31, Year 1
(Perpetual Inventory System: Billings above Cost)

	Adjusted trial balances				Eliminations	Combined	
	Home office		Branch		Debit (Credit)		
	Debit	Credit	Debit	Credit		Debit	Credit
Income statement							
Sales		400,000		80,000			480,000
Cost of goods sold	235,000		67,500		(a) (22,500)	280,000	
Operating expenses	90,000		23,000			113,000	
Subtotals	325,000	400,000	90,500	80,000		393,000	480,000
Net income (to statement of retained earnings below)	75,000		10,500		(b) 22,500	87,000	
Totals	400,000	400,000	90,500	90,500		480,000	480,000
Statement of retained earnings							
Retained earnings, Jan. 1, Year 1		70,000					70,000
Net income (from above)		75,000		10,500	(b) (22,500)		87,000
Dividends	40,000					40,000	
Retained earnings, Dec. 31, Year 1 (to balance sheet below)						117,000	
Totals						157,000	157,000
Balance sheet							
Cash	24,000		5,000			29,000	
Accounts receivable (net)	40,000		18,000			58,000	
Inventories, Dec. 31, Year 1	45,000		22,500		(a) (7,500)	60,000	
Allowance for overvaluation of inventories:							
Branch X		30,000			(a) 30,000		
Investment in Branch X	56,000				(c) (56,000)		
Equipment	150,000					150,000	
Accumulated depreciation		10,000					10,000
Accounts payable		20,000					20,000
Home office				56,000	(c) 56,000		
Common stock, $10 par		150,000					150,000
Retained earnings (from above)							117,000
Totals	355,000	355,000	56,000	56,000	-0-	297,000	297,000

(a) To reduce ending inventories and cost of goods sold of branch to cost, and to eliminate balance in Allowance for Overvaluation of Inventories: Branch X account.

(b) To increase net income of branch by portion of merchandise markup that was realized.

(c) To eliminate reciprocal accounts.

Treatment of beginning inventories priced above cost

The working paper on page 103 shows how the ending inventories and the related allowance for overvaluation of inventories were handled. However, because this was the first year of operations for the branch, no beginning inventories were involved.

Perpetual Inventory System   Under the perpetual inventory system, no special problems arise when the beginning inventories of the branch include an element of unrealized gross profit. The working paper eliminations would be similar to those illustrated below.

Periodic Inventory System   We shall continue the illustration for Smaldino Company for a second year of operations (Year 2) to demonstrate the handling of beginning inventories carried by the branch at an amount above cost. However, we shall assume that both the home office and Branch X adopted the periodic inventory system in Year 2. When the periodic inventory system is used, the home office credits Shipments to Branch (a contra account to Purchases) for the cost of merchandise shipped and Allowance for Overvaluation of Inventories for the markup over cost. The branch debits Shipments from Home Office (analogous to Purchases account) for the billed price of merchandise received.

The beginning inventories for Year 2 were carried by Branch X at $22,500, or 150% of the cost of $15,000. Assume that during Year 2 the home office shipped to Branch X merchandise that cost $80,000 and was billed at $120,000, and that Branch X sold merchandise that was billed at $112,500 for $150,000. The journal entries to record the shipments and sales under a periodic inventory system are illustrated below:

Shipments to branch at a price above cost (periodic inventory system)	Home Office Accounting Records		Branch Accounting Records	
	Investment in		Shipments from	
	Branch X 120,000		Home Office 120,000	
	Shipments to		Home	
	Branch X . . .	80,000	Office	120,000
	Allowance for			
	Overvaluation			
	of Inventories:			
	Branch X . . .	40,000		
	None		Cash (or Accounts	
			Receivable) 150,000	
			Sales	150,000

The branch inventories at the end of Year 2 amounted to $30,000 at billed price, representing cost of $20,000 plus a 50% markup. The flow of merchandise for Branch X during Year 2 is summarized at the top of page 105.

SMALDINO COMPANY
Flow of Merchandise for Branch X
During Year 2

	Cost	Markup	Billed price
Beginning inventories	$15,000	$ 7,500	$ 22,500
Add: Shipments from home office	80,000	40,000	120,000
Available for sale	$95,000	$47,500	$142,500
Less: Ending inventories	(20,000)	(10,000)	(30,000)
Merchandise sold	$75,000	$37,500	$112,500

The activities of the branch for Year 2 are reflected in the three home office ledger accounts below.

In the home office accounting records at the end of Year 2, the balance required in the Allowance for Overvaluation of Inventories: Branch X account is $10,000, that is, the billed price of $30,000 less cost of $20,000

End-of-period balances in home office accounting records

Investment in Branch X

Date	Explanation	Debit	Credit	Balance
	Balance, Dec. 31, Year 1			45,500 dr
	Merchandise billed to branch at 50%			
	above cost	120,000		165,500 dr
	Cash received from branch		113,000	52,500 dr
	Operating expenses billed to branch	4,500		57,000 dr
	Net income for Year 2 reported by			
	branch	10,000		67,000 dr

Allowance for Overvaluation of Inventories: Branch X

Date	Explanation	Debit	Credit	Balance
	Balance, Dec. 31, Year 1 (see page 101)			7,500 cr
	Markup of merchandise shipped to branch			
	during Year 2 (50% of cost)		40,000	47,500 cr
	Realization of 50% markup on mer-			
	chandise sold by branch during Year 2	37,500		10,000 cr

Income: Branch X

Date	Explanation	Debit	Credit	Balance
	Net income reported for Year 2 by branch		10,000	10,000 cr
	Realization of 50% markup on mer-			
	chandise sold by branch during Year 2		37,500	47,500 cr
	Net income of branch (as adjusted)			
	closed to Income Summary account	47,500		-0-

Branch Accounting Records

Inventories, Dec. 31, Year 2	30,000	
Sales	150,000	
Inventories, Dec. 31, Year 1		22,500
Shipments from Home Office		120,000
Operating Expenses		27,500
Income Summary		10,000

To record ending inventories and to close beginning inventories, revenue, and expense accounts.

Income Summary	10,000	
Home Office		10,000

To close Income Summary account.

Home Office Accounting Records

Investment in Branch X	10,000	
Income: Branch X		10,000

To record net income reported by branch.

Allowance for Overvaluation of Inventories: Branch X	37,500	
Income: Branch X		37,500

To recognize as realized income the markup of merchandise applicable to goods sold by branch during Year 2.

Income: Branch X	47,500	
Income Summary		47,500

To close branch income to Income Summary account.

Inventories, Dec. 31, Year 2	70,000	
Sales	500,000	
Shipments to Branch X	80,000	
Inventories, Dec. 31, Year 1		45,000
Purchases		400,000
Operating Expenses		120,000
Income Summary		85,000

To record ending inventories and to close beginning inventories, revenue, and expense accounts.

Income Summary	132,500	
Retained Earnings		132,500

To close Income Summary account.

Retained Earnings	60,000	
Dividends		60,000

To close Dividends account.

for merchandise in the ending inventories. The allowance account, therefore, is reduced from its present balance of $47,500 to $10,000. This reduction of $37,500 represents the 50% markup of merchandise above cost that was realized by the branch during Year 2 and is credited to the Income: Branch X account.

The Home Office account in the branch general ledger shows the following activity for Year 2:

Reciprocal account in branch ledger

	Home Office			
Date	Explanation	Debit	Credit	Balance
	Balance, Dec. 31, Year 1			45,500 cr
	Merchandise received from home office		120,000	165,500 cr
	Cash sent to home office	113,000		52,500 cr
	Operating expenses billed by home office		4,500	57,000 cr
	Net income for Year 2		10,000	67,000 cr

The working paper for combined financial statements under the periodic inventory system appears on pages 108 and 109.

Closing Entries   The closing entries for the branch and the adjusting and closing entries for the home office at the end of Year 2 are illustrated on page 106.

Reconciliation of reciprocal ledger accounts

At the end of an accounting period, the balance of the Investment in Branch account in the home office accounting records may not agree with the balance of the Home Office account in the branch accounting records, because certain transactions may have been recorded by one office but not by the other. The situation is comparable to that of reconciling the ledger account for Cash in Bank with the balance in the monthly bank statement. The lack of agreement between the reciprocal account balances causes no difficulty during an accounting period, but at the end of the period the reciprocal account balances must be brought into agreement before combined financial statements are prepared.

As an illustration of the procedure for reconciling reciprocal account balances at the year-end, assume that the home office and branch accounting records of Mercer Company contain the data on December 31, Year 10, shown on page 110.

Comparison of the two reciprocal accounts discloses the four reconciling items described below:

(1) *A debit of $8,000 in the Investment in Branch A account without a related credit in the Home Office account.*

On December 29, the home office shipped merchandise costing $8,000 to the branch. The home office debits its account with the branch on the

SMALDINO COMPANY

Working Paper for Combined Financial Statements of Home Office and Branch X

For Year Ended December 31, Year 2

(Periodic Inventory System: Billings above Cost)

	Adjusted trial balances				Eliminations	Combined	
	Home office		Branch		Debit		
	Debit	Credit	Debit	Credit	(Credit)	Debit	Credit
Income statement							
Sales		500,000		150,000			650,000
Inventories, Dec. 31, Year 1	45,000		22,500		(b) (7,500)	60,000	
Purchases	400,000					400,000	
Shipments to Branch X		80,000			(a) 80,000		
Shipments from Home Office			120,000		(a) (120,000)		
Inventories, Dec. 31, Year 2		70,000		30,000	(c) 10,000		90,000
Operating expenses	120,000		27,500			147,500	
Subtotal	565,000	650,000	170,000	180,000		607,500	740,000
Net income (to statement of retained earnings below)	85,000		10,000		(d) 37,500	132,500	
Totals	650,000	650,000	180,000	180,000	-0-	740,000	740,000
Statement of retained earnings							
Retained earnings, Dec. 31, Year 1		117,000					117,000
Net income (from above)		85,000		10,000	(d) (37,500)		132,500
Dividends	60,000					60,000	
Retained earnings, Dec. 31, Year 2 (to balance sheet below)						189,500	
Totals						249,500	249,500

Balance sheet

	Home office	Branch X	Eliminations		Combined
Cash	30,000	9,000			39,000
Accounts receivable (net)	64,000	28,000			92,000
Inventories, Dec. 31, Year 2	70,000	30,000	(c)	(10,000)	90,000
Allowance for overvaluation of inventories:					
Branch X	47,500		(a) (b)	40,000 / 7,500	
Investment in Branch X	57,000		(e)	(57,000)	158,000
Equipment	158,000				
Accumulated depreciation	15,000				15,000
Accounts payable	24,500				24,500
Home office		57,000	(e)	57,000	150,000
Common stock, $10 par	150,000				
Retained earnings (from above)					189,500
Totals	439,000	67,000	67,000	-0-	379,000

(a) To eliminate reciprocal accounts for merchandise shipments.
(b) To reduce beginning inventories of branch to cost.
(c) To reduce ending inventories of branch to cost.
(d) To increase net income of branch by portion of merchandise markup that was realized.
(e) To eliminate reciprocal accounts.

Investment in Branch A (in accounting records of Home Office)

Date	Explanation	Debit	Credit	Balance
Year 10				
Nov. 30	Balance			62,500 dr
Dec. 10	Cash received from branch		20,000	42,500 dr
Dec. 27	Collection of branch accounts receivable		1,000	41,500 dr
Dec. 29	Merchandise shipped to branch	8,000		49,500 dr

Home Office (in accounting records of Branch A)

Date	Explanation	Debit	Credit	Balance
Year 10				
Nov. 30	Balance			62,500 cr
Dec. 7	Cash sent to home office	20,000		42,500 cr
Dec. 28	Acquired equipment	3,000		39,500 cr
Dec. 30	Collection of home office accounts receivable		2,000	41,500 cr

date merchandise is shipped, but the branch credits its account with the home office when the merchandise is received, perhaps a few days later. The required journal entry on December 31, Year 10, in the **branch accounting records**, assuming use of the perpetual inventory system, appears below.

Inventories 8,000
    Home Office 8,000
To record shipment of merchandise in transit from home office.

In determining its ending inventories, the branch must add to the inventories on hand the $8,000 of merchandise in transit. This merchandise will appear in the branch balance sheet and also as part of the total inventories in the combined financial statements.

(2) A credit of $1,000 in the Investment in Branch A account without a related debit in the Home Office account.

On December 27, accounts receivable of the branch were collected by the home office. The collection was recorded by the home office by a debit to Cash and a credit to Investment in Branch A. No journal entry was made by the branch; therefore, the following journal entry is required **in the branch accounting records** on December 31, Year 10:

Home Office 1,000
    Accounts Receivable 1,000
To record collection of accounts receivable by home office.

(3) **A debit of $3,000 in the Home Office account without a related credit in the Investment in Branch A account.**

On December 28, the branch acquired equipment for $3,000. Because the equipment used by the branch is carried in the home office accounting records, the journal entry made by the branch was a debit to Home Office and a credit to Cash. No journal entry was made by the home office; therefore, the following journal entry is required on December 31, Year 10, **in the home office accounting records:**

Equipment: Branch A	3,000	
Investment in Branch A		3,000
To record equipment acquired by branch		

(4) **A credit of $2,000 in the Home Office account without a related debit in the Investment in Branch A account.**

On December 30, accounts receivable of the home office were collected by the branch. The collection was recorded by the branch by a debit to Cash and a credit to Home Office. No journal entry was made by the home office; therefore, the following journal entry is required **in the home office accounting records** on December 31, Year 10:

Investment in Branch A	2,000	
Accounts Receivable		2,000
To record collection of accounts receivable by branch.		

The effect of the foregoing end-of-period journal entries is to update the reciprocal accounts, as shown by the reconciliation below:

MERCER COMPANY — HOME OFFICE AND BRANCH A
Reconciliation of Reciprocal Accounts
December 31, Year 10

	Investment in Branch A account (in home office accounting records)	Home Office account (in branch accounting records)
Balances before adjustments	$49,500 dr	$41,500 cr
Add: (1) Merchandise shipped to branch by home office		8,000
(4) Home office accounts receivable collected by branch	2,000	
Less: (2) Branch accounts receivable collected by home office . . .		(1,000)
(3) Equipment acquired by branch	(3,000)	
Balances after adjustments	$48,500 dr	$48,500 cr

Transactions between branches

Efficient operations may on occasion require that assets be transferred from one branch to another. Normally a branch does not carry a reciprocal account with another branch but records the transfer in the Home Office account. For example, if Branch A ships merchandise to Branch B, Branch A debits Home Office and credits Inventories (assuming that the perpetual inventory system is used). Upon receipt of the merchandise, Branch B debits Inventories and credits Home Office. The home office records the transfer between branches by a debit to Investment in Branch B and a credit to Investment in Branch A.

The transfer of merchandise from one branch to another does not justify increasing the carrying amount of inventories by the freight costs incurred because of the indirect routing. The amount of freight costs properly included in inventories at a branch is limited to the cost of shipping the merchandise directly from the home office to its present location. Excess freight costs should be recorded as expenses of the home office.

To illustrate the accounting for excess freight costs on interbranch transfers of merchandise, assume the following data. The home office shipped merchandise costing $6,000 to Branch D and paid freight costs of $400. Subsequently, the home office instructed Branch D to transfer this merchandise to Branch E. Freight costs of $300 were paid by Branch D to carry out this order. If the merchandise had been shipped directly from the home office to Branch E, the freight costs would have been $500. The journal entries required in the three sets of accounting records (assuming that the perpetual inventory system is used) are shown on page 113.

Recording excess freight costs on merchandise transferred from one branch to another as an expense is an example of the accounting principle that "losses" should be given prompt recognition. The excess freight costs from such shipments generally result from inefficient planning of original shipments and should not be included in inventories.

In treating excess freight costs of interbranch transfers as expenses attributable to the home office, we have assumed that the home office makes the decisions directing all shipments. If branch managers are given authority to order transfers of merchandise between branches, the excess freight costs should be recorded as expenses attributable to the branches.

Start-up costs of opening new branches

The establishment of a new branch often requires the incurring of considerable cost before a significant flow of revenue can be generated. Operating losses in the first few months are very likely. Some business enterprises would prefer to capitalize these start-up losses on the grounds that such losses are necessary to successful operation at a new location. However, most enterprises recognize start-up costs in connection with the opening of a new branch as an expense of the accounting period in which the costs are incurred.

The decision should be based on the principle that net income is measured by matching expired costs against realized revenue. If costs can be

In Home Office accounting records:

Investment in Branch D	6,400	
Inventories		6,000
Cash		400

To record shipment of merchandise and payment of freight costs.

Investment in Branch E	6,500	
Excess Freight Expense — Interbranch Transfers	200	
Investment in Branch D		6,700

To record transfer of merchandise from Branch D to Branch E. Interbranch freight of $300 paid by Branch D caused total freight costs on this merchandise to exceed direct shipment costs by $200 ($400 + $300 − $500 = $200).

In Branch D accounting records:

Inventories	6,000	
Freight In	400	
Home Office		6,400

To record receipt of merchandise from home office with freight costs paid in advance by home office.

Home Office	6,700	
Inventories		6,000
Freight In		400
Cash		300

To record transfer of merchandise to Branch E by order of home office and payment of freight costs of $300.

In Branch E accounting records:

Inventories	6,000	
Freight In	500	
Home Office		6,500

To record receipt of merchandise from Branch D transferred by order of home office and normal freight costs billed by home office.

shown to benefit future accounting periods, they should be deferred and allocated to those periods. Seldom is there positive assurance that a new branch will achieve a profitable level of operations in later years.

REVIEW QUESTIONS

1 Explain the usual distinctions between a *sales agency* and a *branch*.

2 Palmer Company has several sales agencies and wishes to determine the profitability of each. Describe the principal accounting procedures that you would recommend

be performed by the home office and by the individual sales agencies to achieve this goal.

3 Some branches maintain complete accounting records and prepare financial statements in much the same way as an autonomous business enterprise. Other branches perform only limited accounting functions, with most accounting activity concentrated in the home office. Assuming that a branch has a fairly complete set of accounting records, what criterion or principle would you suggest be used in deciding whether various types of expenses applicable to the branch should be recorded by the home office or by the branch?

4 Explain the use of *reciprocal accounts* in home office and branch accounting systems in conjunction with a periodic inventory system.

5 The branch and home office reciprocal accounts of Meadow Company are not in balance at the year-end by a substantial amount. What factors might have caused this?

6 Canyon Company operates a number of branches but centralizes its accounting records in the home office and maintains rigorous control of branch operations. The home office finds that Branch D has ample inventories of a certain item of merchandise but that Branch E is almost out of this item. The home office therefore instructs Branch D to ship merchandise with a cost of $5,000 to Branch E. What journal entry should Branch D make, and what principle should guide the treatment of freight costs? (Assume that Branch D uses the perpetual inventory system.)

7 The president of Valley Company informs you that a branch store is being opened and requests your advice as follows: "I have been told that we may bill merchandise shipped to the branch at cost, at selling price, or anywhere in between. Do professional accountants really have that much latitude in the application of generally accepted accounting principles?"

8 The policies of Hillmart Company provide that equipment in use by its branches shall be carried in the accounting records of the home office. Acquisitions of new equipment may be made either by the home office or by a branch with the approval of the home office. Slauson Branch, with the approval of the home office, acquired new equipment at a cost of $8,000. Prepare journal entries for the Slauson Branch and the home office to record the acquisition of this equipment.

9 Groves Company operates ten branches in addition to its main store, and bills merchandise shipped to the branches at 10% above cost. All plant assets are carried in the home office accounting records. The home office also conducts a regular advertising program that benefits all branches. Each branch maintains its own accounting records and prepares separate financial statements. In the home office, the accounting department prepares (**a**) financial statements for the main store; (**b**) revised financial statements for each branch; and (**c**) combined financial statements for the enterprise as a whole.

Explain the purpose of the financial statements prepared by the branches, the home office financial statements, the revised financial statements for the branches, and the combined financial statements.

EXERCISES

Ex. 3-1 Select the best answer for each of the following multiple-choice questions:

1 If the home office of Lacey Company maintains the accounting records for the plant assets of the Northern Branch, and the branch acquired equipment for $5,000 cash, the appropriate journal entry for the branch is:

a Debit the Home Office account and credit a plant asset account for $5,000
b Debit the Home Office account and credit Cash for $5,000
c Debit a plant asset account and credit the Home Office account for $5,000
d Debit Cash and credit the Home Office account for $5,000

2 The home office of Lauro Company, which bills merchandise shipped to the Southern Branch at an amount in excess of cost, prepared the following journal entry at the end of the fiscal year:

Income: Southern Branch	82,000	
Investment in Southern Branch		82,000

The most probable explanation for the journal entry is:

a To record net income reported by branch
b To close branch net loss (as adjusted)
c To record net loss reported by branch
d To close branch net income (as adjusted)

3 A possible shortcoming of billing at cost the merchandise shipped from a home office to a branch is:

a All gross profit on the sale of merchandise is attributed to the home office
b The branch has difficulty in applying the retail method of inventory
c Gross profit information is concealed from branch personnel
d Gross profit of the home office is understated
e None of the foregoing

4 The fiscal year of Robards Company, located in Vancouver, ends September 30. On September 30, Year 1, the home office of Robards shipped merchandise costing $18,000 to the Saskatoon Branch at a billed price of $24,000 and prepared an appropriate journal entry for the shipment. The Saskatoon Branch had not received the merchandise on September 30, Year 1. Both the home office and the Saskatoon Branch use the perpetual inventory system. The end-of-period adjustments for Robards Company on September 30, Year 1, should include:

a A debit to Inventories and a credit to Home Office in the branch accounting records
b A debit to Investment in Saskatoon Branch and a credit to Inventories in the home office accounting records
c A debit to Home Office and a credit to Inventories in the branch accounting records
d Some other journal entry

Ex. 3-2 Prepare journal entries in the home office and Branch P accounting records for each of the following transactions (omit explanations):

a Home office transferred cash of $5,000 and merchandise (at cost) of $10,000 to Branch P. Both the home office and the branch use the perpetual inventory system.
b Home office allocated operating expenses of $1,500 to Branch P.
c Branch P informed the home office that it had collected $416 on a note payable to the home office. Principal amount of the note was $400.
d Branch P made sales of $12,500, terms 2/10, n/30, and incurred operating expenses of $2,500. The cost of goods sold was $8,000, and the operating expenses were paid in cash.
e Branch P reported a net income of $500. (Debit Income Summary in branch accounting records.)

Ex. 3-3 Tillman Textile Company has a single branch in Toronto. On March 1, Year 1, the accounting records of the company include an Allowance for Overvaluation of Inventories: Toronto Branch account with a balance of $32,000. During March, merchandise costing $36,000 was shipped to the Toronto Branch and billed at a price representing a 40% markup on the billed price. On March 31, the branch prepared an income statement indicating a net loss of $11,500 for March, with ending inventories at billed price of $25,000.

a What was the cost of the branch inventories on March 1, assuming a uniform markup on all shipments to the branch?

b Prepare the journal entry to adjust the Allowance for Overvaluation of Inventories: Toronto Branch account on March 31 in the accounting records of the home office.

c What was the correct net income or net loss for the Toronto Branch for the month of March as indicated by the foregoing information?

Ex. 3-4 The home office bills its only branch at 25% above cost for all merchandise shipped to the branch. Both the home office and the branch use the periodic inventory system. During Year 5, the home office shipped merchandise to the branch at a billed price of $30,000. Branch inventories for Year 5 were as follows:

	Jan. 1	Dec. 31
Purchased from home office (at billed price)	$15,000	$19,500
Purchased from outsiders	6,800	8,670

a Prepare the journal entries (including adjusting entries) that should appear in the accounting records of the home office for Year 5 to reflect the foregoing information.

b Assuming that the home office holds merchandise costing $29,500, including $2,500 held on consignment, show how the inventories should be reported in a combined balance sheet for the home office and the branch at the end of Year 5.

Ex. 3-5 Gustafson Company bills its only branch for merchandise at 30% above cost. The branch sells the merchandise at 10% above billed price. Shortly after the close of business on January 28, some of the branch merchandise was destroyed by fire. The following additional information is available:

Inventories, Jan. 1 (at billed price from home office)	$15,600
Inventories, Jan. 28 of merchandise not destroyed (at selling price)	7,150
Shipments from home office from Jan. 1 to Jan. 28 (at billed price)	71,500
Sales from Jan. 1 to Jan. 28	51,840
Sales returns from Jan. 1 to Jan. 28 (merchandise actually returned)	3,220
Sales allowances from Jan. 1 to Jan. 28 (price adjustments)	300

a Compute the estimated cost (to the home office) of the merchandise destroyed by fire.

b Prepare the journal entry in the accounting records of the branch to recognize the uninsured fire loss. Both the home office and the branch use the perpetual inventory system.

Ex. 3-6 The ledger accounts on page 117 appear in the accounting records of the Corman Branch on December 31. The branch collects noninterest-bearing notes receivable as an accommodation to the home office and deposits the proceeds in a home office bank account.

a Reproduce the Investment in Corman Branch account in the home office accounting records, assuming that all intracompany transactions are recorded in a single reciprocal account by the home office.

b Prepare the journal entries required to bring the branch accounting records up to date, assuming that the branch should use a single reciprocal account to record intracompany transactions.

Home Office

Date	Explanation	Debit	Credit	Balance
Jan. 1	Balance			22,180 cr
	Merchandise received from home office		18,300	40,480 cr
	Supplies received from home office		610	41,090 cr
	Cash remitted to home office	8,100		32,990 cr
	Merchandise returned to home office	630		32,360 cr
	Acquisition of fixtures	3,000		29,360 cr

Home Office Notes Collected

Date	Explanation	Debit	Credit	Balance
Jan. 1	Balance			1,350 cr
	Notes collected		800	2,150 cr
	Cash deposited in home office bank account	1,550		600 cr

Income Summary

Date	Explanation	Debit	Credit	Balance
	Revenue		21,900	21,900 cr
	Expenses	19,040		2,860 cr

CASES

Case 3-1   You are engaged in the audit of Deloitte Corporation, which opened its first branch office in Year 10. During the audit the president, George Deloitte, raises the question of the accounting treatment of the branch office operating loss for its first year, which is material in amount.

Deloitte proposes to capitalize the operating loss as a start-up cost to be amortized over a five-year period, stating that branch offices of other companies engaged in the same industry generally suffer a first-year operating loss that is invariably capitalized, and you are aware of this practice. Therefore, according to Deloitte, the loss should be capitalized so that the accounting will be conservative and consistent with established industry practices.

Instructions
a Discuss Deloitte's use of the terms *conservative* and *consistent* from the standpoint of accounting terminology. Discuss the accounting treatment you would recommend.
b What disclosure, if any, would be required in the financial statements of Deloitte Corporation?

Case 3-2 Merritt Company operates a number of branches as well as a main store. Each branch stocks a complete line of merchandise obtained almost entirely from the home office. The branches also handle their own billing, approve customer credit, and make cash collections. Each branch has its own bank account, and each maintains complete accounting records. All noncurrent assets at the branches, consisting chiefly of furniture and office equipment, are carried in the home office accounting records and are depreciated by the straight-line method at 10% a year.

On July 1, Year 1, the Regina Branch acquired office equipment on the orders of the newly appointed branch manager. The equipment had a list price of $2,400, but was acquired on the instalment plan with no cash down payment and 24 monthly payments of $110 beginning August 1, Year 1. No journal entry was made for this transaction by the branch until August 1, when the first monthly payment was recorded by a debit to Miscellaneous Expenses. The same journal entry was made for the next four monthly payments made during Year 1. On December 2 the branch manager became aware, during a meeting at the home office, that equipment could be acquired by the branches only with prior approval by the home office. Regardless of whether the home office or the branches acquired plant assets, such assets were to be carried in the home office accounting records. To avoid criticism, the Regina Branch manager immediately disposed of the office equipment acquired July 1 by sale for $1,500 cash to an independent store. The manager then paid the balance due on the instalment contract using a personal cheque and the $1,500 cheque received from sale of the equipment. In consideration of the advance payment of the remaining instalments on December 3, the equipment dealer agreed to a $100 reduction in the total balance of the contract. No journal entry was made for the disposal of the equipment or the settlement of the liability.

Assume that you are a professional accountant engaged to audit the financial statements of Merritt Company. During your visit to the Regina Branch you analyze the Miscellaneous Expenses account and investigate the five monthly debits of $110. This investigation discloses the acquisition and subsequent disposal of the office equipment. After some hesitation, the branch manager gives you a full explanation of the events.

Instructions
a Would you, as an independent auditor, take any action on this matter? Indicate the major issues involved rather than the accounting details. Give reasons for your answer.
b Prepare the journal entries that should have been made for the entire series of events in the accounting records of the Regina Branch. Assume that Merritt Company accepts responsibility for the branch manager's actions.
c Prepare the journal entries that should have been made in the home office accounting records for the entire series of events, assuming that the home office was informed of each event and accepts responsibility for all actions by the branch manager.
d As an independent situation from b and c, prepare journal entries to correct the accounting records with a minimum of work. One compound journal entry in each set of accounting records is suggested. Assume that interest expense belongs in the branch accounting records. Also assume that Merritt wishes to show in the branch accounting records a liability to the branch manager for personal "loans," if any, and will consider later any disciplinary action to be taken. The accounting records have not been closed for Year 1.

PROBLEMS

3-1 Included in the accounting records of the home office and West Branch, respectively, of Simms Company were the following ledger accounts for the month of January:

Investment in West Branch (in Home Office accounting records)

Date	Explanation	Debit	Credit	Balance
Jan. 1	Balance			39,200 dr
9	Shipment of merchandise	4,000		43,200 dr
21	Receipt of cash		1,600	41,600 dr
27	Collection of branch accounts receivable		800	40,800 dr
31	Shipment of merchandise	3,200		44,000 dr

Home Office (in West Branch accounting records)

Date	Explanation	Debit	Credit	Balance
Jan. 1	Balance			39,200 cr
10	Receipt of merchandise		4,000	43,200 cr
19	Remittance of cash	1,600		41,600 cr
28	Acquisition of furniture	1,200		40,400 cr
30	Return of excess merchandise	1,500		38,900 cr
31	Remittance of cash	500		38,400 cr

Instructions

a Prepare a working paper to reconcile the reciprocal accounts to the corrected balances on January 31.

b Prepare journal entries on January 31, for the (1) home office, and (2) West Branch of Simms Company to bring the accounting records up to date. Both the home office and the branch use the perpetual inventory system.

3-2 Harvey's Hobby Shop established the Rodeo Drive Branch on January 2, Year 3. During the first year of operations, Harvey's Hobby Shop shipped to the branch merchandise that cost $200,000. Billings were made at prices 20% above cost. Freight costs of $10,000 were paid by the home office. Sales by the branch $300,000 and operating expenses were $64,000, all for cash. On December 31, Year 3, the branch took a physical inventory that showed merchandise on hand of $48,000 at billed prices. Both the home office and the branch use the periodic inventory system.

Instructions Prepare journal entries for the branch and the home office to record the foregoing transactions, ending inventories, and other related adjusting and closing entries on December 31, Year 3. (Allocate a proportional amount of freight costs to the ending inventories of the branch.)

3-3 Digi's Designs bills shipments of merchandise to its Ottawa Branch at 140% of cost. During the first year after the branch was established, the following were among the transactions completed:

(1) The home office shipped merchandise with a cost of $100,000 to the Ottawa Branch.

(2) The Ottawa Branch sold for $80,000 cash merchandise that was billed by the home office at $70,000, and incurred operating expenses of $20,000 (all paid in cash).

(3) The physical inventories taken by the Ottawa Branch at the end of the first year were $68,600 at billed prices.

Instructions

a Assuming that the perpetual inventory system is used both by the home office and by the Ottawa Branch, prepare for the first year:

(1) All journal entries, including closing entries, in the accounting records of the Ottawa Branch.
(2) All journal entries, including the adjustment of the inventories overvaluation account, in the accounting records of the home office.

b Assuming that the periodic inventory system is used both by the home office and by the Ottawa Branch, prepare for the first year:

(1) All journal entries, including the closing entry, in the accounting records of the Ottawa Branch.
(2) All journal entries, including the adjustment of the inventories overvaluation account, in the accounting records of the home office.

3-4 Summerland Corporation operates a branch in Quebec to which it bills merchandise at prices 30% above cost. The branch obtains merchandise only from the home office and sells the merchandise at prices averaging 15% above the prices billed by the home office. Both the home office and the branch maintain perpetual inventory records and both close their accounting records on December 31.

On March 10, Year 9, a fire at the branch destroyed a part of the inventories. Immediately after the fire, a physical inventory taken of the merchandise on hand and not damaged showed it to have a selling price of $11,960. On January 1, Year 9, the inventories of the branch at billed price had been $15,600. Shipments from the home office during the period January 1 to March 10 were billed to the Quebec Branch in the amount of $57,200. The branch accounting records show that sales during this period were $41,472, before sales returns of $808.

Instructions Prepare the journal entries necessary to record the uninsured loss from fire in the (**a**) branch accounting records, and (**b**) home office accounting records. Show supporting computations for all amounts. Assume that the loss was reported by the branch to the home office and that it was recorded in the intracompany reciprocal accounts.

3-5 On December 31, Year 5, the Investment in Erie Branch account in the general ledger of the home office of Isotope Company shows a debit balance of $40,000. You ascertain the following facts in analyzing this account:

(1) On December 31, merchandise billed at $5,800 was in transit from the home office to the branch. The periodic inventory system is used by both the home office and the branch.
(2) The branch collected home office accounts receivable of $275; the home office was not notified.
(3) On December 29, the home office mailed a cheque for $2,000 to the branch, but the accountant for the home office recorded the cheque as a debit to the Charitable Contributions account; the branch had not received the cheque as of December 31.
(4) Branch net income for December was recorded erroneously by the home office at $840 instead of $480. The credit was recorded by the home office in the Income: Erie Branch account.
(5) The branch returned supplies costing $220 to the home office; the home office had not recorded the receipt of the supplies. The home office records acquisitions of supplies in the Inventory of Supplies account.

Instructions

a Assuming that all other transactions have been recorded properly, prepare a working paper to determine the unadjusted balance of the Home office account in the general ledger of the branch on December 31, Year 5.

b Prepare the journal entries for the home office to bring its accounting records up to date. Closing entries have not been made.

c Prepare the journal entries for the Erie Branch to bring its accounting records up to date.

d Prepare a reconciliation on December 31, Year 5, of the Investment in Erie Branch account in the accounting records of the home office and the Home Office account in the accounting records of the Erie Branch. Use a single column for each account and start with the unadjusted balances.

3-6 On January 4, Year 5, Hong Kong Toy Company opened its first branch with instructions to Sylvia Cho, the branch manager, to perform the functions of granting credit, billing customers, accounting for receivables, and making cash collections. The branch paid its operating expenses by cheques drawn on its bank account. The branch obtained merchandise solely from the home office; billings for these shipments were at cost to the home office. The adjusted trial balances for the home office and the branch on December 31, Year 5, were as follows:

HONG KONG TOY COMPANY
Adjusted Trial Balances
December 31, Year 5

	Home office		Branch	
	Debit	Credit	Debit	Credit
Cash	$ 42,000		$ 14,600	
Notes receivable	7,000			
Accounts receivable (net)	80,400		37,300	
Inventories	95,800		24,200	
Furniture and equipment (net)	48,100			
Investment in branch	82,700			
Accounts payable		$ 41,000		
Common stock, $2 par		200,000		
Home office				$ 82,700
Retained earnings, Dec. 31, Year 4		25,000		
Sales		360,000		101,100
Cost of goods sold	200,500		85,800	
Operating expenses	69,500		21,900	
Totals	$626,000	$626,000	$183,800	$183,800

The physical inventories on December 31, Year 5, were in agreement with the perpetual records of the home office and the branch.

Instructions

a Prepare a seven-column working paper for combined financial statements of the home office and branch.

b Prepare the closing journal entries on December 31, Year 5, in the accounting records of the branch.

c Prepare the adjusting and closing journal entries pertaining to branch operations in the accounting records of the home office.

3-7 You are engaged to make an audit for the year ended December 31, Year 1, of Vernon Company, which carries on merchandising operations at both a home office and a branch. The unadjusted trial balances of the home office and the branch are given below.

VERNON COMPANY

Unadjusted Trial Balances

December 31, Year 1

	Home office Dr (Cr)	Branch Dr (Cr)
Cash	$ 20,000	$ 7,975
Inventories, Jan. 1, Year 1	23,000	11,550
Miscellaneous assets (net)	200,000	48,450
Investment in branch	60,000	
Allowance for overvaluation of branch inventories,		
Jan. 1, Year 1	(1,000)	
Purchases	190,000	
Shipments from home office		104,500
Freight in from home office		5,225
Operating expenses	42,000	24,300
Current liabilities	(35,000)	(8,500)
Home office		(51,000)
Sales	(155,000)	(142,500)
Shipments to branch	(110,000)	
Common stock, $2.50 par	(200,000)	
Retained earnings, Jan. 1, Year 1	(34,000)	
Totals	$ -0-	$ -0-

The audit on December 31, Year 1, disclosed the following:

(1) The branch office deposits all cash receipts in a local bank for the account of the home office. The audit working papers for the cash cutoff include the following:

Amount	Date deposited by branch	Date recorded by home office
$1,050	Dec. 27, Year 1	Dec. 31, Year 1
1,100	Dec. 30, Year 1	Not recorded
600	Dec. 31, Year 1	Not recorded
300	Jan. 2, Year 2	Not recorded

(2) The branch pays operating expenses incurred locally from an imprest bank account that is maintained with a balance of $2,000. Cheques are drawn once a week on this imprest account, and the home office is notified of the amount needed to replenish the account. On December 31, Year 1, an $1,800 reimbursement cheque was in transit from the home office to the branch office.

(3) The branch receives all its merchandise from the home office. The home office bills the merchandise at 10% above cost. On December 31, Year 1, a shipment with a billed price of $5,500 was in transit to the branch. Freight costs typically are 5% of billed price. Freight costs are considered to be inventoriable costs. Both the home office and the branch use the periodic inventory system.

(4) Beginning inventories in the trial balance are shown at the respective costs to the home office and to the branch. The inventories on December 31, Year 1, were as follows:

Home office, at cost $30,000

Branch, at billed price (excluding shipment in transit and freight)   9,900

Instructions

a Prepare journal entries to adjust the accounting records of the home office on December 31, Year 1.

b Prepare journal entries to adjust the accounting records of the branch on December 31, Year 1.

c Prepare a working paper for combined financial statements of the home office and the branch (use the form on pages 108 and 109). Determine the amounts for the adjusted trial balances for the home office and the branch by incorporating the journal entries in **a** and **b** with the amounts in the unadjusted trial balances.

3-8 The reciprocal ledger accounts below and on page 124 are included in the accounting records of the home office and the Elko Branch of Elsinore Company on April 30, Year 2.

Investment in Elko Branch

Date	Explanation	Debit	Credit	Balance
Year 2				
Feb. 1	Balance			124,630 dr
6	Shipment of merchandise,			
	160 cases @ $49	7,840		132,470 dr
17	Note receivable collected by branch	2,500		134,970 dr
Mar. 31	Cash deposited by branch		2,000	132,970 dr
Apr. 2	Merchandise returned by branch		450	132,520 dr
26	Loss on disposal of branch equipment	780		133,300 dr
28	Operating expenses charged to branch	1,200		134,500 dr
29	Corrected loss on disposal of branch			
	equipment from $780 to $250		530	133,970 dr

You have been retained by the company to assist it with some accounting work preliminary to the preparation of financial statements for the quarter ended April 30, Year 2. Additional information available to you follows:

(1) Branch equipment is carried in the accounting records of the home office; the home office notifies the branch periodically as to the amount of depreciation applicable to equipment used by the branch. Gains or losses on disposal of branch equipment are reported to the branch and included in the branch income statement.

(2) Because of the error in recording the shipment from the home office on February 8, Year 2, the sale of the 160 cases has been debited improperly to cost of goods sold at $46.75 a case.

(3) The branch frequently makes collections of home office accounts receivable, and the home office also collects receivables belonging to the branch. On April 30, Year 2, the branch collected accounts receivable of $350 belonging to the home office, but the branch employee who recorded the collection mistakenly treated the accounts receivable as belonging to the branch.

Home Office

Date	Explanation	Debit	Credit	Balance
Year 2				
Feb. 1	Balance			124,630 cr
8	Merchandise from home office,			
	160 cases @ $49		7,480	132,110 cr
14	Received shipment directly from supplier,			
	invoice to be paid by home office		2,750	134,860 cr
15	Note receivable collected for home office		2,500	137,360 cr
Mar. 30	Deposited cash in account of home office	2,000		135,360 cr
31	Returned merchandise to home office	450		134,910 cr
Apr. 29	Paid repair bill for home office	375		134,535 cr
30	Excess merchandise returned to home			
	office (billed at cost)	5,205		129,330 cr
30	Net income for quarter (preliminary)		9,210	138,540 cr

(4) The branch recorded the preliminary net income of $9,210 by a debit to Income Summary and a credit to Home Office, although the revenue and expense accounts had not been closed.

Instructions

a Reconcile the reciprocal accounts to the correct balances on April 30, Year 2. Use a four-column working paper (debit and credit columns for the Investment in Elko Branch account in the home office accounting records and debit and credit columns for the Home Office account in the branch accounting records). Start with the unadjusted balances on April 30, Year 2, and work to corrected balances, inserting full explanations of all adjusting or correcting items.

b Prepare individual journal entries for the branch to bring its accounting records up to date, assuming that corrections still can be made to revenue and expense accounts. The branch uses the perpetual inventory system. Do not prepare closing entries.

c Prepare individual journal entries for the home office to bring its accounting records up to date. Assume that the home office uses the perpetual inventory system and has not prepared closing entries. Do not prepare closing entries.

3-9 The unadjusted general ledger trial balances on December 31, Year 3, for Ontario Fruits, Inc., and its Bear Valley Branch are shown at the top of page 125. Your audit disclosed the following:

(1) On December 23, Year 3, the branch manager acquired equipment for $4,000, but failed to notify the home office. The branch accountant, knowing that equipment is carried in the home office general ledger, recorded the proper journal entry in the branch accounting records. It is the company's policy not to record any depreciation on equipment acquired in the last half of a year.

(2) On December 27, Year 3, Loblaw Company, a customer of the Bear Valley Branch, erroneously paid its account of $2,000 to the home office. The accoun-

ONTARIO FRUITS, INC.
Unadjusted Trial Balances
December 31, Year 3

	Home office Dr (Cr)	Bear Valley Branch Dr (Cr)
Cash	$ 18,000	$ 18,000
Accounts receivable (net)	35,000	12,000
Inventories, Jan. 1, Year 3 (at cost to home office)	70,000	15,000
Equipment (net)	90,000	
Investment in Bear Valley Branch	30,000	
Accounts payable	(36,000)	(13,500)
Accrued liabilities	(14,000)	(2,500)
Home office		(19,000)
Common stock, $10 par	(50,000)	
Retained earnings, Jan. 1, Year 3	(48,000)	
Sales	(429,000)	(95,000)
Purchases	290,000	24,000
Shipments from home office		45,000
Operating expenses	44,000	16,000
Totals	$ -0-	$ -0-

tant made the correct journal entry in the home office general ledger but did not notify the branch.

(3) On December 30, Year 3, the branch remitted cash of $5,000, which was not received by the home office as of December 31, Year 3.

(4) On December 31, Year 3, the branch erroneously recorded the December allocated expenses from the home office as $500 instead of $1,500.

(5) On December 31, Year 3, the home office shipped merchandise billed at $3,000 to the branch; the shipment was not received by the branch as of December 31, Year 3.

(6) The inventories on December 31, Year 3, excluding the shipment in transit, are: home office — $60,000 (at cost); branch — $20,000 (consisting of $18,000 from home office at billed price and $2,000 from suppliers). Both the home office and the branch use the periodic inventory system.

(7) The home office billed shipments to the branch at 20% above cost, although the billing should have been at cost. The Sales account was credited for the invoice price by the home office.

Instructions

a Prepare journal entries to bring the accounting records of the home office up to date and to correct any errors on December 31, Year 3. Record ending inventories by an offsetting credit to the Income Summary account.

b Prepare journal entries to bring the accounting records of the branch up to date and to correct any errors on December 31, Year 3. Record ending inventories at cost to the home office by an offsetting credit to the Income Summary account.

c Prepare a working paper to summarize the operations of Ontario Fruits, Inc., for the year ended December 31, Year 3. Disregard income taxes and use the following column heads:

Revenue and expenses	Home office	Branch	Combined

3-10 Franco Meglio's, a single proprietorship, sells merchandise at its home office location and also through a branch in Moreno Springs. The home office bills merchandise shipped to the branch at 125% of cost, and is the only supplier for the branch. Shipments of merchandise to the branch have been recorded improperly by credits to Sales for the billed price. Both the home office and the branch use the perpetual inventory system.

Meglio engages you to audit its financial statements for the year ended December 31, Year 5. This lis the first time the proprietorship has utilized the services of an independent accountant. You are provided with the following unadjusted trial balances:

FRANCO MEGLIO'S
Unadjusted Trial Balances
December 31, Year 5

	Home office Dr (Cr)	Moreno Springs Branch Dr (Cr)
Cash	$ 39,000	3,000
Accounts receivable (net)	20,000	22,000
Inventories	30,000	8,000
Investment in Moreno Springs Branch	45,000	
Equipment (net)	150,000	
Accounts payable	(23,000)	
Accrued liabilities		(2,000)
Long-term note payable	(51,000)	
Franco Meglio, capital, Jan. 1, Year 5	(192,000)	
Franco Meglio, drawing	42,000	
Home office		(10,000)
Sales	(350,000)	(150,000)
Cost of goods sold	220,000	93,000
Operating expenses	70,000	36,000
Totals	$ -0-	$ -0-

Additional information disclosed by your examination includes the following:

(1) On January 1, Year 5, inventories of the home office amounted to $25,000 and inventories of the branch amounted to $6,000. During Year 5, the branch was billed for $105,000 for shipments from the home office.

(2) On December 31, Year 5, the home office billed the branch for $12,000, representing the branch's share of operating expenses paid by the home office. This billing has not been recorded by the branch.

(3) All cash collections made by the branch are deposited in a local bank to the account of the home office. Deposits of this nature included the following:

Amount	Date deposited by branch	Date recorded by home office
$5,000	Dec. 28, Year 5	Dec. 31, Year 5
3,000	Dec. 30, Year 5	Not recorded
7,000	Dec. 31, Year 5	Not recorded
2,000	Jan. 2, Year 6	Not recorded

(4) Operating expenses incurred locally by the branch are paid from an imprest bank account that is reimbursed periodically by the home office. Just prior to the end of Year 5, the home office forwarded a reimbursement cheque in the amount of $3,000, which was not received by the branch as of December 31, Year 5.

(5) A shipment of merchandise from the home office to the branch is in transit on December 31, Year 5.

Instructions

a Prepare journal entries to adjust the accounting records of the home office on December 31, Year 5. Establish an allowance for overvaluation of branch inventories.

b Prepare journal entries to adjust the accounting records of the branch on December 31, Year 5.

c Prepare a working paper for combined financial statements of the home office and the branch (use the form illustrated on page 97. Determine the amounts for the adjusted trial balances for the home office and the branch by incorporating the journal entries in **a** and **b** with the amounts in the unadjusted trial balances.

d After the working paper in **c** is completed, prepare all required adjusting and closing entries in the accounting records of the home office.

3-11 Comparative balance sheets for the home office of Jordan Corporation follow:

JORDAN CORPORATION — HOME OFFICE

Balance Sheets

	Dec. 31, Year 5	Dec. 31, Year 4
Assets		
Cash	$ 23,000	$ 25,600
Accounts receivable	95,000	80,000
Allowance for doubtful accounts	(3,000)	(2,400)
Inventories	100,000	112,000
Equipment (net)	200,000	180,000
Investment in Wells Branch	110,000	
Investment in Wells, Inc. (100%)		80,000
Total assets	$525,000	$475,200
Liabilities & Shareholders' Equity		
Accounts payable	$ 88,000	$ 95,300
Accrued liabilities	3,500	2,700
Common stock, $5 par	200,000	200,000
Retained earnings	233,500	177,200
Total liabilities & shareholders' equity	$525,000	$475,200

The home office acquired equipment for $50,000 cash in Year 5, and equipment with a carrying amount of $10,000 was sold at a loss of $3,000. The loss was debited to the Retained Earnings account by mistake. Dividends of $32,000 were declared and paid during Year 5, and net income for Year 5 was $91,300, including $40,000 earned by the branch. The branch remitted $10,000 to the home office at the end of Year 5. Comparative balance sheets for Wells Branch and Wells Inc., are as shown at the top of page 128.

WELLS BRANCH AND WELLS, INC.
Balance Sheets

	Dec. 31, Year 5	Dec. 31, Year 4
Assets		
Cash	$ 28,000	$ 15,000
Accounts receivable (no allowance)	25,000	20,000
Inventories	70,500	65,000
Short-term prepayments	1,500	2,000
Total assets	$125,000	$102,000
Liabilities & Shareholders' Equity		
Accounts payable	$ 15,000	$ 22,000
Common stock, no par		10,000
Retained earnings		70,000
Home office	110,000	
Total liabilities & shareholders' equity	$125,000	$102,000

The branch was operated as a wholly owned subsidiary corporation (Wells, Inc.) until January 1, Year 5, at which time the corporation was liquidated and reorganized as a branch.

Instructions

a Prepare comparative combined (or consolidated) balance sheets for Jordan Corporation on December 31, Year 4, and on December 31, Year 5. In the consolidation of the financial statements of the two corporations, the Investment in Wells, Inc., (in Jordan's accounting records) is eliminated against the shareholders' equity accounts of Wells, Inc.

b Prepare a statement of changes in financial position for Jordan Corporation on the working capital concept for Year 5, assuming that the accounts of Wells Inc., were consolidated with the accounts of Jordan Corporation on December 31, Year 4. Do not include the composition of working capital in the statement of changes in financial position.

c Prepare a statement of changes in financial position for Jordan Corporation on the cash concept for Year 5, assuming that the accounts of Wells, Inc., were consolidated with the accounts of Jordan Corporation on December 31, Year 4. Do not include the composition of working capital in the statement of changes in financial position.

BUSINESS COMBINATIONS AND CONSOLIDATED FINANCIAL STATEMENTS

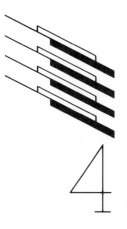

4 BUSINESS COMBINATIONS

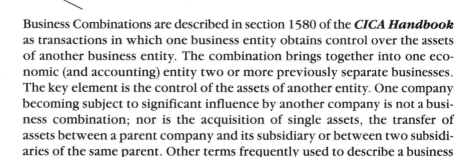

Business Combinations are described in section 1580 of the **CICA Handbook** as transactions in which one business entity obtains control over the assets of another business entity. The combination brings together into one economic (and accounting) entity two or more previously separate businesses. The key element is the control of the assets of another entity. One company becoming subject to significant influence by another company is not a business combination; nor is the acquisition of single assets, the transfer of assets between a parent company and its subsidiary or between two subsidiaries of the same parent. Other terms frequently used to describe a business combination are take-overs, acquisitions, mergers and amalgamations.

Business combinations have been frequent and numerous in the United States and Canada. Statistics issued by W. T. Grimm & Co., a financial consulting firm that compiles data on business combinations, show that as many as 4,000 or more business combinations have been completed in some recent years in the United States. A recent Canadian survey showed that over a four year period, a total of 272 business combinations were disclosed in the financial statements of 325 companies.[1]

In the material that follows we will use the following terms in our discussions of business combinations:

1 **Combined company.** The accounting entity that results from a business combination.
2 **Combining companies.** The business enterprises that enter into a business combination.
3 **Combinor.** A combining company which initiates the take-over of another combining company (the **combinee** or the take-over target).

---

1 See *Financial Reporting in Canada*, 16th Edition 1985, CICA (Toronto), p. 22.

4 *Acquirer.* A combining company which distributes cash or assets for the assets or voting shares of another combining company (*the acquiree*); or whose shareholders as a group end up with control of the voting shares of the combined company. The terms acquirer and acquiree are used in conjunction with the purchase method of accounting for business combinations.

In the first section of this chapter we discuss reasons for the popularity of business combinations and techniques for arranging them. Then, the two methods of accounting for business combinations, that is, *purchase* and *pooling of interests*, are explained and illustrated. In the final section we evaluate the theory of purchase accounting and pooling-of-interests accounting.

BUSINESS COMBINATIONS: WHY AND HOW?

Why do business enterprises enter into a business combination? Although a number of reasons have been cited, probably the overriding one for *combinors* in recent years has been *growth*. Business enterprises have major operating objectives other than growth, but that goal increasingly has motivated combinor managements to undertake business combinations. Advocates of this *external* method of achieving growth point out that it is much more rapid than growth through *internal* means. There is no question that expansion and diversification of product lines, or enlarging the market share for current products, is achieved readily through a business combination with another enterprise. However, the disappointing experiences of many combinors engaging in business combinations suggest that much can be said in favour of more gradual and reasoned growth through internal means, using available management and financial resources.

Other reasons often advanced in support of business combinations are obtaining new management strength or better use of existing management, and achieving manufacturing or other operating economies. In addition, a business combination may be undertaken for the income tax advantages available to one or more parties to the combination.

Government intervention

One danger faced by companies that undertake business combinations is the possibility of government intervention. Governments are concerned that business combinations may result in the lessening of competition and/or the creation of monopoly-like situations. In the United States, business combinations frequently have been attacked by the Federal Trade Commission or the Antitrust Division of the Department of Justice under the provisions of the Clayton Act.

In Canada, the equivalent legislation is the Combines Investigation Act. The Canadian legislation has, however, proved to be somewhat a paper tiger because there have been very few, if any, business combinations reversed by the courts in applying the provisions of this act.

One piece of Canadian legislation that has, in some manner, resulted in the curbing of business combinations is the Investment Canada Act. This act was passed ostensibly to restrict the large amount of foreign ownership in Canadian companies. The Act established the Investment Canada Agency which has the power to review proposed foreign investments in Canadian companies, and either reject the investment or suggest modifications that will yield greater benefits to Canada.

The breadth of the preceding legislation has led to government surveillance of all types of business combinations: **horizontal** (combinations involving enterprises in the same industry), **vertical** (combinations between an enterprise and its customers or suppliers), and **conglomerate** (combinations between enterprises in unrelated industries or markets).

Methods for arranging business combinations

The three common methods for carrying out a business combination are statutory amalgamation, acquisition of capital stock, and acquisition of assets.

Statutory Amalgamation As the name implies, a statutory amalgamation is executed under the provisions of the applicable provincial and federal companies acts in Canada. A business combination can be effected whereby two or more companies combine and continue as one corporate entity. The shareholders of the combining companies become shareholders of the combined company, which is either one of the combining companies or a new company. The combined company's assets and liabilities are the assets and liabilities of the combining companies. The non-surviving combining companies are wound up and therefore cease to exist. Ratification of the share exchange by two thirds of the shareholders of each of the combining companies is often required.

Acquisition of Capital Stock One corporation (the **combinor**) may issue capital stock, cash, debt, or a combination thereof to acquire all or part of the voting capital stock of another corporation (the **combinee**). When there is an acquisition of capital stock the combinor is often described as the **investor** and the combinee the **investee**. This stock acquisition program may function through direct acquisition in the stock market, through negotiations with the principal shareholders of a closely held corporation, or through a tender offer. A **tender offer** is a publicly announced intention to acquire, for a stated amount of cash or shares of capital stock, a maximum number of shares of the combinee's capital stock "tendered" by holders thereof to an agent, such as a trust company. The price per share stated in the tender offer usually is well above the prevailing market price of the combinee's capital stock. If more than 50% of the combinee's voting capital stock is acquired, that corporation becomes **affiliated** with the combinor as a **subsidiary** but is not liquidated and remains a separate legal entity. Business combinations arranged through capital stock acquisitions require authorization by the combinor's board of directors, and may require ratification by the combinee's shareholders.

Acquisition of Assets   A business enterprise may acquire all or most of the assets of another enterprise for cash, debt, capital stock, or a combination thereof. The transaction must be approved by the boards of directors and stockholders of the combining companies. The selling enterprise may continue its existence as a separate entity or it may be liquidated; it does not become an *affiliate* of the combinor.

Establishing the price for a business combination

An important early step in planning a combination is deciding on an appropriate price to pay. The amount of cash or debt securities, or the number of shares of capital stock, to be issued in a business combination usually is determined by variations of the following methods:

1 Capitalization of expected average annual earnings of the combinee at a desired rate of return
2 Determination of current fair value of the combinee's net assets (including goodwill)

The price for a business combination consummated for cash or debt is usually expressed in terms of the total dollar amount of the consideration issued. When capital stock is issued in a business combination, the price is expressed as a ratio of the number of shares of the combinor's capital stock to be exchanged for each share of the combinee's capital stock.

Illustration of Exchange Ratio   The negotiating officers of Palmer Corporation have agreed with the shareholders of Simpson Company to acquire all 20,000 outstanding shares of Simpson common stock for a total price of $1,800,000. Palmer's common stock presently is trading on the open market at $60 a share. Shareholders of Simpson agree to accept 30,000 shares of Palmer's common stock at a value of $60 a share in exchange for their stock holdings in Simpson. The exchange ratio is expressed as 1.5 shares of Palmer's common stock for each share of Simpson's common stock, in accordance with the following computation:

Computation of exchange ratio in business combination	*Number of shares of Palmer Corporation common stock to be issued* *30,000*
	Number of shares of Simpson Company common stock to be exchanged *20,000*
	Exchange ratio: 30,000 ÷ 20,000 . . . . *1.5:1*

METHODS OF ACCOUNTING FOR BUSINESS COMBINATIONS

Purchase accounting

The majority of business combinations involve an *identified acquirer* and one or more acquirees. (It should be noted that in most cases the acquirer and the combinor are the same company. However, in combinations where voting stock is exchanged, it is possible for a combinee to be identified as the acquirer. This situation is known as a "***reverse take-over***.")

When an acquirer has been identified, many accountants consider it logical to account for the business combination as the acquisition of assets, regardless of how the combination is consummated. Thus, assets (including goodwill) acquired in a business combination for cash would be recorded at the amount of cash paid, and assets acquired in a business combination involving the issuance of capital stock would be recorded at the current fair value of the assets or of the capital stock, whichever was more clearly evident. This approach is known as ***purchase accounting*** for business combinations, and was widely used prior to the increase in popularity of pooling-of-interests accounting, which occurred mainly in the United States.

Section 1580, "Business Combinations," set forth the concept of purchase accounting as follows:[2]

Under the purchase method, the acquiring company's interest in assets acquired and the liabilities assumed is accounted for in the acquiring company's financial statements at cost to the acquiring company. The reported income of the acquiring company includes the results of operations of the acquired company from the date of acquisition only.

Determination of cost of an acquiree

The cost of an acquiree in a business combination accounted for by the purchase method is the total of the consideration paid by the acquirer, the acquirer's *direct* "out-of-pocket" costs of the combination, and any ***contingent consideration*** that is determinable on the date of the business combination.

Amount of Consideration   This is the total amount of cash paid, the current fair value of other assets distributed, the discounted present value of debt securities issued, and the current fair value of equity securities issued by the acquirer. Where the fair value of consideration given cannot be determined, the fair value of the net assets acquired should be used to determine the purchase cost.

Out-of-Pocket Costs   Included in this category are legal fees and finder's fees. A *finder's fee* is paid to the investment banking firm or other organizations or individuals that investigated the acquiree, assisted in determining the price of the business combination, and otherwise rendered services to bring about the combination.

Costs of registering and issuing debt securities in a business combination are debited to Bond Issue Costs; they are not part of the cost of the acquiree. Costs of registering and issuing equity securities are not direct costs of the business combination, but are offset against the proceeds from the issuance

2 *CICA Handbook*, CICA (Toronto), Section 1580.07.

of the securities. Indirect out-of-pocket costs of the combination are expensed as incurred by the combining companies.

Contingent Consideration   Contingent consideration is additional cash, other assets, or securities that may be issuable in the future contingent upon future events, such as a specified level of earnings or a designated market price for a security issued to complete the business combination. Contingent consideration that is *determinable* on the consummation date of a combination is recorded as part of the cost of the combination; contingent consideration *not determinable* on the date of the combination is recorded as an additional cost of the combination when the contingency is resolved and the additional consideration is paid or issued (or becomes payable or issuable), except that additional consideration based on share prices reaching some specified amount **does not change the total cost of the combination.**

Illustration of Contingent Consideration   The contract for Norton Company's acquisition of the net assets of Robinson Company provided that Norton would pay $800,000 cash for Robinson's net assets (including goodwill), which would be set up in the Robb Division of Norton Company. The following contingent consideration also was included in the contract:

1 Norton was to pay Robinson $100 a unit for all sales by Robb Division of a slow-moving product that had been written down to scrap value by Robinson prior to the business combination. No portion of the $800,000 price for Robinson's net assets involved the slow-moving product.
2 Norton was to pay Robinson 25% of any pre-tax accounting income of Robb Division for each of the four years subsequent to the business combination.

On January 2, Year 1, the date of completion of the business combination, Robinson Company had firm, noncancellable sales orders for 500 units of the slow-moving product. The sales orders and all the slow-moving product were transferred to Norton by Robinson.

Norton's cost of the net assets acquired from Robinson should include $50,000 ($100 × 500 = $50,000) for the *determinable* contingent consideration attributable to the backlog of sales orders for the slow-moving product. However, because any pre-tax accounting income of Robb Division for the next four years cannot be determined on January 2, Year 1, no provision for the 25% contingent consideration is included in Norton's cost on January 2, Year 1, the total of which amounts to $850,000.

Allocation of cost of an acquiree

The cost of the acquisition is compared with the acquirer's interest in the fair values of the identifiable assets acquired and liabilities assumed. If the cost is greater than the acquirer's interest in the fair values of the net assets acquired, this cost excess is recorded as goodwill. If the cost is less than the acquirer's interest in the fair value of the net assets acquired, this fair value excess, sometimes referred to as "negative goodwill," is used to revise or adjust certain fair values previously determined. The accounting treatment of "negative goodwill" is further discussed on page 141.

Section 1580 provided guidelines for arriving at the fair value of individual assets and liabilities as follows:[3]

(a) Marketable securities at current net realizable values.
(b) Receivables based on the amounts to be received, less allowances for uncollectibility and collection costs, if necessary.
(c) Inventories:
   (i) Finished goods and merchandise at estimated selling prices less the sum of (a) costs of disposal and (b) a reasonable profit allowance for the selling effort;
   (ii) Work in process at estimated selling prices of finished goods less the sum of (a) costs to complete, (b) costs of disposal and (c) a reasonable profit allowance for the completing and selling effort based on profit for similar finished goods;
   (iii) Raw materials at current replacement costs.
(d) Plant and equipment:
   (i) to be used, at current replacement costs for similar capacity unless the expected future use of the assets indicates a lower value to the acquirer;
   (ii) to be sold or held for later sale rather than used, at current net realizable value; and
   (iii) to be used temporarily, at current net realizable value with depreciation to be recognized in the periods of use.
   Replacement cost may be determined directly if a market for used assets exists; otherwise, an estimate of depreciated replacement cost should be used. The accumulated depreciation of the acquired company should not be carried forward by the acquiring company. Current net realizable value will have to take into account factors such as whether there is a demand for such plant and equipment; whether it will have to be dismantled, thereby incurring dismantling costs; whether such demand is within the particular locality, thereby avoiding heavy transportation costs, etc.
(e) Intangible assets which can be identified and named, including contracts, patents, franchises, customer and supplier lists, and favourable leases, at estimated or appraised values.
(f) Other assets, including land, natural resources and non-marketable securities, at estimated or appraised values.
(g) Long-term liabilities, accruals, debts, etc., based on the amount required to discharge the obligation.
(h) Other liabilities and commitments, including unfavourable leases (as lessee), contracts and commitments, and plant closing expense incident to the acquisition, based on the amount required to discharge the obligation.
Discounting may be considered to be an aid in valuation where an asset would not be realized or an obligation would not be discharged in the current operating cycle.

Goodwill   Goodwill frequently is recorded in business combinations, because the total cost of the acquisition exceeds the acquirer's share of the current fair value of identifiable net assets of the acquiree. The *Handbook* required that goodwill acquired after April, 1974 be written off against income on a straight line basis. The period of the amortization is the lesser

3 Ibid., Section 1580.45.

of the estimated life of the goodwill or forty years. This particular requirement was not made retroactive. As a result, some companies disclose their accounting policy in the following fashion: "Goodwill purchased after April, 1974 is being amortized over a 40 year period. Goodwill purchased prior to April, 1974 is not being amortized because, in the opinion of management, there has been no loss in value." These companies are really saying that they are not amortizing a portion of their purchased goodwill because they do not wish to reduce their net income, and because GAAP does not requre them to amortize.

Negative Goodwill   *Negative goodwill* occurs in some business combinations known as *bargain purchases*. In these cases the acquirer's interest in the fair values of the net assets acquired exceeds the cost. A bargain purchase is most likely to occur for an acquiree with a history of losses, or when stock prices are extremely low. Following the rationale that purchased net assets cannot be recorded at an amount greater than their cost, *Section 1580* required that the excess of the acquirer's interest in the fair value of the net assets acquired over their cost be applied to reduce the values assigned to *nonmonetary assets*. It is implied that the values previously assigned to individual nonmonetary assets need re-examination and that these assets are the ones most susceptible to valuation difficulties. If it is not evident that any particular nonmonetary assets should be revalued, then the fair value excess would be applied to reduce the values assigned to all nonmonetary assets (presumably on the basis of their relative fair values).

Illustration of purchase accounting with goodwill

On December 31, Year 1, Mason Company (acquiree) was merged into Saxon Corporation (the acquirer or surviving company). Both companies used the same accounting principles for assets, liabilities, revenue, and expenses and both have a December 31 fiscal year. Saxon exchanged 300,000 shares of its no par common stock (current fair value $13 a share) for all 100,000 issued and outstanding shares of Mason's no par common stock. In addition, Saxon paid the following out-of-pocket costs associated with the business combination:

Acquirer's out-of-pocket costs of business combination CA audit fees for Securities Commission registration statement	$ 60,000
Legal fees:	
For the business combination	10,000
For Securities Commission registration statement	50,000
Finder's fee	56,250
Printer's charges for printing securities	23,000
Securities Commission registration statement fee	750
Total out-of-pocket costs of business combination	$200,000

There was no contingent consideration in the merger contract. This statutory amalgamation will result in Mason Company being dissolved.

Immediately prior to the merger, Mason Company's condensed balance sheet was as follows:

<table>
<tr><td style="vertical-align:top">Acquiree's balance
sheet prior to business
combination</td><td>

MASON COMPANY (Acquiree)

Balance Sheet (prior to business combination)
December 31, Year 1

Assets

Current assets (excluding inventory)	$ 400,000
Inventory	600,000
Plant assets (net)	3,000,000
Other assets	600,000
Total assets	$4,600,000

Liabilities & Shareholders' Equity

Current liabilities	$ 500,000
Long-term debt	1,000,000
Common stock, no par	1,800,000
Retained earnings	1,300,000
Total liabilities & shareholders' equity	$4,600,000

</td></tr>
</table>

Using the guidelines in *Section 1580*, "Business Combinations," the board of directors of Saxon Corporation determined the current fair values of Mason Company's identifiable assets and liabilities (identifiable net assets) as follows:

<table>
<tr><td style="vertical-align:top">Acquiree's identifiable
net assets</td><td>

Current assets (excluding inventory)	$ 400,000
Inventory	750,000
Plant assets (net)	3,400,000
Other assets	600,000
Current liabilities	(500,000)
Long-term debit (discounted present value)	(950,000)
Identifiable net assets of acquiree	$3,700,000

</td></tr>
</table>

The condensed journal entries on page 140 are required for Saxon Corporation (the acquirer) to record the merger with Mason Company on December 31, Year 1, as a purchase-type business combination.

Mason Company (the acquiree) prepares the condensed journal entry at the top of page 141 to record the liquidation of the company on December 31, Year 1.

Acquirer's journal
entries for a
purchase-type business
combination

SAXON CORPORATION (Acquirer)
Journal Entries
December 31, Year 1

Investment in Mason Company Common Stock

   (300,000 shares × $13) 3,900,000

   Common Stock   3,900,000

To record merger with Mason Company as a purchase.

Investment in Mason Company Common Stock

   ($10,000 + $56,250) 66,250

Common stock ($200,000 − $66,250) 133,750

   Cash   200,000

To record payment of costs incurred in merger with Mason
Company. Legal and finder's fees in connection with the merger
are recorded as an investment cost; costs of issuing shares are
recorded as a reduction in the proceeds received from issuance
of common stock.

Current Assets (excluding inventory) 400,000

Inventory 750,000

Plant Assets (net) 3,400,000

Other Assets 600,000

Discount on Long-Term Debt 50,000

Goodwill 266,250

   Current Liabilities   500,000

   Long-Term Debt   1,000,000

   Investment in Mason Company Common Stock   3,966,250

To allocate cost of Mason Company investment to identifiable
assets and liabilities, with the remainder to goodwill. Amount
of goodwill is computed as follows:

   Total cost of investment

      ($3,900,000 + $66,250) $3,966,250

   Less: Carrying amount of
          identifiable net assets
          ($4,600,000 −
          $1,500,000) $3,100,000

     Excess (deficiency) of current
     fair values of identifiable
     net assets over carrying
     amounts:

       Inventory 150,000

       Plant assets (net) 400,000

       Long-term debt   50,000   3,700,000

   Amount of goodwill .... $ 266,250

MASON COMPANY (Acquiree)

Journal Entry

December 31, Year 1

Current Liabilities	500,000	
Long-Term Debt	1,000,000	
Common Stock	1,800,000	
Retained Earnings	1,300,000	
Current Assets (excluding inventory)		400,000
Inventory		600,000
Plant Assets (net)		3,000,000
Other Assets		600,000

To record liquidation of company in conjunction with merger
with Saxon Corporation.

Illustration of purchase accounting with "negative goodwill"

On December 31, Year 1, Davis Corporation acquired the net assets of Fairmont Corporation for $400,000 cash, in a purchase-type business combination. Davis paid legal fees of $40,000 in connection with the combination. The condensed balance sheet of Fairmont Corporation prior to the business combination, with related current fair value data, is presented below:

Balance sheet of
acquiree on date of
business combination

FAIRMONT CORPORATION

Balance Sheet

December 31, Year 1

	Carrying amount	Current fair value
Assets		
Cash and accounts receivable	$ 190,000	$ 200,000
Investment in government bonds	50,000	60,000
Plant assets (net)	870,000	900,000
Intangible assets (net)	90,000	100,000
Total assets	$1,200,000	$1,260,000
Liabilities & Shareholders' Equity		
Current liabilities	$ 240,000	$ 240,000
Long-term debt	500,000	520,000
Total liabilities	$ 740,000	$ 760,000
Common stock, no par	$ 600,000	
Deficit	(140,000)	
Total shareholders' equity	$ 460,000	
Total liabilities & shareholders' equity	$1,200,000	

Thus, Davis Corporation acquired identifiable net assets with a current fair value of $500,000 ($1,260,000 − $760,000 = $500,000) for a total cost of $440,000 ($400,000 + $40,000 = $440,000). The $60,000 excess of current fair value of the net assets over their cost to Davis ($500,000 − $440,000 = $60,000) is prorated to the nonmonetary assets in the ratio of their respective current fair values, as follows:

<table>
<tr><td style="vertical-align:top">Allocation of excess of current fair value over cost of identifiable net assets to nonmonetary assets</td><td>To plant assets: $60,000 × $\dfrac{\$900,000}{\$900,000 + \$100,000}$ ....</td><td>$54,000</td></tr>
<tr><td></td><td>To intangible assets: $60,000 × $\dfrac{\$100,000}{\$900,000 + \$100,000}$ ....</td><td>6,000</td></tr>
<tr><td></td><td>Total excess of current fair value of identifiable net assets over acquirer's cost ....</td><td>$60,000</td></tr>
</table>

No part of the $60,000 excess is allocated to the cash and receivables or to investments in government bonds because these assets are monetary.

The journal entries below record Davis Corporation's acquisition of the net assets of Fairmont Corporation and payment of the legal fees of $40,000.

<table>
<tr><td style="vertical-align:top">Acquirer's journal entries for a purchase-type business combination</td><td colspan="2" style="text-align:center">DAVIS CORPORATION (Acquirer)
Journal Entries
December 31, Year 1</td></tr>
<tr><td></td><td>Investment in Net Assets of Fairmont Corporation ....</td><td>400,000</td><td></td></tr>
<tr><td></td><td>   Cash ....</td><td></td><td>400,000</td></tr>
<tr><td></td><td colspan="3">To record acquisition of net assets of Fairmont Corporation.</td></tr>
<tr><td></td><td>Investment in Net Assets of Fairmont Corporation ....</td><td>40,000</td><td></td></tr>
<tr><td></td><td>   Cash ....</td><td></td><td>40,000</td></tr>
<tr><td></td><td colspan="3">To record payment of legal fees incurred in acquisition of net assets of Fairmont Corporation.</td></tr>
<tr><td></td><td>Cash and Accounts Receivable ....</td><td>200,000</td><td></td></tr>
<tr><td></td><td>Investments in government bonds ....</td><td>60,000</td><td></td></tr>
<tr><td></td><td>Plant Assets ($900,000 − $54,000) ....</td><td>846,000</td><td></td></tr>
<tr><td></td><td>Intangible Assets ($100,000 − $6,000) ....</td><td>94,000</td><td></td></tr>
<tr><td></td><td>   Current Liabilities ....</td><td></td><td>240,000</td></tr>
<tr><td></td><td>   Long-Term Debt ....</td><td></td><td>500,000</td></tr>
<tr><td></td><td>   Premium on Long-Term Debt ($520,000 − $500,000) ....</td><td></td><td>20,000</td></tr>
<tr><td></td><td>   Investment in Net Assets of Fairmont Corporation ....</td><td></td><td>440,000</td></tr>
<tr><td></td><td colspan="3">To allocate cost of net assets acquired to identifiable net assets, with excess of current fair value of the net assets over their cost prorated to nonmonetary assets.</td></tr>
</table>

Pooling-of-interests accounting

The major premise of the pooling-of-interests method was that certain business combinations *involving the issuance of capital stock* were more in the nature of a *combining of stockholder interests* than an *acquisition of assets* or *raising of capital*. Combining of stockholder interests was evidenced by combinations involving common stock exchanges between corporations of approximately equal size. The shareholders and managements of these corporations continued their relative interests and activities in the combined company as they previously did in the separate corporations. Because neither of the like-size combining companies could be considered the *acquirer*, the pooling-of-interests method of accounting provided for carrying forward the combined assets, liabilities, and retained earnings of the combining companies at their *carrying amounts* in the accounting records of the combining companies. The current fair value of the capital stock issued to effect the business combination and the current fair value of the combinee's net assets are disregarded in a pooling of interests.

Illustration of pooling-of-interests accounting

The Saxon Corporation–Mason Company business combination described on page 138 would be accounted for as a pooling of interests by the journal entries below in Saxon Corporation's accounting records.

SAXON CORPORATION (Combinor)		
Journal Entries		
December 31, Year 1		
Current Assets (excluding inventory)	400,000	
Inventory	600,000	
Plant Assets (net)	3,000,000	
Other Assets	600,000	
Current Liabilities		500,000
Long-Term Debt		1,000,000
Common Stock		1,800,000
Retained Earnings		1,300,000
To record merger with Mason Company as a pooling of interests.		
Common stock	200,000	
Cash		200,000
To record payment of out-of-pocket costs incurred in merger with Mason Company.		

Combinor's journal entries for a pooling-type business combination

Because a pooling-type business combination is a combining of stockholder interests rather than an acquisition of assets, an Investment in Mason Company Common Stock account is not used in the journal entries. Instead, in the first journal entry, Mason's assets, liabilities, and retained earnings are assigned their carrying amounts in Mason's premerger balance sheet (see page 139).

The common stock issued by Saxon Corporation is recorded at an amount equal to the common stock on Mason Company's balance sheet. The total out-of-pocket costs of the business combination are recorded as a reduction of the proceeds received for the issuance of common stock.

Special problems with par value shares

The preceding illustrations have assumed that the combining companies have no par value shares. The Canada Business Corporations Act requires a corporation's shares to have no par value. Many of the provincial companies acts have similar provisions. As a result par value shares are becoming rare in Canada. However, not all provinces prohibit the issuance of shares with a par value.

If the combining companies in a pooling business combination have par value shares, there is an additional accounting problem with regard to attaching a dollar value to the shares issued. For example, assume that Saxon and Mason companies have the following shareholders' equities:

	Saxon	Mason	Total
Common stock $5 par value	$1,500,000	$1,000,000	$2,500,000
Contributed surplus	2,000,000	800,000	2,800,000
Retained earnings	700,000	1,300,000	2,000,000
Total shareholders' equity	$4,200,000	$3,100,000	$7,300,000

 Under pooling of interests accounting we combine the shareholder's equities of the combining companies. After the business combination Saxon's shareholders' equity will total $7,300,000. But will the components of Saxon's shareholders' equity be as shown in the total column? The answer is no! Because the common stock issued by Saxon Corporation must be recorded at par (300,000 shares × $5 = $1,500,000), we use the difference ($1,500,000 − $1,000,000 = $500,000) to reduce the amount of contributed surplus of Mason that is recorded by Saxon as part of the combination.

Saxon Corporation's summarized journal entry to record the business combination is as shown at the top of page 145 (assume that there are no direct out-of-pocket costs):

 Supposing Saxon Corporation's stock has a $10 par value. The 300,000 shares issued in the business combination would have to be recorded at $3,000,000. The total paid in capital (common stock plus contributed surplus) of Mason is 1,800,000. The difference of 1,200,000 would first be used to reduce the contributed surplus of Saxon. If the contributed surplus of Saxon was insufficient to absorb the difference, the retained earnings account would be reduced.

Combiner's journal
entry for a pooling-type
business combination
with par value shares

SAXON CORPORATION (Combinor)
Journal Entry
December 31, Year 1

Net Assets ($4,600,000 − $1,500,000)	3,100,000	
Common Stock, $5 par value		1,500,000
Contributed Surplus		300,000
Retained Earnings		1,300,000

To record the merger with Mason Company as a pooling of
interests. (Note: assume no out-of-pocket costs)

If Saxon's stock had a par value of $1, then the share issue would be
recorded at $300,000. This is $700,000 less than the capital stock account
of Mason and contributed surplus would be increased by this amount. The
contributed surplus of Mason ($800,000) and the retained earnings of Mason
($1,300,000) would also be recorded by Saxon.

Popularity of pooling accounting

In the United States the pooling method of accounting for business combinations was sanctioned initially by the AICPA in *Accounting Research
Bulletin No. 40*, "Business Combinations," issued in 1950. However, *ARB
No. 40* provided few criteria for identifying the business combinations that
qualified for pooling accounting, and was therefore unsatisfactory as a
guide for this accounting method. Consequently, in 1957 *ARB No. 48*,
"Business Combinations," superseded the previous pronouncement with
an expanded discussion of the pooling method. *ARB No. 48* continued to
permit pooling accounting for most business combinations involving an
exchange of equity securities. However, *ARB No. 48* also failed to provide
definitive guidelines for identifying the business combinations that qualified
for pooling accounting. As a result, a substantial number of business
combinations arranged during the 1950s and 1960s were accounted for as
poolings, despite the fact that the "combining of stockholder interests"
aspect was absent.

During this time period there were no Canadian pronouncements with
regard to business combinations. As a result Canadian accountants looked
to the AICPA pronouncements for guidance. During the 1950s and 1960s
pooling was used in Canada, but the proportion of business combinations
accounted for as poolings was substantially less than that experienced in the
United States.

Why had pooling accounting become so popular? Some of the reasons
are apparent from the comparison on page 146 of the combined Saxon
Corporation journal entries illustrated previously for the merger with Mason
Company:

Differences in Net Assets The first difference to consider in comparing
the foregoing journal entries is that the net assets recorded under the

Comparison of
combinor's journal
entries — purchase and
pooling

	Purchase accounting	Pooling accounting
Current Assets		
(excluding inventory)	400,000	400,000
Inventory	750,000	600,000
Plant Assets (net)	3,400,000	3,000,000
Other Assets	600,000	600,000
Discount on Long-Term Debt . . .	50,000	
Goodwill	266,250	
Current Liabilities	500,000	500,000
Long-Term Debt	1,000,000	1,000,000
Common Stock	3,766,250	1,600,000
Retained Earnings		1,300,000
Cash	200,000	200,000
To record merger with Mason Company.		

purchase method ($3,766,250) exceed the pooling-method net assets
($2,900,000) by $866,250. The composition of the $866,250 is summa-
rized below:

Excess of purchase asset values over pooling asset values:	
Inventory	$150,000
Plant assets	400,000
Goodwill	266,250
Excess of pooling liability values over purchase liability values:	
Long-term debt	50,000
Excess of purchase net assets values over pooling net assets values	$866,250

If we assume that the $400,000 difference in plant assets is attributable to
depreciable assets, total expenses of Saxon Corporation for years subsequent to December 31, Year 1, will be $866,250 larger under purchase
accounting than under pooling accounting. Assume, for example, that the
$150,000 difference in inventories will be allocated to cost of goods sold on
a fifo basis; the average economic life of plant assets is 10 years; the goodwill is to be amortized over a 40-year period; and the long-term debt has a
remaining five-year term to maturity.[4] Saxon Corporation's **pre-tax income**
for the year ending December 31, Year 2, would be nearly $207,000 less
under purchase accounting than under pooling accounting, attributable to
the following larger expenses under purchase accounting:

---

4 For simplicity, the discount on long-term debt is amortized by the straight-line method. Theoretically, the
effective interest method described in *Intermediate Accounting* of this series could be used when the
difference between the two methods is material in amount.

Cost of goods sold	$150,000
Depreciation ($400,000 × $\frac{1}{10}$)	40,000
Amortization of goodwill ($266,250 × $\frac{1}{40}$)	6,656
Interest expense ($50,000 × $\frac{1}{5}$)	10,000
Excess of Year 2 pre-tax income under pooling accounting rather than under	
purchase accounting	$206,656

It should also be noted that the income statements of Saxon Corporation and Mason Company would be combined in pooling accounting for the *entire* year ended December 31, Year 1 (as described in a subsequent section of this chapter).

In summary, the favourable effect of pooling accounting on post-combination earnings has been the main reason for the popularity of this accounting method.

Differences in Total Shareholder's Equity   The increase in Saxon Corporation's shareholder equity is $866,250 less ($3,766,250 − $2,900,000 = $866,250) under pooling accounting than under purchase accounting. Although retained earnings is $1,300,000 higher, the capital stock is $2,166,250 lower under pooling. If corporate law makes this $1,300,000 difference in retained earnings available as a basis for dividend declaration another advantage of the pooling method is readily apparent.

Impact of Divergent Price-Earnings Ratios   Even more dramatic than the preceding advantages inherent in the pooling-of-interests method of accounting is the potential impact on the market price of Saxon Corporation's common stock if the price-earnings ratios for Saxon's and Mason's common stock differed significantly prior to the merger. Suppose, for example, that Saxon Corporation and Mason Company had the following financial measurements prior to the business combination:

	Saxon Corporation	Mason Company
Year ended Dec. 31, Year 1:		
Net income	$78,000	$375,000
Earnings per share	0.26	$3.75
On Dec. 31, Year 1:		
Number of shares of common stock outstanding	300,000†	100,000†
Market price per share	$13	$30
Price earnings ratio	50	8
†Outstanding during entire year.		

After consummation of the business combination as a pooling, Saxon Corporation's income statement for the year ended December 31, Year 1, reports the combined enterprise's net income as $453,000 — the total of the separate net incomes of the constituent companies. "Pooled" earnings per share for Saxon thus is increased to approximately $0.76. This increased amount of earnings per share is computed by dividing combined earnings of $453,000 by 600,000 (300,000 + 300,000 = 600,000), the *effective* number of shares of Saxon's common stock outstanding during the year ended December 31, Year 1. If the price-earnings ratio for Saxon's common stock continued unchanged, the stock's market price would increase after the merger to $38 a share ($0.76 × 50 = $38), a 192% increase. Saxon Corporation probably would attain the reputation of an "exciting growth company," and Saxon's directors likely would seek out other prospects for pooling-type business combinations.

The 192% increase in the market price of Saxon's common stock is used here to illustrate how accounting numbers might influence the stock market. The actual increase would not be so dramatic because sophisticated investors presumably would see through this "accounting magic." Naive investors might still be fooled by this ploy.

Abuses of pooling accounting

The attractive features of pooling accounting described in the preceding section, together with the absence of firm guidelines for poolings in *ARB No. 48*, led to a number of serious abuses of the method. Among these abuses were retroactive poolings; retrospective poolings; part-pooling, part-purchase accounting; treasury stock issuances; issuances of unusual securities; creation of "instant earnings"; and contingent payouts.

Retroactive Poolings   After *ARB No. 48* was issued, some accountants interpreted its provisions as permitting pooling accounting for many business combinations that already had been accounted for as purchases under *ARB No. 40*. Accordingly, a significant number of business combinations recorded as purchases in the late 1950s and early 1960s were *restated retroactively* as poolings in subsequent years. Such restatements raised questions in the minds of users of financial statements as to the integrity of both the initial and the revised accounting for the business combinations.

Retrospective Poolings   The theory that the combining companies in a pooling business combination were *effectively combined* in accounting periods preceding the actual business combination led to the practice of *retrospective poolings*. This technique involved the consummation of pooling business combinations after the close of a combinor's fiscal year but prior to the issuance of its annual financial statements. The income statement that ultimately was issued included the operating results of the subsequently pooled combinee on a retrospective basis. Thus, a desired earnings per share amount might have been attained simply by a working paper adjustment.

Part-Pooling, Part-Purchase Accounting   Some business combinations involving the issuance of common stock as well as cash and debt were accounted for as *poolings* to the extent of the stock issuance, and as *purchases* for the remainder of the consideration. This hybrid method was inconsistent with any orderly structure of accounting theory.

Treasury Stock Issuances   Pooling accounting required the exchange of common stock between the combining companies. One method devised to avoid the potential dilution of earnings per share resulting from common stock issuances was the cash acquisition of treasury stock, and its subsequent reissuance in a pooling-type business combination. If substance is emphasized over form, such a combination is effected for *cash*, not for *previously unissued stock*.

Issuances of Unusual Securities   As another means of minimizing the dilutive effects of common stock issuances in poolings, many unusual securities were devised to consummate business combinations. These securities, usually in the form of either preferred stock or a special class of common stock, were in most cases convertible to the combinor's voting common stock. In substance, these unusual securities were not equivalent to voting common stock, yet the business combinations involving these securities frequently were treated as poolings.

Creation of ''Instant Earnings''   The discussion on pages 146 to 148, comparing the purchase and pooling journal entries for Saxon Corporation, pointed out how pooling accounting could *instantly increase earnings per share* for the year of a business combination. Another technique for creating instant earnings was the sale of a combinee's assets shortly after the pooling combination. Because the selling price generally exceeded the carrying amounts of the assets, a one-time gain was created. The selling price usually paralleled the current fair value of the combinor's capital stock issued in the pooling combination. Thus, the instant earnings were fictitious because the gain in effect represented proceeds from the capital stock issued to effect the combination.

Contingent Payouts   If the ''combining of stockholder interests'' feature of a pooling combination were genuine, there would be no unresolved contingencies with respect to the number of shares of common stock to be issued in the combination. Nevertheless, a large number of business combinations involving contingent issuances of additional shares of common stock were accounted for as poolings.

Abuses of purchase accounting

Purchase accounting was not free of abuses during the 1950s and 1960s. The principal abuse of purchase accounting was the failure to allocate the cost of an acquiree to the identifiable net assets acquired and to goodwill. Instead, an ''Excess of Cost over Net Assets Acquired'' account was created and presented in the post-combination balance sheet as an intangible asset — usually not subject to amortization. Consequently, reported earnings subsequent to these purchase-type combinations were the same as though pooling accounting had been used. Also, as in pooling-type business combinations, "instant earnings" often were created by the sale of understated identifiable assets shortly after the purchase-type combination.

Action by the AICPA

In 1970 the AICPA's Accounting Principles Board reacted to the abuses of pooling accounting and purchase accounting by tightening the rules permitting pooling to be used and by limiting drastically the range of situations in which pooling would be allowed. *APB Opinion No. 16*, "Business Combinations," provided 12 conditions for business combinations that were to be accounted for as poolings. The opinion required that all of the conditions were to be satisfied for pooling to be appropriate.

Action by the CICA

In December 1973 the Accounting Research Committee issued *Section 1580* of the *Handbook*. This section provided the conditions under which pooling of interest would be allowed in Canada. The section asked *if an acquirer can be identified* in a business combination. If the *answer is yes*, the *purchase method* must be used. If the *answer is no*, then *pooling* must be used.

The ARC provided guidelines for identifying an acquirer as follows:

1 If cash, assets, or debt securities are the means of payment, the company making the payment has been identified as the acquirer.
2 If voting shares have been issued as the means of payment, then an examination of the holdings of the shareholder groups of each of the combining companies in the shares outstanding of the combined company is required as follows:
   a If *a shareholder group* of one of the combining companies *holds more than 50% of the total shares outstanding* of the combined company, an acquirer has been identified.
   b If an acquirer cannot be identified in this manner, an examination is made of the composition of the board of directors and/or the management of the combined company to see if an acquirer can be identified. The implication is that if one of the combining companies appears to dominate this composition, that company has been identified as the acquirer.

The ARC concluded that only in rare situations would it be impossible to identify an acquirer, and therefore the *use of pooling* in business combinations *would also be rare*.

In the Saxon-Mason illustration that we have used, the pooling method would be appropriate given the facts presented. Saxon had 300,000 shares outstanding prior to the business combination and then issued 300,000 shares to the shareholders of Mason. As no shareholder group holds more than 50% of the voting shares of the combined company pooling is the suggested method. However, if examination of the Board of Directors or the management of the combined company indicated a domination by Saxon then an acquirer would be identified and the purchase method would have to be used.

Presentation of business combinations in financial statements

Under both purchase accounting and pooling accounting, the balance sheet for a combined enterprise issued as of the date of a business combination accomplished through a statutory amalgamation or acquisition of assets includes all the assets and liabilities of the combining companies. (The *consolidated* balance sheet issued following a combination that results in a parent-subsidiary relationship is described in Chapter 5.) The form of the combined company's income statement for the accounting period in which a combination is carried out depends on whether purchase or pooling accounting is used to record the combination.

Purchase The income statement of the combined company for the accounting period in which a purchase-type business combination occurred includes the operating results of the acquiree *after the date of the combination only.* For example, under purchase accounting, Saxon Corporation's postmerger income statement for the year ended December 31, Year 1, would be identical to Saxon's premerger income statement shown in the pooling accounting illustration below.

Pooling The income statement of the combined company for the accounting period in which a pooling-type business combination took place includes the results of operations of the combining companies *as though the combination had been completed at the beginning of the period.* Comparative financial statements for preceding periods must be restated in order to show financial information for the new reporting entity for all periods. Intercompany transactions prior to the combination must be eliminated from the combined income statements in a manner comparable to that described in Chapter 3 for branches.[5]

Income statements of combining companies prior to business combination	SAXON CORPORATION AND MASON COMPANY Income Statements For Year Ended December 31, Year 1		
		Saxon Corporation	Mason Company
	Sales	$10,000,000	$5,000,000
	Costs and expenses:		
	Cost of goods sold	$ 8,355,000	$3,000,000
	Operating expenses	1,300,000	962,000
	Interest expense	150,000	100,500
	Income taxes expense	117,000	562,500
	Total costs and expenses	$ 9,922,000	$4,625,000
	Net income	$ 78,000	$ 375,000

5 *CICA Handbook*, CICA (Toronto), Section 1580.

This presentation stems from the concept that a business combination accounted for as a pooling is a ***combining of stockholder interests*** rather than an ***acquisition of assets***. Because stockholder interests are combined, previous financial statements showing changes in those interests also are combined.

To illustrate, assume that the income statements of Saxon Corporation and Mason Company for the year ended December 31, Year 1 (prior to completion of their merger described earlier in this chapter), were as shown on page 151. Assume also that Mason's interest expense includes $25,000 paid to Saxon on a loan that was repaid prior to December 31, Year 1, and that Saxon's sales revenue includes $25,000 (an immaterial amount) interest revenue received from Mason.

The working paper for the postmerger income statement of Saxon Corporation under pooling accounting is illustrated below. The amounts in the Combined column are reported in Saxon's published postmerger income statement for the year ended December 31, Year 1.

SAXON CORPORATION
Working Paper for Combined Income Statement (Pooling of Interests)
For Year Ended December 31, Year 1

	Saxon Corporation	Mason Company	Eliminations	Combined
Sales	10,000,000	5,000,000	(a) (25,000)	14,975,000
Costs and expenses:				
Cost of goods sold	8,355,000	3,000,000		11,355,000
Operating expenses	1,300,000	962,000		2,262,000
Interest expense	150,000	100,500	(a) (25,000)	225,500
Income taxes expense	117,000	562,500		679,500
Total costs and expenses .	9,922,000	4,625,000	(25,000)	14,522,000
Net income	78,000	375,000	-0-	453,000

Explanation of combination eliminations:
(a) To eliminate intercompany interest received by Saxon Corporation from Mason Company.

Disclosure of business combinations in notes to financial statements

Because of the complex nature of business combinations and their effects on the financial position and operating results of the combined enterprise, extensive disclosure is required for the periods in which they occur. The following notes illustrate the required disclosures for a purchase and a pooling of interests:

Purchase On April 2, Year 2, the Company acquired substantially all the assets, including inventory, of Combinee Company for $8,400,000 cash and an agreement to make future payments through July, Year 5, contingent on sales of one of the acquired brands.

The acquisition has been accounted for as a purchase, and is summarized as follows:

Net assets acquired at assigned values:

Current assets	$8,231,000	
Fixed assets	5,700,000	
Other assets	320,000	$14,251,000
Current liabilities	$3,500,000	
Long term debt	2,750,000	6,250,000
		$8,001,000
Goodwill		399,000
		$8,400,000

The contingent consideration will be recorded when and if it becomes payable.

The results of operations of Combinee are included in the consolidated statement of income since the date of acquisition. Had the acquisition taken place on January 1, Year 1, unaudited pro forma sales for the years ended December 31, Year 2 and Year 1, would be $793,627,000 and $777,715,000, respectively, with unaudited pro forma net income of $9,879,000 and $12,015,000, respectively, and unaudited pro forma earnings per share of $1.17 and $1.40, respectively.

Pooling of Interests In November, Year 2, the Company and Combinee Company amalgamated to continue as the Company. This amalgamation has been accounted for as a pooling of interests, and, accordingly, all financial data for accounting periods prior to the merger have been restated to combine the operations of the two companies. The amalgamation was effected by the issue of 6,477,000 shares of the Company's common stock for 100% of the 8,265,000 outstanding shares of Combinee Company. After the amalgamation the relative holdings by shareholders are as follows:

Shareholders of the Company	6,477,000
Shareholders of Combinee Company	6,477,000
Total shares outstanding	12,954,000

The shares of the Company traded at an average price of $13 during the six-month period preceding the amalgamation.

The net assets contributed by the amalgamating companies at book value on Oct. 31, are as follows:

	The Company (millions)	Combinee Company (millions)	Total (millions)
Total assets	$820.6	$571.1	$1,391.7
Total liabilities	370.1	180.9	551.0
Net assets	$450.5	$390.2	$ 840.7

Net revenue and net income of the separate companies for the 39 weeks ended November 3, Year 2 (interim period nearest the combination date), and fiscal Year 1 are as follows:

	Net revenue (millions)	Net income (millions)
39 weeks ended Nov. 3, Year 2 (unaudited):		
Combinor, as previously reported	$1,848.7	$ 43.2
Combinee	137.2	10.4
Combined	$1,985.9	$ 53.6
Fiscal year ended Feb. 3, Year 1:		
Combinor, as previously reported	$2,582.6	$ 90.0
Combinee	150.1	11.4
Combined	$2,732.7	$101.4

APPRAISAL OF ACCOUNTING STANDARDS FOR BUSINESS COMBINATIONS

The accounting standards for business combinations described and illustrated in the preceding pages of this chapter may be criticized on grounds that they are not consistent with the conceptual framework of accounting.

Criticism of purchase accounting

The principal criticisms of purchase accounting centre on the recognition of goodwill. Many accountants take exception to the *residual* basis for valuing goodwill established in Section 1580. These critics contend that part of the amounts thus assigned to goodwill probably apply to other *identifiable* intangible assets. Accordingly, goodwill in a business combination should be valued *directly* by of methods described in *Intermediate Accounting* of this series. Any remaining cost not directly allocated to all identifiable tangible and intangible assets and to goodwill would be apportioned to those assets based on the amounts assigned in the first valuation process.

The mandatory amortization of goodwill, prescribed in Section 1580, is considered by some accountants to be inappropriate for goodwill attributable to a business combination. These accountants recommend treating the amount assigned to goodwill in a business combination as a reduction of shareholders' equity of the combined enterprise.

The accounting described on page 141 for the excess of current fair values over total cost in a bargain-purchase business combination also has been challenged. Critics maintain there is no theoretical support for the arbitrary reduction of previously determined current fair values of assets by an apportioned amount of the bargain-purchase excess. They suggest amortizing this "negative goodwill" in the same manner as positive goodwill.

Other accountants question whether current fair values of the acquirer's net assets — especially goodwill — should be ignored in accounting for a purchase-type business combination. They maintain it is inconsistent to reflect current fair values for net assets of the *acquiree only*, in view of the significance of many combinations involving large constituent companies.

Criticism of pooling accounting

The principal objections raised to pooling accounting are summarized below:

1 Despite the framework for pooling accounting established in Section 1580, this accounting method is founded upon a delicate assumption. This assumption — that some business combinations involving exchanges of voting common stock result in a combining of shareholder interests rather than an acquisition of assets — is difficult to support in accounting theory. Two *Accounting Research Studies* recommended abolishing the pooling accounting method for business combinations between independent constituent companies.[6]

2 The assets of the combinee in a pooling-type business combination are not accounted for at their cost to the combinor. In the illustrated pooling accounting for the merger of Saxon Corporation and Mason Company (pages 143 to 146), the net assets of Mason were recorded in Saxon's accounting records at $3,100,000, the carrying amounts in Mason's accounting records. This amount is $866,250 less than the *cost* of Mason's net assets of $3,966,250 as reflected in the purchase accounting illustration.

3 A consequence of the misstatement of asset values is that net income for each accounting period subsequent to a pooling-type business combination is misstated.

The foregoing are powerful criticisms, and are difficult to refute. Despite its alleged flaws, purchase accounting for business combinations appears conceptually superior in every respect to pooling-of-interests accounting.

Recent development in the United States

In recognition of the unsatisfactory state of accounting for business combinations, the Financial Accounting Standards Board initiated a study of the subject shortly after the Board's inception. A lengthy *FASB Discussion Memorandum*, "An Analysis of Issues Related to Accounting for Business Combinations and Purchased Intangibles," was issued in 1976. However, the FASB deferred further efforts on the study, pending completion of the project to develop a conceptual framework for financial accounting and reporting (described in *Intermediate Accounting* of this series). In 1981, the FASB removed the business combinations and purchased intangibles project from its agenda "because of (its) low priority in relation to other existing and potential projects."[7] The action of the Board may be questioned, in light of the criticisms of current accounting standards for business combinations described in the foregoing section.

---

6 Arthur R. Wyatt, *Accounting Research Study No. 5*, "A Critical Study of Accounting for Business Combinations," AICPA (New York: 1963), p. 105; George R. Catlett and Norman O. Olson, *Accounting Research Study No. 10*, "Accounting for Goodwill," AICPA (New York: 1968), pp. 106, 109.

7 *Status Report*, FASB (Stamford: Apr. 10, 1981), p. 3.

REVIEW QUESTIONS

1 Define a **business combination**.

2 What is a **statutory amalgamation**?

3 Identify two methods that may be used, individually or jointly, to determine an appropriate price to pay for a combinee in a business combination.

4 State how each of the following out-of-pocket costs of a purchase-type business combination should be accounted for:
 a Printing costs for proxy statement mailed to combinor's shareholders in advance of special meeting to ratify terms of the merger
 b Legal fees for negotiating the merger
 c CA firm's fees for auditing Securities Commission registration statement covering shares of common stock issued in the merger
 d Printing costs for securities issued in the merger
 e Legal fees for Securities Commission registration statement covering shares of common stock issued in the merger
 f CA firm's fees for advice on income tax aspects of the merger

5 The word "goodwill" often appears in connection with business combinations. Explain the meaning of **goodwill** and **negative goodwill**.

6 a Define **contingent consideration** in a business combination.
 b If a plan for a business combination includes a provision for contingent consideration, is pooling accounting appropriate for the combination? Explain.

7 How is the cost of an acquiree allocated in a purchase-type business combination?

8 If a business combination meets the CICA Handbook conditions for pooling, what is the accounting effect as compared with a purchase interpretation?

9 Comment on the following quotation:

It is our judgment that the weight of logic and consistency supports the conclusion that business combinations between independent entities are exchange transactions involving a transfer of assets and that the accounting action to account for exchange transactions is necessary to reflect properly the results of business combinations.

10 Discuss some of the reasons for the popularity of pooling accounting for business combinations.

11 Identify five abuses of pooling accounting during the 1960s.

12 How do the journal entries to Contributed Surplus differ in purchase accounting and pooling accounting?

13 Differentiate **retrospective poolings** from **retroactive poolings**.

14 Critics have charged that pooling accounting creates **instant earnings**. How is this accomplished?

15 What information is disclosed in notes to the financial statements of a combined enterprise following a pooling-type business combination?

16 How has purchase accounting for business combinations been criticized?

EXERCISES

Ex. 4-1 Select the best answer for each of the following multiple-choice questions:

1 Which of the following is the appropriate basis for valuing plant assets acquired in a purchase-type business combination carried out by an exchange of cash for common stock?
   a Current fair value
   b Carrying amount
   c Original cost plus any excess of purchase price over carrying amount of the plant assets acquired
   d Original cost

2 How should long-term debt assumed in a business combination be valued under each of the following methods?

	Purchase	Pooling of interests
a	Carrying amount	Carrying amount
b	Carrying amount	Current fair value
c	Current fair value	Current fair value
d	Current fair value	Carrying amount

3 Combinor Corporation issued nonvoting preferred stock with a current fair value of $4,000,000 in exchange for all the outstanding common stock of Combinee Company. On the date of the exchange, Combinee had identifiable net assets with a carrying amount of $2,000,000 and a current fair value of $2,500,000. In addition, Combinor issued preferred stock valued at $400,000 to an individual as a finder's fee in arranging the merger business combination. As a result of this transaction, Combinor should record an increase in net assets of:
   a $2,000,000   b $2,500,000   c $2,900,000   d $4,400,000
   e Some other amount

4 Goodwill from a business combination:
   a Should be expensed in the year of the combination
   b Is an asset that is not subject to amortization
   c Is an intangible asset
   d Occurs in a pooling of interests

5 Which of the following is a potential abuse that can arise when a business combination is accounted for as a pooling of interests?
   a Assets of the combinee may be overvalued when the price paid by the combinor is allocated among specific assets
   b Liabilities of the combinee may be undervalued when the price paid by the combinor is allocated among specific liabilities
   c An undue amount of cost may be assigned to goodwill, thus potentially allowing for an overstatement of pooled earnings
   d Earnings of the combined enterprise may be increased because of the combination only, and not as a result of efficient operations

Ex. 4-2 Gamma Corporation was organized in a statutory amalgamation to combine the resources of Alpha Company and Beta, Inc., in a business combination accounted for by the pooling method. On January 2, Year 1, Gamma issued 65,000 shares of its $10 par common stock in exchange for all the outstanding common stock of Alpha and Beta. The shareholders' equity of Alpha and Beta on January 2, Year 1, were as follows:

	Alpha Company	Beta, Inc.	Totals
Common stock, $1 par	$150,000	$450,000	$600,000
Contributed surplus	20,000	55,000	75,000
Retained earnings	110,000	210,000	320,000
Total shareholders' equity	$280,000	$715,000	$995,000

Compute the balance of Gamma's Contributed Surplus immediately after the business combination. Disregard out-of-pocket costs of the business combination.

Ex. 4-3 On March 31, Year 3, Combinor Corporation acquired the identifiable net assets of Combinee Company for $800,000 cash. On the date of the business combination, Combinee had $100,000 of liabilities. The current fair values of Combinee's assets on March 31, Year 3, were as follows:

Current assets	$ 400,000
Noncurrent assets	600,000
Total current fair value	$1,000,000

Out-of-pocket costs of the business combination may be disregarded.

Prepare journal entries for Combinor on March 1, Year 3, to record its business combination with Combinee. (State your assumptions.)

Ex. 4-4 Synde Corporation (the survivor) issued its preferred stock with a current fair value of $1,000,000 in exchange for all the outstanding common stock of Moro Company, which had identifiable net assets with a carrying amount of $500,000 and a current fair value of $600,000. In addition, Synde issued preferred stock valued at $120,000 to an investment banker as a finder's fee for arranging the merger business combination.

Compute the total increase in Synde's net assets resulting from the business combination with Moro.

Ex. 4-5 Webb Corporation paid $100,000 cash for the net assets of Lorne Company, which consisted of the following:

	Carrying amount	Current fair value
Current monetary assets	$20,000	$ 28,000
Plant assets (net)	80,000	110,000
Liabilities	(20,000)	(18,000)
Net assets	$80,000	$120,000

Compute the amount at which Webb should record the plant assets acquired from Lorne.

Ex. 4-6 The condensed balance sheet of Leno Company on March 31, Year 8, is given at the top of page 159.

On March 31, Year 8, Kinder Corporation paid $700,000 cash for all the net assets of Leno (except cash) in a business combination qualifying for purchase accounting. The carrying amounts of Leno's other current assets and current liabilities were the same as their current fair values. However, current fair values of Leno's plant assets and long-term debt were $920,000 and $190,000, respectively.

Also on March 31, Kinder paid the following out-of-pocket costs for the business combination with Leno:

Legal fees	$ 10,000
Finder's fee	70,000
Fee for audit of Leno Company's March 31, Year 8, financial statements ..	20,000
Total out-of-pocket costs of business combination	$100,000

LENO COMPANY

Condensed Balance Sheet
March 31, Year 8

Assets

Cash	$ 20,000
Other current assets	140,000
Plant assets (net)	740,000
Total assets	$900,000

Liabilities & Shareholders' Equity

Current liabilities	$ 80,000
Long-term debt	200,000
Common stock	300,000
Retained earnings	320,000
Total liabilities & shareholders' equity	$900,000

Compute the amount of goodwill or "negative goodwill" in the business combination of Kinder Corporation and Leno Company.

Ex. 4-7 The condensed balance sheet of Munoz Company on February 28, Year 7, with related current fair values of assets and liabilities, appears below.

MUNOZ COMPANY

Balance Sheet
February 28, Year 7

	Carrying amount	Current fair value
Assets		
Current assets	$ 500,000	$ 580,000
Plant assets (net)	1,000,000	1,150,000
Other assets	300,000	350,000
Total assets	$1,800,000	
Liabilities & Shareholders' Equity		
Current liabilities	$ 300,000	300,000
Long-term debt	400,000	380,000
Common stock, $1 par	500,000	
Contributed surplus	200,000	
Retained earnings	400,000	
Total liabilities & shareholders' equity	$1,800,000	

On February 28, Year 7, Seville Corporation issued 600,000 shares of its $1 par common stock (current fair value $25 a share) to Maria Munoz, sole stockholder of Munoz Company, for all 500,000 shares of Munoz Company common stock owned by her, in a merger business combination qualifying for pooling accounting. Because the merger was negotiated privately and Maria Munoz signed a "letter agreement" not to dispose of the Seville common stock she received, the Seville stock was not subject to Securities Commission registration requirements. Thus, only $5,000 in legal fees was incurred to effect the merger; these fees were paid in cash by Seville on February 28, Year 7.

Prepare journal entries to record the business combination in the accounting records of Seville Corporation.

Ex. 4-8 On November 1, Year 4, Sullivan Corporation issued 50,000 shares of its common stock in exchange for all the common stock of Mears Company in a statutory amalgamation. Out-of-pocket costs of the business combination may be disregarded. Sullivan tentatively recorded the shares of common stock issued at par and debited Investment in Mears Company Common Stock for $500,000. Mears Company was liquidated and became Mears Division of Sullivan.

The net income of Sullivan and Mears Company or Mears Division during Year 4 was as follows:

	Jan. 1–Oct. 31	Nov. 1–Dec. 31
Sullivan Corporation	$420,000	$80,000*
Mears Company	350,000	
Mears Division of Sullivan Corporation		50,000

*Excludes any portion of Mears Division net income.

Condensed balance sheet and other data for Year 4 follow:

	Sullivan Corporation		Mears Company	Mears Division of Sullivan Corporation
	Oct. 31	Dec. 31	Oct. 31	Dec. 31
Assets	$3,500,000	$4,080,000	$4,000,000	$4,150,000
Liabilities	500,000	500,000	1,000,000	1,100,000
Common stock, $10 par	2,000,000	2,500,000	2,000,000	
Retained earnings	1,000,000	1,080,000*	1,000,000	
Market price per share of				
common stock	100	130	20	

*Excludes any portion of Mears Division net income.

Neither company paid dividends during Year 4. In recent months, Sullivan's common stock has been selling at about 40 times earnings; prior to November 1, Year 4, Mears Company common stock had been selling at 10 times earnings.

Answer the following questions, **assuming that the differences between current fair values and carrying amounts of Mears Company's identifiable net assets apply to land**. Show supporting computations.

a Assuming that the merger is accounted for as a pooling, what is Sullivan's net income for Year 4?

b What is the amount of the Year 4 earnings per share for Sullivan on a pooling basis?

c If the merger had been accounted for as a purchase, what would Sullivan's net income have been for Year 4?

d What is Sullivan's earnings per share for Year 4 on a purchase basis?

e What is the amount of retained earnings on a pooling basis at the end of Year 4?

f What is the amount of retained earnings on a purchase basis at the end of Year 4?

g Which method of accounting would be required under Section 1580 of the *CICA Handbook*?

CASES

Case 4-1 When a business combination is effected by an exchange of common stock, the transaction is accounted for either as a purchase or as a pooling of interests. The methods are not optional, and may yield significantly different results as to financial position and results of operations of the combined enterprise.

Instructions Discuss the supportive arguments for each of the following methods of accounting for business combinations:
a Purchase method
b Pooling-of-interests method

Do not discuss the rules for distinguishing between a purchase and a pooling of interests.

Case 4-2 The boards of directors of Carter Corporation, Fulton Company, Russell, Inc., and Towne Corporation are meeting jointly to discuss plans for a statutory amalgamation. Each of the corporations has one class of common stock outstanding; Fulton also has one class of preferred stock outstanding. Although terms have not as yet been settled, Carter will be the surviving corporation. Because the directors want to conform to generally accepted accounting principles, they have asked you to attend the meeting as an advisor.

Instructions Consider each of the following questions independently of the others and answer each in accordance with generally accepted accounting principles. Explain your answers.
a Assume that the business combination will be consummated August 31, Year 5. Explain the philosophy underlying the accounting and how the balance sheet accounts of each of the four corporations will appear in Carter's balance sheet on September 1, Year 5, if the business combination is accounted for as a:
(1) Pooling
(2) Purchase
b Assume that the business combination will be consummated August 31, Year 5. Explain how the income statement accounts of each of the four corporations will be accounted for in Carter's income statement for the year ended December 31, Year 5, if the combination is accounted for as a:
(1) Pooling
(2) Purchase
c Some of the directors believe that the terms of the business combination should be agreed on immediately and that the method of accounting to be used may be chosen at some later date. Others believe that the terms of the business combination and the accounting method to be used are closely related. Which position is correct? Explain.
d Carter and Towne are comparable in size; Russell and Fulton are much smaller. How do these facts affect the choice of accounting method for the business combination?
e Fulton was formerly a subsidiary of Garson Corporation, which has no other relationship to any of the four companies discussing the business combination. Garson voluntarily spun off Fulton 18 months ago. What effect, if any, do these facts have on the choice of accounting method for the business combination?
f Carter holds 2,000 of Fulton's 10,000 outstanding shares of preferred stock and 15,000 of Russell's 100,000 outstanding shares of common stock. All of Carter's holdings were acquired during the first three months of Year 5. What effect, if any, do these facts have on the choice of accounting method?

g Because the directors feel that one of Towne's major divisions will not be compatible with the operations of the combined enterprise, they anticipate that it will be sold as soon as possible after the business combination is consummated. They expect to have no trouble in finding a buyer. What effect, if any, do these facts have on the choice of accounting method?

Case 4-3 You have been engaged to examine the financial statements of Solamente Corporation for the fiscal year ended May 31, Year 6. You discover that on June 1, Year 5, Mika Company was merged into Solamente in a business combination qualifying for purchase accounting. You also find that both Solamente and Mika (prior to its liquidation) incurred legal fees, accounting fees, and printing costs for the business combination; both companies debited those costs to an intangible asset ledger account entitled "Cost of Business Combination." In its journal entry to record the business combination with Mika, Solamente increased its Cost of Business Combination account by an amount equal to the balance in Mika's comparable ledger account.

Instructions Evaluate Solamente's accounting for the out-of-pocket costs of the business combination with Mika.

Case 4-4 After extended negotiations, Combinor Corporation acquired from Combinee Company most of the latter's assets on June 30, Year 3. At the time of the acquisition, Combinee's accounting records (adjusted to June 30, Year 3) reflected the descriptions and amounts that appear below for the assets acquired.

You ascertain that the valuation accounts were Allowance for Doubtful Accounts, Allowance for Price Decline in Inventories, and Accumulated Depreciation.

	Cost	Valuation accounts	Carrying amounts
Accounts receivable	$ 83,600	$ 3,000	$ 80,600
Inventories	107,000	5,200	101,800
Land	20,000		20,000
Buildings	207,500	73,000	134,500
Machinery and equipment	205,000	41,700	163,300
Goodwill	50,000		50,000
Totals	$673,100	$122,900	$550,200

During the extended negotiations, Combinee held out for a consideration of approximately $600,000 (depending upon the level of accounts receivable and inventories). However, on June 30, Year 3, Combinee agreed to accept Combinor's offer of $450,000 cash plus 1% of Combinor's net sales (as defined in the contract) of the next five years, with payments at the end of each year. Combinee expects that Combinor's total net sales during this five-year period will exceed $15,000,000.

Instructions
a How should Combinor Corporation account for the buisness combination? Explain.
b Discuss the propriety of recording goodwill in the accounting records of Combinor Corporation for the business combination.

Case 4-5 On February 15, Year 6, negotiating officers of Shane Corporation agreed with George Merlo, sole shareholder of Merlo Company and Merlo Industries, Inc., to acquire all his common stock ownership in the two companies as follows:

(1) 10,000 shares of Shane's $1 par common stock (current fair value $25 a share) would be issued to George Merlo on February 28, Year 6, for his 1,000 shares of $10 par common stock of Merlo Company. In addition, 10,000 shares of Shane common stock would be issued to George Merlo on February 28, Year 11, if aggregate net income of Merlo Company for the five-year period then ended exceeded $300,000.

(2) $250,000 cash would be paid to George Merlo on February 28, Year 6, for his 10,000 shares of $1 par common stock of Merlo Industries, Inc. In addition $250,000 in cash would be paid to George Merlo on February 28, Year 11, if aggregate net income of Merlo Industries, Inc., for the five-year period then ended exceeded $300,000.

Both Merlo Company and Merlo Industries, Inc., are to be merged into Shane on February 28, Year 6, and are to continue operations after that date as divisions of Shane. George Merlo also agreed not to compete with Shane for the period March 1, Year 6, through February 28, Year 11. Because the merger was negotiated privately and George Merlo signed a "letter agreement" not to dispose of the Shane common stock he received, the business combination was not subject to the jurisdiction of any securities commission. Out-of-pocket costs of the business combination were negligible.

Selected financial statement data of the three constituent companies as of February 28, Year 6 (prior to the merger), were as follows:

	Shane Corporation	Merlo Company	Merlo Industries, Inc.
Total assets	$25,000,000	$ 500,000	$ 600,000
Shareholders' equity	10,000,000	200,000	300,000
Net sales	50,000,000	1,500,000	2,500,000
Earnings per share	5	30	3

The controller of Shane prepared the following condensed journal entries to record the merger on February 28, Year 6:

Assets	500,000	
Liabilities		300,000
Common Stock		10,000
Common Stock to Be Issued		10,000
Contributed Surplus		180,000
To record merger with Merlo Company as a pooling.		

Assets	650,000	
Goodwill	150,000	
Liabilities		300,000
Payable to George Merlo		250,000
Cash		250,000
To record merger with Merlo Industries, Inc., as a purchase, with assets and liabilities of Merlo Industries, Inc., recorded at current fair values and goodwill to be amortized over a 40-year economic life.		

Instructions Do you concur with the controller's journal entries? Discuss.

PROBLEMS

4-1 The balance sheet of Combinee Company on October 31, Year 5, was as follows:

COMBINEE COMPANY
Balance Sheet
October 31, Year 5

Assets

Cash	$ 60,000
Other current assets	420,000
Plant assets (net)	920,000
Total assets	$1,400,000

Liabilities & Shareholders' Equity

Current liabilities	$ 180,000
Long-term debt	250,000
Common stock, no par	520,000
Retained earnings	450,000
Total liabilities & shareholders' equity	$1,400,000

After a thorough study, Combinor Corporation's board of directors established the following current fair values for Combinee's identifiable net assets other than cash:

Other current assets	$ 500,000
Plant assets (net)	1,000,000
Current liabilities	180,000
Long-term debt	250,000

Accordingly, on October 31, Year 5, Combinor issued 100,000 shares of its no par (current fair value $13) common stock for all the net assets of Combinee in a business combination qualifying for purchase accounting. Also on October 31, Year 5, Combinor paid the following out-of-pocket costs in connection with the combination:

Finder's fee and legal fees	$180,000
Costs associated with issuing shares	120,000
Total out-of-pocket costs of business combination	$300,000

Instructions Prepare journal entries in the accounting records of Combinor Corporation on October 31, Year 5, to record the business combination with Combinee Company.

4-2 Condensed balance sheets of Conner Company and Capsol Company on July 31, Year 9, were as shown at the top of page 165.

On July 31, Year 9, Conner and Capsol entered into a statutory amalgamation. The new company, Consol Corporation, issued 75,000 shares of no par common stock for all the outstanding common stock of Conner and Capsol. Out-of-pocket costs of the business combination may be disregarded.

	Conner Company	Capsol Company
Total assets	$700,000	$670,000
Total liabilities	$300,000	$300,000
Common stock, no par	280,000	380,000
Retained earnings (deficit)	120,000	(10,000)
Total liabilities & shareholders' equity	$700,000	$670,000

Instructions

a Prepare a journal entry to record the business combination in the accounting records of Consol as a pooling.

b Prepare a journal entry to record the business combination in the accounting records of Consol as a purchase. Assume that Capsol is the acquirer; that current fair values of identifiable assets are $800,000 for Conner and $700,000 for Capsol; that each company's liabilities are fairly stated at $300,000; and that the current fair value of Consol's common stock is $14 a share.

4-3 The condensed balance sheets of Stole Corporation, the combinor, prior to and subsequent to its March 1, Year 4, merger with Moore Company, appear below.

STOLE CORPORATION

Balance Sheets Prior to and Subsequent to Business Combination
March 1, Year 4

	Prior to business combination	Subsequent to business combination
Assets		
Current assets	$ 500,000	$ 850,000
Plant assets (net)	1,000,000	1,800,000
Total assets	$1,500,000	$2,650,000
Liabilities & Shareholders' Equity		
Current Liabilities	$ 350,000	$ 600,000
Long-term debt	100,000	150,000
Common stock, no par	710,000	1,210,000
Retained earnings	340,000	690,000
Total liabilities & shareholders' equity	$1,500,000	$2,650,000

Prior to the business combination, Moore had total assets of $1,200,000 and total liabilities of $300,000. Out-of-pocket costs of the business combination were paid by Stole on March 1, Year 4.

Instructions Reconstruct the journal entries that Stole prepared on March 1, Year 4, to record the business combination with Moore.

4-4 On October 31, Year 9, Stevens Corporation issued 20,000 shares of its no par (current fair value $20) common stock for all the outstanding common stock of

Morgan Company in a statutory amalgamation. Out-of-pocket costs of the business combination paid by Stevens on October 31, Year 9, were as follows:

Direct costs of the business combination	$20,870
Costs of registering and issuing common stock	31,130
Total out-of-pocket costs of business combination	$52,000

Morgan's balance sheet on October 31, Year 9, follows:

MORGAN COMPANY
Balance Sheet
October 31, Year 9

Assets

Inventories	$140,000
Other current assets	80,000
Plant assets (net)	380,000
Total assets	$600,000

Liabilities & Shareholders' Equity

Payable to Stevens Corporation	$ 75,000
Other liabilities	225,000
Common stock, no par	170,000
Retained earnings	130,000
Total liabilities & shareholders' equity	$600,000

Other information:
(1) The current fair values of Morgan's other current assets and all its liabilities equalled the carrying amounts on October 31, Year 9.
(2) Current fair values of Morgan's inventories and plant assets were $160,000 and $420,000, respectively, on October 31, Year 9.
(3) Stevens's October 31, Year 9, balance sheet included an asset entitled Receivable from Morgan Company in the amount of $75,000.

Instructions   Prepare Stevens Corporation's journal entries on October 31, Year 9, to record the business combination with Morgan Company:
a As a purchase
b As a pooling of interests

4-5   The balance sheet on March 31, Year 7, and the related current fair value data for Ambrose Company are as follows:

AMBROSE COMPANY
Balance Sheet
March 31, Year 7

	Carrying amount	Current fair value
Assets		
Current assets	$ 500,000	$ 575,000
Plant assets (net)	1,000,000	1,200,000
Patent (net)	100,000	50,000
Total assets	$1,600,000	

Current liabilities	$ 300,000	$ 300,000
Long-term debt	400,000	450,000
Common stock, no par	100,000	
Retained earnings	800,000	
Total liabilities & shareholders' equity	$1,600,000	

Note: The current assets are all monetary.

On April 1, Year 7, Baxter Corporation issued 50,000 shares of its no par common stock (current fair value $14 a share) and $225,000 cash for the net assets of Ambrose Company, in a business combination qualifying for purchase accounting. Of the $125,000 out-of-pocket costs paid by Baxter on April 1, Year 7, $50,000 were legal fees and finders' fees related to the business combination.

Instructions Prepare journal entries to record the business combination in the accounting records of Baxter Corporation.

4-6 Molo Company merged into Stave Corporation in a business combination completed April 30, Year 5. Out-of-pocket costs paid by Stave on April 30, Year 5, in connection with the combination were as follows:

Finder's fee and legal fees relating to the business combination	$15,000
Cost associated with securities issued to complete the business combination	10,000
Total out-of-pocket costs of business combination	$25,000

The individual balance sheets of the constituent companies immediately prior to the merger were as follows:

STAVE CORPORATION AND MOLO COMPANY
Balance Sheets
April 30, Year 5

	Stave Corporation	Molo Company
Assets		
Current assets	$ 4,350,000	$ 3,000,000
Plant assets (net)	18,500,000	11,300,000
Patents	450,000	200,000
Deferred charges	150,000	
Total assets	$23,450,000	$14,500,000
Liabilities & Shareholders' Equity		
Liabilities	$ 2,650,000	$ 2,100,000
Common stock, $20 par	8,000,000	
Common stock, $5 par		3,750,000
Contributed Surplus	8,200,000	3,200,000
Retained earnings	4,600,000	5,450,000
Total liabilities & shareholders' equity	$23,450,000	$14,500,000

You have obtained the following additional information:

(1) The current fair values of the identifiable assets and liabilities of Stave Corporation and Molo Company were as follows on April 30, Year 5:

STAVE CORPORATION AND MOLO COMPANY

Current Fair Values of Identifiable Net Assets

April 30, Year 5

	Stave Corporation	Molo Company
Current assets	$ 4,950,000	$ 3,400,000
Plant assets (net)	22,000,000	14,000,000
Patents	570,000	360,000
Deferred charges	150,000	
Liabilities	(2,650,000)	(2,100,000)
Identifiable net assets	$25,020,000	$15,660,000

(2) There were no intercompany transactions prior to the business combination.

(3) Molo Company was liquidated on completion of the merger.

Instructions Prepare journal entries in the accounting records of Stave Corporation to record the business combination with Molo Company under each of the
following independent assumptions:

a Stave exchanged 400,000 shares of previously unissued common stock for all the
outstanding common stock of Molo, therefore meeting the CICA conditions for
pooling.

b Stave paid $3,100,000 cash and issued 16% debentures at face amount of
$16,900,000 for all the outstanding common stock of Molo. The current fair
value of the debentures is equal to their face amount.

4-7 As of the close of business August 31, Year 2, Mullin Company merged into Samos
Corporation in a business combination meeting the conditions for pooling accounting listed in *Section 1580*, "Business Combinations." Premerger income statements of the constituent companies for the year ended August 31, Year 2, were as
follows:

SAMOS CORPORATION AND MULLIN COMPANY

Income Statements

For Year Ended August 31, Year 2

	Samos Corporation	Mullin Company
Revenue:		
Net sales	$800,000	$550,000
Interest	20,000	
Rent		50,000
Total revenue	$820,000	$600,000
Costs and expenses:		
Cost of goods sold	$480,000	$300,000
Operating expenses	75,000	50,000
Interest expense	15,000	10,000
Income taxes expense	150,000	144,000
Total costs and expenses	$720,000	$504,000
Net income	$100,000	$ 96,000

During the year prior to the merger, Mullin had obtained from and repaid to Samos a $100,000, 15%, 90-day loan; Samos had rented for the entire year a sales office owned by Mullin with a monthly rent of $500 plus 1% of net sales; and Samos had sold to Mullin at Samos's regular markup, goods costing $120,000, all of which Mullin sold during the year ended August 31, Year 2, to outside customers at Mullin's regular markup.

Instructions

a Prepare the working paper eliminations (in journal entry form) for Samos Corporation's postmerger income statement for the year ended August 31, Year 2.

b Prepare a working paper for the postmerger combined income statement of Samos Corporation for the year ended August 31, Year 2.

4-8 On June 30, Year 2, Capsule Company and Compari Company entered into a statutory amalgamation. A new company, Cap-Com Corporation, issued 100,000 shares of its 500,000 authorized shares of no-par common stock as follows:

(1) 50,000 shares for all 10,000 outstanding shares of Capsule's no par common stock

(2) 50,000 shares for all 15,000 outstanding shares of Compari's no par common stock

CAPSULE COMPANY AND COMPARI COMPANY
Balance Sheets
June 30, Year 2

	Capsule Company	Compari Company
Assets		
Current assets	$ 225,000	$300,000
Receivable from Cap-Com Corporation	25,000	
Plant assets (net)	700,000	500,000
Other assets	60,000	10,000
Total assets	$1,010,000	$810,000
Liabilities & Shareholders' Equity		
Current liabilities	$ 160,000	$ 80,000
Long-term debt	200,000	90,000
Common stock	100,000	165,000
Retained earnings	550,000	475,000
Total liabilities & shareholders' equity	$1,010,000	$810,000

CAPSULE COMPANY AND COMPARI COMPANY
Statements of Income and Retained Earnings
For Year Ended June 30, Year 2

Net sales	$2,000,000	$3,000,000
Costs and expenses:		
Cost of goods sold	$1,200,000	$2,000,000
Operating expenses	400,000	500,000
Interest expense	15,000	10,000
Income taxes expense	231,000	294,000
Total costs and expenses	$1,846,000	$2,804,000
Net income	$ 154,000	$ 196,000
Retained earnings, beginning of year	396,000	279,000
Retained earnings, end of year	$ 550,000	$ 475,000

Costs of $25,000 associated with the statutory amalgamation (legal and audit fees, printing charges, issue costs) were paid in cash on June 30, Year 2 (prior to the amalgamation), by Capsule on behalf of Cap-Com. There were no other intercompany transactions.

Condensed financial statements of Capsule and Compari for the year ended June 30, Year 2, prior to the consolidation are shown on page 169.

Capsule costs its inventories on the fifo basis; Compari uses lifo cost for inventories. As part of the amalgamation contract, Compari agreed to change its inventories valuation method from lifo to fifo. Relevant data for Compari are as follows:

	Lifo cost	Fifo cost
Inventories, June 30, Year 2	$100,000	$150,000
Inventories, June 30, Year 1	90,000	130,000

Instructions

a Prepare the adjusting journal entry on June 30, Year 2, to change Compari Company's inventories from lifo cost to fifo cost. (*Note:* A change from lifo to another inventory costing method requires the retroactive adjustment of retained earnings.)

b Prepare the June 30, Year 2, journal entry of Cap-Com Corporation to record the statutory amalgamation as a pooling. Do not include revenue and expenses in the journal entry.

c Compute the pooled net income of Cap-Com Corporation for the year ended June 30, Year 2.

4-9 Coolidge Corporation agreed to pay $850,000 cash and issue 50,000 shares of its $10 par ($20 market value a share) common stock on September 30, Year 4, to Hoover Company for all the net assets of Hoover except cash. In addition, Coolidge agreed that if the market value of its common stock was not $20 a share or more on September 30, Year 5, a sufficient number of additional shares of common stock would be issued to Hoover to make the aggregate market value of its Coolidge common shareholdings equal to $1,000,000 on that date.

The balance sheet of Hoover on September 30, Year 4, with related current fair values of assets and liabilities, is presented at the top of page 171.

Out-of-pocket costs of the business combination paid by Coolidge on September 30, Year 4, were as follows:

Audit fees — Securities Commission registration statement	$ 30,000
Finder's fee (2% of aggregate consideration)	35,000
Legal fees — business combination	15,000
Legal fees — Securities Commission registration statement	20,000
Printing costs — securities and Securities Commission	
registration statement	25,000
Securities Commission registration fee	350
Total out-of-pocket costs of business combination	$125,350

Instructions

a Prepare the September 30, Year 4, journal entries in the accounting records of Coolidge Corporation to reflect the foregoing transactions.

b Assume that on September 30, Year 5, the market value of Coolidge Corporation's common stock was $16 a share. Prepare a journal entry to record the issuance of additional shares of Coolidge common stock to Hoover Company on that date and the payment of cash in lieu of fractional shares, if any.

HOOVER COMPANY

Balance Sheet

September 30, Year 4

	Carrying amount	Current fair value
Assets		
Cash	$ 100,000	$ 100,000
Accounts receivable (net)	300,000	300,000
Inventories	600,000	680,000
Short-term prepayments	20,000	20,000
Investment in Truman Company 12% debentures	100,000	180,000
Land	500,000	650,000
Other plant assets (net)	1,000,000	1,250,000
Patent (net)	80,000	100,000
Total assets	$2,700,000	
Liabilities & Shareholders' Equity		
Current liabilities	$ 700,000	$ 700,000
Long-term debt	500,000	480,000
Common stock, $5 par	600,000	
Contributed surplus	400,000	
Retained earnings	500,000	
Total liabilities & shareholders' equity	$2,700,000	

4-10 The board of directors of Simeon Corporation is considering a merger with Masha Company. The most recent financial statements and other financial data for the two companies, both of which use the same accounting principles and practices, are shown below and at the top of page 172.

SIMEON CORPORATION AND MASHA COMPANY

Balance Sheets

October 31, Year 8

	Simeon Corporation	Masha Company
Assets		
Current assets	$ 500,000	$ 200,000
Plant assets (net)	1,000,000	900,000
Other assets	300,000	200,000
Total assets	$1,800,000	$1,300,000
Liabilities & Shareholders' Equity		
Current liabilities	$ 400,000	$ 150,000
Long-term debt	500,000	750,000
Common stock	700,000	200,000
Retained earnings	200,000	200,000
Total liabilities & shareholders' equity	$1,800,000	$1,300,000

SIMEON CORPORATION AND MASHA COMPANY

Statements of Income and Retained Earnings
For Year Ended October 31, Year 8

	Simeon Corporation	Masha Company
Net sales	$5,000,000	$3,900,000
Costs and expenses:		
Costs of goods sold	$3,500,000	$2,600,000
Operating expenses	1,180,000	950,000
Interest expense	200,000	250,000
Total costs and expenses	$4,880,000	$3,800,000
Net income	$ 120,000	$ 100,000
Retained earnings, beginning of year	80,000	100,000
Retained earnings, end of year	$ 200,000	200,000
Earnings per share	$4.00	$5.00
Price-earnings ratio	5	5

Simeon's directors estimate that the out-of-pocket costs of the merger will be as follows:

Finder's fee and legal fees for the merger	$ 5,000
Costs associated with issuing shares	7,000
Total out-of-pocket costs of merger	$12,000

The fair values of Masha's liabilities on October 31, Year 8, are equal to their carrying amounts. Current fair values of Masha's assets on that date are as follows:

Current assets (difference from balance sheet amount of $200,000 attributable to inventories carried at fifo cost that were sold during year ended Oct. 31, Year 9)	$230,000
Plant assets (difference from balance sheet amount of $900,000 attributable to land — $60,000 and to depreciable assets with a five-year remaining economic life — $40,000)	1,000,000
Other assets (difference from balance sheet amount of $200,000 attributable to leasehold with a remaining term of four years)	220,000

Simeon's board of directors is considering two alternative plans for effecting the merger, as follows:

Plan 1 Issue 30,000 shares of common stock for all the outstanding common stock of Masha in a business combination meeting the conditions for pooling accounting enumerated in Section 1580, "Business Combinations."

Plan 2 Issue 15,000 shares of common stock with a current fair value of $20 a share, $100,000 cash, and a 15%, three-year note for $200,000 for all the outstanding common stock of Masha. The current fair value of the note is equal to its face amount.

Under either plan, Masha would be liquidated but would continue operations as a division of Simeon.

Instructions To assist Simeon Corporation's board of directors in their evaluation of the two plans, compute or prepare the following for each plan as though the merger had been effected on October 31, Year 8.

a Net income and earnings per share (rounded to the nearest cent) of Simeon for the year ended October 31, Year 8.

b Net income and earnings per share (rounded to the nearest cent) of Simeon for the year ending October 31, Year 9, assuming the same sales and cost patterns for the year ended October 31, Year 8. Goodwill, if any, is to be amortized over 40 years.

c Pro forma balance sheets following the business combination on October 31, Year 8.

4-11 The following information pertains to the shareholders' equity sections of three companies as at December 31, Year 1.

	Company X	Company Y	Company Z
Common shares (NPV)	$ 75,000	$ 48,000	$60,000
Retained earnings	92,500	70,000	35,000
Total	$167,500	$118,000	$95,000
Common shares outstanding	15,000 shares	12,000 shares	16,500 shares

It is proposed that on January 1, Year 2, Company X will issue shares to the shareholders of Company Y and Company Z for 100% of their holdings as follows:

to the shareholders of Company Y — 13,500 shares

to the shareholders of Company Z — 12,000 shares

Company X shares traded at $14.00 per share on December 31, Year 1.

Company X will incur the following expenses:

Costs of registering and issuing shares	$12,000
Other expenses associated with the takeover	30,000
Total	$42,000

Instructions

1 Prepare a summarized pro-forma balance sheet of Company X as at January 1, Year 2, using the purchase method of accounting for the business combination.

2 Prepare a summarized pro-forma balance sheet of Company X as at January 1, 1982, using the pooling of interest method of accounting for the business combination.

3 Which method would be required to account for this combination in Canada? Show supporting computations.

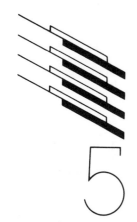

5 CONSOLIDATED FINANCIAL STATEMENTS: ON DATE OF PURCHASE BUSINESS COMBINATION

In Chapter 4 we used the terms *investor* and *investee* in our discussion of business combinations involving an acquirer's purchase of common stock of an acquiree corporation. If the investor acquires more than 50% of the voting common stock of the investee, *a parent-subsidiary relationship* is established. The investee becomes a *subsidiary* of the acquiring *parent company* (investor) but remains a separate legal entity.

Strict adherence to the legal aspects of such a business combination would require the issuance of separate financial statements for the parent company and the subsidiary on the date of the combination, and also for all subsequent accounting periods of the affiliation. However, such strict adherence to legal form would ignore the substance of most parent-subsidiary relationships. A parent company and its subsidiary usually are a single *economic entity*. In recognition of this fact, *consolidated financial statements* are issued to report the financial position and operating results of a parent company and its subsidiaries as though they comprised a single accounting entity.

Nature of consolidated financial statements

Consolidated financial statements are similar to the combined financial statements described in Chapter 3 for a home office and its branches. Assets, liabilities, revenue, and expenses of the parent company and its subsidiaries are totalled; intercompany transactions and balances are eliminated; and the final consolidated amounts are reported in the consolidated balance sheet, statements of income and retained earnings, and statement of changes in financial position.

However, the separate legal entity status of the parent and subsidiary corporations necessitates consolidation eliminations that generally are more complex than the combination eliminations described in Chapter 3 for a home office and its branches. Before illustrating consolidation eliminations, we shall examine some basic principles of consolidation.

Should all subsidiaries be consolidated?

Section 3050 of the *CICA Handbook*, "Long-term Investments," suggested that because a *parent* company's management *controls* the resources of the parent and its subsidiaries it is more informative to the shareholders of the parent company to prepare consolidated financial statements. The section required the consolidation of all subsidiaries, but allowed for *certain exceptions* as follows:

1 If a subsidiary is bankrupt or in receivership, *control* by the parent *no longer exists*.
2 If a subsidiary is located in a foreign country which has imposed restrictions on asset transfers, *earnings are not likely to accrue to the parent*.
3 If the parent plans, or is required by government action, to dispose of a subsidiary, the parent's *control is temporary*.
4 If a subsidiary is a bank or insurance company whose financial statements are not prepared in accordance with GAAP, the *combining of non-GAAP statements* with statements prepared in accordance with GAAP *would not be proper*.
5 If the components of a subsidiary's financial statements are dissimilar to those of the parent and other subsidiaries, interpretation of the consolidated results may be difficult, and as a result *consolidation would not be the most informative presentation*.

The 16th edition of *Financial Reporting in Canada*, the CICA's annual survey of accounting practices in the published financial statements of 325 companies, reported the following:

1 A total of 270 companies consolidated all subsidiaries; however, 26 companies excluded some subsidiaries from the consolidated financial statements. (The remaining 29 companies reported no subsidiaries.)
2 The major reasons for exclusion were dissimilarity of financial statement components, impairment of parent's control and earnings not likely to accrue to the parent.
3 A total of 14 companies disclosed the existence of finance subsidiaries, 6 of which did not consolidate these subsidiaries.

It appears that some companies are using the dissimilarity of financial statement components as reasons for excluding their finance subsidiaries. Traditionally it has been argued that finance subsidiaries with assets composed mainly of long- and short-term receivables should not be consolidated with subsidiaries whose asset structure is dominated by plant and inventory. The Handbook provisions do not explicitly permit the exclusion of finance subsidiaries, but the "dissimilarity of components" clause is obviously being used to achieve this result. An examination of the concept of control as the basis for the preparation of consolidated financial statements sheds some doubt on the validity of this treatment.

The meaning of control

Section 3050 indicated that an investor's direct or indirect ownership of more than 50% of an investee's voting common stock was required as evidence of control in a parent-subsidiary relationship. However, as was outlined in the discussion of allowed exceptions, there are situations where it is obvious that control does not exist or is difficult to implement. Exclusion from consolidation in these cases, and particularly when statements are not prepared in accordance with generally accepted accounting principles, seems to be a reasonable approach.

Where control is not impaired there would seem to be no theoretical justification to allow exclusion of subsidiaries solely because their financial statements are dissimilar. In the authors' opinion the argument that finance-related subsidiaries should not be consolidated with the manufacturing or retailing operations of the other companies in the group is difficult to justify when one considers the wide variety of production, marketing, and service enterprises that are consolidated in a conglomerate or highly diversified family of corporations.

It is important to recognize that a parent company's control of a subsidiary may be achieved *indirectly*. For example, if Plymouth Corporation owns 85% of the outstanding voting common stock of Selwyn Company and 45% of Talbot Company's common stock, and Selwyn also owns 45% of Talbot's common stock, both Selwyn and Talbot are controlled by Plymouth, because it effectively controls 90% of Talbot. This effective control consists of 45% owned directly and 45% indirectly.

Criticism of the concept of control

Some accountants have challenged the definition of *control* described in the preceding section, which emphasizes *legal form*. These accountants maintain that an investor owning less than 50% of an investee's voting common stock *in substance* may control the affiliate, especially if the remaining common stock is scattered among a large number of shareholders who do not attend shareholder meetings or give proxies. Effective control of an investee also is possible if the individuals composing management of the investor corporation own a substantial number of shares of common stock of the investee or successfully solicit proxies from the investee's other shareholders. These arguments merit further study in the search for a less arbitrary definition of *control* than the one described in the preceding section.

Unconsolidated subsidiaries in consolidated financial statements

Section 3050 required the use of the *equity method* of accounting for most unconsolidated subsidiaries in consolidated financial statements. In those situations where the parent's control has been impaired and earnings no longer accrue to the parent, the cost method was required. The equity method of accounting, which is discussed in depth in Chapter 6, reflects the parent company's share of the earnings or losses of an unconsolidated subsidiary on a single line in the consolidated income statement. Use of the equity method of accounting results in an amount for consolidated net income identical to the amount that would have resulted from consolidating the subsidiary.

CONSOLIDATION OF WHOLLY OWNED SUBSIDIARY ON DATE OF PURCHASE-TYPE BUSINESS COMBINATION

To illustrate consolidated financial statements for a parent company and a wholly owned purchased subsidiary, assume that on December 31, Year 1, Palm Corporation issued 10,000 shares of its common stock (current fair value $45 a share) to shareholders of Starr Company for all 40,000 outstanding common shares of Starr. There was no contingent consideration. Out-of-pocket costs of the business combination paid by Palm on December 31, Year 1, consisted of the following:

Finder's and legal fees relating to business combination	$50,000
Costs associated with issuing shares	35,000
Total out-of-pocket costs of business combination	$85,000

Acquirer's out-of-pocket costs of business combination

Because Palm Corporation had 30,000 shares outstanding prior to the take-over, the business combination qualifies for purchase accounting. Starr Company is to continue its corporate existence as a wholly owned subsidiary of Palm Corporation. Both business enterprises have a December 31 fiscal year and use the same accounting principles and procedures; thus, no adjusting entries are required for either enterprise prior to the combination.

Financial statements of Palm Corporation and Starr Company for their fiscal year ended December 31, Year 1, prior to consummation of the business combination, are shown on page 178.

The December 31, Year 1, current fair values of Starr Company's identifiable assets and liabilities were the same as their carrying amounts, except for the three assets listed below:

	Current fair values, Dec. 31, Year 1
Inventories	$135,000
Plant assets (net)	365,000
Patent	25,000

Current fair values of selected assets of acquiree

Because Starr is continuing as a separate corporation and generally accepted accounting principles do not normally sanction write-ups of assets of a going concern, Starr does not prepare journal entries for the business combination.[1] Palm Corporation records the combination as a purchase on December 31, Year 1, with the journal entries on page 179.

---

[1] Sections 3060 and 3270 of the *CICA Handbook* allow the use of appraised values for fixed assets under certain circumstances.

PALM CORPORATION AND STARR COMPANY
Separate Financial Statements
For Year Ended December 31, Year 1

	Palm Corporation	Starr Company
Income Statements		
Revenue		
Net sales	$ 990,000	$600,000
Interest revenue	10,000	
Total revenue	$1,000,000	$600,000
Costs and expenses		
Cost of goods sold	$ 635,000	$410,000
Operating expenses	80,000	30,000
Interest expense	50,000	30,000
Income taxes expense	141,000	78,000
Total costs and expenses	$ 906,000	$548,000
Net income	$ 94,000	$ 52,000
Statements of Retained Earnings		
Retained earnings, beginning of year	$ 65,000	$100,000
Add: Net income	94,000	52,000
Subtotal	$ 159,000	$152,000
Less: Dividends	25,000	20,000
Retained earnings, end of year	$ 134,000	$132,000
Balance Sheets		
Assets		
Cash	$ 100,000	$ 40,000
Inventories	150,000	110,000
Other current assets	110,000	70,000
Receivable from Starr Company	25,000	
Plant assets (net)	450,000	300,000
Patent		20,000
Total assets	$ 835,000	$540,000
Liabilities & Shareholders' Equity		
Payable to Palm Corporation		$ 25,000
Income taxes payable	$ 66,000	10,000
Other liabilities	285,000	115,000
Common stock, no par	350,000	
Common stock, no par		258,000
Retained earnings	134,000	132,000
Total liabilities & shareholders' equity	$ 835,000	$540,000

Acquirer's journal
entries for
purchase-type business
combination on
December 31, Year 1

PALM CORPORATION (Acquirer)
Journal Entries
December 31, Year 1

Investment in Starr Company Common Stock (10,000 × $45)	450,000	
Common Stock		450,000

To record issuance of 10,000 shares of common stock for all the outstanding common stock of Starr Company in a purchase-type business combination.

Investment in Starr Company Common Stock	50,000	
Common stock	35,000	
Cash		85,000

To record payment of out-of-pocket costs of business combination
with Starr Company. Finder's and legal fees relating to the combination are recorded as additional costs of the investment; costs associated with issuing shares are recorded as an offset to the previously
recorded proceeds from the issuance of common stock.

The first journal entry above is similar to the entry illustrated in Chapter 4 (page 140) for a merger accounted for as a purchase. An Investment in Common Stock account is debited with the current fair value of the acquirer's common stock issued to effect the business combination, and the capital stock account is credited in the usual manner for any common stock issuance. In the second journal entry, the **direct** out-of-pocket costs of the business combination are debited to the Investment in Common Stock account, and the costs that are associated with issuing the common shares are applied to reduce the proceeds of the common share issuance.

Unlike the journal entries for a merger accounted for as a purchase illustrated in Chapter 4, the foregoing journal entries do not include any debits or credits to record individual assets and liabilities of Starr Company in the accounting records of Palm Corporation. The reason is that Starr was not **liquidated** as in a statutory amalgamation; it maintains its status as a separate legal entity.

After the foregoing journal entries have been posted, the affected ledger accounts of Palm Corporation (the acquirer) appear as shown on page 180.

Working Paper for Consolidated Balance Sheet   Purchase accounting for the business combination of Palm Corporation and Starr Company requires a fresh start for the consolidated entity. This reflects the theory that a business combination that meets the requirements for purchase accounting is an **acquisition** of the acquiree's net assets (assets less liabilities) by the acquirer. The operating results of Palm and Starr prior to the date of their business combination are those of two separate **economic**—as well as **legal** — entities. Accordingly, a consolidated balance sheet is the only **consolidated** financial statement issued by Palm on December 31,

Ledger accounts of
acquirer affected by
business combination

Cash

Date	Explanation	Debit	Credit	Balance
12/31/1	Balance forward			100,000 dr
12/31/1	Out-of-pocket costs of business combination		85,000	15,000 dr

Investment in Starr Company Common Stock

Date	Explanation	Debit	Credit	Balance
12/31/1	Issuance of common stock in business combination	450,000		450,000 dr
12/31/1	Direct out-of-pocket costs of business combination	50,000		500,000 dr

Common Stock, No Par

Date	Explanation	Debit	Credit	Balance
12/31/1	Balance forward			350,000 cr
12/31/1	Issuance of common stock in business combination		450,000	800,000 cr
12/31/1	Out-of-pocket costs of business combination	35,000		765,000 cr

Year 1, the date of the purchase-type business combination of Palm and Starr.

Preparation of a consolidated balance sheet usually requires the use of a *working paper for consolidated balance sheet*. The form of the working paper, with the individual balance sheet amounts included for both Palm Corporation and Starr Company, is presented on page 181.

Developing the Elimination   Palm Corporation's Investment in Starr Company Common Stock account in the working paper for consolidated balance sheet is similar to a home office's Investment in Branch account, as described in Chapter 3. However, Starr Company is a *separate corporation*, not a *branch*; therefore, Starr has the two conventional shareholders' equity accounts rather than the Home Office reciprocal account used by a branch.[2] Accordingly, the elimination for the *intercompany* accounts of Palm and Starr must *decrease to zero* the Investment in Starr Company Common Stock account of Palm and the two shareholders' equity accounts of Starr. Decreases in assets are effected by *credits*, and decreases in share-

---

2 If Starr's shares had a par value there could be three shareholders' equity accounts.

Wholly owned subsidiary on date of purchase-type business combination

PALM CORPORATION AND SUBSIDIARY
Working Paper for Consolidated Balance Sheet
December 31, Year 1

	Palm Corporation	Starr Company	Eliminations increase (decrease)	Consolidated
Assets				
Cash	15,000	40,000		
Inventories	150,000	110,000		
Other current assets	110,000	70,000		
Intercompany receivable (payable)	25,000	(25,000)		
Investment in Starr Company common stock	500,000			
Plant assets (net)	450,000	300,000		
Patent		20,000		
Goodwill				
Total assets	1,250,000	515,000		
Liabilities & Shareholders' Equity				
Income taxes payable	66,000	10,000		
Other liabilities	285,000	115,000		
Common stock	765,000	258,000		
Retained earnings	134,000	132,000		
Total liabilities & shareholders' equity ..	1,250,000	515,000		

holders' equity accounts are effected by **debits**; therefore, the elimination for Palm Corporation and subsidiary on December 31, Year 1 (the date of the purchase-type business combination), is begun as follows (a journal entry format is used to facilitate review of the elimination):

Common Stock — Starr	258,000	
Retained Earnings — Starr	132,000	
	(390,000)	
Investment in Starr Company Common Stock — Palm		500,000

The footing of $390,000 of the debit items of the foregoing partial elimination represents the carrying amount of the net assets of Starr Company and is $110,000 less than the credit item of $500,000, which represents the cost of Palm Corporation's investment in Starr. As indicated on page 177, part of the $110,000 difference is attributable to the excess of current fair values over carrying amounts of certain *identifiable* assets of Starr. This excess is summarized below (the current fair values of all other assets and liabilities are equal to their carrying amounts):

Differences between current fair values and carrying amounts of acquiree's identifiable assets	Current fair values	Carrying amounts	Excess of current fair values over carrying amounts
Inventories	$135,000	$110,000	$25,000
Plant assets (net)	365,000	300,000	65,000
Patent	25,000	20,000	5,000
Totals	$525,000	$430,000	$95,000

We already have indicated that generally accepted accounting principles preclude the write-up of a going concern's assets. Thus, to conform to the requirements of purchase accounting for business combinations, the foregoing excess of current fair values over carrying amounts must be incorporated in the consolidated balance sheet of Palm Corporation and subsidiary by means of the elimination. *Increases* in assets are recorded by *debits*; thus, the elimination for Palm Corporation and subsidiary begun above is continued below (in journal entry format).

Use of elimination to reflect the acquirer's interest in the current fair values of the acquiree's identifiable net assets

Common Stock — Starr	258,000	
Retained Earnings — Starr	132,000	
Inventories — Starr	25,000	
Plant Assets (net) — Starr	65,000	
Patent — Starr	5,000	
	485,000	
Investment in Starr Company Common Stock — Palm		500,000

The revised footing of $485,000 of the debit items of the foregoing partial elimination is equal to the current fair value of the *identifiable* tangible and intangible net assets of Starr Company. Thus, the $15,000 difference ($500,000 − $485,000 = $15,000) between the cost of Palm Corporation's investment in Starr and Palm Corporation's interest in the current fair value of Starr's identifiable net assets represents *goodwill* of Starr, in accordance with purchase accounting theory for business combinations, described in Chapter 4 (pages 134 to 142). Consequently, the December 31, Year 1, elimination for Palm Corporation and subsidiary is completed with a $15,000 *debit* to Goodwill — Starr.

Completed Elimination and Working Paper for Consolidated Balance Sheet The completed elimination for Palm Corporation and subsidiary (in journal entry format) and the related working paper for consolidated balance sheet appear on page 183.

Completed working
paper elimination for
wholly owned
purchased subsidiary on
date of business
combination

PALM CORPORATION AND SUBSIDIARY

Working Paper Elimination
December 31, Year 1

(a) Common Stock — Starr	258,000
Retained Earnings — Starr	132,000
Inventories — Starr	25,000
Plant Assets (net) — Starr	65,000
Patent — Starr	5,000
Goodwill — Starr	15,000
Investment in Starr Company Common Stock — Palm	500,000

To eliminate intercompany investment and equity accounts of subsidiary on date of business combination; and to allocate excess
of cost over carrying amount of identifiable assets acquired, with
remainder to goodwill.

Wholly owned subsidiary on date of purchase-type business combination.

PALM CORPORATION AND SUBSIDIARY

Working Paper for Consolidated Balance Sheet
December 31, Year 1

	Palm Corporation	Starr Company	Eliminations increase (decrease)		Consolidated
Assets					
Cash	15,000	40,000			55,000
Inventories	150,000	110,000	(a)	25,000	285,000
Other current assets	110,000	70,000			180,000
Intercompany receivable					
(payable)	25,000	(25,000)			
Investment in Starr Com-					
pany common stock ...	500,000		(a)	(500,000)	
Plant assets (net)	450,000	300,000	(a)	65,000	815,000
Patent		20,000	(a)	5,000	25,000
Goodwill			(a)	15,000	15,000
Total assets	1,250,000	515,000		(390,000)	1,375,000
Liabilities & Shareholders' Equity					
Income taxes payable ...	66,000	10,000			76,000
Other liabilities	285,000	115,000			400,000
Common stock, no par ...	765,000				765,000
Common stock, no par ...		258,000	(a)	(258,000)	
Retained earnings	134,000	132,000	(a)	(132,000)	134,000
Total liabilities & share-					
holders' equity	1,250,000	515,000		(390,000)	1,375,000

The following features of the working paper for consolidated balance sheet on the date of the purchase-type business combination should be emphasized:

1   The elimination is not entered in either the parent company's or the subsidiary's accounting records; it simply is a part of the working paper for preparation of a consolidated balance sheet.

2   The elimination is used to reflect the parent company's interest in the differences between current fair values and carrying amounts of the subsidiary's identifiable net assets because the subsidiary did not write up its assets to current fair values on the date of the business combination.

3   The Eliminations column in the working paper for consolidated balance sheet reflects *increases* and *decreases*, rather than *debits* and *credits*. Debits and credits are not appropriate in a working paper dealing with *financial statements* rather than *trial balances*.

4   *Intercompany receivables* and *payables* are placed on the same line of the working paper for consolidated balance sheet and are combined to produce consolidated amounts of zero.

5   The respective corporations are identified in the components of the elimination. The reason for precise identification is explained in Chapter 8 dealing with the eliminations of intercompany profits.

6   The consolidated capital stock account is that of the parent company only. Subsidiaries' capital stock accounts *always* are eliminated in the process of consolidation.

7   Consolidated retained earnings on the date of the purchase-type business combination includes only the retained earnings of the parent company. This treatment is consistent with the theory that purchase accounting reflects a fresh start in an acquisition of net assets (assets less liabilities), not a combining of existing shareholder interests.

8   The amounts in the Consolidated column of the working paper for consolidated balance sheet reflect the financial position of a *single economic entity* comprising *two legal entities*, with all *intercompany* balances of the two entities eliminated.

Consolidated Balance Sheet   The amounts in the Consolidated column of the working paper for consolidated balance sheet are presented in the customary fashion in the *consolidated balance sheet* (opposite) of Palm Corporation and subsidiary. In the interest of brevity, notes to financial statements and other required disclosures are omitted.

In addition to the foregoing *consolidated* balance sheet on December 31, Year 1, Palm Corporation's published financial statements for the year ended December 31, Year 1, include the *unconsolidated* income statement and statement of retained earnings illustrated on page 178.

CONSOLIDATION OF PARTIALLY OWNED SUBSIDIARY ON DATE OF PURCHASE-TYPE BUSINESS COMBINATION

The consolidation of a parent company and its *partially owned* subsidiary differs from the consolidation of a wholly owned subsidiary in two major respects —the amounts used to revalue the net assets of the subsidiary, and the recognition of minority interest. These points are further discussed on

PALM CORPORATION AND SUBSIDIARY

Consolidated Balance Sheet
December 31, Year 1

Assets

Current assets:		
Cash		$ 55,000
Inventories		285,000
Other		180,000
Total current assets		$ 520,000
Plant assets (net)		815,000
Intangible assets:		
Goodwill	$15,000	
Patent	25,000	40,000
Total assets		$1,375,000

Liabilities & Shareholders' Equity

Liabilities:		
Income tax payable		$ 76,000
Other		400,000
Total liabilities		$ 476,000
Shareholders' equity:		
Common stock, no par	$765,000	
Retained earnings	134,000	899,000
Total liabilities & shareholders' equity		$1,375,000

page 189. **Minority interest** is a term applied to the claims of shareholders other than the parent company against the net income or losses and net assets of the subsidiary. The minority interest in the subsidiary's net income or losses is reported in the consolidated income statement, and the minority interest in the subsidiary's net assets is reported in the consolidated balance sheet.

To illustrate the consolidation techniques for a purchase-type business combination involving a partially owned subsidiary, assume the following facts. On December 31, Year 1, Post Corporation issued 57,000 shares of its common stock (current fair value $20 a share) to shareholders of Sage Company in exchange for 38,000 of the 40,000 outstanding shares of Sage's common stock in a purchase-type business combination. Thus, Post acquired a 95% interest (38,000 ÷ 40,000 = 0.95) in Sage, which became Post's subsidiary. There was no contingent consideration. Out-of-pocket costs of the combination, paid in cash by Post on December 31, Year 1, were as follows:

Acquirer's out-of-pocket costs of business combination

Finder's and legal fees relating to business combination	$ 52,250
Costs associated with issuing shares	72,750
Total out-of-pocket costs of business combination	$125,000

Financial statements of Post Corporation and Sage Company for their fiscal year ended December 31, Year 1 prior to the business combination, are presented below. There were no intercompany transactions prior to the combination.

POST CORPORATION AND SAGE COMPANY
Separate Financial Statements
For Year Ended December 31, Year 1

	Post Corporation	Sage Company
Income Statements		
Net sales	$5,500,000	$1,000,000
Costs and expenses		
Cost of goods sold	$3,850,000	$ 650,000
Operating expenses	600,000	100,000
Interest expense	75,000	40,000
Income taxes expense	585,000	126,000
Total costs and expenses	$5,110,000	$ 916,000
Net income	$ 390,000	$ 84,000
Statements of Retained Earnings		
Retained earnings, beginning of year	$ 810,000	$ 290,000
Add: Net income	390,000	84,000
Subtotal	$1,200,000	$ 374,000
Less: Dividends	150,000	40,000
Retained earnings, end of year	$1,050,000	$ 334,000
Balance Sheets		
Assets		
Cash	$ 200,000	$ 100,000
Inventories	800,000	500,000
Other current assets	550,000	215,000
Plant assets (net)	3,500,000	1,100,000
Goodwill	100,000	
Total assets	$5,150,000	$1,915,000
Liabilities & Shareholders' Equity		
Income taxes payable	$ 100,000	$ 76,000
Other liabilities	2,450,000	870,000
Common stock, no par	1,550,000	
Common stock, no par		635,000
Retained earnings	1,050,000	334,000
Total liabilities & shareholders' equity	$5,150,000	$1,915,000

The December 31, Year 1, current fair values of Sage Company's identifiable assets and liabilities were the same as their carrying amounts, except for the assets listed below.

	Current fair values, Dec. 31, Year 1
Inventories	$ 526,000
Plant assets (net)	1,290,000
Leasehold	30,000

Current fair values of selected assets of acquiree

Sage Company does not prepare journal entries related to the business combination, because Sage is continuing as a separate corporation, and generally accepted accounting principles do not permit the write-up of assets of a going concern. Post records the combination with Sage as a purchase by means of the following journal entries on December 31, Year 1:

Acquirer's journal entries for purchase-type business combination

POST CORPORATION (Acquirer)
Journal Entries
December 31, Year 1

Investment in Sage Company Common stock (57,000 × $20)	1,140,000	
Common stock		1,140,000

To record issuance of 57,000 shares of common stock for 38,000 of the 40,000 outstanding shares of Sage Company common stock in a purchase-type business combination.

Investment in Sage Company Common Stock	52,250	
Common Stock	72,750	
Cash		125,000

To record payment of out-of-pocket costs of business combination with Sage Company. Finder's and legal fees relating to the combination are recorded as additional costs of the investment; costs associated with issuing shares are recorded as an offset to the previously recorded proceeds from the issuance of common stock.

After the foregoing journal entries have been posted, the affected ledger accounts of Post Corporation are as illustrated as follows:

Ledger accounts
of acquirer affected
by business combination

Cash

Date	Explanation	Debit	Credit	Balance
12/31/1	Balance forward			200,000 dr
12/31/1	Out-of-pocket costs of			
	business combination		125,000	75,000 dr

Investment in Sage Company Common Stock

Date	Explanation	Debit	Credit	Balance
12/31/1	Issuance of common stock in			
	business combination	1,140,000		1,140,000 dr
12/31/1	Direct out-of-pocket costs			
	of business combination	52,250		1,192,250 dr

Common Stock, No Par

Date	Explanation	Debit	Credit	Balance
12/31/1	Balance forward			1,550,000 cr
12/31/1	Issuance of common stock in			
	business combination		1,140,000	2,690,000 cr
12/31/1	Out-of-pocket costs of			
	business combination	72,750		2,617,250 cr

Developing the Elimination The preparation of the elimination for a parent company and a partially owned purchased subsidiary parallels that for a wholly owned purchased subsidiary described earlier in this chapter. First, the *intercompany* accounts are reduced to zero, as follows (in journal entry format):

Elimination of
intercompany accounts
of parent company and
purchased subsidiary on
date of business
combination

Common Stock — Sage	635,000	
Retained Earnings — Sage	334,000	
	(969,000)	
Investment in Sage Company Common Stock — Post		1,192,250

The footing of $969,000 of the debit items of the above partial elimination represents the carrying amount of the net assets of Sage Company and is $223,250 less than the credit item of $1,192,250. This $223,250 difference is the excess of the total of the cost of Post Corporation's investment in Sage Company and the *minority interest* in Sage Company's net assets over the carrying amounts of Sage's identifiable net assets. Part of this

$223,250 difference is attributable to the excess of current fair values over carrying amounts of certain identifiable net assets of Sage, which is computed as follows, from the data provided on page 187 (the current fair values of all other assets and liabilities are equal to their carrying amounts):

<table>
<tr><td rowspan="2" style="text-align:right">Difference between
current fair values and
carrying amounts of
acquiree's identifiable
assets</td><td></td><td>Current
fair value</td><td>Carrying
amount</td><td>Excess of
current fair
values over
carrying
amounts</td></tr>
<tr><td>Inventories ....</td><td>$ 526,000</td><td>$ 500,000</td><td>$ 26,000</td></tr>
<tr><td></td><td>Plant assets (net) ....</td><td>1,290,000</td><td>1,100,000</td><td>190,000</td></tr>
<tr><td></td><td>Leasehold ....</td><td>30,000</td><td></td><td>30,000</td></tr>
<tr><td></td><td>Totals ....</td><td>$1,846,000</td><td>$1,600,000</td><td>$246,000</td></tr>
</table>

If Sage Company was a 100% owned subsidiary we would use all of the excess of current fair values over carrying amounts to revalue the net assets of Sage in the consolidation process. This was the case in our last example (p. 182). But Sage Company is only a 95% owned subsidiary. Therefore we use only 95% of the excess to revalue the subsidiary's net assets in the consolidation process as follows:

<table>
<tr><td rowspan="2" style="text-align:right">Calculation of
amount of excess of
fair values over
carrying amounts used
for consolidation</td><td></td><td>Excess of
current fair
values over
carrying amounts</td><td>Acquirer's
95%
interest</td><td>Amount
used for
consolidation</td></tr>
<tr><td>Inventories ....</td><td>$ 26,000</td><td>0.95</td><td>$ 24,700</td></tr>
<tr><td></td><td>Plant assets (net) ....</td><td>190,000</td><td>0.95</td><td>180,500</td></tr>
<tr><td></td><td>Leasehold ....</td><td>30,000</td><td>0.95</td><td>28,500</td></tr>
<tr><td></td><td>Totals ....</td><td>$246,000</td><td></td><td>$233,700</td></tr>
</table>

As discussed previously, the foregoing differences are not entered in Sage Company's accounting records. Thus, to conform to the requirements of purchase accounting, the differences must be reflected in the consolidated balance sheet of Post Corporation and subsidiary by means of the elimination, which is continued below:

<table>
<tr><td rowspan="6" style="text-align:right">Use of elimination to
reflect the acquirer's
interest in the
differences between
fair values and
carrying amounts of
identifiable net assets
of acquiree on date of
business combination</td><td>Common Stock — Sage ....</td><td>635,000</td><td></td></tr>
<tr><td>Retained Earnings — Sage ....</td><td>334,000</td><td></td></tr>
<tr><td>Inventories — Sage ....</td><td>24,700</td><td></td></tr>
<tr><td>Plant Assets (net) — Sage ....</td><td>180,500</td><td></td></tr>
<tr><td>Leasehold — Sage ....</td><td>28,500</td><td></td></tr>
<tr><td></td><td>1,202,700</td><td></td></tr>
<tr><td></td><td>Investment in Sage Company Common Stock — Post ....</td><td></td><td>1,192,250</td></tr>
</table>

The revised footing of $1,202,700 of the debit items of the above partial elimination represents the carrying value of Sage Company's identifiable net assets plus Post Company's interest in the difference between current fair values and carrying values of these same net assets on December 31, Year 1.

Two items now must be recognized to complete the elimination for Post Corporation and subsidiary. First, the **minority interest** in the identifiable net assets (at carrying values) of Sage company is recognized by a ***credit***. The minority interest is computed below:

Computation of minority interest in the carrying value of the acquiree's net assets	

Carrying value of Sage Company's net assets ($635,000 + $334,000)	$969,000
Minority interest ownership in Sage Company's identifiable net assets	
(100% minus Post Corporation's 95% interest)	0.05
Minority interest in Sage Company's identifiable net assets	
($969,000 × 0.05)	$ 48,450

Second, the goodwill acquired by Post Corporation in the business combination with Sage Company is recognized by a ***debit***. The goodwill is computed below:

Computation of goodwill acquired by acquirer	

Cost of Post Corporation's 95% interest in Sage Company	$1,192,250
Less: Current fair value of Sage Company's identifiable net assets acquired by	
Post [($969,000 + $246,000 = $1,215,000) × 0.95]	1,154,250
Goodwill acquired by Post Corporation	$ 38,000

It is important to note that because the value of the goodwill is based on the difference between the parent's cost and the parent's interest in the current fair value of the subsidiary's net assets, and because the value of the minority interest in the subsidiary's net assets is based on the carrying amounts, it is necessary to use only the parent's interest in the difference between current fair values and carrying values in the consolidation process.

The working paper elimination for Post Corporation and subsidiary may now be completed as shown at the top of page 191.

The purchase discrepancy

The previous discussion has used a process of incomplete unbalanced working paper entries as a means of analyzing the consolidation process. At each stage in the process the required balancing figure is examined and an additional incomplete working paper entry is prepared, until the final balanced entry emerges. In situations where the parent owns 100% of the subsidiary this process might be all that is necessary. However, in situations where the parent's control is less than 100%, the calculation becomes more complicated.

Completed working
paper elimination for
partially owned
purchased subsidiary
on date of business
combination

POST CORPORATION AND SUBSIDIARY
Working Paper Elimination
December 31, Year 1

(a)	Common Stock — Sage	635,000	
	Retained Earnings — Sage	334,000	
	Inventories — Sage	24,700	
	Plant Assets (net) — Sage	180,500	
	Leasehold — Sage	28,500	
	Goodwill — Sage	38,000	
	Investment in Sage Company Common Stock — Post		1,192,250
	Minority Interest in Net Assets of Subsidiary		48,450

To eliminate intercompany investment and equity accounts of
subsidiary on date of business combination; to allocate the
parent company's share of the excess of cost over carrying
amount of identifiable assets acquired, with remainder to
goodwill; and to establish minority interest in net assets
of subsidiary on date of business combination.

At this point we introduce the following alternative calculation as a means
of determining the amounts to be used in the working paper elimination:

Calculation of the
purchase discrepancy
and its allocation;
and the calculation of
minority interest

Cost of 95% interest in Sage			$1,192,250
Carrying amount of Sage's net assets			
Common stock		$635,000	
Retained earnings		334,000	
Total shareholders' equity		$969,000	
Post's ownership interest		0.95	920,550
Purchase discrepancy (difference between cost and Post's			
interest in the carrying value of Sage's net assets)			$ 271,700
Allocated to revalue the net assets of Sage for consolidation			
purposes:			
Inventory	$ 26,000 × 0.95 =	$ 24,700	
Plant assets (net)	190,000 × 0.95 =	180,500	
Leasehold	30,000 × 0.95 =	28,500	233,700
Balance — Goodwill			$ 38,000
Minority Interest (based on carrying values of Sage's net assets)			
Shareholders' equity of Sage			$ 969,000
Minority interest percentage			0.05
Minority interest in Sage Company			$ 48,450

The first step is the ***calculation of the purchase discrepancy***, which
is the difference between the parent's cost of its investment in the subsidiary and the parent's interest in the carrying values of the subsidiary's net
assets.

The second step is the *allocation of the purchase discrepancy* to revalue the identifiable net assets of the subsidiary. You will note that the parent's interest in the difference between the fair value and carrying value of specific identifiable net assets is the amount used in the revaluation.

The third step is the *calculation of goodwill* (or negative goodwill). If the amount used to revalue the specific identifiable net assets of the subsidiary is less than the purchase discrepancy, the resultant difference is goodwill. If the amount used to revalue the specific identifiable net assets of the subsidiary is greater than the purchase discrepancy, negative goodwill results. This latter case would require a further calculation in which this negative balance would be used to reduce the amounts of nonmonetary assets of the subsidiary.

The fourth step is the calculation of the **minority interest** based on the carrying values of the net assets of the subsidiary.

It is possible for a purchase discrepancy to be negative. In this situation the parent's interest in the carrying values of the subsidiary's net assets would be greater than the parent's investment cost. A negative purchase discrepancy is not the same as negative goodwill, nor does it necessarily imply that there will be negative goodwill. If the fair values of the subsidiary's net assets are less than their carrying values, the amounts used to revalue the specific identifiable net assets of the subsidiary downward could be greater than the negative purchase discrepancy, resulting in positive goodwill.

Working Paper for Consolidated Balance Sheet   The working paper for the consolidated balance sheet on December 31, Year 1, for Post Corporation and subsidiary is shown on page 193.

Nature of minority interest

The appropriate classification and presentation of minority interest in consolidated financial statements has been a perplexing problem for accountants. Over the years, two theories for consolidated financial statements have been developed to account for minority interest — the *parent company theory* and the *entity theory*. One authority has described these two theories as follows:[3]

> The "parent company" concept views consolidated statements as an extension of parent company statements, in which the investment account of the parent is replaced by the individual assets and liabilities underlying the parent's investment, and subsidiaries are viewed as almost the equivalent of branches. When subsidiary ownership is not complete, the consolidation process segregates the minority interest in the partially owned subsidiary. *The minority interest is considered to be an outside group and a liability as far as the parent shareholder is concerned.*

. . . .

3 *Consolidated Financial Statements*, Accountants International Study Group (Plaistow, England: 1973), p. 7.

Partially owned subsidiary on date of purchase-type business combination

POST CORPORATION AND SUBSIDIARY
Working Paper for Consolidated Balance Sheet
December 31, Year 1

	Post Corporation	Sage Company	Eliminations increase (decrease)		Consolidated
Assets					
Cash	75,000	100,000			175,000
Inventories	800,000	500,000	(a)	24,700	1,324,700
Other current assets	550,000	215,000			765,000
Investment in Sage Company common stock	1,192,250		(a)	(1,192,250)	
Plant assets (net)	3,500,000	1,100,000	(a)	180,500	4,780,500
Leasehold			(a)	28,500	28,500
Goodwill	100,000		(a)	38,000	138,000
Total assets	6,217,250	1,915,000		(920,550)	7,211,700
Liabilities & Shareholders' Equity					
Income taxes payable . . .	100,000	76,000			176,000
Other liabilities	2,450,000	870,000			3,320,000
Minority interest in net assets of subsidiary . . .			(a)	48,450	48,450
Common stock	2,617,250				2,617,250
Common stock		635,000	(a)	(635,000)	
Retained earnings	1,050,000	334,000	(a)	(334,000)	1,050,000
Total liabilities & shareholders' equity . .	6,217,250	1,915,000		(920,550)	7,211,700

In contrast to the parent company concept, the "entity" concept views consolidated statements as those of an economic entity with *two classes of proprietary interest* — the major or dominant interest and the minority interest. It holds that in consolidation these interests should be treated consistently. The consolidated statements are not viewed as an extension of parent company statements; rather, they are viewed as an expression of the financial position and operating results of a distinct "consolidated entity" consisting of a number of related companies whose relationship arises from common control (based on powers conferred by share ownership). When related companies are viewed as parts of such an entity, the minority interest, instead of representing an accountability to an outside group by the parent, represents "*a part of capital.*"

As indicated in the foregoing quotation, the ***parent company theory*** of consolidated financial statements views the minority interest in net assets of a subsidiary as a ***liability***. This liability is increased each accounting period subsequent to the date of a purchase-type business combination by an ***expense*** representing the minority's share of the subsidiary's net income (or decreased by the minority's share of the subsidiary's net loss). Dividends declared by the subsidiary to minority shareholders decrease the liability to them. Consolidated net income is reported ***net*** of the minority's share of the subisidiary's net income, as illustrated in Chapter 6.

In the ***entity theory***, the minority interest in the subsidiary's net assets is included in the shareholders' equity section of the consolidated balance sheet. The consolidated income statement presents the minority interest in the subsidiary's net income as a ***subdivision of total consolidated net income***, similar to the distribution of net income of a partnership (see page 16).

In the authors' opinion, the entity theory of reporting minority interest overemphasizes the ***legal aspects*** of the separate corporate organizations involved in a parent–subsidiary relationship. In substance, minority shareholders are a special class of owners of the consolidated entity who exercise ***no ownership control whatsoever*** over the operations of either the parent company or the subsidiary.

Section 1600.63 of the ***Handbook*** required only that minority interest be shown outside of shareholders' equity but did not specify that it be included with liabilities. Canadian practice varies. Some companies show minority interest between liabilities and shareholders' equity. Others include minority interest in the total of liabilities. From a student's perspective, it is useful to view minority interest as "another ownership equity" separate and distinct from the equity of the controlling group. Consequently, the presentation of minority interest between liabilities and shareholders' equity will be stressed throughout this book.

Consolidated balance sheet for partially owned subsidiary

The consolidated balance sheet of Post Corporation and its partially owned subsidiary, Sage Company, is shown on page 195. The consolidated amounts are taken from the working paper for consolidated balance sheet on page 193.

The inclusion of minority interest in net assets of subsidiary between liabilities and shareholders' equity in the consolidated balance sheet of Post Corporation and subsidiary is consistent with current practice. It should be noted that there is no ledger account for minority interest in net assets of subsidiary, in either the parent company's or the subsidiary's accounting records.

Alternative methods for valuing minority interest and goodwill

The computation of minority interest in subsidiary and goodwill on page 190 is based on two premises. First, the current fair values of the subsid-

POST CORPORATION AND SUBSIDIARY
Consolidated Balance Sheet
December 31, Year 1
Assets

Current assets:

Cash		$ 175,000
Inventories		1,324,700
Other		765,000
Total current assets		$2,264,700
Plant assets (net)		4,780,500
Intangible assets:		
Goodwill	$ 138,000	
Leasehold	28,500	166,500
Total assets		$7,211,700

Liabilities & Shareholders' Equity

Liabilities:

Income taxes payable		$ 176,000
Other		3,320,000
Total liabilities		$3,496,000
Minority interest in net assets of subsidiary		48,450
Shareholders' equity:		
Common stock, no par	$2,617,250	
Retained earnings	1,050,000	3,667,250
Total liabilities & shareholders' equity		$7,211,700

iary's identifiable net assets should be reflected in the consolidated financial statements only to the extent (percentage) that they have been purchased by the parent. This results in a dual basis of valuation — carrying value plus parent's percentage of the difference between fair value and carrying value. Second, only the subsidiary goodwill *acquired* by the parent company should be recognized, in accordance with the cost principle for valuing assets. This computational method is consistent with the *parent company theory* of consolidated financial statements.

Two alternatives to the procedure described above have been suggested. The first alternative would value the identifiable net assets of the subsidiary on a single basis—current fair value. Under this alternative, the total difference between current fair values and carrying amounts of Sage Company's identifiable net assets summarized on page 189 would be reflected in the aggregate debits to inventories, plant assets, and leasehold in the working paper elimination for Post Corporation and subsidiary on December 31, Year 1. The minority interest in net assets of subsidiary would be based on the *current fair values* of Sage Company's identifiable net assets, rather than on their *carrying amounts*, and would be computed as follows: $1,215,000 × 0.05 = $60,750. Goodwill would be $38,000, as in the preceding illustration. Supporters of this alternative, which also is consistent with the *parent company theory* of consolidated financial statements, argue that 100% of the current fair values of an acquiree's identifiable net assets should be reflected in consolidated financial statements. The related minority interest should be reflected in consolidated financial statements at the current fair values of the subsidiary's identifiable net assets.

The other alternative for valuing minority interest in net assets of subsidiary and goodwill is to obtain a current fair value for *100%* of a partially owned purchased subsidiary's *total* net assets, either through independent measurement of the minority interest or by *inference* from the cost of the parent company's investment in the subsidiary. Independent measurement of the minority interest might be accomplished by reference to quoted market prices of publicly traded common stock owned by minority shareholders of the subsidiary. The computation of minority interest and goodwill of Sage Company by inference from the cost of Post Corporation's investment in Sage is illustrated below:

<table>
<tr><td rowspan="7">Computation of minority interest and goodwill of partially owned purchased subsidiary based on implied total current fair value of subsidiary</td><td>Total cost of Post Corporation's investment in Sage Company . . . .</td><td>$1,192,250</td></tr>
<tr><td>Post's percentage ownership of Sage . . . .</td><td>95%</td></tr>
<tr><td>Implied current fair value of 100% of Sage's total net assets</td><td></td></tr>
<tr><td>($1,192,250 ÷ 0.95) . . . .</td><td>$1,255,000</td></tr>
<tr><td>Minority interest ($1,255,000 × 0.05) . . . .</td><td>$ 62,750</td></tr>
<tr><td>Goodwill ($1,255,000 − $1,215,000, the current fair value of Sage's</td><td></td></tr>
<tr><td>*identifiable* net assets) . . . .</td><td>$ 40,000</td></tr>
</table>

Supporters of this approach, which is consistent with the *entity theory* of consolidated financial statements, contend that a *single valuation method* should be used for all net assets of a purchased subsidiary — including goodwill — regardless of the existence of a minority interest in the subsidiary. They further maintain that the goodwill should be recorded at its implied value, rather than at the amount purchased by the parent, as is done for a wholly owned purchased subsidiary, in accordance with the theory of purchase accounting for business combinations.

This approach has some merit when the parent's percentage ownership is large. It might be valid to assume that if the parent company paid $1,192,250 for a 95% interest, the cost of 100% would have been approximately $1,255,000. However, in situations where the parent's percentage ownership is much smaller, say for example 55%, this approach loses validity. It also loses validity in situations where the parent's percentage ownership occurs in a series of small purchases and control is achieved after a total of 50.1% of the subsidiary's stock has been acquired.

A summary of the three methods for valuing minority interest and goodwill of a partially owned purchased subsidiary (derived from the December 31, Year 1, business combination of Post Corporation and Sage Company) appears on page 197.

The authors have chosen to reflect, in subsequent chapters of this book, the method illustrated in the elimination on page 191 (method 1 above), not

Comparison of three
methods for valuing
minority interest and
goodwill of partially
owned purchased
subsidiary

	Total identifiable net assets	Minority interest in net assets of subsidiary	Goodwill
1 Identifiable net assets recognized at current fair value only to extent of parent company's interest; balance of net assets and minority interest in net assets of subsidiary reflected at carrying amounts (a)	$1,202,700*	$48,450	$38,000
2 Identifiable net assets recognized at current fair value; minority interest in net assets of subsidiary based on the current fair values of identifiable net assets (a)	$1,215,000	$60,750	$38,000
3 Current fair value, through independent measurement or inference, assigned to total net assets of subsidiary, including goodwill (b)	1,215,000	62,750	40,000

* $969,000 + ($246,000 × 0.95) = $1,202,700
(a) Consistent with **parent company theory** of consolidated financial statements.
(b) Consistent with **entity theory** of consolidated financial statements.

for its conceptual superiority, but because its usage is required by the CICA Handbook.[4]

"Negative goodwill" in consolidated balance sheet

A purchase-type business combination that results in a parent company–subsidiary relationship may involve an excess of the parent's interest in the current fair values of the subsidiary's identifiable net assets over the cost of the parent's investment in the subsidiary's common stock. If so, the accounting principles described in Chapter 4 (page 141) are applied. The excess of current fair values over cost is applied pro rata to reduce the amounts initially assigned to nonmonetary assets.

Illustration of "Negative Goodwill": Wholly Owned Subsidiary   On December 31, Year 1, Plowman Corporation acquired all the outstanding common stock of Silbert Company for $850,000 cash, including direct out-of-pocket costs of the purchase-type business combination. Shareholders' equity of Silbert totalled $800,000, consisting of common stock, $500,000; and retained earnings, $300,000. The current fair values of Silbert's

4 See *CICA Handbook*, Sections 1580.44 and 1600.15.

identifiable net assets were the same as their carrying amounts, except for the following:

Current fair values of selected assets of acquiree

	Current fair values	Carrying amounts	Current fair value excess
Inventories	$ 350,000	$ 325,000	$25,000
Investments in marketable securities	62,000	55,000	7,000
Plant assets (net)	980,000	940,000	40,000
Intangible assets (net)	70,000	52,000	18,000
Totals	$1,462,000	$1,372,000	$90,000

The marketable securities are assumed to be monetary. The calculation and allocation of the purchase discrepancy is as follows:

Calculation and allocation of the purchase discrepancy

Cost of 100% interest in Silbert		$850,000
Carrying value of Silbert's net assets:		
Common stock	$500,000	
Retained earnings	300,000	
Total shareholders' equity	$800,000	
Plowman's ownership interest	1.00	800,000
Purchase discrepancy		$ 50,000
Allocated to revalue the net assets of Silbert:		
Inventories	$ 25,000	
Investments in marketable securities	7,000	
Plant assets (net)	40,000	
Intangible assets (net)	18,000	90,000
"Negative goodwill"		$ 40,000
Allocated to reduce nonmonetary assets (basis relative current fair values)		
Inventories ($40,000 × 0.25)	$ 10,000	
Plant assets ($40,000 × 0.70)	28,000	
Intangible assets (net) ($40,000 × 0.05)	2,000	40,000
Balance		$ 0

Calculations of ratio of relative current fair values of nonmonetary assets

Inventories	$350,000/$1,400,000 =	25%
Plant assets	$980,000/$1,400,000 =	70%
Intangible assets	$70,000/$1,400,000 =	5%
Total		100%

The December 31, Year 1, working paper elimination for Plowman Corporation and subsidiary is shown below:

Working paper
elimination for wholly
owned purchased
subsidiary with
"negative goodwill"
on date of business
combination

PLOWMAN CORPORATION AND SUBSIDIARY
Working Paper Elimination
December 31, Year 1

(a) Common Stock — Silbert	500,000	
Retained Earnings — Silbert	300,000	
Inventories — Silbert ($25,000 − $10,000)	15,000	
Investments in Marketable Securities — Silbert	7,000	
Plant Assets (net) — Silbert ($40,000 − $28,000)	12,000	
Intangible Assets (net) — Silbert ($18,000 − $2,000)	16,000	
Investment in Silbert Company Common Stock — Plowman . . .		850,000

To eliminate intercompany investment and equity accounts of
subsidiary on date of business combination; and to allocate
$40,000 excess of current fair values of subsidiary's identifi-
able net assets over cost to subsidiary's nonmonetary assets in
ratio of relative current fair values.

Illustration of "Negative Goodwill": Partially Owned Subsidiary   Let
us change the Plowman Corporation–Silbert Company business combination
described in the foregoing section by assuming that Plowman acquired
98%, rather than **100%**, of Silbert's common stock for $833,000 ($850,000
× 0.98 = $833,000) on December 31, Year 1, with all other facts remaining
unchanged. The calculation and allocation of the purchase discrepancy, and
the calculation of minority interest, is as follows:

Calculation and
allocation of the
purchase discrepancy;
and the calculation
of minority interest

Cost of 98% interest in Silbert		$833,000
Carrying value of Silbert's net assets:		
Shareholders' equity	$800,000	
Plowman's ownership interest	0.98	784,000
Purchase discrepancy		$ 49,000
Allocated to revalue the net assets of Silbert		
Inventories ($25,000 × 0.98)	$ 24,500	
Investments in marketable securities ($7,000 × 0.98)	6,860	
Plant assets (net) ($40,000 × 0.98)	39,200	
Intangible assets (net) ($18,000 × 0.98)	17,640	88,200
"Negative goodwill"		$ 39,200
Allocated to reduce nonmonetary assets (basis relative current		
fair values)		
Inventories ($39,200 × 0.25)	$ 9,800	
Plant assets ($39,200 × 0.70)	27,440	
Intangible assets (net) ($39,200 × 0.05)	1,960	39,200
Balance		$ 0
Minority interest:		
Shareholders' equity of Silbert		$800,000
Minority interest percentage		0.02
Minority interest in Silbert Company		$16,000

The working paper elimination for Plowman Corporation and subsidiary on December 31, Year 1, is as shown below:

PLOWMAN CORPORATION AND SUBSIDIARY
Working Paper Elimination
December 31, Year 1

(a) Common Stock — Silbert	500,000	
Retained Earnings — Silbert	300,000	
Inventories — Silbert ($24,500 – $9,800)	14,700	
Investments in Marketable Securities — Silbert	6,860	
Plant Assets (net) — Silbert ($39,200 – $27,440)	11,760	
Intangible Assets (net) — Silbert ($17,640 – $1,960)	15,680	
Investment in Silbert Company Common Stock — Plowman		833,000
Minority Interest in Net Assets of Subsidiary		16,000

To eliminate intercompany investment and equity accounts of subsidiary on date of business combination; to allocate parent company's share of excess ($39,200) of current fair values of subsidiary's identifiable net assets over cost to subsidiary's nonmonetary assets in the ratio of relative current fair values and to establish minority interest in net assets of subsidiary on date of business combination.

Subsidiary company formed by the parent

In some cases the subsidiary is not acquired through a share purchase, but rather by the parent company forming the subsidiary company. When the subsidiary issues shares immediately after incorporation, the parent company receives all or a portion of the issue. On this formation date, the carrying value and the fair value of the subsidiary's net assets are obviously equal and there is no goodwill. It should also be obvious that the subsidiary has no retained earnings at this time.

If the parent owns less than 100% of the subsidiary, the consolidated financial statements will show a minority interest based on net asset carrying amounts. Therefore, the working paper elimination entries are much simpler than our previous examples and consist of eliminating the parent's investment account, the subsidiary's capital stock account(s), and the establishment of any minority interest.

Subsidiary with recorded goodwill on acquisition date

Occasionally goodwill exists in the records of an acquiree on the date of a business combination. At some past date the acquiree was an acquirer in a business combination and recorded goodwill as the difference between the cost of the acquisition and the fair value of the net identifiable assets acquired. Now this company has itself been acquired and is a subsidiary of another company. A question arises as to the treatment of the goodwill that exists on the balance sheet of a company on the date that it becomes a subsidiary of another company.

Section 1580.42 of the Handbook indicated that the amount of goodwill is determined after the acquisition cost has been allocated to identifiable net assets, and that any *existing goodwill is not carried forward*. This implies that *goodwill is not an identifiable asset* to be valued separately but instead is an asset valued at a residual amount.

In the preparation of a consolidated balance sheet on the date of purchase type business combination the existing goodwill of the subsidiary is written off against the shareholders' equity of the subsidiary by a working paper entry. The following example will illustrate this point.

On December 31, Year 1, P Company acquired 90% of the outstanding shares of S Company at a total cost of $92,000. On this date the current fair values of the identifiable net assets of S Company were equal to their carrying amounts. The summarized balance sheet of S Company on December 31, Year 1, was as follows:

<table>
<tr><td>Balance sheet of subsidiary with recorded goodwill on date of acquisition by parent</td><td colspan="2">S COMPANY
Balance Sheet
December 31, Year 1</td></tr>
<tr><td></td><td>Net Assets (total assets − total liabilities) . . . .</td><td>$ 95,000</td></tr>
<tr><td></td><td>Goodwill . . . .</td><td>5,000</td></tr>
<tr><td></td><td>Total . . . .</td><td>$100,000</td></tr>
<tr><td></td><td>Shareholder's Equity</td><td></td></tr>
<tr><td></td><td>Common Stock . . . .</td><td>$ 70,000</td></tr>
<tr><td></td><td>Retained earnings . . . .</td><td>30,000</td></tr>
<tr><td></td><td>Total . . . .</td><td>$100,000</td></tr>
</table>

The calculation and allocation of the purchase discrepancy and the calculation of the minority interest is as follows:

<table>
<tr><td rowspan="2">Calculation and allocation of the purchase discrepancy; and the calculation of minority interest</td><td>Cost of 90% interest in S Company . . . .</td><td></td><td></td><td>$ 92,000</td></tr>
<tr><td>Carrying value of S Company's net assets:</td><td></td><td></td><td></td></tr>
<tr><td></td><td>Common stock . . . .</td><td></td><td>$70,000</td><td></td></tr>
<tr><td></td><td>Retained earnings . . . .</td><td>$30,000</td><td></td><td></td></tr>
<tr><td></td><td>Less: Goodwill write off for consolidation purposes . .</td><td>5,000</td><td>25,000</td><td></td></tr>
<tr><td></td><td>Total . . . .</td><td></td><td>$95,000</td><td></td></tr>
<tr><td></td><td>P Company's ownership interest . . . .</td><td></td><td>0.90</td><td>85,500</td></tr>
<tr><td></td><td>Purchase discrepancy . . . .</td><td></td><td></td><td>$ 6,500</td></tr>
<tr><td></td><td>Allocated to revalue net assets of S Company (current</td><td></td><td></td><td></td></tr>
<tr><td></td><td>fair values equal carrying amounts) . . . .</td><td></td><td></td><td>0</td></tr>
<tr><td></td><td>Balance — Goodwill . . . .</td><td></td><td></td><td>$ 6,500</td></tr>
<tr><td></td><td>Minority Interest:</td><td></td><td></td><td></td></tr>
<tr><td></td><td>Shareholders' equity of S Company . . . .</td><td></td><td></td><td>$100,000</td></tr>
<tr><td></td><td>Less: Existing goodwill . . . .</td><td></td><td></td><td>5,000</td></tr>
<tr><td></td><td></td><td></td><td></td><td>$ 95,000</td></tr>
<tr><td></td><td>Minority interest percentage . . . .</td><td></td><td></td><td>0.10</td></tr>
<tr><td></td><td>Minority interest in S Company . . . .</td><td></td><td></td><td>$ 9,500</td></tr>
</table>

The working paper elimination for P Company and subsidiary is as follows:

Working paper elimination
for subsidiary with recorded goodwill on date of
acquisition

P COMPANY AND SUBSIDIARY
Working Paper Elimination
December 31, Year 1

(a)	Retained Earnings — S Company	5,000	
	Goodwill — S Company		5,000
	To write off the existing goodwill of S Company for consolidation		
	purposes.		
(b)	Common stock — S Company	70,000	
	Retained Earnings — S Company ($30,000 − $5,000)	25,000	
	Goodwill — S Company	6,500	
	Investment in S Company Common Stock — P Company		92,000
	Minority interest in Net Assets of subsidiary		9,500
	To eliminate intercompany investment and equity accounts of sub-		
	sidiary on date of business combination; to allocate the parent		
	company's share of the excess of cost over carrying amount of net		
	identifiable assets acquired, with remainder to goodwill; and to		
	establish minority interest in net assets of subsidiary on date of		
	business combination.		

If P Company directs S Company to write off its $5,000 goodwill as at January 1, Year 2, no further problems will occur in the consolidation process. If, however, S Company does not write off its recorded goodwill the preparation of consolidated financial statements on December 31, Year 2, and all future years will require working paper entries to write off any goodwill that still exists in the subsidiary's records and to reverse any amortization of that goodwill that has been recorded by the subsidiary.

Footnote disclosure of consolidation policy

The "Summary of Significant Accounting Policies" footnote should include a description of consolidation policy reflected in consolidated financial statements. The following excerpt from an annual report of a publicly owned corporation is typical:

Principles of Consolidation — The consolidated financial statements include the accounts of the Company and its subsidiaries, all of which are wholly owned. All significant intercompany accounts are eliminated in consolidation.

The excess of net assets of acquired subsidiaries over cost is being amortized over ten-year periods from their respective dates of acquisition.

Advantages and shortcomings of consolidated financial statements

Consolidated financial statements are useful principally to shareholders and prospective investors of the parent company. These users of consolidated financial statements are provided with comprehensive financial information for the economic unit represented by the parent company and its subsidiaries, without regard for legal separateness of the constituent companies.

Creditors of each consolidated company and minority shareholders of subsidiaries find only limited use for consolidated financial statements, because such statements do not show the financial position or operating results of the individual companies forming the consolidated group. In addition, creditors of the constituent companies cannot ascertain the asset coverages for their respective claims. But perhaps the most telling criticism of consolidated financial statements in recent years has come from financial analysts. These critics have pointed out that consolidated financial statements of diversified companies (conglomerates) are impossible to classify into a single industry. Thus, say the financial analysts, consolidated financial statements of a conglomerate cannot be used for comparative purposes. The problem of financial reporting by diversified companies is considered in Chapter 11.

REVIEW QUESTIONS

1 The use of consolidated financial statements for reporting to shareholders is common. Under some conditions, however, it is the practice to exclude certain subsidiaries from consolidation. List the conditions under which subsidiaries should be excluded from consolidated financial statements.

2 The principal limitation of consolidated financial statements is their lack of separate information about the assets, liabilities, revenue, and expenses of the individual companies included in the consolidation. List the problems that users of consolidated financial statements encounter as a result of this limitation.

3 What criteria could influence a parent company in its decision to include a subsidiary in consolidated financial statements, or to exclude the subsidiary? Explain.

4 Discuss the similarities and dissimilarities between consolidated financial statements for parent company and subsidiaries, and combined financial statements for segments (branches) of a single legal entity.

5 Are eliminations for the preparation of consolidated financial statements recorded in the accounting records of the parent company or of the subsidiary? Explain.

6 If a business combination resulting in a parent-subsidiary relationship is accounted for as a purchase, the identifiable net assets of the subsidiary must be reflected at the parent's interest in their current fair values in the consolidated balance sheet on the date of the business combination. Does this require the subsidiary to record the current fair values of the identifiable net assets in its accounting records? Explain.

7 The controller of Pastor Corporation, which has just become the parent of Sexton Company in a purchase-type business combination, inquires if a consolidated income statement is required for the year ended on the date of the combination. What is your reply? Explain.

8 Differentiate between a *working paper for consolidated balance sheet* and a *consolidated balance sheet*.

9 Describe three methods that have been proposed for valuing minority interest and related goodwill in the consolidated balance sheet of a parent company and its partially owned purchased subsidiary.

10 Compare the *parent company theory* and the *entity theory* of consolidated financial statements as they relate to the classification of minority interest in net assets of subsidiary in the consolidated balance sheet.

11 What does the *CICA Handbook* say about the classification of minority interest in the consolidated balance sheet?

12 Outline the calculation and allocation of the purchase discrepancy.

13 If a purchase discrepancy is negative, does this mean that there will be negative goodwill? Explain.

14 Minority interest and goodwill could be valued by inference. Describe this procedure and comment on its shortcomings.

EXERCISES

Ex. 5-1 Select the best answer for each of the following multiple-choice questions:

1 On the date of a purchase-type business combination resulting in a parent company-subsidiary relationship, consolidated retained earnings includes the retained earnings of:
a Both the parent company and the subsidiary
b The parent company only
c The subsidiary only
d Both the parent company and the subsidiary, plus an amount to balance the journal entry to record the business combination.

2 On November 4, Year 4, Pegler Corporation paid $500,000 cash and issued 100,000 shares with a current fair value of $10 a share for all 50,000 outstanding shares of Stadler Company, which became a subsidiary of Pegler. Also on November 4, Year 4, Pegler paid $50,000 for finder's and legal fees related to the business combination and $80,000 for costs associated with the Securities Commission registration statement for the common stock issued in the combination. The net result of Pegler's journal entries to record the combination is to:
a Debit Investment in Stadler Company Common stock for $1,500,000
b Credit common stock for $1,000,000
c Debit Expenses of Business Combination for $130,000
d Credit Cash for $630,000

3 Under the CICA Handbook method of determining minority interest in the net assets of a partially owned purchased subsidiary on the date of the business combination, the minority interest percentage is applied to the:
a Carrying amount of subsidiary's total net assets
b Current fair value of subsidiary's identifiable net assets
c Carrying amount of subsidiary's identifiable net assets
d Current fair value of subsidiary's total net assets

4 Consolidated financial statements *always should exclude* from consolidation any subsidiaries:

a In foreign countries
b In bankruptcy proceedings
c That are finance companies
d That are controlled indirectly

5 On June 30, Year 8, Porus Corporation acquired for cash at $10 a share all 100,000 shares of Sorus Company. The total current fair value of identifiable assets of Sorus was $1,200,000 on June 30, Year 8, including the appraised value of Sorus Company's plant assets (its only nonmonetary assets) of $250,000. The consolidated balance sheet of Porus Corporation and subsidiary on June 30, Year 8, should include:

a A deferred credit (negative goodwill) of $50,000
b Goodwill of $50,000
c A deferred credit (negative goodwill) of $200,000
d Goodwill of $200,000
e None of the foregoing

Ex. 5-2 Painter Corporation acquired 80% of the outstanding common shares of Santiago Company on October 31, Year 6, for $800,000, including out-of-pocket costs of the business combination. The working paper elimination (in journal entry form) on that date was as follows (explanation omitted):

PAINTER CORPORATION AND SUBSIDIARY
Working Paper Elimination
October 31, Year 6

Common Stock — Santiago	110,000	
Retained Earnings — Santiago	490,000	
Inventories — Santiago ($50,000 × 0.80)	40,000	
Plant Assets (net) — Santiago ($100,000 × 0.80)	80,000	
Goodwill — Painter	200,000	
Investment in Santiago Company Common Stock —		
Painter		800,000
Minority Interest in Net Assets of Subsidiary		
($600,000 × 0.20)		120,000

Assuming that a value is to be imputed for 100% of Santiago's net assets (including goodwill) from Painter's $800,000 cost, compute the debit to Goodwill and the credit to Minority Interest in Net Assets of Subsidiary in the foregoing working paper elimination.

Ex. 5-3 On March 31, Year 2, Port Corporation acquired for $8,000,000 cash all the outstanding common shares of Starboard Company when Starboard's balance sheet showed net assets of $6,400,000. Out-of-pocket costs of the business combination may be disregarded. Starboard's identifiable net assets had current fair values different from carrying amounts as follows:

	Carrying amounts	Current fair values
Plant assets (net)	$10,000,000	$11,500,000
Other assets	1,000,000	700,000
Long-term debt	6,000,000	5,600,000

Compute the amount of goodwill, if any, to be included in the consolidated balance sheet of Port Corporation and subsidiary on March 31, Year 2.

Ex. 5-4 Paige Corporation acquired 70% of the outstanding common shares of Stone Company on July 31, Year 8. The unconsolidated balance sheet of Paige immediately after the purchase-type business combination and the consolidated balance sheet of Paige Corporation and subsidiary are as follows:

PAIGE CORPORATION AND SUBSIDIARY
Unconsolidated and Consolidated Balance Sheets
July 31, Year 8

	Unconsolidated	Consolidated
Assets		
Current assets	$106,000	$146,000
Investment in Stone Company common stock	100,000	
Plant assets (net)	270,000	367,000
Goodwill		11,100
Total assets	$476,000	$524,100
Liabilities & Shareholders' Equity		
Current liabilities	$ 15,000	$ 28,000
Minority interest in net assets of subsidiary		35,100
Common stock	350,000	350,000
Retained earnings	111,000	111,000
Total liabilities & shareholders' equity	$476,000	$524,100

Of the excess payment for the investment in Stone Company common stock, $7,000 was allocated to Stone's plant assets and the balance was allocated to goodwill. Current assets of Stone include a $2,000 receivable from Paige that arose before the business combination.

a Compute the total current assets in Stone Company's separate balance sheet on July 31, Year 8.

b Compute the total shareholders' equity in Stone Company's separate balance sheet on July 31, Year 8.

c Show how the goodwill of $11,100 included in the consolidated balance sheet was computed.

Ex. 5-5 Combinor Corporation and Combinee Company have been operating separately for five years. Each company has a minimal amount of liabilities and a simple capital structure consisting solely of common stock. Combinor, in exchange for its unissued common stock, acquired 80% of the outstanding common stock of Combinee. Combinee's identifiable net assets had a current fair value of $800,000 and a carrying amount of $600,000. The current fair value of the Combinor common stock issued in the business combination was $700,000.

Compute the minority interest in net assets of subsidiary and the goodwill that would appear in the consolidated balance sheet of Combinor Corporation and subsidiary, under three alternative methods of computation as illustrated on page 197.

Ex. 5-6 Shown on page 207 are the December 31, Year 3, balance sheets of two companies prior to their business combination.

POCO CORPORATION AND SMALL COMPANY
Separate Balance Sheets
December 31, Year 3

	Poco Corporation	Small Company
Assets		
Cash	$ 3,000	$ 100
Inventories (at fifo cost, which approximates current		
fair value)	2,000	200
Plant assets (net)	5,000	700*
Total assets	$10,000	$1,000
Liabilites & Shareholders' Equity		
Current liabilities	$ 600	$ 100
Common stock	4,000	300
Retained earnings	5,400	600
Total liabilities & shareholders' equity	$10,000	$1,000

* Current fair value on Dec. 31, Year 3, is $1,400.

a On December 31, Year 3, Poco Corporation acquired all the outstanding common shares of Small Company for $2,000 cash. Compute the amount of goodwill that should appear in the consolidated balance sheet of Poco Corporation and subsidiary on December 31, Year 3.

b On December 31, Year 3, Poco Corporation acquired all the outstanding common shares of Small Company for $1,600 cash. Compute the amount of plant assets that should appear in the consolidated balance sheet of Poco Corporation and subsidiary on December 31, Year 3.

Ex. 5-7 On November 1, Year 4, Parker Corporation issued 10,000 shares of its no par ($30 current fair value) common stock for 85 of the 100 outstanding shares of Sacco Company's no par common stock, in a purchase-type business combination. Out-of-pocket costs of the business combination were as follows:

Legal and finder's fees associated with the business combination	$36,800
Costs incurred for issuing shares	20,000
Total out-of-pocket costs of business combination	$56,800

On November 1, Year 4, the current fair values of Sacco's identifiable net assets were equal to their carrying amounts. On that date, Sacco's shareholders' equity consisted of the following:

Common stock	$150,000
Retained earnings	70,000
Total shareholders' equity	$220,000

Prepare the journal entries in Parker Corporation's accounting records to record the business combination with Sacco Company.

Ex. 5-8 The condensed individual and consolidated balance sheets of Perth Corporation and its subsidiary, Sykes Company, on the date of their business combination appear on page 208.

PERTH CORPORATION AND SUBSIDIARY
Individual and Consolidated Balance Sheets
June 30, Year 3

	Perth Corporation	Sykes Company	Consolidated
Assets			
Cash	$ 100,000	$ 40,000	$ 140,000
Inventories	500,000	90,000	610,000
Other current assets	250,000	60,000	310,000
Investment in Sykes Company common stock	440,000		
Plant assets (net)	1,000,000	360,000	1,440,000
Goodwill	100,000		120,000
Total assets	$2,390,000	$550,000	$2,620,000
Liabilities & Shareholders' Equity			
Income taxes payable	$ 40,000	$ 35,000	$ 75,000
Other liabilities	580,600	195,000	775,600
Common stock	1,449,400	410,000	1,449,400
Retained earnings (deficit)	320,000	(90,000)	320,000
Total liabilities & shareholders' equity .	$2,390,000	$550,000	$2,620,000

Reconstruct the working paper elimination (in journal entry form) indicated by the above data.

Ex. 5-9 Simplex Company's balance sheet on December 31, Year 6, was as follows:

SIMPLEX COMPANY
Balance Sheet
December 31, Year 6

Assets

Cash	$ 100,000
Accounts receivable (net)	200,000
Inventories	510,000
Plant assets (net)	900,000
Total assets	$1,710,000

Liabilities & Shareholders' Equity

Current liabilities	$ 310,000
Long-term debt	500,000
Common stock	300,000
Retained earnings	600,000
Total liabilities & shareholders' equity	$1,710,000

On December 31, Year 6, Protex Corporation acquired all the outstanding common shares of Simplex for $1,500,000 cash, including direct out-of-pocket costs. On that date, the current fair value of Simplex's inventories was $450,000 and the current fair value of Simplex's plant assets was $1,000,000. The current fair values of all other assets and liabilities of Simplex were equal to their carrying amounts.

a Compute the amount of goodwill that should appear in the December 31, Year 6, consolidated balance sheet of Protex Corporation and subsidiary.

b Compute the amount of consolidated retained earnings that should appear in the December 31, Year 6, consolidated balance sheet of Protex Corporation and subsidiary, assuming that Protex's unconsolidated balance sheet on that date included retained earnings of $2,500,000.

Ex. 5-10 The working paper elimination on August 31, Year 5, for the consolidated balance sheet of Payton Corporation and subsidiary is shown below. On that date, Payton acquired most of the outstanding common shares of Sutton Company for cash.

PAYTON CORPORATION AND SUBSIDIARY

Working Paper Elimination
August 31, Year 5

Common Stock — Sutton	95,250	
Retained Earnings — Sutton	50,100	
Inventories — Sutton	3,432	
Plant Assets (net) — Sutton	25,080	
Patent — Sutton	3,960	
Goodwill — Sutton	5,280	
Investment in Sutton Company Common Stock — Payton		165,660
Minority Interest in Net Assets of Subsidiary		17,442

To eliminate intercompany investment and equity accounts of subsidiary on date of business combination; to allocate excess of cost over parent's interest in current fair values of identifiable net assets acquired to goodwill; and to establish minority interest in net assets of subsidiary on date of purchase-type business combination.

Answer the following questions (show supporting computations):

a What percentage of the outstanding common shares of the subsidiary was acquired by the parent company?

b What was the aggregate current fair value of the subsidiary's identifiable net assets on August 31, Year 5?

c What amount would be assigned to goodwill under the method that infers a total current fair value for the subsidiary's total net assets, based on the parent company's investment?

d What amount would be assigned to minority interest in subsidiary under the method described in *c*?

CASES

Case 5-1 The minority interest in a subsidiary might be presented several ways in a consolidated balance sheet.

Instructions Discuss the propriety of reporting the minority interest in the consolidated balance sheet:

a As a liability

b As a part of shareholders' equity

c In a separate classification between liabilities and shareholders' equity

Case 5-2 On January 2, Year 2, the board of directors of Photo Corporation assigned to a voting trust 15,000 shares of the 60,000 shares of Soto Company common stock owned by Photo. The trustee of the voting trust controls 40,000 of Soto's 100,000 shares of issued common stock. The term of the voting trust is three years.

Instructions Are consolidated financial statements appropriate for Photo Corporation and Soto Company for the three years ending December 31, Year 4? Explain.

Case 5-3 On July 31, Year 5, Paley Corporation transferred all right, title, and interest in several of its current research and development projects to Carla Saye, sole shareholder of Saye Company, in exchange for 55 of the 100 shares of Saye Company common stock owned by Carla Saye. On the same date, Martin Morgan, who is not related to Paley Corporation, Saye Company, or Carla Saye, acquired for $45,000 cash the remaining 45 shares of Saye Company common stock owned by Carla Saye. Carla Saye notified the directors of Paley Corporation of the sale of the stock to Morgan.

Because Paley had expensed the costs related to the research and development when the costs were incurred, Paley's controller prepared the following journal entry to record the business combination with Saye Company:

Investment in Saye Company Common Stock (55 × $1,000)   55,000

  Gain on Disposal of Intangible Assets   55,000

To record transfer of research and development projects to Carla

Saye in exchange for 55 shares of Saye Company common stock.

Valuation of the investment is based on an unrelated cash sale of

Saye Company common stock on this date.

Instructions
a Do you concur with the foregoing journal entry? Explain.
b Should the $55,000 gain appear in consolidated financial statements of Paley Corporation and subsidiary on July 31, Year 5? Explain.

Case 5-4 On May 31, Year 6, Patrick Corporation acquired at 100, $500,000 face amount of Stear Company's 10-year, 12%, convertible debentures due May 31, Year 11. The debentures were convertible to 50,000 shares of Stear's voting common stock, of which 40,000 shares were issued and outstanding on May 31, Year 6. The controller of Patrick, who also is one of three Patrick officers who serve on the five-member board of directors of Stear, proposes to issue consolidated financial statements for Patrick Corporation and Stear Company on May 31, Year 6.

Instructions Do you agree with the Patrick controller's proposal? Explain, including in your discussion appropriate financial statement disclosure of the "related party" status of Patrick Corporation and Stear Company.

Case 5-5 In Year 6, Pinch Corporation, a chain of discount stores, began a program of business combinations with its suppliers. On May 31, Year 6, the close of its fiscal year, Pinch paid $8,500,000 cash and issued 100,000 shares of its common stock (current fair value $20 a share) for all 10,000 outstanding shares of Silver Company. Silver was a furniture manufacturer whose products were sold in Pinch's stores. Total shareholders' equity of Silver on May 31, Year 6, was $9,000,000. Out-of-pocket costs attributable to the business combination itself (as opposed to the Securities Commission registration statement for the 100,000 shares of Pinch's common stock) paid by Pinch on May 31, Year 6, totalled $100,000.

In the consolidated balance sheet of Pinch Corporation and subsidiary on May 31, Year 6, the $1,600,000 difference between the parent company's cost and the carrying amounts of the subsidiary's identifiable net assets was allocated in accordance with purchase accounting as follows:

Inventories	$ 250,000
Plant assets	850,000
Patents	300,000
Goodwill	200,000
Total excess of cost over carrying amounts of subsidiary's	
net assets	$1,600,000

Under terms of the indenture for a $1,000,000 debenture bond liability of Silver, Pinch is obligated to maintain Silver as a separate corporation and to issue a separate balance sheet for Silver each May 31. Pinch's controller contends that Silver's balance sheet on May 31, Year 6, should show net assets of $10,600,000—their cost to Pinch. Silver's controller disputes this valuation, claiming that generally accepted accounting principles require issuance of a historical cost balance sheet for Silver on May 31, Year 6.

Instructions
a Present arguments in favour of the Pinch controller's position.
b Present arguments in favour of the Silver controller's position.
c Which position do you approve? Explain.

PROBLEMS

5-1 On September 30, Year 1, Planck Corporation issued 100,000 common shares (current fair value $12 a share) for 18,800 shares of the 20,000 outstanding shares of Soper Company. The $150,000 out-of-pocket costs of the business combination paid by Planck on September 30, Year 1, were allocable as follows: 60% to legal fees and finder's fee directly related to the business combination, and 40% to the Securities Commission registration statement for Planck's common shares issued in the business combination. There was no contingent consideration.

Immediately prior to the business combination, balance sheets of the constituent companies were as follows:

PLANCK CORPORATION AND SOPER COMPANY

Separate Balance Sheets
September 30, Year 1

	Planck Corporation	Soper Company
Assets		
Cash	$ 200,000	$ 100,000
Accounts receivable (net)	400,000	200,000
Inventories (net)	600,000	300,000
Plant assets (net)	1,300,000	1,000,000
Total assets	$2,500,000	$1,600,000
Liabilities & Shareholders' Equity		
Current liabilities	$ 800,000	$ 400,000
Long-term debt		100,000
Common stock	1,200,000	
Common stock		400,000
Retained earnings	500,000	700,000
Total liabilities & shareholders' equity	$2,500,000	$1,600,000

Current fair values of Soper's identifiable net assets differed from their carrying amounts as follows:

	Current fair values, Sept. 30, Year 1
Inventories	$ 340,000
Plant assets (net)	1,100,000
Long-term debt	90,000

Instructions

a Prepare journal entries for Planck Corporation on September 30, Year 1, to record the business combination with Soper Company as a purchase.

b Prepare a working paper for consolidated balance sheet and related working paper elimination (in journal entry form) for Planck Corporation and subsidiary on September 30, Year 1. Balances in the working papers should reflect the journal entries in *a*.

5-2 Balance sheets of Pageant Corporation and Symbol Company on May 31, Year 4, together with current fair values of Symbol's identifiable net assets, are shown below:

PAGEANT CORPORATION AND SYMBOL COMPANY
Separate Balance Sheets
May 31, Year 4

		Symbol Company	
	Pageant Corporation	Carrying amounts	Current fair values
Assets			
Cash	$ 550,000	$ 10,000	$ 10,000
Accounts receivable (net)	700,000	60,000	60,000
Inventories	1,400,000	120,000	140,000
Plant assets (net)	2,850,000	610,000	690,000
Total assets	$5,500,000	$800,000	
Liabilities & Shareholders' Equity			
Current liabilities	$ 500,000	$ 80,000	$ 80,000
Long-term debt	1,000,000	400,000	440,000
Common stock	2,700,000	140,000	
Retained earnings	1,300,000	180,000	
Total liabilities & shareholders' equity	$5,500,000	$800,000	

On May 31, Year 4, Pageant acquired all 10,000 outstanding shares of Symbol Company by paying $300,000 cash to Symbol's shareholders and $50,000 cash for finder's and legal fees relating to the business combination. There was no contingent consideration, and Symbol became a subsidiary of Pageant.

Instructions

a Prepare journal entries to record the business combination of Pageant Corporation and Symbol Company on May 31, Year 4.

b Prepare a working paper for consolidated balance sheet of Pageant Corporation and subsidiary on May 31, Year 4, and the related working paper elimination (in journal entry form). Balances in the working papers should reflect the journal entries in *a*. Round your computations to the nearest dollar.

5-3 On April 30, Year 6, Powell Corporation issued 30,000 shares of its no-par common stock with a current fair value of $20 a share for 80% of Seaver Company's common stock. There was no contingent consideration; out-of-pocket costs of the business combination, paid by Seaver on behalf of Powell on April 30, Year 6, were as follows:

Finder's and legal fees relating to business combination	$40,000
Costs associated with issuing shares	30,000
Total out-of-pocket costs of business combination	$70,000

Balance sheets of the constituent companies on April 30, Year 6, prior to the business combination, are shown below:

POWELL CORPORATION AND SEAVER COMPANY
Separate Balance Sheets
April 30, Year 6

	Powell Corporation	Seaver Company
Assets		
Cash	$ 50,000	$ 150,000
Accounts receivable (net)	230,000	200,000
Inventories	400,000	350,000
Plant assets (net)	1,300,000	560,000
Total assets	$1,980,000	$1,260,000
Liabilities & Shareholders' Equity		
Current liabilities	$ 310,000	$ 250,000
Long-term debt	800,000	600,000
Common stock, no-par	500,000	
Common stock, no-par		460,000
Retained earnings (deficit)	370,000	(50,000)
Total liabilities & shareholders' equity	$1,980,000	$1,260,000

Current fair values of Seaver's identifiable net assets were the same as their carrying amounts, except for the following:

	Current fair values, Apr. 30, Year 6
Inventories	$440,000
Plant assets (net)	780,000
Long-term debt	620,000

Instructions
a Prepare a journal entry for Seaver Company on April 30, Year 6, to record its payment of out-of-pocket costs of the business combination on behalf of Powell Corporation.
b Prepare journal entries for Powell Corporation to record the purchase-type business combination with Seaver Company on April 30, Year 6.
c Prepare a working paper for consolidated balance sheet of Powell Corporation and subsidiary on April 30, Year 6, and the related working paper elimination (in journal entry form). Balances in the working papers should reflect the journal entries in *a* and *b*.

5-4 On July 31, Year 10, Pell Corporation issued 20,000 shares (current fair value $10 a share) for 90% of the outstanding shares of Swift Company, which is to remain a separate corporation. Out-of-pocket costs of the business combination, paid by Pell on July 31, Year 10, are shown below:

Finder's and legal fees related to business combination	$20,000
Costs associated with issuing shares	10,000
Total out-of-pocket costs of business combination	$30,000

The constituent companies' balance sheets on July 31, Year 10, prior to the business combination, follow:

PELL CORPORATION AND SWIFT COMPANY
Separate Balance Sheets
July 31, Year 10

	Pell Corporation	Swift Company
Assets		
Current assets	$ 800,000	$150,000
Plant assets (net)	2,400,000	300,000
Goodwill		20,000
Total assets	$3,200,000	$470,000
Liabilities & Shareholders' Equity		
Current liabilities	$ 400,000	$120,000
Long-term debt	1,000,000	200,000
Common stock	1,200,000	
Common stock		75,000
Retained earnings	600,000	75,000
Total liabilities & shareholders' equity	$3,200,000	$470,000

Swift's goodwill resulted from its July 31, Year 4, acquisition of the net assets of Solo Company.

Swift's assets and liabilities having July 31, Year 10, current fair values different from their carrying amounts were as follows:

	Carrying amounts	Current fair values
Inventories	$ 60,000	$ 65,000
Plant assets (net)	300,000	340,000
Long-term debt	200,000	190,000

There were no intercompany transactions prior to the business combination, and there was no contingent consideration in connection with the combination.

Instructions

a Prepare Pell Corporation's journal entries on July 31, Year 10, to record the business combination with Swift Company as a purchase.

b Prepare the working paper elimination (in journal entry form) and the related working paper for consolidated balance sheet of Pell Corporation and subsidiary on July 31, Year 10. Balances in the working papers should reflect the journal entries in *a*.

5-5 On October 31, Year 4, Pagel Corporation acquired 83% of the outstanding common shares of Sayre Company in exchange for 50,000 shares of Pagel's no par ($10 current fair value a share) common stock. There was no contingent consideration. Out-of-pocket costs of the business combination paid by Pagel on October 31, Year 4, were as follows:

Legal and finder's fees related to business combination	$34,750
Costs associated with issuing shares	55,250
Total out-of-pocket costs of business combination	$90,000

There were no intercompany transactions between the constituent companies prior to the business combination. Sayre is to be a subsidiary of Pagel. The separate balance sheets of the constituent companies prior to the business combination follow:

PAGEL CORPORATION AND SAYRE COMPANY
Separate Balance Sheets
October 31, Year 4

	Pagel Corporation	Sayre Company
Assets		
Cash	$ 250,000	$ 150,000
Inventories	860,000	600,000
Other current assets	500,000	260,000
Plant assets (net)	3,400,000	1,500,000
Patents (net)		80,000
Total assets	$5,010,000	$2,590,000
Liabilities & Shareholders' Equity		
Income taxes payable	$ 40,000	$ 60,000
Other current liabilities	390,000	854,000
Long-term debt	950,000	1,240,000
Common stock	3,000,000	
Common stock		100,000
Retained earnings	630,000	336,000
Total liabilities & shareholders' equity	$5,010,000	$2,590,000

Current fair values of Sayre's identifiable net assets were the same as their carrying amounts on October 31, Year 4, except for the following:

Inventories	$ 620,000
Plant assets (net)	1,550,000
Patents (net)	95,000
Long-term debt	1,225,000

Instructions
a Prepare Pagel Corporation's journal entries on October 31, Year 4, to record the business combination with Sayre Company as a purchase.
b Prepare the working paper eliminations (in journal entry form) on October 31, Year 4, and the related working paper for the consolidated balance sheet of Pagel Corporation and subsidiary. Balances in the working papers should reflect the journal entries in *a*.

5-6 On January 31, Year 3, Porcino Corporation issued $50,000 cash, 6,000 shares of no par common stock (current fair value $15 a share), and a 5-year, 14%, $50,000 promissory note payable for all 10,000 shares of Secor Company's outstanding common stock, which were owned by Lawrence Secor. The only out-of-pocket costs paid by Porcino to complete the business combination were legal fees of $10,000, because Porcino's common stock issued in the combination was not subject to any registration requirements. There was no contingent consideration, and 14% was a fair rate of interest for the promissory note issued by Porcino in connection with the business combination.

Balance sheets of Porcino and Secor on January 31, Year 3, prior to the business combination, were as follows:

PORCINO CORPORATION AND SECOR COMPANY
Separate Balance Sheets
January 31, Year 3

	Porcino Corporation	Secor Company
Assets		
Inventories	$ 380,000	$ 60,000 —
Other current assets	640,000	130,000
Plant assets (net)	1,520,000	470,000 —
Intangible assets (net)	160,000	40,000 —
Total assets	$2,700,000	$700,000
Liabilities & Shareholders' Equity		
Current liabilities	$ 420,000	$200,000
Long-term debt	650,000	300,000
Common stock	1,020,000	
Common stock		310,000
Retained earnings (deficit)	610,000	(110,000)
Total liabilities & shareholders' equity	$2,700,000	$700,000

Current fair values of Secor's identifiable net assets that differed from their carrying amounts on January 31, Year 3, were as follows:

	Current fair values
Inventories	$ 70,000
Plant assets (net)	540,000
Intangible assets (net)	60,000
Long-term debt	350,000

Instructions
a Prepare journal entries for Porcino Corporation on January 31, Year 3, to record its business combination with Secor Company.

b Prepare a working paper for consolidated balance sheet of Porcino Corporation and subsidiary on January 31, Year 3, and the related working paper elimination (in journal entry form). Balances in the working papers should reflect the journal entries in *a*. Round your computations to the nearest dollar.

5-7 On June 30, Year 7, Pandit Corporation issued a $300,000 note payable, due $60,000 a year with interest at 15% beginning June 30, Year 8, for 8,500 of the 10,000 outstanding shares of no par common stock of Singh Company. Legal fees of $20,000 incurred by Pandit in connection with the business combination were paid on June 30, Year 7.

Balance sheets of the constituent companies, immediately following the business combination, are shown below:

PANDIT CORPORATION AND SINGH COMPANY
Separate Balance Sheets
June 30, Year 7

	Pandit Corporation	Singh Company
Assets		
Cash	$ 80,000	$ 60,000
Accounts receivable (net)	170,000	90,000
Inventories	370,000	120,000
Investment in Singh Company common stock	320,000	
Plant assets (net)	570,000	240,000
Goodwill	50,000	
Total assets	$1,560,000	$510,000
Liabilities & Shareholders' Equity		
Accounts payable	$ 320,000	$160,000
15 % note payable, due $60,000 annually	300,000	
Common stock	650,000	230,000
Retained earnings	290,000	120,000
Total liabilities & shareholders' equity	$1,560,000	$510,000

Other information
1 An independent audit of Singh Company's financial statements for the year ended June 30, Year 7, disclosed that Singh had omitted from its June 30, Year 7, inventories merchandise shipped FOB shipping point by a vendor on June 30, Year 7, at an invoiced amount of $35,000.
2 Current fair values of Singh's net assets reflected in Singh's balance sheet on June 30, Year 7, differed from carrying amounts as follows:

	Current fair values
Inventories	$150,000
Plant assets (net)	280,000

Instructions
a Prepare a journal entry to correct the inventory misstatement in Singh Company's financial statements for the year ended June 30, Year 7.

b Prepare a working paper elimination (in journal entry form) and a working paper for the consolidated balance sheet of Pandit Corporation and subsidiary on June 30, Year 7. The amounts for Singh Company should reflect the adjusting journal entry prepared in *a*. Round your computations to the nearest dollar.

5-8 Shown below are the balance sheets of Pliny Corporation and Sylla Company on December 31, Year 6, prior to their business combination:

PLINY CORPORATION AND SYLLA COMPANY

Separate Balance Sheets
December 31, Year 6

	Pliny Corporation	Sylla Company
Assets		
Inventories	$ 800,000	$ 300,000
Other current assets	1,200,000	500,000
Long-term investments in marketable securities		200,000
Plant assets (net)	2,500,000	900,000
Intangible assets (net)	100,000	200,000
Total assets	$4,600,000	$2,100,000
Liabilities & Shareholders' Equity		
Current liabilities	$1,400,000	$ 300,000
10% note payable, due June 30, Year 16	2,000,000	
12% bonds payable, due Dec. 31, Year 11		500,000
Common stock	800,000	600,000
Retained earnings	400,000	700,000
Total liabilities & shareholders' equity	$4,600,000	$2,100,000

On December 31, Year 6, Pliny paid $100,000 cash and issued $1,500,000 face amount of 14%, 10-year bonds for all the outstanding common shares of Sylla, which became a subsidiary of Pliny. On the date of the business combination, 16% was a fair rate of interest for the bonds of both Pliny and Sylla, which paid interest on June 30 and December 31. There was no contingent consideration involved in the business combination, but Pliny paid the following out-of-pocket costs on December 31, Year 6:

Finder's and legal fees relating to business combination	$50,000
Costs associated with the registration statement for Pliny's bonds	40,000
Total out-of-pocket costs of business combination	$90,000

In addition to the 12% bonds payable, Sylla had identifiable net assets with current fair values that differed from carrying amounts on December 31, Year 6, as follows:

	Current fair values
Inventories	$330,000
Long-term investments in marketable securities	230,000
Plant assets (net)	940,000
Intangible assets (net)	220,000

Instructions
a Prepare journal entries for Pliny Corporation to record the business combination with Sylla Company on December 31, Year 6. Use the appendix in back of the

book to compute present value, rounded to nearest dollar, of the 14% bonds issued by Pliny.

b Prepare a working paper for consolidated balance sheet for Pliny Corporation and subsidiary on December 31, Year 6, and the related working paper elimination (in journal entry form). Use the appendix in back of the book to compute present value, rounded to nearest dollar, of the 12% bonds payable of Sylla. Amounts in the working papers should reflect the journal entries in *a*.

5-9 You have been engaged to examine the financial statements of Parthenia Corporation and subsidiary for the year ended June 30, Year 6. The working paper for consolidated balance sheet of Parthenia and subsidiary on June 30, Year 6, prepared by Parthenia's inexperienced accountant, is below.

PARTHENIA CORPORATION AND SUBSIDIARY

Working Paper for Consolidated Balance Sheet
June 30, Year 6

	Parthenia Corporation	Storey Company	Eliminations increase (decrease)	Consolidated
Assets				
Cash	60,000	50,000		110,000
Accounts receivable (net)	120,000	90,000		210,000
Inventories	250,000	160,000		410,000
Investment in Storey Company common stock	220,000		(a) (220,000)	
Plant assets (net)	590,000	500,000		1,090,000
Goodwill	60,000			60,000
Total assets	1,300,000	800,000	(220,000)	1,880,000
Liabilities & Shareholders' Equity				
Current liabilities	200,000	280,000		480,000
Long-term debt	500,000	300,000		800,000
Common stock, $5 par	100,000			100,000
Common stock, $10 par		50,000	(a) (50,000)	
Contributed Surplus	200,000	70,000	(a) (70,000)	200,000
Retained earnings	300,000	100,000	(a) (100,000)	300,000
Total liabilities & shareholders' equity .	1,300,000	800,000	(220,000)	1,880,000

In the course of your examination, you review the following June 30, Year 6, journal entries in the accounting records of Parthenia Corporation:

Investment in Storey Company Common Stock	220,000
Goodwill	60,000
Cash	280,000

To record acquisition of 4,000 shares of Storey Company's outstanding common stock in a purchase-type business combination,
and to record acquired goodwill as follows:

Cash paid for Storey common stock	$280,000
Less: Shareholders' equity of Storey, June 30,	
Year 6	220,000
Goodwill acquired	$ 60,000

Expenses of Business Combination	10,000
Cash	10,000

To record payment of legal fees in connection with business
combination with Storey Company.

Your inquiries of directors and officers of Parthenia and your review of supporting documents disclosed the following current fair values for Storey's identifiable
net assets that differ from carrying amounts on June 30, Year 6:

	Current fair values
Inventories	$180,000
Plant assets (net)	530,000
Long-term debt	260,000

Instructions

a Prepare a journal entry or entries to correct Parthenia Corporation's accounting
for its June 30, Year 6, business combination with Storey Company.

b Prepare a corrected working paper for consolidated balance sheet of Parthenia
Corporation and subsidiary on June 30, Year 6, and related working paper elimination (in journal entry form). Amounts in the working papers should reflect the
journal entries in **a**.

5-10 The balance sheets of Par Ltd. and Sub Ltd. on December 31, Year 0 are:

	Par Ltd.	Sub Ltd.
Cash	$100,000	$ 9,000
Accounts Receivable	25,000	
Inventory		21,000
Total current assets	125,000	30,000
Plant and Equipment	165,000	51,000
Trademarks	10,000	7,000
	$300,000	$88,000
Current liabilities	$ 50,000	$10,000
Long-term liabilities	70,000	20,000
Total	120,000	30,000
Common stock	100,000	30,000
Retained earnings	80,000	28,000
	$300,000	$88,000

The fair values of the identifiable assets and liabilities of Sub Ltd. at December 31, Year 0 are:

Cash		$ 9,000
Inventory		26,000
Plant and equipment		60,000
Trade marks		14,000
		$109,000
Current liabilities	10,000	
Long-term liabilities	19,000	29,000
		$ 80,000

Assume the following took place on January 1, Year 1. (Par Ltd. acquired the stock from the shareholders of Sub Ltd.)

Case 1. Par Ltd. paid $95,000 to acquire all of the common stock of Sub Ltd.

Case 2. Par Ltd. paid $80,000 to acquire all of the common stock of Sub Ltd.

Case 3. Par Ltd. paid $70,000 to acquire all of the common stock of Sub Ltd. (Any excess of fair values over the $70,000 cost is to be deducted from plant and equipment).

Case 4. Par Ltd. paid $76,000 to acquire 80% of the common stock of Sub Ltd.

Case 5. Par Ltd. paid $63,000 to acquire 90% of the common stock of Sub Ltd.(Any excess of fair values over the $63,000 cost is to be allocated to nonmonetary assets.)

Instructions
For each of the five cases, prepare a consolidated balance sheet as at January 1, Year 1.

6 CONSOLIDATED FINANCIAL STATEMENTS: SUBSEQUENT TO DATE OF ACQUISITION OF A SUBSIDIARY: EQUITY METHOD

In Chapter 4, the two methods of accounting for business combinations, purchase and pooling, were illustrated and discussed. In Chapter 5, the preparation of consolidated financial statements on the date of a business combination was illustrated using the purchase method of accounting. This method is by far the predominant method used in Canada and pooling is rarely seen. In this chapter, and the chapters that follow, our discussion of the preparation of consolidated financial statements will be limited to business combinations accounted for under the purchase method.

We now focus our attention to consolidated financial statements prepared subsequent to the date of a business combination. Because we are using the purchase method, in which one company (the parent) is the acquirer, we shall refer to this date as the ***date of acquisition***. Subsequent to the date of acquisition, the parent company must account for the operating results of the subsidiary: the subsidiary's net income or loss, and dividends declared and paid by the subsidiary. In addition a number of intercompany transactions that frequently occur in a parent-subsidiary relationship must be accounted for. These transactions will be discussed in later chapters.

ACCOUNTING FOR OPERATING RESULTS OF WHOLLY OWNED PURCHASED SUBSIDIARIES

In accounting for the operating results of consolidated purchased subsidiaries, a parent company may choose either the ***equity method*** or the ***cost method*** of accounting.

Equity method

In the equity method of accounting, the parent company records its share of the subsidiary's net income or net loss, adjusted for the amortization of the purchase discrepancy on the date of acquisition, as well as its share of dividends declared by the subsidiary. Thus, the equity method of accounting for a subsidiary's operating results is similar to home office accounting for a branch's operations, as described in Chapter 3.

Proponents of the equity method of accounting maintain that the method is consistent with the accrual basis of accounting, because it recognizes increases or decreases in the carrying amount of the parent company's investment in the subsidiary when they are *realized* by the subsidiary as net income or net loss, not when they are *paid* by the subsidiary as dividends. Thus, proponents claim, the equity method stresses the *economic substance* of the parent company-subsidiary relationship because the two companies constitute a single economic entity for accounting purposes. Proponents of the equity method also claim that dividends declared by a subsidiary cannot constitute *revenue* to the parent company, as maintained by advocates of the cost method; instead, dividends are a liquidation of a portion of the parent company's investment in the subsidiary.

Cost Method

In the cost method of accounting, the parent company accounts for the operations of a subsidiary only to the extent that dividends are declared by the subsidiary. Dividends declared by the subsidiary from net income subsequent to the business combination are *revenue* to the parent company; dividends declared by the subsidiary in excess of post-combination net income constitute a reduction of the parent company's investment in the subsidiary. Net income or net loss of the subsidiary is *not recorded* by the parent company when the cost method of accounting is used.

Supporters of the cost method contend that the method appropriately recognizes the *legal form* of the parent company-subsidiary relationship. Parent company and subsidiary are separate legal entities; accounting for a subsidiary's operations should recognize the separateness, according to proponents of the cost method. Thus, a parent company realizes revenue from an investment in a subsidiary when the subsidiary declares a dividend, not when the subsidiary reports net income. The cost method of accounting is illustrated in Chapter 7.

Choosing between equity method and cost method

A particular company is free to choose either equity or cost as a bookkeeping method of recording the purchase of an investment in the shares of another company, and the revenues that the investment earns. When the *CICA Handbook* requires the use of the two methods, it is referring to their usage in financial reporting and is not dictating bookkeeping practices. The Handbook requirements will be discussed in Chapter 7.

Consolidated financial statement amounts are the same, regardless of whether a parent company uses the equity method or the cost method to account for a subsidiary's operations. However, the working paper eliminations used in the two methods are different, as illustrated in subsequent sections of this chapter and in Chapter 7.

Illustration of equity method for wholly owned subsidiary for first year after acquisition

We now continue the accounting for the Palm-Starr business combination example introduced in Chapter 5 in which Palm Corporation acquired 100% of the outstanding common shares of Starr Company on December 31, Year 1. The purchase discrepancy (not illustrated in our previous discussion of this particular example) is calculated as follows:

Cost of 100% interest in Starr — Dec. 31, Year 1		$500,000
Carrying amount of Starr's net assets		
Common stock	$258,000	
Retained earnings	132,000	
Total shareholders' equity	$390,000	
Palm's ownership interest	1.00	390,000
Purchase discrepancy		$110,000
Allocated to revalue the net assets of Starr		
Inventory $25,000 × 1.00	$ 25,000	
Plant assets (net) 65,000 × 1.00	65,000	
Patent 5,000 × 1.00	5,000	95,000
Balance — Goodwill		$ 15,000

Readers should review the journal entries in Chapter 5 (pages 182 to 183) to verify the details of this calculation.

Assume that Starr reported net income of $60,000 (income statement is on page 229) for the year ended December 31, Year 2. Assume further that on December 20, Year 2, Starr's board of directors declared a cash dividend of $0.60 a share on the 40,000 outstanding shares of common stock owned by Palm. The dividend was payable January 8, Year 3, to shareholders of record December 29, Year 2.

Starr's December 20, Year 2, journal entry to record the dividend declaration is as follows:

Year 2			
Dec. 20	Dividends (40,000 × $0.60)	24,000	
	Intercompany Dividends Payable		24,000
	To record declaration of dividend payable Jan. 8, Year 3, to		
	shareholders of record Dec. 29, Year 2.		

Starr's credit to the Intercompany Dividends Payable account indicates that the liability for dividends payable to the parent company *must be eliminated* in the preparation of consolidated financial statements for the year ended December 31, Year 2.

Under the equity method of accounting, Palm Corporation prepares the following journal entries to record the dividend and net income of Starr for the year ended December 31, Year 2:

PALM CORPORATION

General Journal

Year 2			
Dec. 20	Intercompany Dividends Receivable	24,000	
	Investment in Starr Company Common Stock		24,000
	To record dividend declared by Starr Company, payable		
	Jan. 8, Year 3, to shareholders of record Dec. 29, Year 2.		
Dec. 31	Investment in Starr Company Common Stock	60,000	
	Intercompany Investment Income		60,000
	To record 100% of Starr Company's net income for the year		
	ended Dec. 31, Year 2.		

The first journal entry records the dividend declared by the subsidiary in the Intercompany Dividends Receivable account, and is the counterpart of the subsidiary's journal entry to record the declaration of the dividend. The credit to the Investment in Starr Company Common Stock account in the first journal entry reflects an underlying premise of the equity method of accounting: dividends declared by a subsidiary represent a return of a portion of the parent company's investment in the subsidiary.

The second journal entry records the parent company's 100% share of the subsidiary's net income for Year 2. The subsidiary's net income *accrues* to the parent company under the equity method of accounting, similar to the accrual of interest on a note receivable.

Adjustment of Subsidiary's Net Income Because Palm Corporation's business combination with Starr Company was accounted for as a *purchase*, Palm must prepare a third equity-method journal entry on December 31, Year 2, to adjust Starr's net income for depreciation and amortization attributable to the parent's share of the differences between the current fair values and carrying amounts of Starr's net assets on the date of the Palm-Starr business combination. In other words, Palm must prepare a journal entry to amortize the purchase discrepancy. Because such differences are not recorded by the subsidiary, the subsidiary's *net income is overstated* from the point of view of the consolidated entity.

The allocation of the purchase discrepancy is further expanded to show the components of net plant assets as well as the estimated economic lives as follows:

Inventories		$ 25,000
Plant assets (net):		
Land	$15,000	
Building (economic life 15 years)	30,000	
Machinery (economic life 10 years)	20,000	65,000
Patent (economic life 5 years)		5,000
Goodwill (economic life 30 years)		15,000
Total		$110,000

Palm Corporation prepares the following additional journal entry to reflect the effects of amortization of the purchase discrepancy on Starr's net income for the year ended December 31, Year 2:

Parent company's equity-method journal entry to record the amortization of the purchase discrepancy

PALM CORPORATION

General Journal

Year 2

Dec. 31	Intercompany Investment Income	30,500	
	Investment in Starr Company Common Stock		30,500

To amortize the purchase discrepancy on Dec. 31, Year 1, as follows:

Inventories — to cost of goods sold	$25,000
Building — depreciation ($30,000 ÷ 15)	2,000
Machinery — depreciation ($20,000 ÷ 10) . .	2,000
Patent — amortization ($5,000 ÷ 5)	1,000
Goodwill — amortization ($15,000 ÷ 30) . . .	500
Total amortization applicable to Year 2 . . .	$30,500

After the three foregoing journal entries are posted, Palm Corporation's Investment in Starr Company Common Stock and Intercompany Investment Income ledger accounts appear below.

Ledger accounts of parent company using equity method of accounting for wholly owned purchased subsidiary

Investment in Starr Company Common Stock

Date	Explanation	Debit	Credit	Balance
12/31/1	Issuance of common stock in business combination	450,000		450,000 dr
12/31/1	Direct out-of-pocket costs of business combination	50,000		500,000 dr
12/20/2	Dividend declared by Starr		24,000	476,000 dr
12/31/2	Net income of Starr	60,000		536,000 dr
12/31/2	Amortization of the purchase discrepancy		30,500	505,500 dr

Intercompany Investment Income

Date	Explanation	Debit	Credit	Balance
12/31/2	Net income of Starr		60,000	60,000 cr
12/31/2	Amortization of the purchase discrepancy	30,500		29,500 cr

Developing the Elimination Palm Corporation's use of the equity method of accounting for its investment in Starr Company resulted in a balance in the investment account that is a mixture of two components: (1) the parent's share of the carrying amount of Starr's identifiable net assets, and (2) the unamortized portion of the purchase discrepancy. These components are analyzed as follows:

PALM CORPORATION
Analysis of Investment in Starr Company Common Stock Account
For Year Ended December 31, Year 2

	Carrying amount	Purchase discrepancy	Total	
Beginning balances	$390,000	$110,000	$500,000	
Net income of Starr	60,000		60,000	Intercompany
Amortization of the				investment
purchase				income,
discrepancy		(30,500)	(30,500)	$29,500
Dividend declared				
by Starr	(24,000)		(24,000)	
Ending balances	$426,000	$ 79,500	$505,500	

The $426,000 ending balance of the Carrying Amount column agrees with the total shareholders' equity of Starr Company on December 31, Year 2 (see Balance Sheet section of working paper for consolidated financial statements on page 229), as follows:

Subsidiary's shareholders' equity at end of Year 2

Common stock $258,000
Retained earnings 168,000
  Total shareholders' equity $426,000

The $79,500 ending balance of the purchase discrepancy column agrees with the December 31, Year 2, total of the unamortized balances for each of the respective components, as shown below:

Purchase discrepancy amortization schedule one year subsequent to business combination

	Balance, Dec. 31, Year 1 (p. 225)	Amortization for Year 2 (p. 226)	Balance, Dec. 31, Year 2
Inventories	$ 25,000	$(25,000)	
Plant assets (net):			
Land	$ 15,000		$15,000
Building	30,000	$ (2,000)	28,000
Machinery	20,000	(2,000)	18,000
Total plant assets ...	$ 65,000	$ (4,000)	$61,000
Patent	5,000	(1,000)	4,000
Goodwill	15,000	(500)	14,500
Totals	$110,000	$(30,500)	$79,500

The working paper elimination subsequent to the date of acquisition must include accounts that appear in the constituent companies' income statements and statements of retained earnings, as well as in their balance sheets, because **all three basic financial statements must be consoli dated for accounting periods subsequent to the date of a business combination.** (A consolidated statement of changes in financial position is prepared from the three basic **consolidated** financial statements and other information, as explained in Chapter 10.) The accounts that must be included in the elimination are the subsidiary's shareholders' equity, certain assets, costs and expenses, and dividends; and the investment and intercompany investment income of the parent company. Assuming that Starr Company allocates machinery depreciation and patent amortization entirely to cost of goods sold, goodwill amortization entirely to operating expenses, and building depreciation 50% each to cost of goods sold and operating expenses, the working paper elimination for Palm Corporation and subsidiary on December 31, Year 2, is as follows:

Working paper
elimination for wholly
owned subsidiary
subsequent to date
of acquisition

PALM CORPORATION AND SUBSIDIARY
Working Paper Elimination
December 31, Year 2

(a) Common Stock — Starr	258,000
Retained Earnings — Starr	132,000
Intercompany Investment Income — Palm	29,500
Plant Assets (net) — Starr ($65,000 − $4,000)	61,000
Patent — Starr ($5,000 − $1,000)	4,000
Goodwill — Starr ($15,000 − $500)	14,500
Cost of Goods Sold — Starr	29,000
Operating Expenses — Starr	1,500
Investment in Starr Company Common Stock —	
Palm	505,500
Dividends — Starr	24,000

To carry out the following:

(1) Eliminate intercompany investment and equity accounts of subsidiary **at beginning of year**, and subsidiary dividend.

(2) Provide for Year 2 depreciation and amortization on the purchase discrepancy allocated to Starr's net assets as follows:

	Cost of goods sold	Operating expenses
Inventories sold	$25,000	
Building depreciation	1,000	$1,000
Machinery depreciation	2,000	
Patent amortization	1,000	
Goodwill amortization		500
Totals	$29,000	$1,500

(3) Allocate the unamortized purchase discrepancy to appropriate assets of Starr.

Equity method: Wholly owned subsidiary subsequent to date of acquisition

PALM CORPORATION AND SUBSIDIARY

Working Paper for Consolidated Financial Statements

For Year Ended December 31, Year 2

	Palm Corporation	Starr Company	Eliminations increase (decrease)	Consolidated
Income Statement				
Revenue				
Net sales	1,100,000	680,000		1,780,000
Intercompany investment income	29,500		(a) (29,500)	
Total revenue	1,129,500	680,000	(29,500)	1,780,000
Costs and expenses				
Cost of goods sold	700,000	450,000	(a) 29,000	1,179,000
Operating expenses	151,000	80,000	(a) 1,500	232,500
Interest expense	49,000			49,000
Income taxes expense	120,000	90,000		210,000
Total costs and expenses	1,020,000	620,000	30,500*	1,670,500
Net income	109,500	60,000	(60,000)	109,500
Statement of Retained Earnings				
Retained earnings, beginning of year	134,000	132,000	(a) (132,000)	134,000
Net income	109,500	60,000	(60,000)	109,500
Subtotal	243,500	192,000	(192,000)	243,500
Dividends	30,000	24,000	(a) (24,000)	30,000
Retained earnings, end of year	213,500	168,000	(168,000)	213,500
Balance Sheet				
Assets				
Cash	15,900	72,100		88,000
Intercompany receivable (payable)	24,000	(24,000)		
Inventories	136,000	115,000		251,000
Other current assets	88,000	131,000		219,000
Investment in Starr Company common stock	505,500		(a) (505,500)	
Plant assets (net)	440,000	340,000	(a) 61,000	841,000
Patent		16,000	(a) 4,000	20,000
Goodwill			(a) 14,500	14,500
Total assets	1,209,400	650,100	(426,000)	1,433,500
Liabilities & Shareholders' Equity				
Income taxes payable	40,000	20,000		60,000
Other liabilities	190,900	204,100		395,000
Common stock, no par	765,000			765,000
Common stock, no par		258,000	(a) (258,000)	
Retained earnings	213,500	168,000	(168,000)	213,500
Total liabilities & shareholders' equity	1,209,400	650,100	(426,000)	1,433,500

*An increase in total costs and expenses and a decrease in net income.

Working Paper for Consolidated Financial Statements   The working paper for consolidated financial statements for Palm Corporation and subsidiary for the year ended December 31, Year 2, is on page 229. The intercompany receivable and payable is the $24,000 dividend payable by Starr to Palm on December 31, Year 2. (The advances by Palm to Starr that were outstanding on December 31, Year 1, were repaid by Starr January 2, Year 2.)

The following aspects of the working paper for consolidated financial statements of Palm Corporation and subsidiary should be emphasized:

1   The intercompany receivable and payable, placed in adjacent columns on the same line, are offset without a formal elimination.

2   The elimination cancels all intercompany transactions and balances not dealt with by the offset technique described in **1** above.

3   The elimination cancels the subsidiary's retained earnings balance *at the beginning of the year* (the date of acquisition), so that the three basic financial statements of the two companies each may be consolidated in turn. (All financial statements of a parent company and a subsidiary are consolidated subsequent to the date of acquisition.)

It should be noted that the dividends declared by the subsidiary have no effect on consolidated retained earnings. The subsidiary's net income has been taken into account by the parent's equity method journal entry and is included in the parent's net income (and therefore is part of consolidated retained earnings). Dividends are distributions of net income to shareholders. When a wholly owned subsidiary pays a dividend the result is simply a transfer of cash from the subsidiary to the parent with the consolidated entity's cash and retained earnings remaining unchanged.

4   It assumed that the fifo method is used by Starr Company to account for inventories; thus, the $25,000 difference attributable to Starr's beginning inventories is allocated to cost of goods sold.

5   One of the effects of the elimination is to reduce the purchase discrepancy on the date of acquisition. The effect of the reduction is as follows:

Purchase discrepancy on date of acquisition (Dec. 31, Year 1)	$110,000
Less: Reduction in elimination (a) ($29,000 + $1,500)	30,500
Unamortized difference, Dec. 31, Year 2	$ 79,500

The joint effect of Palm Corporation's use of the equity method of accounting and the annual elimination will be to extinguish $64,500 of the $79,500 difference above through Palm's Investment in Starr Company Common Stock account. The $15,000 balance applicable to Starr's land will not be extinguished, unless the land is sold.

6   The parent company's use of the equity method of accounting results in the following equalities:

Parent company net income = consolidated net income

Parent company retained earnings = consolidated retained earnings

These equalities exist when the equity method of accounting is used *even if there are intercompany profits accounted for in the determination of consolidated net assets.* Intercompany profits are discussed in Chapter 8.

7   Purchase accounting theory requires the exclusion, from consolidated retained earnings, of a subsidiary's retained earnings on date of a business combination

Palm Corporation's use of the equity method of accounting meets this requirement. Palm's ending retained earnings balance in the working paper, which is equal to consolidated retained earnings, includes Palm's $29,500 share of the subsidiary's adjusted net income for the year ended December 31, Year 2, the first year of the parent-subsidiary relationship.

8 Despite the equalities indicated above, **consolidated financial statements** are superior to **parent company financial statements** for the presentation of financial position and operating results of parent and subsidiary companies. The effect of the consolidation process for Palm Corporation and subsidiary is to reclassify Palm's $29,500 share of its subsidiary's adjusted net income to the revenue and expense components of that net income. Similarly, Palm's $505,500 investment in the subsidiary is replaced by the assets and liabilities comprising the subsidiary's net assets. This concept is illustrated below.

Intercompany investment income (Palm's income statement) .... $ 29,500

is replaced with the following components of
Starr's net income adjusted by
the purchase discrepancy amortization:

	Starr's Income Statement	Purchase Discrepancy Amortization	
Revenue	$ 680,000		$680,000
Cost of goods sold	(450,000)	($29,000)	(479,000)
Operating expenses	(80,000)	(1,500)	(81,500)
Income tax expense	(90,000)		(90,000)
Total	$ 60,000	($30,500)	$ 29,500

Investment in Starr Company common stock (Palm's balance sheet) $505,500

is replaced with the following components of Starr's
balance sheet, revalued by the allocation of the
unamortized purchase discrepancy, and by the
unamortized balance of Starr's goodwill:

	Starr's Balance Sheet	Allocation of Unamortized Purchase Discrepancy	
Cost	$ 72,100		$ 72,100
Inventories	115,000		115,000
Other current assets	131,000		131,000
Plant assets (net)	340,000	$61,000	401,000
Patent	16,000	4,000	20,000
Goodwill		14,500	14,500
Intercompany payable	(24,000)		(24,000)
Income tax payable	(20,000)		(20,000)
Other liabilities	(204,100)		(204,100)
Total	$ 426,000	$79,500	$ 505,500

PALM CORPORATION AND SUBSIDIARY
Consolidated Income Statement
For Year Ended December 31, Year 2

Net sales		$1,780,000
Costs and expenses:		
Cost of goods sold	$1,179,000	
Operating expenses	232,500	
Interest expense	49,000	
Income taxes expense	210,000	
Total costs and expenses		1,670,500
Net income		$ 109,500
Earnings per share of common stock (40,000 shares outstanding)		$2.74

PALM CORPORATION AND SUBSIDIARY
Consolidated Statement of Retained Earnings
For Year Ended December 31, Year 2

Retained earnings, beginning of year	$134,000
Add: Net income	109,500
Subtotal	$243,500
Less: Dividends ($0.75 a share)	30,000
Retained earnings, end of year	$213,500

PALM CORPORATION AND SUBSIDIARY
Consolidated Balance Sheet
December 31, Year 2

Assets

Current assets:		
Cash		$ 88,000
Inventories		251,000
Other		219,000
Total current assets		$ 558,000
Plant assets (net)		841,000
Intangible assets:		
Goodwill	$14,500	
Patent	20,000	34,500
Total assets		$1,433,500

Liabilities & Shareholders' Equity

Liabilities:		
Income taxes payable		$ 60,000
Other		395,000
Total liabilities		$ 455,000
Shareholders' equity:		
Common stock, no par	$765,000	
Retained earnings	213,500	978,500
Total liabilities & shareholders' equity		$1,433,500

Consolidated Financial Statements The consolidated income statement, statement of retained earnings, and balance sheet of Palm Corporation and subsidiary for the year ended December 31, Year 2, appear on page 232. The amounts in the consolidated financial statements are taken from the Consolidated column in the working paper on page 229.

Illustration of equity method for wholly owned subsidiary for second year after acquisition

In this section, we continue the Palm Corporation–Starr Company example to demonstrate application of the equity method of accounting for a wholly owned subsidiary for the second year following the date of acquisition. On December 17, Year 3, Starr Company declared a dividend of $40,000, payable January 6, Year 4, to Palm Corporation, the shareholder of record December 28, Year 3. For the year ended December 31, Year 3, Starr reported net income of $90,000.

The purchase discrepancy amortization schedule for Year 3 is shown below:

Purchase discrepancy amortization schedule two years subsequent to date of acquisition		Balances Dec. 31, Year 2 (Page 225)	Amortization for Year 3	Balances Dec. 31, Year 3
Plant assets (net):				
Land..................................		$15,000		$15,000
Building.............................		28,000	$(2,000)	26,000
Machinery..........................		18,000	(2,000)	16,000
Total plant assets...................		$61,000	$(4,000)	$57,000
Patent...............................		4,000	(1,000)	3,000
Goodwill............................		14,500	(500)	14,000
Totals..............................		$79,500	$(5,500)	$74,000

After the posting of appropriate Year 3 journal entries under the equity method of accounting, selected ledger accounts for Palm Corporation appear as shown at the top of page 234.

Developing the Elimination The working paper elimination for December 31, Year 3, is developed in much the same way as the elimination for December 31, Year 2, as shown on pages 234 to 235.

Working Paper for Consolidated Financial Statements The December 31, Year 3, elimination for Palm Corporation and subsidiary are illustrated in the working paper for consolidated financial statements on page 236.

Investment in Starr Company Common Stock

Date	Explanation	Debit	Credit	Balance
12/31/1	Issuance of common stock in business combination	450,000		450,000 dr
12/31/1	Direct out-of-pocket costs of business combination	50,000		500,000 dr
12/20/2	Dividend declared by Starr		24,000	476,000 dr
12/31/2	Net income of Starr	60,000		536,000 dr
12/31/2	Amortization of the purchase discrepancy		30,500	505,500 dr
12/17/3	Dividend declared by Starr		40,000	465,500 dr
12/31/3	Net income of Starr	90,000		555,500 dr
12/31/3	Amortization of the purchase discrepancy		5,500*	550,000 dr

Intercompany Investment Income

Date	Explanation	Debit	Credit	Balance
12/31/2	Net income of Starr		60,000	60,000 cr
12/31/2	Amortization of the purchase discrepancy	30,500		29,500 cr
12/31/2	Closing entry	29,500		-0-
12/31/3	Net income of Starr		90,000	90,000 cr
12/31/3	Amortization of the purchase discrepancy	5,500*		84,500 cr

* Building depreciation ($30,000 ÷ 15) $2,000
Machinery depreciation ($20,000 ÷ 10) 2,000
Patent amortization ($5,000 ÷ 5) 1,000
Goodwill amortization ($15,000 ÷ 30) 500
    Total amortization applicable to Year 3 . . . . $5,500

PALM CORPORATION AND SUBSIDIARY
Working Paper Elimination
December 31, Year 3

(a)	Common Stock — Starr	258,000	
	Retained Earnings — Starr	168,000	
	Intercompany Investment Income — Palm	84,500	
	Plant Assets (net) — Starr ($61,000 − $4,000)	57,000	
	Patent — Starr ($4,000 − $1,000)	3,000	
	Goodwill — Starr ($14,500 − $500)	14,000	
	Cost of Goods Sold — Starr	4,000	
	Operating Expenses — Starr	1,500	
	Investment in Starr Company Common Stock — Palm		550,000
	Dividends — Starr		40,000

To carry out the following:

(1) *Eliminate intercompany investment and equity accounts of subsidiary **at beginning of year**, and subsidiary dividend.*

(2) *Provide for Year 3 depreciation and amortization on the purchase discrepancy allocated to Starr's net assets as follows:*

	Cost of goods sold	Operating expenses
Building depreciation	$1,000	$1,000
Machinery depreciation	2,000	
Patent amortization	1,000	
Goodwill amortization		500
Totals	$4,000	$1,500

(3) *Allocate unamortized purchase discrepancy to appropriate assets of Starr.*

ACCOUNTING FOR OPERATING RESULTS OF PARTIALLY OWNED SUBSIDIARIES

Accounting for the operating results of a partially owned subsidiary requires the computation of the minority interest in net income or net losses of the subsidiary. Thus, the consolidated income statement of a parent company and its partially owned subsidiary includes an expense, minority interest in net income (or loss) of subsidiary.

 Students will recall that in Chapter 5 they were urged to view minority interest as an ownership equity distinct and separate from the equity of the controlling group. While minority interest is usually shown as an expense on the consolidated income statement, it is really a distribution of net income rather than a determinant of net income. The minority interest in the net assets of the subsidiary appears on the consolidated balance sheet between liabilities and shareholders' equity.

Illustration of equity method for partially owned subsidiary for first year after date of acquisition

The Post Corporation-Sage Company consolidated entity described in Chapter 5 (pages 184 to 188) is used in this section to illustrate the equity method of accounting for the operating results of a partially owned subsidiary. Post owns 95% of the 40,000 outstanding common shares of Sage.

Assume that Sage Company on November 24, Year 2, declared a $1 a share dividend, payable December 16, Year 2, to shareholders of record December 1, Year 2, and that Sage reported net income of $90,000 for the year ended December 31, Year 2.

Equity method: wholly owned subsidiary subsequent to date of acquisition

PALM CORPORATION AND SUBSIDIARY
Working Paper for Consolidated Financial Statements
For Year Ended December 31, Year 3

	Palm Corporation	Starr Company	Eliminations Increase (decrease)		Consolidated
Income Statement					
Revenue					
Net sales	1,400,000	750,000			2,150,000
Intercompany investment					
income	84,500		(a)	(84,500)	
Total revenue	1,484,500	750,000		(84,500)	2,150,000
Costs and expenses					
Cost of goods sold	840,500	455,000	(a)	4,000	1,299,500
Operating expenses	369,000	70,000	(a)	1,500	440,500
Income tax expense	115,000	135,000			250,000
Total costs and expenses	1,324,500	660,000		5,500	1,990,000
Net income	160,000	90,000		(90,000)	160,000
Statement of Retained Earnings					
Retained earnings, beginning of year	213,500	168,000	(a)	(168,000)	213,500
Net income	160,000	90,000		(90,000)	160,000
Subtotal	373,500	258,000		(258,000)	373,500
Dividends	30,000	40,000	(a)	(40,000)	30,000
Retained earnings, end of year	343,500	218,000		(218,000)	343,500
Balance Sheet Assets					
Cash	5,500	30,000			35,500
Intercompany receivable (payable)	40,000	(40,000)			
Inventories	160,000	120,000			280,000
Other current assets	65,000	110,000			175,000
Investment in Starr company common stock	550,000		(a)	(550,000)	
Plant assets (net)	523,000	394,000	(a)	57,000	974,000
Patent		12,000	(a)	3,000	15,000
Goodwill			(a)	14,000	14,000
Total assets	1,343,500	626,000		(476,000)	1,493,500
Liabilities & Shareholders' Equity					
Income taxes payable	35,000	40,000			75,000
Other liabilities	200,000	110,000			310,000
Common stock, no par	765,000				765,000
Common stock, no par		258,000	(a)	(258,000)	
Retained earnings	343,500	218,000		(218,000)	343,500
Total liabilities & shareholders' equity	1,343,500	626,000		(476,000)	1,493,500

The journal entries below record the above dividend in Sage's accounting records. The journal entries in the middle of this page are required in the accounting records of Post Corporation.

Partially owned subsidiary's journal entries for declaration and payment of dividend

Year 2			
Nov. 24	Dividends (40,000 × $1)	40,000	
	Dividends Payable ($40,000 × 0.05)		2,000
	Intercompany Dividends Payable		
	($40,000 × 0.95)		38,000
	To record declaration of dividend payable Dec. 16, Year 2,		
	to shareholders of record Dec. 1, Year 2.		
Dec. 16	Dividends Payable	2,000	
	Intercompany Dividends Payable	38,000	
	Cash		40,000
	To record payment of dividend declared Nov. 24, Year 2,		
	to shareholders of record Dec. 1, Year 2.		

Parent company's equity-method journal entries to record operating results of partially owned subsidiary

POST CORPORATION
General Journal

Year 2			
Nov. 24	Intercompany Dividends Receivable	38,000	
	Investment in Sage Company Common Stock		38,000
	To record dividend declared by Sage Company, payable		
	Dec. 16, Year 2, to shareholders of record Dec. 1, Year 2.		
Dec. 16	Cash	38,000	
	Intercompany Dividends Receivable		38,000
	To record receipt of dividend from Sage Company.		
31	Investment in Sage Company Common Stock		
	($90,000 × 0.95)	85,500	
	Intercompany Investment Income		85,500
	To record 95% of net income of Sage Company for the		
	year ended Dec. 31, Year 2.		

As pointed out on page 225, a purchase-type business combination involves a restatement of net asset values of the subsidiary. Sage Company's reported net income of $90,000 does not reflect cost expirations attributable to Sage's restated net asset values, *because the restatements were not recorded in Sage's accounting records*. Consequently, the amortization of the $271,700 purchase discrepancy on the date of acquisition must be accounted for by Post Corporation. Assume, as in Chapter 5 (page 191), that the purchase discrepancy was allocable to Sage's net assets as shown at the top of page 238.

Expanded allocation of
the purchase discrepancy
on date of acquisition

Inventories		$ 24,700
Plant assets (net):		
Land	57,000	
Building (economic life 20 years)	76,000	
Machinery (economic life 5 years)	47,500	180,500
Leasehold (economic life 6 years)		28,500
Goodwill (economic life 40 years)		38,000
Total		$271,700

Post Corporation prepares the following additional journal entry on December 31, Year 2, under the equity method of accounting to reflect the amortization of the purchase discrepancy:

Parent company's equity-
method journal entry to
record amortization of the
purchase discrepancy

Intercompany Investment Income		43,700
Investment in Sage Company Common Stock		43,700
To amortize the December 31, Year 1 purchase discrepancy		
as follows:		
Inventories — to cost of goods sold	$24,700	
Building — depreciation ($76,000 ÷ 20)	3,800	
Machinery — depreciation ($47,500 ÷ 5)	9,500	
Leasehold — amortization ($28,500 ÷ 6)	4,750	
Goodwill — amortization ($38,000 ÷ 40)	950	
Total amortization	$43,700	

After the preceding journal entry is posted, Post Corporation's Investment in Sage Company Common Stock and Intercompany Investment Income ledger accounts appear as follows:

Ledger accounts of parent
company under equity
method of accounting for
partially owned subsidiary

Investment in Sage Company Common Stock

Date	Explanation	Debit	Credit	Balance
12/31/1	Issuance of common stock in			
	business combination	1,140,000		1,140,000 dr
12/31/1	Out-of-pocket costs of business			
	combination	52,250		1,192,250 dr
11/24/2	Dividend declared by Sage		38,000	1,154,250 dr
12/31/2	Net income of Sage	85,500		1,239,750 dr
12/31/2	Amortization of the purchase			
	discrepancy		43,700	1,196,050 dr

Intercompany Investment Income

Date	Explanation	Debit	Credit	Balance
12/31/2	Net income of Sage		85,500	85,500 cr
12/31/2	Amortization of the purchase			
	discrepancy	43,700		41,800 cr

Developing the Eliminations   Post Corporation's use of the equity method of accounting for its investment in Sage Company resulted in a balance in the investment account that is a mixture of two components: (1) the carrying amount of Sage's identifiable net assets, (2) the purchase discrepancy. These components are analyzed below:

POST CORPORATION

Analysis of Investment in Sage Company Common Stock Account

For Year Ended December 31, Year 2

	Carrying amount Calculation	Total	Purchase discrepancy	Total
Beginning balances	$969,000 × 0.95	$920,550	$271,700	$1,192,250
Net income of Sage	90,000 × 0.95	85,500		85,500 } Intercompany
Amortization of the				} investment
purchase discrepancy ...			(43,700)	(43,700) } income $41,800
Dividend declared by Sage .	(40,000 × 0.95)	(38,000)		(38,000)
Ending balances	$1,019,000 × 0.95	$968,050	$228,000	$1,196,050

The minority interest in Sage's net assets is analyzed below. Note that the minority interest is based on the carrying amounts of the net assets of Sage.

POST CORPORATION

Analysis of Minority Interest in Net Assets of Sage Company

For Year Ended December 31, Year 2

	Carrying amount Calculation	Total
Beginning balances	$969,000 × 0.05	$48,450 } Minority interest in
Net income of Sage	90,000 × 0.05	4,500 } net income of
Dividend declared by Sage	(40,000 × 0.05)	(2,000) } subsidiary, $4,500
Ending balances	1,019,000 × 0.05	$50,950

The $1,019,000 ($968,050 + $50,950 = $1,019,000) total of the ending balances of the Carrying Amount columns of the two foregoing analyses agrees with the total shareholders' equity of Sage Company on December 31, Year 2 (see Balance Sheet section of working paper for consolidated financial statements on page 242), as follows:

Subsidiary's shareholders' equity at end of Year 2	Common stock, no par	$ 635,000
	Retained earnings	384,000
	Total shareholders' equity	$1,019,000

The $228,000 total of the ending balance of the purchase discrepancy column of the Investment in Sage account agrees with the December 31,

Year 2, total of the unamortized purchase discrepancy as shown in the schedule below:

Purchase discrepancy amortization schedule one year subsequent to date of acquisition

	Balances Dec. 31, Year 1 (page 238)	Amortization for Year 2 (page 238)	Balances Dec. 31, Year 2
Inventories	$ 24,700	$(24,700)	
Plant assets (net):			
Land	$ 57,000		$ 57,000
Building	76,000	$ (3,800)	72,200
Machinery	47,500	(9,500)	38,000
Total plant assets	$180,500	$(13,300)	$167,200
Leasehold	28,500	(4,750}	23,750
Goodwill	38,000	(950)	37,050
Totals	$271,700	$(43,700)	$228,000

Assuming that Sage Company allocates machinery depreciation and leasehold amortization entirely to cost of goods sold, building depreciation 50% each to cost of goods sold and operating expenses, and goodwill amortization entirely to operating expenses, the working paper eliminations for Post Corporation and subsidiary on December 31, Year 2, are as shown on page 241.

Working Paper for Consolidated Financial Statements   The working paper for consolidated financial statements for Post Corporation and subsidiary for the year ended December 31, Year 2, is shown on page 242.

The following aspects of the working paper for consolidated financial statements of Post Corporation and subsidiary should be emphasized:

1 Elimination (*a*) cancels Sage's retained earnings *at the beginning of the year*. This step is essential for the preparation of all three basic consolidating financial statements.

2 The parent company's use of the equity method of accounting results in the following equalities:

Parent company net income = consolidated net income
Parent company retained earnings = consolidated retained earnings

These equalities exist in the equity method of accounting even if there are intercompany profits eliminated for the determination of consolidated net assets. Intercompany profits are discussed in Chapter 8.

3 One of the effects of elimination (*a*) is to reduce the purchase discrepancy on the date of acquisition. The effect of the reduction is as follows:

Purchase discrepancy on date of acquisition
(Dec. 31, Year 1) $271,700
  Less: Reduction in elimination (a) $40,850 + $2,850) 43,700
  Unamortized balance, Dec. 31, Year 2 . . . . $228,000

Working paper eliminations
for partially owned
purchased subsidiary
subsequent to date of
acquisition

POST CORPORATION AND SUBSIDIARY
Working Paper Eliminations
December 31, Year 2

(a)	Common Stock — Sage	635,000
	Retained Earnings — Sage	334,000
	Intercompany Investment Income — Post	41,800
	Plant Assets (net) — Sage ($180,500 − $13,300)	167,200
	Leasehold — Sage ($28,500 − $4,750)	23,750
	Goodwill — Sage ($38,000 − $950)	37,050
	Cost of Goods Sold — Sage	40,850
	Operating Expenses — Sage	2,850
	Investment in Sage Company Common Stock — Post ..	1,196,050
	Dividends — Sage	40,000
	Minority Interest in Net Assets of Subsidiary	
	($48,450 − $2,000)	46,450

To carry out the following:

(1) Eliminate intercompany investment and equity accounts
of subsidiary **at beginning of year**, and subsidiary
dividends.

(2) Provide for Year 2 depreciation and amortization on the
purchase discrepancy allocated to Sage's identifiable net
assets as follows:

	Cost of goods sold	Operating expenses
Inventories sold	$24,700	
Building depreciation	1,900	$1,900
Machinery depreciation	9,500	
Leasehold amortization	4,750	
Goodwill amortization		950
Totals	$40,850	$2,850

(3) Allocate the unamortized purchase discrepancy to
appropriate assets.

(4) Establish minority interest in net assets of subsidiary at
beginning of year ($48,450), less minority share of
dividends declared by subsidiary during year
($40,000 × 0.05 = $2,000).

(b)	Minority Interest in Net Income of Subsidiary	4,500
	Minority Interest in Net Assets of Subsidiary	4,500

To establish minority interest in subsidiary's net income for
Year 2 as follows:

Net income of subsidiary	$90,000
Minority share: $90,000 × 0.05	$ 4,500

Equity method: Partially owned subsidiary subsequent to date of acquisition

POST CORPORATION AND SUBSIDIARY
Working Paper for Consolidated Financial Statements
For Year Ended December 31, Year 2

3 tiered format

	Post Corporation	Sage Company	Eliminations increase (decrease)		Consolidated
Income Statement					
Revenue					
Net sales	5,611,000	1,089,000			6,700,000
Intercompany investment income	41,800		(a)	(41,800)	
Total revenue	5,652,800	1,089,000		(41,800)	6,700,000
Costs and expenses					
Cost of goods sold	3,925,000	700,000	(a)	40,850	4,665,850
Operating expenses	556,000	129,000	(a)	2,850	687,850
Interest and income taxes expense	710,000	170,000			880,000
Minority interest in net income of subsidiary			(b)	4,500	4,500
Total costs and expenses	5,191,000	999,000		48,200 †	6,238,200
Net Income	461,800	90,000		(90,000)	461,800
Statement of Retained Earnings					
Retained earnings, beginning of year	1,050,000	334,000	(a)	(334,000)	1,050,000
Net Income	461,800	90,000		(90,000)	461,800
Subtotal	1,511,800	424,000		(424,000)	1,511,800
Dividends	158,550	40,000	(a)	(40,000)	158,550
Retained earnings, end of year	1,353,250	384,000		(384,000)	1,353,250
Balance Sheet					
Assets					
Inventories	861,000	439,000			1,300,000
Other current assets	639,000	371,000			1,010,000
Investment in Sage Company common stock	1,196,050		(a)	(1,196,050)	
Plant assets (net)	3,600,000	1,150,000	(a)	167,200	4,917,200
Leasehold			(a)	23,750	23,750
Goodwill	95,000		(a)	37,050	132,050
Total assets	6,391,050	1,960,000		(968,050)	7,383,000
Liabilities & Shareholders' Equity					
Liabilities	2,420,550	941,000			3,361,550
Minority interest in net assets of subsidiary			(a)	46,450	
			(b)	4,500	50,950
Common stock, no par	2,617,250				2,617,250
Common stock, no par		635,000	(a)	(635,000)	
Retained earnings	1,353,250	384,000		(384,000)	1,353,250
Total liabilities & shareholders' equity	6,391,050	1,960,000		(968,050)	7,383,000

†An increase in total costs and expenses and a decrease in net income.

The joint effect of Post's use of the equity method of accounting and the annual eliminations will be to extinguish $171,000 of the remaining $228,000 difference through Post's Investment in Sage Company Common Stock account. The $57,000 balance applicable to Sage's land will not be extinguished, unless the land is sold.

4 The minority interest in net assets of subsidiary on December 31, Year 2, may be verified as follows:

Sage Company's total shareholders' equity, Dec. 31, Year 2 . . . . $1,019,000

Minority interest in net assets of subsidiary ($1,019,000 × 0.05) . . . $ 50,950

5 The minority interest in net income of subsidiary is recognized in elimination (*b*) in the amount of $4,500 (5% of the net income of Sage Company) as an increase in minority interest in net assets of subsidiary and a decrease in the amount of consolidated net income.

Consolidated Financial Statements   The consolidated income statement, statement of retained earnings, and balance sheet of Post Corporation and subsidiary for the year ended December 31, Year 2, appear on page 244. The amounts in the consolidated financial statements are taken from the Consolidated column in the working paper on page 242.

Illustration of equity method for partially owned subsidiary for second year after acquisition

In this section, we continue the Post Corporation–Sage Company example to demonstrate application of the equity method of accounting for a partially owned subsidiary for the second year following acquisition. On November 22, Year 3, Sage Company declared a dividend of $50,000, payable December 17, Year 3, to shareholders of record December 1, Year 3. For the year ended December 31, Year 3, Sage reported net income of $105,000. Post's share of the dividend was $47,500 ($50,000 × 0.95 = $47,500), and Post's share of Sage's reported net income was $99,750 ($105,000 × 0.95 = $99,750).

The purchase discrepancy amortization schedule for Year 3 is shown below:

Purchase discrepancy amortization schedule two years subsequent to date of acquisition		Balances Dec. 31, Year 2 (Page 240)	Amortization for Year 3	Balances Dec. 31, Year 3
Plant assets (net):				
Land		$ 57,000		$ 57,000
Building		72,200	$ (3,800)	68,400
Machinery		38,000	(9,500)	28,500
Total plant assets		$167,200	$(13,300)	$153,900
Leasehold		23,750	(4,750)	19,000
Goodwill		37,050	(950)	36,100
Totals		$228,000	$(19,000)	$209,000

POST CORPORATION AND SUBSIDIARY
Consolidated Income Statement
For Year Ended December 31, Year 2

Net sales		$6,700,000
Costs and expenses:		
Cost of goods sold	4,665,850	
Operating expenses	687,850	
Interest and income taxes expense	880,000	
Minority interest in net income of subsidiary	4,500	
Total costs and expenses		6,238,200
Net income		$ 461,800
Earnings per share of common stock (1,057,000 shares outstanding)		$0.44

POST CORPORATION AND SUBSIDIARY
Consolidated Statement of Retained Earnings
For Year Ended December 31, Year 2

Retained earnings, beginning of year	$1,050,000
Add: Net income	461,800
Subtotal	$1,511,800
Less: Dividends ($0.15 a share)	158,550
Retained earnings, end of year	$1,353,250

POST CORPORATION AND SUBSIDIARY
Consolidated Balance Sheet
December 31, Year 2

Assets

Current assets:		
Inventories		$1,300,000
Other		1,010,000
Total current assets		$2,310,000
Plant assets (net)		4,917,200
Intangible assets:		
Goodwill	$132,050	
Leasehold	23,750	
Total assets		155,800
		$7,383,000

Liabilities & Shareholders' Equity

Liabilities		$3,361,550
Minority interest in net assets of subsidiary		50,950
Shareholders' equity:		
Common stock, no par	$2,617,250	
Retained earnings	1,353,250	
		3,970,500
Total liabilities & shareholders' equity		$7,383,000

After the posting of appropriate Year 3 journal entries under the equity method of accounting, selected ledger accounts for Post Corporation appear as shown below.

Investment in Sage Company Common Stock

Date	Explanation	Debit	Credit	Balance
12/31/1	Issuance of common stock in business combination	1,140,000		1,140,000 dr
12/31/1	Direct out-of-pocket costs of business combination	52,250		1,192,250 dr
11/24/2	Dividend declared by Sage		38,000	1,154,250 dr
12/31/2	Net income of Sage	85,500		1,239,750 dr
12/31/2	Amortization of the purchase discrepancy		43,700	1,196,050 dr
11/22/3	Dividend declared by Sage		47,500	1,148,550 dr
12/31/3	Net income of Sage	99,750		1,248,300 dr
12/31/3	Amortization of the purchase discrepancy		19,000*	1,229,300 dr

Intercompany Investment Income

Date	Explanation	Debit	Credit	Balance
12/31/2	Net income of Sage		85,500	85,500 cr
12/31/2	Amortization of the purchase discrepancy	43,700		41,800 cr
12/31/2	Closing entry	41,800		-0-
12/31/3	Net income of Sage		99,750	99,750 cr
12/31/3	Amortization of the purchase discrepancy	19,000*		80,750 cr

*Building depreciation ($76,000 ÷ 20)	$ 3,800
Machinery depreciation ($47,500 ÷ 5)	9,500
Leasehold amortization ($28,500 ÷ 6)	4,750
Goodwill amortization ($38,000 ÷ 40)	950
Total	$19,000

Developing the Eliminations The working paper eliminations for December 31, Year 3, are developed in much the same way as for the eliminations for December 31, Year 2, as illustrated on page 246.

Working Paper for Consolidated Financial Statements The December 31, Year 3, eliminations for Post Corporation and subsidiary are illustrated in the working paper for consolidated financial statements on page 247.

Working paper eliminations for partially owned subsidiary subsequent to date of acquisition

Handwritten margin notes:
- ① This is s/s at begining of current period
- ② we eliminate the equity pick up
- ③ Ju record allocation of purchase descrepency + amortization & depreciation
- ④ we get rid of Investment account - balance as of end of period
- ⑤ get rid of dividends
- ⑥ we record minority interest, There's a formula
- ⑦ see (6) we record minority interest of net income.
- These seven piece of info are carried over and placed in W/S.

POST CORPORATION AND SUBSIDIARY
Working Paper Eliminations
December 31, Year 3

(a)	Common Stock — Sage	635,000	
	Retained Earnings — Sage	384,000	
	Intercompany Investment Income — Post	80,750	
	Plant Assets (net) — Sage ($167,200 – $13,300)	153,900	
	Leasehold — Sage ($23,750 – $4,750)	19,000	
	Goodwill — Sage ($37,050 – $950)	36,100	
	Cost of Goods Sold — Sage	16,150	
	Operating Expenses — Sage	2,850	

Investment in Sage Company Common Stock — Post . .	1,229,300
Dividends — Sage	50,000
Minority Interest in Net Assets of Subsidiary	
($50,950 – $2,500)	48,450

To carry out the following:

(1) Eliminate intercompany investment and equity accounts of subsidiary **at beginning of year**, and subsidiary dividend.

(2) Provide for Year 3 depreciation and amortization on the purchase discrepancy allocated to Sage's identifiable net assets as follows:

	Cost of goods sold	Operating expenses
Building depreciation	1,900	$1,900
Machinery depreciation	9,500	
Leasehold amortization	4,750	
Goodwill amortization		950
Totals	$16,150	$2,850

(3) Allocate the unamortized purchase discrepancy to appropriate assets.

(4) Establish minority interest in net assets of subsidiary at beginning of year ($50,950), less minority share of dividends declared by subsidiary during year ($50,000 × 0.05 = $2,500).

(b)	Minority Interest in Net Income of Subsidiary	5,250	
	Minority Interest in Net Assets of Subsidiary		5,250.

To establish minority interest in subsidiary's net income for Year 3 as follows:

Net income of subsidiary	$105,000
Minority share: $105,000 × 0.05	$ 5,250

POST CORPORATION AND SUBSIDIARY
Working Paper for Consolidated Financial Statements
For Year Ended December 31, Year 3

	Post Corporation	Sage Company	Eliminations increase (decrease)		Consolidated
Income Statement					
Revenue					
Net sales	5,530,000	1,100,000			6,630,000
Intercompany investment income	80,750		(a)	(80,750)	
Total revenue	5,610,750	1,100,000		(80,750)	6,630,000
Costs and expenses					
Cost of goods sold	3,817,000	730,000	(a)	16,150	4,563,150
Operating expenses	851,150	120,000	(a)	2,850	974,000
Interest and income tax expense	590,000	145,000			735,000
Minority interest in net income of subsidiary			(b)	5,250	5,250
Total costs and expenses	5,258,150	995,000		24,250	6,277,400
Net Income	352,600	105,000		(105,000)	352,600
Statement of Retained Earnings					
Retained earnings, beginning of year	1,353,250	384,000	(a)	(384,000)	1,353,250
Net Income	352,600	105,000		(105,000)	352,600
Subtotal	1,705,850	489,000		(489,000)	1,705,850
Dividends	158,550	50,000	(a)	(50,000)	158,550
Retained earnings, end of year	1,547,300	439,000		(439,000)	1,547,300
Balance Sheet					
Assets					
Inventories	900,000	470,000			1,370,000
Other current assets	243,250	190,000			433,250
Investment in Sage Company common stock	1,229,300		(a)	(1,229,300)	
Plant assets (net)	4,200,000	1,414,000	(a)	153,900	5,767,900
Leasehold			(a)	19,000	19,000
Goodwill	92,000		(a)	36,100	128,100
Total assets	6,664,550	2,074,000		(1,020,300)	7,718,250
Liabilities & Shareholders' Equity					
Liabilities	2,500,000	1,000,000			3,500,000
Minority interest in net assets of subsidiary			(a)	48,450	
			(b)	5,250	53,700
Common stock, no par	2,617,250				2,617,250
Common stock, no par		635,000	(a)	(635,000)	
Retained earnings	1,547,300	439,000		(439,000)	1,547,300
Total liabilities & shareholders' equity	6,664,550	2,074,000		(1,020,300)	7,718,250

The changes in minority interest during Year 3, and the December 31, Year 3, balance of the minority interest in net assets of subsidiary may be verified as follows:

	Sage Company shareholders' equity	Minority shareholders' ownership percentage (0.05)
Capital stock	$ 635,000	$31,750
Retained earnings Jan. 1, Year 3	384,000	19,200
Balance Jan. 1, Year 3	$1,019,000	$50,950
Net Income, Year 3	105,000	5,250
Subtotal	$1,124,000	$56,200
Dividends	50,000	2,500
Balance Dec. 31, Year 3	$1,074,000	$53,700

When the parent company uses the equity method, the unamortized purchase discrepancy may be verified as follows:

Investment in Sage Company common stock —
Dec. 31, Year 3 . . . . $1,229,300
Shareholders' equity Sage — Dec. 31, Year 3 . . . . $1,074,000
Post's ownership percentage 0.95   1,020,300
Unamortized purchase discrepancy — Dec. 31, Year 3 . . . . . $ 209,000

Concluding comments on equity method of accounting

In today's accounting environment, the equity method of accounting for a subsidiary's operations is preferable to the cost method (illustrated in Chapter 7) for the following reasons:

1 The equity method emphasizes *economic substance* of the parent company-subsidiary relationship, while the cost method emphasizes *legal form*. More and more, modern accounting stresses substance over form.

2 The equity method permits the use of *parent company journal entries* to reflect many items that must be included in *consolidation eliminations* in the cost method (see Chapter 7). Formal journal entries in the accounting records provide a better record than do working paper eliminations.

3 The equity method facilitates issuance of non-consolidated financial statements for the parent company. Generally accepted accounting principles require the equity method of accounting for unconsolidated subsidiaries in separate parent-company financial statements in many situations.[1]

4 Even when intercompany profits (discussed in Chapter 8) exist in assets or liabilities to be consolidated, the parent company's net income and combined retained

1 See Chapter 7, pages 282–284 for a discussion of reporting requirements for unconsolidated subsidiaries.

earnings account balances are identical in the equity method to the related consolidated amounts. Thus, the equity method provides a useful self-checking technique

REVIEW QUESTIONS

1 The equity method of accounting produces parent company net income that equals consolidated net income. The equity method also results in parent company retained earnings of the same amount as consolidated retained earnings. Why, then, are consolidated financial statements considered superior to the separate financial statements of the parent company when the parent company uses the equity method? Explain.

2 Plumstead Corporation's 92%-owned subsidiary declared a dividend of $3 a share on its 50,000 outstanding shares of common stock. How would Plumstead record this dividend under
   a The equity method of accounting?
   b The cost method of accounting?

3 Discuss some of the advantages that result from the use of the equity method, rather than the cost method, of accounting for a subsidiary's operating results.

4 Minority interest appears as an expense on a consolidated income statement. Is this really an expense? In which company's ledger, parent or subsidiary, would you expect to find this account? Explain.

5 If the *CICA Handbook* requires an investment in a subsidiary company to be accounted for by the equity method, is it possible for a parent company to account for that investment by the cost method without violating the Handbook's pronouncements? Explain.

6 A consolidated retained earnings statement shows the balance at the beginning of the year, the net income for the year, the dividends declared during the year, and the balance at the end of the year. Are dividends declared by the subsidiary during the year, included in the total dividends that appear in the consolidated retained earnings statement? Explain.

7 A purchase discrepancy allocated to revalue the land of a subsidiary company on acquisition date will always appear on subsequent consolidated balance sheets. Do you agree? Explain.

8 Purchase accounting theory requires the exclusion of a subsidiary's retained earnings on the date of acquisition from consolidated retained earnings. Would this be true if the pooling of interest theory was used? Explain.

EXERCISES

Ex. 6-1   Select the best answer for each of the following multiple-choice questions:

1 Which of the following ledger accounts is used in both the equity method and the cost method of accounting for the operating results of a subsidiary?
   a Intercompany Investment Income
   b Intercompany Dividends Receivable
   c Intercompany Dividends Revenue
   d Minority Interest in Net Income of Subsidiary

2 Dividends declared by a subsidiary that are payable to minority shareholders of the subsidiary are credited by the subsidiary to:

a Minority interest in net income of subsidiary

b Minority interest in net assets of subsidiary

c Dividends payable

d Intercompany dividends payable

3 Plover Corporation accounts for its 80%-owned subsidiary, Swallow Company, under the equity method of accounting. For the fiscal year ended March 31, Year 5, Swallow reported net income of $100,000, but declared no dividends. Amortization of the purchase discrepancy for the year ended March 31, Year 5, totalled $40,000. Plover's closing entry for the year ended March 31, Year 5, should include:

a A credit of $40,000 to Intercompany Investment Income

b A debit of $60,000 to Retained Earnings

c A debit of $60,000 to Intercompany Investment Income

d A credit of $40,000 to Retained Earnings

Ex. 6-2 The working paper elimination (in journal entry form) for Purling Corporation and Subsidiary on October 31, Year 6, the date of the business combination, was:

PURLING CORPORATION AND SUBSIDIARY

Working Paper Elimination

October 31, Year 6

(a)	Common Stock — Stagg	250,000	
	Retained Earnings — Stagg	200,000	
	Plant Assets — Stagg (depreciable)	250,000	
	Goodwill — Stagg	60,000	
	Investment in Stagg Company Common Stock —		
	Purling		760,000

To eliminate intercompany investment, and equity accounts of subsidiary on date of business combination; and to allocate the purchase discrepancy to identifiable assets acquired, with remainder to goodwill.

During the year ended October 31, Year 7, Stagg Company reported net income of $50,000, and on October 31, Year 7, Stagg declared dividends of $20,000, payable November 16, Year 7. Stagg depreciates plant assets by the straight-line method at a 10% rate and amortizes intangible assets by the straight-line method over a 40-year life. Stagg includes plant assets depreciation in cost of goods sold and goodwill amortization in operating expenses.

a Prepare Purling Corporation's October 31, Year 7, journal entries to record the operating results and dividend of Stagg Company under the equity method of accounting. Omit explanations.

b Prepare the October 31, Year 7, working paper elimination for Purling Corporation and subsidiary, in journal entry form. Omit explanation.

Ex. 6-3 Pinson Corporation owns a 90% interest in a purchased subsidiary, Solomon Company, which is accounted for by the equity method. During Year 5, Pinson had income, exclusive of intercompany investment income, of $145,000, and Solomon had net income of $120,000. Solomon declared and paid a $40,000 dividend during Year 5. There were no differences between the current fair values and carrying amounts of Solomon's identifiable net assets on the date of the business combination.

Compute the consolidated net income of Pinson Corporation and subsidiary for Year 5.

Ex. 6-4 On March 31, Year 1, Pitt Corporation acquired for cash 90% of the outstanding common stock of Scow Company. The $100,000 excess of Pitt's investment over 90% of the current fair value (and carrying amount) of Scow's identifiable net assets was allocable to goodwill having an estimated economic life of 25 years on March 31, Year 1. For the fiscal year ended March 31, Year 2, Scow reported a net loss of $130,000 and declared no dividends.

What amount should Pitt Corporation record in its Intercompany Investment Income account under the equity method of accounting for the fiscal year ended March 31, Year 2? Show computations.

Ex. 6-5 Following are all details of three ledger accounts of a parent company that uses the equity method of accounting for its subsidiary's operating results:

Intercompany Dividends Receivable

Aug. 16, Year 8	36,000	Aug. 27, Year 8	36,000

Investment in Subsidiary Common Stock

Sept. 1, Year 7	630,000	Aug. 16, Year 8	36,000
Aug. 31, Year 8	72,000	Aug. 31, Year 8	5,000

Intercompany Investment Income

Aug. 31, Year 8	5,000	Aug. 31, Year 8	72,000

What is the most logical explanation for each of the transactions recorded in the above ledger accounts?

Ex. 6-6 On January 2, Year 6, Parr Corporation acquired 75% of the outstanding common stock of Spade Company for $345,000 cash, including out-of-pocket costs. The investment is accounted for by the equity method. On that date, Spade's identifiable net assets (carrying amount and current fair value) were $300,000. Parr has determined that the excess of the cost of its investment in Spade's identifiable net assets has an indeterminant economic life.

Spade's net income for the year ended December 31, Year 6, was $160,000. During Year 6, Parr received $60,000 cash dividends from Spade. There were no other transactions between the two enterprises.

Compute the balance of Parr Corporation's Investment in Spade Company Common Stock account (after adjustment) on December 31, Year 6.

Ex. 6-7 Seal Company, wholly owned subsidiary of Presto Corporation, reported net income of $90,000 and paid dividends of $35,000 for the first year following the business combination. Goodwill computed in accordance with purchase accounting amounted to $64,000 on the date of the business combination, and had an estimated economic life of 20 years. Exclusive of Seal's operations, Presto had net income of $180,000 for the first year following the business combination.

Compute the net income of Presto Corporation under (**a**) the equity method, and (**b**) the cost method of accounting for the operating results of Seal Company.

Ex. 6-8 The balance of Putnam Corporation's Investment in Salisbury Company Common Stock ledger account on September 30, Year 6, was $265,000. The 20% minority interest in net assets of subsidiary in the consolidated balance sheet of Putnam

Corporation and subsidiary on September 30, Year 6, was $60,000. For the fiscal year ended September 30, Year 7, Salisbury reported net income of $50,000 and declared and paid dividends of $18,750. Amortization for the fiscal year ended September 30, Year 7, in the consolidated income statement, was as follows:

Differences between current fair values and carrying amounts of
   Salisbury's identifiable net assets on date of business combination $4,500
Goodwill   1,000

Compute the following:

a Balance of Putnam's Investment in Salisbury Company Common Stock ledger account on September 30, Year 7
b Balance of Putnam's Intercompany Investment Income ledger account on September 30, Year 7, before closing entries
c Amount of the unamortized purchase discrepancy on September 30, Year 7
d Minority interest in net income of subsidiary in consolidated income statement of Putnam Corporation and subsidiary for year ended September 30, Year 7
e Minority interest in net assets of subsidiary in consolidated balance sheet of Putnam Corporation and subsidiary on September 30, Year 7

CASES

Case 6-1   The most common method of accounting for the operating results of subsidiaries is the equity method.

Instructions   Answer the questions shown below with respect to the equity method of accounting:
a Under what circumstances should the equity method of accounting be applied?
b At what amount should the initial investment be recorded, and what events subsequent to the initial investment (if any) would change this amount?
c How is investment income recognized under the equity method of accounting, and how is the amount determined?

Case 6-2   Financial accounting usually emphasizes the economic substance of events even though the legal form may differ and suggest different treatment. For example, under the accrual basis of accounting, expenses are recognized when incurred (substance) rather than when cash is paid (form).
   Although the feature of substance over form exists in most generally accepted accounting principles and practices, there are times when form prevails over substance.

Instructions   For each of the following topics, discuss the underlying theory in terms of both substance and form, that is, substance over form and possibly form over substance. Each topic should be discussed independently.
a Consolidated financial statements
b Equity method of accounting for investments in common stock of subsidiaries and influenced investees

Case 6-3   You have recently been hired for the position of controller of Precision Corporation, a manufacturing enterprise that has begun a program of expansion through business combinations. On February 1, Year 4, two weeks prior to your controllership appointment, Precision completed the acquisition of 85% of the outstanding common shares of Sloan Company for $255,000 cash, including out-of-pocket costs. You are engaged in a discussion with Precision's chief accountant concerning the appropriate accounting method for Precision's interest in Sloan Company's operating results. The chief accountant strongly supports the cost method of accounting, offering the following arguments:

1 The cost method recognizes that Precision and Sloan are separate legal entities.
2 The existence of a minority interest in Sloan requires emphasis on the legal separateness of the two companies.
3 A parent company recognizes revenue under the cost method only when the subsidiary declares dividends. Such dividend revenue is consistent with the revenue realization principle of financial accounting. The Intercompany Investment Income account recorded in the equity method of accounting does not fit the definition of realized revenue.
4 Use of the equity method of accounting might result in Precision's declaring dividends to its shareholders out of "paper" retained earnings that belong to Sloan.
5 The cost method is consistent with other aspects of historical-cost accounting, because working paper eliminations, rather than journal entries in ledger accounts, are used to recognize amortization of differences between current fair values and carrying amounts of Sloan's identifiable net assets.

Instructions Prepare a rebuttal to each of the chief accountant's arguments.

PROBLEMS

6-1 The working paper elimination for Pakistan Corporation and subsidiary on March 31, Year 7, the date of the purchase-type business combination, was as follows:

PAKISTAN CORPORATION AND SUBSIDIARY
Working Paper Elimination
March 31, Year 7

(a)	Common Stock	150,000	
	Retained Earnings — Sikkim	150,000	
	Inventories — Sikkim (fifo cost)	20,000	
	Land — Sikkim	50,000	
	Other Plant Assets — Sikkim (economic life 10 years)	80,000	
	Goodwill — Sikkim (economic life 40 years)	40,000	
	Investment in Sikkim Company Common Stock — Pakistan		490,000

To eliminate intercompany investment and equity accounts of subsidiary on date of business combination; and to allocate excess of cost over carrying amounts to identifiable assets acquired, with remainder to goodwill.

For the fiscal year ended March 31, Year 8, Sikkim Company reported net income of $60,000. Sikkim declared a cash dividend of $20,000 on March 1, Year 8, and paid the dividend on March 15, Year 8. (Sikkim had not declared or paid dividends during the year ended March 31, Year 7.) Sikkim uses the straight-line method for depreciation expense and amortization expense, both of which are included in operating expenses.

Instructions
a Prepare journal entries in the accounting records of Pakistan Corporation to record the operating results of Sikkim Company for the year ended March 31, Year 8, under the equity method of accounting.
b Prepare three-column ledger accounts for Pakistan Corporation's Investment in Sikkim Company Common Stock and Intercompany Investment Income accounts, and post the journal entries in a.

c Prepare a working paper elimination for Pakistan Corporation and subsidiary on March 31, Year 8, in journal entry form.

 6-2 Placer Corporation's October 31, Year 4, journal entries to record the operations of its 80%-owned purchased subsidiary, Sybarite Company, during the first fiscal year following the business combination, were as follows:

PLACER CORPORATION

Journal Entries

October 31, Year 4

Intercompany Dividends Receivable	16,000	
Investment in Sybarite Company Common Stock		16,000
To record $1 a share dividend declared by Sybarite Company,		
payable Nov. 7, Year 4, to shareholders of record Oct. 31,		
Year 4.		
Investment in Sybarite Company Common Stock	40,000	
Intercompany Investment Income		40,000
To record 80% of Sybarite Company's reported net income for		
the year ended Oct. 31, Year 4.		
Intercompany Investment Income	29,000	
Investment in Sybarite Company Common Stock		29,000

To amortize the purchase discrepancy on Oct. 31, Year 3:

Inventories — to cost of goods sold	$20,000
Plant assets — depreciation ($80,000 ÷ 10) . . .	8,000
Goodwill — (20,000 ÷ 20 years)	1,000
Total	$29,000

Other information:

(1) Placer acquired 16,000 shares of Sybarite's common stock on October 31, Year 3, at a total cost, including out-of-pocket costs, of $240,000. The minority interest in net assets of subsidiary on that date was $30,000.

(2) On October 31, Year 4, the balances of Sybarite's Common Stock and Retained Earnings ledger accounts were in the ratio of 4:5 respectively.

(3) Sybarite allocates depreciation expense 75% to cost of goods sold and 25% to operating expenses, and goodwill amortization to operating expenses.

Instructions

a Calculate the purchase discrepancy and its allocation on Oct. 31, Year 3.

b Prepare working paper eliminations for Placer Corporation and subsidiary on October 31, Year 4. (Suggestion: Use T accounts to determine balances in key accounts of the parent company and subsidiary.)

6-3 On January 2, Year 6, Pilot Corporation made the following investments:

(1) Acquired for cash 80% of the outstanding common stock of Stewart Company at $70 a share. The shareholders' equity of Stewart on January 2, Year 6, consisted of the following:

Common stock, $50 par	$50,000
Retained earnings	20,000
Total shareholders' equity	$70,000

(2) Acquired for cash 70% of the outstanding common stock of Skate Company at $40 a share. The shareholders' equity of Skate on January 2, Year 6, consisted of the following:

Common stock, $50 par	$ 60,000
Contributed surplus	20,000
Retained earnings	40,000
Total shareholders' equity	$120,000

Out-of-pocket costs of the two business combinations may be disregarded. An analysis of the retained earnings of each company for Year 6 follows:

	Pilot Corporation	Stewart Company	Skate Company
Balances, beginning of year	$240,000	$20,000	$40,000
Net income (loss)	104,600*	36,000	(12,000)
Cash dividends declared and paid, Dec. 31,			
Year 6	(40,000)	(16,000)	(9,000)
Balances, end of year	$304,600*	$40,000	$19,000

* Before giving effect to journal entries in a(2), below.

Instructions
a Prepare journal entries for Pilot Corporation to record the following for Year 6:
   (1) Investments in subsidiaries' common stock
   (2) Parent company's share of subsidiaries' net income or net loss
   (3) Parent company's share of subsidiaries' dividends declared (Do not prepare journal entries for receipt of cash.)
b Compute the amount of minority interest in each subsidiary's net assets on December 31, Year 6.
c Compute the amount that should be reported as consolidated retained earnings of Pilot Corporation and subsidiaries on December 31, Year 6. Show supporting computations.

6-4 Analyses of the Investment in State Company Common Stock ledger account of Pablo Corporation (State's parent company), the minority interest in net assets of State Company, and the purchase discrepancy allocated to State Company's identifiable net assets on May 31, Year 3, the date of the Pablo-State business combination, are as follows for the fiscal year ended May 31, Year 4:

PABLO CORPORATION
Analysis of Investment in State Company Common Stock Account
For Year Ended May 31, Year 4

	Carrying amount	Purchase Discrepancy	Total
Beginning balances	$400,000	$130,000	$530,000
Net income of State	80,000		80,000 } Intercompany
Amortization of the			investment
purchase discrepancy		(9,200)	(9,200) income, $70,800
Dividends declared by State .	(30,000)		(30,000)
Ending balances	$450,000	$120,800	$570,800

PABLO CORPORATION

Analysis of Minority Interest in Net Assets of State Company

For Year Ended May 31, Year 4

	Carrying amount
Beginning balances	$100,000
Minority interest in net income of subsidiary	20,000
Dividends declared by State	(7,500)
Ending balances	$112,500

PABLO CORPORATION

Purchase Discrepancy Amortization Schedule

For Year Ended May 31, Year 4

	Balances May 31, Year 3	Amortization for Year 4	Balances May 31, Year 4
Plant assets (net):			
Land	31,200		31,200
Buildings	28,800	3,200	25,600
Machinery	20,000	4,000	16,000
Total plant assets	80,000	7,200	72,800
Goodwill	50,000	2,000	48,000
Totals	130,000	9,200	120,800

State Company had 10,000 shares of no par value common stock outstanding on May 31, Year 4, that had been issued for $5 a share when State was organized. State includes depreciation expense on plant assets in cost of goods sold. Goodwill amortization is to be included in operating expenses on the consolidated income statement. Dividends were declared by State on May 31, Year 4.

Instructions

a Reconstruct Pablo Corporation's journal entries for the year ended May 31, Year 4, to record the operating results of State Company under the equity method of accounting.

b Prepare working paper eliminations for Pablo Corporation and subsidiary, in journal entry form, on May 31, Year 4.

6-5 Parch Corporation acquired 82% of Steppe Company's outstanding common stock for $328,000 cash on March 31, Year 8. Out-of-pocket costs of the business combination may be ignored. Steppe's shareholders' equity accounts on March 31, Year 8, were as follows:

Common stock, no par (25,000 shares)	$125,000
Retained earnings	135,000
Total shareholders' equity	$260,000

All of Steppe's identifiable net assets were fairly valued at their March 31, Year 8, carrying amounts except for the following:

	Carrying amounts	Current fair values
Land	$100,000	$120,000
Building (net) (10-year economic life)	200,000	250,000
Patent (net) (8-year economic life)	60,000	80,000

Any goodwill resulting from the business combination is amortized over the maximum period of 40 years. Steppe uses the straight-line method for depreciation and amortization. Steppe includes depreciation expense in cost of goods sold and amortization expense in operating expenses.

During the year ended March 31, Year 9, Steppe reported net income of $1.20 a share and declared and paid no dividends. There were no intercompany transactions between Parch and Steppe.

Instructions

a Prepare Parch Corporation's journal entries to record Steppe Company's operating results for the fiscal year ended March 31, Year 9, under the equity method of accounting.

b Prepare the working paper eliminations for Parch Corporation and subsidiary on March 31, Year 9.

6-6 Pavich Corporation acquired 75% of the outstanding common stock of Sisler Company on October 1, Year 6, for $547,500, including direct out-of-pocket costs. Sisler's shareholders' equity on October 1, Year 6, was as follows:

Common stock	$350,000
Retained earnings	200,000
Total shareholders' equity	$550,000

Current fair values of Sisler's identifiable net assets exceeded their carrying amounts as follows:

	Excess of current fair values over carrying amounts
Inventories	$30,000
Plant assets (net) (economic life 10 years)	50,000
Patents (net) (economic life 5 years)	20,000

Pavich amortizes goodwill over a 40-year economic life, and both Pavich and Sisler include depreciation expense in cost of goods sold and amortization expense in operating expenses. Both companies use the straight-line method for depreciation and amortization.

For the two fiscal years ended September 30, Year 8, Sisler reported net income and declared and paid dividends as follows:

Year ended Sept. 30,	Net income	Dividends
Year 7	$ 80,000	$10,000
Year 8	120,000	75,000

Instructions

a Prepare journal entries for Pavich Corporation on September 30, Year 7, and September 30, Year 8, to record under the equity method of accounting the operating results of Sisler Company for the two fiscal years ended on those dates.

Do not prepare entries for the declaration of Sisler's dividends; assume the dividends were received by Pavich on September 30 of each year.

b Prepare working paper eliminations for Pavich Corporation and subsidiary on September 30, Year 7, and September 30, Year 8.

6-7 The working paper elimination for Plumm Corporation and its wholly owned subsidiary, Stamm Company, on the date of the business combination was as follows:

PLUMM CORPORATION AND SUBSIDIARY
Working Paper Elimination
November 30, Year 1

Common Stock — Stamm	280,000	
Retained Earnings — Stamm	220,000	
Inventories — Stamm	20,000	
Goodwill — Stamm	40,000	
Investment in Stamm Company Common Stock — Plumm		560,000

To eliminate intercompany investment and equity accounts of subsidiary on date of business combination, and to allocate the purchase discrepancy to identifiable assets acquired, with remainder to goodwill having an economic life of 40 years.

Financial statements of Plumm and Stamm for the fiscal year ended November 30, Year 2, were as follows:

PLUMM CORPORATION AND STAMM COMPANY
Financial Statements
For Year Ended November 30, Year 2

	Plumm Corporation	Stamm Company
Income Statements		
Revenue:		
Net sales	$800,000	$415,000
Intercompany investment income	69,000	
Total revenue	$869,000	$415,000
Costs and expenses:		
Cost of goods sold	$500,000	$110,000
Operating expenses	200,000	80,000
Income taxes expense	60,000	135,000
Total costs and expenses	$760,000	$325,000
Net income	$109,000	$ 90,000
Statements of Retained Earnings		
Retained earnings, beginning of year	$640,000	$220,000
Net income	109,000	90,000
Subtotal	$749,000	$310,000
Dividends	60,000	30,000
Retained earnings, end of year	$689,000	$280,000

Balance Sheets
Assets

Investment in Stamm Company common stock	$ 599,000	
Other	1,840,000	$960,000
Total assets	$2,439,000	$960,000

Liabilities & Shareholders' Equity

Liabilities	$ 650,000	$400,000
Common stock	1,100,000	280,000
Retained earnings	689,000	280,000
Total liabilities & shareholders' equity	$2,439,000	$960,000

Instructions

a Reconstruct the journal entries for Plumm Corporation on November 30, Year 2, under the equity method of accounting, to record the operating results of Stamm Company for the fiscal year ended November 30, Year 2, including Stamm's dividend declared and paid on that date. (Do not prepare a journal entry for the declaration of the dividend.)

b Prepare a working paper for consolidated financial statements of Plumm Corporation and subsidiary for the fiscal year ended November 30, Year 2, and the related working paper elimination. Include goodwill amortization in operating expenses.

6-8 On June 30, Year 6, Petal Corporation acquired for cash of $19 a share, including out-of-pocket costs, all the outstanding common stock of Sepal Company. Both companies continued to operate as separate entities and both companies have calendar years. Petal adopted the equity method of accounting for Sepal's operating results.

(1) On June 30, Year 6, Sepal's balance sheet was as follows:

SEPAL COMPANY
Balance Sheet
June 30, Year 6
Assets

Cash	$ 700,000
Accounts receivable (net)	600,000
Inventories	1,400,000
Plant assets (net)	3,300,000
Other assets	500,000
Total assets	$6,500,000

Liabilities & Shareholders' Equity

Accounts payable and other current liabilities	$ 700,000
Long-term debt	2,600,000
Other liabilities	200,000
Common stock (1,000,000 shares)	1,400,000
Retained earnings	1,600,000
Total liabilities & shareholders' equity	$6,500,000

(2) On June 30, Sepal's assets and liabilities having current fair values that were different from carrying amounts were as follows:

	Current fair values
Plant assets (net)	$16,400,000
Other assets	200,000
Long-term debt	2,200,000

The differences between current fair values and carrying amounts resulted in a debit or credit to depreciation or amortization for the consolidated financial statements for the six-month period ended December 31, Year 6, as follows:

Plant assets (net)	$500,000 debit
Other assets	10,000 credit
Long-term debt	5,000 debit
Total	$495,000 debit

(3) The amount paid by Petal in excess of the current fair value of the identifiable net assets of Sepal is attributable to expected future earnings of Sepal and will be amortized over the maximum allowable period.

(4) The Year 6 net income or net loss for each company was as follows:

	Petal Corporation	Sepal Company
Jan. 1 to June 30	$ 250,000	$ (750,000)
July 1 to Dec. 31	1,070,000	1,250,000

The $1,070,000 net income of Petal includes Petal's equity in the adjusted net income of Sepal for the six months ended December 31, Year 6.

(5) On December 31, Year 6, the balance sheets for both companies were as follows:

PETAL CORPORATION AND SUBSIDIARY
Balance Sheets
December 31, Year 6

	Petal Corporation	Sepal Company
Assets		
Cash	$ 3,500,000	$ 625,000
Accounts receivable (net)	1,400,000	1,500,000
Inventories	1,000,000	2,500,000
Investment in Sepal Company common stock	19,720,000	
Plant assets (net)	2,000,000	3,100,000
Other assets	100,000	475,000
Total assets	$27,720,000	$8,200,000
Liabilities & Shareholders' Equity		
Accounts payable and other current liabilities	$ 1,500,000	$1,100,000
Long-term debt	4,000,000	2,600,000
Other liabilities	750,000	250,000
Common stock	15,000,000	1,400,000
Retained earnings	6,470,000	2,850,000
Total liabilities & shareholders' equity	$27,720,000	$8,200,000

Instructions Prepare the consolidated balance sheet of Petal Corporation and its wholly owned subsidiary, Sepal Company, on December 31, Year 6. Do not use a working paper, but show supporting computations.

6-9 The financial statements of Princeton Corporation and Stonier Company, Princeton's wholly owned subsidiary, were as follows for the year ended December 31, Year 6:

PRINCETON CORPORATION AND STONIER COMPANY
Financial Statements
For Year Ended December 31, Year 6

	Princeton Corporation	Stonier Company
Income Statements		
Revenue:		
Net sales	$1,000,000	$ 880,000
Intercompany investment income	76,000	
Total revenue	$1,076,000	$ 880,000
Costs and expenses:		
Cost of goods sold	$ 800,000	$ 600,000
Operating expenses	90,000	80,000
Income taxes expense	66,000	120,000
Total costs and expenses	$ 956,000	$ 800,000
Net income	$ 120,000	$ 80,000
Statements of Retained Earnings		
Retained earnings, beginning of year	$ 842,000	$ 230,000
Net income	120,000	80,000
Subtotal	$ 962,000	$ 310,000
Dividends	50,000	50,000
Retained earnings, end of year	$ 912,000	$ 260,000
Balance Sheet		
Assets		
Current assets	$ 840,000	$ 450,000
Investment in Stonier Company common stock ...	438,000	
Plant assets (net)	1,622,000	830,000
Intangible assets (net)	100,000	60,000
Total assets	$3,000,000	$1,340,000
Liabilities & Shareholders' Equity		
Liabilities	$ 946,000	$ 930,000
Common stock	1,100,000	150,000
Retained earnings	954,000	260,000
Total liabilities & shareholders' equity	$3,000,000	$1,340,000

There were no changes in the common stock account of Stonier since December 31, Year 3, the date of the Princeton-Stonier business combination. Stonier's Retained Earnings account since the business combination date but prior to closing entries of December 31, Year 6, is shown at the top of page 262.

Retained Earnings

Date	Explanation	Debit	Credit	Balance
12/31/3	Balance			150,000 cr
12/31/4	Close net income		80,000	230,000 cr
12/31/4	Close Dividends account	40,000		190,000 cr
12/31/5	Close net income		100,000	290,000 cr
12/31/5	Close Dividends account	60,000		230,000 cr

Princeton Corporation's Investment in Stonier Company Common Stock is shown below.

Investment in Stonier Company Common Stock

Date	Explanation	Debit	Credit	Balance
12/31/3	Total costs of business combination	370,000		370,000 dr
12/20/4	Dividend declared by Stonier		40,000	330,000 dr
12/31/4	Net income of Stonier	80,000		410,000 dr
12/31/4	Amortization of the purchase discrepancy		34,000(1)	376,000 dr
12/20/5	Dividend declared by Stonier		60,000	316,000 dr
12/31/5	Net income of Stonier	100,000		416,000 dr
12/31/5	Amortization of the purchase discrepancy		4,000(2)	412,000 dr
12/20/6	Dividend declared by Stonier		50,000	362,000 dr
12/31/6	Net income of Stonier	80,000		442,000 dr
12/31/6	Amortization of the purchase discrepancy		4,000(2)	438,000 dr

(1) Cost of goods sold, $30,000; depreciation of plant assets, $4,000
(2) Depreciation of plant assets, $4,000

On December 31, Year 3, the date of the Princeton-Stonier purchase-type business combination, a $20,000 excess of current fair values of Stonier's identifiable net assets over the total cost of Princeton's investment was applied to reduce the current fair value excess attributable to Stonier's plant assets from $60,000 to $40,000. This amount was being amortized by the straight-line method in Princeton's equity-method journal entries over the ten-year economic life of Stonier's plant assets. Stonier includes depreciation expense in operating expenses.

Instructions   Prepare a working paper for consolidated financial statements of Princeton Corporation and subsidiary on December 31, Year 6, and the related working paper elimination.

6-10   On January 1, Year 1, Parent Company acquired 90% of the common shares of Subsidiary Corp. at a total cost of $500,000. The following information was taken from the records of Subsidiary Corp. on January 1, Year 1:

	Carrying Value	Fair Value
Misc. Assets	$ 800,000	$ 800,000
Inventory (fifo)	150,000	175,000
Land	110,000	140,000
Equipment	225,000	240,000
	$1,285,000	$1,355,000
Misc. Liabilities	835,000	835,000
Net Assets	$ 450,000	$ 520,000

Subsidiary Corporation records depreciation on its equipment using the reducing balance method at a 20% rate. Any goodwill is to be amortized over the maximum allowable period on a straight-line basis. During the three-year period ending December 31, Year 3, Subsidiary Corporation's net income totalled $84,000 and dividends totalling $45,000 were declared and paid. Parent Company uses the equity method to account for its investment.

Instructions
a Prepare a purchase discrepancy amortization schedule for the three-year period ending December 31, Year 3.
b Compute the balance in the account "Investment in Subsidiary Corp. Common Stock" on December 31, Year 3.
c Verify the total unamortized purchase discrepancy on December 31, Year 3, by using the amounts computed in part **b**.
d Compute the minority interest on December 31, Year 3.

6-11 Balance sheet and income statement data for two affiliated companies for the current year are given below.

BALANCE SHEET DATA
as of December 31, Year 4

	Able Company	Baker Company
Cash	$ 40,000	$ 21,000
Receivables	92,000	84,000
Inventories	56,000	45,000
Land	20,000	60,000
Plant and equipment	200,000	700,000
Accumulated depreciation	(80,000)	(350,000)
Investment in Baker Company (equity)	344,240	
Advances to Baker Company	100,000	
Total assets	$772,240	$560,000
Accounts payable	$130,000	$ 96,500
Advances payable		100,000
Common stock	400,000	200,000
Beginning retained earnings	229,580	154,000
Net income for the year	34,660	17,500
Dividends	(22,000)	(8,000)
Total liabilities & shareholders' equity	$772,240	$560,000

INCOME STATEMENT DATA
Year ended December 31, Year 4

Sales revenues	$600,000	$400,000
Interest revenues	6,700	
Intercompany investment income	11,360	
Total revenues	618,060	$400,000
Cost of goods sold	$334,000	$225,000
Depreciation expense	20,000	70,000
Selling and administrative expense	207,000	74,000
Interest expense	1,700	6,000
Income taxes expense	20,700	7,500
Total expenses	$583,400	$382,500
Net Income	$ 34,660	$ 17,500

Additional Information:

1 Able Company acquired an 80% interest in Baker Company on January 1, Year 1, for $272,000. On that date the following information was noted about specific net assets of Baker:

	Book Value	Fair Value
Inventory	$20,000	$50,000
Land	25,000	45,000
Equipment (est. life 15 years)	60,000	78,000

2 On January 1, Year 1, Baker had a retained earnings balance of $30,000.
3 Any Goodwill is to be amortized over a 20-year period.
4 Able carries its investment at equity.

Instructions
Prepare the following:
a Consolidated Income Statement.
b Consolidated Retained Earnings Statement.
c Consolidated Balance Sheet.

7

CONSOLIDATED FINANCIAL STATEMENTS SUBSEQUENT TO DATE OF ACQUISITION OF A SUBSIDIARY: COST METHOD

In Chapter 6, we illustrated the working paper procedures necessary for the preparation of consolidated financial statements subsequent to the date of acquisition when the parent company accounts for its investment in a subsidiary by the equity method. In this chapter we will use the same two illustrations of a parent and its subsidiary except that we assume that the parent accounts for its investment in subsidiary by *the cost method*.

Illustration of cost method for wholly owned subsidiary for the first two years after acquisition

Palm Corporation acquired 100% of the outstanding common shares of Starr Company on December 31, Year 1. The purchase discrepancy and its allocation on this date is as follows (repeated from Chapter 6, page 224):

Cost of 100% interest in Starr — Dec. 31, Year 1		$ 500,000
Carrying amount of Starr's net assets		
Common stock	$ 258,000	
Retained earnings	132,000	
Total shareholders' equity	$ 390,000	
Palm's ownership interest	1.00	390,000
Purchase discrepancy		$ 110,000
Allocated to revalue the net assets of Starr		
Inventory $25,000 × 1.00	$ 25,000	
Plant assets (net) 65,000 × 1.00	65,000	
Patent 5,000 × 1.00	5,000	95,000
Balance — Goodwill.		$ 15,000

Calculation and allocation of the purchase discrepancy on acquisition date

Starr's financial statements for the first two years following the date of acquisition disclosed the following:

Year ended December 31	Net income	Dividends declared
Year 2	$ 60,000	24,000
Year 3	90,000	40,000

The purchase discrepancy amortization schedule for Years 2 and 3 is as follows:

Purchase discrepancy amortization schedule

	Balances Dec. 31, Year 1	Amortization Year 2	Balances Dec. 31, Year 2	Amortization Year 3	Balances Dec. 31, Year
Inventories . . .	$ 25,000	$(25,000)			
Plant assets					
(net)					
Land	$ 15,000		$ 15,000		$ 15,000
Building	30,000	$ (2,000)	28,000	$ (2,000)	26,000
Machinery . .	20,000	(2,000)	18,000	(2,000)	16,000
Total plant assets . . .	$ 65,000	$ (4,000)	$ 61,000	$ (4,000)	$ 57,000
Patent	5,000	(1,000)	4,000	(1,000)	3,000
Goodwill	15,000	(500)	14,500	(500)	14,000
Totals . . .	$110,000	$(30,500)	$ 79,500	$ (5,500)	$ 74,000

Consolidation in first year after acquisition

Because Palm Corporation uses the cost method, rather than the equity method, to account for Starr Company's operating results for the year ended December 31, Year 2, Palm would not prepare journal entries to reflect Starr's net income for the year, or to amortize the purchase discrepancy. Instead, its only entry is to record Starr's dividend declaration on December 20, Year 2 as follows:

Intercompany Dividends Receivable	24,000	
Intercompany Dividends Revenue		24,000

To record dividend declared by Starr Company payable
Jan. 8, Year 3, to shareholders of record Dec. 29, Year 2.

Calculations required when the cost method is being used

As outlined in Chapter 6, when the parent company uses the equity method the parent's net income is equal to consolidated net income. When the parent uses the cost method, this statement is not true and therefore it is *necessary to calculate what consolidated net income will be* before attempting the consolidated income statement working paper. Before making this calculation let us *describe what consolidated net income is.* Consolidated net income is made up of the following:

Description of the components of consolidated net income

Net Income of the parent from its own operations (i.e. excluding any net income or dividends of the subsidiary)	$ xxx
Plus: the parent's share of the net income of the subsidiary	xxx
Less: the amortization of the purchase discrepancy	(xxx)
Total equals consolidated net income	$ xxx

When the parent company uses the equity method, its net income has been increased by its share of the reported net income of the subsidiary and has been decreased by the amortization of the purchase discrepancy, and therefore equals consolidated net income. However, when the parent company uses the cost method, its net income has been increased only by its share of the dividends declared by the subsidiary. We therefore must calculate consolidated net income for Year 2 as follows (Palm's financial statements are on page 269):

Calculation of consolidated net income for Year 2

Palm's net income (cost method)		$ 104,000
Less: intercompany dividend revenue		24,000
Palm's net income, own operations		$ 80,000
Starr's net income	$ 60,000	
Palm's ownership percentage	1.00	
Palm's share of Starr's net income	$ 60,000	
Less: amortization of the purchase discrepancy for the year	30,500	29,500
Consolidated net income		$ 109,500

You will note that if Palm had used the equity method its reported net income for Year 2 would be $109,500. The calculation illustrated above simply *restates Palm's reported income (computed using the cost method) to what it would have been had Palm used the equity method to account for its investment in Starr.* The working paper eliminations for Palm Corporation and subsidiary on December 31, Year 2 are as shown on page 268.

The working paper for consolidated financial statements for Palm Corporation and subsidiary for the year ended December 31, Year 2 appears on page 269.

The following points relative to the cost method working paper for Palm Corporation and subsidiary should be noted:

1 The consolidated amounts in the cost method working paper for consolidated financial statements are identical to the consolidated amounts in the equity method working paper (page 229). This outcome results from the differing eliminations used in the two methods.

2 Elimination (a) simply adjusts Palm Company's accounts to what they would hav been under the equity method. The calculation of consolidated net income (pag 267) provides the details of the adjustment.

3 Once Palm's records have been adjusted to the equity method, the equity metho eliminations (elimination (b)) with their underlying reasons as described in Chapte 6 (page 228) are used.

4 Because we are preparing consolidated financial statements on December 3 Year 2, which is one year after the date of the business combination, the retaine earnings of Palm Corporation at the beginning of the year are equal to consol dated retained earnings.

Working paper
elimination for wholly
owned subsidiary
subsequent to date of
acquisition

PALM CORPORATION AND SUBSIDIARY

Working Paper Elimination

December 31, Year 2

(a) Intercompany Dividend Revenue — Palm 24,000

Investment in Starr Company Common

    Stock — Palm 5,500

    Intercompany Investment Income — Palm 29,50

To adjust Palm Corporation's accounts to

equity method balances and descriptions.

(b) Common Stock — Starr 258,000

Retained Earnings — Starr 132,000

Intercompany Investment Income — Palm 29,500

Plant Assets (net) — Starr ($65,000 − $4,000) 61,000

Patent — Starr ($5,000 − $1,000) 4,000

Goodwill — Starr ($15,000 − $500) 14,500

Cost of Goods Sold — Starr 29,000

Operating Expenses — Starr 1,500

    Investment in Starr Company Common Stock —

        Palm 505,50

        Dividends — Starr 24,00

To carry out the following:

(1) Eliminate intercompany investment and equity
accounts of subsidiary **at beginning of year,** and subsidiary dividend.

(2) Provide for Year 2 depreciation and amortization on
the purchase discrepancy allocated to Starr's net
assets as follows:

	Cost of goods sold	Operating expenses
Inventories sold	$25,000	
Building depreciation	1,000	$1,000
Machinery depreciation .	2,000	
Patent amortization	1,000	
Goodwill amortization .		500
Totals	$29,000	$1,500

(3) Allocate the unamortized purchase discrepancy to appropriate assets of Starr.

Equity method: Wholly owned subsidiary subsequent to date of acquisition

PALM CORPORATION AND SUBSIDIARY
Working Paper for Consolidated Financial Statements
For Year Ended December 31, Year 2

	Palm Corporation	Starr Company	Eliminations increase (decrease)	Consolidated
Income Statement				
Revenue				
Net sales	1,100,000	680,000		1,780,000
Intercompany dividend revenue	24,000		(a) (24,000)	
Intercompany investment income			(a) 29,500	
			(b) (29,500)	
Total revenue	1,124,000	680,000	(24,000)	1,780,000
Costs and expenses				
Cost of goods sold	700,000	450,000	(b) 29,000	1,179,000
Operating expenses	151,000	80,000	(b) 1,500	232,500
Interest expense	49,000			49,000
Income tax expense	120,000	90,000		210,000
Total costs and expenses	1,020,000	620,000	30,500	1,670,500
Net income	104,000	60,000	(54,500)	109,500
Statement of Retained Earnings				
Retained earnings, beginning of year	134,000	132,000	(b) (132,000)	134,000
Net income	104,000	60,000	(54,500)	109,500
Subtotal	238,000	192,000	(186,500)	243,500
Dividends	30,000	24,000	(b) (24,000)	30,000
Retained earnings, end of year	208,000	168,000	(162,500)	213,500
Balance Sheet				
Assets				
Cash	15,900	72,100		88,000
Intercompany receivable (payable)	24,000	(24,000)		
Inventories	136,000	115,000		251,000
Other current assets	88,000	131,000		219,000
Investment in Starr Company common stock . .	500,000		(a) 5,500	
			(b) (505,500)	
Plant assets (net)	440,000	340,000	(b) 61,000	841,000
Patent		16,000	(b) 4,000	20,000
Goodwill			(b) 14,500	14,500
Total assets	1,203,900	650,100	(420,500)	1,433,500
Liabilities & Shareholders' Equity				
Income taxes payable	40,000	20,000		60,000
Other liabilities	190,900	204,100		395,000
Common stock, no par	765,000			765,000
Common stock, no par		258,000	(b) (258,000)	
Retained earnings	208,000	168,000	(162,500)	213,500
Total liabilities & shareholders' equity	1,203,900	650,100	(420,500)	1,433,500

Consolidation in second year after acquisition

The only journal entry prepared by Palm Corporation for the Year 3 operating results of Starr Company under the cost method of accounting is to accrue its share of the dividends declared by Starr on December 17, Year 3 as follows:

Intercompany Dividends Receivable	40,000	
Intercompany Dividends Revenue		40,000

To record dividend declared by Starr Company payable Jan. 6, Year 4, to shareholders of record Dec. 28, Year 3.

The Year 3 financial statements of Palm Corporation and Starr Company are shown on page 273. Because the cost method is being used by Palm *it is necessary to make two calculations* before making the working paper elimination entries. We *first calculate consolidated net income* for Year 3 as follows:

Calculation of consolidated net income for Year 3

Palm's net income (cost method)		$ 115,500
Less: intercompany dividend revenue		40,000
Palm's net income, own operations		75,500
Starr's net income	$ 90,000	
Palm's ownership percentage	1.00	
Palm's share of Starr's net income	$ 90,000	
Less: amortization of the purchase discrepancy for the year ...	5,500	84,500
Consolidated net income		$ 160,000

This calculation is again simply adjusting Palm's net income under the cost method, to what it would have been under the equity method.

Because we are consolidating more than one year subsequent to the date of acquisition *an additional calculation is required.* If Palm Corporation had been using the equity method its retained earnings balance on January 1, Year 3 would be equal to consolidated retained earnings. Palm is using the cost method and therefore its retained earnings on January 1, Year 3 is not equal to consolidated retained earnings. A calculation of consolidated retained earnings on January 1, Year 3 is necessary as shown at the top of page 271.

This calculation is *adjusting Palm's retained earnings under the cost method to what it would have been under the equity method*. Further elaboration about the details of the calculation is as follows:

Calculation of consolidated
retained earnings Jan. 1,
Year 3

Palm's retained earnings — beginning of year		$ 208,000
Starr's retained earnings — beginning of year	$ 168,000	
Starr's retained earnings — acquisition date	$ 132,000	
Increase since acquisition	$ 36,000	
Palm's ownership percentage	1.00	
Palm's share of Starr's increase	$ 36,000	
Less: amortization of purchase		
discrepancy to beginning of year	30,500	5,500
Consolidated retained earnings —		
beginning of year		$ 213,500

1 Consolidated retained earnings on the date of a business combination (i.e. the date of acquisition) consists only of the retained earnings of the parent company (under the purchase method of accounting).

2 Consolidated net income in any one year subsequent to the date of acquisition consists of the net income of the parent company, plus the parent's share of the net income of the subsidiary, less the purchase discrepancy amortization for the year.

3 It therefore logically follows that the consolidated retained earnings balance at any time subsequent to the date of acquisition must contain the parent's share of the subsidiary's net income earned since the date of the business combination, less the total purchase discrepancy amortization to date.

4 If the parent uses the equity method, the parent's retained earnings balance at any one time contains the parent's share of the subsidiary's net income less the purchase discrepancy amortization and is equal to consolidated retained earnings.

5 If the parent uses the cost method, the parent's retained earnings *contain only the parent's share of the subsidiaries' dividends* declared since the date of the business combination.

6 The sum of net incomes minus the sum of dividends, both measured from the date of acquisition, is equal to *the change in retained earnings* measured from the same date. This change in retained earnings is an increase if the sum of the net income is greater than the sum of the dividends.

7 When we add the parent's share of the subsidiary's retained earnings increase to the retained earnings of the parent company (which contains its share of the subsidiary's dividends under the cost method), the resultant retained earnings amount includes the parent's share of the subsidiary's net income earned since the date of the combination. A deduction of the total purchase discrepancy amortization to date gives a retained earnings balance that is equal to consolidated retained earnings.

The working paper eliminations for Palm Corporation and subsidiary on December 31, Year 3 are as shown on page 272.

Working Paper for Consolidated Financial Statements The working paper for consolidated financial statements for Palm Corporation and subsidiary for the year ended December 31, Year 3 appears on page 273.

The following points relative to the cost method working papers should be noted:

1 Elimination (a) adjusts Palm Corporation's accounts to what they would have been under the equity method. The details of the adjustment are provided by the calculations of consolidated net income for Year 3 and consolidated retained earnings at the beginning of Year 3 (pages 270 and 271).

2 Once the accounts of Palm have been adjusted to the equity method in elimination (a) then the equity method eliminations as described in Chapter 6 (pages 234 and 235) are entered (elimination (b)).

Working paper elimination for wholly owned subsidiary, second year subsequent to date of acquisition

PALM CORPORATION AND SUBSIDIARY		
Working Paper Elimination		
December 31, Year 3		
(a) Intercompany Dividend Revenue — Palm	40,000	
Investment in Starr Company Common		
Stock — Palm ($44,500 + $5,500).	50,000	
Intercompany Investment Income — Palm		84,500
Retained Earnings — Palm (beginning of year)		5,500
To adjust Palm Corporation's accounts to		
equity method balances and descriptions.		
(b) Common Stock — Starr	258,000	
Retained Earnings — Starr	168,000	
Intercompany Investment Income — Palm	84,500	
Plant Assets (net) — Starr ($61,000 − $4,000)	57,000	
Patent — Starr ($4,000 − $1,000)	3,000	
Goodwill — Starr ($14,500 − $500)	14,000	
Costs of Goods Sold — Starr	4,000	
Operating Expenses — Starr	1,500	
Investment in Starr Company Common Stock —		
Palm		550,000
Dividends — Starr		40,000

To carry out the following:

(1) Eliminate intercompany investment and equity accounts of subsidiary **at beginning of year,** and subsidiary dividend.

(2) Provide for Year 3 depreciation and amortization on the purchase discrepancy allocated to Starr's net assets as follows:

	Cost of goods sold	Operating expenses
Building depreciation	$1,000	$1,000
Machinery depreciation . . .	2,000	
Patent amortization	1,000	
Goodwill amortization		500
Totals	$4,000	$1,500

(3) Allocate unamortized purchase discrepancy to appropriate assets of Starr.

Cost method: Wholly owned subsidiary subsequent to date of acquisition

PALM CORPORATION AND SUBSIDIARY
Working Paper for Consolidated Financial Statements
For Year Ended December 31, Year 3

	Palm Corporation	Starr Company	Eliminations increase (decrease)	Consolidated
Income Statement				
Revenue				
Net sales	1,400,000	750,000		2,150,000
Intercompany dividend revenue	40,000		(a) (40,000)	
			(a) 84,500	
Intercompany investment income			(b) (84,500)	
Total revenue	1,440,000	750,000	(40,000)	2,150,000
Costs and expenses				
Cost of goods sold	840,500	455,000	(b) 4,000	1,299,500
Operating expenses	369,000	70,000	(b) 1,500	440,500
Income tax expense	115,000	135,000		250,000
Total costs and expenses	1,324,500	660,000	5,500	1,990,000
Net income	115,500	90,000	(45,500)	160,000
Statement of Retained Earnings				
			(a) 5,500	
Retained earnings, beginning of year	208,000	168,000	(b) (168,000)	213,500
Net income	115,500	90,000	(45,500)	160,000
Subtotal	323,500	258,000	(208,000)	373,500
Dividends	30,000	40,000	(b) (40,000)	30,000
Retained earnings, end of year.	293,500	218,000	(168,000)	343,500
Balance Sheet				
Assets				
Cash	5,500	30,000		35,500
Intercompany receivable (payable)	40,000	(40,000)		
Inventories	160,000	120,000		280,000
Other current assets	65,000	110,000		175,000
Investment in Starr Company common stock . .	500,000		(a) 50,000	
			(b) (550,000)	
Plant assets (net)	523,000	394,000	(b) 57,000	974,000
Patent		12,000	(b) 3,000	15,000
Goodwill			(b) 14,000	14,000
Total assets	1,293,500	626,000	(426,000)	1,493,500
Liabilities & Shareholders' Equity				
Income taxes payable	35,000	40,000		75,000
Other liabilities	200,000	110,000		310,000
Common stock, no par	765,000			765,000
Common stock, no par		258,000	(b) (258,000)	
Retained earnings	293,500	218,000	(168,000)	343,500
Total liabilities & shareholders' equity	1,293,500	626,000	(426,000)	1,493,500

Illustration of cost method for partially owned purchased subsidiary for first two years after the business combination

We return to the Post Corporation – Sage Company business combination which involves a partially owned subsidiary. Post acquired 95% of Sage's outstanding common shares at a total cost (including out-of-pocket costs) of $1,192,250 on December 31, Year 1. The purchase discrepancy and its allocation on this date is as follows (repeated from Chapter 5 page 191):

Calculation of the pur-
chase discrepancy and its
allocation

Cost of 95% interest in Sage		1,192,250
Carrying amount of Sage's net assets		
Common stock	$ 635,000	
Retained earnings	334,000	
Total shareholders' equity	$ 969,000	
Post's ownership interest	0.95	920,550
Purchase discrepancy		$ 271,700
Allocated to revalue the net assets of Sage:		
Inventory	$ 26,000 × 0.95 =	$ 24,700	
Plant assets (net)	190,000 × 0.95 =	180,500	
Leasehold	30,000 × 0.95 =	28,500	233,700
Balance — Goodwill		$ 38,000

Sage's financial statements for the first two years following the business combination disclosed the following:

Year ended December 31	Net income	Dividends declared
Year 2	$ 90,000	$40,000
Year 3	105,000	50,000

The purchase discrepancy amortization schedule for Years 2 and 3 is as follows:

Purchase discrepancy
amortization schedule

	Balances Dec. 31, Year 1	Amortization Year 2	Balances Dec. 31, Year 2	Amortization Year 3	Balances Dec. 31, Year 3
Inventories	$ 24,700	$ (24,700)			
Plant assets (net):					
Land	$ 57,000		$ 57,000		$ 57,000
Building	76,000	$ (3,800)	72,200	$ (3,800)	68,400
Machinery . . .	47,500	(9,500)	38,000	(9,500)	28,500
Total plant					
assets . . .	$180,500	$ (13,300)	$167,200	$ (13,300)	$153,900
Leasehold	28,500	(4,750)	23,750	(4,750)	19,000
Goodwill	38,000	(950)	37,050	(950)	36,100
Totals	$271,700	$ (43,700)	$228,000	$ (19,000)	$209,000

Consolidation in first year after acquisition

Using the cost method to account for its investment in Sage, Post Corporation makes the following entry in Year 2 to record Sage's dividend declaration:

Intercompany Dividends Receivable	38,000	
Intercompany Dividends Revenue		38,000
To record dividend declared by Sage Company, payable		
Dec. 16, Year 2, to shareholders of record Dec. 1, Year 2.		

Post's journal entry for receipt of the dividend from Sage would be the same under the cost method as under the equity method of accounting illustrated previously in Chapter 6.

Calculation of Year 2 consolidated net income

Because the parent has used the cost method, **we must calculate consolidated net income for Year 2** as an aid to making the working paper eliminations. We are consolidating one year subsequent to the date of acquisition and therefore the parent's retained earnings at the beginning of year are equal to consolidated retained earnings. Year 2 consolidated net income is calculated as follows (Post's financial statements are on page 277):

Calculation of consolidated net income for Year 2

Post's net income (cost method)		$ 458,000
Less: intercompany dividend revenue		38,000
Post's net income, own operations		$ 420,000
Sage's net income	$ 90,000	
Post's ownership percentage	0.95	
Post's share of Sage's net income	$ 85,500	
Less: amortization of the purchase discrepancy		
for the year	43,700	41,800
Consolidated net income		$ 461,800

This calculation restates Post's cost method net income of $458,000 to what its net income would be under the equity method ($461,800). The working paper eliminations for Post Corporation and subsidiary on December 31, Year 2 are as shown on page 276.

Elimination (a) adjusts Post's cost method accounts to their equity method balances and descriptions. Once Post's accounts have been restated to the equity method (on the working paper only) the identical eliminations described in Chapter 6 (page 241) are used (eliminations (b) and (c)).

The working paper for consolidated financial statements for Post Corporation and subsidiary for the year ended December 31, Year 2 appears on page 277.

POST CORPORATION AND SUBSIDIARY
Working Paper Eliminations
December 31, Year 2

(a) Intercompany Dividend Revenue — Post	38,000	
Investment in Sage Company Common		
Stock — Post ($41,800 − $38,000)	3,800	
Intercompany Investment Income — Post		41,800
To adjust Post Corporation's accounts to		
equity method balances and descriptions.		
(b) Common Stock — Sage	635,000	
Retained Earnings — Sage	334,000	
Intercompany Investment Income — Post	41,800	
Plant Assets (net) — Sage	167,200	
Leasehold — Sage	23,750	
Goodwill — Sage	37,050	
Cost of Goods Sold — Sage	40,850	
Operating Expenses — Sage	2,850	
Investment in Sage Company		
Common Stock — Post		1,196,050
Dividends — Sage		40,000
Minority Interest in Net Assets		
of Subsidiary ($48,450 − $2,000)		46,450
To carry out the following:		

(1) Eliminate intercompany investment, and shareholders' equity accounts of subsidiary **at beginning of year,** and subsidiary dividends.

(2) Provide for Year 2 depreciation and amortization on the purchase discrepancy allocated to Sage's identifiable net assets as follows:

	Cost of goods sold	Operating expenses
Inventories sold	$24,700	
Building depreciation	1,900	$ 1,900
Machinery depreciation	9,500	
Leasehold amortization	4,750	
Goodwill amortization		950
Totals	$40,850	$ 2,850

(3) Allocate the unamortized purchase discrepancy to appropriate assets.

(4) Establish minority interest in net assets of subsidiary at beginning of year ($48,450), less minority share of dividends declared by subsidiary during year ($40,000 × 0.05 = $2,000).

(c) Minority Interest in Net Income of Subsidiary	4,500	
Minority Interest in Net Assets of Subsidiary . . .		4,500
To establish minority interest in subsidiary's net		
income for Year 2 ($90,000 × 0.05 = $4,500).		

Handwritten: 43,500

Handwritten: 85,500 − 43,700 = 41,800

POST CORPORATION AND SUBSIDIARY
Working Paper for Consolidated Financial Statements
For Year Ended December 31, Year 2

	Post Corporation	Sage Company	Eliminations increase (decrease)		Consolidated
Income Statement					
Revenue					
Net sales	5,611,000	1,089,000			6,700,000
Intercompany dividend revenue	38,000		(a)	(38,000)	
Intercompany investment income			(a)	41,800	
			(b)	(41,800)	
Total	5,649,000	1,089,000		(38,000)	6,700,000
Costs and expenses					
Cost of goods sold	3,925,000	700,000	(b)	40,850	4,665,850
Operating expenses	556,000	129,000	(b)	2,850	687,850
Interest and income tax expense	710,000	170,000			880,000
Minority interest in net income of subsidiary .			(c)	4,500	4,500
Total costs and expenses	5,191,000	999,000		48,200	6,238,200
Net income	458,000	90,000		(86,200)	461,800
Statement of Retained Earnings					
Retained earnings, beginning of year	1,050,000	334,000	(b)	(334,000)	1,050,000
Net income	458,000	90,000		(86,200)	461,800
Subtotal	1,508,000	424,000		(420,200)	1,511,800
Dividends	158,550	40,000	(b)	(40,000)	158,550
Retained earnings, end of year.	1,349,450	384,000		(380,200)	1,353,250
Balance Sheet					
Assets					
Inventories	861,000	439,000			1,300,000
Other current assets	639,000	371,000			1,010,000
			(a)	3,800	
Investment in Sage Company common stock . .	1,192,250		(b)	(1,196,050)	
Plant assets (net)	3,600,000	1,150,000	(b)	167,200	4,917,200
Leasehold			(b)	23,750	23,750
Goodwill	95,000		(b)	37,050	132,050
Total assets	6,387,250	1,960,000		(964,250)	7,383,000
Liabilities & Shareholders' Equity					
Liabilities	2,420,550	941,000			3,361,550
Minority interest in net assets of subsidiary . . .			(b)	46,450	
			(c)	4,500	50,950
Common stock, no par	2,617,250				2,617,250
Common stock, no par		635,000	(b)	(635,000)	
Retained earnings	1,349,450	384,000		(380,200)	1,353,250
	6,387,250	1,960,000		(964,250)	7,383,000

Illustration of cost method for Post Corporation and subsidiary for second year after business combination

Under the cost method, Post Corporation makes a journal entry to record Sage's Year 3 dividend declaration as follows:

Intercompany Dividends Receivable	*47,500*	
Intercompany Dividends Revenue		*47,500*
To record dividend declared by Sage Company, payable		
Dec. 17, Year 3, to shareholders of record December 1,		
Year 3.		

Post's journal entry to record the receipt of the dividend from Sage on Dec. 17, Year 3 is not illustrated.

The Year 3 financial statements of Post Corporation and Sage Company are shown on page 280. Before making the working paper elimination entries *it is necessary to calculate both Year 3 consolidated net income and the consolidated retained earnings balance at the beginning of the year.*

Calculation of Year 3 Consolidated Net Income

Post's net income (cost method)		$ 319,350
Less: intercompany dividend revenue		47,500
Post's net income, own operations		$ 271,850
Sage's net income	$ 105,000	
Post's ownership percentage	0.95	
Post's share of Sage's net income	$ 99,750	
Less: amortization of the purchase		
discrepancy for the year	19,000	80,750
Consolidated net income		$ 352,600

Calculation of Beginning of Year Consolidated Retained Earnings

Post's retained earnings — beginning of year		$1,349,450
Sage's retained earnings — beginning of year	$ 384,000	
Sage's retained earnings — acquisition date	334,000	
Increase since acquisition	$ 50,000	
Post's ownership percentage	0.95	
Post's share of Sage's increase	47,500	
Less: amortization of purchase discrepancy		
to beginning of year	43,700	3,800
Consolidated retained earnings — beginning of year		$1,353,250

Bookkeeping take approach = Cost
makes 2 adj to make T/B = Equity - then proceed or Equity

Eliminate
Dividend Shrae
substitute
Investment income

adj the R/E
merely Investment
arrive at
would have been
if equity BLCK
had been followed

Post Corporation and Subsidiary
Working Paper Eliminations
December 31, Year 3

ists out of
_T/B_

Equity PU

(a) Intercompany Dividend Revenue — Post	47,500	
Investment in Sage Company Common		
Stock — Post ($33,250 + $3,800)	37,050	
Intercompany Investment Income — Post . . .		80,750
Retained Earnings — beginning of year — Post .		3,800

R/E vrder
Equity)

To adjust Post Corporation's accounts to equity
method balances and descriptions.

(b) Common Stock — Sage	635,000	
Retained Earnings — Sage	384,000	
Intercompany Investment Income — Post	80,750	
Plant Assets (Net) — Sage	153,900	
Leasehold — Sage	19,000	
Goodwill — Sage	36,100	
Cost of Goods Sold — Sage	16,150	
Operating Expenses — Sage	2,850	
Investment in Sage Company		
Common Stock — Post		1,229,300
Dividends — Sage		50,000
Minority Interest in Net Assets		
of Subsidiary ($50,950 − $2,500)		48,450

To carry out the following:

(1) Eliminate intercompany investment, and equity accounts of subsidiary at beginning
of year, and subsidiary dividends.

(2) Provide for Year 3 depreciation and amortization on the purchase discrepancy allocated to Sage's identifiable net assets as follows:

	Cost of goods sold	Operating expenses
Building depreciation	$ 1,900	$ 1,900
Machinery depreciation	$ 9,500	
Leasehold amortization	4,750	
Goodwill amortization		950
Totals	16,150	2,850

(3) Allocate unamortized purchase discrepancy to appropriate assets.

(4) Establish minority interest in net assets of subsidiary at beginning of year ($50,950),
less minority share of dividends declared by subsidiary during year ($50,000 ×
0.05 = $2,500).

(c) Minority Interest in Net Income of Subsidiary	5,250	
Minority Interest in Net Assets of Subsidiary		5,250

To establish minority interest in subsidiary's
net income for Year 3 ($105,000 × 0.05 = $5,250).

Cost method: Partially owned subsidiary subsequent to date of acquisition

POST CORPORATION AND SUBSIDIARY
Working Paper for Consolidated Financial Statements
For Year Ended December 31, Year 3

	Post Corporation	Sage Company	Eliminations increase (decrease)		Consolidated
Income Statement					
Revenue					
Net sales	5,530,000	1,100,000			6,630,000
Intercompany dividend revenue	47,500		(a)	(47,500)	
Intercompany investment income			(a)	80,750	
			(b)	(80,750)	
Total	5,577,500	1,100,000		(47,500)	6,630,000
Costs and expenses					
Cost of goods sold	3,817,000	730,000	(b)	16,150	4,563,150
Operating expenses	851,150	120,000	(b)	2,850	974,000
Interest and income tax expense	590,000	145,000			735,000
Minority interest in net income of subsidiary .			(c)	5,250	5,250
Total	5,258,150	995,000		24,250	6,277,400
Net income	319,350	105,000		(71,750)	352,600
Statement of Retained Earnings					
			(a)	3,800	
Retained earnings, beginning of year	1,349,450	384,000	(b)	(384,000)	1,353,250
Net income	319,350	105,000		(71,750)	352,600
Subtotal	1,668,800	489,000		(451,950)	1,705,850
Dividends	158,550	50,000	(b)	(50,000)	158,550
Retained earnings, end of year.	1,510,250	439,000		(401,950)	1,547,300
Balance Sheet					
Assets					
Inventories	900,000	470,000			1,370,000
Other current assets	243,250	190,000			433,250
Investment in Sage Company			(a)	37,050	
common stock	1,192,250		(b)	(1,229,300)	
Plant assets (net)	4,200,000	1,414,000	(b)	153,900	5,767,900
Leasehold			(b)	19,000	19,000
Goodwill	92,000		(b)	36,100	128,100
Total assets	6,627,500	2,074,000		(983,250)	7,718,250
Liabilities & Shareholders' Equity					
Liabilities	2,500,000	1,000,000			3,500,000
Minority interest in net assets of subsidiary . . .			(b)	48,450	
			(c)	5,250	53,700
Common stock, no par	2,617,250				2,617,250
Common stock, no par		635,000	(b)	(635,000)	
Retained earnings	1,510,250	439,000		(401,950)	1,547,300
	6,627,500	2,074,000		(983,250)	7,718,250

These two calculations adjust Post's Year 3 cost method net income and beginning of the year retained earnings to their equity method amounts. The working paper eliminations for Post Corporation and subsidiary on December 31, Year 3 are shown on page 279.

Elimination (a) adjusts Post's cost method accounts to equity method balances and descriptions. Eliminations (b) and (c) are identical to the eliminations described in Chapter 6 (page 246).

It should now be obvious that *only three accounts on the financial statements of the parent company change when the two methods (cost and equity) are used*. These accounts are as follows:

1 Investment in Subsidiary
2 Retained Earnings
3 Intercompany Dividend Revenue (under the cost method) becomes Intercompany Investment Income (under the equity method).

All three accounts will have different balances under each method. When the cost method has been used, the working paper procedure is to adjust the parent's accounts to the equity method, and then proceed with the equity method working paper eliminations.

The working paper for consolidated financial statements for Post Corporation and subsidiary appears on page 280.

Accounting for long-term investments

Our discussions to date have focussed on business combinations and the preparation of consolidated financial statements. Canadian accounting principles in this area are found in three sections of the *CICA Handbook.* These sections are *Section 3050 "Long-term Investments," Section 1580 "Business Combinations," and Section 1600 "Consolidated Financial Statements and the Equity Method of Accounting."* While each is basically separate and distinct from the others, they all relate to our present (and future) discussions regarding consolidated financial statements. A fourth *Section 3055 "Investments in Corporate and Unincorporated Joint Ventures"* which is also related, but less directly, is discussed in detail in Chapter 11.

The diagram on page 282 outlines the interrelationships of the Handbook sections. We will now examine the relevant portions of each of these sections to illustrate how they fit into the overall scheme.

Section 3050 "Long-term Investments"   This section discusses the financial reporting requirements for an investment which is considered to be long-term. (The distinction between long-term and temporary is basically one of intent by the investor to hold the investment for more than one year beyond the current fiscal year. Handbook Section 3010 discusses the accounting treatment for temporary investments.) Section 3050 indicates that a long-term investment is either (1) an investment in a subsidiary of the investor, (2) an investment in which the investor has significant influence over the investee, or (3) a portfolio investment.

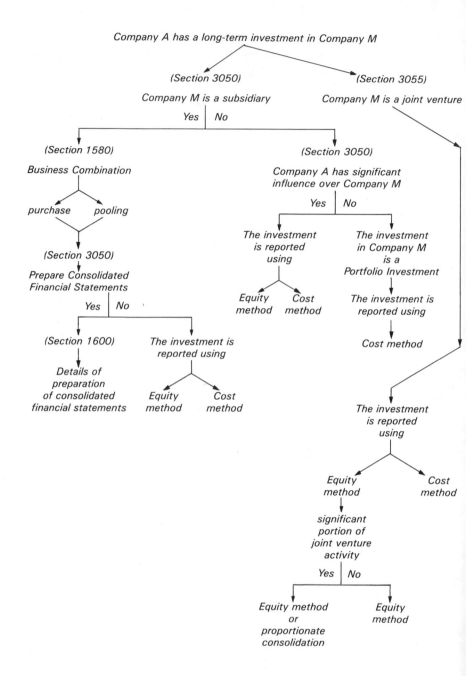

An investment in a subsidiary If the investor controls, directly or indirectly, more than 50% of the voting shares of the investee, the investee is a subsidiary of the investor. The handbook recommendations are as follows:

Consolidated financial statements recognize that, even though a parent and its subsidiaries are separate legal entities, the companies together constitute a single economic group. A single economic group exists when the management of the parent company is able to control the resources of the parent and its subsidiaries. The fact that a subsidiary operates in a different industry does not contradict the premise that the parent and subsidiary together are a single economic group. (3050.04)

Shareholders of the parent company need to be informed about the resources and results of operations of the group as a whole. Consolidated financial statements show all the assets, related liabilities and income of the parent and subsidiaries as a single economic group. With few exceptions, such presentation is more informative to the shareholders of the parent company than separate financial statements of the parent company and of its subsidiaries. (3050.05)

When a company has one or more subsidiaries, that company's financial statements should be prepared on a consolidated basis, except in the situations outlined in paragraphs 3050.08, 3050.10, 3050.12 and 3050.14. (3050.06)

A subsidiary should be excluded from consolidation if (a) increases in the equity of the subsidiary are not likely to accrue to the parent, or (b) control by the parent over the subsidiary's assets or operations is seriously impaired. In these circumstances the investment should be accounted for by the cost method. (3050.08)

A subsidiary should be excluded from consolidation when control by the parent company is temporary because a formal plan exists to dispose of the investment in the subsidiary. The parent company's investment should be accounted for at the lower of the estimated net realizable value and the carrying value of the investment resulting from the use of the equity method. (3050.10)

A parent's investment in a subsidiary that is a bank or an insurance company the financial statements of which are neither prepared in accordance with generally accepted accounting principles nor conformed, for the purposes of consolidation, to this basis should be accounted for by a modified form of the equity method. This method would be identical to the equity method except that the subsidiary's earnings would not be adjusted to conform to generally accepted accounting principles. The financial statements of the parent company should include financial information concerning the excluded subsidiary similar to that set out in paragraph 3050.14. (3050.12)

When the financial statement components of a subsidiary are such that consolidation would not provide the more informative presentation to the shareholders of the parent company, the investment in the subsidiary should be accounted for by the equity method. The financial statements of the parent company should include either separate financial statements of the subsidiary, combined financial statements of similar subsidiaries or, provided all information significant to the consolidated statements is disclosed, condensed financial statements (including notes) of the subsidiary. There should be an explanation of the nature and amount of any adjustments of the net income or loss of the excluded subsidiary, as shown in its financial statements, to arrive at the amount included in the parent's income statement in respect of this subsidiary. (3050.14)

When one or more subsidiaries are excluded from consolidation, the reason for the exclusion should be stated. (3050.15)

As our discussion in Chapter 5 indicated, paragraph 14 seems to allow an escape clause from the overall provision that the consolidation of subsidiaries is the most informative presentation.

A further paragraph (3050.18) also allows a parent company to present non-consolidated statements in order to comply with the statutory reporting requirements of government bodies. It is assumed that consolidated financial statements will be prepared for purposes of reporting to shareholders, and therefore this paragraph allows the auditor to express an unqualified opinion on this second set of statements prepared for other purposes, such as income tax reporting. Wholly-owned subsidiaries that are themselves parent companies are also allowed to prepare non-consolidated statements. In both instances the parent company is required to disclose the method used (cost or equity) to account for the investment in the subsidiary.

Significant influence investments and portfolio investments   While an investment may not allow the investor to control the investee, it may be sufficient to allow the investor to exercise significant influence over the operations of the investee. If this is the case the Handbook provides:

An investor that is able to exercise significant influence over an investee should account for the investment by the equity method, except in the situation outlined in paragraph 3050.23. (3050.21)

When an investor ceases to be able to exercise significant influence, the investment should be accounted for by the cost method. Also, when the investor is able to exercise significant influence but circumstances similar to those requiring exclusion of a subsidiary from consolidation prevail (paragraph 3050.08), the investment should be accounted for by the cost method. (3050.23)

This section describes the equity method as the process whereby the investor takes up its pro rata share of the earnings of the investee "*computed by the consolidation method.*" This requires the yearly amortization of the purchase discrepancy and adjustments for unrealized intercompany profits and losses, and gains and losses from holding intercompany bonds, even though the investee is not a subsidiary of the investor.

If the investee is not a subsidiary, nor subject to significant influence by the investor, then the section implies that it must be a *portfolio investment* to be accounted for by the *cost method.* However there is one more possibility. Under Section 3055 the investee could be a joint venture. Accounting for investments in joint ventures is discussed in Chapter 11.

Section 3050 further requires that a loss due to the decline in the market value of a long-term investment below its carrying value should be recognized. This applies to all three types of investments discussed in this section. If the investee is a subsidiary which is consolidated, the assets of the subsidiary should be written down for consolidation purposes to reflect the decline in value. For example a sustained period of losses of a subsidiary may suggest that any consolidated goodwill associated with that subsidiary should be written off.

Section 1580 "Business Combinations"   A business combination occurs when one company gains control over the net assets of another company. A subsidiary is a company that is controlled by a parent company, and therefore is a business combination. On the date of acquisition of the subsidiary, the parent must apply the provisions of this section to determine if the combination is to be accounted for as a *purchase* or a *pooling.* These provisions, and the two methods of accounting, were discussed in Chapter 4. It should be noted that significant influence investments, portfolio investments, and joint venture investments *are not business combinations* as defined in this section, because control over net assets does not exist.

Section 1600 "Consolidated Financial Statements and the Equity Method of Accounting"   This section is basically a "how-to-do-it section." The consolidation procedures that we have examined in Chapter 5 to 7 and those that we will examine in Chapters 8 to 10, are found here. However this is not a section to be read by a student attempting to learn consolidations for the first time. The procedures are described only in very broad terms, and the section is intended to be used as a guide by accountants who are already familiar with the consolidation process.

The initial paragraph in this section states that the provisions deal with "the preparation of consolidated financial statements where the related business combination was accounted for by the purchase method." The implication is that if consolidated financial statements are to be prepared for a business combination accounted for under the pooling method, the provisions described in this section would not apply. Many of this section's provisions could only apply to a purchase combination. The write-off of the purchase discrepancy for consolidated purposes is an obvious example. However the handling of *intercompany receivables and payables, intercompany revenues and expenses, and unrealized gains and losses on intercompany asset transfers* are, in the opinion of the authors, *examples of provisions that would also apply to the consolidation of a pooled subsidiary.* It would also appear logical to assume that if a pooled subsidiary was not consolidated under the provisions of Section 3050, then the financial statement presentation of the investment required by this section (equity or cost) would also apply.

REVIEW QUESTIONS

1 ''Consolidated financial statement balances will be the same, regardless of whether a parent company uses the equity method or the cost method to account for a subsidiary's operations.'' Why is this quotation true?

2 Both Parnell Corporation and Plankton Company have wholly owned subsidiaries. Parnell Corporation's general ledger has an Intercompany Dividend Revenue account, and an Intercompany Investment Income account appears in Plankton Company's ledger. Do both companies use the same method of accounting for their subsidiaries' operating results? Explain.

3 What are the components of consolidated net income?

4 Outline the calculation of the following, when the parent company uses the cost method:
   a consolidated net income
   b consolidated retained earnings

5 What is the initial working paper entry when the parent has used the cost method to account for its investment?

6 What accounts on the financial statements of the parent company will have balances that are different under the cost and equity methods?

7 Under what circumstances is it acceptable for a parent company to report its non-consolidated subsidiary under **a** equity method; **b** cost method?

8 Which of the following investments would come under the provisions of Section 1580 of the **CICA Handbook:**
   a joint venture
   b significant influence
   c portfolio
   d subsidiary? Explain.

9 What is the modified form of the equity method as described in Section 3050.12 of the **CICA Handbook?**

10 What paragraph in the **CICA Handbook** is probably being used by companies that do not consolidate their finance subsidiaries?

EXERCISES

Ex. 7-1 When Pierce Company purchased 95% of Sill Company on January 1, Year 1, the $60,000 purchase discrepancy was allocated entirely to goodwill to be amortized over the maximum period allowable. Pierce Company uses the cost method to account for its investment. Pierce reported a Year 1 net income of $25,000 and declared no dividends. Sill Company reported net income of $40,000 and paid dividends of $9,000 in Year 1. The shareholders' equity of Sill amounted to $100,000 on January 1, Year 1.
Compute:
a Consolidated net income, Year 1
b Minority interest on the Year 1 consolidated income statement
c Investment in Sill Company common stock on December 31, Year 1 (equity method)

Ex. 7-2 Panta Corporation purchased 80% of Santo Company on January 1, Year 1 for $500,000. Santo had common stock of $400,000 and retained earnings of $100,000 on that date.

On January 1, Year 1, the inventory of Santo was undervalued by $30,000 and a patent with an estimated remaining life of 5 years was overvalued by $65,000. Any goodwill is to be amortized over 20 years. On December 31, Year 4, Panta had retained earnings amounting to $90,000 while Santo had retained earnings of $225,000. Panta uses the cost method. Compute the following on December 31, Year 4:

a Consolidated retained earnings
b Minority interest
c Investment in Santo (equity method)
d Consolidated goodwill
e Proof of consolidated goodwill using the Investment in Santo (equity method) from part (c)

Ex. 7-3 Summarized balance sheets of Pedro Company and its subsidiary Santo Corporation on December 31, Year 4 are as follows:

	Pedro Company	Santo Corporation	Consolidated
Current assets	160,000	700,000	860,000
Investment in Santo (at cost)	640,000		
Other assets	600,000	900,000	1,500,000
	1,400,000	1,600,000	2,360,000
Liabilities	800,000	200,000	1,000,000
Minority interest			280,000
Common stock	900,000	600,000	900,000
Retained earnings (deficit)	(300,000)	800,000	180,000
	1,400,000	1,600,000	2,360,000

On the date that Pedro acquired its interest in Santo there was no purchase discrepancy and the carrying values of Santo's net assets were equal to market values. During the year Pedro reported a net loss of $60,000 while Santo reported a net income of $140,000. No dividends were declared by either company in Year 4. Pedro uses the cost method to account for its investment.

Instructions Compute the following:
a The percentage of Santo shares owned by Pedro Company
b Consolidated net income for Year 4
c Pedro Company's December 31, Year 3 retained earnings if the equity method had been in use
d The retained earnings of Santo Corporation on the date that Pedro acquired its interest in Santo

Ex. 7-4 Peony Company purchased an 85% interest in Spirea Corporation on December 31, Year 1, for $650,000. On that date Spirea Corporation had common stock of $500,000 and retained earnings of $100,000. The purchase discrepancy was allocated $78,200 to inventory with the balance to goodwill (estimated life, 10 years). Spirea reported a net income of $30,000 in Year 2 and $52,000 in Year 3. While no dividends were declared in Year 2, Spirea declared $15,000 dividends in Year 3.

Peony Company uses the cost method and reported a net income of $28,000 in Year 2 and a net loss of $45,000 in Year 3. Peony's retained earnings on December 31, Year 3 amounted to $91,000.

Instructions Compute the following:
a Minority interest in net income for Year 2 and Year 3
b Consolidated net income for Year 2 and Year 3

c Consolidated retained earnings on December 31, Year 3
d Minority interest on December 31, Year 3
e Investment in Spirea Corporation common shares on December 31, Year 3 (equity method)
f Consolidated goodwill on December 31, Year 3

Ex 7-5 The following entry was entered in the consolidated financial statements working paper for the current year.

Intercompany dividend revenue	95,000	
Investment in subsidiary company	74,100	
Intercompany investment income		161,500
Retained earnings — beginning of year		7,600

The 80% owned subsidiary company had a retained earnings balance of $150,000 at the end of the current year. The purchase discrepancy had been fully amortized prior to the start of the current year.

a What is the purpose of the working paper entry?
b Prepare a retained earnings statement for the subsidiary company for the current year.
c What is the amount of the minority interest that will appear on the consolidated income statement for the current year?

Ex 7-6 The following statements of net income and retained earnings were prepared by Pinto Corporation and Savoy Company on December 31 of the current year.

	Pinto Corporation	Savoy Company
Sales	$ 900,000	$ 500,000
Dividend income	60,000	
Total	$ 960,000	$ 500,000
Cost of sales	$ 600,000	$ 300,000
Operating expenses	200,000	80,000
Total	$ 800,000	$ 380,000
Net income	$ 160,000	$ 120,000
Retained earnings, January 1	301,000	584,000
	$ 461,000	$ 704,000
Dividends	150,000	80,000
Retained earnings, December 31	$ 311,000	$ 624,000

Pinto obtained its 75% interest in Savoy 8 years ago when Savoy had retained earnings amounting to $53,000. The purchase discrepancy on acquisition date was allocated entirely to equipment with an estimated remaining life of 10 years, and amounted to $80,000. Pinto uses the cost method.

Prepare the following statements for the current year ended December 31:

a Consolidated income statement.
b Consolidated retained earnings.

CASES

Case 7-1 On January 2, Year 6, Petro Corporation issued 200,000 shares of its common stock in exchange for all of the 100,000 shares of Swiss Company's outstanding common stock in a pooling-type business combination. The current fair value of Petro's common stock was $40 a share on the date of the combination. The balance sheets of Petro and Swiss immediately before the combination contained the following information:

Petro Corporation

Common stock	$ 9,000,000
Retained earnings	11,000,000
Total shareholders' equity	$20,000,000

Swiss Company

Common stock	$ 3,000,000
Retained earnings	4,000,000
Total shareholders' equity	$ 7,000,000

Additional information is as follows:

(1) Net income for the year ended December 31, Year 6, was $1,150,000 for Petro and $350,000 for Swiss. The net income for Petro does not include its share of Swiss Company's net income.
(2) During Year 6, Petro declared and paid $900,000 in dividends to its shareholders and Swiss declared and paid $220,000 in dividends to Petro.
(3) Petro uses the equity method, but has not recorded its share of Swiss net income for the year, nor any purchase discrepancy amortization.
(4) Any purchase discrepancy will be amortized over 40 years.

Instructions

a Prepare the shareholders' equity section of the consolidated balance sheet of Petro Corporation and subsidiary on December 31, Year 6. Prepare a supporting analysis for consolidated retained earnings.

b Assume that this is a purchase-type business combination and repeat the requirements of part **a**.

Case 7-2 A few days after the 31 December year end of Stanford Resources Ltd., the company's accountant presented the President, Mr. Bill Johnson, with preliminary Year 3 financial statements with comparative figures for Year 2. Although many of the balances had not yet been finalized, Johnson wanted a rough idea of the Year 3 results. The following two items eventually captured his attention:

	Year 3	Year 2
Receivable from Bromly Company	75,000	–
Investment in Bromly Company	980,000	–

The President wants to know how these two items should be presented on the finalized 31 December Year 3 balance sheet of Stanford Resources Ltd.

Instructions Outline your response to Mr. Johnson.

PROBLEMS

7-1 On December 31, Year 1 the financial statements on page 290 were prepared. Company P uses the cost method to account for its investment.

Other information:

Company P purchased 80% of the stock of Company S January 1, Year 1 for $15,200. At that date the equipment of Company S had a fair market value of $12,000 with an estimated remaining life of 8 years. The book values of all other assets and liabilities of Company S were equal to fair market values. Any goodwill is to be amortized over a 20-year period.

Instructions: Prepare a working paper for consolidated financial statements on December 31, Year 1.

INCOME STATEMENT FOR YEAR 1

	Company P	Company S
Sales	48,000	30,000
Dividend Income from S	2,000	
Total Revenue	50,000	30,000
Cost of Sales	26,500	14,700
Expenses (Misc.)	5,000	8,000
Total Expenses	31,500	22,700
Net Income	18,500	7,300

RETAINED EARNINGS STATEMENT FOR YEAR 1

	Company P	Company S
Balance January 1	85,000	6,000
Net Income	18,500	7,300
	103,500	13,300
Dividends	6,000	2,500
Balance December 31	97,500	10,800

BALANCE SHEET DECEMBER 31, YEAR 1

	Company P	Company S
Assets (Misc.)	137,300	11,300
Inventory	12,000	7,000
Equipment (Net)	30,000	14,000
Investment in S–at cost	15,200	
	194,500	32,300
Liabilities	47,000	11,500
Capital stock	50,000	10,000
Retained Earnings	97,500	10,800
	194,500	32,300

7-2 Perch Corporation acquired 82% of State Company's outstanding common stock for $328,000 cash on March 31, Year 8. Out-of-pocket costs of the business combination may be ignored. State's shareholders' equity accounts on March 31, Year 8, were as follows:

Common stock, no par (25,000 shares)	$125,000
Retained earnings	135,000
Total shareholders' equity	$260,000

All of State's identifiable net assets were fairly valued at their March 31, Year 8, carrying amounts except for the following:

	Carrying amounts	Current fair values
Land	$100,000	$120,000
Building (net) (10-year economic life)	200,000	250,000
Patent (net) (8-year economic life)	60,000	80,000

Any goodwill resulting from the business combination is amortized over the maximum period of 40 years. State uses the straight-line method for depreciation and amortization. State includes depreciation expense in cost of goods sold and amortization expense in operating expenses.

During the year ended March 31, Year 9, State reported net income of $1.20 a share and declared and paid no dividends. Perch has used the cost method to account for its investment in State Company.

Instructions Prepare the working paper eliminations for Perch Corporation and subsidiary on March 31, Year 9.

7-3 Pavlich Corporation acquired 75% of the outstanding common stock of Sister Company on October 1, Year 6, for $547,500, including direct out-of-pocket costs. Sister's shareholders' equity on October 1, Year 6, was as follows:

Common stock	$350,000
Retained earnings	200,000
Total shareholders' equity	$550,000

Current fair values of Sister's identifiable net assets exceeded their carrying amounts as follows:

	Excess of current fair values over carrying amounts
Inventories	$30,000
Plant assets (net) (economic life 10 years)	50,000
Patents (net) (economic life 5 years)	20,000

Pavlich amortizes goodwill over a 40-year economic life, and both Pavlich and Sister include depreciation expense in cost of goods sold and amortization expense in operating expenses. Both companies use the straight-line method for depreciation and amortization.

For the two fiscal years ended September 30, Year 8, Sister reported net income and declared and paid dividends as follows:

Year ended Sept. 30,	Net income	Dividends
Year 7	$ 80,000	$10,000
Year 8	120,000	75,000

Pavlich accounts for its investment in Sister Company by the cost method.

Instructions Prepare working paper eliminations for Pavlich Corporation and subsidiary on September 30, Year 7 and September 30, Year 8.

7-4 Ping Corporation acquired 80% of the outstanding common shares of Stang Company on December 31, Year 2, for $120,000. On that date, Stang had one class of common shares outstanding at a par value of $100,000 and retained earnings of $30,000. Ping had a $50,000 deficit in retained earnings.

Ping acquired the Stang common stock from Stang's major stockholder primarily to acquire control of signboard leases owned by Stang. The leases will expire on December 31, Year 7, and Ping's executives estimated that the leases, which cannot be renewed, were worth at least $20,000 more than their carrying amount when the Stang common stock was acquired. Stang includes signboard leases amortization in other expenses.

The financial statements for both companies for the year ended December 31, Year 6, are as follows:

PING CORPORATION AND SUBSIDIARY
Financial Statements
For Year Ended December 31, Year 6

	Ping Corporation	Stang Company
Income Statements		
Net sales	$420,000	$300,000
Costs and expenses:		
Cost of goods sold	$315,000	$240,000
Other expenses	65,000	35,000
Total costs and expenses	$380,000	$275,000
Net income	$ 40,000	$ 25,000
Statements of Retained Earnings		
Retained earnings, beginning of year	$ 15,000	$ 59,000
Net income	40,000	25,000
Subtotal	$ 55,000	$ 84,000
Dividends		9,000
Retained earnings, end of year	$ 55,000	$ 75,000
Balance Sheets		
Assets		
Current assets	$172,000	$199,100
Investment in Stang Company common stock	120,000	
Land	25,000	10,500
Building and equipment	200,000	40,000
Accumulated depreciation	(102,000)	(7,000)
Signboard leases (net)		8,400
Total assets	$415,000	$251,000
Liabilities & Shareholders' Equity		
Dividends payable		$ 9,000
Other current liabilities	$ 60,000	67,000
Common stock, $1 par	300,000	100,000
Retained earnings	55,000	75,000
Total liabilities & shareholders' equity	$415,000	$251,000

Stang declared a 9% cash dividend on December 20, Year 6, payable January 16, Year 7, to shareholders of record December 31, Year 6. Ping carries its investment at cost and had not recorded Stang's dividend on December 31, Year 6. Neither company paid dividends during Year 6.

Instructions

a Prepare adjusting entries for Ping Corporation on December 31, Year 6, to convert its accounting for Stang Company to the equity method of accounting.

b Prepare the working paper for consolidated financial statements of Ping Corporation and subsidiary on December 31, Year 6, and the related working paper eliminations. Balances for Ping Corporation should reflect the adjusting entries in *a*.

7-5 The working paper elimination for Plow Corporation and its 90% owned subsidiary, Starr Company, on the date of the business combination was as at the top of page 293. Financial statements of Plow and Starr for the fiscal year ended November 30, Year 2, were as shown at the bottom of page 293.

PLOW CORPORATION AND SUBSIDIARY
Working Paper Elimination
November 30, Year 1

Common Stock — Starr	280,000	
Retained Earnings — Starr	220,000	
Inventories — Starr	18,000	
Goodwill — Starr	36,000	
Investment in Starr Company Common Stock — Plow . . .		504,000
Minority interest in net assets of subsidiary		50,000

To eliminate intercompany investment and equity accounts of subsidiary on date of
business combination, and to allocate the purchase discrepancy to identifiable assets
acquired, with remainder to goodwill having an economic life of 40 years; and to establish minority interest in net assets of subsidiary on date of business combination.

PLOW CORPORATION AND STARR COMPANY
Financial Statements
For Year Ended November 30, Year 2

	Plow Corporation	Starr Company
Income Statements		
Revenue:		
Net Sales	$800,000	$415,000
Intercompany dividend income	27,000	
Total revenue	$ 827,000	$415,000
Costs and expenses:		
Cost of goods sold	$500,000	$110,000
Operating expenses	200,000	80,000
Income taxes expense	60,000	135,000
Total costs and expenses	$760,000	$325,000
Net income	$ 67,000	$ 90,000
Statements of Retained Earnings		
Retained earnings, beginning of year	$640,000	$220,000
Net income	67,000	90,000
Subtotal	$707,000	$310,000
Dividends	60,000	30,000
Retained earnings, end of year	$647,000	$280,000
Balance Sheets		
Assets		
Investment in Starr Company common stock	$ 504,000	
Other	1,893,000	$960,000
Total assets	$2,397,000	$960,000
Liabilities & Shareholders' Equity		
Liabilities	$ 650,000	$400,000
Common stock, $1 par	1,100,000	280,000
Retained earnings	647,000	280,000
Total liabilities & shareholders' equity	$2,397,000	$960,000

Instructions Prepare a working paper for consolidated financial statements o Plow Corporation and subsidiary for the fiscal year ended November 30, Year 2 and the related working paper elimination. Include goodwill amortization in opera ing expenses.

7-6 The following financial statements were prepared on December 31, Year 6.

Balance Sheet

	Pearl Company	Silver Company
Inventory	$1,600,000	$ 220,000
Plant and Equipment	3,000,000	2,690,000
Accumulated Depreciation	(750,000)	(310,000)
Investment in Silver Company — at cost	2,500,000	
	$6,350,000	$2,600,000
Capital Stock	$3,000,000	$1,000,000
Contributed Surplus	850,000	600,000
Retained Earnings	2,500,000	1,000,000
	$6,350,000	$2,600,000

Income Statement

	Pearl Company	Silver Company
Sales	$4,000,000	$1,000,000
Dividend Income	150,000	
Total Revenue	$4,150,000	$1,000,000
Cost of Sales	$2,500,000	$ 400,000
Misc. Expenses	320,000	70,000
Depreciation Expense	80,000	10,000
Income Tax Expense	250,000	120,000
Total	$3,150,000	$ 600,000
Net Income	$1,000,000	$ 400,000

Retained Earnings Statement

	Pearl Company	Silver Company
Balance January 1	$2,000,000	$ 800,000
Net Income	1,000,000	400,000
Subtotals	$3,000,000	$1,200,000
Dividends	500,000	200,000
Balance December 31	$2,500,000	$1,000,000

Other information:

Pearl Company purchased 75% of the outstanding voting stock of Silver Company for $2,500,000 on July 1, Year 2, at which time Silver Company's retained earnings was $400,000. The purchase discrepancy on this date was allocated as follows:

30% to undervalued inventory

40% to equipment; remaining life 8 years

Balance is Goodwill to be amortized over 15 years

Instructions Prepare a working paper for consolidated financial statements on December 31, Year 6.

7-7 Balance sheet and income statement data for two affiliated companies for the current year are given below:

BALANCE SHEET DATA
as of December 31, Year 4

	Able Company	Baker Company
Cash	$ 40,000	$ 21,000
Receivables	92,000	84,000
Inventories	56,000	45,000
Land	20,000	60,000
Plant and equipment	200,000	700,000
Accumulated depreciation	(80,000)	(350,000)
Investment in Baker Company (cost)	272,000	
Advances to Baker Company	100,000	
Total assets	$700,000	$560,000
Accounts payable	$130,000	$ 96,500
Advances payable		$100,000
Common stock	400,000	200,000
Beginning retained earnings	162,300	154,000
Net income for the year	29,700	17,500
Dividends	(22,000)	(8,000)
Total liabilities & shareholders' equity	$700,000	$560,000

INCOME STATEMENT DATA
Year ended December 31, Year 4

	Able Company	Baker Company
Sales revenues	$600,000	$400,000
Interest revenues	6,700	
Intercompany dividend revenue	6,400	
Total revenues	$613,100	$400,000
Cost of goods sold	$334,000	$225,000
Depreciation expense	20,000	70,000
Selling and administrative expense	207,000	74,000
Interest expense	1,700	6,000
Income taxes expense	20,700	7,500
Total expenses	$583,400	$382,500
Net Income	$ 29,700	$ 17,500

Other Information:
(1) Able Company acquired an 80% interest in Baker Company on January 1, Year 1 for $272,000. On that date the following information was noted about specific net assets of Baker:

	Book Value	Fair Value
Inventory	$20,000	$50,000
Land	25,000	45,000
Equipment (est. life 15 years)	60,000	78,000

(2) On January 1, Year 1, Baker had a retained earnings balance of $30,000.
(3) Any Goodwill is to be amortized over a 20-year period.
(4) Able carries its investment at cost.

Instructions Prepare the following:

a Consolidated Income Statement

b Consolidated Retained Earnings Statement

c Consolidated Balance Sheet

7-8 On January 2, Year 1, Ayr Ltd. purchased 80 percent of the outstanding shares o
York Ltd. for $4,120,000 in cash. On that date, York Ltd.'s balance sheet and the fai
market value of its identifiable assets and liabilities were as follows:

	Book Value	Fair Value
Cash	$ 500,000	$ 500,000
Accounts Receivable	1,500,000	1,500,000
Inventory	2,000,000	2,200,000
Plant and Equipment (net)	4,500,000	4,500,000
Patents (net)	1,000,000	1,500,000
	$9,500,000	
Accounts Payable	$2,000,000	$2,000,000
Bonds Payable 10%	3,000,000	3,300,000
Common Stock	2,000,000	
Retained Earnings	2,500,000	
	$9,500,000	

The patents had a remaining life of 10 years and the bonds mature on December 31
Year 10. Both companies use fifo and both companies amortize goodwill ove
20 years.

On December 31, Year 3, the trial balances of the two companies are as follows

	Ayr Ltd.	York Ltd.
Cash	$ 400,000	$ 600,000
Accounts Receivable	$ 1,000,000	$ 1,300,000
Inventory	4,600,000	1,900,000
Plant and Equipment (net)	8,000,000	5,000,000
Patents (net)		700,000
Investment in York Ltd. (cost)	4,120,0000	
Cost of Goods Sold	5,000,000	3,000,000
Depreciation Expense	900,000	400,000
Patent Amortization Expense		100,000
Interest Expense	480,000	300,000
Other Expenses	3,280,000	1,000,000
Dividends	300,000	100,000
	$28,080,000	$14,400,000
Accounts Payable	$ 3,000,000	$ 1,400,000
Bonds Payable	4,000,000	3,000,000
Common Stock	5,000,000	2,000,000
Retained Earnings	6,000,000	3,000,000
Sales	10,000,000	5,000,000
Dividend Revenue	80,000	
	$28,080,000	$14,400,000

Instructions:

a Prepare consolidated financial statements on December 31, Year 3.

b If Ayr Ltd. had used the equity method, what accounts on the trial balances would have amounts different than those shown?

c Compute the equity method balances of these accounts.

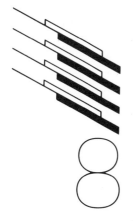

CONSOLIDATED FINANCIAL STATEMENTS: INTERCOMPANY REVENUES AND EXPENSES, INTERCOMPANY PROFITS AND LOSSES IN NONDEPRECIABLE ASSETS

The preparation of **consolidated financial statements** for external reporting purposes treats the separate legal entities of a parent and its subsidiaries as a single economic entity. The companies within this single entity are often called **affiliated companies.** Consolidated financial statements should reflect only transactions between the entity and those outside the entity, and should not include transactions between affiliated companies. However, affiliated companies often sell their products to each other, loan surplus cash to each other, and charge each other for services provided. These **intercompany transactions** that take place within the economic entity must be eliminated in the preparation of consolidated financial statements if these statements are to reflect only transactions with those outside the entity. The elimination of intercompany receivables and payables was previously illustrated (Chapter 5). Two other types of intercompany transactions that are eliminated are:

1 Intercompany revenues and expenses, and
2 Intercompany profits in assets.

Before we illustrate the **elimination of these intercompany transactions** we will examine an alternative way of presenting minority interest in the consolidated income statement.

An alternative presentation of minority interest

Our previous examples have presented the **minority interest** in the net income of a subsidiary among the expenses in the consolidated income statement. An alternative way would be to show minority interest as an **allocation of net income** rather than as a determinant of net income. The following example will illustrate this point.

Parent Company owns 90% of Subsidiary Company. Any purchase discrepancy has been fully amortized in prior years. Parent Company uses the equity method to account for its investment but has made no entry during the current year. The two company's summarized income statements for the current year (Year 1) are as follows:

Income statements of parent and subsidiary

	Parent Company	Subsidiary Company
Sales	$20,000	$8,000
Cost of goods sold	$13,000	$4,300
Expenses	3,600	2,000
Total costs & expenses	$16,600	$6,300
Net income	$ 3,400	$1,700

We can calculate **consolidated net income** for the current year in the following manner:

Calculation of Year 1 consolidated net income

Parent Company net income		$3,400
Subsidiary Company net income	$1,700	
Parent Company's share of Subsidiary Company's net income	.9	1,530
Consolidated net income		$4,930

From this calculation we can see that the minority interest in the net income of Subsidiary Company will be $170 (10% of $1,700). A consolidated income statement for the current year, prepared without using a working paper, is as follows:

Consolidated income statement prepared without a working paper

PARENT COMPANY AND SUBSIDIARY
Consolidated Income Statement
For Year 1

Sales ($20,000 + $8,000)	$28,000
Cost of goods sold ($13,000 + $4,300)	$17,300
Expenses ($3,600 + $2,000)	5,600
Minority interest (10% × 1,700)	170
Total costs and expenses	$23,070
Net income	$ 4,930

The calculations shown in brackets are used to show how the amounts on the income statement have been arrived at, and would not appear on the financial statement. You will note that minority interest has been shown in the conventional manner. An *alternative way to present minority interest* would be:

PARENT COMPANY AND SUBSIDIARY
Consolidated Income Statement
For Year 1

Sales	$28,000
Cost of goods sold	$17,300
Expenses	5,600
Total costs and expenses	$22,900
Net income — consolidated entity	$ 5,100
Less: Minority interest	170
Net income	$ 4,930

This presentation of minority interest does not significantly alter the consolidated income statement. Total costs and expenses has changed, but net income is unchanged. A new line "Net income — consolidated entity" has been introduced. The presentation of minority interest in this form illustrates the following useful points:

1 The *consolidated entity,* made up of Parent Company and Subsidiary Company earned a *total net income* of $5,100 during the current year.
2 The consolidated entity's net income consists of the net incomes of the *parent* and the *subsidiary* as follows (refer to the calculation of consolidated net income on page 299):

Parent Company net income	$3,400
Subsidiary Company net income	$1,700
Entity's net income	$5,100

3 There are two "*equities*" on a consolidated balance sheet:
  (a) the equity of the *minority shareholders* (in this case represented by 10% of the subsidiary's issued shares), which appears as one amount, and
  (b) the equity of the *controlling shareholders* (the shareholders of the parent) the details of which appear under the heading "Shareholders' Equity."
4 The net income earned by the consolidated entity is allocated to the two "equities" as follows:

Minority interest (to minority interest equity)	$ 170
Consolidated net income (to consolidated retained earnings)	4,930
Total entity net income	$5,100

We again remind the reader that *conventional financial reporting would show minority interest among the expenses on the consol-*

dated income statement. Presentation in this manner tends to disguise the concept of total entity net income and the two "equities" that make up the consolidated entity. In future examples we will illustrate the allocation of the entity's net income to the two equities as a useful device to aid you in the understanding of the consolidation concepts involved in the elimination of intercompany transactions.

INTERCOMPANY REVENUE AND EXPENSES

Intercompany sales and purchases

The following example will be used to illustrate the overall concept of the *elimination of intercompany sales and purchases in the preparation of a consolidated income statement.*

Let your imagination stray a bit and suppose that you went shopping at your local supermarket, and upon paying for your purchases, you noticed that a silver dollar was included in the change that you received from the cashier. You took the silver dollar to a coin dealer and found out that it was a rare coin which was worth substantially more than its face value. The dealer offered you $41 for the coin and you accepted the offer. It is obvious that you made a $40 profit on the sale of the silver dollar to the dealer. An income statement showing only this transaction would appear as follows:

Income statement for coin transaction	
Sales	$41
Cost of Goods Sold	1
Net income (profit)	$40

Now let your imagination stray even further and assume that the following events took place between the time you received the silver dollar from the supermarket and the time you sold it to the coin dealer.

Your pants have four pockets. Let's call them pocket 1, pocket 2, pocket 3, and pocket 4. Pocket 1 received the coin from the supermarket and sold it to pocket 2 for $10. Pocket 2 sold the coin to pocket 3 for $15. Pocket 3 sold the coin to pocket 4 for $25, and then pocket 4 sold the coin to the dealer for $41. Has any part of the transaction changed as far as you (as an entity) are concerned? The answer of course is no. You still had sales of $41, cost of goods sold of $1, and a net income of $40. But assume that your pockets each recorded their share of the transaction, and prepared income statements as follows:

	Pocket 1	Pocket 2	Pocket 3	Pocket 4
Income statements of pockets				
Sales	10	15	25	41
Cost of goods sold	1	10	15	25
Net income	$ 9	$ 5	$10	$16

Notice that the arrows indicate the interpocket transactions that took place. Notice also that the sum of the net incomes of your four pockets is equal to your net income of $40. We should therefore be able to prepare an income statement for you (as an entity) by combining the components of the income statements of your four pockets as follows:

outside
transaction

Sales ($10 + $15 + $25 + $41) $91
Cost of goods sold ($1 + $10 + $15 + $25) 51
Net income $40

However, sales and cost of goods sold are not the correct amounts because they contain the interpocket sales and purchases. They should reflect only sales to and purchases from **outside** the entity. If we eliminate the interpocket sales and purchases we will have an income statement that reflects transactions that you as an entity incurred with others outside the entity. This statement can be prepared as follows:

	Total of four pockets	Eliminate interpocket sales & purchases	Total
Sales	$91	$50	$41
Cost of goods sold	51	50	1
Net income	$40	$ 0	$40

Notice that if we eliminate an equal amount of revenue and expense from an income statement the resultant net income remains unchanged.

Your four pockets in this example are similar in all respects to a parent company and its subsidiary companies. Let us assume that a parent company (P) has holdings in three subsidiaries as follows: P owns 80% of S1, 90% of S2 and 75% of S3. The coin transactions previously illustrated were carried out by P and its three subsidiaries. These were the only transactions that took place during the current year. At the year end the parent and its subsidiaries prepared the following income statements:

	P	S1	S2	S3
Sales	$10	$15	$25	$41
Cost of goods sold	1	10	15	25
Net income	$ 9	$ 5	$10	$16

We are assuming that P uses the equity method but has made no entries during the current year and all purchase discrepancies have been fully amortized in prior years.

Before preparing a consolidated income statement, we can calculate *consolidated net income* as follows:

	S1	S2	S3	Total	
P's net income					$ 9
Subsidiary net income	$ 5	$10	$16	$31	
P's ownership	.8	.9	.75		
Share of subsidiary net income	$ 4	$ 9	$12		25
Consolidated net income					$34

Suppose we prepare a consolidated income statement without eliminating intercompany sales and purchases in the following manner:

P AND SUBSIDIARIES

**Consolidated Income Statement
For Current Year**

Sales (10 + 15 + 25 + 41)	$91
Cost of goods sold (1 + 10 + 15 + 25)	51
Net income — consolidated entity	$40
Less minority interest (see calculation below)	6
Net income	$34

Calculation of minority interest

S1 (20% × $5)	$1
S2 (10% × $10)	$1
S3 (25% × $16)	$4
Total	$6

Note that the net income of the consolidated entity is made up of the net incomes of the parent and its three subsidiaries. But we have not eliminated the intercompany sales and purchases that took place during the year. If we eliminate these intercompany transactions the net income earned by the consolidated entity will not change. Minority interest and consolidated net income are only *allocations* of the entity's net income and so they also will not be affected by the elimination of these intercompany sales and purchases. The consolidated income statement after the elimination of intercompany sales and purchases would be as follows:

Consolidated income
statement after elimination
of intercompany sales and
purchases

Sales	(91–50)	$41
Cost of Goods Sold	(51–50)	1
Net income — consolidated entity		$40
Less minority interest		6
Net Income		$34

Other examples of intercompany revenue and expenses

Suppose the parent company *loans* $100,000 to the subsidiary company and receives a note payable on demand with interest at 10%. The transactions would be recorded as follows:

Parent Company		Subsidiary Company	
Note Receivable .. $100,000		Cash $100,000	
Cash	$100,000	Note payable ...	$100,000

Journal entries of parent company and subsidiary to record intercompany loan transactions

To record intercompany borrowings on January 1 of the current year.

Cash .... $ 10,000		Interest expense .. $ 10,000	
Interest Revenue	$ 10,000	Cash	$ 10,000

To record the intercompany payment of interest on December 31 of the current year.

From the consolidated entity's point of view all that has happened is the transfer of cash from one bank account to another. No revenue has been earned, no expense has been incurred, and there are no receivables or payables. The elimination of $10,000 interest revenue and interest expense on the consolidated income statement does not change the net income of the consolidated entity. If total net income is not affected, then the amount allocated to the minority and controlling interest is also not affected. On the consolidated balance sheet we eliminate $100,000 from notes receivable and notes payable. An equal elimination of assets and liabilities on a balance sheet leaves the amounts of the two equities (minority interest and controlling interest) unchanged.

Note also that if the roles were reversed and it was the subsidiary that loaned $100,000 to the parent company, the eliminations on the consolidated income statement and balance sheet would be the same and would have no effect on the amount of the minority interest appearing on each statement.

Intercompany Management Fees   Often the parent company will charge its subsidiary companies a yearly *management fee* as a means of allocating head office costs to all the companies within the group. (We will not discuss the pros and cons of this procedure here. Readers who are interested in the reasons for, and effectiveness of, allocations of this nature are advised to consult any management accounting textbook.) From an external reporting point of view we have intercompany revenue and expenses which must be eliminated on the consolidated income statement.

Intercompany Rentals   Occasionally buildings or equipment owned by one company are used by another company within the group. Rather than transfer legal title, the companies agree on a yearly *rental* to be charged, resulting in the necessity to eliminate the intercompany rental revenues and expenses from the consolidated income statement.

In summary, the following intercompany revenues and expenses are eliminated from the consolidated income statement:

(1) Intercompany sales and purchases
(2) Intercompany interest revenue and expense
(3) Intercompany management fee revenue and expense
(4) Intercompany rental revenue and expense

These items are eliminated to stop the double counting of revenue and expenses but have **no effect on the calculation of the minority interest** in the net income of the subsidiary companies.

INTERCOMPANY PROFITS IN ASSETS

If one affiliated company sells assets to another affiliated company there is a possibility that the profit or loss recorded on the transaction has not been realized from the point of view of consolidated entity. If the purchasing affiliate has sold these assets outside the group all profits (losses) recorded are realized. If, however, all or a portion of these assets have not been sold outside the group, we must eliminate the remaining intercompany profit (loss) from the consolidated statements. The intercompany profit (loss) will be realized for consolidation purposes during the accounting period in which the particular asset is sold to outsiders. The sale to outsiders may also result in an additional profit (loss) which is not adjusted in the consolidation process. *Three types of unrealized intercompany profits (losses)* are eliminated:

(1) profits in inventory
(2) profits in non-depreciable assets
(3) profits in depreciable assets

The first two will be discussed in this chapter, the latter in Chapter 9. The examples that follow will illustrate the *boldback* of unrealized intercompany profits *in one accounting period* and the *realization* of the profit *in a subsequent period.* The holdback and realization of intercompany losses will not be illustrated, but the same principles will apply.

Unrealized intercompany inventory profits — subsidiary selling

Refer to the illustration of the consolidated income statement of Parent Company and its subsidiary on page 300. Let us assume that there were intercompany transactions during Year 1 which were overlooked when the consolidated income statement was prepared. These transactions were as follows:

1 During Year 1 Subsidiary Company made sales to Parent Company amounting to $6,000 at a gross profit rate of 30%.
2 At the end of Year 1 Parent Company's inventory contained items purchased from Subsidiary Company for $2,000.

3 Subsidiary Company paid (or accrued) income tax on its taxable income at a rate of 40%.

The income statements of Parent Company and Subsidiary Company for Year 1 were as follows (details of income tax expense have been added):

	Parent Company	Subsidiary Company
Sales	$20,000	$8,000
Cost of goods sold	13,000	4,300
Miscellaneous expense	1,400	900
Income tax expense	2,200	1,100
Total costs and expenses	$16,600	$6,300
Net income	$ 3,400	$1,700

Note that the subsidiary recorded a gross profit of $1,800 (30% × $6,000) from its sales to the parent during the year and paid income tax of $720 (40% × $1,800) on this profit. If the parent had sold all of its intercompany purchases to customers outside the consolidated entity, then this gross profit of $1,800 would be considered **realized** as far as the entity is concerned. But the parent's inventory contains items purchased from the subsidiary for $2,000. There is an **unrealized** intercompany gross profit of $600 (30% × $2,000) in this inventory. From the **consolidated entity's** point of view this $600 profit will be realized when the parent sells the items to outsiders. This $600 profit must be held back from consolidated income in Year 1. Furthermore, the $240 tax expense relating to this profit must also be held back from the consolidated income statement. **Income tax allocation** is used whenever there is a timing difference between taxable income and accounting income. When this $600 gross profit is realized on a future consolidated income statement, income tax expense will be increased to match the tax expense with the profit.

We will now prepare (without a working paper) the Year 1 consolidated income statement with adjustments for the intercompany transactions that took place.

The intercompany transactions that require elimination are summarized as follows:

Intercompany sales and purchases	$6,000
Unrealized profit in ending inventory	
Gross profit	$ 600
Income tax (40%)	240
Aftertax profit	$ 360

Before preparing a consolidated income statement it is useful to calculate consolidated net income as follows:

Parent Company net income		$3,400
Subsidiary Company net income	$1,700	
Less: profit in ending inventory	360	
Adjusted net income	$1,340	
Parent Company's share	.9	1,206
Consolidated net income		$4,606

The *aftertax intercompany profit* is deducted from Subsidiary Company's net income because the subsidiary was the selling company in the transaction, and its net income contains this profit being held back for consolidation purposes.

The consolidated income statement is prepared by adding the revenue and expenses of the two companies and eliminating the intercompany transactions as follows:

PARENT COMPANY AND SUBSIDIARY
Consolidated Income Statement
Year 1

Sales (20,000 + 8,000 − 6,000)[a]	$22,000
Cost of goods sold (13,000 + 4,300 − 6,000[a] + 600)[b]	$11,900
Miscellaneous expense (1,400 + 900)	2,300
Income tax expense (2,200 + 1,100 − 240)[c]	3,060
Total costs and expenses	$17,260
Net income − consolidated entity	$ 4,740
Less: Minority interest (10% × 1,340)	134
Net income	$ 4,606

Net income − consolidated entity consists of:	
Parent's net income	$ 3,400
Subsidiary's adjusted net income	$ 1,340
Entity's net income	$ 4,740

The eliminations made on the income statement require further elaboration:

1 The elimination of intercompany sales and purchases are equal reductions of revenues and expenses which do not change the net income of the consolidated entity nor the amount allocated to the minority and controlling equities. This elimination is labelled (a).

2 To hold back the gross profit of $600 from the consolidated entity's net income, cost of goods sold is increased by $600. The elimination entry for the gross profit is labelled (b). The reasoning is as follows:
    (a) Cost of goods sold is made up of opening inventory, plus purchases, minus ending inventory.
    (b) The ending inventory contains the $600 gross profit.
    (c) If we subtract the $600 profit from the ending inventory the resultant amount represents cost to the consolidated entity.

(d) A reduction of $600 from ending inventory increases cost of goods sold by $600.

(e) This increase of cost of goods sold reduces the net income earned by the entity by $600.

3 Because the entity's before-tax net income has been reduced by $600, it is necessary to reduce the income tax expense by $240 (the tax paid on the profit held back). The elimination entry for income tax is labelled (c).

4 A reduction of income tax expense increases the net income of the consolidated entity.

5 A $600 increase in cost of goods sold together with a $240 reduction in income tax expense results in the aftertax profit of $360 being removed from the entity's net income.

Intercompany inventory profit elimination on the consolidated balance sheet

Simplistically, a consolidated balance sheet is prepared by adding together the assets and liabilities of the parent and subsidiary companies. The hold-back for consolidated purposes of $360 aftertax profit in the consolidated income statement must also be reflected in the preparation of the December 31, Year 1 consolidated balance sheet. The consolidated income statement eliminations reduced the entity's net income by $360, which was allocated to the two equities as follows:

<table>
<tr><td style="text-align:right">Allocation of aftertax
inventory profit being held
back to two equities</td><td>*To minority interest (10% × $360)* ....</td><td>*$ 36*</td></tr>
<tr><td></td><td>*To controlling interest (90% × $360)* ....</td><td>*324*</td></tr>
<tr><td></td><td>*Total allocated to the two equities* ....</td><td>*$360*</td></tr>
</table>

While the reduction allocated to the controlling interest is reflected in the consolidated retained earnings statement and thus ends up in the consolidated balance sheet, the reduction allocated to the minority interest does not flow to the balance sheet through any similar type of statement. The minority interest appearing on the consolidated balance sheet requires a calculation as follows:

<table>
<tr><td style="text-align:right">Calculation of minority
interest as at Dec., 31,
Year 1</td><td>*Shareholders' equity of Subsidiary Company on Dec. 31, Year 1* ....</td><td>*$XXX*</td></tr>
<tr><td></td><td>*Less: profit in ending inventory* ....</td><td>*360*</td></tr>
<tr><td></td><td>*Adjusted shareholders' equity* ....</td><td>*$XXX*</td></tr>
<tr><td></td><td>*Minority interest share* ....</td><td>*.10*</td></tr>
<tr><td></td><td>*Minority interest* ....</td><td>*$XXX*</td></tr>
</table>

If the equity side of the balance sheet has been reduced by $360 the **asset side must also be reduced** by a similar total amount. The elimination of the unrealized profit from the asset side would be accomplished as follows

Elimination of inventory
profit and adjustment
for tax effects on asset
side of consolidated
balance sheet

PARENT COMPANY AND SUBSIDIARY
Consolidated Balance Sheet
December 31, Year 1

Assets

Inventory (P + S − $600)[b]	$XXX
Deferred income tax (+ $240)[c]	240
Total assets	$XXX

The reasons for these eliminations can be further explained as follows:

1 The holdback of the $600 gross profit on the consolidated income statement was accomplished by reducing the amount of ending inventory in the cost of goods sold calculation. (A reduction in ending inventory increases cost of goods sold). The ending inventory in the cost of goods sold calculation is the asset inventory on the consolidated balance sheet. Removing the $600 gross profit from the asset results in the consolidated inventory being reflected at cost to the entity. This elimination is labelled (b).

2 On the consolidated income statement we reduced income tax expense by $240, representing the tax paid on the gross profit. As far as the consolidated entity is concerned this $240 is an asset, and it will become an expense when the inventory is sold to outsiders. This deferred tax asset is "added into" the assets on the consolidated balance sheet by the elimination labelled (c). (The illustration assumes that neither the parent nor the subsidiary had deferred income taxes on their individual balance sheets.)

3 A reduction of $600 from inventory and a $240 increase in deferred income taxes results in a net reduction to consolidated assets of $360, which equals the $360 reduction that has taken place on the equity side.

Equity Method Journal Entries   Parent Company would make the following journal entries in Year 1 if it used the equity method to account for its investment in Subsidiary Company:

Dec. 31	Investment in Subsidiary Company	$1,530	
	Intercompany investment income		$1,530
	To record 90% of Subsidiary Company's reported		
	net income for Year 1 ($1,700 × .9 = $1,530).		
Dec. 31	Intercompany investment income	324	
	Investment in Subsidiary Company		324
	To hold back 90% of the intercompany inventory		
	profit recorded by Subsidiary Company in Year 1		
	($360 × .9 = $324).		

The intercompany investment income would appear on the parent company's income statement as follows:

PARENT COMPANY

Income Statement

Year 1

Sales	$20,000
Intercompany investment income (1,530–324)	1,206
Total revenue	$21,206
Cost of goods sold	$13,000
Miscellaneous expense	1,400
Income tax expense	2,200
Total costs and expenses	$16,600
Net income	$ 4,606

The use of the equity method *always results in the parent's net income being equal to consolidated net income.*

Realization of intercompany inventory profits

Our previous example illustrated the *holdback* of an unrealized intercompany inventory profit *in Period 1*. We will continue our example of Parent Company and Subsidiary Company for *Period 2*. Let us assume that during this period there were no intercompany transactions and that on December 31, Year 2 the inventory of Parent Company contained no items purchased from Subsidiary Company. In other words, the intercompany inventory profit that existed on December 31, Year 1 has been *realized* in Year 2 because Parent Company has sold its Year 2 opening inventory. While Parent Company is still using the equity method, it has not as yet made the equity method journal entries in Year 2. The income statements prepared by the two companies for Year 2 were as follows:

	Parent Company	Subsidiary Company
Sales	$25,000	$12,000
Cost of goods sold	$16,000	$ 5,500
Miscellaneous expense	2,350	1,400
Income tax expense	2,600	2,000
Total costs and expenses	$20,950	$ 8,900
Net income	$ 4,050	$ 3,100

Consolidated net income for Year 2 is calculated as follows:

Parent Company net income		$4,050
Subsidiary Company net income	$3,100	
Add: Profit in opening Inventory	360	
Adjusted net income	$3,460	
Parent Company's share	.9	3,114
Consolidated net income		$7,164

The aftertax intercompany inventory profit of $360, which was **held back in Year 1**, is being **realized in Year 2**, and is **added to the net income of Subsidiary Company** because the subsidiary was the company that originally recorded the profit.

In preparing a consolidated income statement for Year 2, we prepare elimination entries for the intercompany transaction to bring the original intercompany gross profit into the income statement and increase income tax expense for the tax on this profit. The Year 2 consolidated income statement can be prepared (without a working paper) as follows:

<table>
<tr><td rowspan="10" style="vertical-align:top">Year 2 consolidated income statement prepared without working paper

</td><td colspan="2" align="center">**PARENT COMPANY AND SUBSIDIARY**</td></tr>
<tr><td colspan="2" align="center">*Consolidated Income Statement*</td></tr>
<tr><td colspan="2" align="center">*Year 2*</td></tr>
<tr><td>Sales (25,000 + 12,000) . . . .</td><td align="right">$37,000</td></tr>
<tr><td>Cost of goods sold (16,000 + 5,500 − 600)[a] . . . .</td><td align="right">$20,900</td></tr>
<tr><td>Miscellaneous expense (2,350 + 1,400) . . . .</td><td align="right">3,750</td></tr>
<tr><td>Income tax expense (2,600 + 2,000 + 240)[b] . . . .</td><td align="right">4,840</td></tr>
<tr><td>Total costs and expenses . . . .</td><td align="right">$29,490</td></tr>
<tr><td>Net income — consolidated entity . . . .</td><td align="right">$ 7,510</td></tr>
<tr><td>Less: Minority interest (10% × 3,460) . . . .</td><td align="right">346</td></tr>
<tr><td>Net income . . . .</td><td align="right">$ 7,164</td></tr>
</table>

In comparing this consolidated income statement with the calculation of consolidated net income on page 310 you will note that the **entity's net income is made up of the two components** as follows:

<table>
<tr><td rowspan="3" style="vertical-align:top">Components of entity's net income</td><td>Parent's net income . . . .</td><td align="right">$4,050</td></tr>
<tr><td>Subsidiary's adjusted net income . . . .</td><td align="right">3,460</td></tr>
<tr><td>Entity's net income . . . .</td><td align="right">$7,510</td></tr>
</table>

The elimination entries are explained as follows:

1. There were no intercompany sales or purchases in Year 2, and therefore no elimination is required on the income statement.
2. To realize the gross profit of $600 in Year 2, cost of goods sold is decreased by $600 by the elimination labelled (a). The reasoning behind this is as follows:
   (a) Cost of goods sold is made up of opening inventory, plus purchases, minus ending inventory.
   (b) The opening inventory contains the $600 gross profit. After we reduce it by $600, the opening inventory is at cost to the entity.
   (c) A reduction of $600 from opening inventory decreases cost of goods sold by $600.
   (d) This decrease in cost of goods sold increases the before-tax net income earned by the entity by $600.
3. Using the concepts of tax allocation we increase income tax expense by $240 in order to match the tax expense with the $600 gross profit being realized. The **increase in tax expense** is accomplished by the elimination entry labelled (b).

Note that the deferred tax asset on the December 31, Year 1 consolidated balance sheet (see page 309) becomes an expense on the Year 2 consolidated income statement, because the December 31, Year 1 inventory was sold in Year 2.

4 A $600 decrease in cost of goods sold together with a $240 increase in income tax expense, results in the aftertax intercompany Year 1 *profit* of $360 *being realized for consolidation purposes in Year 2*.

The December 31, Year 2 consolidated balance sheet requires no intercompany profit adjustments in its preparation. The inventory of Parent Company contains no unrealized profit, and therefore there is no deferred tax asset. All intercompany profits recorded by Subsidiary Company have been realized for consolidation purposes.

The elimination entry adjustments on the Year 2 consolidated income statement increased the entity's net income by $360. This increase was allocated to the two equities as follows:

Allocation of aftertax inventory profit being realized to two equities	*To minority interest (10% × $360)*	*$ 36*
	To controlling interest (90% × $360)	*324*
	Total allocated to two equities	*$360*

The December 31, Year 1 consolidated retained earnings was reduced by $324 but this is *offset* by the $324 increase in Year 2 consolidated net income, so that the December 31, Year 2 retained earnings is not affected. The minority interest on the consolidated balance sheet is also not affected and would be calculated as follows:

Calculation of minority interest as at Dec. 31, Year 2	*Shareholders' equity of Subsidiary Company on December 31, Year 2*	*$XXX*
	Minority interest portion	*.10*
	Minority interest	*$XXX*

Equity method journal entries

Parent Company would make the following equity method journal entries in Year 2.

Parent Company's Year 2 equity method journal entries	*Dec. 31*	*Investment in Subsidiary Company*	*2,790*	
		Intercompany investment income		*2,790*
		To record 90% of Subsidiary Company's reported net income for Year 2 ($3,100 × .9 = $2,790).		
	Dec. 31	*Investment in Subsidiary*	*324*	
		Intercompany investment income		*324*
		To realize in Year 2 the intercompany inventory profit held back in Year 1 ($360 × .9 = $324).		

Intercompany investment income of $3,114 ($2,790 + $324) would appear on *Parent Company's* income statement for Year 2 and would result in a total *net income* of $7,164 ($4,050 + $3,114) which, of course, *is equal to consolidated net income*.

Intercompany profit in inventories and amount of minority interest

Accountants have given considerable thought to intercompany profits in purchases and sales transactions of partially owned subsidiaries. There is general agreement that all the unrealized intercompany profit in a partially owned subsidiary's ending inventories should be eliminated for consolidated financial statements. *This holds true whether the sales to the subsidiary are downstream from the parent company or are made by a wholly owned subsidiary of the same parent*.

There has been no such agreement on the treatment of intercompany profit in the parent company's or a subsidiary's inventories from upstream or lateral sales by a partially owned subsidiary. Two alternative approaches have been suggested:

1 The first approach is elimination of intercompany profit only to the extent of the parent company's ownership interest in the selling subsidiary's common stock. This approach is based on the "parent company theory" of consolidated financial statements (see Chapter 5, pages 192 to 194), in which the minority interest is considered to be a *liability* of the consolidated entity. If the minority shareholders are considered *outside creditors*, intercompany profit in the parent company's ending inventories has been *realized* to the extent of the minority shareholders' interest in the selling subsidiary's common stock.

2 The second approach is elimination of all the intercompany profit. The "entity theory" of consolidated financial statements (see Chapter 5, page 193), in which the minority interest is considered to be a *part of consolidated stockholders' equity*, underlies this approach. If minority shareholders are *part owners* of consolidated assets, their share of intercompany profits in inventories has not been realized.

The following paragraphs from Section 1600 of the Handbook indicate the position taken by the CICA:

Intercompany gains and losses. To the extent that assets transferred within the consolidated group are still on hand, their carrying values may include unrealized intercompany gains or losses. The amount of such gains or losses would include the gain or loss on disposal of fixed assets and the profit and loss on sale of inventory items. The existence of intercompany losses may indicate a permanent decline in the value of the relevant assets. It may be necessary to recognize this decline in value by writing down such assets. In certain circumstances, some of the costs incurred in transferring assets within the consolidated group, such as freight costs, may appropriately increase the assets' carrying value. If income taxes have been paid or provided on the intercompany profits on assets remaining within the group, they are accounted for as deferred income taxes. **(1600.27)**

Complete elimination of unrealized intercompany gains or losses and adjustments of applicable income taxes is necessary so that assets may be presented at historical cost to the consolidated entity. There is a view that, where a minority interest exists, a proportion of any intercompany transaction may be considered to have been at arm's length, and that the proportion of the gains or losses relating to the minority interest would be recognized in computing income. This view is inconsistent with the fact that the parent and its subsidiary are related and therefore not operating at arm's length. For this reason, unrealized intercompany gains or losses should be entirely eliminated. (For treatment of gains or losses on transactions between a venturer and a joint venture, see INVESTMENTS IN CORPORATE AND UNINCORPORATED JOINT VENTURES, Section 3055.) **(1600.28)**

Unrealized intercompany gains or losses arising subsequent to the date of an acquisition on assets remaining within the consolidated group should be eliminated. The amount of elimination from assets should not be affected by the existence of a minority interest. **(1600.30)**

An intercompany gain or loss recognized by the parent or by a wholly-owned subsidiary company is eliminated. An intercompany gain or loss recognized by a subsidiary company in which there is a minority interest might be either eliminated entirely against the majority interest or divided proportionately between the majority and minority interests. Allocating a portion of the elimination of an intercompany gain or loss to the minority interest may not be consistent with the legal position of such shareholders. However, allocation is appropriate because consolidated financial statements are prepared primarily for the parent company shareholders and it follows that the effect on consolidated net income is based solely on the proportion of the subsidiary company's shares held by the parent. **(1600.31)**

Where there is an unrealized intercompany gain or loss recognized by a subsidiary company in which there is a minority interest, such gain or loss should be eliminated proportionately between the majority and minority interest in that company's income. **(1600.32)**

Consequently, intercompany profits or losses in inventories resulting from **upstream or lateral sales of merchandise by a partially owned subsidiary** must be considered in the determination of minority interest in net income of the subsidiary, and in the computation of retained earnings of the subsidiary. The subsidiary's net income must be **increased** by the **realized** intercompany profit in the purchasing affiliate's **beginning** inventories and **decreased** by the **unrealized** intercompany profit in the purchasing affiliate's **ending** inventories. Failure to do so would attribute the entire intercompany profit effects to the **consolidated** net income.

Should net profit or gross profit be eliminated?

Some accountants have discussed the propriety of eliminating intercompany **net profit**, rather than **gross profit**, in inventories of the consolidated entity. There is little theoretical support for such a proposal. First, elimination of intercompany net profit would in effect capitalize operating (selling and administrative) expenses in consolidated inventories. Selling expenses are always period costs, and only in unusual circumstances are some administrative expenses capitalized in inventories as product costs. Second, determination of net profit for particular merchandise requires many assumptions as to allocations of common costs.

Unrealized Intercompany Inventory Profits — Parent Selling

In our previous example the **subsidiary** was the **selling company** in the unrealized intercompany profit transaction. This resulted in the $360 after-tax profit elimination being allocated to the minority and controlling equities. Recall that our example was based on the concept that we had forgotten to take into account intercompany transactions when we originally prepared the consolidated income statement. We then corrected this statement by eliminating the intercompany revenues and expenses and the unrealized intercompany profit.

Suppose we had said that it was the **parent company** that sold the inventory to the subsidiary. A calculation of consolidated net income for each of the two years should point out where the differences would lie. Year 1 consolidated net income would be calculated as follows:

Parent Company net income		$3,400
Less: profit in ending inventory		360
Adjusted net income — Parent Company		$3,040
Subsidiary Company net income	$1,700	
Parent Company's share	.9	1,530
Consolidated net income		$4,570

Calculation of Year 1 consolidated net income if parent sold inventory to subsidiary

The fact that the **consolidated entity's net income remains unchanged** can be verified with the following calculation:

Parent's adjusted net income	$3,040
Subsidiary's net income	1,700
Entity's net income	$4,740

Proof that entity's net income is the same, regardless which company sold the inventory

The consolidated income statement eliminations for intercompany sales and purchases, unrealized gross profit in inventory and the adjustment to income tax expense would not change. However, minority interest would be $170 (10% of $1,700). The elimination of the aftertax profit would not affect the calculation of minority interest because the parent was the selling company. The $360 holdback is allocated entirely to the controlling equity.

On the consolidated balance sheet the elimination entries to adjust inventory and deferred income taxes are also the same as before. However, the *minority interest* calculation on the balance sheet *is not affected by the inventory profit holdback* because it has been allocated entirely to consolidated retained earnings.

Year 2 consolidated net income would be calculated as follows:

<table>
<tr><td rowspan="6" style="text-align:left">**Calculation of Year 2 consolidated net income if parent sold inventory to subsidiary**</td><td>Parent Company net income ....</td><td></td><td>$4,050</td></tr>
<tr><td>Add: profit in opening inventory ....</td><td></td><td>360</td></tr>
<tr><td>Adjusted net income — Parent Company ....</td><td></td><td>$4,410</td></tr>
<tr><td>Subsidiary Company net income ....</td><td>$3,100</td><td></td></tr>
<tr><td>Parent Company's share ....</td><td>.9</td><td>2,790</td></tr>
<tr><td>Consolidated net income ....</td><td></td><td>$7,200</td></tr>
</table>

The consolidated entity's net income for Year 2 has not changed and is made up of:

<table>
<tr><td rowspan="3" style="text-align:left">**Proof that entity's net income is the same regardless which company sold the inventory**</td><td>Parent's adjusted net income ....</td><td>$4,410</td></tr>
<tr><td>Subsidiary's net income ....</td><td>3,100</td></tr>
<tr><td>Entity's net income ....</td><td>$7,510</td></tr>
</table>

It follows then that the elimination entries on the Year 2 consolidated income statement would be the same as those for Year 1, but the amount of minority interest would be $310 (10% of $3,100).

In summary, the holdback and subsequent realization of intercompany profits in assets is allocated to the minority and controlling equities only if the subsidiary was the original seller in the intercompany transaction. *If the parent was the original seller, the allocation is entirely to the controlling equity*.

Parent's equity method journal entries

Parent Company would make the entries shown at the top of page 317 in Year 1.

An astute reader will conclude that because the parent was the selling company the second entry is removing the profit from accounts that did not originally contain it. This of course is true. However, it is the intercompany Investment Income account on the income statement of Parent Company that creates the equality between Parent Company's net income under the

Parent Company's Year 1 equity method journal entries if parent sold inventory to subsidiary	*Dec. 31*	*Investment in Subsidiary Company*	*$1,530*	
		Intercompany investment income		*$1,530*
		To record 90% of Subsidiary Company's reported net income for Year 1 ($1,700 × .9 = $1,530).		
	Dec. 31	*Intercompany investment income*	*$ 360*	
		Investment in Subsidiary Company		*$ 360*
		To hold back the intercompany inventory profit recorded by Parent Company in Year 1.		

equity method and consolidated net income. In the same manner the Investment in Subsidiary Company account on the Parent Company's balance sheet creates the equality between Parent Company's retained earnings under the equity method and consolidated retained earnings. Therefore all adjustments that affect consolidated net income are reflected in these two accounts.

In Year 2 Parent Company would make the following entries:

Parent Company's Year 2 equity method journal entries if parent sold inventory to subsidiary	*Dec. 31*	*Investment in Subsidiary Company*	*$2,790*	
		Intercompany investment income		*$2,790*
		To record 90% of Subsidiary Company's reported net income for Year 2 ($3,100 × .9 = $2,790).		
	Dec. 31	*Investment in Subsidiary*	*$ 360*	
		Intercompany investment income		*$ 360*
		To realize in Year 2 the intercompany inventory profit held back in Year 1.		

Unrealized intercompany land profits

The holdback and realization of an intercompany profit in land is accomplished in a more straightforward manner on the consolidated income statement. Suppose that in Year 1 there was an intercompany sale of land on which a before-tax profit of $600 was recorded, that $240 tax was accrued, and that on December 31, Year 1, the land was still held by the purchasing company. (We are assuming that this was not a capital gain for tax purposes.)

The selling company would make the following entry to record the intercompany transaction.

Cash	*$2,600*	
Land		*$2,000*
Gain on sale of land		*$ 600*

The purchasing company would record the intercompany transaction as follows:

Land	$2,600	
Cash		$2,600

In the preparation of the consolidated financial statements the profit elimination and the related income tax adjustment would take place as follows:

<table>
<tr><td rowspan="4" style="vertical-align:top">Elimination of inter-
company land gain, and
tax effects in preparation
of Year 1 consolidated
income statement</td></tr>
</table>

PARENT COMPANY AND SUBSIDIARY

Consolidated Income Statement

Year 1

Gain on sale of land ($600 − $600)	$ 0
Income tax expense (P + S − 240)	$XXX
Net income − consolidated entity	$XXX
Less: minority interest	XXX
Net income	$XXX

It should be obvious that holdback of the gain and the reduction of income tax expense has reduced the entity's net income by $360. If the subsidiary was the selling company the $360 aftertax profit held back would be used to calculate minority interest in the consolidated income, and thus would be allocated to the two equities. *If the parent was the selling company, minority interest would not be affected* and the entire profit holdback would be allocated to the controlling equity.

PARENT COMPANY AND SUBSIDIARY

Consolidated Balance Sheet

December 31, Year 1

Assets

Land ($2,600 − $600)	$2,000
Deferred income tax (+ $240)	240
Total assets	$XXX

The balance sheet eliminations for a land profit are very similar to those for an inventory profit. In this case the before-tax profit is deducted from land, whereas in the former case it was deducted from inventory. The addition of deferred income tax to the consolidated balance sheet is the same for both types of profit. *The effect on the minority interest calculation depends on whether or not the subsidiary was the selling company*.

Realization of Intercompany Land Profits

An unrealized intercompany inventory profit held back for consolidated purposes in Year 1 is considered realized in Year 2. It is assumed that the FIFO method of inventory costing is being used and that any inventory on hand at the beginning of a year has been sold by the end of that year. This would be true in most instances.

When are intercompany land profits considered *realized* for consolidation purposes? The answer is when the land is sold to outsiders, which may be many years later. At the end of each successive year prior to the sale to outsiders the preparation of the consolidated balance sheet requires the same adjustments as those of Year 1. Consolidated income statements require no adjustment until the year of the sale outside, because in each year prior to that event, the income statements of both affiliates will not contain any transactions with regard to the land.

In this case let us assume that the land was sold outside during Year 8 at a profit of $1,300. The company making the sale in Year 8 would record the following journal entry:

Cash	$3,900	
Land		$2,600
Gain on sale of land		$1,300

While the selling company recorded a gain of $1,300 the gain to the entity is $1,900 ($1,300 + $600). On the Year 8 consolidated income statement the gain held back in Year 1 is realized and the income tax expense adjusted as follows:

Realization of intercompany land gain in preparation of Year 8 consolidated income statement

PARENT COMPANY AND SUBSIDIARY
Consolidated Income Statement
Year 8

Gain on sale of land ($1,300 + $600)	$1,900
Income tax expense (P + S + $240)	XXX
Net income — consolidated entity	$ XXX
Less: minority interest	XXX
Net income	$ XXX

The entity's net income is increased by $360 ($600 − $240). If the subsidiary was the original selling company the minority interest in the Year 8 net income will be affected, whereas the whole $360 will be allocated to the controlling interest if the parent was the original seller.

Equity Method Journal Entries   Parent Company's equity journal entries for the land gain in Years 1 and 8 would be identical to the entries illustrated previously for inventory in Years 1 and 2, depending of course on *which company was the original seller* in the intercompany profit transaction.

COMPREHENSIVE ILLUSTRATION OF WORKING PAPER FOR CONSOLIDATED FINANCIAL STATEMENTS — EQUITY METHOD

Our illustrations of the elimination of intercompany revenues, expenses and unrealized nondepreciable asset profits were accomplished without the use of working papers. This approach was used *to focus attention on the concepts involved* in each type of elimination and their effects on each of the financial statements. To examine the effects on all of the statements together, we will now return to an example using working papers. The comprehensive illustration that follows incorporates many of the concepts explained and illustrated in Chapters 5 through 8. The illustration is for Peter Corporation and its partially owned subsidiary, Salt Company, for the year ended December 31, Year 3.

Details about the two companies and the intercompany transactions that have been incurred are as follows:

1 Peter purchased 80% of the outstanding shares of Salt on January 1, Year 1 at a cost of $65,000. On acquisition date Salt had retained earnings of $10,000, and the carrying amounts of its net assets were equal to current fair values. Any goodwill is to be amortized over a 10 year life.

2 Both companies sell merchandise to each other. Peter sells to Salt at a gross profit of 35%, while Salt earns a gross profit of 40% from its sales to Peter.

3 The December 31, Year 2 inventory of Peter contained purchases made from Salt amounting to $7,000. There were no intercompany purchases in the inventory of Salt on this date.

4 During Year 3 the following intercompany transactions took place:
   (a) Salt made a $25,000 payment to Peter for management fees, which was recorded under the category "other expenses."
   (b) Salt made sales of $75,000 to Peter. The December 31, Year 3 inventory of Peter contained merchandise purchased from Salt amounting to $16,500.
   (c) Peter made sales of $100,000 to Salt. The December 31, Year 3 inventory of Salt contained merchandise purchased from Peter amounting to $15,000.
   (d) On July 1, Year 3, Peter borrowed $60,000 from Salt and signed a note bearing interest at 12% per annum. The interest on this note was paid on December 31, Year 3.
   (e) During the year Salt sold land to Peter and recorded a gain of $20,000 on the transaction. This land is being held by Peter on December 31, Year 3.

5 Since acquisition Peter has used the equity method to account for its investment in Salt.

6 Both companies pay income tax at a rate of 40%.

The Year 3 financial statements of the two companies appear on pages 324 and 325. Before commencing the working papers, it is useful to make certain calculations and list the eliminations that must be made.

The calculation, allocation and amortization of the purchase discrepancy is as follows:

Calculation of purchase
discrepancy, its alloca-
tion, and amortization to
Dec. 31, Year 3

Cost of 80% of Salt Jan. 1, Year 1		$65,000
Carrying amounts of Salt's net assets:		
Common stock	$50,000	
Retained earnings	10,000	
Total Shareholders' Equity	$60,000	
Peter's ownership interest	0.80	48,000
Purchase discrepancy		$17,000
Allocated to revalue net assets of Salt		0
Balance — Goodwill — Jan. 1, Year 1		$17,000
Amortized for consolidation purposes:		
Year 1	$ 1,700	
Year 2	1,700	
Year 3	1,700	5,100
Balance — Goodwill — Dec. 31, Year 3		$11,900

The following intercompany items require eliminations:

Intercompany receivables and payables

Notes receivable and payable	$ 60,000

Calculation of items to be
eliminated in preparation
of Year 3 consolidated
financial statements

Intercompany revenues and expenses

Management fees	$ 25,000
Sales and purchases	
Peter to Salt	$100,000
Salt to Peter	$ 75,000
Total	$175,000
Interest revenue and expense (12% × 60,000 × 1/2 year)	$ 3,600

Unrealized intercompany profits	Before Tax	40% Tax	After Tax
Opening inventory — Salt selling (7,000 × 40%)	$ 2,800	$ 1,120	$ 1,680
Ending inventory			
Salt selling (16,500 × 40%)	$ 6,600	$ 2,640	$ 3,960
Peter selling (15,000 × 35%)	$ 5,250	2,100	3,150
Total	$11,850	$ 4,740	$ 7,110
Land — Salt selling	$20,000	$ 8,000	$12,000

Note that the **unrealized profits** have been labelled as **to the company
that made the intercompany profit**. Therefore the land profit — Salt
selling is in the land account of Peter. Furthermore, in order to simplify the

calculations we have assumed that this profit was taxed at the full 40% rate. If this profit was a capital gain for tax purposes, the rate would be 20%.

The **ledger accounts** for Peter Corporation's Investment in Salt Company and Salt Company's Retained Earnings are presented on page 323. Review of these accounts should aid in understanding the illustrative working paper for consolidated financial statements on pages 324 and 325 and the related working paper eliminations on pages 326 and 327.

Following are important features of the working paper for consolidated financial statements and related working paper eliminations for the year ended December 31, Year 3.

1 Intercompany investment income of Peter Corporation for Year 3 is computed as follows:

<table>
<tr><td style="text-align:right; font-style:italic">Calculation of balance in
intercompany investment
income account</td><td>Salt's net income ($24,000 × .080) ....</td><td>$19,200</td></tr>
<tr><td></td><td>Add: Opening inventory profit — Salt selling</td><td></td></tr>
<tr><td></td><td>($1,680 × 0.80) ....</td><td>1,344</td></tr>
<tr><td></td><td>Less: Closing inventory — Salt selling ($3,960 × 0.80) ....</td><td>(3,168)</td></tr>
<tr><td></td><td>Closing inventory profit — Peter selling ....</td><td>(3,150)</td></tr>
<tr><td></td><td>Land gain — Salt selling ($12,000 × 0.80) ....</td><td>(9,600)</td></tr>
<tr><td></td><td>Amortization of purchase discrepancy ....</td><td>(1,700)</td></tr>
<tr><td></td><td>Total ....</td><td>$ 2,926</td></tr>
</table>

2 The following equalities exist because of the parent company's use of the equity method:

Parent company net income = consolidated net income
Parent company retained earnings = consolidated retained earnings

3 The portion of elimination (a) that has been labelled (i) (ii) (iii) represents adjustments for intercompany profits and the related income tax effects on both the income statement and the balance sheet. The unlabelled portion of elimination (a) represents concepts discussed in prior chapters and is explained in the narrative. Note that in calculating minority interest in net assets at the beginning of the year, the intercompany profit in opening inventory is deducted from beginning of the year shareholders' equity of the subsidiary. This profit was held back from Year 2 consolidated net income and because the subsidiary was the original selling company, the profit holdback was allocated to the minority and controlling equities.

4 Elimination (a) labelled (i) is the holdback of the intercompany gain on the sale of land by the subsidiary. The before-tax gain of $20,000 is removed from income and the asset land. The tax paid on this gain of $8,000 (40% × $20,000) is removed from income tax expense and becomes the asset deferred income tax. This elimination affects the calculation of minority interest in net income because the subsidiary was the selling company.

5 Elimination (a) labelled (ii) is the holdback of the intercompany profits in inventory. Increasing cost of sales $11,850 decreases before-tax net income by the same amount. The asset inventory is also decreased by this profit. The $4,740 (40% of $11,850) income tax paid on this profit is removed from income tax expense and is added to the asset deferred income tax. This inventory profit will be realized in the Year 4 consolidated income statement. Note that the total

inventory profit resulted from the parent selling to the subsidiary and the subsidiary selling to the parent (see page 321 for calculations). Minority interest in net income is affected only by the portion of the profit where the subsidiary was the original selling company.

6 Elimination (a) labelled (iii) realizes in Year 3 the intercompany inventory profit that was held back in Year 2. A decrease in cost of goods sold of $2,800 increases net income before tax by this amount. Income tax expense is increased by $1,120 (40% of $2,800) to match income tax expense with the inventory profit being realized. The December 31, Year 2 consolidated balance sheet contained a deferred income tax asset of $1,120. This amount now becomes an expense on the Year 3 consolidated income statement. Because the subsidiary was the original selling company this elimination affects the calculation of the minority interest in net income.

7 Elimination (b) establishes the minority interest in the net income of the subsidiary. The calculation is shown in the narrative.

PETER CORPORATION LEDGER
Investment in Salt Company

Date	Explanation	Debit	Credit	Balance
1/1/1	Acquisition cost	65,000		65,000 dr
12/31/1	Dividend of Salt		12,000	53,000 dr
12/31/1	Net income of Salt	40,000		93,000 dr
12/31/1	Amortization of purchase discrepancy		1,700	91,300 dr
12/31/2	Dividend of Salt		12,000	79,300 dr
12/31/2	Net income of Salt	33,600		112,900 dr
12/31/2	Amortization of purchase discrepancy		1,700	111,200 dr
12/31/2	Hold back inventory profit ($1,680 × 0.80) ..		1,344	109,856 dr
12/31/3	Dividend of Salt		12,000	97,856 dr
12/31/3	Net income of Salt	19,200		117,056 dr
12/31/3	Realize inventory profit ($1,680 × 0.80)	1,344		118,400 dr
12/31/3	Hold back inventory profit ($3,960 × 0.80) ..		3,168	115,232 dr
12/31/3	Hold back inventory profit		3,150	112,082 dr
12/31/3	Hold back land gain ($12,000 × 0.80)		9,600	102,482 dr
12/31/3	Amortization of purchase discrepancy		1,700	100,782 dr

SALT COMPANY LEDGER
Retained Earnings

Date	Explanation	Debit	Credit	Balance
1/1/1				10,000 cr
12/31/1	Close net income		50,000	60,000 cr
12/31/1	Close dividends	15,000		45,000 cr
12/31/2	Close net income		42,000	87,000 cr
12/31/2	Close dividends	15,000		72,000 cr
12/31/3	Close net income		24,000	96,000 cr
12/31/3	Close dividends	15,000		81,000 cr

Equity method: Partially owned subsidiary subsequent to acquisition

PETER CORPORATION AND SUBSIDIARY

Working Paper for Consolidated Financial Statements
For Year Ended December 31, Year 3

	Peter Corporation	Salt Company	Eliminations increase (decrease)	Consolidated
Income Statement				
Net sales	900,000	250,000	(c) (175,000)	975,000
Management fee revenue . . .	25,000		(c) (25,000)	
Interest revenue		3,600	(c) (3,600)	
Gain on land sale		20,000	(a) (20,000)	
Intercompany investment income	2,926		(a) (2,926)	
Total revenue	927,926	273,600	(226,526)	975,000
Cost of goods sold	540,000	162,000	(a) (2,800) (a) 11,850 (c) (175,000)	536,050
Interest expense	3,600		(c) (3,600)	
Other expense	196,400	71,600	(c) (25,000)	243,000
Income tax expense	80,000	16,000	(a) (8,000) (a) 1,120 (a) (4,740)	84,380
Goodwill amortization expense			(a) 1,700	1,700
Minority interest in net income			(b) 1,944	1,944
Total costs and expenses	820,000	249,600	(202,526)	867,074
Net income	107,926	24,000	(24,000)	107,926

Working Paper for Consolidated Financial Statements
For Year Ended December 31, Year 3

	Peter Corporation	Salt Company	Eliminations increase (decrease)		Consolidated
Statement of Retained Earnings					
Retained earnings, beginning					
of year	197,856	72,000	(a)	(72,000)	197,856
Net income	107,926	24,000		(24,000)	107,926
Subtotal	305,782	96,000		(96,000)	305,782
Dividends	50,000	15,000	(a)	(15,000)	50,000
Retained earnings,					
end of year	255,782	81,000		(81,000)	255,782
Balance Sheet					
Notes receivable		60,000	(d)	(60,000)	
Inventory	32,000	27,000	(a)	(11,850)	47,150
Land	175,000	19,000	(a)	(20,000)	174,000
Other assets	320,000	65,000			385,000
Investment in Salt Company .	100,782		(a)	(100,782)	
Goodwill			(a)	11,900	11,900
			{ (a)	4,740 }	
Deferred income tax			{ (a)	8,000 }	12,740
Total assets	627,782	171,000		(167,992)	630,790
Notes payable	60,000		(d)	(60,000)	
Other liabilities	212,000	40,000			252,000
Minority interest in net			{ (a)	21,064 }	
assets			{ (b)	1,944 }	23,008
Common stock	100,000				100,000
Common stock		50,000	(a)	(50,000)	
Retained earnings	255,782	81,000		(81,000)	255,782
Total liabilities and					
shareholders' equity ...	627,782	171,000		(167,992)	630,790

(a)	Common Stock — Salt	$ 50,000	
	Retained Earnings — Salt	72,000	
	Intercompany Investment Income — Peter	2,926	
	Goodwill — Salt	11,900	
	Goodwill Amortization Expense — Salt	1,700	
(i)	Gain on Sale of Land	20,000	
(i)	Deferred Income Tax	8,000	
(ii)	Cost of Goods Sold	11,850	
(ii)	Deferred Income Tax	4,740	
(iii)	Income Tax Expense	1,120	
	Investment in Salt Company — Peter		$100,782
	Dividends — Salt		15,000
	Minority Interest in Net Assets		21,064
(i)	Land		20,000
(i)	Income Tax Expense		8,000
(ii)	Inventory		11,850
(ii)	Income Tax Expense		4,740
(iii)	Cost of Goods Sold		2,800

To carry out the following:

(1) Eliminate intercompany investment and equity accounts of subsidiary at beginning of year, and subsidiary dividends.

(2) Provide Year 3 amortization of the purchase discrepancy, and allocate the unamortized portion to appropriate assets.

(3) Establish minority interest in net assets of subsidiary at beginning of year, less minority share of dividends of subsidiary during year as follows:

Shareholders' equity, beginning of year	$122,000	
Less: opening inventory profit	1,680	
Adjusted shareholders' equity	$120,320	
Less: dividends	15,000	
	$105,320	
Minority share ($105,320 × 0.20)	$ 21,064	

(4) To hold back and realize intercompany profits in Year 3,
and adjust for income tax effects.

(b) Minority Interest in Net Income .... $ 1,944

    Minority Interest in Net Assets .... $ 1,944

To establish minority interest in subsidiary's adjusted net
income for Year 3 as follows:

Net income of subsidiary		$ 24,000
Add: opening inventory profit		1,680
		$ 25,680
Less: ending inventory profit	$ 3,960	
land gain	12,000	15,960
Adjusted net income of		
subsidiary		$ 9,720
Minority share ($9,720 × 0.20) ..		$ 1,944

[handwritten: only unrealized on upstream transactions]

(c) Net Sales .... $175,000 *[handwritten: Elimination of intercompany Sales]*

    Management Fee Revenue 25,000

    Interest Revenue 3,600

      Cost of Goods Sold $175,000

      Other Expense 25,000

      Interest Expense 3,600

To eliminate intercompany revenues and expenses for Year 3.

(d) Notes Payable 60,000

    Notes Receivable 60,000

To eliminate intercompany receivables and payables at
Dec. 31, Year 3.

8 Eliminations (c) and (d) eliminate intercompany revenues and expenses, an intercompany receivables and payables. These eliminations were listed after th entries which established the minority interest, to further reinforce the concep that *they do not affect the calculation of minority interest*. Note also tha the offset method for intercompany receivables and payables illustrated in pre vious chapters has not been used. Either the offset method or the eliminatio entry method will produce the same results.

9 When cost of goods sold was adjusted for intercompany profits the eliminatio entry did not specify whether it was the parent's account or the subsidiary' account that was affected. This was done purposely. Specific labelling woul only confuse the issue. It is important to focus attention only on the compan that *recorded* the intercompany profit, not on the company whose account contain it. In a similar manner it is not necessary to focus attention on whic company's accounts are affected by the elimination of intercompany revenue and expenses, but rather that consolidated revenues and expenses are bein reduced to stop double counting. In many cases it is obvious which company' accounts are being adjusted.

10 Minority interest in net assets at December 31, Year 3 may be verified as follows

Verification of minority interest as at Dec. 31, Year 3			
Shareholders' equity of Salt, Dec. 31, Year 3			
Common Stock			$ 50,00
Retained Earnings			81,00
Total			$131,00
Less: Closing inventory profit		$ 3,960	
Land profit		12,000	
Adjusted net assets of Salt, Dec. 31, Year 3			$115,04
Minority Interest ($115,040 × 0.20)			$ 23,00

11 The consolidated amounts in the working paper for consolidated financia statements represent the financial position and operating results of Peter Corpora tion and subsidiary resulting from the consolidated entity's transactions with *outsiders*. All intercompany transactions, profits, and balances have been elim nated in the computation of the consolidated amounts.

COMPREHENSIVE ILLUSTRATION OF WORKING PAPER FOR CONSOLIDATED FINANCIAL STATEMENTS — COST METHOD

The illustration for Peter Corporation and its subsidiary Salt Company fo the year ended December 31, Year 3 is repeated. All facts about the two companies and the intercompany transactions that were incurred are unchanged, except that Peter Corporation has used the *cost method* to account for its investment since acquisition date. The financial statement of the two companies appear on pages 330 and 331. Notice that the follow ing accounts of Peter Corporation have changed.

1 Intercompany investment income ($2,926) has been replaced with intercompany dividend revenue ($12,000).
2 Peter's net income is now $117,000 and is not equal to consolidated net income
3 Investment in Salt Company is stated at acquisition cost ($65,000).
4 Peter's retained earnings at the beginning and the end of Year 3 do not equa consolidated retained earnings on those dates.

The calculation and amortization of the purchase discrepancy, and the calculation of intercompany transactions requiring elimination, would be the same as previously illustrated (page 321). The working paper procedure under the cost method requires an *initial elimination entry* to adjust the parent company's accounts to equity method balances and descriptions. Once the parent's accounts have been adjusted, the equity method eliminations proceed as usual. It is necessary to make *two additional calculations* to aid in preparing the initial working paper entry. Consolidated net income is calculated as follows:

Calculation of consolidated net income for Year 3 when parent uses the cost method			

Income of Peter			$117,000
Less: Intercompany dividends		$12,000	
Amortization of purchase discrepancy		1,700	
Profit in closing inventory		3,150	16,850
Adjusted net income			$100,150
Income of Salt		24,000	
Add: Profit in opening inventory		1,680	
		25,680	
Less: Profit in ending inventory	$ 3,960		
Land gain	12,000	15,960	
Adjusted net income		$ 9,720	
Peter's ownership		0.80	7,776
Consolidated net income			$107,926

Consolidated retained earnings on January 1, Year 3 is calculated as follows:

Calculation of consolidated retained earnings as at Jan. 1, Year 3, when parent uses the cost method

Retained earnings of Peter Jan. 1, Year 3		$153,000
Less: Amortization of purchase discrepancy to January 1,		
Year 3 ($1,700 + $1,700)		3,400
Adjusted retained earnings		$149,600
Retained earnings of Salt Jan. 1, Year 3	$72,000	
Retained earnings of Salt — acquisition	10,000	
Increase	$62,000	
Less: Profit in opening inventory	1,680	
Adjusted increase	$60,320	
Peter's ownership	0.80	48,256
Consolidated retained earnings Jan. 1, Year 3		$197,856

From the consolidated net income calculation we can determine that intercompany investment income would be made up of the following:

Adjusted net income of Salt ($9,720 × 0.80)		$ 7,776
Less: Amortization of purchase discrepancy	$ 1,700	
Profit in ending inventory	3,150	4,850
Total		$ 2,926

Cost method: Partially owned subsidiary subsequent to acquisition

PETER CORPORATION AND SUBSIDIARY
Working Paper for Consolidated Financial Statements
For Year Ended December 31, Year 3

	Peter Corporation	Salt Company	Eliminations increase (decrease)	Consolidated
Income Statement				
Net sales	900,000	250,000	(d) (175,000)	975,00
Management fee revenue	25,000		(d) (25,000)	
Interest revenue		3,600	(d) (3,600)	
Gain on land sale		20,000	(b) (20,000)	
Intercompany dividend revenue	12,000		(a) (12,000)	
Intercompany investment income			(a) 2,926 (b) (2,926)	
Total revenue	937,000	273,600	(235,600)	975,00
Cost of goods sold	540,000	162,000	(b) (2,800) (b) 11,850 (d) (175,000)	536,05
Interest expense	3,600		(d) (3,600)	
Other expense	196,400	71,600	(d) (25,000)	243,00
Income tax expense	80,000	16,000	(b) (8,000) (b) 1,120 (b) (4,740)	84,38
Goodwill amortization expense			(a) 1,700	1,70
Minority interest in net income			(c) 1,944	1,94
Total costs and expenses	820,000	249,600	(202,526)	867,07
Net income	117,000	24,000	(33,074)	107,92

Cost method: Partially owned subsidiary subsequent to acquisition

PETER CORPORATION AND SUBSIDIARY
Working Paper for Consolidated Financial Statements
For Year Ended December 31, Year 3

	Peter Corporation	Salt Company	Eliminations increase (decrease)		Consolidated
Statement of Retained Earnings					
Retained earnings, beginning			(a)	44,856	
of year	153,000	72,000	(b)	(72,000)	197,856
Net income	117,000	24,000		(33,074)	107,926
Subtotal	270,000	96,000		(60,218)	305,782
Dividends	50,000	15,000	(b)	(15,000)	50,000
Retained earnings,					
end of year	220,000	81,000		(45,218)	255,782
Balance Sheet					
Notes receivable		60,000	(e)	(60,000)	
Inventory	32,000	27,000	(b)	(11,850)	47,150
Land	175,000	19,000	(b)	(20,000)	174,000
Other assets	320,000	65,000			385,000
			(a)	35,782	
Investment in Salt Company . .	65,000		(b)	(100,782)	
Goodwill			(a)	11,900	11,900
			(b)	4,740	
Deferred income tax			(b)	8,000	12,740
Total assets	592,000	171,000		(132,210)	630,790
Notes payable	60,000		(e)	(60,000)	
Other liabilities	212,000	40,000			252,000
Minority interest in net			(b)	21,064	
assets			(c)	1,944	23,008
Common stock	100,000				100,000
Common stock		50,000	(b)	(50,000)	
Retained earnings	220,000	81,000		(45,218)	255,782
Total liabilities and					
shareholders' equity . . .	592,000	171,000		(132,210)	630,790

The consolidated retained earnings calculation indicates that Peter's retained earnings would be $44,856 ($197,856 − $153,000) higher had the equity method been used. With this information we can prepare the initial working paper entry as follows:

(a)	Investment in Salt Company — Peter	$35,782	
	Intercompany dividend revenue — Peter	12,000	
	Intercompany investment income — Peter		$ 2,92
	Retained earnings, beginning of year — Peter		44,85

To adjust Peter Corporation's accounts to equity method balances and descriptions.

Once this entry is entered into the working paper the parent's account have been adjusted to the equity method and the remaining working pape entries would be entered (see pages 326 and 327). Previous entry (a) woul be labelled (b); entry (b) would be labelled (c), and so on. All consolidate financial statement amounts remain the same. The consolidated incom statement using the alternative presentation of minority interest discusse previously in this chapter would appear as follows:

Consolidated income statement with alternative
presentation of minority
interest

PETER CORPORATION AND SUBSIDIARY
Consolidated Income Statement
Year ended December 31, Year 3

Net Sales	$975,00
Cost of Goods Sold	$536,05
Other Expense	243,00
Goodwill amortization expense	1,70
Income tax expense	84,38
Total costs and expenses	$865,13
Net income — consolidated entity	$109,87
Less: Minority interest	1,94
Net income	$107,92

The calculation of consolidated net income (page 329) indicates tha entity's net income is composed of:

Adjusted net income — Peter	$100,15
Adjusted net income — Salt	9,72
Net income — consolidated entity	$109,87

REVIEW QUESTIONS

1 The alternative method of presenting minority interest on a consolidated income statement presents information not shown on conventional consolidated income statements. Explain.

2 In what way are an individual's pants with four pockets similar to a parent company with three subsidiaries? Explain with reference to intercompany revenues and expenses.

3 List the types of intercompany revenue and expenses that are eliminated in the preparation of a consolidated income statement and indicate the effect that each elimination has on the amount of minority interest in net income.

4 From a single entity point of view, intercompany revenue and expenses and intercompany borrowings do nothing more than transfer cash from one bank account to another. Explain.

5 If an intercompany profit is recorded on the sale of an asset to an affiliate within the consolidated entity in period one, when should this profit be considered realized? Explain.

6 The reduction of a $1,000 intercompany gross profit from ending inventory should be accompanied by a $400 increase to deferred income taxes in consolidated assets. Do you agree? Explain.

7 A parent company rents a sales office to its wholly owned subsidiary under an operating lease requiring rent of $2,000 a month. What adjustments to income tax expense should accompany the elimination of the parent's $24,000 rent revenue and the subsidiary's $24,000 rent expense in the preparation of a consolidated income statement? Explain.

8 Intercompany losses recorded on the sale of assets to an affiliate within the consolidated entity should be eliminated in the preparation of consolidated financial statements in all cases. Do you agree with this statement? Explain.

9 Is an intercompany gain on the sale of land ever realized? Explain.

10 Describe the effects that the elimination of intercompany sales and intercompany profits in ending inventory will have on the various elements of the consolidated financial statements.

EXERCISES

Ex. 8-1 X Company owns 75% of Y Company, and uses the equity method to account for its investment. Y's opening inventory contained an intercompany profit of $8,000, while X's ending inventory contained an intercompany profit of $12,000. Y Company reported a net income of $50,000 for the year. Assume a 40% tax rate.
a Prepare X Company's equity method journal entries for the year.
b Calculate the minority interest in net income that would appear on the consolidated income statement.

Ex. 8-2 Palimino Corporation acquired a 70% interest in Sokal Company in Year 2. For the years ended December 31, Year 3 and Year 4, Sokal had net income of $80,000 and $90,000, respectively. During Year 3, Sokal sold merchandise to Palimino for $10,000 at a gross profit of $2,000. The merchandise was resold during Year 4 by Palimino to outsiders for $15,000.
   Compute the minority interest in Sokal's net income for Year 3 and Year 4. Assume a 40% tax rate.

Ex. 8-3 The following consolidated income statement of a parent and its 90% owned sul sidiary was prepared by an accounting student before reading this chapter:

Consolidated Income Statement

Sales	$500,000
Rental revenue	24,000
Interest revenue	50,000
Total revenue	$574,000
Cost of goods sold	350,000
Rental expense	24,000
Interest expense	35,000
Miscellaneous administration expense	45,000
Minority interest in net income	9,000
Income tax expense	42,000
Total costs and expenses	$505,000
Net income	$ 69,000

The following items were overlooked when the statement was prepared:

(1) The opening inventory of the parent contained an intercompany profit of $5,000

(2) During the year intercompany sales were made at a 30% gross profit rate a follows:

By the parent	$100,000
By the subsidiary	$ 80,000

(3) At the end of the year one-half of the items purchased from the parent remaine in the inventory of the subsidiary.

(4) All of the rental revenue and 70% of the interest revenue was intercompany an appeared on the income statement of the parent.

(5) Assume a 40% rate for income tax.

Prepare a correct consolidated income statement in the alternative form illus trated in this chapter.

Ex. 8-4 The consolidated balance sheet of Pearl Company and its 85% owned subsidiary Shand Company showed deferred income taxes of $31,600 at December 31, Year 5 which was arrived at as follows:

	Intercompany Profit	Income tax 40%
Inventory	$10,000	$ 4,000
Land	14,000	5,600
Trademark	55,000	22,000

During Year 6, one-quarter of the land was sold to outsiders. On December 31, Year 6 the inventories of Pearl contained items purchased from Shand for $35,000, and the inventories of Shand contained purchases made from Pearl for $50,000. Both com panies record gross profits at the rate of 35% on their intercompany sales. Income tax rates remained unchanged during the year. The trademark, which was purchased from Shand in Year 2, is considered to have an unlimited life.

a Calculate the total change (increase or decrease) that will be made to income tax expense on the Year 6 consolidated income statement.

b Calculate the amount of deferred income taxes that will appear on the December 31, Year 6 consolidated balance sheet.

Ex. 8-5 Elko Corporation acquired a 90% interest in the common stock of Mara Corporation at the beginning of Year 1. The $40,000 purchase discrepancy on that date was allocated 30% to inventory with the remainder to goodwill with an estimated life of 10 years. The retained earnings of Mara Corporation at date of acquisition was $18,000, and Elko has carried its investment under the cost method. Both companies have a 40% income tax rate.

The following information, extracted from the accounting records of the two companies, relates to operations during Year 3:

	Elko Corporation	Mara Corporation
Net income (including dividend revenues)	$125,000	$66,000
Dividends paid during Year 3	60,000	30,000
Retained earnings at the end of Year 3 (after books have		
been closed)	375,000	95,000
Intercompany profits on sales made by Mara Corporation to		
Elko Corporation, included in Elko's inventory:		
At the beginning of Year 3	15,000	
At the end of Year 3	12,000	

a Prepare a statement of consolidated retained earnings for Year 3, including supporting schedules showing how all figures were derived.

b Prepare a schedule showing the change in the minority interest in the retained earnings of Mara Corporation during Year 3.

Ex. 8-6 Brown Company purchased a 70% interest in Green Company several years ago in order to obtain retail outlets for its major products. Since that time Brown has sold to Green Company a substantial portion of its merchandise requirements. At the beginning of the current year Green Company's inventory of $690,000 was composed 80% of goods purchased from Brown at markups averaging 30% on Brown Company's cost. Sales from Brown to Green during the current year were $5,600,000. The estimated intercompany profit in Green's ending inventory was $194,000.

Brown Company owns buildings and land used in Green Company's retail operations and rented to Green Company. Rentals paid by Green Company to Brown Company during the current year amounted to $743,000. At the end of the current year, Brown sold to Green for $250,000 land to be used in the development of a shopping centre which had cost Brown $203,500. The gain was included in Brown Company's net income for the current year. Brown also holds a one-year, 6% note of Green Company on which it has accrued interest revenues of $22,500 during the current year.

During the current year Brown Company reported net income of $568,100 and Green Company reported net income of $248,670. Brown uses the cost method to account for its investment.

Calculate the current year's consolidated net income (assume a 40% tax rate).

Ex. 8-7 L Company owns a controlling interest in M Company and Q Company. L purchased an 80% interest in M at a time when M company reported retained earnings of $500,000. L purchased a 70% interest in Q at a time when Q Company reported retained earnings of $50,000.

An analysis of the changes in retained earnings of the three companies during the current year appears below:

	L Company	M Company	Q Company
Retained earnings balance at beginning of the current year	$ 976,000	$ 843,000	$682,000
Net income	580,000	360,000	240,000
Dividends paid or declared	(250,000)	(200,000)	(150,000)
Retained earnings balance at end of the current year	$1,306,000	$1,003,000	$772,000

Q Company sells parts to L Company, which after further processing and assembly are sold by L to M Company where they become a part of the finished product sold by M. Intercompany profits included in inventories at the beginning and end of the current year are estimated as follows:

	Beginning inventory	Ending inventory
Intercompany profit in inventory:		
On sales from Q to L	$90,000	$ 35,000
On sales from L to M	52,000	118,000

L uses the cost method to account for its investments, and income tax allocation at a 40% rate when it prepares consolidated financial statements.

a Calculate consolidated net income for the current year.

b Prepare a statement of consolidated retained earnings for the current year.

CASES

Case 8-1 As independent auditor of a new client, Aqua Water Corporation, you are reviewing the working paper for consolidated financial statements prepared by Arthur Brady, Aqua Water's accountant. Aqua Water distributes water to homeowners in a suburb of a large city. Aqua Water purchases the water from its subsidiary, Aqua Well Company. Aqua Water organized Aqua Well five years ago and acquired all its common stock for cash on that date.

During the course of your audit, you have learned the following:

(1) Both Aqua Water and Aqua Well are public utilities subject to the jurisdiction of the province's Public Utilities Commission.

(2) Aqua Well charges Aqua Water for the transmission of water from wells to consumers. The transmission charge, at the customary utility rate, was approved by the province's Public Utilities Commission.

(3) Aqua Well charges Aqua Water separately for the volume of water delivered to Aqua Water's customers.

(4) Your audit working papers show the following audited amounts for the two companies' separate financial statements:

	Aqua Water Corporation	Aqua Well Company
Total revenue	$3,500,000	$ 300,000
Net income	300,000	50,000
Total assets	5,700,000	1,000,000
Shareholders' equity	2,500,000	600,000

The working paper for consolidated financial statements prepared by Aqua Water Corporation's accountant appears in order, except that Aqua Well's Transmission Revenue account of $60,000 does not eliminate Aqua Water's Transmission Expense account of the same amount. The accountant explained that, because the transmission charge by Aqua Well is at the customary utility rate approved by the province's Public Utilities Commission, the charge should not be treated as intercompany revenue and expense. Furthermore, Brady points out, the working paper for consolidated financial statements does eliminate Aqua Well's Water Sales account of $200,000 against Aqua Water's Water Purchases account of the same amount.

Instructions Do you concur with the accountant's (Brady's) position? Explain.

Case 8-2 The existence of intercompany profits in consolidated inventories as a result of sales of merchandise by a partially owned subsidiary to its parent company has given rise to the following three viewpoints as to how such profits should be treated for consolidated financial statements:
a Only the parent company's share of intercompany profits in inventories should be eliminated.
b The entire amount of intercompany profits in inventories should be eliminated against the equities of the controlling and minority groups in proportion to their interests.
c The entire amount of intercompany profits in inventories should be eliminated against consolidated retained earnings.

Instructions Present arguments to support each viewpoint.

Case 8-3 Sawhill Company, one of two wholly owned subsidiaries of Peasley Corporation, is in liquidation. On October 31, Year 8, the close of a fiscal year, Sawhill sold accounts receivable with a carrying amount of $50,000 to Shelton company, the other wholly owned subsidiary of Peasley Corporation, for a gain of $10,000. Shelton debited the $10,000 to a deferred charge account, which is to be amortized to expense in proportion to the amounts collected on the receivables Shelton acquired from Sawhill. The $10,000 gain appeared in the consolidated income statement of Peasley Corporation and Shelton Company for the year ended October 31, Year 8; Sawhill Company was not included in the consolidated financial statements on that date because it was in liquidation. Peasley uses the equity method of accounting for its investments in both Shelton and Sawhill.

Instructions Evaluate the accounting described above.

PROBLEMS

8-1 On January 2, Year 1, Big Limited acquired 70 percent of the outstanding voting shares of Mak Limited. The purchase discrepancy on that date was allocated in the following manner:

Inventory	$100,000	
Land	50,000	
Plant and equipment	60,000	estimated life 5 years
Patent	40,000	estimated life 8 years
Goodwill	30,000	estimated life 10 years
Total	$280,000	

The Year 5 income statements and retained earnings statements for the two companies were as follows:

	Big	Mak
Sales	$4,000,000	$2,100,000
Intercompany investment income	204,700	—
Rental revenue	—	70,000
Total revenue	4,204,700	$2,170,000
Cost of goods sold	$2,000,000	$ 800,000
Selling and administrative expense	550,000	480,000
Interest expense	250,000	140,000
Depreciation	450,000	225,000
Patent Amortization	—	25,000
Rental expense	35,000	—
Income tax	300,000	200,000
Total expenses	$3,585,000	$1,870,000
Net income	$ 619,700	$ 300,000

	Big	Mak
Retained earnings, January 1	$2,000,000	$ 900,000
Add: Net income	619,700	300,000
	$2,619,700	$1,200,00
Less: Dividends	100,000	50,000
Retained earnings, December 31	$2,519,700	$1,150,000

Additional information

(1) Mak regularly sells merchandise to Big. Intercompany sales in Year 5 totalled $400,000.

(2) Intercompany profits in the inventories of Big were as follows:

January 1, Year 5	$75,000
December 31, Year 5	$40,000

(3) Big's entire rental expense relates to equipment rented from Mak.

(4) Big uses the equity method to account for its investment and uses income tax allocation at the rate of 40% when it prepares consolidated statements.

Instructions Prepare the following consolidated financial statements for Year 5:
(a) Income statement;
(b) Retained earnings statement.

8-2 The combined income and retained earnings statements of Par Company and its subsidiaries, Subone Company and Subtwo Company, were prepared as at December 31, Year 6 and are shown at the top of page 339.

Additional information

(1) Par Company purchased its 80% interest in Subone company on January 1, Year 1. On this date Subone had a retained earnings balance of $40,000 and the purchases discrepancy amounting to $15,000 was allocated entirely to plant and equipment with an estimated remaining life of 8 years.

	Par Company	Subone Company	Subtwo Company
Revenues			
Sales	$450,000	$270,000	$190,000
Dividends	43,750	—	—
Rent	—	130,000	—
Interest	10,000	—	—
Total Revenue	$503,750	$400,000	$190,000
Expenses			
Cost of sales	$300,000	$163,000	$145,000
General & administrative	50,000	20,000	15,000
Interest	—	10,000	—
Depreciation	18,000	28,000	—
Rent	25,000	—	14,000
Income Tax	27,000	75,000	7,000
Total expenses	$420,000	$296,000	$181,000
Net Income	$ 83,750	$104,000	$ 9,000
Retained earnings Jan. 1, Year 6	700,000	92,000	75,000
	$783,750	$196,000	$ 84,000
Dividends	80,000	50,000	5,000
Retained earnings Dec. 31, Year 6	$703,750	$146,000	$ 79,000

(2) Par Company purchased its 75% interest in Subtwo Company on Dec. 31, Year 3. On this date, Subtwo had a retained earnings balance of $80,000. The purchase discrepancy amounting to $19,000 was allocated to goodwill; however, because Subtwo had failed to report adequate profits, the goodwill was entirely written off for consolidated purposes by the end of Year 5.

(3) Par Company has established a policy that any intercompany sales will be made at a gross profit rate of 30%.

(4) On January 1 of Year 6 the inventory of Par contained goods purchased from Subone for $15,000.

(5) During Year 6 the following intercompany sales took place:

Par to Subone	$ 90,000
Subone to Subtwo	120,000
Subtwo to Par	150,000

(6) On December 31, Year 6 the inventories of each of the three companies contained items purchased on an intercompany basis in the following amounts.

Inventory of	Amount
Par Company	$90,000
Subone Company	22,000
Subtwo Company	40,000

(7) In addition to its merchandising activities, Subone Company is in the office equipment rental business. Both Par and Subtwo rent office equipment from Subone and the rental expense on their Year 6 income statements is entirely from this type of transaction.

(8) During Year 6 Subone paid $10,000 interest to Par for intercompany advances.

(9) Par Company uses the cost method to account for investments and uses tax allocation at a rate of 40% when it prepares consolidated financial statements.

Instructions Prepare a combined consolidated income and retained earnings statement for Year 6.

8-3 The income statements of the Evans Company and the Falcon Company for the current year are shown below:

	Evans Company	Falcon Company
Sales revenues	$450,000	$600,000
Dividend revenues	32,000	
Rent revenues	33,600	
Interest revenues		18,000
Total revenues	$515,600	$618,000
Cost of goods sold	$288,000	$353,000
Operating expenses	104,000	146,000
Interest expense	30,000	
Income taxes	31,700	43,500
Total expenses	$453,700	$542,500
Net income	$ 61,900	$ 75,500
Beginning retained earnings	632,000	348,000
Dividends	(30,000)	(40,000)
Ending retained earnings	$663,900	$383,500

Evans Company owns 80% of the outstanding common stock of Falcon Company, purchased at the time the latter company was organized.

Evans Company sells parts to Falcon Company at a price which is 25% above cost. Total sales from Evans to Falcon during the year were $85,000. Included in Falcon's inventories were parts purchased from Evans amounting to $21,250 in beginning inventories and $28,750 in the ending inventory.

Falcon Company sells back to Evans Company certain finished goods, at a price which gives Falcon an average gross profit of 30% on these intercompany sales. Total sales from Falcon to Evans during the year were $177,000. Included in the inventories of Evans Company were parts acquired from Falcon amounting to $11,000 in beginning inventories and $3,000 in ending inventories.

Falcon Company rents an office building from Evans Company, paying $2,800 per month in rent. Evans Company has borrowed $600,000 through a series of 5% notes, of which Falcon company holds $360,000 as notes receivable. Use income tax allocation at a 40% rate.

Instructions
a Prepare a consolidated income statement.
b Prepare a consolidated statement of retained earnings.

8-4 The partial trial balance of Company P and Company S at December 31, Year 5 was:

	Company P		Company S	
	Dr.	Cr.	Dr.	Cr.
Investment in Company S	$90,000			
Common stock		$150,000		$60,000
Retained earnings (charged with dividends, no other changes during the year)		101,000		34,000

44 000
(48 000)
44 000

Additional information

(1) The investment in the shares of S Company which represents a 90% interest was acquired January 2, Year 1 for $90,000. At this time, the shareholders' equity of this company was: capital stock, $60,000; retained earnings, $20,000.

(2) Net incomes of the two companies for the year were:

P Company $60,000
S Company $48,000

(3) During Year 5, sales of Company P to Company S were $10,000, and sales of Company S to Company P were $50,000. Rates of gross profit on intercompany sales in Year 4 and Year 5 were 40% of sales.

(4) On December 31, Year 4 the inventory of Company P included $7,000 of merchandise purchased from Company S, and the inventory of Company S included $3,000 of merchandise purchased from Company P. On December 31, Year 5, the inventory of Company P included $20,000 of merchandise purchased from Company S and inventory of Company S included $5,000 of merchandise purchased from Company P.

(5) During the year ended December 31, Year 5, Company P paid dividends of $12,000 and Company S paid dividends of $10,000.

(6) At the time that P purchased the stock of S, it was felt that the purchase price reflected unrecorded goodwill of S. This goodwill is being amortized for consolidation purposes over a period of 5 years.

(7) In Year 3, land which originally cost $45,000 was sold by Company S to Company P for $50,000.

(8) Assume a corporate tax rate of 40%.

Instructions Prepare the following:
a A statement of consolidated retained earnings for the year ended December 31, Year 5.
b Your calculations of the amount of minority interest that would appear in the consolidated balance sheet at December 31, Year 5.

8-5 Company H has controlling interests in three subsidiaries as shown in the data below:

	Company H	Subsidiaries		
		Company L	Company J	Company K
Retained earnings at acquisition		$30,000	$40,000	$25,000
% ownership		95%	90%	85%
Retained earnings Jan. 1, Year 5	$12,000	50,000	43,000	30,000
Net income (loss) during Year 5		20,000	(5,000)	30,000
Dividends paid during Year 5	10,000	5,000	3,000	15,000
Inter-company sales		50,000	70,000	

Company K had items in its inventory on Jan. 1, Year 5 on which Company L had made a profit of $5,000.

Company J had items in its inventory on Dec. 31, Year 5 on which Company K had made a profit of $10,000.

Company J rents premises from Company L at an annual rental of $8,500.

The parent company has no income (other than from its investments) and no expenses. It uses the *equity method* of recording its investments, but has made no entries during Year 5. Assume a 40% tax rate.

Instructions Prepare the following:
a Entries that Company H would make in Year 5.
b Your calculations of consolidated net income for Year 5.
c A statement of consolidated retained earnings for Year 5.

 8-6 The balance sheets at the end of the current year, and the income statements for the current year, for the Purvis and Slater Companies are given below:

BALANCE SHEETS

	Purvis Company	Slater Company
Cash	$ 13,000	$ 47,000
Receivables	31,000	106,000
Inventories	80,000	62,000
Investment in Slater Company	257,340	
Other assets	91,000	157,000
Total assets	$472,340	$372,000
Current liabilities	$160,000	$ 83,000
Capital stock	200,000	150,000
Beginning retained earnings	101,260	126,000
Net income	36,080	63,000
Dividends	(25,000)	(50,000)
Total liabilities & capital	$472,340	$372,000

INCOME STATEMENT DATA

	Purvis Company	Slater Company
Sales revenues	$340,000	$820,000
Intercompany investment income	40,080	
Interest revenues		1,250
Gain on sale of land	13,000	
Total revenues	$393,080	$821,250
Beginning inventory	$ 44,000	$ 93,600
Purchases	237,000	583,400
Ending inventory	(80,000)	(62,000)
Cost of goods sold	$201,000	$615,000
Operating expenses	135,600	100,450
Interest expense	6,500	
Income taxes	13,900	42,800
Total expenses	$357,000	$758,250
Net income	$ 36,080	$ 63,000

Purvis Company owns 90% of the stock of Slater Company, purchased for $225,000 six years ago when Slater's retained earnings were $56,000. Since that date the Purvis Company has amortized 60% of the excess of the cost of the investment over the carrying value of the underlying net assets of Slater. The management of Purvis regarded this excess payment as the cost of goodwill associated with affiliation, and authorized amortization over a period of 10 years.

Purvis Company owes Slater Company $25,000 on a three-year, 5% note. During the current year Purvis Company sold to Slater land at a price $13,000 in excess of Purvis's cost. This was not a capital gain for tax purposes.

Purvis Company buys all its merchandise from Slater and has done so for several years. The average gross profit realized by Slater on these sales is approximately the same as on sales to outsiders and has remained stable for the last two years. Purvis has used the equity method, and uses income tax allocation for consolidated statement preparation at a rate of 40%.

Instructions Prepare consolidated financial statements for the current year.

8-7 On January 1, Year 3, the Plenty Company purchased 80 percent of the outstanding voting shares of the Sparse Company for $1.6 million in cash. On that date, the Sparse Company's balance sheet and the fair values of its identifiable assets and liabilities were as follows:

	Carrying Value	Fair Value
Cash	$ 25,000	$ 25,000
Accounts receivable	310,000	290,000 *(20000)*
Inventories	650,000	600,000 *(50,000)*
Plant and equipment (net)	2,015,000	2,050,000 *35000*
Total assets	$3,000,000	
Current liabilities	$ 300,000	$ 300,000
Long-term liabilities	1,200,000	1,100,000 *100,000*
Common stock	500,000	
Retained earnings	1,000,000	
Total liabilities and shareholders' equity	$3,000,000	

On January 1, Year 3, the Sparse Company's plant and equipment had a remaining useful life of 8 years and its long-term liabilities mature on January 1, Year 7. Goodwill, if any, is to be amortized over 40 years.

The balance sheets as at December 31, Year 9, and the retained earnings statements for the year ending December 31, Year 9 for the two companies are as follows:

Balance Sheets as at December 31, Year 9

	Plenty	Sparse
Cash	$ 500,000	$ 40,000
Accounts receivable	1,700,000	500,000
Inventories	2,300,000	1,200,000
Plant and equipment (net)	8,200,000	4,000,000
Investment in Sparse (at cost)	1,600,000	
Land	700,000	260,000
Total assets	$15,000,000	$6,000,000
Current liabilities	$ 600,000	$ 200,000
Long-term liabilities	3,000,000	3,000,000
Common stock	1,000,000	500,000
Retained earnings	10,400,000	2,300,000
Total liabilities and shareholders' equity	$15,000,000	$6,000,000

Retained Earnings for Year 9

	Plenty	Sparse
Balance January 1, Year 9	$ 9,750,000	$2,000,000
Net Income, Year 9	1,000,000	400,000
Subtotal	$10,750,000	$2,400,000
Dividends, Year 9	350,000	100,000
Balance December 31, Year 9	$10,400,000	$2,300,000

Additional information:

(1) The inventories of both companies have a maximum turnover period of 1 year. Receivables have a maximum turnover period of 62 days.

(2) On July 1, Year 7, Plenty sold a parcel of land to Sparse for $100,000. Plenty had purchased this land in Year 4 for $150,000. On September 30, Year 9, Sparse sold the property to another company for $190,000.

(3) During Year 9, $2 million of Plenty's sales were to Sparse. Of these sales, $500,000 remain in the December 31, Year 9 inventories of Sparse. The December 31, Year 8 inventories of Sparse contained $312,500 of merchandise purchased from Plenty. Plenty's sales to Sparse are priced to provide it with a gross profit of 20 percent.

(4) During Year 9, $1.5 million of Sparse's sales were to Plenty. Of these sales $714,280 remain in the December 31, Year 9 inventories of Plenty. The December 31, Year 8 inventories of Plenty contained $857,140 of merchandise purchased from Sparse. Sparse's sales to Plenty are priced to provide it with a gross profit of 25 percent.

(5) Dividends declared on December 31, Year 9 were:

Plenty	$350,000
Sparse	$100,000

(6) All amortization and depreciation charges of both companies are calculated on a straight-line basis.

(7) Assume a 40% tax rate for both companies.

Instructions:
a Prepare the consolidated retained earnings statement.
b Prepare the consolidated balance sheet.

8-8 The following are the financial statements of Post Corporation and its subsidiary Sage Company as at 31 December, Year 3.

BALANCE SHEETS — DECEMBER 31, YEAR 3

	Post Corporation	Sage Ltd.
Cash	$ 12,200	$ 12,900
Accounts receivable	17,200	9,100
Notes receivable		55,000
Inventory	32,000	27,000
Land	175,000	19,000
Plant and Equipment	520,000	65,000
Accumulated depreciation	(229,400)	(17,000)
Investment in Sage — at cost	65,000	
	$592,000	$171,000
Accounts payable	$212,000	$ 40,000
Notes payable .,........................	55,000	
Capital stock	100,000	50,000
Retained earnings January 1	158,000	72,000
Net income	117,000	24,000
Dividends	(50,000)	(15,000)
	$592,000	$171,000

INCOME STATEMENTS — YEAR 3

	Post Corporation	Sage Ltd.
Sales	$900,000	$240,000
Management fee revenue	26,500	
Interest revenue		6,800
Gain on land sale		30,000
Dividend revenue	10,500	
Total	$937,000	$276,800
Cost of goods sold	$540,000	$162,000
Interest expense	20,000	
Other expense	180,000	74,800
Income tax expense	80,000	16,000
Total	$820,000	$252,800
Net income	$117,000	$ 24,000

Additional information

(1) Post purchased 70% of the outstanding shares of Sage on 1 January, Year 1 at a cost of $65,000 and has used the cost method to account for its investment. On that date Sage had retained earnings of $15,000, and fair values were equal to carrying values for all its net assets except: Inventory — overvalued by 12,000; Equipment — undervalued by 18,000. The equipment had an estimated remaining life of 5 years and the company has a policy of amortizing goodwill over a 10 year period.

(2) Both companies sell merchandise to each other at a gross profit rate of 25%.

(3) The 31 December, Year 2 inventory of Post contained purchases made from Sage amounting to $14,000. There were no intercompany purchases in the inventory of Sage on this date.

(4) During Year 3 the following intercompany transactions took place:

   (a) Sage made a payment of $26,500 to Post for management fees, which was recorded under the category "other expenses."
   (b) Sage made sales of $90,000 to Post. The December 31, Year 3 inventory of Post contained merchandise purchased from Sage amounting to $28,000.
   (c) Post made sales of $125,000 to Sage. The December 31, Year 3 inventory of Sage contained merchandise purchased from Post amounting to $18,000.
   (d) On July 1, Year 3 Post borrowed $55,000 from Sage and signed a note bearing interest at 12% per annum. The interest on this note was paid on 31 December, Year 3.
   (e) During the year Sage sold land to Post and recorded a gain of $30,000 on the transaction. This land is being held by Post on 31 December, Year 3.

(5) Both companies pay income tax at 40% on their taxable incomes.

Instructions Prepare the following consolidated financial statements for Year 3:
a Income statement
b Retained earnings statement
c Balance sheet

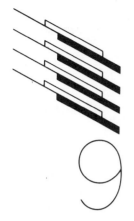

CONSOLIDATED FINANCIAL STATEMENTS: INTERCOMPANY PROFITS AND LOSSES IN DEPRECIABLE ASSETS, INTERCOMPANY BONDHOLDINGS

In Chapter 8 we illustrated the holdback and realization of an intercompany profit in inventory and land. In both cases the before-tax profit of $600 and the corresponding income tax of $240 were held back in the year of the intercompany transaction and realized in the year of sale to outsiders. We will now examine the holdback and realization of an intercompany profit in a depreciable asset.

INTERCOMPANY PROFITS IN DEPRECIABLE ASSETS

We return to the example of Parent Company and its 90% ownership of Subsidiary Company illustrated in Chapter 8. The income statements for the two companies for Year 1 are as follows:

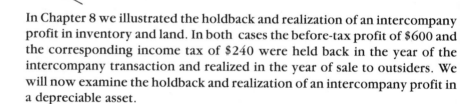

<table>
<tr><td style="text-align:left">**Year 1 income statements of parent and subsidiary**</td><td></td><td>**Parent Company**</td><td>**Subsidiary Company**</td></tr>
<tr><td>Sales</td><td></td><td>$20,000</td><td>$7,400</td></tr>
<tr><td>Gain on sale of equipment</td><td></td><td></td><td>600</td></tr>
<tr><td>Total</td><td></td><td>$20,000</td><td>$8,000</td></tr>
<tr><td>Cost of goods sold</td><td></td><td>$13,000</td><td>$4,300</td></tr>
<tr><td>Depreciation expense</td><td></td><td>700</td><td></td></tr>
<tr><td>Miscellaneous expense</td><td></td><td>700</td><td>900</td></tr>
<tr><td>Income tax expense</td><td></td><td>2,200</td><td>1,100</td></tr>
<tr><td>Total costs and expenses</td><td></td><td>$16,600</td><td>$6,300</td></tr>
<tr><td>Net Income</td><td></td><td>$ 3,400</td><td>$1,700</td></tr>
</table>

Notice that although the details shown on each income statement have been changed, the net incomes of the two companies are unchanged.

On July 1, Year 1, the subsidiary sold office equipment to the parent and recorded a profit of $600 on the transaction. This intercompany sale of equipment was recorded in the following manner by the two companies:

Parent Company		Subsidiary Company	
Equipment 2,100		Cash 2,100	
Cash	2,100	Equipment	1,500
		Gain on sale of	
		equipment	600

We are assuming that on July 1, Year 1 the subsidiary purchased the equipment for $1,500 with the intention of using it, but instead immediately sold it to the parent at a profit of $600. It is also assumed that this transaction was not a capital gain for tax purposes and therefore the subsidiary paid $240 (40% × $600) income tax on this profit. We further assume that the equipment is being depreciated over an estimated useful life of one and a half years, and that this is the only depreciable asset held by either company. On December 31, Year 1, the parent company recorded depreciation expense in the following manner:

Depreciation expense $700
   Accumulated depreciation $700
To record one-half year's depreciation on the equipment (2,100 ÷ 1½ × ½ year)

Note that if the subsidiary had sold the equipment at its cost, the parent's depreciation expense for Year 1 would have been 500 (1,500 ÷ 1½ × ½ year). This is the amount of depreciation expense that should appear on the income statement of the entity (i.e. on the consolidated income statement) for Year 1, because this amount is based on **the historical cost** of the equipment to the entity.

When we prepare a consolidated income statement we will have to make four eliminations. These eliminations can be described as follows:

a Eliminate the gain on sale of equipment of $600. This results in the entity's before-tax income being reduced by $600.

b Corresponding with the first elimination we reduce income tax expense by $240 (40% × $600). These first two eliminations result in the entity's aftertax net income being reduced by $360 ($600 − $240) and are identical to the land gain eliminations illustrated in Chapter 8.

c Eliminate the portion of the gain contained in depreciation expense. The intercompany profit of $600 is being depreciated over 1½ years. In Year 1, $200 (600 ÷ 1½ × ½ year) depreciation expense was recorded on this profit. When we reduce depreciation expense by $200 in preparing the consolidated income statement the resultant amount of $500 ($700 − $200) represents the entity's depreciation expense based on the equipment's cost.

d A reduction of $200 depreciation expense increases the entity's before-tax income by $200. Therefore, the corresponding entry for elimination (c) is to increase income tax expense by $80 (40% × $200). Note that entries (c) and (d) result in the entity's aftertax net income being increased by $120 ($200 − $80).

Entries **(c)** and **(d)** illustrate how the realization of an intercompany profit in a depreciable asset takes place on the consolidated income statement. ***The reduction of depreciation expense***, by the amount of the intercompany profit therein, <u>increases the</u> entity's net income ***and therefore realizes for consolidation purposes a portion of the intercompany profit*** that was previously held back. From the point of view of the consolidated entity, the intercompany gain element of the acquiring affiliate's annual depreciation expense represents a realization of a portion of the intercompany gain by the selling affiliate. Depreciation, in this view, is in effect ***an indirect sale of a portion of the equipment to the customers of the acquiring affiliate***. The selling prices of the acquiring affiliate's products or services are established at amounts to cover all costs of producing the product or services, including depreciation expense.

We will now prepare (without a working paper) the consolidated income statement for Year 1 adjusted for the intercompany transactions. The intercompany transactions that require elimination are as follows:

Unrealized intercompany profits	*Before Tax*	*40% Tax*	*After Tax*
Equipment gain — subsidiary selling			
— July 1, Year 1	*$600*	*$240*	*$360*
Less: Realized by depreciation — Year 1	*200*	*80*	*120*
Balance Dec. 31, Year 1	*$400*	*$160*	*$240*

Calculation of Year 1 adjustments for intercompany equipment profit

Preparation of Year 1 consolidated income statement without a working paper

Parent Company and Subsidiary Consolidated Income Statement Year 1	
Sales ($20,000 + $7,400)	*$27,400*
Gain on sale of equipment ($600 − $600[a])	*0*
Total	*$27,400*
Cost of goods sold ($13,000 + $4,300)	*$17,300*
Depreciation expense ($700 − $200[c])	*500*
Miscellaneous expense ($700 + $900)	*1,600*
Income tax expense ($2,200 + $1,100 − $240[b] + $80[d])	*3,140*
Total costs and expenses	*$22,540*
Net income — consolidated entity	*4,860*
Less: Minority interest (10% × $1,460)	*146*
Net income	*$ 4,714*

The net income of the consolidated entity ($3,400 + $1,460 = $4,860) and the calculation of minority interest in net income can be verified by the following calculation of consolidated net income.

Parent Company net income		$3,400
Subsidiary Company net income	$1,700	
Less: equipment gain	360	
	$1,340	
Add: equipment gain realized by depreciation	120	
Adjusted net income	$1,460	
Parent Company's share	.9	1,314
Consolidated net income		$4,714

The intercompany gain on equipment must also be eliminated in the preparation of the consolidated balance sheet on December 31, Year 1. The elimination of the gain on the assets side of the balance sheet is accomplished as follows:

Elimination of equipment
gain and tax adjustment
on Year 1 consolidated
balance sheet

**Parent Company and Subsidiary
Consolidated Balance Sheet
December 31 Year 1
Assets**

Equipment ($2,100 − $600[a])	$1,500	
Less: Accumulated depreciation ($700 − $200[b])	500	$1,000
Deferred Income Tax (+ $240[c] − $80[d])		160
Total Assets		$ XXX

The reasons for the balance sheet eliminations are as follows:

a The before-tax profit of $600 is included in the equipment balance of $2,100. Removing this profit restates the equipment to the original cost to the entity of $1,500.

b The amount of the accumulated depreciation contains the depreciation taken to date on the original cost ($500) plus the depreciation taken to date on the profit ($200). By reducing the accumulated depreciation by $200 the resultant amount represents depreciation on original cost. Note that a reduction to equipment of $600 together with a reduction in accumulated depreciation of $200 results in a reduction in the net book value of equipment of $400, which is the before-tax profit being held back as at December 31, Year 1. (See the calculation on page 348).

c The $240 increase in deferred income taxes represents the tax adjustment for elimination (a).

d The $80 decrease in deferred income taxes represents the tax adjustment for elimination (b).

Note that a reduction of $400 in the net book value of the equipment together with an increase in deferred taxes of $160 (40% × $400) results in total assets being reduced by $240, which is the aftertax profit being held back as at December 31, Year 1. (See calculation on page 348.)

A re-examination of the consolidated income statement and the calculation of consolidated net income (page 348 and above) indicates that the entity's net income was reduced by $240 and that this reduction was allocated to the two equities as follows:

<table>
<tr><td rowspan="3">**Allocation of net equipment profit held back as at Dec. 31, Year 1 to the two equities**</td><td>*To minority interest (10% × $240)* ....</td><td>*$ 24*</td></tr>
<tr><td>*To controlling interest (90% × $240)* ....</td><td>*216*</td></tr>
<tr><td>*Total allocated to the two equities* ....</td><td>*$240*</td></tr>
</table>

The amount of the reduction allocated to the controlling interest is in the net income on the consolidated income statement and flows to the consolidated balance sheet through the consolidated retained earnings statement. The amount allocated to minority interest **does not flow to the balance sheet** through any similar type of statement and therefore **has to be taken into account in the minority interest calculation**. The amount of minority interest appearing on the consolidated balance sheet on December 31, Year 1 requires the following calculation:

<table>
<tr><td rowspan="5">**Calculation of minority interest as at Dec. 31, Year 1**</td><td>*Shareholders' Equity of Subsidiary Company on Dec. 31, Year 1* ....</td><td>*$XXX*</td></tr>
<tr><td>*Less: Net equipment profit being held back on Dec. 31, Year 1* ....</td><td>*240*</td></tr>
<tr><td>*Adjusted Shareholders' Equity* ....</td><td>*$XXX*</td></tr>
<tr><td>*Minority Interest %* ....</td><td>*.10*</td></tr>
<tr><td>*Minority Interest* ....</td><td>*$XXX*</td></tr>
</table>

Equity Method Journal Entries

Parent Company would make the following equity method journal entries in Year 1:

<table>
<tr><td rowspan="13">**Parent company's Year 1 equity method journal entries**</td><td>*Dec. 31*</td><td>*Investment in Subsidiary Company* ....</td><td>*1,530*</td><td></td></tr>
<tr><td></td><td>*Intercompany Investment Income* ....</td><td></td><td>*1,530*</td></tr>
<tr><td></td><td>*To record 90% of Subsidiary Company's reported*</td><td></td><td></td></tr>
<tr><td></td><td>*net income for Year 1 ($1,700 × .9 = $1,530)*</td><td></td><td></td></tr>
<tr><td>*Dec. 31*</td><td>*Intercompany Investment Income* ....</td><td>*324*</td><td></td></tr>
<tr><td></td><td>*Investment in Subsidiary Company* ....</td><td></td><td>*324*</td></tr>
<tr><td></td><td>*To record the holdback of 90% of the intercompany*</td><td></td><td></td></tr>
<tr><td></td><td>*equipment gain recorded by Subsidiary Company*</td><td></td><td></td></tr>
<tr><td></td><td>*on July 1, Year 1 ($360 × .9 = $324)*</td><td></td><td></td></tr>
<tr><td>*Dec. 31*</td><td>*Investment in Subsidiary Company* ....</td><td>*108*</td><td></td></tr>
<tr><td></td><td>*Intercompany Investment Income* ....</td><td></td><td>*108*</td></tr>
<tr><td></td><td>*To record 90% of the portion of the equipment gain*</td><td></td><td></td></tr>
<tr><td></td><td>*realized by depreciation in Year 1 ($120 × .9 = $108)*</td><td></td><td></td></tr>
</table>

Intercompany investment income of $1,314 ($1,530 − $324 + $108) would appear on Parent Company's Year 1 income statement resulting in a total parent's net income of $4,714 ($3,400 + $1,314), which is equal to consolidated net income (see page 348).

Realization of Remaining Equipment Gain — Year 2

The equipment sold to the parent on July 1, Year 1 had a remaining life of 1½ years on that date. In the preparation of the Year 1 consolidated income statement, both the holdback of the intercompany gain and the realization of one third of the gain took place. In Year 2 the realization of the remaining two thirds of the gain takes place in the preparation of the consolidated income statement. Thus the intercompany gain is fully realized at the end of Year 2, only because the equipment had a 1½ year remaining life on the date of the intercompany sale.

The Year 2 income statements for the two companies are as follows (Parent Company has not yet recorded the equity method journal entries for the year):

Year 2 income statements of parent and subsidiary

	Parent Company	Subsidiary Company
Sales	$25,000	$12,000
Cost of goods sold	$16,000	$ 5,500
Depreciation expense	1,400	
Miscellaneous expense	950	1,400
Income tax expense	2,600	2,000
Total costs and expenses	$20,950	$ 8,900
Net income	$ 4,050	$ 3,100

The intercompany transactions that require elimination in the preparation of the Year 2 consolidated financial statements are as follows:

Calculation of Year 2 adjustments for intercompany equipment profit

Unrealized Intercompany Profits	Before Tax	40% Tax	After Tax
Equipment gain July 1, Year 1	$600	$240	$360
Less: realized by depreciation — Year 1	200	80	120
Balance Dec. 31, Year 1	$400	$160	$240
Less: realized by depreciation — Year 2	400	160	240
Balance Dec. 31, Year 2	$ 0	$ 0	$ 0

The Year 1 transactions described above have been taken into account in preparation of the Year 1 consolidated financial statements and in the Year 1 equity method journal entries of the parent company. We are preparing the Year 2 consolidated income statement and therefore we are only concerned with the gain realized by depreciation in Year 2. The preparation of the consolidated income statement (without working papers) is accomplished in the following manner.

Parent Company and Subsidiary
Consolidated Income Statement
Year 2

Sales ($25,000 + 12,000)	$37,000
Cost of goods sold (16,000 + 5,500)	$21,500
Depreciation expense (1400 − 400[a])	1,000
Miscellaneous expense (950 + 1,400)	2,350
Income tax expense (2,600 + 2,000 + 160[b])	4,760
Total costs and expenses	$29,610
Net income − consolidated entity	$ 7,390
Less: Minority interest (10% × 3,340)	334
Net income	$ 7,056

The net income of the consolidated entity and the amount used in the minority interest calculation is verified by the calculation of consolidated net income as follows:

Parent Company net income		$4,050
Subsidiary net income	$3,100	
Add: equipment gain realized by depreciation	240	
Adjusted net income	$3,340	
Parent Company's share	.9	3,006
Consolidated net income		$7,056

The two eliminations are explained as follows:

a Depreciation expense is reduced by the portion of the gain contained therein. A reduction of $400 to depreciation expense increases the entity's before-tax net income by that amount. This elimination entry realizes $400 of the original intercompany gain in before-tax dollars and restates consolidated depreciation to the amount based on the entity's cost.

b The corresponding entry for elimination (a) is the increase to income tax expense of $160 (40% × $400). By using income tax allocation, we match the income tax expense with the amount of the gain being realized. On the December 31, Year 1 consolidated balance sheet a deferred tax asset appeared in relation to the equipment gain. This entry reduces that asset by $160, and treats it as an expense in Year 2.

The preparation of a consolidated balance sheet on December 31, Year 2 also requires elimination entries with respect to the equipment gain. This is accomplished in the manner shown at the top of page 353.

The elimination entries on the balance sheet are explained as follows:

a The reduction of $600 in equipment removes the intercompany gain and restates the equipment to historical cost to the entity ($1,500).

b This equipment is fully depreciated on December 31, Year 2, and therefore the accumulated depreciation balance of $2,100 contains the $600 intercompany gain. By reducing the accumulated depreciation by $600 the resultant balance ($1,500) is based on historical cost to the entity.

Elimination of equipment
gain on Year 2
consolidated balance
sheet

Parent Company and Subsidiary
Consolidated Balance Sheet
December 31, Year 2

Assets

Equipment ($2,100 − $600[a]) $1,500

Less: accumulated depreciation ($2,100 − $600[b]) .... 1,500 $ 0

Total assets .... $XXX

Note that if both the equipment and the accumulated depreciation have been reduced by $600, total consolidated assets have not been changed. In other words all intercompany gains held back previously have been realized as at December 31, Year 2. If there are no intercompany gains being held back there will be no deferred income tax on the consolidated balance sheet. The deferred income taxes of $160 appearing on the December 31, Year 1 consolidated balance sheet became an expense on the Year 2 consolidated income statement.

There are no adjustments required on the equity side of the December 31, Year 2 consolidated balance sheet, because there is no reduction in assets. Recall that in the preparation of the Year 2 consolidated income statement, $240 of the intercompany equipment gain was realized. This was allocated to the two equities as follows:

Allocation of equipment
gain realized in Year 2
to the two equities

To minority interest (10% × $240) .... $ 24

To controlling interest (90% × $240) 216

Total allocated $240

Recall also (see page 350) that in the preparation of the Year 1 consolidated income statement, $240 was held back and allocated in the same manner. The amounts held back in Year 1 *have been offset* by the amounts realized in Year 2, so that the December 31, Year 2 balances of the two equities are not affected.

Equity Method Journal Entries

Parent Company would make the following journal entries in Year 2, if it accounts for its investment by the equity method:

Dec. 31   Investment in Subsidiary Company 2,790

     Intercompany Investment Income 2,790

     To record 90% of Subsidiary Company's reported net

     income for Year 2 ($3,100 × .9 = $2,790).

Dec. 31   Investment in Subsidiary Company 216

     Intercompany investment income 216

     To record 90% of the portion of the equipment gain

     realized by depreciation in Year 2 ($240 × .9 = $216).

Intercompany investment income amounting to $3,006 ($2,790 + $216) would appear on Parent Company's Year 2 income statement, resulting in a net income of $7,056 which is equal to consolidated net income.

Comparison of Realization of Inventory and Equipment Profits Over Two-Year Period

In Chapter 8 the holdback and realization of an intercompany profit in inventory was illustrated. In this chapter we have illustrated the holdback and realization of an intercompany gain in equipment. In both cases the aftertax profit (gain) was $360 (60% × $600), and the subsidiary was the selling company. The following **summarizes the effect** on the entity's net income over a two-year period.

Effect of inventory profit on entity's net income over a two-year period

Intercompany Inventory Profit			
	Year 1	*Year 2*	*Total*
Parent Company net income	$3,400	$4,050	$ 7,450
Subsidiary Company net income	1,700	3,100	4,800
Total	$5,100	$7,150	$12,250
Aftertax profit (holdback) realized	(360)	360	0
Net income — consolidated entity	$4,740	$7,510	$12,250
Allocated to the two equities:			
Minority interest	134	346	480
Consolidated retained earnings	4,606	7,164	11,770
Total	$4,740	$7,510	$12,250

Effect of equipment gain on entity's net income over a two-year period

Intercompany Equipment Gain			
	Year 1	*Year 2*	*Total*
Parent Company net income	$3,400	$4,050	$ 7,450
Subsidiary Company net income	1,700	3,100	4,800
Total	$5,100	$7,150	$12,250
Aftertax gain (held back) realized	(360)	240	0
	120		
Net income — consolidated entity	$4,860	$7,390	$12,250
Allocated as follows:			
Minority interest	$ 146	$ 334	$ 480
Consolidated retained earnings	4,714	7,056	11,770
Total	$4,860	$7,390	$12,250

The two-year summaries shown above in part illustrate a number of significant points in relation to consolidated financial statements.

1 The consolidated entity's net income is measured at the end of time periods that are usually one year in length.

2 During this measurement process, the holdback and subsequent realization of profits (losses) resulting from intercompany transactions takes place.

3 The *realization* of previously held back profits (losses) *occurs during the period* in which the acquiring company either *sells the asset* containing the profit (loss) to outsiders, *or depreciates the asset*, therefore selling the services provided by the asset to outsiders.

4 If we examine a time period longer than one year, and if, at the end of that period, the assets of the constituent companies do not contain intercompany profits, the following truism becomes evident:

The consolidated entity's net income for this longer period consists of
(a) the reported net income of the parent company, exclusive of intercompany investment or dividend income, plus
(b) the reported net income of the subsidiary company (or companies), minus
(c) the purchase discrepancy amortization.

In the above illustration we assumed that the purchase discrepancy had been fully amortized for consolidation purposes prior to Year 1, and that the parent company had omitted making the required equity journal entries in each of the two years.

5 The entity's net income measurement for this longer time period, and its allocation to the two equities, *is not affected by the fact that assets were sold at intercompany profits (losses) during the period*. (See the two-year total column.)

6 When consolidated statements are prepared at the end of an *intervening time period* (for example Year 1, Year 2) we have to determine whether there were profits (losses) recorded by any of the constituent companies that were not realized by the end of the period, and whether there were profits (losses) from prior periods, or the current period, that were realized during the period.

7 *The profit holdbacks and realizations* are used in the measurement of the entity's net income, and are *adjustments to the reported net income of the selling constituent* in the allocation of that net income.

In Chapter 8 we also illustrated the holdback and realization of a $360 aftertax intercompany gain in land. In this case the realization process took place in Year 8 but the overall concepts discussed above remain the same.

Working Paper Illustration — Plant Assets

We will now turn to a working paper example to illustrate the holdback and subsequent realization of intercompany profits in depreciable assets. Penn Company owns 80% of Sill Corporation and accounts for its investment by the equity method. The acquisition date purchase discrepancy was allocated entirely to goodwill which has been fully amortized for consolidation purposes prior to Year 5. There were no unrealized intercompany profits in assets on December 31, Year 4. During Year 5 the following intercompany transactions took place:

1 On January 1, Year 5 Penn sold used equipment to Sill and recorded a $14,000 gain on the transactions calculated as follows:

Calculation of inter-
company gain on sale of
equipment, parent selling

Selling price of equipment		$44,000
Carrying amount		
Cost	$60,000	
Accumulated depreciation — Dec. 31, Year 4	30,000	30,000
Gain on sale of equipment		$14,000

The equipment had an estimated remaining life of 8 years on this date.

2 Ten years prior to the beginning of Year 5, Sill developed a patent at a cost of $34,000, which it had been amortizing over the maximum legal life of 17 years. On October 1, Year 5, Sill sold the patent to Penn and recorded a $7,500 gain calculated as follows:

<table>
<tr><td rowspan="7">**Calculation of inter-
company gain on sale of
patent, subsidiary selling**</td><td>*Selling price of patent* . . . .</td><td></td><td></td><td>*$20,000*</td></tr>
<tr><td>*Carrying amount*</td><td></td><td></td><td></td></tr>
<tr><td>*Cost* . . . .</td><td></td><td>*$34,000*</td><td></td></tr>
<tr><td>*Amortization:*</td><td></td><td></td><td></td></tr>
<tr><td>*To Jan. 1, Year 5 (10 × $2,000)* . . . .</td><td>*$20,000*</td><td></td><td></td></tr>
<tr><td>*Year 5* . . . .</td><td>*1,500*</td><td>*21,500*</td><td>*$12,500*</td></tr>
<tr><td>*Gain of sale of patent* . . . .</td><td></td><td></td><td>*$ 7,500*</td></tr>
</table>

Penn is amortizing this patent over its remaining legal life of 6¼ years.

3 Both gains were assessed income tax at a rate of 40%.

The financial statements of both companies as at December 31, Year 5 appear on page 358. The unrealized profits and the income tax effects that require elimination in the preparation of the Year 5 consolidated financial statement are as follows:

<table>
<tr><td rowspan="2">**Calculation of adjustments
required in the preparation
of Year 5 consolidated
financial statements**</td><td>*Unrealized intercompany profits*</td><td>*Before
Tax*</td><td>*40%
Tax*</td><td>*After
Tax*</td></tr>
<tr><td></td><td></td><td></td><td></td></tr>
<tr><td></td><td>*Equipment (Penn selling)*</td><td></td><td></td><td></td></tr>
<tr><td></td><td>*Jan. 1, Year 5 gain* . . . .</td><td>*$14,000*</td><td>*$5,600*</td><td>*$8,400*</td></tr>
<tr><td></td><td>*Depreciation Year 5 (14,000 ÷ 8)* . . . .</td><td>*1,750*</td><td>*700*</td><td>*1,050*</td></tr>
<tr><td></td><td>*Balance Dec. 31, Year 5* . . . .</td><td>*$12,250*</td><td>*$4,900*</td><td>*$7,350*</td></tr>
<tr><td></td><td>*Patent (Sill selling)*</td><td></td><td></td><td></td></tr>
<tr><td></td><td>*Oct. 1, Year 5 gain* . . . .</td><td>*$ 7,500*</td><td>*$3,000*</td><td>*$4,500*</td></tr>
<tr><td></td><td>*Amortization Year 5* . . . .</td><td>*300*</td><td>*120*</td><td>*180*</td></tr>
<tr><td></td><td>*(7,500 ÷ 6¼ × ¼)*</td><td></td><td></td><td></td></tr>
<tr><td></td><td>*Balance Dec. 31, Year 5* . . . .</td><td>*$ 7,200*</td><td>*$2,880*</td><td>*$4,320*</td></tr>
<tr><td></td><td>*Deferred income taxes December 31, Year 5*</td><td></td><td></td><td></td></tr>
<tr><td></td><td>*Equipment profit* . . . .</td><td>*$ 4,900*</td><td></td><td></td></tr>
<tr><td></td><td>*Patent profit* . . . .</td><td>*$ 2,880*</td><td></td><td></td></tr>
<tr><td></td><td>*Total* . . . .</td><td>*$ 7,780*</td><td></td><td></td></tr>
</table>

The ledger accounts reflecting Penn Company's investment in Sill Corporation accounted for under the equity method appear on page 357. The account Investment in Sill Company reflects only the Year 5 transactions. Because the purchase discrepancy has been fully amortized prior to Year 5, the January 1, Year 5 balance in this account represents 80% of

PENN COMPANY LEDGER
Investment in Sill Corporation

Date	Explanation	Debit	Credit	Balance
1/1/5	Balance			283,200 Dr
12/31/5	Dividend of Sill (80% × $8000)		6,400	276,800 Dr
12/31/5	Net income of Sill (80% × $25,000)	20,000		296,800 Dr
12/31/5	Equipment profit held back		8,400	288,400 Dr
12/31/5	Equipment profit realized	1,050		289,450 Dr
12/31/5	Patent profit (80% × $4,500) held back . . .		3,600	285,850 Dr
12/31/5	Patent profit realized (80% × 180) held back	144		285,994 Dr

Intercompany Investment Income

Date	Explanation	Debit	Credit	Balance
12/31/5	Net income of Sill		20,000	20,000 Cr
12/31/5	Equipment profit held back	8,400		11,600 Cr
12/31/5	Equipment profit realized		1,050	12,650 Cr
12/31/5	Patent profit held back	3,600		9,050 Cr
12/31/5	Patent profit realized		144	9,194 Cr

the capital stock and retained earnings of Sill Corporation on this date ($200,000 + $154,000 = $354,000 × 0.80 = $283,200).

The working paper for the Year 5 consolidated financial statements and the related working paper eliminations appear on pages 358 and 359.

The following features of the elimination entries require further elaboration.

1 Because the parent uses the equity method:

Penn Company net income = consolidated net income
Penn Company retained earnings = consolidated retained earnings

2 In this particular illustration there is no purchase discrepancy to amortize or allocate.

3 The portion of elimination (a) that has been labelled (i to iv) represents the adjustments for the Year 5 equipment and patent intercompany profit transactions. The unlabelled portion is fully explained in the narrative.

4 Elimination (a) (i) is the holdback of the equipment profit on January 1, Year 5. The tax effect is netted in (a) (iv).

5 Elimination (a) (ii) recognizes the portion of the equipment profit realized by depreciation in Year 5. The tax effect is netted in (a) (iv).

6 Elimination (a) (iii) recognizes **both the holdback** of the patent profit on Oct. 1, Year 5, and **the amount realized by amortization** in Year 5. Note that consolidated patent amortization expense of $2,000 was recorded by both companies and represents one year's amortization of the original patent cost ($34,000). The tax effect is netted in (a) (iv).

Equity method: Partially owned subsidiary subsequent to acquisition

PENN COMPANY AND SUBSIDIARY
Working Paper for Consolidated Financial Statements
For Year Ended December 31, Year 5

	Penn Company	Sill Corporation	Eliminations Increase (Decrease)		Consolidated
Income Statement					
Miscellaneous revenues	500,000	300,000			800,000
Intercompany investment income	9,194		(a)	(9,194)	
Gain on sale of equipment	14,000		(a)	(14,000)	
Gain on sale of patent		7,500	(a)	(7,500)	
Total revenue	523,194	307,500		(30,694)	800,000
Miscellaneous costs and					
expenses	309,600	185,000			494,600
Depreciation expense	120,000	80,000	(a)	(1,750)	198,250
Patent amortization expense	800	1,500	(a)	(300)	2,000
Income taxes expense	33,000	16,000	(a)	(7,780)	41,220
Minority interest in net income . .			(b)	4,136	4,136
Total costs and expenses	463,400	282,500		(5,694)	740,206
Net income	59,794	25,000		(25,000)	59,794
Statement of Retained Earnings					
Retained earnings, beginning of					
year	162,000	154,000	(a)	(154,000)	162,000
Net income	59,794	25,000		(25,000)	59,794
Subtotal	221,794	179,000		(179,000)	221,794
Dividends	25,000	8,000	(a)	(8,000)	25,000
Retained earnings, end of year . .	196,794	171,000		(171,000)	196,794
Balance Sheet					
Miscellaneous assets	271,600	131,000			402,600
			(c)	30,000	
Plant and equipment	200,000	700,000	(a)	(14,000)	916,000
			(c)	30,000 *	
Accumulated depreciation	(80,000)	(250,000)	(a)	1,750 **	(358,250)
Patent (net)	19,200		(a)	(7,200)	12,000
Investment in Sill Corporation . . .	285,994		(a)	(285,994)	
Deferred income tax			(a)	7,780	7,780
Total assets	696,794	581,000		(297,664)	980,130
Miscellaneous liabilities	100,000	210,000			310,000
			(a)	69,200	
Minority interest in net assets . . .			(b)	4,136	73,336
Common stock	400,000				400,000
Common stock		200,000	(a)	(200,000)	
Retained earnings	196,794	171,000		(171,000)	196,794
Total liabilities and					
shareholders' equity	696,794	581,000		(297,664)	980,130

*increase

**decrease

PENN COMPANY AND SUBSIDIARY
Working Paper Eliminations
December 31, Year 5

(a) Common Stock — Sill	200,000	
Retained Earnings — Sill	154,000	
Intercompany Investment Income — Penn	9,194	
(i) Gain on Sale of Equipment	14,000	
(ii) Accumulated Depreciation	1,750	
(iii) Gain on Sale of Patent	7,500	
(iv) Deferred income tax	7,780	
Investment in Sill Corporation — Penn		285,994
Dividends — Sill		8,000
Minority Interest in Net Assets		69,200
(i) Plant and Equipment		14,000
(ii) Depreciation Expense		1,750
(iii) Patent		7,200
(iii) Patent Amortization Expense		300
(iv) Income Taxes Expense		7,780

To carry out the following:

(1) Eliminate the intercompany investment accounts, and equity accounts of subsidiary at beginning of year, and subsidiary dividends.

(2) Establish minority interest in net assets of subsidiary at beginning of year, less minority share of dividends of subsidiary during year as follows:

Shareholders' Equity — beginning of year	$354,000	
Less: dividends	8,000	
	$346,000	
Minority share ($346,000 × 0.20)	$ 69,200	

(3) To holdback and realize intercompany profit in Year 5 and adjust for income tax effects.

(b) Minority Interest in Net Income	4,136	
Minority Interest in Net Assets		4,136

To establish minority interest in subsidiary's adjusted net income for Year 5 as follows:

Net income of subsidiary	$ 25,000	
Less: patent profit	4,500	
	$ 20,500	
Add: patent profit realized by amortization	180	
Adjusted net income of subsidiary	$ 20,680	
Minority share ($20,680 × 0.20)	$ 4,136	

(c) Plant and Equipment	30,000	
Accumulated depreciation		30,000

To re-establish the accumulated depreciation of the equipment on the date of the intercompany purchase by the subsidiary.

7 Elimination (a) (iv) adjusts income tax expense for the Year 5 holdback and realization of both the equipment and patent profit, and records the December 31, Year 5 deferred income asset based on the unrealized profits being held back at the end of the year (see calculation on page 356). Alternatively we could have recorded the tax effects of (i), (ii) and (iii) separately.

8 When Penn sold the equipment to Sill on January 1, Year 5, the balance in the accumulated depreciation account was removed by Penn's journal entry. Entry (c) *re-establishes this amount* so that on the December 31, Year 5 consolidated balance sheet the plant assets and the accumulated depreciation amounts are based on the original historical cost to the entity.

9 *Minority interest* in net assets at December 31, Year 5 *may be verified as follows:*

Verification of minority interest as at Dec. 31, Year 5

Shareholders' equity of Sill Dec. 31, Year 5	
Common Stock	$200,000
Retained Earnings	171,000
Total	$371,000
Less: net patent gain Dec. 31, Year 5	4,320
Adjusted shareholders' equity	$366,680
Minority Interest ($366,680 × 0.20)	$ 73,336

INTERCOMPANY BONDHOLDINGS

Our discussions to date have been focussed on gains (losses) resulting from the intercompany sale of inventory, land and depreciable assets. The treatment of these gains (losses) in the preparation of consolidated financial statements can be summarized as follows: *Gains (losses)* resulting from the intercompany sale of assets *are realized subsequent* to the *recording of the intercompany transaction* by the selling affiliate.

Occasionally one affiliate will purchase all or a portion of the bonds issued by another affiliate. In the preparation of consolidated financial statements the elimination of the intercompany accounts (investment in bonds and bonds payable; interest revenue and interest expense) may result in a gain (loss) being reflected in the preparation of consolidated financial statements. The treatment of this type of gain (loss) can be summarized in the following manner: *Gains (losses)* arising because of the elimination of intercompany bond holding accounts *are realized prior* to the *recording of these gains (losses)* by the affiliates. Before we examine how these gains and losses occur in the elimination of the intercompany accounts, let us look at intercompany bondholding situations that do not result in gains or losses.

Intercompany bondholdings — no gain or loss

Not all intercompany bondholdings result in gains or losses being reflected in the consolidated statements. For example, let us assume that one affiliate issued $10,000 in bonds, and that another affiliate acquired the whole issue.

(The amounts used are unrealistically low for a bond issue, but are realistic in relation to the size of Parent Company and Subsidiary Company, the two companies that we have been using in our illustrations. Furthermore, the concepts will be the same regardless of the size of the amounts used.) Immediately after the issue the records of the two companies would show the following accounts:

Intercompany bondholdings in the accounts of the two affiliates

Acquiring affiliate's records	Issuing affiliate's records
Investment in bonds $10,000	Bonds payable $10,000

From the entity's point of view the two accounts are similar to intercompany receivables and payables and would be eliminated by the following working paper entry in the preparation of the consolidated balance sheet:

Working paper elimination entry — consolidated balance sheet

Bonds Payable	10,000	
Investment in Bonds		10,000

It is important to **note that the eliminations are equal, and because of this fact, there is no gain or loss** resulting from the working paper elimination of these two intercompany accounts. At the end of each succeeding year this working paper elimination will be repeated until the bonds mature. After that date, the two accounts would no longer exist in the affiliate's records and further working paper eliminations would not be required.

The consolidated balance sheet is not the only statement requiring working paper eliminations. If we assume that the bonds pay interest at the rate of 10%, then the income statement of the issuing affiliate will show interest expense of $1,000 while the income statement of the acquiring affiliate will show interest revenue of $1,000. These intercompany revenue and expense accounts would be eliminated by the following working paper entry in the preparation of the consolidated income statement:

Working paper elimination entry — consolidated income statement

Interest Revenue	1,000	
Interest Expense		1,000

Again it is important to **note that amounts are equal, and because of this fact there is no gain or loss** resulting from this working paper elimination. The consolidated income statement working paper elimination would be repeated each successive year until the bonds mature.

Our example has assumed that the bonds were issued at par. Suppose the bonds were issued to the purchasing affiliate at a premium or discount.

Provided that both affiliates use the same methods to amortize the issue premium or discount, and the purchase premium or discount, the amounts in the intercompany accounts on all successive balance sheets and income statements *will be equal. The important concept of equal elimination* on both statements would still be true.

In prior chapters, we have illustrated the fact that the *equal elimination* of intercompany receivables and payables *does not change* the amount of the two equities on the consolidated balance sheet. Furthermore, *the equal elimination* of intercompany revenues and expenses *does not change* the net income of the consolidated entity, and therefore can have no effect on the amount of that net income that is allocated to the two equities. As a result it does not matter which affiliate is the parent company and which is a subsidiary, or whether both affiliates are subsidiary companies because in all cases the working paper eliminations would be similar to those illustrated.

Intercompany bondholdings — resulting in gains or losses

When the market rate of interest is different than the coupon rate on the date of a bond issue, the bonds will be issued at a price which is different than par. If current interest rates are higher (lower) than the coupon rate the bonds will be issued at a discount (premium). Subsequent to the issue bond market prices will rise (fall) if the market interest rate falls (rises). It is *the market price differential* on the date of an intercompany purchase that *is the cause of the gains or losses resulting from intercompany bondholdings.* Let us change our example slightly to illustrate how this occurs.

Parent Company has a $10,000 bond issue outstanding which pays 10% interest annually on December 31. The bonds were originally issued at a premium which is being amortized by the company on a straight-line basis. On December 31, Year 1 this unamortized issue premium amounts to $200. The bonds mature on December 31, Year 5.

On December 31, Year 1 Subsidiary Company purchases all of the outstanding bonds of Parent Company on the open market at a cost of $9,600. Immediately after Subsidiary Company's bond acquisition, the records of the two companies would show the following accounts.

Intercompany bondholdings in the accounts of the two affiliates	Subsidiary Company's records		Parent Company's records	
	Investment in bonds		Bonds payable	$10,000
	of Parent Company	$10,000	Add: unamortized	
	Less: discount on		issue premium	200
	purchase	400		
	Net	$ 9,600	Net	$10,200

The net amounts reflect our assumption of how the asset and the liability would be presented on the respective balance sheets of the two companies on December 31, Year 1. The preparation of the consolidated balance sheet on this date would require the elimination of the two intercompany amounts by the following working paper entry.

PARENT COMPANY AND SUBSIDIARY
Partial Working Paper Elimination
December 31, Year 1

(a) *Bonds Payable*	*10,200*	
Investment in bonds of Parent Company		*9,600*
Gain on bond retirement		*600*
To eliminate the intercompany bond accounts and to recognize		
the resulting gain on the retirement of bonds.		

The eliminations of the asset and liability would appear on the consolidated balance sheet working paper. The balancing amount of the elimination entry, ***gain on bond retirement, appears on the consolidated income statement*** working paper. From the consolidated entity's point of view the bonds of the entity have been purchased on the open market and retired. The retirement gain can be calculated in the following manner:

Calculation of gain on bond retirement

Carrying amount of the bond liability	*$10,200*
Cost of investment in bonds	*9,600*
Gain on bond retirement	*$ 600*

It should be noted that if Parent Company had acquired and retired its own bonds in the same manner, it would have recorded a gain on bond retirement of the same amount. This gain would appear on Parent Company's income statement, and would also appear on the consolidated income statement. The actual event was different (Subsidiary Company purchased the bonds), but because the two companies are a single economic entity, the gain will still appear on the consolidated income statement. The only difference is the gain on the consolidated income statement does not appear on the income statement of the parent. Instead *it appears on the consolidated income statement as a result of the unequal elimination of the intercompany asset and liability* accounts in the preparation of the consolidated balance sheet.

An examination of the makeup of the asset and liability accounts (see page 362) will indicate why there is a gain of $600. If the bonds had originally been issued at par (face value), and if the bonds had been acquired on the open market at a price equal to par, there would be no gain on retirement. *It is the unamortized issue premium and the discount*

on the bond purchase that cause the gain. This premium and discou~~n~~
will be amortized by the two companies in Years 2 to 5, and thus will ~~b~~
reflected in the individual income statements of the two companies in tho~~s~~
future periods. This will become more evident when we examine th~~e~~
consolidation procedures in Year 2. The important point to note at th~~is~~
stage is that *the constituent companies will pay tax* on this gain *i~~n~~*
future periods when the *actual recording of the gain* takes place. Th~~e~~
consolidated entity is realizing the gain in Year 1 and therefore this timi~~ng~~
difference requires income tax allocation. Assuming a 40% tax rate th~~e~~
following additional working paper elimination entry would be require~~d~~

PARTIAL WORKING PAPER ELIMINATION
December 31, Year 1

(b) Income tax expense   240

    Deferred income tax   24

  To record the deferred income liability and expense on the Year 1

  intercompany bond gain (40% × $600 = $240).

The effect of elimination (a) and (b) on the Year 1 consolidated income is t~~o~~
increase the net income of the ~~equity~~ _{entity} by $360 ($600 − $240) = $360). Th~~e~~
entity's net income consists of the net income of the parent, plus the n~~et~~
income of the subsidiary, and therefore the aftertax increase must affect on~~e~~
or the other, or perhaps both.

There are *four possible approaches* that could be taken:

1 Allocate the gain to the issuing company because the company purchasing th~~e~~
bonds is acting as an agent for the issuing company.
2 Allocate the gain to the purchasing company because its investment led to th~~e~~
retirement of the bonds for consolidation purposes.
3 Allocate the gain to the parent company, because its management controls th~~e~~
actions of all the affiliated companies in the group. This would only be a separat~~e~~
alternative if both parties to the transaction were subsidiaries of that parent.
4 Allocate the gain between the issuing and purchasing companies because eac~~h~~
will record its portion of the gain in future periods.

An allocation of the gain would not be required in the case of 100%
owned subsidiaries because there would be no minority interest on th~~e~~
consolidated financial statements. The approach adopted is very importan~~t~~
in the situation where the subsidiaries are less than 100% owned becaus~~e~~
approaches 1, 2 and 4 could result in all or a portion of the gain bein~~g~~
allocated to the subsidiary company and would therefore affect minorit~~y~~
interest. The *CICA Handbook* is silent regarding the approach to be taken~~.~~
However, an exposure draft issued prior to the release of Section 160~~0~~
indicated a preference for alternative 4. When Section 1600 was release~~d~~
the preference indicated in the exposure draft had been deleted. In th~~e~~
illustrations that follow any gain (losses) from the elimination of intercom~~-~~
pany bondholding will be allocated to the purchasing and issuing affiliate~~s~~
(approach 4) because it is *conceptually superior* to the others.

Calculation of the Portion of the Gain
Allocated to the Affiliates

From the point of view of the purchasing affiliate the *cost* of the acquisition *is compared with the par value* of the bonds acquired, the difference being a gain or loss. From the point of view of the issuing affiliate, *it cost* an amount equal to the *par value* of bonds to retire *the carrying value* of the liability, with the difference also resulting in a gain or loss.

The gain and its allocation can be calculated in the following manner:

Par (face) value of bond liability	$10,000
Cost of investment in bonds	9,600
Gain allocated to purchasing affiliate	$ 400
Carrying amount of bond liability	$10,200
Par (face) value of bond liability	10,000
Gain allocated to issuing affiliate	$ 200

Allocation of bond gain to purchasing and issuing companies

Notice that the gain to the entity of $600 is made up of the two gains allocated to the affiliates ($400 + $200 = $600). Both the entity's gain and the amounts allocated are expressed in before-tax dollars. *The following chart is useful in calculating* the aftertax amounts *needed in the allocation* of the entity's aftertax net income to the two equities.

Bond gain allocation chart Dec. 31, Year 1

	Entity			Parent Company			Subsidiary Company		
	Before tax	40% tax	After tax	Before tax	40% tax	After tax	Before tax	40% tax	After tax
Gain on bond retirement — Dec. 31, Year 1	$600	$240	$360	$200	$80	$120	$400	$160	$240

On December 31, Year 1, the two companies prepared the following income statements (we are still assuming that there is no purchase discrepancy amortization and that the parent has not yet recorded the entries required by the equity method):

Year 1 income statements of parent and subsidiary

	Parent Company	Subsidiary Company
Miscellaneous revenue	$20,000	$8,000
Miscellaneous costs and expenses	$13,450	$5,200
Interest expense	950	
Income tax expense	2,200	1,100
Total costs and expenses	$16,600	$6,300
Net Income	$ 3,400	$1,700

The net incomes are the same as all previous examples in this chapter and Chapter 8. The details of revenue and expense have been changed so that we can focus our attention on the specific topic under discussion. Note that the parent's interest expense ($950) is made up of the $1,000 interest paid minus $50 amortization of the original bond issue premium.

The consolidated income statement for Year 1 would be prepared (without a working paper) in the following manner:

<table>
<tr><td style="width:22%">Preparation of Year 1 consolidated income statement without a working paper</td><td colspan="2" style="text-align:center">Parent Company and Subsidiary
Consolidated Income Statement
Year 1</td></tr>
<tr><td></td><td>Miscellaneous revenue ($20,000 + $8,000) ....</td><td style="text-align:right">$28,00(</td></tr>
<tr><td></td><td>Gain on bond retirement .... (a)</td><td style="text-align:right">60(</td></tr>
<tr><td></td><td>   Total ....</td><td style="text-align:right">$28,60(</td></tr>
<tr><td></td><td>Miscellaneous costs and expenses ($13,450 + $5,200) ....</td><td style="text-align:right">$18,65(</td></tr>
<tr><td></td><td>Interest expense ($950 + $0) ....</td><td style="text-align:right">95(</td></tr>
<tr><td></td><td>Income tax expense ($2,200 + $1,100 + $240[b]) ....</td><td style="text-align:right">3,54(</td></tr>
<tr><td></td><td>   Total costs and expenses ....</td><td style="text-align:right">$23,14(</td></tr>
<tr><td></td><td>Net income — consolidated equity ....</td><td style="text-align:right">$ 5,46(</td></tr>
<tr><td></td><td>Less: minority interest (10% × $1,940) ....</td><td style="text-align:right">19(</td></tr>
<tr><td></td><td>Net income ....</td><td style="text-align:right">$ 5,26(</td></tr>
</table>

The net income of the consolidated entity ($3,520 + $1,940 = $5,460) and the amounts used in the calculation of the minority interest in net income can be verified by the following calculation of consolidated net income:

<table>
<tr><td style="width:22%">Calculation of Year 1 consolidated net income</td><td>Parent Company net income ....</td><td></td><td style="text-align:right">$3,40(</td></tr>
<tr><td></td><td>Add: bond gain allocated ....</td><td></td><td style="text-align:right">12(</td></tr>
<tr><td></td><td>Adjusted net income ....</td><td></td><td style="text-align:right">$3,52(</td></tr>
<tr><td></td><td>Subsidiary Company net income ....</td><td style="text-align:right">$1,700</td><td></td></tr>
<tr><td></td><td>Add: bond gain allocated ....</td><td style="text-align:right">240</td><td></td></tr>
<tr><td></td><td>Adjusted net income ....</td><td style="text-align:right">$1,940</td><td></td></tr>
<tr><td></td><td>Parent Company's share ....</td><td style="text-align:right">.9</td><td style="text-align:right">1,74(</td></tr>
<tr><td></td><td>Consolidated net income ....</td><td></td><td style="text-align:right">$5,26(</td></tr>
</table>

Elimination entries (a) and (b) were illustrated on pages 363 and 364 and require no further elaboration. The use of the chart allocating the gain in aftertax dollars (page 365) in the preparation of the consolidated income statement and the calculation of consolidated net income can be explained as follows:

1 The entity column reflects the amounts used in the preparation of the consolidated income statement. Note that the aftertax column is not directly used.

2 Both of the allocation columns (Parent Company and Subsidiary Company) are used in the calculation of consolidated net income, but only in aftertax amounts. This is because they are used to adjust the aftertax net incomes of the two constituents. The before-tax and tax columns are presented only as balancing amounts.

The preparation of the consolidated balance sheet on December 31, Year 1 can be described as follows (refer to the working paper entries on pages 363 and 364):

1 Part of entry (a) was to the consolidated balance sheet. Assets were decreased by $9,600 and liabilities were decreased by $10,200. Obviously the balance sheet will not balance. If the liability and owners' equity side was increased by $600, the net decrease in liabilities and shareholders' equity would be $9,600, which would be equal to the $9,600 decrease in assets.

2 Part of the $600 increase required is found in entry (b). A deferred tax liability amounting to $240 appears on the consolidated balance sheet as a result of this working paper entry.

3 The remainder of the $600 required comes from the allocation of the entity's net income to the two equities. The entity's net income was increased by $360 ($600 − $240 = $360) as a result of entries (a) and (b). The calculation of consolidated net income shows that this was allocated to the two equities as follows:

Allocation of Dec. 31, Year 1 bond gain to the two equities

	Total	Minority Interest	Controlling Interest
Gain allocated to Parent	$120		$120
Gain allocated to Subsidiary	240	$24	216
Total	$360	$24	$336

4 In summary, the $600 increase required to balance the liability and shareholders' equity side is made up of:

Allocation of increase to liability and equity side of balance sheet

Increase to deferred income tax liability	$240
Increase to minority interest	24
Increase to consolidated retained earnings	336
Total	$600

Equity method journal entries

Parent Company, using the equity method to account for its investment in Subsidiary Company, would make the journal entries in Year 1 as shown at the top of page 368.

Intercompany investment income of $1,866 ($1,530 + $120 + $216) would appear on Parent Company's Year 1 income statement resulting in a total Parent's net income of $5,266 ($3,400 + $1,866).

Dec. 31   Investment in Subsidiary Company   1,530
      Intercompany Investment Income . . . .—. .   1,53⦁
    To record 90% of Subsidiary Company's reported net
    income for Year 1 ($1,700 × .9 = $1,530).

Dec. 31   Investment in Subsidiary Company   120
      Intercompany Investment Income . . . .   12⦁
    To record the gain from intercompany bondholdings
    allocated to Parent Company.

Dec. 31   Investment in Subsidiary Company   216
      Intercompany Investment Income . . . .   21⦁
    To record 90% of the gain from intercompany bondholdings
    allocated to Subsidiary Company ($240 × .9 = $216).

Accounting for gain in subsequent years

We will now focus our attention on Year 2 to illustrate the accounting for intercompany bondholdings in years subsequent to the intercompany transactions that resulted in a gain (or loss). At the end of Year 2 the two companies prepared the following income statements:

	Parent Company	Subsidiary Company
Miscellaneous revenue	$25,000	$10,900
Interest revenue		1,100
Total	$25,000	$12,000
Miscellaneous costs and expenses	$17,400	$ 6,900
Interest expense	950	
Income tax expense	2,600	2,000
Total costs and expenses	$20,950	$ 8,900
Net income	$ 4,050	$ 3,100

In Year 2 interest revenue and expense was recorded by the two companies as follows:

Journal entries made in
Year 2 by both companies
to record interest revenue
and expense

Parent Company	Subsidiary Company
Interest expense 1,000	Cash 1,000
Cash 1,000	Interest revenue 1,000
To record payment of Year 2 Interest.	To record receipt of Year 2 Interest.
	Investment in Bonds of
Bond issue premium . . . 50	Parent Company 100
Interest expense 50	Interest revenue 100
To amortize issue premium	To amortize discount on the purchase
($200 ÷ 4 = $50).	of bonds ($400 ÷ 4 = $100).

Notice that the entry recording the amortization of the issue premium and the purchase discount *increased* the respective net incomes of the two companies. Thus in Year 2 Parent Company recorded one quarter of the original gain allocated to it in Year 1 ($200 × ¹/₄ = $50), and in the same manner Subsidiary Company also recorded one quarter of the original gain allocated to it in Year 1 (400 × ¹/₄ = $100). Because the bonds mature four years after the date of the intercompany purchase, and because the original gain on bond retirement was created because of the existence of the unamortized issue premium and the discount on the intercompany purchase of bonds ($200 + $400 = $600), the *concept of the realization of the gain* on the consolidated financial statements *prior to the recording of the gain* by the constituent companies becomes evident.

Both Subsidiary Company's interest revenue of $1,100 ($1,000 + $100 = $1,100) and Parent Company's interest expense of $950 (1,000 − $50 = $950) represent intercompany revenues and expenses which are eliminated on the Year 2 consolidated income statement with the following *incomplete* working paper entry:

PARENT COMPANY AND SUBSIDIARY

Partial Working Paper Eliminations
December 31, Year 2

Interest Revenue	1,100	
Interest Expense		950
To eliminate Year 2 intercompany interest revenue and expense.		

In past examples the elimination of intercompany revenues and expenses (sales and purchases, rental revenue and expense etc.) has had no effect on the net income of the entity, because the amounts eliminated were always *equal*. Referring back to the journal entries made by both companies (page 368) you will see that *this equal component is still present*. We are still eliminating $1,000 interest revenue and expense in the working paper elimination. However, *in addition*, we are also eliminating the portions of the gain on bond retirement that were recorded by both companies as a result of the amortization of the premium and discount in Year 2. Failure to do so would result in the gain on bond retirement being recorded twice over the life of the bonds. It is because *we do not allow this portion of the gain* to be reflected in the Year 2 consolidated income statement that we have an *unequal elimination* of intercompany revenue and expense on the working paper elimination entry. The elimination of $1,100 intercompany interest revenue and $950 intercompany interest expense *decreases* the before tax *net income* of the entity by $150. We will describe this reduction of the entity's before-tax net income as the *"interest elimination loss."*

The *realization of a gain* on bond retirement on the consolidated income statement in the year of acquisition of intercompany bonds *will always result in an "interest elimination loss,"* affecting the entity's before-tax net income in all *subsequent consolidated income statements* until the bonds mature. This "interest elimination loss" *does not appear* as such on the consolidated income statement, because it results from eliminating an amount of intercompany interest revenue that is larger than the amount of intercompany interest expense eliminated. Conversely, **the realization of a loss** on bond retirement in the year of acquisition of intercompany bonds, **will always result in an "interest elimination gain"** on all **subsequent consolidated income statements**, because the amount of interest expense eliminated will always be larger than the amount of interest revenue eliminated.

As stated previously, the entity's Year 2 before-tax net income has been decreased by $150. This results from eliminating the portion of the gain on bond retirement recorded by the constituent companies in Year 2. Both companies paid (or accrued) income tax on their portion of the gain recorded in Year 2, a total of $60 ($150 × 40%). Recall that the entire gain was realized for consolidated purposes in Year 1 and an income tax provision was made at that time. This is clearly another example of a timing difference. We must therefore decrease income tax expense in the preparations of the consolidated income statement. The **complete** income statement working paper elimination entry is as follows:

Complete partial working paper elimination Dec. 31, Year 2	Interest revenue	1,100
	Interest expense	950
	Income tax expense	60
	To eliminate Year 2 intercompany interest revenue and expense and to adjust for the income tax effect of the elimination.	

The addition of the income tax expense entry still leaves us with an **unequal** elimination on the consolidated income statement. However, this "interest elimination loss" is now in aftertax dollars and amounts to $90 ($1,100 − $950 − $60 = $90). A reconstruction of the **intercompany bond chart** for the life of the bonds will illustrate how this loss is allocated to the two constituents each year.

Bond chart from Dec. 31, Year 1 to Dec. 31, Year 5

	Entity			Parent Company			Subsidiary Company		
	Before tax	40% tax	After tax	Before tax	40% tax	After tax	Before tax	40% tax	After tax
Gain on bond Dec. 31, Year 1	$600	$240	$360	$200	$80	$120	$400	$160	$240
Interest elimination loss — Year 2	150	60	90	50	20	30	100	40	60
Balance — gain — Dec. 31, Year 2 ...	$450	$180	$270	$150	$60	$90	$300	$120	$180
Interest elimination loss — Year 3 ...	150	60	90	50	20	30	100	40	60
Balance — gain — Dec. 31, Year 3 ...	$300	$120	$180	$100	$40	$60	$200	$80	$120
Interest elimination loss — Year 4 ...	150	60	90	50	20	30	100	40	60
Balance — gain — Dec. 31, Year 4 ...	$150	$60	$90	$50	$20	$30	$100	$40	$60
Interest elimination loss — Year 5 ...	150	60	90	50	20	30	100	40	60
Balance Dec. 31, Year 5	0	0	0	0	0	0	0	0	0

We can further illustrate this concept by examining the two company's accounts from the date of the intercompany purchase to the date of maturity of the bonds.

Comparison of the intercompany interest accounts over the life of the bonds

Year Ended Dec. 31	Subsidiary Company's Interest Revenue	Parent Company's Interest Expense	Difference
Year 2	$ 950	$1,100	$150
Year 3	950	1,100	150
Year 4	950	1,100	150
Year 5	950	1,100	150
Totals	$3,800	$4,400	$600

The difference column is the before-tax "interest elimination loss" resulting from the elimination of the two intercompany interest accounts on each year's consolidated income statement.

The Year 2 consolidated income statement is prepared (without a working paper) in the following manner:

Preparation of Year 2 consolidated income statement without a working paper

Parent Company and Subsidiary
Consolidated Income Statement
Year 2

Miscellaneous revenue ($25,000 + $10,900)	$35,900
Interest revenue ($0 + $1,100 − $1,100)	0
Total	$35,900
Miscellaneous costs and expenses ($17,400 + $6,900)	$24,300
Interest expense ($950 + $0 − $950)	0
Income tax expense ($2,600 + $2,000 − $60)	4,540
Total costs and expenses	$28,840
Net income — Consolidated entity	$ 7,060
Less: Minority interest (10% × $3,040)	304
Net income	$ 6,756

The following calculation of consolidated net income illustrates the makeup of the entity's net income and the amounts used to calculate minority interest:

Calculation of Year 2 consolidated net income

Parent Company net income		$4,050
Less: interest elimination loss allocated		30
Adjusted net income		$4,020
Subsidiary Company net income	$3,100	
Less: interest elimination loss allocated	60	
Adjusted net income	$3,040	
Parent Company's share	.9	2,736
Consolidated net income		$6,756

On December 31, Year 2 the Investment in Bonds of Parent Company on the balance sheet of Subsidiary Company will show a balance of $9,700 ($9,600 + $100 = $9,700) and Bonds Payable on the balance sheet of Parent Company will show a balance of $10,150 ($10,200 − 50 = $10,150). In the preparation of the consolidated balance sheet on December 31, Year 2 the two intercompany accounts are eliminated by the following incomplete working paper entry:

PARENT COMPANY AND SUBSIDIARY
Partial Working Paper Eliminations
December 31, Year 2

Bonds Payable	10,150	
Investment in Bonds of Parent Company		9,700
To eliminate the intercompany bond accounts on Dec. 31, Year 2.		

This entry is somewhat similar to the entry made on December 31, Year (see page 363) except that the before-tax amount now required to balance is a gain of $450 instead of the $600 gain required a year ago. Furthermore the $450 does not appear as such on the consolidated income statement. Recall that the $600 gain appeared on the Year 1 consolidated income statement. *A gain on bond retirement appears* as such *only once*, in the year that the intercompany purchase takes place. Recall also that a portion of the gain is being recorded by the constituent companies each year subsequent to the intercompany purchase, and is eliminated on each subsequent consolidated income statement so that it is not realized twice. A referral to the bond chart (page 370) indicates that the entity's deferred income tax liability is $180 as at December 31, Year 2. We can now complete the balance sheet working paper entry by adding the deferred tax component as follows:

PARENT COMPANY AND SUBSIDIARY
Partial Working Paper Elimination
December 31, Year 2

Bonds payable	10,150	
Investment in Bonds of Parent Company		9,700
Deferred Income Tax		180
To eliminate the intercompany bond accounts and to set up		
the deferred income tax liability on Dec. 31, Year 2.		

We need a $270 increase to equity in order to have the balance sheet in balance. The bond chart (page 370) shows the entity's position at this amount on December 31, Year 2. Using the allocation columns we can see that the entity's gain position is allocated to the two equities as follows:

Allocation of Dec. 31, Year 2 bond gain to the two equities	Total	Minority Interest	Controlling Interest
Gain allocated to Parent	$ 90		$90
Gain allocated to Subsidiary	180	18	162
Total	$270	$18	$252

The gain allocated to controlling interest flows to the consolidated balance sheet by way of the consolidated income and retained earnings statements. No such statement contains the flow of the gain to minority interest and therefore we must take this into account when we calculate the minority interest as at December 31, Year 2 as follows:

Calculation of minority interest on Dec. 31, Year 2	
Shareholders' equity of Subsidiary — Dec. 31, Year 2	$XXX
Add: Bond gain as at Dec. 31, Year 2	180
Adjusted shareholders' equity	$XXX
Minority Interest %	.10
Minority interest Dec. 31, Year 2	$XXX

Equity method journal entries

Parent Company would make the following journal entries in Year 2:

Dec. 31 Investment in Subsidiary Company	2,790	
Intercompany Investment Income		2,790
To record 90% of Subsidiary Company's reported net income		
for Year 2 ($3,100 × .9 = $2,790).		
Dec. 31 Intercompany Investment Income	30	
Investment in Subsidiary Company		30
To record the "interest elimination loss" allocated to Parent		
Company.		
Dec. 31 Intercompany Investment Income	54	
Investment in Subsidiary Company		54
To record 90% of the "interest elimination loss" allocated to		
Subsidiary Company ($60 × .9 = $54).		

The intercompany investment income of $2,706 ($2,790 − $30 − $54) would appear on Parent Company's Year 1 income statement, resulting in a total Parent's net income of $6,756 ($4,050 + $2,706) which equals consolidated net income.

Gains (losses) not allocated to the two equities

On page 364 we outlined four approaches that could be taken in allocating the bond gains (losses). We have used approach 4 in our illustrations. Because the **CICA Handbook** is silent on this matter any one of approaches 1 to 3 could also be used. If any of these approaches were used the entire gain (loss) would be allocated to only one of the affiliated companies. If this was the case the bond chart (page 370) would only need the entity columns.

Gains (losses) allocated to two equities — loss to one, gain to the other.

Suppose that the issuing affiliate had $10,000 in bonds outstanding with a carrying value of $10,700, and the purchasing affiliate paid $10,100 to acquire all of the issue on the open market. From the entity's view there is a before-tax gain on bond retirement of $600, calculated as follows:

<table>
<tr><td>Calculation of entity's gain on bond retirement</td><td>Carrying amount of bonds ....</td><td>$10,700</td></tr>
<tr><td></td><td>Cost of investment in bonds ....</td><td>10,100</td></tr>
<tr><td></td><td>Gain on bond retirement ....</td><td>$ 600</td></tr>
</table>

If we allocate the gain to the two affiliates (approach 4) we see that the **issuing affiliate** is allocated **a gain** of $700 while the **purchasing affiliate** is allocated **a loss** of $100. This can be verified by the following calculation:

<table>
<tr><td rowspan="6">Allocation of bond gain to the two affiliates</td><td>Carrying amount of bond liability ....</td><td>$10,700</td></tr>
<tr><td>Par value of bond liability ....</td><td>10,000</td></tr>
<tr><td>Gain to issuing affiliate ....</td><td>$ 700</td></tr>
<tr><td>Cost of investment in bonds ....</td><td>$10,100</td></tr>
<tr><td>Par value of bond liability ....</td><td>10,000</td></tr>
<tr><td>Loss to purchasing affiliate ....</td><td>$ 100</td></tr>
</table>

In subsequent years the entity's "interest elimination loss" will be allocated as a **loss** to the issuing affiliate and a **gain** to the purchasing affiliate.

Effective Yield Method of Amortization

Our previous examples have assumed that both companies use the straight-line method to amortize the premiums and discounts. This method leads to fairly easy calculations because the yearly amortizations are equal. If either or both of the companies use the effective yield method of amortization the calculations become more complex, but the concepts remain the same. Remember that it is the *reversal of the affiliate's amortization of premiums or discounts that causes the interest elimination losses or gains in years subsequent* to the date of the intercompany purchase.

Intercompany Bond Illustration Using Working Papers

We will complete our discussion of intercompany bondholdings with a working paper example that illustrates the following:

1 An intercompany bond acquisition on January 1, results in a loss on bond retirement.
2 The amount of the intercompany bondholding is less than 100%.
3 The allocation of the bond loss results in a gain to one company and a loss to the other company.
4 Because the acquisition took place on January 1, the consolidated income statement contains both the loss on bond retirement and the resultant interest elimination gain.
5 The interest elimination gain is allocated as a loss to one company and a gain to the other company.

The illustration is for Parson Corporation and its 75% owned subsidiary, Sloan Company, for the year ended December 31, Year 5.

Details about the two companies and the intercompany bond transactions that have occurred are as follows:

1 Parson purchased 75% of the outstanding shares of Sloan on January 1, Year 1, at a cost of $98,000. On this date Sloan's retained earnings amounted to $40,000. The purchase discrepancy was allocated entirely to goodwill with an estimated remaining life of 10 years.
2 Sloan has a 10%, $100,000 bond issue outstanding that was originally issued at a premium. These bonds mature on December 31, Year 8. On January 1, Year 5 the unamortized premium amounted to $1,200. Sloan uses the straight-line method of amortization.
3 On January 1, Year 5 Parson acquired $60,000 face value of Sloan's outstanding bonds at a cost of $61,500. Parson also uses the straight-line method of amortization.
4 Any *gains or losses* on intercompany bondholdings *are to be allocated* to the purchasing and issuing affiliates.
5 Both companies pay income tax at a rate of 40%.
6 Parson uses the *cost method* to account for its investment in Sloan.

The Year 5 financial statements of both companies appear on page 379. Before attempting the working paper eliminations it is necessary to make some detailed calculations.

The calculation, allocation and amortization of the purchase discrepancy is as shown at the top of page 376.

An intercompany acquisition of bonds took place on January 1, Year 5. The loss on bond retirement in before-tax dollars and its allocation on this date is calculated as shown in the middle of page 376.

Calculation, allocation, and amortization of purchase discrepancy, Dec. 31, Year 5	Cost of 75% of Sloan Jan. 1, Year 1		$ 98,00(
	Carrying amount of Sloan's net assets:		
	Common stock	$ 80,000	
	Retained earnings	40,000	
	Total shareholders' equity	$120,000	
	Parson's ownership interest	0.75	90,00(
	Purchase discrepancy — Jan. 1, Year 1		$ 8,00(
	Allocated to revalue Sloan's net assets		(
	Balance — Goodwill — Jan. 1, Year 1		$ 8,00(
	Amortized for consolidation purposes:		
	Years 1 to 4	$ 3,200	
	Year 5	800	4,00(
	Balance — Goodwill — Dec. 31, Year 5		$ 4,00(

Calculation of bond loss and allocation in before-tax dollars	Cost of 60% of Sloan's bonds — Jan. 1		$61,50(
	Carrying amount of bond liability		
	10% bonds payable	$100,000	
	Bond premium	1,200	
	Total	$101,200	
	Amount acquired by Parson	60%	60,72(
	Loss to entity		78(
	Allocation of bond loss:		
	Cost of bonds		$61,50(
	Par value of bonds		60,00(
	Loss to Parsons		$ 1,50(
	Par value of bonds		$60,00(
	Carrying amount of bonds		60,72(
	Gain to Sloan		72(

You will note that the entity's before-tax loss occurred on January 1, Year 5, the date of the acquisition and retirement (for consolidation purposes) of 60% of Sloan's bonds, and that this *loss will appear as a separate item* on the Year 5 consolidated income statement. Our past discussions have indicated that any subsequent elimination of intercompany interest revenue and expenses must result in a before-tax gain to the entity. This "gain" resulting from an unequal elimination of intercompany revenue and expense will also be reflected in the Year 5 consolidated income statement but *will not appear as a separate item*.

The cause of the unequal elimination is the reversal of each company's amortization of the issue and acquisition premiums for consolidation purposes. An examination of the relevant ledger accounts of both companies relative to the intercompany bonds (see page 377) will illustrate this concept. It is important to note that only 60% of the amounts in Sloan's accounts are intercompany. Thus we can see that the elimination of $5,625

PARSON CORPORATION LEDGER

Investment in Sloan Company Bonds

Date	Explanation	Debit	Credit	Balance
1/ 1/5 Acquisition of $60,000 face amount		61,500		61,500 dr
12/31/5 Amortization of acquisition premium			375	61,125 dr

Interest Revenue

Date	Explanation	Debit	Credit	Balance
12/31/5 Interest received			6,000	6,000 cr
12/31/5 Amortization of acquisition premium		375		5,625 cr

Subsidiary company's ledger accounts

SLOAN COMPANY LEDGER

10% Bonds Payable

Date	Explanation	Debit	Credit	Balance
12/31/5 Balance				100,000 cr

Premium on Bonds

Date	Explanation	Debit	Credit	Balance
1/ 1/5 Balance				1,200 cr
12/31/5 Amortization		300		900 cr

Interest Expense

Date	Explanation	Debit	Credit	Balance
12/31/5 Payment of Interest		10,000		10,000 dr
12/31/5 Amortization of premium			300	9,700 dr

interest revenue, and $5,820 ($9,700 × 60% = $5,820) interest expense, *increases* the entity's before-tax net income by $195. This represents one quarter of the January 1 loss to the entity ($780 ÷ 4 = $195). All amounts discussed so far are in before-tax dollars. We can now prepare the following intercompany bond chart in order to summarize the year's transactions, allocate them to the two companies, and reflect the income tax effects:

Chart summarizing Year 5 intercompany bondholding transactions

	Entity			Parson Corporation			Sloan Corporation		
	Before tax	40% tax	After tax	Before tax	40% tax	After tax	Before tax	40% tax	After tax
Jan. 1/5 Bond loss (gain)	$780	$312	$468	$1,500	$600	$900	$(720)	$(288)	$(432)
Year 5 Int. elim. gain (loss)	195	78	117	375	150	225	(180)	(72)	(108)
Dec. 31/5 Balance loss (gain)	$585	$234	$351	$1,125	$450	$675	$(540)	$(216)	$(324)

Parson Corporation accounts for its investment in Sloan Company by *the cost method*. When this method has been used the working paper procedure is to *convert the parent's accounts to the equity method* and then prepare elimination entries. In order to convert to equity *two calculations* have to be made. The calculation of Year 5 consolidated net income is as follows:

Income of Parson		$139,128
Less: Intercompany dividends	$ 7,500	
Amortization of purchase discrepancy	800	
Jan. 1 bond loss allocated	900	9,200
		$129,928
Add: Year 5 interest elimination gain allocated		225
Adjusted net income		$130,150
Income of Sloan	$36,700	
Less: Year 5 interest elimination loss allocated	108	
	$36,592	
Add: Jan. 1, bond gain allocated	432	
Adjusted net income	$37,024	
Parson's ownership %	0.75	27,768
Consolidated net income		$157,918

The calculation of consolidated retained earnings on January 1, Year 5 is as follows:

Retained earnings of Parsons Jan. 1, Year 5		$245,000
Less: amortization of purchase discrepancy to Jan. 1, Year 5		3,200
Adjusted retained earnings		$241,800
Retained earnings of Sloan Jan. 1, Year 5	$90,000	
Retained earnings of Sloan — acquisition	40,000	
Increase	$50,000	
Parson's ownership %	0.75	37,500
Consolidated retained earnings Jan. 1, Year 5		$279,300

Using the amounts contained *in both calculations* we can prepare the *initial working paper entry to convert from cost to equity*. The consolidated financial statement working paper and the working paper elimination entries appear on pages 379 and 380 to 381.

The following are important features of the working paper and the related eliminations:

1 Elimination (b) uses the same concepts developed in all previous illustrations. The portion of the elimination labelled (i) (ii) (iii) (iv) represents the adjustments for the Year 5 intercompany bond transactions and accounts.

2 Elimination (b) (i) brings the Jan. 1 loss on retirement of bonds on to the consolidated income statement.

Cost method: Partially owned subsidiary subsequent to acquisition

PARSON CORPORATION AND SUBSIDIARY

Working Paper for Consolidated Financial Statements
For Year Ended December 31, Year 5

	Parson Corporation	Sloan Company	Eliminations Increase (Decrease)		Consolidated
Income statement					
Miscellaneous revenues	650,000	200,000			850,000
Interest revenue	5,625		(b)	(5,625)	
Intercompany dividend revenue . . .	7,500		(a)	(7,500)	
Intercompany investment income			(a) (b)	26,293 (26,293)	
Total revenue	663,125	200,000		(13,125)	850,000
Miscellaneous costs and expenses	432,000	129,600			561,600
Goodwill amortization expense . . .			(b)	800	800
Interest expense		9,700	(b)	(5,820)	3,880
Loss on bond retirement			(b)	780	780
Income taxes expense	92,000	24,000	(b)	(234)	115,766
Minority interest in net income . . .			(c)	9,256	9,256
Total costs and expenses	524,000	163,300		4,782	692,082
Net income	139,125	36,700		(17,907)	157,918
Statement of Retained Earnings			(a)	34,300	
Retained earnings, beginning of year	245,000	90,000	(b)	(90,000)	279,300
Net income	139,125	36,700		(17,907)	157,918
Subtotal	384,125	126,700		(73,607)	437,218
Dividends	70,000	10,000	(b)	(10,000)	70,000
Retained earnings, end of year . . .	314,125	116,700		(63,607)	367,218
Balance Sheet					
Miscellaneous assets	605,000	372,600			977,600
Investment in Sloan Company	98,000		(a) (b)	53,093 (151,093)	
Investment in bonds of Sloan	61,125		(b)	(61,125)	
Deferred income tax			(b)	234	234
Goodwill			(b)	4,000	4,000
Total assets	764,125	372,600		(154,891)	981,834
Miscellaneous liabilities	300,000	75,000			375,000
Bonds payable		100,000	(b)	(60,000)	40,000
Premium on bonds		900	(b)	(540)	360
Minority interest in net assets			(b) (c)	40,000 9,256	49,256
Common stock	150,000				150,000
Common stock		80,000	(b)	(80,000)	
Retained earnings	314,125	116,700		(63,607)	367,218
Total liabilities and shareholders' equity	764,125	372,600		(154,891)	981,834

PARSON CORPORATION AND SUBSIDIARY
Working Paper Eliminations
December 31, Year 5

(a) Investment in Sloan Company — Parson	53,093	
Intercompany Dividend Revenue — Parson	7,500	
Intercompany Investment Income — Parson		26,293
Retained Earnings — beginning of year — Parson		34,300
To adjust Parson's accounts to equity method		
balances and descriptions.		
(b) Common Stock — Sloan	80,000	
Retained Earnings — Sloan	90,000	
Intercompany Investment Income — Parson	26,293	
Goodwill — Sloan	4,000	
Goodwill Amortization Expense — Sloan	800	
(i) Loss on Bond Retirement	780	
(ii) Interest Revenue	5,625	
(iii) Deferred Income Tax	234	
(iv) Premium on Bonds	540	
(iv) Bonds Payable	60,000	
Investment in Sloan Company — Parson		151,093
Dividends — Sloan		10,000
Minority Interest in Net Assets		40,000
(ii) Interest Expense		5,820
(iii) Income Tax Expense		234
(iv) Investment in Bonds of Sloan		61,125

To carry out the following:

(1) Eliminate the intercompany investment accounts, and
    equity accounts of subsidiary at beginning of year, and
    subsidiary dividends.

(2) Provide Year 5 amortization of the purchase discrepancy,
    and allocate unamortized portion to goodwill.

(3) Establish minority interest in net assets of subsidiary at
    beginning of year, less minority share of dividends of
    subsidiary during the year as follows:

Shareholders' Equity — beginning of year	$170,000
Less: dividends	10,000
	$160,000
Minority share ($160,000 × 0.25)	$ 40,000

(continued)

3 Elimination (b) (ii) eliminates the intercompany interest revenue and expense. The elimination of $195 more expense than revenue *creates the interest elimination gain* referred to on the bond chart. Note that this *"gain" is hidden* in the consolidated income statement. Note also that only 60% of the interest expense is intercompany. The remaining 40% represents the entity's interest expense.

PARSON CORPORATION AND SUBSIDIARY
Working Paper Eliminations
December 31, Year 5 (continued)

(4) Realize the entity's loss on bond retirement on Jan. 1,
Year 5, and eliminate intercompany interest revenue
and expense for the year and adjust for income tax, and
eliminate the intercompany bond asset and liability
accounts on Dec. 31, Year 5.

(c) Minority Interest in Net Income	9,256	
Minority Interest in Net Assets		9,256

To establish minority interest in subsidiary's
adjusted net income for Year 5 as follows:

Net income of subsidiary	$ 36,700
Add: Allocation of Jan. 1 bond loss (the	
allocation to subsidiary is a gain)	432
	37,132
Less: Allocation of Year 5 interest elimination	
gain (the allocation to subsidiary is	
a loss)	108
Adjusted net income of subsidiary	$ 37,024
Minority share ($37,024 × 0.25)	$ 9,256

4 Elimination (b) (iii) adjusts for the income tax effects of (i) and (ii). This net amount appears on the bond chart.

5 Elimination (b) (iv) eliminates the Dec. 31, Year 5 balances of the intercompany bondholdings. Only 60% of the bond liability accounts are eliminated. The remaining 40% represents the liability of the entity.

6 We can ***verify the amount of minority interest*** on the consolidated balance sheet by the following calculation:

Verification of minority interest on Dec. 31, Year 5

Shareholders' equity of Sloan Dec. 31, Year 5	
Common stock	$ 80,000
Retained earnings	116,700
Total	$196,700
Add: Net bond gain allocated	324
Adjusted shareholders' equity	$197,024
Minority interest ($197,024 × 0.25)	$ 49,256

7 If the equity method had been used, Parson's retained earnings would be equal to consolidated retained earnings. We can ***verify consolidated retained earnings*** as at December 31, Year 5 as follows:

Retained earnings of Parson Dec. 31, Year 5		$314,125
Less: amortization of purchase discrepancy to Dec. 31, Year 5		
($3,200 + $800)	$ 4,000	
net Dec. 31, Year 5 bond loss allocated	675	4,675
Adjusted retained earnings		$309,450
Retained earnings of Sloan Dec. 31, Year 5	$116,700	
Retained earnings of Sloan — acquisition	40,000	
Increase	$ 76,700	
Add: net Dec. 31, Year 5 bond gain allocated	324	
Adjusted increase	$ 77,024	
Parson's ownership %	0.75	$ 57,768
Consolidated retained earnings Dec. 31, Year 5		$367,218

REVIEW QUESTIONS

1 Explain how an intercompany gain of $2,700 on the sale of a depreciable asset is held back on the consolidated income statement in the year of sale and realized on subsequent consolidated income statements. What income tax adjustments should be made in each instance?

2 The realization of intercompany inventory and depreciable asset profits are really adjustments made in the preparation of consolidated income statements to arrive at historical cost numbers. Explain why this is so.

3 An intercompany inventory profit is realized when the inventory is sold outside the entity. Is this also the case with respect to an intercompany profit in a depreciable asset? Explain.

4 An intercompany gain on a depreciable asset resulting from a sale by the parent company is subsequently realized by an adjustment to the subsidiary's depreciation expense in the preparation of consolidated income statements. Should this adjustment be taken into account in the calculation of minority interest in net income? Explain.

5 Consolidated income statements report the earnings of a single economic entity. Will the total reported earnings of this entity, measured at the end of a period of time greater than one year, be affected by the fact that intercompany sales of assets at a profit occurred during this period of time? Explain.

6 Four approaches could be used to allocate gains (losses) on the elimination of intercompany bondholdings in the preparation of consolidated financial statements. Outline these four approaches. Which approach is conceptually superior? Why?

7 An "interest elimination gain (loss)" does not appear as a distinguishable item on a consolidated income statement. Explain.

8 The adjustment for the holdback of an intercompany gain in assets requires a corresponding adjustment to a consolidated deferred tax asset. The adjustment for a gain from intercompany bondholdings requires a corresponding adjustment to a consolidated deferred tax liability. In both cases the tax adjustment is made because of a gain. Why is the tax adjustment different? Explain.

9 Some intercompany gains (losses) are realized for consolidation purposes subsequent to their actual recording by the affiliates, while others are recorded by the

affiliates subsequent to their realization for consolidation purposes. Explain by referring to the type of gains (losses) that apply to each case.

EXERCISES

Ex. 9-1   P Company owns 90% of S Company and uses the equity method to account for its investment. On July 1, Year 2 S sold a patent to P at a profit of $40,000. This patent had a remaining life of 8 years at this time. For the years December 31, Year 2 and Year 3, S Company reported net incomes of $50,000 and $65,000 respectively. Assume a 40% tax rate.

Instructions   Calculate the amount of minority interest in net income for Years 2 and 3.

Ex. 9-2   X Company owns 80% of Y Company and uses the equity method to account for its investment. On January 1, Year 2 the investment in Company Y account had a balance of $86,900, and Y Company's capital stock and retained earnings totalled $100,000. The unamortized purchase discrepancy had an estimated remaining life of 6 years at this time. The following intercompany asset transfers took place in Years 2 and 3: January 1, Year 2, sale of asset to X at a profit of $45,000; April 30, Year 3, sale of asset to Y at a profit of $60,000. Both assets purchased are being depreciated over 5 years. In Year 2 Y reported a net income of $125,000 and dividends paid of $70,000, while in Year 3 its net income and dividends were $104,000 and $70,000 respectively.

Instructions   Calculate the December 31 Year 3 balance in the account investment in Y. (Assume a 40% tax rate.)

Ex. 9-3   Peggy Company owns 75% of Sally Inc., and uses the cost method to account for its investment. The following data was taken from the Year 4 income statements of the two companies:

	Peggy Company	*Sally Inc.*
Gross profit	$580,000	$270,000
Miscellaneous expenses	110,000	85,000
Depreciation expense	162,000	97,000
Income tax expense	123,000	35,000
Total expense	$395,000	$217,000
Net income	185,000	53,000

In Year 2 Sally sold equipment to Peggy at a profit of $15,000. Peggy has been depreciating this equipment over a 5 year period. Use income tax allocation at a rate of 40%.

Instructions   Using only the information supplied above
a Calculate consolidated net income for Year 4
b Prepare a consolidated income statement for Year 4
c Calculate the amount of the asset "deferred income tax" that would appear on the Year 4 consolidated balance sheet.

Ex. 9-4   Use the information and instructions of Exercise 9-3 except assume that the equipment was sold by Peggy to Sally.

Ex. 9-5   Alpha Corporation owns 90% of the common stock of Beta Corporation and uses the equity method to account for its investment.

On January 1, Year 4 Alpha Corporation purchased $160,000 par of Beta Corporation's 10% bonds for $152,000. Beta's bond liability on this date consisted of $800,000 par 10% bonds due January 1, Year 8, and unamortized discount of $16,000. Interest payment dates are June 30 and December 31.

Both companies have a December 31 year end. Alpha Corporation uses income tax allocation at 40% tax rate when it prepares consolidated financial statements.

Beta Corporation reported a net income of $114,000 in Year 4 and declared a dividend of $30,000 on December 31.

Required

1 Calculate the amount of the gain or loss that will appear as a separate item on the Year 4 consolidated income statement, as a result of the bond transaction that occurred during the year.

2 Prepare the equity journal entries that Alpha Corporation would make on December 31, Year 4.

3 Calculate the amount of the bond liability that will appear on the December 31, Year 4 consolidated balance sheet.

Ex. 9-6 Parent Co. owns 75% of Sub. Co. and uses the cost method to account for its investment. The following are summarized income statements for the year ended December 31, Year 7. (Sub. Co. did not declare or pay dividends in Year 7.)

INCOME STATEMENTS — YEAR 7

	Parent Co.	Sub. Co.
Interest revenue	$ 8,750	$ —
Other misc. revenues	900,000	500,000
Total revenue	$908,750	$500,000
Interest expense	$ —	$ 44,000
Other misc. expense	$600,000	350,000
Income tax expense	124,000	42,000
Total expenses	$724,000	$436,000
Net income	$184,750	$ 64,000

Other Information

On July 1, Year 7, Parent Co. purchased 40% of the outstanding bonds of Sub. Co. for $152,500. On that date Sub. Co. had $400,000 of 10% bonds payable outstanding which mature in 5 years. The bond discount on the books of Sub. Co. on July 1, Year 7 amounted to $20,000. Interest is payable January 1 and July 1. Any gains (losses) are to be allocated to each company.

Required

Prepare a consolidated income statement for Year 7 using a 40% tax rate.

Ex. 9-7 The comparative consolidated income statements of a parent and its 75% owned subsidiary were prepared *incorrectly* as at December 31 (page 385, top). The following items were overlooked when the statements were prepared:

1 The Year 5 gain on sale of assets resulted from the subsidiary selling equipment to the parent on September 30. The parent immediately leased the equipment back to the subsidiary at an annual rental of $12,000. This was the only intercompany rent transaction that occurred each year. The equipment had a remaining life of 5 years on the date of sale.

CONSOLIDATED INCOME STATEMENTS

	Year 5	Year 6
Miscellaneous revenues	$750,000	$825,000
Gain on sale of assets	8,000	42,000
Rental revenue	3,000	12,000
Total	$761,000	$879,000
Miscellaneous expense	$399,800	$492,340
Rent expense	52,700	64,300
Depreciation expense	75,000	80,700
Income tax expense	81,000	94,500
Minority interest in net income	32,500	5,160
Total	$641,000	$737,000
Net income	$120,000	$142,000

2 The Year 6 gain on sale of assets resulted from the January 1 sale of a building, with a remaining life of 7 years, by the subsidiary to the parent.

3 Both gains were taxed at a rate of 40%.

Instructions   Prepare correct consolidated income statements for Years 5 and 6.

Ex. 9-8   Parent Company purchased 80% of Subsidiary Company on January 1, Year 1 when Subsidiary Company had a retained earnings balance of $10,000. The resultant purchase discrepancy of $48,000 was allocated to Goodwill and is being amortized over a 40 year life. Parent Company uses the cost method to account for its investment. An analysis of the Retained Earnings account for Year 7 appears below.

	Parent Company	Subsidiary Company
Balance Jan. 1	$ 6,000	$ 20,000
Net income (loss)	4,000	(1,000)
	$10,000	$ 19,000
Dividends		8,000
Balance Dec. 31	$10,000	$ 11,000

Other Information

On July 1, Year 3 Parent Company sold equipment to Subsidiary Company at a profit of $19,000. This equipment had a remaining estimated life of 5 years on this date.

Parent Company has purchased a substantial portion of its merchandise requirements from Subsidiary Company since control was acquired. Unrealized Profits in Parent Company's inventory are as follows:

Beginning inventory	$16,500
Ending inventory	9,500

Instructions   Prepare a statement of consolidated retained earnings for Year 7 (assume a corporate tax rate of 40%).

Ex. 9-9   Palmer Corporation owns 70% of the common stock of Scott Corporation and uses the equity method to account for its investment.

Scott Corporation purchased $80,000 par of Palmer Corporation's 10 percent bonds on October 1, Year 5 for $76,000. Palmer's bond liability on October 1, Year 5 consisted of $400,000 par of 10 percent bonds due on October 1, Year 9, with unamortized discount of $8,000. Interest payment dates are April 1 and October 1 of each year and straight-line amortization is used. Intercompany bond gains (losses) are to be allocated to each affiliate.

Both companies have a December 31 year end. Scott Corporation's financial statements for Year 5 indicate that it earned a net income of $70,000 and that on December 31, Year 5 it declared a dividend of $15,000.

Required

a Prepare the equity journal entries that Palmer Corporation would make in Year 5. (Assume a 40% tax rate.)

b Compute the amount of the bond liability that will appear on the December 31, Year 5 consolidated balance sheet.

Ex. 9-10 The following item appeared on the Year 6 consolidated income statement of Park Corporation Ltd:

Loss on retirement of bonds of affiliated company   *$20,000*

No such item appeared on the separate income statements of Park Corporation or its subsidiaries in Year 6. The bonds "retired" mature in 10 years.

Required

a Describe the transaction that caused this item to appear on the Year 6 income statement.

b Describe how this transaction probably affected other items on the Year 6 consolidated financial statements.

c Outline the effect that this transaction will have on subsequent consolidated income statements.

PROBLEMS

9-1 Financial statements of Proctor Ltd. and its 80% owned subsidiary Silex Ltd. as at December 31, Year 5 are presented below:

BALANCE SHEETS — DECEMBER 31, YEAR 5

	Proctor	Silex
Cash	$ 18,100	$ 20,600
Accounts receivable	60,000	55,000
Inventories	35,000	46,000
Investment in Silex — at cost	129,200	—
Land, building & equipment	198,000	104,000
Accumulated depreciation	(86,000)	(30,000)
	$ 354,300	$ 195,600
Accounts payable	$ 56,000	$ 70,100
Dividends payable	5,000	5,500
Capital stock	225,000	50,000
Retained earnings January 1	45,500	68,000
Net income	42,800	13,000
Dividends	(20,000)	(11,000)
	$ 354,300	195,600

INCOME STATEMENTS — YEAR ENDED DECEMBER 31, YEAR 5

	Proctor	Silex
Sales	$ 535,400	$ 270,000
Dividend & misc. income	9,900	—
Total	$ 545,300	$ 270,000
Cost of sales	364,000	206,000
Selling expense	78,400	24,100
Admin. expense (including depreciation)	46,300	20,700
Income taxes	13,800	6,200
	$ 502,500	$ 257,000
Net income	$ 42,800	$ 13,000

Other Information

1 Proctor acquired its 80% interest in Silex on January 1, Year 1. The retained earnings of Silex were $12,000 on that date and there have been no subsequent changes in the capital stock accounts. On January 1, Year 1 fair values were equal to carrying values except for the following:

	Carrying Value	Fair Value
Inventory	$50,000	$32,000
Patent	0	14,000

2 The patent of Silex had remaining legal life of 8 years on January 1, Year 1 and goodwill (if any) was to be amortized over a 10 year period.

3 On January 1, Year 5, the inventories of Proctor contained items purchased from Silex on which Silex had made a profit of $1,900. During Year 5 Silex sold goods to Proctor for $92,000 of which $21,000 remained unpaid at the end of the year. Silex made a profit of $3,300 on goods remaining in Proctor's inventory at December 31, Year 5.

4 On January 1, Year 3, Silex sold equipment to Proctor at a price which was $10,500 in excess of its book value. The equipment had an estimated remaining life of 6 years on that date.

5 Proctor sold a tract of land to Silex in Year 2 at a profit of $7,000.

6 Assume a corporate tax rate of 40%.

Required
Prepare the following consolidated financial statements:
a Income statement
b Retained earnings statement
c Balance sheet

9-2 Income statements of two affiliated companies for the year ended December 31, Year 6 are given on page 388.

Additional Information

1 M Company uses the equity method to account for its investment in K Company.

2 M Company acquired its 80% interest in K Company on January 1, Year 1. On

	M Company	K Company
Sales	$600,000	$350,000
Rent revenue	—	50,000
Interest revenue	6,700	—
Income from subsidiary	30,070	—
Gain on land sale	—	8,000
Total revenue	$636,770	$408,000
Cost of goods sold	$334,000	$225,000
Depreciation expense	20,000	70,000
Administrative expense	207,000	74,000
Interest expense	1,700	6,000
Provision for income taxes	20,700	7,500
Total expenses	$583,400	$382,500
Net income	$ 53,370	$ 25,500

that date the purchase discrepancy of $25,000 was allocated entirely to goodwill and is being amortized over a 20 year period.

3 M Company made an advance of $100,000 to K Company on July 1, Year 6. This loan is due on call and requires the payment of interest at 12% per year.

4 M Company rents marine equipment from K Company. During Year 6 $50,000 rent was paid and was charged to administrative expense.

5 In Year 4 M Company sold land to K Company and recorded a profit of $10,000 on the sale, K Company held the land until October Year 6 when it was sold to an unrelated company.

6 During Year 6 K Company made sales to M Company totalling $90,000. The December 31, Year 6 inventories of M Company contain an unrealized profit of $5,000. The January 1, Year 6 inventories of M Company contained an unrealized profit of $12,000.

7 On January 1, Year 4 M Company sold machinery to K Company and recorded a profit of $13,000. The remaining useful life on that date was 5 years. Assume straight line depreciation.

8 Tax allocation is to be used and you are to assume a 40% average corporate tax rate for this purpose.

Instructions Prepare a consolidated income statement for Year 6.

9-3 Condensed financial statements of Para and Medic Companies prepared on December 31 of Year 3 are given on page 389.

Additional information

1 Para acquired 85% of Medic's common stock on January 1 of Year 1 for $150,000. At the date of acquisition, Medic reported a retained earnings balance of $20,000 and its net assets were believed to be carried on its records at reasonable valuations with the exception of inventory which was undervalued in the amount of $15,000 and land which was undervalued in the amount of $8,000. Any goodwill is to be amortized over a period of 10 years.

2 Para accounts for its investment in Medic by the cost method.

3 Interest revenues are 100% intercompany.

4 Medic's sales during Year 3 include $60,000 of sales to Para. Goods purchased

BALANCE SHEETS
DECEMBER 31 OF YEAR 3

Assets	Para Company	Medic Company
Cash	$ 14,000	$ 16,800
Receivables	25,000	21,000
Inventories	45,000	50,000
Property, plant and equipment	195,000	260,000
Accumulated depreciation	(35,000)	(40,000)
Other assets	79,600	
Investment in Medic stock	150,000	
Total	$ 473,600	$ 307,800

Liabilities & Shareholder's Equity		
Current liabilities	$ 36,400	$ 37,800
Long term liabilities		102,500
Common stock	350,000	125,000
Retained earnings, January 1	77,600	25,000
Net income	34,600	29,500
Dividends	(25,000)	(12,000)
Total	$ 473,600	$ 307,800

INCOME STATEMENTS
YEAR 3

	Para Company	Medic Company
Sales revenues	$ 460,200	$ 270,000
Dividend income	10,200	
Interest revenues	2,200	
Total	$ 472,600	$ 270,000
Cost of goods sold	$ 350,000	$ 173,000
Depreciation expense	18,000	28,000
General and administrative expenses	57,000	19,000
Interest expense		9,500
Income taxes	13,000	11,000
Total	$ 438,000	$ 240,500
Net income	$ 34,600	$ 29,500

from Medic and included in Para's inventories were $20,000 at the beginning of Year 3 and $30,000 at the end of Year 3. Medic's cost on sales to Para averages 70% of selling price. At the end of Year 3, Para owed Medic $9,100 on open account.

5 At the beginning of Year 2, Para sold equipment to Medic for $70,000. The book value of the equipment on Para's records at date of sale was $55,000. Medic has depreciated the equipment on a straight line basis at the rate of 20% per year.

6 Para uses tax allocation for consolidation purposes. Assume a 40% corporate tax rate.

Instructions   Prepare in good form the following:
a Consolidated income statement
b Consolidated retained earnings statement
c Consolidated balance sheet.

9-4 On December 31, Year 1, the Pridmore Company purchased 80 percent of the outstanding voting shares of the Stubbin Company for $964,000 in cash. The balance sheet of the Stubbin Company on that date and the fair values of its tangible assets and liabilities were as follows:

	Book Value	Fair Value
Cash and accounts receivable	$ 200,000	$175,000
Inventories	300,000	300,000
Plant and equipment	600,000	700,000
Accumulated depreciation	(100,000)	
Total assets	$1,000,000	
Current liabilities	$ 100,000	$100,000
Long-term liabilities	200,000	150,000
No par common stock	500,000	
Retained earnings	200,000	
Total equities	$ 1,000,000	

The difference between the fair value and book value of cash and accounts receivable of the subsidiary at December 31, Year 1 was adjusted by Stubbin in Year 2. At the acquisition date, the plant and equipment had an estimated remaining useful life of ten years with no net salvage value. The long-term liabilities mature on December 31, Year 6. Any goodwill arising from the business combination will be amortized over 20 years. The Pridmore Company uses the cost method to account for its investment in Stubbin. Both the Pridmore Company and the Stubbin Company use the straight-line method to calculate all depreciation and amortization.

The Statements of income and change in retained earnings of the two companies for the year ending December 31, Year 5 were as follows:

	Pridmore	Stubbin
Sales of merchandise	$6,000,000	$1,000,000
Other revenues	200,000	20,000
Total revenues	$6,200,000	$1,020,000
Cost of goods sold	$2,500,000	$ 400,000
Depreciation expense	500,000	80,000
Interest expense	400,000	20,000
Other expenses (Including income tax)	1,300,000	190,000
Total expenses	$4,700,000	$ 690,000
Net income	$1,500,000	$ 330,000
Retained earnings — 1/1/Year 5	4,200,000	300,000
Dividends	(200,000)	(50,000)
Retained earnings — 31/12/Year 5	$5,500,000	$ 580,000

Other Information

1 On December 31, Year 4, Stubbin Company sold a warehouse to Pridmore for $63,000. It had been purchased on January 1, Year 3 for $100,000 and had an estimated 20 year life on that date with no salvage value.

2 During Year 4, Stubbin sold merchandise which it had purchased for $120,000 to Pridmore for $250,000. None of this merchandise had been resold by Pridmore by December 31, Year 4. Both companies account for inventories on the first-in, first-out basis.

3 Pridmore had sales of $200,000 to Stubbin during Year 4 which gave rise to a

gross profit of $125,000. This inventory was resold by Stubbin during Year 4 for $225,000.

4 During Year 5, Stubbin sold merchandise which had been purchased for $160,000 to Pridmore Company for $300,000. Since the sales occurred in December of Year 5, all of this merchandise remained in the December 31, Year 5 inventories of Pridmore and had not been paid for by Pridmore.

5 During September of Year 5, Pridmore had sales of $280,000 to Stubbin which increased Pridmore's gross profit by $160,000. By December 31, Year 5, one-half of this merchandise had been sold to the public by Stubbin.

6 On January 1, Year 5, Pridmore sold to Stubbin for $28,000 a machine which had cost $40,000. On January 1, Year 5 it had been depreciated for six years of its estimated eight year life. This sale was not considered an extraordinary transaction by Pridmore.

7 During Year 5, Pridmore Company charged Stubbin Company $25,000 for management fees.

8 Assume a 40% corporate tax rate.

Required
a Prepare a consolidated income statement for the Pridmore Company and its subsidiary, the Stubbin Company, for the year ending December 31, Year 5 in accordance with the recommendations of the *CICA Handbook*.
b Prepare a consolidated statement of retained earnings for the Pridmore Company and its subsidiary, the Stubbin Company, for the year ending December 31, Year 5. (SMA adapted)

9-5 On January 1, Year 1, Porter Inc. purchased 85 percent of the outstanding voting shares of Sloan Ltd. for $3,025,000 in cash. On this date, Sloan had no par common stock outstanding in the amount of $2,200,000 and retained earnings of $1,100,000. The identifiable assets and liabilities of Sloan had fair values that were equal to their carrying values except for the following:
  (i) Plant and equipment (net) had a fair value $200,000 greater than its carrying value. The remaining useful life on January 1, Year 1, was 20 years with no anticipated salvage value.
  (ii) Accounts receivable had a fair value $75,000 less than carrying value.
  (iii) Long-term liabilities had a fair value $62,500 less than carrying value. These liabilities mature on June 30, Year 9.
It is the policy of Porter to amortize all goodwill balances over 5 years. Both Porter and Sloan use the straight-line method for amortization and depreciation.

Other Information

1 Between January 1, Year 1, and December 31, Year 3, Sloan earned $345,000 and paid dividends of $115,000.

2 On January 1, Year 2, Sloan sold a patent to Porter for $165,000. On this date, the patent had a carrying value on the books of Sloan of $185,000, and a remaining useful life of 5 years.

3 On September 1, Year 3, Porter sold land to Sloan for $93,000. The land had a carrying value on the books of Porter of $72,000. Sloan still owned this land on December 31, Year 4.

4 For the year ending December 31, Year 4, the Statements of Income revealed the following:

	Porter	Sloan
Total revenues	$2,576,000	$973,000
Cost of goods sold	$1,373,000	$467,000
Depreciation expense	483,000	176,000
Other expenses	352,000	153,000
Total expenses	$2,208,000	$796,000
Net income	$ 368,000	$177,000

Porter records its investment in Sloan using the cost method and includes dividend income from Sloan in its total revenues.

5 Porter and Sloan paid dividends of $125,000 and $98,000 respectively in Year 4.

6 Sloan issued no common stock subsequent to January 1, Year 1. Selected balance sheet accounts for the two companies as at December 31, Year 4 were:

	Porter	Sloan
Accounts receivable (net)	$ 987,000	$ 133,000
Inventories	1,436,000	787,000
Plant and equipment (net)	3,467,000	1,234,000
Patents (net)	263,000	-0-
Land	872,000	342,000
Long-term liabilities	1,876,000	745,000
Retained earnings	4,833,000	1,409,000

7 During Year 4, Porter's merchandise sales to Sloan were $150,000. The unrealized profits in Sloan's inventory on January 1 and December 31, Year 4, were $14,000 and $10,000 respectively. At December 31, Year 4, Sloan still owed Porter $5,000 for merchandise purchases.

8 During Year 4, Sloan's merchandise sales to Porter were $55,000. The unrealized profits in Porter's inventory on January 1 and December 31, Year 4, were $1,500 and $2,500 respectively. At December 31, Year 4, Porter still owed Sloan $2,000 for merchandise purchases.

9 Use income tax allocation at a rate of 40%.

Required

a Compute the balances that would appear in the Consolidated Balance Sheet of Porter and Sloan as at December 31, Year 4, for the following:
   i) Patent (net)
   ii) Goodwill
   iii) Minority interest
   iv) Retained earnings
   v) Deferred income taxes

b Porter has decided not to prepare consolidated financial statements and will report its investment in Sloan by the equity method. Calculate the total revenues, including investment income, that would be disclosed in the Income Statement of Porter for the year ended December 31, Year 4.

(SMA adapted)

9-6   The selected ledger accounts on page 393 were taken from the trial balance of a parent and its subsidiary company as at December 31, Year 9.

Other Information

1 Company P purchased its 90% interest in Company S in Year 1, on the date that

	P Company	S Company
Investment in bonds of P		$ 39,000
Investment in stock of S (CICA equity)	$139,899	
Sales	630,000	340,000
Interest income		1,850
Investment income	15,339	
Gain on sale of land	7,000	
Capital stock	300,000	100,000
Retained earnings	85,000	50,000
Bonds payable 8%	198,000	
Cost of sales	485,000	300,000
Interest expense	17,000	
Selling and admin. expense	50,000	20,000
Income tax expense	34,000	8,740
Dividends	10,000	8,000

Company S was incorporated and has followed the CICA equity method to account for its investment since that date.

2 On April 1, Year 5, land that had originally cost $15,000 was sold by S Company to P Company for $21,000. P purchased the land with the intention of developing it; but in Year 9 it decided that the location was not suitable and the land was sold to a chain of drug stores.

3 On January 1, Year 2 P Company issued $200,000 face value bonds due in 10 years. The proceeds from the bond issue amounted to $190,000.

4 On July 1, Year 9, S Company purchased $40,000 of these bonds on the open market at a cost of $38,750. Intercompany bond holding gains (losses) are allocated between the two affiliates.

5 S Company had $75,000 in sales to P company during Year 9.

6 Use income tax allocation at a 40% tax rate.

Instructions
a Prepare a statement of consolidated net income for Year 9.
b Prepare a consolidated statement of retained earnings for Year 9.

9-7 The Preston Company purchased 70% of the capital stock of Silver Company on January 1, Year 6 for $480,000 when the latter company's capital stock and retained earnings were $500,000 and $40,000 respectively. On this date an appraisal of the assets of Silver Company disclosed the following differences.

	Carrying Value	Fair Value
Inventory	$120,000	$108,000
Land	150,000	200,000
Plant and equipment	700,000	770,000

The plant and equipment had an estimated life of 20 years on this date and any goodwill is to be amortized over 8 years.

The balance sheets of Preston and Silver, prepared on December 31, Year 11, follow.

	December 31, Year 11	
	Preston Company	Silver Company
Cash	$ 41,670	$ 57,500
Accounts receivable	215,350	170,000
Inventory	225,000	180,000
Investment in Silver Co. stock (equity method)	541,510	—
Investment in Silver Co. bonds	227,000	—
Land	100,000	150,000
Plant and equipment	625,000	940,000
Less: Accumulated depreciation	(183,000)	(220,000)
Patent (net of amortization)	31,500	—
	$1,824,030	$1,277,500
Accounts payable	56,030	100,000
Bonds payable (Due Year 20)	—	477,500
Capital stock	750,000	500,000
Retained earnings	1,018,000	200,000
	$1,824,030	$1,277,500

Other Information

1 On January 1, Year 1 Silver issued $500,000 of $8^{1}/_{2}$% bonds at 90, maturing in 20 years (on December 31, Year 20).

2 On January 1, Year 11 Preston acquired $200,000 of Silver's bonds on the open market at a cost of $230,000.

3 On July 1, Year 8 Silver sold a patent to Preston for $63,000. The patent had a carrying value on Silver's books of $42,000 on this date and an estimated remaining life of 7 years.

4 Preston uses tax allocation (rate 40%) and allocates bond gains between affiliates when it consolidates Silver.

5 Preston uses the equity method to account for its investment.

Instructions Prepare a consolidated balance sheet as at December 31, Year 11

9-8   The balance sheets at December 31, Year 8, of Park Company and Savoy Company are as shown on page 395.

Additional information

1 Park acquired 90% of Savoy for $201,900 on July 1, Year 1 and accounts for its investment under the cost method. At that time the shareholders equity of Savoy amounted to $175,000 and the assets of Savoy were undervalued by the following amounts.

Inventory	$12,000
Buildings	$20,000 remaining life 9 years
Patents	$15,000 remaining life 10 years

The directors of Park decided to amortize any goodwill over a 7 year period.

2 Park sells goods to Savoy on a regular basis at a gross profit of 30%. During Year 8

BALANCE SHEETS DECEMBER 31, YEAR 8

	Park Company	Savoy Company
Cash	$ 13,000	$ 48,800
Receivables	31,000	106,000
Inventories	80,000	62,000
Investment in stock of Savoy	201,900	
Plant and equipment	740,000	460,000
Accumulated depreciation	(625,900)	(348,400)
Patents		4,500
Investment in bonds of Park		39,100
	$440,000	$372,000
Current liabilities	$ 55,500	$ 53,000
Dividends payable	6,000	30,000
Bonds payable 6%	98,500	
Capital stock	200,000	150,000
Retained earnings Jan. 1	64,000	126,000
Net income	41,000	63,000
Dividends	(25,000)	(50,000)
	$440,000	$372,000

these sales totalled $150,000. On January 1, Year 8 the inventory of Savoy contained goods purchased from Park amounting to $18,000, while the December 31, Year 8 inventory contained goods purchased from Park amounting to $22,000.

3 On August 1, Year 6 Savoy sold land to Park at a profit of $16,000. During Year 8 Park sold one-quarter of the land to an unrelated company.

4 Park had $100,000 6% bonds outstanding on January 1, Year 8 maturing in 4 years. On that date Savoy acquired $40,000 of these bonds on the open market at a cost of $38,800.

The Year 8 income statements of the two companies show the following with respect to bond interest.

	Park	Savoy
Interest expense	$6,500	
Interest revenue		$2,700

5 Savoy owes Park $22,000 on open account on December 31, Year 8.

6 Assume a 40% corporate tax rate and allocate bond gains (losses) between the two companies.

Instructions

1 Prepare the following statements:
   a Consolidated balance sheet
   b Consolidated retained earnings statement

2 Prepare the Year 8 journal entries that would be made on the books of Park Company if the equity method was used to account for the investment.

9-9   On January 2, Year 1 Jackson Ltd. purchased 80 percent of the outstanding shares of Brown Ltd. for $2,000,000. At that date Brown Ltd. had common stock of $500,000 and retained earnings of $1,250,000. Jackson Ltd. acquired the Brown Ltd. stock to

obtain control of copyrights held by Brown. These copyrights, with a remaining li
of eight years, had a fair value of $500,000 in excess of their carrying value. Exce
for the copyrights, the carrying values of the recorded assets and liabilities of Brow
were equal to their fair values. On December 31, Year 4 the trial balances of the tw
companies are as follows:

	Jackson Ltd.	Brown Ltd.
Cash	$ 1,000,000	$ 500,000
Accounts receivable	2,000,000	356,000
Inventory	3,000,000	2,250,000
Plant and equipment	14,000,000	2,500,000
Copyrights (net)		400,000
Investment in Brown (cost)	2,000,000	
Investment in Jackson bonds		244,000
Cost of goods sold	2,400,000	850,000
Other expenses	962,000	300,000
Interest expense	38,000	
Income tax expense	600,000	350,000
Dividends	600,000	250,000
	$26,600,000	$8,000,000
Accounts payable	$ 2,492,000	$2,478,500
Accumulated depreciation:		
Plant and equipment	4,000,000	1,000,000
Bonds payable	500,000	
Premium on bonds payable	8,000	
Common stock	4,500,000	500,000
Retained earnings, January 1	10,000,000	2,000,000
Sales	4,900,000	2,000,000
Dividend revenue	200,000	
Interest revenue		21,500
	$26,600,000	$8,000,000

Additional Information

1 The Year 4 net incomes of the two companies are as follows:
   Jackson Ltd. $1,100,000
   Brown Ltd.   521,500

2 Both companies use straight-line depreciation and amortization. Any goodwill i
   to be written off over 20 years.

3 On January 2, Year 2 Brown sold equipment to Jackson for $500,000. The equip
   ment had a net book value of $400,000 at the time of the sale. The remainin
   useful life of the equipment was 5 years.

4 The Year 4 opening inventories of Jackson contained $500,000 of merchandis
   purchased from Brown during Year 3. Brown Ltd. had recorded a gross profit o
   $200,000 on this merchandise.

5 During Year 4 Brown's sales to Jackson totalled $1,000,000. These sales wer
   made at a gross profit rate of 40%.

6 Jackson's ending inventory contains $300,000 of merchandise purchased from Brown.

7 Other expenses include depreciation expense and copyright amortization expense.

8 On January 2, Year 2 Jackson issued 8 percent, 7 year bonds with a face value of $500,000 for $514,000. Interest is paid annually on December 31. On January 2, Year 4, Brown purchased one half of this issue in the open market at a cost of $242,500. Intercompany bond gains (losses) are to be allocated between the two affiliates.

9 Tax allocation will be at a rate of 40%.

Instructions

a Prepare the following consolidated financial statements:
   (1) Income statement
   (2) Retained earnings statement
   (3) Balance sheet
b Calculate the December 31, Year 4 balance in the account "Investment in Brown" if Jackson Ltd. had used the equity method to account for its investment.

10 CONSOLIDATED FINANCIAL STATEMENTS: SPECIAL PROBLEMS

In this chapter we consider the following special problems that arise in the preparation of consolidated financial statements:

1 Changes in parent company's ownership interest in a subsidiary
2 Subsidiary with preferred shares outstanding
3 Indirect shareholdings
4 Statement of changes in financial position

CHANGES IN PARENT COMPANY OWNERSHIP INTEREST IN A SUBSIDIARY

A parent company's ownership interest will change if:

1 The parent company purchases additional holdings in its subsidiary; or
2 The parent company sells some of its holdings in its subsidiary; or
3 The subsidiary issues additional common shares to the public.

When the parent's ownership changes, the percentage of subsidiary common stock held by minority shareholders also changes. This percentage change in minority interest does not present any particular problems in the preparation of consolidated financial statements. The major consolidation problem involved with ownership changes is the effect such changes have on the *valuation of subsidiary net assets* in the consolidated financial statements. When the parent's ownership percentage increases, there will be an additional purchase discrepancy which must be allocated to revalue the net assets of the subsidiary as of the date of increase. When the parent's ownership percentage decreases, *a reduction in the unamortized purchase discrepancy* occurs. We will examine the calculation of the reduction first and then look at a situation where the parent's percentage increases by block purchases and then decreases as a result of its own actions or actions of its subsidiary.

Effect on purchase discrepancy of parent company sale of a portion of its subsidiary common shareholdings

Assume that P Company purchased 60% of the outstanding common shares of S Company at a cost of $150,000. On this date S Company's shareholder's equity was as follows:

Shareholders' equity of subsidiary on date of business combination

S COMPANY	
Shareholder's Equity	
Common stock (10,000 shares)	$100,000
Retained earnings	90,000
	$190,000

The carrying values of all of S Company's net assets were equal to current fair values, except for specialized equipment, which was undervalued by $9,000. The calculation and allocation of the purchase discrepancy is as follows:

Calculation and allocation of purchase discrepancy

Cost of 60% of S Company		$150,000
Carrying amount of S's net assets:		
Common stock	$100,000	
Retained earnings	90,000	
Total shareholders' equity	$190,000	
P's ownership interest	0.60	114,000
Purchase discrepancy		$ 36,000
Allocated:		
Equipment (9,000 × 0.60)		5,400
Balance — Goodwill		$ 30,600

Now let us assume that on the same day that P Company purchased 6,000 shares in Company S, it sold 600 shares on the open market for $18,000. (This is not a very realistic assumption, but we use it to illustrate the effect that such a transaction will have on the purchase discrepancy.)

Note that after the sale, P Company's ownership percentage is 54% (5,400 shares ÷ 10,000 shares = 54%). Note also that P Company has disposed of 10% of its investment in S Company (600 shares ÷ 6,000 shares = 10%). Another way of calculating the percentage of investment disposed is as follows:

Ownership before sale 60%
Ownership after sale 54%
Change 6%
Percentage of investment sold: 6 ÷ 60 = 10%.

P Company would make the following journal entry to record the sale of 600 shares:

Parent's entry for sale of
portion of investment in
subsidiary

Cash 18,000
   Investment in Company S (10% × $150,000) 15,000
   Gain on Sale of Shares 3,000

The $3,000 gain in sale would appear on P Company's current income statement and would also appear on the consolidated income statement. Now let us recalculate the purchase discrepancy immediately after the sale of 600 shares:

Purchase discrepancy after
sale by parent of 10% of
investment

Investment in Company S ($150,000 − $15,000) $135,000
Shareholders' equity — Company S $190,000
P's ownership interest 0.54   102,600
Purchase discrepancy .... $ 32,400

The purchase discrepancy has been reduced by 10% of its original amount. The effect of this reduction on the amounts allocated to revalue S Company's net assets can be shown as follows:

Effect of sale on
components of purchase
discrepancy

	Purchase Discrepancy Prior to Sale	Reduction Due to Sale of 10%	Purchase Discrepancy After Sale
Equipment	$ 5,400	$ 540	$ 4,860
Goodwill	30,600	3,060	27,540
Total	$36,000	$3,600	$32,400

This 10% reduction in the purchase discrepancy should cause no real surprise. Remember that the $36,000 original purchase discrepancy was "buried" in the investment in S Company amount of $150,000. When Parent Company's journal entry to record the sale removed 10% from the investment account, it also removed 10% of the purchase discrepancy.

The example illustrated was probably unrealistic because the sale took place on the same date that the parent purchased the subsidiary. However, the effect would be the same if the sale had occurred subsequent to the date of acquisition, except that the **unamortized purchase discrepancy** would be reduced by 10% rather than the original purchase discrepancy. This concept will be illustrated in a later example. (See page 406).

Block acquisitions of subsidiary (step purchases)

The consolidation illustrations that we have used in previous chapters have assumed that the parent company achieved its control in a subsidiary by making a single purchase of the subsidiary's common shares. This is not always the case. In some instances a parent company will achieve its ownership interest through a series of block acquisitions (sometimes described as step purchases). The consolidation problems are basically the same whether control was achieved in the first purchase, with any additional purchase(s) simply increasing the parent's ownership interest, or whether control was not present after the first purchase but was achieved with subsequent purchases. For each purchase, a purchase discrepancy is calculated and allocated to revalue the net assets of the subsidiary, with the balance allocated to goodwill. We will illustrate this concept with an example.

Purchase of first block of shares

On January 1, Year 1, Par Company purchased 60% of the outstanding common shares of Sub Company at a cost of $150,000. On this date Sub Company's shareholders' equity was as follows:

Shareholders' equity of subsidiary on acquisition date

SUB COMPANY
Shareholders' Equity
January 1, Year 1

Common stock (10,000 Shares)	$100,000
Retained earnings	90,000
	$190,000

The carrying amounts of Sub Company's net assets were equal to current fair values except for specialized equipment which was undervalued by $9,000. This equipment had an estimated remaining life of 5 years, and any goodwill is amortized over a 10-year period. The purchase discrepancy calculation and allocation is the same as that shown on page 399 because all amounts used in the two illustrations are identical. On December 31, Year 1, Sub Company reported a net income of $30,000 and paid dividends amounting to $8,000. Before recording Par Company's equity method journal entries for Year 1, the amortization of the purchase discrepancy would be calculated as follows:

	Balance January 1 Year 1	Amortization Year 1	Unamortized Balance December 31 Year 1
Equipment	$ 5,400	$1,080	$ 4,320
Goodwill	30,600	3,060	27,540
Total	$36,000	$4,140	$31,860

Par Company's journal entries using the equity method to account for its investment are:

Investment in Sub Company	18,000	
Intercompany Investment Income		18,000
To record 60% of Sub Company's net income for		
Year 1 ($30,000 × 0.60 = $18,000).		
Cash	4,800	
Investment in Sub Company		4,800
To record dividends received from		
Sub Company in Year 1 ($8,000 × 0.60 = $4,800)		
Intercompany Investment Income	4,140	
Investment in Sub Company		4,140
To record the amortization of the		
purchase discrepancy for Year 1.		

Consolidated financial statements for Year 1 would be prepared in the same manner as was illustrated in previous chapters.

Purchase of second block of shares

On January 1, Year 2, Par Company purchased an additional 3,000 shares of Sub Company for $78,200. This represents 30% of Sub Company's outstanding shares and the parent's total ownership interest is now 90%. On this date the carrying amount of Sub Company's net assets were equal to current fair values except for the specialized equipment which was now undervalued by $12,000. This equipment now had an estimated life of 4 years. Goodwill is to be amortized over 10 years. The purchase discrepancy and its allocation for the second block is calculated as indicated at the top of page 403:

On December 31, Year 2, Sub Company reported a net income of $35,000 and paid dividends amounting to $10,000. The purchase discrepancy amortization schedule for Year 2 would be prepared in the manner shown on page 403.

Calculation and allocation
of purchase discrepancy
— second block

Cost of 30% of Sub Company .... *dividends*		$78,200
Carrying amount of Sub's net assets:		
Common stock .... *.*	$100,000	
Retained earnings ($90,000 + $30,000 − $8,000)	112,000	
Total shareholders' equity	$212,000	
Par's ownership interest	0.30	63,600
Purchase discrepancy		$14,600
Allocated:		
Equipment ($12,000 × 0.30)		3,600
Balance — Goodwill		$11,000

	First Purchase		Second Purchase		Total
	Equip.	*Goodwill*	*Equip.*	*Goodwill*	
Balance December 31, Year 1 ...	$4,320	$27,540			$31,860
Purchase January 1, Year 2			$3,600	$11,000	14,600
	$4,320	$27,540	$3,600	$11,000	$46,460
Amortization, Year 2	1,080	3,060	900	1,100	6,140
Balance December 31, Year 2 ...	$3,240	$24,480	$2,700	$ 9,900	$40,320

Par Company's equity method journal entries for Year 2 would be as follows:

Investment in Sub Company	31,500	
Intercompany investment income		31,500
To record 90% of Sub Company's net income		
for Year 2 ($35,000 × 0.90 = $31,500).		
Cash	9,000	
Investment in Sub Company		9,000
To record dividends received from Sub		
Company in Year 2 ($10,000 × 0.90 = $9,000).		
Intercompany investment income	6,140	
Investment in Sub Company		6,140
To record the amortization of the purchase		
discrepancy for Year 2.		

On December 31, Year 2, the account "Investment in Sub Company" on Par Company's books would have a balance of $253,620 calculated as follows:

Cost of first purchase (60%) January 1, Year 1	$150,000
Year 1 equity method journal entries:	
Sub Company net income ($30,000 × 0.60)	18,000
Sub Company dividends ($8,000 × 0.60)	(4,800)
Purchase discrepancy amortization	(4,140)
Balance December 31, Year 1	$159,060
Cost of second purchase (30%) January 1, Year 2	78,200
Year 2 equity method journal entries:	
Sub Company net income ($35,000 × 0.90)	31,500
Sub Company dividends ($10,000 × 0.90)	(9,000)
Purchase discrepancy amortization	(6,140)
Balance December 31, Year 2	$253,620

The preceding example has assumed that there were no intercompany transactions involving unrealized profits during the two-year period. When this is the case, the elimination of the parent's ownership interest in the shareholders' equity of the subsidiary against the investment in subsidiary account will always yield a balance equal to the unamortized purchase discrepancy. This can be illustrated as follows:

Investment in Sub Company — December 31, Year 2		$253,620
Shareholders' equity of Sub Company:		
Common stock	$100,000	
Retained earnings		
Balance January 1, Year 1	$90,000	
Net income Years 1 and 2	65,000	
($30,000 + $35,000)		
Dividends Years 1 and 2	(18,000)	
($8,000 + $10,000)		
Balance December 31, Year 2	137,000	
Total	$237,000	
Par's ownership interest	0.90	213,300
Balance — unamortized purchase discrepancy . .		$ 40,320

The details of the allocation of the unamortized purchase discrepancy are shown in the schedule on page 403. The working paper for the consolidated balance sheet and related working paper elimination entries for Par Company and subsidiary on December 31, Year 2 are shown on page 405.

A working paper for the preparation of consolidated income statement for Year 2 has not been illustrated. The procedures would be the same as those of previous chapters except that purchase discrepancy amortization allocated to depreciation and goodwill amortization expenses is made up of two amounts as shown at the bottom of page 405.

PAR COMPANY AND SUBSIDIARY

Working Paper for Consolidated Balance Sheet
December 31, Year 2

	Par Company	Sub Company	Eliminations increase (decrease)	Consolidated
Assets				
Current assets	300,000	75,000		375,000
Investment in Sub Company	253,620		(253,620)	
Equipment (net)		92,000	5,940	97,940
Other assets (net)	400,000	150,000		550,000
Goodwill			34,380	34,380
Total assets	953,620	317,000	(213,300)	1,057,320
Liabilities & Shareholders' Equity				
Liabilities (Miscellaneous)	328,490	80,000		408,490
Minority interest in net assets				
of subsidiary			23,700	23,700
Common stock	250,000	100,000	(100,000)	250,000
Retained earnings	375,130	137,000	(137,000)	375,130
Total liabilities & shareholders'				
equity	953,620	317,000	(213,300)	1,057,320

PAR COMPANY AND SUBSIDIARY

Working Paper Eliminations
December 31, Year 2

Common stock — Sub Company	100,000	
Retained earnings — Sub Company	137,000	
Equipment ($3,240 + $2,700)	5,940	
Goodwill ($24,480 + $9,900)	34,380	
Investment in Sub Company		253,620
Minority interest ($237,000 × 0.10)		23,700

To eliminate intercompany investment and equity accounts of Sub Company, to allocate unamortized purchase discrepancy to identifiable net assets and goodwill, and to establish minority interest in net assets of Sub Company.

Amortization of purchase discrepancy for Year 2 reflected on consolidated income statement	

Depreciation expense ($1,080 + $900)	$1,980
Goodwill amortization expense ($3,060 + $1,100)	4,160
Total	$6,140

In summary, the only new consolidation concept involved with block acquisitions is the revaluation of the subsidiary's net assets at the time each block is acquired. *Section 1600.13* of the *Handbook* describes the process as follows:

> Where an investment in a subsidiary is acquired through two or more purchases, the parent company's interest in the subsidiary's identifiable assets and liabilities should be determined as follows:
> (a) the assignable costs of the subsidiary's identifiable assets and liabilities should be determined as at each date on which an investment was acquired;
> (b) the parent company's interest in the subsidiary's identifiable assets and liabilities acquired at each step in the purchase should be based on the assignable costs of all such assets and liabilities at that date.

The *Handbook* also suggests that this process should commence the first time that the equity method becomes appropriate and, in addition, that it would be practical to treat numerous small purchases, especially those made over short periods of time, as a single purchase.

Reduction in parent's interest in subsidiary

The effect of a reduction in a parent's ownership interest on a single block purchase discrepancy was illustrated earlier in this chapter (page 400). We will now carry on our illustration of Par Company and its subsidiary Sub Company to examine the effects of a reduction of ownership interest on a multiple block purchase. We will examine two alternative ways that a reduction of ownership interest could occur: (1) the parent sells a portion of its holdings in its subsidiary, and (2) the subsidiary issues additional common shares to the public. In each alternative, we assume that the ownership change took place on January 1, Year 3.

Alternative One: Parent sells a portion of its holdings

On January 1, Year 3, Par Company sold 900 shares of its holdings in Sub Company for $30,000. This represents 10% of its investment (900 shares ÷ 9,000 shares) and as a result its ownership interest has declined from 90% to 81% (8,100 shares ÷ 10,000 shares).

Par Company would make the following journal entry on January 1, Year 3 to record the sale of 900 shares:

<table>
<tr><td>Parent's entry for sale of portion of investment in subsidiary</td><td>Cash ....</td><td>30,000</td><td></td></tr>
<tr><td></td><td>Investment in Sub Company ($253,620 × 0.10) ....</td><td></td><td>25,362</td></tr>
<tr><td></td><td>Gain on sale of investment ....</td><td></td><td>4,638</td></tr>
<tr><td></td><td>To record the sale of 900 shares of Sub Company.</td><td></td><td></td></tr>
</table>

We observed in our previous example that a 10% reduction in the investment account results in a 10% reduction in the unamortized purchase discrepancy. In this example there are two unamortized purchase discrepancies because there were two purchases of stock. Does the reduction affect the first, or the second, or both? The answer is that the reduction affects both, because **Section 1600.42** of the **Handbook** requires that the reduction of the carrying amount of the investment should be based on the average carrying value. Therefore, because we have reduced the investment account by 10%, we have also reduced the two unamortized purchase discrepancies by 10%.

On December 31, Year 3, Sub Company reported a net income of $40,000 and paid dividends amounting to $15,000. The following purchase discrepancy amortization schedule would be made on December 31, Year 3:

Schedule showing effect of sale on unamortized purchase discrepancy, and Year 3 amortization

	First Purchase		Second Purchase		Total
	Equip.	Goodwill	Equip.	Goodwill	
Balance December 31, Year 2	$3,240	$24,480	$2,700	$9,900	$40,320
10% disposal January 1, Year 3 ...	324	2,448	270	990	4,032
Balance after disposal	$2,916	$22,032	$2,430	$8,910	$36,288
Amortization — Year 3	972	2,754	810	990	5,526
Balance December 31, Year 3 ...	$1,944	$19,278	$1,620	$7,920	$30,762

Note that the Year 3 amortization is based on the years of life remaining from the original estimates, which is three years for equipment, eight years for the first purchase goodwill, and nine years for the second purchase goodwill. Alternatively, the amortization amounts could be calculated by taking 90% of the amortization amounts shown in the schedule on page 403. (If 10% of the investment has been sold, 90% of the original investment is left to amortize, and therefore, the subsequent amounts of amortization are 90% of the original amounts).

Par Company's equity method journal entries for Year 3 would be as follows:

Parent's Year 3 equity method journal entries

Investment in Sub Company	32,400	
Intercompany investment income		32,400
To record 81% of Sub Company's net income		
for Year 3 ($40,000 × 0.81 = $32,400).		
Cash	12,150	
Investment in Sub Company		12,150
To record dividends received from Sub		
Company in Year 3 ($15,000 × 0.81 = $12,150).		
Intercompany investment income	5,526	
Investment in Sub Company		5,526
To record the amortization of the purchase		
discrepancy for Year 3.		

On December 31, Year 3, the account "Investment in Sub Company" would have a balance of $242,982 calculated as follows:

Calculation of balance in parent's investment account, end of Year 3

Balance December 31, Year 2 (9,000 shares)	$253,620
Sale of 10% of investment (900 Shares)	(25,362)
Year 3 equity method journal entries:	
Sub Company net income ($40,000 × 0.81)	32,400
Sub Company dividends ($15,000 × 0.81)	(12,150)
Purchase discrepancy amortization	(5,526)
Balance December 31, Year 3	$242,982

In the preparation of the consolidated balance sheet on December 31, Year 3, the elimination of Sub Company's shareholders' equity against the investment account will result in the unamortized purchase discrepancy as follows:

Calculation of unamortized purchase discrepancy, end of Year 3

Investment in Sub Company — December 31, Year 3		$242,982
Shareholders' equity of Sub Company		
Common stock	$100,000	
Retained earnings		
($137,000 + $40,000 − $15,000)	162,000	
Total	$262,000	
Par's ownership interest	0.81	212,220
Balance — unamortized purchase discrepancy		$ 30,762

The schedule on page 407 shows that this amount would be allocated to equipment $3,564 ($1,944 + $1,620) and to goodwill $27,198 ($19,278 + $7,920) in the preparation of the consolidated balance sheet. Minority interest would appear in the amount of $49,780 ($262,000 × 0.19).

The working paper for the preparation of the Year 3 consolidated income statement is shown on page 409.

The following points regarding the income statement amounts and eliminations should be noted:

1 The gain on sale of investment is not eliminated and therefore appears on the consolidated income statement.

2 Intercompany investment income ($26,874) consists of $32,400 − $5,526 (see page 407).

3 The purchase discrepancy amortization allocated to depreciation ($1,782) consists of $972 + $810 (see page 407).

4 The purchase discrepancy amortization allocated to goodwill ($3,744) consists of $2,754 + $990 (see page 407).

5 Minority interest in net income is $7,600 ($40,000 × 0.19).

Working Paper for Consolidated Income Statement
December 31, Year 3

	Par Company	Sub Company	Eliminations increase (decrease)	Consolidated
Revenues (miscellaneous)	200,000	150,000		350,000
Gain on sale of investment	4,638			4,638
Intercompany investment income	26,874		(26,874)	
Total	231,512	150,000	(26,874)	354,638
Expenses (miscellaneous)	130,000	90,000		220,000
Depreciation expense — equipment ..		20,000	1,782	21,782
Goodwill amortization expense			3,744	3,744
Minority interest in net income			7,600	7,600
Total	130,000	110,000	13,126	253,126
Net income	101,512	40,000	(40,000)	101,512

Alternative Two: Subsidiary issues additional shares to public

We are assuming that alternative one did not take place, and instead, that Sub Company issued an additional 2,500 shares for $83,000 on January 1, Year 3. Sub Company would record this transaction as follows:

Subsidiary's journal entry for share issue	Cash	83,000	
	Common stock		83,000
	To record the issuance of 2,500 common shares.		

Sub Company now has 12,500 common shares issued, and because Par Company did not buy any of the new issue its holdings have remained constant (9,000 shares), but its ownership interest has declined to 72% (9,000 shares ÷ 12,500 shares). This represents a 20% reduction in its investment calculated as follows:

Calculation of reduction in parent's investment	Ownership before share issue	90%
	Ownership after share issue	72%
	Change	18%
	Percentage of investment reduced: 18 ÷ 90 = 20%	

The effect of this reduction on the unamortized purchase discrepancy is the same as if the parent had sold a portion of its holding in the subsidiary (**Handbook Section 1600.46–.47**). In this case 20% of the unamortized purchase discrepancy has been "disposed of" as a result of the share issue. However at this point the only entry made to record the transaction is the entry made by Sub Company. Parent Company must also adjust its investment account to record the effect of this transaction on its investment. The following analysis indicates the amount of the adjustment.

<table>
<tr><td>Calculation of effect on parent of subsidiary share issue</td><td>Loss due to reduction of investment account</td><td></td></tr>
<tr><td></td><td>20% × $253,620 ....</td><td>$50,724</td></tr>
<tr><td></td><td>Gain due to ownership of new assets resulting from subsidiary share issue</td><td></td></tr>
<tr><td></td><td>72% × $83,000 ....</td><td>$59,760</td></tr>
<tr><td></td><td>Net gain to parent due to share issue ....</td><td>$ 9,036</td></tr>
</table>

In our previous example we explained the reasoning for removing 20% from the investment account. The unamortized purchase discrepancy is included in the $253,620 amount and if this discrepancy has been reduced by 20% a logical extension would be to remove 20% from the total investment balance. If the subsidiary had issued the 2,500 shares for no consideration, then the investment account would have to be reduced by $50,724 and a loss equal to that amount would be recorded by Par Company. But Sub Company received $83,000 for its new share issue, and Par Company now controls 72% of the net assets of its subsidiary including the additional cash received as a result of the new share issue. Par Company has gained by the 72% ownership interest in the assets received by Sub Company. It should be obvious that net gain or loss resulting from the transaction depends on the amount that the subsidiary received from its new share issue. Given the facts of this particular example, Par Company would make the following journal entry on January 1, Year 3:

<table>
<tr><td>Parent's journal entry for subsidiary share issue</td><td>Investment in Sub Company ....</td><td>9,036</td><td></td></tr>
<tr><td></td><td>Gain from subsidiary share issue ....</td><td></td><td>9,036</td></tr>
<tr><td></td><td>To record the effect of subsidiary's</td><td></td><td></td></tr>
<tr><td></td><td>issue of 2,500 shares on parent's investment.</td><td></td><td></td></tr>
</table>

As in our previous example, we assume that in Year 3, Sub Company reported a net income of $40,000 and paid $15,000 in dividends. The following purchase discrepancy amortization schedule would be prepared on December 31, Year 3.

Schedule showing effect
of reduction on unamor-
tized purchase discre-
pancy, and Year 3
amortization

| | First Purchase | | Second Purchase | | Total |
	Equip.	Goodwill	Equip.	Goodwill	
Balance December 31, Year 2	$3,240	$24,480	$2,700	$9,900	$40,320
20% "disposed" January 1,					
Year 3	648	4,896	540	1,980	8,064
Balance after disposal	$2,592	$19,584	$2,160	$7,920	$32,256
Amortization — Year 3	864	2,448	720	880	4,912
Balance December 31, Year 3 ...	$1,728	$17,136	$1,440	$7,040	$27,344

Par Company's equity method journal entries for Year 3 would be as follows:

Investment in Sub Company	28,800	
Intercompany investment income		28,800
To record 72% of Sub Company's net income		
for Year 3 ($40,000 × 0.72 = $28,800).		
Cash	10,800	
Investment in Sub Company		10,800
To record dividends received from Sub		
Company in Year 3 (15,000 × 0.72 = 10,800).		
Intercompany investment income	4,912	
Investment in Sub Company		4,912
To record the amortization of the purchase discrepancy for Year 3.		

In the same manner as previous examples the elimination of the parent's interest in the subsidiary's shareholders' equity against the parent's investment account leaves a balance equal to the unamortized purchase discrepancy. This is illustrated at the top of page 412.

The working paper for the consolidated balance sheet on December 31, Year 3 is not illustrated. The schedule above shows how the unamortized purchase discrepancy would be allocated in the preparation of the consolidated balance sheet. Minority interest in the net assets of Sub Company would appear in the amount of $96,600 (345,000 × 0.28).

The working paper for the preparation of the Year 3 consolidated income statement is shown on page 412. It should be noted that the account "gain from subsidiary share issue" on Par Company's income statement is not eliminated in the consolidation process and therefore appears on the Year 3 consolidated income statement. The details of the purchase discrepancy amortization allocated to equipment and goodwill can be found in the schedule above. Minority interest in net income is $11,200 ($40,000 × 0.28).

Calculation of unamortized
purchase discrepancy end
of Year 3

Investment in Sub Company

Balance December 31, Year 2	$ 253,620
Increase due to subsidiary share issue	9,036
Sub Company net income ($40,000 × 0.72)	28,800
Sub Company dividends ($15,000 × 0.72)	(10,800)
Purchase discrepancy amortization	(4,912)
Balance December 31, Year 3	$275,744

Shareholders' equity of Sub Company

Common stock — December 31, Year 2	$100,000	
Share issue — Year 3	83,000	
Common stock December 31, Year 3	$183,000	
Retained earnings December 31, Year 3		
($137,000 + $40,000 − $15,000)	162,000	
Total December 31, Year 3	$345,000	
Par's ownership interest	0.72	248,400
Balance — unamortized purchase discrepancy		$ 27,344

PAR COMPANY AND SUBSIDIARY
Working Paper for Consolidated Income Statement
December 31, Year 3

	Par Company	Sub Company	Eliminations increase (decrease)	Consolidated
Revenues (miscellaneous)	200,000	150,000		350,000
Gain from subsidiary share issue	9,036			9,036
Intercompany investment income . . .	23,888		(23,888)	
Total	232,924	150,000	(23,888)	359,036
Expenses (miscellaneous)	130,000	90,000		220,000
Depreciation expense — equipment . .		20,000	1,584	21,584
Goodwill amortization expense			3,328	3,328
Minority interest in net income			11,200	11,200
Total	130,000	110,000	16,112	256,112
Net income	102,924	40,000	(40,000)	102,924

SUBSIDIARY WITH PREFERRED SHARES OUTSTANDING

Our examples to date have assumed that subsidiary companies have only one class of shares — common shares — in their capital structures. Some subsidiaries, however, have outstanding preferred shares. When this is the case we have an additional consolidation problem in determining the minority interest in the net assets and net income of the subsidiary, based on the preferences associated with the preferred shares.

Illustration of minority interest in subsidiary with preferred stock

Suppose, for example, that on July 1, Year 4, Praeger Corporation paid $200,000 (including direct out-of-pocket costs of the business combination) for 60% of Simmon Company's 10,000 shares of outstanding $1 par, 9% cumulative preferred stock and 80% of Simmon's 50,000 shares of outstanding no par common stock. The preferred shares have a liquidation preference of $1.10 a share and are callable at $1.20 a share plus cumulative preferred dividends in arrears. The shareholders' equity of Simmon on July 1, Year 4, was as follows:

Shareholders' equity of subsidiary on date of business combination	
9% preferred stock, $1 par, 10,000 shares	$ 10,000
Common stock, no par, 50,000 shares	100,000
Contributed surplus	30,000
Retained earnings	50,000
Total shareholders' equity	$190,000

Cumulative preferred dividends were one year in arrears on July 1, Year 4. The current fair values of Simmon's identifiable net assets on July 1, Year 4, were equal to their carrying amounts on that date, except for inventory which was undervalued by $10,000.

The presence of the preferred stock raises two questions:

1 What part if any, does the preferred stock play in the valuation of the net assets of the subsidiary?

2 Which per-share amount — $1 par, $1.10 liquidation preference, or $1.20 call price—should be used to measure the minority interest in Simmon's net assets on July 1, Year 4?

In the opinion of the authors, the following are logical answers to the two questions:

1 The preferred stock does not enter into the valuation of net assets as a result of the business combination. Typically, preferred shareholders have no voting rights; thus, in a business combination, preferred stock may in substance be considered **debt** rather than **owner's equity**. Accordingly, the amount paid by the combinor for the subsidiary's common stock should be the measure of the net asset revaluation and goodwill.

2 The call price should be used to measure the minority interest of the preferred shareholders in Simmon's net assets on July 1, Year 4. The call price generally is the maximum claim on net assets imposed by the preferred share contract. Furthermore, the call price is the amount that Simmon would pay, on a going-concern basis, to liquidate the preferred stock. Use of the preferred stock's liquidation value in the determination of the minority shareholders' interest in the subsidiary's net assets would stress a **quitting-concern** approach, rather than a going-concern principle. Finally, the par of the preferred stock has no real significance as a measure of value for the preferred stock.

Because the problem associated with subsidiary preferred stock is essentially one of determining the amount of minority interest, whenever a consolidated balance sheet is prepared it is necessary to split the shareholders' equity of the subsidiary into its preferred and common stock components. In addition, based on our foregoing discussion regarding asset valuation, the amount of the preferred stock component can be used to determine the amount of the preferred stock acquisition cost. The split up of Simmon's shareholders' equity is illustrated as follows:

	Total	Shareholder's Equity Preferred	Common
9% preferred stock	$ 10,000	$10,000	
Common stock	100,000		$100,000
Contributed surplus	30,000	2,000	28,000
Total contributed capital	$140,000	$12,000	$128,000
Retained earnings	50,000	900	49,100
	$190,000	$12,900	$177,100

The contributed surplus allocated to preferred equity is the call premium per share multiplied by the number of preferred shares outstanding ($.20 × 10,000 shares). The $900 retained earnings allocated to the preferred is the amount of preferred dividends in arrears on this date, because any dividends paid on this date to common shareholders could only occur after the preferred dividends in arrears were fully paid. The subheading "total contributed capital" will prove useful in our further analysis (page 416).

Based on the foregoing analysis, Praeger prepares the following journal entry to record the business combination with Simmon on July 1, Year 4. (Out-of-pocket costs of the combination are not accounted for separately in this illustration.)

Investment in Simmon Company preferred stock		
($12,900 × 0.60)	7,740	
Investment in Simmon Company common stock ($200,000		
– $7,740)	192,260	
Cash		200,000
To record business combination with Simmon Company.		

The calculation at the top of page 415 of the purchase discrepancies on July 1, Year 4 illustrates that the valuation of the net assets of Simmon is based only on the cost of the common share investment.

The calculation of minority interest in the net assets of Simmon on July 1, Year 4, is also shown on page 415.

	Preferred		Common	
Cost of preferred stock	$7,740			
Cost of common stock				$192,260
Book value of stock	$12,900		$177,100	
Parent's ownership interest	0.60	7,740	0.80	141,680
Purchase discrepancy		$ 0		50,580
Allocated				
Inventory $10,000 × 0.80				8,000
Balance— goodwill				$ 42,580

Preferred stock ($12,900 × 0.40)	$ 5,160
Common stock ($177,100 × 0.20)	35,420
Total minority interest	$40,580

The working paper elimination for Praeger and subsidiary on July 1, Year 4 is as follows:

PRAEGER CORPORATION AND SUBSIDIARY
Working Paper Elimination
July 1, Year 4

Preferred stock — Simmon	10,000	
Common stock — Simmon	100,000	
Contributed surplus — Simmon	30,000	
Retained earnings — Simmon	50,000	
Inventory — Simmon	8,000	
Goodwill — Simmon	42,580	
Investment in Simmon Company preferred stock — Praeger		7,740
Investment in Simmon Company common stock — Praeger		192,260
Minority interest in net assets of subsidiary		40,580

To eliminate intercompany investment and related equity
accounts of subsidiary on date of business combination; to
allocate the purchase discrepancy attributable to common stock;
and to provide for minority interest in subsidiary's net assets.

Preferred stock considerations subsequent to date of business combination

Regardless of whether Simmon's preferred dividend is paid or omitted in years subsequent to July 1, Year 4, the preferred dividend affects the computation of the minority interest in the net income of Simmon, and

Praeger's Year 5 journal entries under the equity method of accounting. For example, assume that Simmon had net income of $65,000 and declared and paid total dividends of $26,800 on June 30, Year 5, made up of the preferred dividend in arrears, the current year's preferred dividend, and a common dividend of $0.50 a share. An analysis of the change in Simmon's retained earnings for fiscal Year 5, split between preferred and common, yields the following information:

<table>
<tr><td rowspan="2" style="text-align:right">Change in retained earnings of subsidiary allocated to preferred and common components</td><td></td><td colspan="2" style="text-align:center">Retained Earnings</td><td></td></tr>
<tr><td>Total</td><td>Preferred</td><td>Common</td></tr>
<tr><td>Balance July 1, Year 4 . . . .</td><td>$ 50,000</td><td>$ 900</td><td>$ 49,100</td></tr>
<tr><td>Net income fiscal Year 5 . . . .</td><td>65,000</td><td>900</td><td>64,100</td></tr>
<tr><td>   Subtotal . . . .</td><td>$115,000</td><td>$1,800</td><td>$113,200</td></tr>
<tr><td>Dividends June 30, Year 5 . . . .</td><td>26,800</td><td>1,800</td><td>25,000</td></tr>
<tr><td>Balance June 30, Year 5 . . . .</td><td>$ 88,200</td><td>0</td><td>$ 88,200</td></tr>
</table>

Notice that regardless of the amount of the current year's net income (or loss) a portion equal to the amount of the current year's preferred dividend is allocated to increase the preferred equity because the preferred shares are cumulative. Based on this analysis Praeger makes the journal entries shown on page 417 under the equity method of accounting.

After these journal entries are posted, Praeger's investment accounts will have balances calculated as follows:

<table>
<tr><td rowspan="2" style="text-align:right">Calculation of balance in parent's investment accounts</td><td colspan="2" style="text-align:center">Investment Accounts</td></tr>
<tr><td>Preferred Stock</td><td>Common Stock</td></tr>
<tr><td>Balance July 1, Year 4 . . . .</td><td>$7,740</td><td>$192,260</td></tr>
<tr><td>Share of Simmon's net income . . . .</td><td>540</td><td>51,280</td></tr>
<tr><td>Dividends from Simmon . . . .</td><td>(1,080)</td><td>(20,000)</td></tr>
<tr><td>Purchase discrepancy amortization . . . .</td><td></td><td>(12,258)</td></tr>
<tr><td>Balance June 30, Year 5 . . . .</td><td>$7,200</td><td>$211,282</td></tr>
</table>

The shareholders' equity of Simmon Company on June 30, Year 5, would be split between preferred and common as follows:

<table>
<tr><td rowspan="2" style="text-align:right">Allocation of shareholders' equity of subsidiary into preferred and common components</td><td></td><td colspan="2" style="text-align:center">Shareholders' Equity</td></tr>
<tr><td>Total</td><td>Preferred</td><td>Common</td></tr>
<tr><td>Contributed capital (see page 414) . . . .</td><td>$140,000</td><td>$12,000</td><td>$128,000</td></tr>
<tr><td>Retained earnings (see above) . . . .</td><td>88,200</td><td>0</td><td>88,200</td></tr>
<tr><td>   Total . . . .</td><td>$228,200</td><td>$12,000</td><td>$216,200</td></tr>
</table>

PRAEGER CORPORATION
Journal Entries
June 30, Year 5

Cash 21,080

   Investment in Simmon Company preferred stock 1,080

   Investment in Simmon Company common stock 20,000

To record receipt of dividends declared and paid

by Simmon Company as follows:

	Preferred	Common
Total paid by Simmon	$ 1,800	$25,000
% owned by Praeger	0.60	0.80
Cash received	$ 1,080	$20,000

Investment in Simmon Company preferred stock 540

Investment in Simmon Company common stock 51,280

   Intercompany investment income 51,820

To record share of Simmon Company's net

income as follows:

	Preferred	Common
Net income Year 5	900	64,100
% owned by Praeger	0.60	0.80
	540	51,280

Intercompany investment income 12,258

   Investment in Simmon Company Common Stock 12,258

To provide for Year 5 amortization of the

purchase discrepancy as follows (goodwill is

being amortized over 10 years):

Inventory (to cost of sales)	8,000
Goodwill (42,580 ÷ 10)	4,258
	$12,258

The minority interest in the net assets of Simmon on June 30, Year 5, is calculated as follows:

Preferred stock ($12,000 × 0.40)	$ 4,800
Common stock ($216,200 × 0.20)	43,240
Total minority interest	$48,040

To facilitate the preparation of the June 30, Year 5 consolidated financial statement working papers the following calculation summarizing the changes in minority interest is useful:

	Changes in Minority Interest		
	Preferred	Common	Total
Balance July 1, Year 4	$5,160	35,420	40,580
Net income:			
$900 × 0.40	360		} 13,180
$64,100 × 0.20		12,820	
Dividends:			
$1,800 × 0.40	(720)		} (5,720)
$25,000 × 0.20		(5,000)	
Balance June 30, Year 5	$4,800	$43,240	$48,040

The Year 5 consolidated statement working paper elimination entries are shown below.

PRAEGER CORPORATION AND SUBSIDIARY
Working Paper Eliminations
June 30, Year 5

(a) Preferred stock — Simmon	10,000	
Common stock — Simmon	100,000	
Contributed surplus — Simmon	30,000	
Retained earnings — Simmon	50,000	
Intercompany investment income — Praeger		
($51,820 − $12,258)	39,562	
Goodwill ($42,580 − $4,258)	38,322	
Cost of goods sold	8,000	
Goodwill amortization expense	4,258	
Investment in Simmon Company preferred stock —		
Praeger		7,200
Investment in Simmon Company common stock —		
Praeger		211,282
Minority interest in net assets of		
subsidiary ($40,580 − $5,720)		34,860
Dividends — Simmon		26,800
To eliminate intercompany investment account, and related		
equity accounts of subsidiary at beginning of year; to		
eliminate subsidiary's dividends declared; to record the Year 5		
amortization of the purchase discrepancy; to record the un-		
amortized balance of the purchase discrepancy on June 30,		
Year 5; and to provide for the minority interest in subsidiary		
at beginning of year, less dividends to minority shareholders.		
(b) Minority interest in net income of subsidiary	13,180	
Minority interest in net assets of subsidiary		13,180
To provide for minority interest in net income of subsidiary		
for Year 5.		

Preferred shares acquired subsequently

A parent company may acquire an investment in the preferred shares of its subsidiary subsequent to the date that it acquired its common share investment. When the cost of the investment is different from the carrying value of the preferred equity acquired, a problem arises as to the disposition of the preferred stock purchase discrepancy. As discussed before, this purchase discrepancy should not be used to revalue the net assets of the subsidiary, because preferred share market prices are influenced by interest rate changes and not by changes in the value of the subsidiary company (the exception would be fully participating shares). Therefore, any preferred share purchase discrepancy should be treated as a capital transaction and adjusted to consolidated contributed surplus or retained earnings.

Other Types of Preferred Shares   Treatment similar to that illustrated previously is appropriate for a subsidiary having other types of outstanding preferred shares. If the preferred shares were ***noncumulative***, there would be no parent company accrual of passed dividends. If the preferred shares were ***participating*** (which seldom is the case), the subsidiary's retained earnings would be allocated to the minority interests in preferred stock and common stock according to the terms of the ***participation clause***.

INDIRECT SHAREHOLDINGS

A subsidiary company is a company whose voting shares are controlled directly or indirectly by another company. Control is achieved by the ability to elect a majority of the board of directors and results from direct or indirect holdings of more than 50% of the voting shares. The following diagrams illustrate direct and indirect holdings:

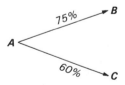

In this case B and C are subsidiaries of A through direct control.

$$E \xrightarrow{\quad 90\% \quad} F \xrightarrow{\quad 70\% \quad} G$$

This example illustrates indirect control. G is a subsidiary of F, but F in turn is a subsidiary of E. Because E can control the voting shares of G through its control of F, G is also a subsidiary of E.

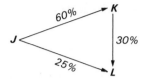

K is a subsidiary of J through direct control. L is also a subsidiary of J through indirect control because 55% of its voting shares are controlled directly and indirectly by J, even though only 43% [25% + (60% × 30%)] of L's net income will flow to J under the equity method of accounting.

Many companies in Canada have intercorporate structures that are far more complex than have been illustrated here. In this section we examine the preparation of consolidated financial statements when the parent's control over the subsidiary is indirect.

Illustration of Indirect Shareholdings   On December 31, Year 2, Placer Corporation acquired 160,000 shares (80%) of the outstanding common stock of Shabot Company for $476,240, and 36,000 shares (45%) of Sur Company's outstanding common stock for $182,000. Both amounts included direct out-of-pocket costs of the common stock acquisitions. On December 31, Year 2, Shabot owned 20,000 shares (25%) of Sur's outstanding common stock; accordingly, Placer acquired indirect control of Sur as well as direct control of Shabot in the business combination.

The diagram of ownership after Placer's December 31, Year 2 acquisition is as follows:

Affiliation diagram

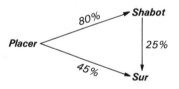

Separate balance sheets of Shabot and Sur on December 31, Year 2 follow:

SHABOT COMPANY AND SUR COMPANY
Separate Balance Sheets
December 31, Year 2

	Shabot Company	Sur Company
Assets		
Current assets	$ 360,400	$190,600
Investment in Sur Company common stock	91,950	
Plant assets (net)	640,650	639,400
Total assets	$1,093,000	$830,000

Liabilities & Shareholders' Equity

Current liabilities	$ 210,200	$ 80,500
Long-term debt	300,000	389,500
Common stock, $1 par	200,000	80,000
Contributed surplus	150,000	120,000
Retained earnings	232,800	160,000
Total liabilities & shareholders' equity	$1,093,000	$830,000

Shabot's Investment in Sur Company Common Stock account appeared as follows on December 31, Year 2:

Investment account of subsidiary investor

Investment in Sur Company Common Stock

Date	Explanation	Debit	Credit	Balance
12/31/1	Acquisition of 20,000 shares	82,000		82,000 dr
12/6/2	Dividends: $0.25 a share		5,000	77,000 dr
12/31/2	Share of net income			
	($60,000 × 0.25)	15,000		92,000 dr
12/31/2	Amortization of goodwill			
	($2,000 ÷ 40)		50	91,950 dr

The ledger account of Shabot indicates that Shabot had applied the equity method of accounting for its investment in Sur, and that the $2,000 excess of the cost of Shabot's investment over the underlying equity of Sur's identifiable net assets was allocated to goodwill having an economic life of 40 years.

The current fair value of the identifiable net assets of both Shabot and Sur equaled their carrying amounts on December 31, Year 2. Accordingly, goodwill acquired by Placer in the business combination with Shabot and Sur was computed as follows:

Goodwill calculation on date of acquisition

	Shabot Company	Sur Company
Cost of investment	$476,240	$182,000
Less: Current fair value of identifiable assets acquired:		
Shabot ($582,800 × 0.80)	466,240	
Sur ($360,000 × 0.45)		162,000
Goodwill (economic life 40 years)	$ 10,000	$ 20,000

Working Paper for Consolidated Balance Sheet on Date of Business Combination

The working paper for consolidated balance sheet of Placer Corporation and subsidiaries on December 31, Year 2, the date of the

purchase-type business combination, appears below, and the related working
paper eliminations are as shown on page 423.

PLACER CORPORATION AND SUBSIDIARIES
Working Paper for Consolidated Balance Sheet
December 31, Year 2

	Placer Corporation	Shabot Company	Sur Company	Eliminations increase (decrease)		Consolidated
Assets						
Current assets	1,400,000	360,400	190,600			1,951,000
Investment in Shabot Company						
common stock	476,240			(a)	(476,240)	
Investment in Sur Company				(b)	(91,950)	
common stock	182,000	91,950		(b)	(182,000)	
Plant assets (net)	3,800,000	640,650	639,400			5,080,050
				(a)	10,000	31,950
Goodwill				(b)	21,950	
Total assets	5,858,240	1,093,000	830,000		(718,240)	7,063,000
Liabilities & Shareholders' Equity						
Current liabilities	600,000	210,200	80,500			890,700
Long-term debt	3,000,000	300,000	389,500			3,689,500
Minority interest in net				(a)	116,560	224,560
assets of subsidiaries				(b)	108,000	
Common stock, $1 par	1,200,000	200,000	80,000	(a)	(200,000)	1,200,000
				(b)	(80,000)	
Contributed surplus	500,000	150,000	120,000	(a)	(150,000)	500,000
				(b)	(120,000)	
Retained earnings	558,240	232,800	160,000	(a)	(232,800)	558,240
				(b)	(160,000)	
Retained earnings of investee						
Total liabilities & share-						
holders' equity	5,858,240	1,093,000	830,000		(718,240)	7,063,000

The following aspects of the working paper eliminations deserve special
emphasis:

1 The investment accounts are eliminated against the shareholders' equity accounts of
   the investee companies, leaving purchase discrepancies which are allocated to
   revalue the net assets of the investee companies (in this case the three purchase
   discrepancies were each allocated to goodwill), and minority interests which
   appear as one amount on the consolidated balance sheet.
2 The goodwill applicable to Sur is made up of the unamortized balance from
   Shabot's previous investment ($1,950), plus the additional goodwill from Plac-

er's December 31, Year 2 investment ($20,000). The goodwill applicable to Shabot ($10,000) results from Placer's December 31, Year 2 investment.

3 Minority interest is based on the carrying values of the investee's net assets multiplied by the percent of voting stock not held within the group (in this case 20% of Shabot and 30% of Sur).

4 Consolidated shareholders' equity is that of the parent company (Placer).

Working paper eliminations in subsequent year

For the year ended December 31, Year 3, Shabot Company had income from its own operations (exclusive of investment income from Sur) of $150,000 and declared dividends of $60,000; Sur Company had net income of $80,000 and declared dividends of $20,000. Placer Corporation's Year 3 net income from its own operations (exclusive of investment income from Shabot and Sur) was $270,000, and dividends of $90,000 were paid during the year. In

---

PLACER CORPORATION AND SUBSIDIARIES
Working Paper Eliminations
December 31, Year 2

(a)	Common stock — Shabot	200,000	
	Contributed surplus — Shabot	150,000	
	Retained earnings — Shabot	232,800	
	Goodwill — Shabot	10,000	
	Investment in Shabot Company common stock —		
	Placer		476,240
	Minority interest in net assets of subsidiaries		
	($582,800 × 0.20)		116,560
	To eliminate intercompany investment and equity ac-		
	counts of Shabot Company on date of business combination;		
	to allocate excess of cost over current fair values (and		
	carrying amounts) of identifiable net assets acquired to		
	goodwill; and to establish minority interest in net assets		
	of Shabot on date of business combination.		
(b)	Common stock — Sur	80,000	
	Contributed surplus	120,000	
	Retained earnings — Sur	160,000	
	Goodwill — Sur ($1,950 + $20,000)	21,950	
	Investment in Sur Company common stock — Placer		182,000
	Investment in Sur Company common stock — Shabot		91,950
	Minority interest in net assets of subsidiaries		
	($360,000 × 0.30)		108,000
	To eliminate intercompany investments and equity ac-		
	counts of Sur Company on date of business combination;		
	to allocate excess of cost over current fair values (and		
	carrying amounts) of identifiable net assets acquired to		
	goodwill; and to establish minority interest in net assets		
	of Sur on date of business combination.		

---

the preparation of the Year 3 financial statements (see page 425), Placer and Shabot have used the equity method to account for their intercompany investments. The following schedule is useful because it illustrates the calculation of consolidated net income and the use of the equity method by Placer and Shabot:

Schedule Showing the Calculation of Consolidated Net Income
Year 3

	Placer	Shabot	Sur	Total
Net income — exclusive of inter-company investment income . . .	$270,000	$150,000	$80,000	$500,000
Less: goodwill amortization				
Shabot	(250)			
Sur	(500)	(50)		(800)
Total	$269,250	$149,950	$80,000	$499,200
Allocate Sur:				
25% to Shabot		20,000	(20,000)	
45% to Placer	36,000		(36,000)	
Shabot net income — equity				
method		$169,950		
Allocate Shabot:				
80% to Placer	135,960	(135,960)		
Unallocated		$ 33,990	$ 24,000	57,990
Placer net income — equity				
method	$ 441,210			
Consolidated net income				$ 441,210

The following points regarding preparation and interpretation of the schedule should be noted:

1 Purchase discrepancy amortizations (in this example all were allocated to goodwill with a 40-year life) are recorded by each company that has an investment in another company in the group. In the schedule they are the first adjustment made. Any adjustments for intercompany asset profits, and gains or losses on intercompany bond transactions would also be made here (as would the deduction for intercompany dividends if the cost method had been used).

2 Because Placer should not record its 80% share of Shabot's net income until Shabot has recorded its 25% share of Sur's net income, Sur's net income is allocated first.

3 Shabot's net income using the equity method can now be determined.

4 After Shabot's net income has been allocated, Placer's net income using the equity method is determined.

5 The portion of Shabot's and Sur's net income that was not allocated is the minority interest in that net income.

6 The total column shows amounts that would appear on the consolidated income statement. Net income—consolidated entity is $499,200. Minority interest in net income of subsidiaries is $57,990.

PLACER CORPORATION AND SUBSIDIARIES
Working Paper for Consolidated Financial Statements
For the Year Ended December 31, Year 3

	Placer Corporation	Shabot Company	Sur Company	Eliminations increase (decrease)	Consolidated
Income Statement					
Miscellaneous revenue	900,000	550,000	200,000		1,650,000
Intercompany investment income — Shabot	135,710			(a) (135,710)	
Intercompany investment income — Sur	35,500	19,950		(b) (35,500) (b) (19,950)	
Total revenue	1,071,210	569,950	200,000	(191,160)	1,650,000
Miscellaneous expenses	630,000	400,000	120,000		1,150,000
Goodwill amortization				(a) 250 (b) 550	800
Minority interest in net income of subsidiaries				(c) 57,990	57,990
Total expenses	630,000	400,000	120,000	58,790	1,208,790
Net income	441,210	169,950	80,000	(249,950)	441,210
Statement of Retained Earnings					
Balance — beginning of year	558,240	232,800	160,000	(a) (232,800) (b) (160,000)	558,240
Net income	441,210	169,950	80,000	(249,950)	441,210
Subtotal	999,450	402,750	240,000	(642,750)	999,450
Dividends	90,000	60,000	20,000	(a) (60,000) (b) (20,000)	90,000
Balance — end of year	909,450	342,750	220,000	(562,750)	909,450
Balance Sheet					
Miscellaneous assets	5,637,000	1,005,850	920,000		7,562,850
Investment in Shabot Company common stock	563,950			(a) (563,950)	
Investment in Sur Company common stock	208,500	106,900		(b) (208,500) (b) (106,900)	
Goodwill				(a) 9,750 (b) 21,400	31,150
Total assets	6,409,450	1,112,750	920,000	(848,200)	7,594,000
Miscellaneous liabilities	3,800,000	420,000	500,000		4,720,000
Minority interest in net assets of subsidiaries				(a) 104,560 (b) 102,000 (c) 57,990	264,550
Common stock, $1 par	1,200,000	200,000	80,000	(a) (200,000) (b) (80,000)	1,200,000
Contributed surplus	500,000	150,000	120,000	(a) (150,000) (b) (120,000)	500,000
Retained earnings	909,450	342,750	220,000	(562,750)	909,450
	6,409,450	1,112,750	920,000	(848,200)	7,594,000

The intercompany investment ledger accounts for Placer and Shabot are shown on page 427. The working papers and elimination entries are on page 425 and below.

PLACER CORPORATION AND SUBSIDIARIES
Working Paper Eliminations
December 31, Year 3

(a)
Common stock — Shabot	200,000	
Contributed surplus — Shabot	150,000	
Retained earnings — Shabot	232,800	
Intercompany investment income — Placer		
($135,960 – $250)	135,710	
Goodwill — Shabot ($10,000 – $250)	9,750	
Goodwill amortization expense	250	
Investment in Shabot Company common stock — Placer		563,950
Dividends — Shabot		60,000
Minority interest in net assets of		
subsidiaries ($116,560 – $12,000)		104,560

To eliminate intercompany investment account, and equity accounts of Shabot at beginning of year, and subsidiary dividends; to establish goodwill at end of year and record amortization expense for the year; and to establish minority interest in net assets of Shabot at beginning of Year ($116,560), less dividends to minority shareholders (60,000 × 0.20 = $12,000).

(b)
Common stock — Sur	80,000	
Contributed surplus — Sur	120,000	
Retained earnings — Sur	160,000	
Intercompany investment income — Placer ($36,000 – $500) ..	35,500	
Intercompany investment income — Shabot ($20,000 – $50) ..	19,950	
Goodwill — Sur [($1,950 – $50) + ($20,000 – $500)]	21,400	
Goodwill amortization expense ($500 + $50)	550	
Investment in Sur Company common stock — Placer		208,500
Investment in Sur Company common stock — Shabot		106,900
Dividends — Sur		20,000
Minority interest in net assets of subsidiaries		
($108,000 – $6,000)		102,000

To eliminate intercompany investment accounts, and equity accounts of Sur at beginning of year, and subsidiary dividends; to establish goodwill at end of year and record amortization expense for the year; and to establish minority interest in net assets of Sur at beginning of year ($108,000) less dividends to minority shareholders ($20,000 × 0.30 = $6,000).

(c)
Minority interest in net income of subsidiaries	57,990	
Minority interest in net assets of subsidiaries		57,990

To establish minority interest in subsidiaries' net income for Year 3
(See page 424)

Investment accounts of
parent company and
subsidiary

PLACER CORPORATION LEDGER
Investment in Shabot Company Common Stock

Date	Explanation	Debit	Credit	Balance
12/31/2	Acquisition of 160,000 shares	476,240		476,240 dr
12/6/3	Dividends: $0.30 a share		48,000	428,240 dr
12/31/3	Share of net income ($169,950 × 0.80)	135,960		564,200 dr
12/31/3	Amortization of goodwill ($10,000 ÷ 40)		250	563,950 dr

Investment in Sur Company Common Stock

Date	Explanation	Debit	Credit	Balance
12/31/2	Acquisition of 36,000 shares	182,000		182,000 dr
12/6/3	Dividends: $0.25 a share		9,000	173,000 dr
12/31/3	Share of net income ($80,000 × 0.45)	36,000		209,000 dr
12/31/3	Amortization of goodwill ($20,000 ÷ 40)		500	208,500 dr

SHABOT COMPANY LEDGER
Investment in Sur Company Common Stock

Date	Explanation	Debit	Credit	Balance
12/31/1	Acquisition of 20,000 shares	82,000		82,000 dr
12/6/2	Dividends: $0.25 a share		5,000	77,000 dr
12/31/2	Share of net income ($60,000 × 0.25)	15,000		92,000 dr
12/31/2	Amortization of goodwill ($2,000 ÷ 40)		50	91,950 dr
12/6/3	Dividends: $0.25 a share		5,000	86,950 dr
12/31/3	Share of net income ($80,000 × 0.25)	20,000		106,950 dr
12/31/3	Amortization of goodwill ($2,000 ÷ 40)		50	106,900 dr

CONSOLIDATED STATEMENT OF CHANGES IN FINANCIAL POSITION

The consolidated financial statements issued by publicly owned companies include a statement of changes in financial position, generally prepared on a working capital concept.[1] Such a statement may be prepared as described in the *Intermediate Accounting* text of this series; however, when the statement is prepared on a consolidated basis, a number of special problems arise. Some of these are described below:

1 Depreciation and amortization expense, as reported in the consolidated income statement, is added to combined net income, *including the minority interest in net income of subsidiary*, in the consolidated statement of changes in financial position. The depreciation and amortization expense in a purchase-type business

---

1 In recent years there has been an increase in the number of companies using a cash or cash equivalent concept. At the time of publication of this book the CICA Accounting Standards Committee had issued an exposure draft to revise *Handbook Section 1540* which recommends the use of cash or cash equivalents.

combination is based on the current fair values of the assets, including any goodwill of subsidiaries on the dates of the business combinations. Net income applicable to minority interests is included in the computation of working capital provided from operations, because 100% of working capital of all subsidiaries is included in a consolidated balance sheet.

2 Only cash dividends declared by the parent company and the cash dividends declared by partially owned subsidiary companies *to minority shareholders* are reported as applications of working capital. Cash dividends declared by subsidiaries to the parent company have no effect on consolidated working capital because cash is transferred entirely *within the affiliated group* of companies. Dividends declared to minority shareholders that are material in amount should be listed separately or disclosed parenthetically in the consolidated statement of changes in financial position.

3 An acquisition by the parent company of additional shares of common stock directly from a subsidiary does not change the amount of consolidated working capital and thus is not reported in a consolidated statement of changes in financial position.

4 An acquisition by the parent company of additional shares of common stock from minority shareholders reduces consolidated working capital. Consequently, such an acquisition is reported in the consolidated statement of changes in financial position as a financial resource (working capital or cash) applied.

5 A sale of part of the investment in a subsidiary company increases consolidated working capital (and the amount of minority interest) and thus is reported as a financial resource provided in the consolidated statement of changes in financial position. A gain or loss from such a sale represents an adjustment to combined net income of the parent company and its subsidiaries in the measurement of working capital provided from operations.

Illustration of consolidated statement of changes in financial position

Parent Corporation has owned 100% of the common stock of Sub Company for several years. Sub has outstanding only one class of common stock, and its total shareholders' equity at the end of Year 10 was $500,000. At the beginning of Year 11, Parent sold 30% of its investment in Sub's common stock to outsiders for $205,000, which was $55,000 more than the carrying amount of the stock in Parent's accounting records. Sub had net income of $100,000 in Year 11 and declared cash dividends of $60,000 near the end of Year 11. During Year 11, Parent issued additional common stock and cash of $290,000 in exchange for plant assets with a current fair value of $490,000.

The effect of the parent's disposal of 30% of its investment on the consolidated balance sheet can be examined in the analysis that follows. Parent Corporation made the following journal entry to record the sale of 30% of its investment at the beginning of Year 11:

Parent's entry for sale of portion of its investment	*Cash*	*205,000*	
	Investment in Sub Company		*150,000*
	Gain on sale of investment		*55,000*

The reduction in the investment account represents 30% of the carrying value prior to the sale. The balance in the investment account prior to the sale was $500,000 ($150,000 ÷ 0.30). An examination of the calculation of the unamortized purchase discrepancy before and after the sale will help to illustrate the effect the transaction had on the consolidated balance sheet.

		Prior to Sale
Investment in Sub Company (equity method)		$500,000
Shareholders' equity of Sub Company	$500,000	
Parent's ownership interest	1.00	500,000
Balance — unamortized purchase discrepancy		0
Minority interest in Sub Company		0

Calculation of purchase discrepancy and minority interest prior to sale

After the sale of 30%, the unamortized purchase discrepancy and minority interest would be calculated as follows:

		After Sale
Investment in Sub Company ($500,000 − $150,000)		$350,000
Shareholders' equity of Sub Company	$500,000	
Parent's ownership interest	0.70	350,000
Balance — unamortized purchase discrepancy		$ 0
Minority interest in Sub Company ($500,000 × 0.30) . . .		$150,000

Calculation of purchase discrepancy and minority interest after sale

There was no minority interest prior to the sale, but the disposal of 30% by Parent Company resulted in a minority interest of $150,000. From the view of the consolidated entity the effect of the transaction can be described in the following journal entry:

Cash	205,000	
Minority interest in Sub Company		150,000
Gain on sale of investment		55,000

Effect of sale on consolidated entity

Working capital increased by $205,000, minority interest increased by $150,000 and the entity's net income increased by the amount of the gain.

The consolidated income statement for Year 11, the consolidated statement of retained earnings for Year 11, and the comparative consolidated balance sheets on December 31, Year 10 and Year 11, are presented on page 430.

A working paper for a consolidated statement of changes in financial position on a working capital concept for Year 11 is shown on page 431. The consolidated statement of changes in financial position for Parent Corporation and subsidiary for Year 11 is on page 432.

PARENT CORPORATION AND SUBSIDIARY
Consolidated Income Statement
For Year Ended December 31, Year 11

Sales and other revenue (including gain of $55,000 on sale of investment in Sub Company common stock)		$2,450,000
Costs and expenses:		
Cost of goods sold	$1,500,000	
Depreciation and amortization expense	210,000	
Other operating expenses	190,000	1,900,000
Income before income taxes		$ 550,000
Income taxes expense		250,000
Combined net income		$ 300,000
Less: Minority interest in net income of subsidiary		30,000
Consolidated net income		$ 270,000
Earnings per share		$ 5.14

PARENT CORPORATION AND SUBSIDIARY
Consolidated Statement of Retained Earnings
For Year Ended December 31, Year 11

Retained earnings, beginning of year	$670,000
Add: Net income	270,000
Subtotal	$940,000
Less: Dividends ($2.91 a share)	160,000
Retained earnings, end of year	$780,000

PARENT CORPORATION AND SUBSIDIARY
Consolidated Balance Sheets
December 31,

	Year 11	Year 10
Assets		
Current assets	$1,200,000	$ 900,000
Plant assets	3,000,000	2,510,000
Less: Accumulated depreciation	(1,300,000)	(1,100,000)
Intangible assets (net)	240,000	250,000
Total assets	$3,140,000	$2,560,000
Liabilities & Shareholders' Equity		
Current liabilities	$ 505,000	$ 490,000
Long-term debt	693,000	600,000
Minority interest in net assets of subsidiary	162,000	
Common stock, $10 par	550,000	500,000
Contributed surplus	450,000	300,000
Retained earnings	780,000	670,000
Total liabilities & shareholders' equity	$3,140,000	$2,560,000

PARENT CORPORATION AND SUBSIDIARY
Working Paper for Consolidated Statement of Changes in Financial Position
(Working Capital Concept)
For Year Ended December 31, Year 11

	Account balances, Dec. 31, Year 10	Analysis of transactions for Year 11			Account balances, Dec. 31, Year 11
			Debit	Credit	
Working capital	410,000	(x)	285,000		695,000
Plant assets	2,510,000	(7)	290,000		3,000,000
		(8)	200,000		
Intangible assets (net)	250,000			(2) 10,000	240,000
Totals	3,170,000				3,935,000
Accumulated depreciation	1,100,000			(2) 200,000	1,300,000
Long-term debt	600,000			(5) 93,000	693,000
Minority interest in net assets of subsidiary . . .		(9)	18,000	(3) 150,000	
				(4) 30,000	162,000
Common stock, $10 par	500,000			(6) 50,000	550,000
Contributed surplus	300,000			(6) 150,000	450,000
Retained earnings	670,000	(9)	160,000	(1) 270,000	780,000
Totals	3,170,000		953,000	953,000	3,935,000
Financial resources provided:					
Operations — net income		(1)	270,000		
Add: Depreciation and amortization expense .		(2)	210,000		From operations, $455,000
Minority interest in net income of					
subsidiary		(4)	30,000		
Less: Gain on sale of investment in Sub					
Company common stock				(3) 55,000	
Sale of investment in Sub Company common stock		(3)	205,000		
Increase in long-term debt		(5)	93,000		
Issuance of common stock in exchange for plant assets		(6)	200,000		
Financial resources applied:					
Acquisition of plant assets for cash				(7) 290,000	
Acquisition of plant assets in exchange for common stock				(8) 200,000	
Declaration of dividends, including $18,000 to minority shareholders of Sub Company .				(9) 178,000	
Total financial resources provided and applied			1,008,000	723,000	
Increase in working capital				(x) 285,000	
Totals			1,008,000	1,008,000	

PARENT CORPORATION AND SUBSIDIARY

Consolidated Statement of Changes in Financial Position
(Working Capital Concept)
For Year Ended December 31, Year 11

Financial resources provided

   Working capital provided from operations:

Operations — Net income, including minority interest of $30,000	$300,000
Add: Depreciation and amortization expense	210,000
Less: Gain on sale of investment in Sub Company common stock	(55,000)
Working capital provided from operations	$455,000
Sale of investment in Sub Company common stock	205,000
Long-term borrowing	93,000
Issuance of common stock in exchange for plant assets	200,000
Total financial resources provided	$953,000

Financial resources applied

Acquisition of plant assets for cash	$290,000	
Acquisition of plant assets in exchange for common		
stock	200,000	
Declaration of cash dividends, including $18,000 to		
minority shareholders of Sub Company	178,000	
Total financial resources applied		668,000
Increase in financial resources: working capital		$285,000

Composition of working capital

	End of Year 11	End of Year 10	Increase (decrease) in working capital
Current assets	$1,200,000	$900,000	$300,000
Less: Current liabilities	505,000	490,000	(15,000)
Working capital	$ 695,000	$410,000	
Increase in working capital			$285,000

The following items in the consolidated statement of changes in financial position warrant special emphasis:

1 The working capital provided from operations *includes* the minority interest in net income of Sub Company.

2 The working capital provided from operations *excludes* the gain of $55,000 from sale of the investment in Sub Company common stock; thus, the entire proceeds of $205,000 are reported as a provision of consolidated working capital.

3 Only the dividends declared to shareholders of Parent Corporation ($160,000) and to minority stockholders of Sub Company ($18,000) are reported as applications of consolidated working capital.

4 The issuance of common stock by Parent Corporation to acquire plant assets is a *financing and investing activity* (as defined in *Handbook Section 1540*) and is reported as both a provision and an application of consolidated working capital, even though no working capital accounts were affected directly by this exchange transaction.

REVIEW QUESTIONS

1 How should a parent company's cash dividends declared but not paid be shown on a consolidated statement of changes in financial position prepared under (a) a working capital concept, (b) a cash concept? Explain.

2 At what stage in the installment acquisition of an eventual subsidiary's outstanding common stock should the parent company ascertain the current fair values of the subsidiary's identifiable net assets? Explain.

3 Why does a parent company realize a gain or a loss when a subsidiary issues common stock to the public at a price per share that differs from the carrying amount per share of the parent company's investment in the subsidiary's common stock? Explain.

4 Explain how the minority interest in net assets of a subsidiary is affected by the parent company's ownership of 70% of the subsidiary's outstanding common shares and 60% of the subsidiary's outstanding 7%, cumulative, preferred shares.

5 How should a subsidiary company's cash dividends declared but not paid be shown on a consolidated statement of changes in financial position prepared under (a) a working capital concept, (b) a cash concept? Explain.

6 How is the minority interest in consolidated net income shown on the consolidated statement of changes in financial position? Explain.

7 Is a gain or a loss realized by a parent company on the sale of part of its investment in common stock of a subsidiary eliminated in the preparation of consolidated financial statements? Explain.

8 A subsidiary company has shareholders' equity made up of preferred and common shares. The parent company owns 100% of the subsidiary's common shares. Will the consolidated financial statements show minority interest? Explain.

EXERCISES

Ex 10-1 On August 1, Year 6, Packard Corporation acquired 2,000 of the 10,000 outstanding shares of Stenn Company's $1 par common stock for $10,000. Stenn's identifiable net assets had a current fair value and carrying amount of $40,000 on that date. Stenn had net income of $3,000 and declared and paid dividends of the same amount for the year ended July 31, Year 7. On August 1, Year 7, Packard acquired 4,500 more shares of Stenn's outstanding common stock for $22,500. The current fair values and carrying amounts of Stenn's identifiable net assets were still $40,000 on that date. Stenn had net income of $7,500 and declared no dividends for the year ended July 31, Year 8.

Prepare journal entries in Packard Corporation's accounting records for the above facts for the two years ended July 31, Year 8.

Ex 10-2 The shareholders' equity section of Stegg Company's August 31, Year 2, balance sheet was as shown on page 434.

On August 31, Year 2, Panay Corporation acquired 50,000 shares of Stegg's outstanding preferred stock and 75,000 shares of Stegg's outstanding common stock for a total cost — including out-of-pocket costs — of $1,030,500. The current fair values of Stegg's identifiable net assets were equal to their carrying amounts on August 31, Year 2.

Answer the following questions (show supporting computations):

a What amount of the $1,030,500 total cost is assignable to Stegg's preferred stock?

b What is the minority interest of preferred shareholders in Stegg's net assets on August 31, Year 2?

c What is the amount of goodwill acquired by Panay August 31, Year 2?

d What is the minority interest of common shareholders in Stegg's net assets on August 31, Year 2?

8% cumulative preferred stock, $1 par, dividends in arrears two years, authorized, issued, and outstanding 100,000 shares, callable at $1.10 a share plus dividends in arrears	$ 100,000
Common stock, $2 par, authorized, issued, and outstanding 100,000 shares	200,000
Contributed surplus — common stock	150,000
Retained earnings	750,000
Total shareholders' equity	$1,200,000

Ex 10-3 On March 31, Year 4, the consolidated balance sheet of Polberg Corporation and its 85%-owned subsidiary, Serrano Company, showed goodwill of $65,400 and minority interest in net assets of subsidiary of $22,800. On April 1, Year 4, Polberg paid $10,000 to minority shareholders who owned 500 shares of Serrano's 10,000 shares of issued common stock. Asset fair values equaled carrying values.

Compute goodwill and minority interest in net assets of subsidiary for inclusion in the consolidated balance sheet of Polberg Corporation and subsidiary on April 1, Year 4.

Ex 10-4 On January 2, Year 3, Prester Corporation organized Shire Company, paying $40,000 for 10,000 shares of Shire's $1 par common stock. On January 3, Year 3, before beginning operations, Shire issued 2,000 shares of its $1 par common stock to the public for net proceeds of $11,000.

Compute the gain or loss to Prester that resulted from Shire's issuance of common shares to the public.

Ex 10-5 Simplex Company, the partially owned subsidiary of Polyglot Corporation, had net income of $342,800 for the year ended May 31, Year 6. Simplex declared a dividend of $12 a share on its 10,000 shares of outstanding 12%, $100 par, cumulative preferred stock, and a dividend of $8 a share on its 80,000 shares of outstanding $1 par common stock. Polyglot owns 7,000 shares of preferred stock and 60,000 shares of common stock of Simplex. There were no dividends in arrears on the preferred shares.

Prepare a schedule to show the allocation of Simplex Company's $342,800 net income for the year ended May 31, Year 6, to consolidated net income and to the minority interest in net income of subsidiary.

Ex 10-6 On January 2, Year 7, Prince Corporation organized Sabine Company with authorized common stock of 10,000 shares, $5 par. Prince acquired 4,000 shares of Sabine's common stock at $8 a share, and Samnite Company, a wholly owned subsidiary of Prince, acquired the 6,000 remaining authorized shares of Sabine's common stock at $8 a share. For the year ended December 31, Year 7, Sabine had net income of $80,000 and declared dividends of $2 a share on December 28, Year 7, payable on January 25, Year 8.

Prepare journal entries under the equity method of accounting to record the operating results of Sabine Company for Year 7 in the accounting records of **a** Prince Corporation, and **b** Samnite Company. Omit explanations.

Ex 10-7 Prieto Corporation declared and paid cash dividends of $250,000 and distributed a
5% stock dividend in Year 5. The market value of the shares distributed pursuant
to the 5% stock dividend was $600,000. Prieto owns 100% of the common stock
of S Company and 75% of the common stock of SS Company. In Year 5, S declared
and paid a cash dividend of $100,000 on the common shares and $25,000 on its
$5 cumulative preferred shares. None of the preferred shares are owned by Prieto.
In Year 5, SS declared and paid cash dividends of $44,000 on its common shares,
the only class of capital stock issued.

Compute the amount that should be reported as working capital applied to payment of dividends in the Year 5 consolidated statement of changes in financial
position for Prieto Corporation and subsidiaries.

Ex 10-8 The consolidated statement of changes in financial position for Paradise Corporation
and its partially owned subsidiaries for Year 2 will be prepared on a working capital
concept. Using the following letters, indicate how each of the 13 items listed
below should be reported in the statement. A given item may be reported more
than one way.

A – O = Add to combined net income in the determination of consolidated working
capital provided from operations

D – O = Deduct from combined net income in the determination of consolidated
working capital provided from operations

FP = A financial resource provided

FA = A financial resource applied

N = Not included or separately disclosed in the consolidated statement of
changes in financial position

1 The minority interest in net income of subsidiaries is $37,500.

2 Paradise issued a bond payable to a subsidiary company in exchange for plant
assets with a current fair value of $180,000.

3 Paradise distributed a 10% stock dividend; the additional shares of common
stock issued had a current fair value of $675,000.

4 Paradise declared and paid a cash dividend of $200,000.

5 Long-term debt of Paradise in the amount of $2 million was converted to common
stock.

6 A subsidiary sold plant assets to outsiders at the carrying amount of $80,000.

7 Paradise's share of the net income of an unconsolidated subsidiary totalled
$28,000. The subsidiary did not declare or pay cash dividends in Year 2.

8 Consolidated depreciation and amortization expense totalled $285,000.

9 A subsidiary company amortized $3,000 of premium on bonds payable owned
by outsiders.

10 Paradise sold its entire holdings in an 80%-owned subsidiary for $3 million.

11 Paradise merged with Sun Company in a pooling-type business combination;
150,000 shares of common stock with a current fair value of $4.5 million were
issued by Paradise for 98% of Sun's common stock.

12 Paradise received cash dividends of $117,000 from its consolidated subsidiaries.

13 The consolidated subsidiaries of Paradise declared and paid cash dividends of
$21,500 to minority shareholders.

Ex 10-9   Company P has made investments in Company X and Company Y as follows:

> January 1, Year 1 — Purchased 80% of the outstanding common shares of Company X
> July 1, Year 2 — Purchased 70% of the outstanding common shares of Company Y
> September 1, Year 3 — Purchased 60% of the outstanding preferred shares of Company Y

There were $100,000, 10% cumulative, redeemable at $110, $100 par value, preferred shares outstanding on September 1, Year 3. The purchase discrepancies of both companies reflected unrecorded goodwill to be amortized over a 10-year period.

During Year 13 Company P manufactured and sold the components of a machine that Company Y was assembling for use by Company X. Company P recorded a profit of $8,000 when it sold the components to Company Y. On January 1, Year 14, Company Y sold the machine to Company X and recorded a profit of $12,000. Company X is depreciating the machine over an estimated life of 5 years.

During Year 14 the subsidiary companies reported net incomes as follows:

Company X	$50,000
Company Y	$ 8,000

On December 31, Year 14 preferred dividends were two years in arrears.

Instructions   Calculate the amount of intercompany investment income that Company P would report in Year 14 under the equity method of accounting (assume a corporate tax rate of 40%).

Ex 10-10   Intercompany shareholdings of an affiliated group during the year ended December 31, Year 2 were as follows:

B Ltd.	G Company:	D Company:
90% of G Company	70% of C Ltd.	60% of E Ltd.
80% of D Company	10% of D Ltd.	

The equity method is being used for intercompany investments, but no entries have been made in Year 2. The net incomes before equity method earnings for Year 2 were as follows:

	Net Income
B Ltd.	$54,000
G Company	32,000
D Company	26,700
C Ltd.	15,400
E Ltd.	11,600

Intercompany profits in the December 31, Year 2 inventories, and the affiliated companies involved were:

Selling Corporation	Profit Made by Selling Corporation
B Ltd.	$5,000
D Company	1,000
C Ltd.	2,400

Use income tax allocation at a 40% rate.

Instructions

a Calculate consolidated net income for Year 2.

b Calculate the amount of minority interest in subsidiary net income that would appear on the Year 2 consolidated income statement.

Ex 10-11 Company X owns 80% of Company Y and 30% of Company Z. Company Y owns 40% of Company Z. Company A owns 90% of Company X. All investments were made at a price equal to carrying values and have been accounted for under the cost method.

The following facts apply to Year 9 operations

	A	X	Y	Z
Net income	$135,000	$120,000	$80,000	$50,000
Dividends paid	60,000	50,000	20,000	10,000

On January 1, Year 9, Company Z sold a piece of equipment to Company Y for $32,000. The net book value of the machine was $20,000 and it has an 8-year remaining life. Assume a 40% corporate tax rate.

Instructions

Prepare a partial consolidated statement of Net Income for Year 9. (Start with: "net income before minority interest".)

Ex 10-12 On January 1, Year 1, P Company acquired 8,000 of the 10,000 outstanding common shares of S Company at a cost of $240,000. The carrying value of S Company's net assets on this date amounted to $280,000. Any purchase discrepancy was allocated $10,000 to land, with the balance to goodwill with a 10-year life.

During Year 1, S Company reported a net income of $60,000 and paid dividends of $27,000.

On July 1, Year 2, S Company issued an additional 2,500 common shares to outsiders for $74,000. On December 31, Year 2, S Company reported a net income of $90,000 (earned uniformly during the year) and paid dividends of $30,000 on this date.

P Company uses the equity method to account for its investment in S.

Instructions

a Compute the balance of P Company's investment in S Company account on December 31, Year 2.

b Calculate the amount of goodwill and the adjustment to land that will appear on the consolidated balance sheet on December 31, Year 2.

c Prepare an independent proof of the unamortized purchase discrepancy at December 31, Year 2.

Ex 10-13 Separate balance sheets of Parker Corporation, Siegel Company, and Spurgeon Company on December 31, Year 3, are shown on page 438.

On January 2, Year 4, Parker acquired 70% of the outstanding common shares of Siegel for $680,000 and 40% of the outstanding common shares of Spurgeon for $330,000. On the same date Siegel also acquired 40% of the outstanding common shares of Spurgeon for $330,000. (Out-of-pocket costs of the business combination may be disregarded). Both Parker and Siegel had borrowed cash from banks on December 31, Year 3, to finance the common stock acquisitions.

The current fair values of both Siegel's and Spurgeon's identifiable net assets were the same as their carrying amounts on January 2, Year 4. Both Parker and Siegel use a 30-year economic life for goodwill.

PARKER CORPORATION, SIEGEL COMPANY, AND SPURGEON COMPANY

Separate Balance Sheets
December 31, Year 3

	Parker Corporation	Siegel Company	Spurgeon Company
Assets			
Current assets	$1,820,800	$ 920,000	$ 650,000
Plant assets (net)	3,260,700	740,000	1,260,000
Total assets	$5,081,500	$1,660,000	$1,910,000
Liabilities & Shareholders' Equity			
Current liabilities	$1,020,200	$ 400,600	$ 240,300
Long-term debt	1,240,700	380,500	930,200
Common stock	1,120,000	600,000	500,000
Retained earnings	1,700,600	278,900	239,500
Total liabilities & shareholders' equity	$5,081,500	$1,660,000	$1,910,000

Instructions

a Prepare journal entries in the accounting records of Parker Corporation and Siegel Company on January 2, Year 4, to record the business combination of Parker, Siegel, and Spurgeon Company.

b Prepare a consolidated balance sheet for Parker Corporation and subsidiaries on January 2, Year 4.

CASES

Case 10-1   Scarbo Company, a wholly owned subsidiary of Poller Corporation, is in need of additional long-term financing. Under instructions from Poller, Scarbo offers 5,000 shares of its previously unissued no par common stock to shareholders of Poller at a price of $10 a share. The offer is fully subscribed by Poller's shareholders, and the common stock is issued for $50,000 cash on June 30, Year 6.

After the common stock issuance, Poller owns 45,000 shares, or 90%, of the 50,000 outstanding shares of Scarbo common stock, and shareholders of Poller own 5,000 shares, or 10%, of Scarbo's outstanding common stock. By comparing Poller's 90% interest in Scarbo's net assets after the common stock issuance with the parent company's 100% interest in the subsidiary's net assets before the stock issuance, Poller's accountant computed a $4,000 gain for entry in Poller's accounting records. The controller of Poller objected to the accountant's entry. The controller pointed out that the 5,000 shares of Scarbo common stock were issued to Poller's shareholders, not to outsiders, and that it is a basic accounting principle that a corporation cannot profit from common stock issuances to its shareholders.

Instructions   Evaluate the objections of Poller Corporation's controller.

Case 10-2   On January 2, Year 3, Phoenix Corporation acquired for cash all the outstanding common shares of Scottsdale Company and 70% of the outstanding common shares of Sonoma Company. Included among the assets of Scottsdale are investments in 80% of the outstanding common shares of Spokane Company and 30% of the outstanding common shares of Sonoma Company.

Instructions Discuss the accounting principles that Phoenix Corporation should use for its investment in Scottsdale Company and in its financial statements issued subsequent to the business combination with Scottsdale.

Case 10-3 On January 2, Year 1, Preble Corporation acquired 15% of the outstanding common shares of Searle Company for cash. On January 2, Year 2, Preble acquired an additional 25% of Searle's outstanding common shares in exchange for Preble's common shares. On January 2, Year 3, Preble acquired the remaining 60% of Searle's outstanding common shares for cash. Both Preble and Searle have December 31 fiscal years.

Instructions Describe how Preble Corporation should apply the equity method of accounting for the operating results of Searle Company.

Case 10-4 Pick Company owns 62% of the outstanding shares of Slick Company. The president of Pick Company has hired you to advise him on the preparation of consolidated financial statements.

The companies wish to raise money for capital expansion.

Two alternatives are being considered by the president:

(1) Pick Company will sell 11,000 shares from its holdings in Slick Company.

(2) Slick Company will issue 11,000 new shares through a brokerage company. The brokerage company has indicated that it has a number of customers who would be willing to buy this offering. In fact it will probably have to pro-rate these shares so that all customers will get some part of the issue.

The president notes that because Slick Company's 100,000 outstanding shares are now trading at $90 per share either alternative will raise the same amount of money.

He also indicates that as far as he is concerned the consolidated balance sheet prepared after the transaction should be identical under either alternative.

Instructions Outline your advice to the president.

PROBLEMS

10-1 The following are condensed balance sheets as at December 31, Year 3 of Port Ltd. and its subsidiary Starr Ltd.

	Port Ltd.	Starr Ltd.
Cash	$ 35,000	$ 20,000
Receivables	25,000	21,000
Inventories	120,000	115,000
Plant and equipment (net)	400,000	200,000
Investment in Starr stock (at cost)	205,000	—
	$785,000	$356,000
Current liabilities	$172,000	$ 120,000
Common stock	400,000	100,000
Retained earnings January 1, Year 3	200,000	89,000
Net income	17,000	52,000
Dividends	(4,000)	(5,000)
	$785,000	$356,000

Additional information

(1) Port acquired 55% of the common stock of Starr on January 1, Year 1 for $150,000 when Starr had retained earnings of $50,000. At that time the recorded

values of all assets approximated fair market value with the exception of inventory which was under-valued by a total of $10,000.

On January 1, Year 2, Port acquired an additional 25% of the common stock of Starr at a cost of $55,000. At that time, a parcel of land owned by Starr was under-valued by a total of $30,000. The retained earnings of Starr on January 1, Year 2 were $80,000.

(2) During Year 3 the parcel of land mentioned in (1) above was sold by Starr to a land development company.

(3) During Year 3 Starr made sales to Port amounting to $80,000. The December 31, Year 3 inventory of Port contained an intercompany gross profit of $9,000.

(4) The January 1, Year 3 inventory of Starr contained an intercompany gross profit of $14,000.

(5) On December 1, Year 3, Starr declared a semi-annual dividend of $2,500 payable on January 15, Year 4. Port recorded its share of this dividend on December 2, Year 3.

(6) At December 31, Year 3, Port owed Starr $9,000 on an intercompany loan. During Year 3, $855 in interest was paid by Port to Starr with regard to this loan.

(7) Any goodwill is to be amortized over a 10-year period.

(8) Port has used the cost method of accounting for its investment in Starr.

(9) Assume a 40% corporate tax rate and use income tax allocation.

Instructions

a Prepare the following Year 3 consolidated financial statements:
   1. Balance Sheet,
   2. Retained Earnings Statement.

b Assume that Port has accounted for its investment by the equity method since its acquisition of Starr. Prepare Port's equity method journal entries for Year 3 only.

c Assume that on January 3, Year 4, Starr issued additional common shares, that Port chose not to subscribe to any of these shares, and that as a result its ownership percentage in Starr declined to 68%. Calculate the amount of goodwill that would appear on a January 4, Year 4 consolidated balance sheet.

10-2   Comparative income statements for P Company, A Company and T Company for the year ended December 31, Year 8 are as follows:

	P Company	A Company	T Company
Sales	$500,000	$347,480	$790,000
Dividend income	35,000	56,000	—
Rental income	—	14,400	—
Total income	$535,000	$417,880	$790,000
Cost of goods sold	$270,000	$180,000	$609,400
Selling and admin. expenses	80,500	120,992	145,752
Rental expense	14,400	—	—
Income tax expense	50,100	46,700	13,900
Total expense	$415,000	$347,692	$769,052
Net income	$120,000	$ 70,188	$ 20,948

Additional information:

(1) A acquired its 80% interest in T on July 1, Year 5. The purchase discrepancy on this date amounted to $39,600 and was allocated entirely to an unrecorded patent of T which had a remaining legal life of 9 years.

(2) P acquired its 70% interest in A on December 31, Year 3. The consolidated balance sheet of P and its subsidiary A as at December 31, Year 3 showed goodwill amounting to $84,000 which was to be amortized over the maximum period allowable.

(3)

	P Company	A Company	T Company
Dividends declared, Year 8	$40,000	$50,000	$70,000

(4) On July 1, Year 8, T sold a machine to P at a selling price of $128,000. It cost T $89,000 to construct this machine and this cost is reflected in T company's cost of sales. The machine has an estimated useful life of five years.

(5) P Company rents office space from A Company for $1,200 per month.

(6) Assume a 40% tax rate and use income tax allocation.

Instructions Prepare a Year 8 consolidated income statement.

10-3 Condensed consolidated comparative balance sheets of Prill Company Ltd., and its 70% owned subsidiary, follow:

	Year 6	Year 5
Assets		
Current assets	$2,400,000	$2,040,000
Plant and equipment	4,800,000	5,100,000
Accumulated depreciation	(1,800,000)	(1,980,000)
Goodwill	360,000	396,000
Total assets	$5,760,000	$5,556,000
Liabilities and shareholders' equity		
Current liabilities	$1,538,400	$1,800,000
Long term liabilities	2,160,000	2,100,000
Minority interest	345,600	336,000
Shareholders' equity	1,716,000	1,320,000
Total liabilities and shareholders' equity	$5,760,000	$5,556,000

Additional information

(1) During Year 6 the subsidiary company paid dividends totaling $96,000.

(2) Consolidated net income for Year 6 was $480,000.

(3) Equipment that was worn out and obsolete was retired during the year. The equipment originally cost $600,000 and had a net book value of $65,000 on the date it was retired.

(4) Prill declared $84,000 in dividends during the year.

(5) There were no changes in Prill's 70% interest during the year.

Instructions Prepare a consolidated statement of changes in financial position for the year (working capital approach).

10-4 On January 1, Year 2, S Company's shareholders' equity was as follows:

Common stock (6,000 shares)	$ 30,000
Retained earnings	105,000
	$135,000

Company P held 5,400 shares of S on January 1, Year 2 and its investment in S Company account had a balance of $189,000 on that date. P accounts for its investment by the equity method. Any purchase difference was allocated to goodwill with a remaining life on January 1, Year 2 of 5 years.

The following events took place subsequent to January 1, Year 2.

(1) During Year 2, S reported a net income of $30,000 and declared dividends of $7,500 on November 10 of the year.

(2) On December 31, Year 2, P sold 900 of the S Company shares it held at a price of $45 per share.

(3) During Year 3, S reported a net income of $57,000 and paid dividends of $12,000 on November 15 of the year.

(4) On December 29, Year 3, S issued an additional 1,500 shares to third parties at a price of $69 per share.

Instructions

a Calculate the amount of goodwill that would appear on the consolidated balance sheet on December 31, Year 3.

b Prepare the journal entry that Company P would make on December 31, Year 2 to record the sale of 900 shares.

c Prepare the journal entry that Company P would make on December 29, Year 3 to record the effect of the issue of 1,500 shares by S Company.

d Prepare an independent proof of the goodwill calculated in part *a*.

10-5 On December 31, Year 7, Pro Company purchased 80% of the common shares of Slow Company for $140,000 and 30% of its cumulative, non-participating, 8% preferred shares for $16,200. The preferred shares were one year in arrears on this date. The fair values of Slow's net assets were equal to book values except for a patent, with a remaining life of four years, which had a book value of $10,000 and a fair value of $8,000. Any goodwill is to be amortized over a 10-year period. Pro uses the cost method to account for its investment in Slow. There were no changes in Slow's share capital in Year 8.

The following balance sheets were prepared on December 31, Year 8.

	Pro Company	Slow Company
Investment in Slow Company:		
Common shares	$140,000	$ —
Preferred shares	16,200	—
Miscellaneous assets	480,000	325,000
	$636,200	$325,000
Miscellaneous liabilities	$316,000	$ 85,000
Common shares, no par	200,000	—
Common shares ($100 par)	—	100,000
Preferred shares ($100 par)	—	50,000
Contributed surplus	—	30,000
Retained earnings Jan 1, Year 8	100,200	40,000
Net income — Year 8	35,000	20,000
Dividends — Year 8	(15,000)	—
	$636,200	$325,000

Instructions

a Calculate consolidated net income for Year 8.

b Prepare a consolidated balance sheet as at December 31, Year 8.

10-6 The condensed balance sheets of P Ltd. and S Ltd. as at December 31, Year 3 are as follows:

	P Ltd.	S Ltd.
Current assets	$223,400	$227,200
Fixed assets	294,000	374,800
1,200 common shares in S Ltd. (at cost)	150,100	–
	$667,500	$602,000
Current liabilities	$167,500	$157,000
Accumulated depreciation	128,000	202,000
5% cumulative preferred shares of		
$100 par value each	–	48,000
Common shares of $100 par value each	300,000	160,000
Retained earnings	72,000	35,000
	$667,500	$602,000

Additional information

(1) P Ltd. acquired its holdings of common shares in S Ltd. as follows:
   900 shares on December 31, Year 1 at a cost of $112,100
   300 shares on December 31, Year 2 at a cost of $38,000
(2) On December 20 of Years 1, 2 and 3, S Ltd. declared dividends of 5% on cumulative preferred shares and $10 per common share to shareholders of record on December 29 of each of the three respective years.
(3) S Ltd. sold to P Ltd. depreciable fixed assets on January 1, Year 3 at a price which was $10,000 in excess of book value. P has depreciated these assets at a rate of 10% straight line. (Assume a 40% tax rate.)
(4) Net incomes for the two companies were as follows:

	Year 3	Year 2	Year 1
P Ltd.	$39,000	$20,000	$34,000
S Ltd.	19,000	20,000	12,000

(5) There have been no changes in S Ltd.'s retained earnings account since Year 1 other than for dividends and net incomes.
(6) The carrying values of S Ltd.'s assets were considered to be representative of market values on the date of each purchase.

Instructions
a Prepare a consolidated balance sheet as at Dec. 31, Year 3.
b Prepare a statement of consolidated retained earnings for Year 3.

10-7 The comparative consolidated financial statements on page 444 were prepared from the records of Parker Corporation and its 90% owned subsidiary Sells Company Ltd.

Additional information

(1) Plant assets amounting to $240,000 were purchased in Year 12.
(2) Parker received $324,000 in dividends from Sells during the year.
(3) Year 12 consolidated depreciation expense was $120,000.
(4) Parker issued additional shares to the public during the year.

Instructions Prepare a consolidated statement of changes in financial position (working capital concept) for the year ended December 31, Year 12.

PARKER CORPORATION

Consolidated Balance Sheets
December 31

Assets	Year 12	Year 11
Cash	$ 276,000	$ 144,000
Accounts receivable	600,000	480,000
Inventory	360,000	600,000
Plant (net)	1,680,000	1,560,000
Goodwill	624,000	696,000
	$3,540,000	$3,480,000
Liabilities and shareholders' equity		
Accounts payable	$ 300,000	$ 360,000
Bonds payable	600,000	1,200,000
Total liabilities	$ 900,000	$1,560,000
Minority interest in net assets	$ 96,000	$ 120,000
Shareholders' equity		
Common stock (no par)	$1,800,000	$1,200,000
Retained earnings	744,000	600,000
Total shareholders' equity	$2,544,000	$1,800,000
Total liabilities and shareholders' equity	$3,540,000	$3,480,000

PARKER CORPORATION

Consolidated Statement of Retained Earnings
For Year Ended December 31, Year 12

Balance — beginning of year	$600,000
Add: Net income	384,000
Subtotal	$984,000
Less: Dividends	240,000
Balance — end of year	$744,000

10-8   On January 1, Year 8, S Company's shareholders' equity was as follows:

Common Stock (par $5)	$20,000
Retained Earnings	70,000
	$90,000

Company P held 3,600 shares of S on January 1, Year 8, and its investment in S Company account had a balance of $126,000 on that date. P accounts for its investment by the equity method. Any purchase difference was allocated to goodwill with a remaining life on January 1, Year 8 of 10 years.

The following events took place subsequent to January 1, Year 8:

(1) On July 1, Year 8, P sold 600 of the S Company shares it held at a price of $30 per share.
(2) During Year 8, S reported a net income of $20,000 (earned equally throughout the year) and declared dividends of $5,000 on December 31.
(3) During Year 9, S reported a net income of $38,000 and paid dividends of $8,000 on November 15.
(4) On December 29, Year 9, S issued an additional 1,000 shares to third parties at a price of $46 per share.

Instructions

a Calculate the amount of goodwill that would appear on the consolidated balance sheet on December 31, Year 9.

b Prepare the journal entry that Company P would make on July 1, Year 8 to record the sale of 600 shares.

c Prepare the journal entry that Company P would make on December 29, Year 9 to record the effect of the issue of 1,000 shares by S Company.

10-9 Pastore Corporation acquired an 80% interest in Seville Company on December 31, Year 5, for a total consideration of $1 million. The acquisition cost consisted of $850,000 cash and $150,000 current fair value of securities of Redeker, Inc., which had been owned by Pastore as a long-term investment. The investment in Seville is accounted for by Pastore under the equity method of accounting. The consolidated balance sheet for the two companies on December 31, Year 5, follows:

PASTORE CORPORATION AND SUBSIDIARY
Consolidated Balance Sheet
December 31, Year 5

Assets

Cash	$ 750,000
Accounts receivable (net)	1,300,000
Inventories	2,250,000
Plant assets	3,850,000
Less: Accumulated depreciation	(1,400,000)
Total assets	$6,750,000

Liabilities & Shareholders' Equity

Notes payable (current)	$1,500,000
Accounts payable	1,000,000
Minority interest in net assets of subsidiary	250,000
Common stock	1,800,000
Retained earnings	2,200,000
Total liabilities & shareholders' equity	$6,750,000

On July 2, Year 6, Pastore sold a 10% interest in Seville for $150,000. After the sale Pastore's ownership interest was 70%. The net income, cash dividends, and depreciation expense for each company for Year 6 are summarized below. The net income of Pastore includes intercompany investment income from Seville and the gain or loss on the sale of Seville's common stock.

	Pastore Corporation	Seville Company
Net income for first half of Year 6	$260,000	$72,500
Net income for second half of Year 6	273,500	82,500
Cash dividends declared and paid in December, Year 6	100,000	30,000
Depreciation expense for Year 6	225,000	55,000

The separate unclassified balance sheets for Pastore Corporation and Seville Company on December 31, Year 6, are given on page 446.

PASTORE CORPORATION AND SEVILLE COMPANY
Separate Balance Sheets
December 31, Year 6
Assets

	Pastore Corporation	Seville Company
Cash	$ 695,000	$ 260,000
Accounts receivable (net)	900,000	500,000
Inventories	1,600,000	750,000
Investment in Seville Company common stock	962,500	
Plant assets	3,500,000	1,250,000
Less: Accumulated depreciation	(1,055,000)	(625,000)
Total assets	$6,602,500	$2,135,000

Liabilities & Shareholders' Equity

	Pastore Corporation	Seville Company
Notes payable	$1,100,000	$ 310,000
Accounts payable	569,000	450,000
Bonds payable	500,000	
Common stock	1,800,000	500,000
Retained earnings	2,633,500	875,000
Total liabilities & shareholders' equity	$6,602,500	$2,135,000

Instructions
a Compute the consolidated net income for Year 6.
b Prepare a consolidated balance sheet on December 31, Year 6, without using a working paper.
c Prepare a consolidated statement of changes in financial position on a working capital concept for Year 6. A working paper is not required.
d Reconcile the amount of minority interest on December 31, Year 5, with the amount of minority interest on December 31, Year 6.

10-10 On January 1, Year 1, X Company acquired 800 shares of Y Company's common stock for $24,000 and 180 shares of its 5 percent cumulative, non-participating preferred stock for $19,800. On this date the shareholders' equity accounts of Y Company were:

Common stock ($10 par value)	$10,000
Preferred stock ($100 par value)	20,000
Retained earnings (Note 1)	12,000

(Note 1 — Preferred dividends were two years in arrears on January 1, Year 1)

The income statements at the top of page 447 are for the two companies for the year ended December 31, Year 5.

Additional information

(1) In Year 5 Y paid dividends totalling $9,000. There were no preferred dividends in arrears on December 31, Year 4.

	P	S
	X Company	**Y Company**
Sales	$600,000	$400,000
Dividend and management fee revenues	27,300	–
Rental revenue	–	11,200
	$627,300	$411,200
Cost of sales	$343,900	$234,700
Depreciation expense	20,000	70,000
Rental expense	5,000	–
Selling and administration expense	207,000	74,000
Interest expense	1,700	6,000
Income tax expense	20,000	9,000
Total expenses	$597,600	$393,700
Net income	$ 29,700	$ 17,500

(2) X uses the cost method to account for its investment in Y.
(3) Y purchases merchandise for resale from X. In Year 5 Y purchased $33,000 in merchandise from X and had items in inventory on December 31, Year 5, on which X had made a profit of $2,500. The January 1, Year 5 inventory contained an intercompany profit of $1,400.
(4) X rents equipment from Y and in Year 5 paid a rental charge of $3,000 and recorded an account payable to Y of $2,000 for the balance of the rentals.
(5) On July 1, Year 3, Y sold a building to X at a profit of $13,000. X is depreciating this building on a straight-line basis over a 10-year life.
(6) Y paid $20,000 to X for management fees in Year 5.
(7) Assume a corporate tax rate of 40%.
(8) Any purchase discrepancy is allocated to goodwill.

Instructions   Prepare a statement of consolidated net income for Year 5.

10-11   The White Company owns 90 percent of the capital stock of Black Company. Black Company owns 80% of the capital stock of Red Company. On January 1, Year 1, the Black Company issued $200,000 of 7 percent, 10-year bonds to nonaffiliates at 96. On January 1, Year 7, the Red Company acquired $60,000 of these bonds at 103. Interest is payable January 1 and July 1.
The following data relate to the Year 7 income statements:

	White	Black	Red
Gross profit	$141,000	$102,800	$122,250
Operating expenses and income taxes	30,000	42,000	50,000
Interest expense	12,000	14,800	16,000
Miscellaneous revenue			
(including interest)	1,000	4,000	3,750
Net income	100,000	50,000	60,000

White and Black account for their investments on the cost basis. No dividends were declared during Year 7.
In Year 8 the companies reported the following:

	White	Black	Red
Net income	$85,000	$45,000	$38,000
Dividends paid	12,000	10,000	8,000

Instructions

a Prepare a statement of consolidated net income for Year 7. (Use income tax allocation at 40%.)

b Calculate consolidated net income for Year 8. (Use income tax allocation at 40%.)

10-12 Balance sheet data of P Company and its three subsidiary companies as at December 31, Year 4 are listed below:

	P Company	A Company	B Company	C Company
Inventories	$ 92,600	$ 40,500	$ 87,000	$ 79,000
Investment in A	151,600			
Investment in B	136,500			
Investment in C				
Preferred stock	50,000			
Common stock	411,300			
Other assets	245,000	282,000	200,000	600,000
	$1,087,000	$322,500	$287,000	$679,000
Liabilities	270,000	72,000	90,000	140,000
Preferred stock $100 par value	325,000			100,000
Common stock $10 par value	380,000	200,000	150,000	400,000
Retained earnings	112,000	50,500	47,000	39,000
	$1,087,000	$322,500	$287,000	$679,000

Details of P Company's acquisitions are as follows:

A Company

P purchased 40% of the stock of A on January 1, Year 1, for $100,000. On January 1, Year 2, P purchased an additional 20% of the stock of A for $51,600. Information as to the fair market value of the net assets of A on both dates is as follows:

	January 1, Year 1		January 1, Year 2	
	Fair Value	Book Value	Fair Value	Book Value
Inventory	$12,000	$10,000	$19,000	$16,000
Vacant land held for future use	14,000	8,000	15,000	8,000

In October, Year 4, A Company sold the vacant land for $31,000 in order to improve its earnings.

B Company

P purchased 12,000 shares (80%) of the stock of B on July 1, Year 2, for $156,000. Retained earnings of B on this date amounted to $25,000 and the book values of B's net assets were equal to fair market values. On December 31, Year 3, P sold 1,500 shares of its holdings in B for $25,000 and reported a gain of $5,500 on the sale. (The Year 3 dividends of B were declared in November. Note: P's gain was calculated using the cost method.)

C Company

P purchased 90% of the common shares of C on January 1, Year 3, for $411,300. All net assets were fairly valued in the books of C on this date with the exception of equipment which was undervalued by $11,000 and had an estimated remaining life of 6 years.

On January 1, Year 4, C issued $100,000 of 8%, cumulative, $100 par value, preferred shares at par. P purchased 50% of the preferred share issue.

Details of changes in the retained earnings of the subsidiary companies are shown below:

	A	B	C
Balance, January 1, Year 1	$20,000	$11,000	$52,000
Net income Year 1	25,000	9,000	3,000
Dividends Year 1	(13,000)	-0-	(1,000)
Balance, December 31, Year 1	$32,000	$20,000	$54,000
Net income Year 2	26,000	10,000	(8,000)
Dividends Year 2	(13,000)	-0-	-0-
Balance December 31, Year 2	$45,000	$30,000	$46,000
Net income Year 3	33,000	12,000	17,000
Dividends Year 3	(13,000)	(4,000)	(5,000)
Balance December 31, Year 3	$65,000	$38,000	$58,000
Net income Year 4	(14,500)	13,000	(19,000)
Dividends Year 4	-0-	(4,000)	-0-
Balance December 31, Year 4	$50,500	$47,000	$39,000

P Company carries all of its investments at cost. Any goodwill is to be amortized over a 10-year period.

Intercompany transactions:

The December 31, Year 4 inventories contain unrealized profits as follows:

P's inventory contains 17,000 profit purchased from C

A's inventory contains 9,000 profit purchased from B

B's inventory contains 12,000 profit purchased from P

Assume a corporate tax rate of 40% and use income tax allocation.

Instructions   Prepare the December 31, Year 4 consolidated balance sheet. (Show complete details of all calculations.)

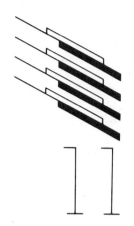

11

ACCOUNTING AND REPORTING OF INVESTMENTS IN JOINT VENTURES; SEGMENT REPORTING; INTERIM REPORTS

In this chapter we deal with three topics that have received considerable attention from accountants in recent years. Investments in joint ventures was the subject of a CICA pronouncement that differed substantially from accounting practice in the U.S.A. Reporting for segments of business enterprise and interim reports have been the subject of pronouncements by professional accounting organizations in both Canada and the U.S.A. All three topics are of considerable significance for accountants who deal with publicly owned business enterprises.

INVESTMENTS IN JOINT VENTURES

In recent years the assembly of resources for some types of business undertaking has been accomplished by means of joint venture arrangements. The high risks and costs associated with certain projects, accompanied by a scarcity of financial resources, have contributed to the use of this form of organization. Often the technological expertise of one company is combined with the marketing and financial expertise of other companies, by the formation of a new organization to undertake some specific project. This new company, which may or may not be incorporated, is called a *joint venture*, and usually has *other companies as its owners (either as shareholders or partners)*. Many examples of this form of organization exist in oil and gas exploration, in large real estate developments and in business expansion in foreign countries. In 1978 the CICA issued *Handbook Section 3055* to deal with the financial reporting of investments in joint ventures. This section is complementary to *Section 3050 Longterm Investments* which was discussed in Chapter 7 (see pages 279 to 283), and has a unique provision that allows the use of the *proportionate consolidation method* in certain instances. Before we examine some of the provisions of this section we will illustrate the preparation of consolidated financial statements prepared under the proportionate consolidation method.

Proportionate consolidation

Proportionate consolidation has existed for many years in the accounting literature under the name of the ***proprietary concept***, but has received little support in practice. It involves preparing consolidated financial statements ***without showing a dollar amount for minority interest*** in net assets and net income. We will illustrate this concept by preparing simple consolidated statements using first full consolidation, then second, the proportionate consolidation method.

Let us assume that Company J owns 90% of the common stock of Company K, that any purchase discrepancy has been fully amortized in prior years, and that J uses the equity method to account for its investment. The current year's financial statements for the two companies are as follows:

BALANCE SHEETS

	Company J	Company K
Miscellaneous assets	$1,500	$1,000
Investment in Company K	540	–
Total assets	$2,040	$1,000
Miscellaneous liabilities	$1,100	$ 400
Shareholders' equity	940	600
Total liabilities and shareholders' equity	$2,040	$1,000

INCOME STATEMENTS

	Company J	Company K
Miscellaneous revenues	$2,000	$ 800
Equity earnings from K	135	–
Total revenue	$2,135	$ 800
Miscellaneous expenses	1,700	650
Net income	$ 435	$ 150

The consolidated financial statements can be prepared without working papers as follows:

Consolidated statements using the full consolidation method

COMPANY J AND SUBSIDIARY
Consolidated Balance Sheet

Miscellaneous assets ($1,500 + $1,000)	$2,500
Miscellaneous liabilities ($1,100 + $400)	$1,500
Minority interest (10% × $600)	60
Shareholders' equity	940
Total	$2,500

COMPANY J AND SUBSIDIARY
Consolidated Income Statement

Miscellaneous revenues ($2,000 + $800)	$2,800
Miscellaneous expenses ($1,700 + $650)	2,350
Net income — consolidated entity	$ 450
Less: minority interest (10% × $150)	15
Net income	$ 435

In the preparation of the consolidated balance sheet, ***Investment in Company K was replaced by 100% of the assets and liabilities of Company K and the minority interest*** in these net assets ($1,000 − $400 − $60 = $540). In a similar manner the consolidated income statement was prepared by ***replacing Equity Earnings from K with 100% of the revenues and expenses of Company K and the minority interest*** in the net income of Company K ($800 − $650 − $15 = $135). If we wish to prepare a consolidated balance sheet of Company J and subsidiary without showing any minority interest in net assets (***the proportionate consolidation method***) the only way it can be accomplished is if ***Investment in Company K is replaced by the parent's ownership interest (90%) in the assets and liabilities of Company K***. The consolidated balance sheet prepared under the proportionate consolidation method, without working papers, is as follows:

Consolidated balance sheet using the proportionate consolidation method

COMPANY J AND SUBSIDIARY
Consolidated Balance Sheet

Miscellaneous assets ($1,500 + [90% × $1,000 = $900])	$2,400
Miscellaneous liabilities ($1,100 + [90% × $400 = $360])	$1,460
Shareholders' equity	$ 940
Total liabilities & shareholder's equity	$2,400

In a similar manner the preparation of the consolidated income statement without showing the minority interest in net income can only be accomplished if ***Equity Earnings from K is replaced by 90% of Company K's revenues and expenses*** in the following manner:

Consolidated income statement using the proportionate consolidation method

COMPANY J AND SUBSIDIARY
Consolidated Income Statement

Miscellaneous revenues ($2,000 + [90% × $800 = $720])	$2,720
Miscellaneous expenses ($1,700 + [90% × $650 = $585])	$2,285
Net income	$ 435

You will note that shareholders' equity and net income remain the same; it is the amount of assets, liabilities, revenues and expenses that differ.

The Handbook description of a joint venture

Section 3055.03 describes a joint venture as "an arrangement whereby two or more parties (the venturers) jointly control a specific business undertaking and contribute resources towards its accomplishment." The distinctive feature of this description is *joint control*. The section adds further clarification by suggesting that joint control is established by an agreement between the venturers (usually in writing), and this means that key operating decisions require the consent of the venturers and that *no one venturer can unilaterally control the joint venture* regardless of the amount of assets contributed by that venturer. For example, a single venturer (Company L) could own more than 50% of the outstanding shares of Company M (which would normally suggest that Company M is a subsidiary), but an agreement among the venturers establishing joint control would mean that Company M is a joint venture, and not a subsidiary.

Accounting for an investment in a joint venture

Section 3055 describes the financial reporting treatment of investments in joint ventures as follows:

Except as outlined in paragraph 3055.13, an investment in a joint venture should be accounted for by the equity method, or when a significant portion of the venturer's activities is carried out through joint ventures, by either the equity method or proportionate consolidation. **(3055.11)**

When the earnings of a joint venture are unlikely to accrue to the venturer, the cost method should be used. **(3055.13)**

Supplementary disclosure is required showing the venturer's share of assets, liabilities, revenues and expenses if either equity or proportionate consolidation is used, or if the cost method is used, the reasons for its use.

The use of proportionate consolidation could result in a joint venture's assets, liabilities, revenues, and expenses appearing on the financial statements of each of its owners. For example, assume a joint venture, Company A, is owned by three venturers as follows:

Company X	40%
Company Y	30%
Company Z	30%
Total	100%

Venturers' ownership interest in a joint venture

If all three venturers conduct a significant proportion of their activities through joint ventures and choose the proportionate consolidation method of reporting, then each venturer's proportion of the assets, liabilities, revenues and expenses of Company A would appear in the three companies' consolidated financial statements.

Intercompany profits in assets

Intercompany profits in assets are fully eliminated from the consolidated statements of a parent and its subsidiaries. If the subsidiary was the selling company, 100% of the profit, net of income tax, is eliminated and allocated to the minority and controlling equities (consolidated retained earnings) on the consolidated balance sheet. If the parent company was the selling company, the entire profit net of income tax is eliminated and allocated to the controlling equity. This is not the case in the proportionate consolidation of a venturer and a joint venture, because of the nature of the proportionate consolidation method and *because of the requirements of Section 3055.*

If the *joint venture sells assets at a profit* to the venturer, and these assets have not been resold to independent third parties, *only the venturer's ownership percentage* of the after-tax profit *can be eliminated*, because there is no minority interest to allocate the remaining percentage to.

If the *venturer sells assets at a profit* to the joint venture, which have not been resold to independent third parties, it would be possible to eliminate 100% of the after-tax profit under the proportionate consolidation method because the entire profit elimination is allocated to the controlling equity. However, *Section 3055* suggests that because the joint venture agreement does not allow a particular venturer to exercise control, *a venturer selling to the joint venture is considered to be dealing at arms-length with the other venturers*, and therefore a portion of the profit equal to the other venturer's ownership interest can be considered realized. However, if any of the other venturers are affiliated with the selling venturer, the portion of the profit equal to the non-affiliated venturers' interest is the amount that should be considered realized. The paragraph describing the treatment of intercompany gains and losses is as follows:

When the substance of a transaction between a venturer and a joint venture is such that a gain or loss has occurred:
(a) any gain should be recognized only to the extent of the interests of the other non-affiliated venturers;
(b) the full amount of any loss should be recognized at the time of the transaction in order to recognize the impairment in the value of the asset transferred. **(3055.22)**

Notice that no elimination of unrealized intercompany losses is required, which is contrary to the procedure that would be followed in the consolidation of a parent and its subsidiaries.

Intercompany revenues and expenses

Although *Section 3055* does not mention the handling of intercompany receivables, payables, revenues and expenses, it is the authors' view that they should also be eliminated in the preparation of proportionate consolidated financial statements. However, due to the nature of this consolidation process, only the venturer's ownership percentage can be eliminated. To eliminate 100% of these items as is done in the full consolidation process would result in negative amounts because only the venturer's proportion of a joint venture's receivables or payables, revenues or expenses is available for elimination under the proportionate method.

Purchase discrepancies

The formation of a joint venture by its venturers cannot result in purchase discrepancies in the investment accounts of the venturers. However, if one of the founding venturers sells its ownership interest, the new venturer could pay an amount different than its interest in the carrying value of the joint venture's net assets, *resulting in a purchase discrepancy*. This purchase discrepancy would be allocated and amortized in the same manner illustrated previously for parent-subsidiary affiliations.

Illustration of the consolidation of a venturer and a joint venture

Explor Ltd. is a joint venture in which A Company has a 45% ownership interest. A Company, an original founder of Explor Ltd., uses the equity method to account for its investment, but has made no entries to its investment account for Year 4. The following are the financial statements of the two companies on December 31, Year 4:

<table>
<tr><td></td><td colspan="2" align="center">**INCOME STATEMENTS — YEAR 4**</td></tr>
<tr><td></td><td align="right">*A Company*</td><td align="right">*Explor Ltd.*</td></tr>
<tr><td>*Sales*</td><td align="right">*$900,000*</td><td align="right">*$300,000*</td></tr>
<tr><td>*Cost of sales*</td><td align="right">*$630,000*</td><td align="right">*$180,000*</td></tr>
<tr><td>*Miscellaneous expenses*</td><td align="right">*100,000*</td><td align="right">*40,000*</td></tr>
<tr><td>*Total*</td><td align="right">*$730,000*</td><td align="right">*$220,000*</td></tr>
<tr><td>*Net income*</td><td align="right">*$170,000*</td><td align="right">*$ 80,000*</td></tr>
</table>

<table>
<tr><td></td><td colspan="2" align="center">**BALANCE SHEETS — DECEMBER 31, YEAR 4**</td></tr>
<tr><td></td><td align="right">*A Company*</td><td align="right">*Explor Ltd.*</td></tr>
<tr><td>*Miscellaneous assets*</td><td align="right">*$654,500*</td><td align="right">*$277,000*</td></tr>
<tr><td>*Inventory*</td><td align="right">*110,000*</td><td align="right">*90,000*</td></tr>
<tr><td>*Investment in Explor Ltd.*</td><td align="right">*85,500*</td><td align="right">*—*</td></tr>
<tr><td>*Total*</td><td align="right">*$850,000*</td><td align="right">*$367,000*</td></tr>
<tr><td>*Miscellaneous liabilities*</td><td align="right">*$130,000*</td><td align="right">*$ 97,000*</td></tr>
<tr><td>*Capital stock*</td><td align="right">*300,000*</td><td align="right">*100,000*</td></tr>
<tr><td>*Retained earnings, January 1*</td><td align="right">*250,000*</td><td align="right">*90,000*</td></tr>
<tr><td>*Net income — Year 4*</td><td align="right">*170,000*</td><td align="right">*80,000*</td></tr>
<tr><td></td><td align="right">*$850,000*</td><td align="right">*$367,000*</td></tr>
</table>

Financial statements of a venturer and a joint venture

During Year 4, A Company sold merchandise totaling $110,000 to Explor Ltd. and recorded a gross profit of 30% on these sales. On December 31, Year 4, the inventory of Explor Ltd. contained items purchased from A Company for $22,000, and Explor Ltd. had a payable of $5,000 to

A Company on this date. A Company will use the proportionate consolidation method to report its investment in Explor Ltd. for Year 4.

The following are the calculations of the amounts used in the elimination of intercompany transactions in the preparation of the consolidated financial statements:

Intercompany sales and purchases

Total for the year	$110,000
A Company's ownership interest	45%
Amount eliminated	$ 49,500

Intercompany receivables and payables

Total at end of year	$ 5,000
A Company's ownership interest	45%
Amount eliminated	$ 2,250

Intercompany profits in inventory

Total at end of year ($22,000 × 30%)	$ 6,600
Profit considered realized — 55%	3,630
Unrealized — 45%	$ 2,970

The following explanations will clarify the calculations made:

1 Because the proportionate consolidation method will use 45% of Explor's financial statement items, we **eliminate only 45% of the intercompany revenues, expenses, receivables and payables**. If we eliminated 100% of these items we would be eliminating more than we are using in the consolidation process.

2 The inventory of Explor Ltd. contains an intercompany profit of $6,600 recorded by A Company. Because there is joint control, A Company has realized $3,630 of this profit by selling to the other unaffiliated ventures, and therefore only **A Company's 45% ownership interest is considered unrealized**.

3 Income tax allocation is required when timing differences occur. Assuming that A Company pays income tax at a rate of 40%, **the income tax effects** of the inventory profit elimination can be calculated as follows:

	Before Tax	40% Tax	After Tax
Inventory profit — A selling	$2,970	$1,188	$1,782

Because A Company has not recorded this year's equity method journal entries, we must calculate consolidated net income for Year 4 as follows:

Income of A Company		$170,000
Less: unrealized inventory profit		1,782
Adjusted net income		$168,218
Income of Explor Ltd.	$80,000	
A's ownership interest	45%	36,000
Consolidated net income		$204,218

A Company has used equity method prior to this year and therefore its retained earnings at the beginning of the year is equal to consolidated retained earnings. We can prepare the consolidated retained earnings statement for Year 4 as follows:

A COMPANY

Consolidated Statement of Retained Earnings
Year Ended December 31, Year 4

Balance January 1	$250,000
Net income	204,218
Balance December 31	$454,218

The preparation of the Year 4 consolidated statements without the use of a working paper is illustrated as follows:

A COMPANY

Consolidated Income Statement
Year Ended December 31, Year 4

(a)	
Sales ($900,000 + [45% × $300,000] − $49,500)	$985,500
Cost of sales $\quad\quad\quad\quad\quad\quad\quad\quad (a)\quad\quad\quad\quad (c)$	
($630,000 + [45% × $180,000] − $49,500 + $2,970)	$664,470
Miscellaneous expenses $\quad\quad\quad\quad\quad\quad (d)$	
($100,000 + [45% × $40,000] − $1,188)	116,812
Total	$781,282
Net income	$204,218

A COMPANY

Consolidated Balance Sheet
December 31, Year 4

Miscellaneous assets $\quad\quad\quad\quad\quad\quad (b)$		
($654,500 + [45% × $277,000] − $2,250)		$776,900
$\quad\quad\quad\quad\quad\quad\quad\quad\quad\quad\quad\quad\quad\quad (c)$		
Inventory ($110,000 + [45% × 90,000] − $2,970)		147,530
Deferred income tax	(d)	1,188
Total assets		$925,618
Miscellaneous liabilities $\quad\quad\quad\quad\quad\quad (b)$		
($130,000 + [45% × $97,000] − $2,250)		$171,400
Shareholders' equity		
Capital stock	$300,000	
Retained earnings	454,218	754,218
Total liabilities and shareholders' equity		$925,618

The amounts used in the preparation are explained as follows:

1 With the exception of shareholders' equity and deferred income tax the first two amounts used come from the individual financial statements and consist of 100% of A Company plus 45% of Explor Ltd.

2 The adjustment labelled (a) is the elimination of intercompany revenues and expenses.

3 The adjustment labelled (b) is the elimination of intercompany receivables and payables.

4 The adjustment labelled (c) is the elimination of the before tax unrealized inventory profit.

5 The adjustment labelled (d) is the elimination of the income tax on the unrealized inventory profit. It is assumed that miscellaneous expenses includes income tax expense.

6 The investment account and shareholders' equity of Explor Ltd. were eliminated in the following manner:

<table>
<tr><td>Elimination of investment account and shareholders' equity of joint venture at January 1, Year 4</td><td>Investment in Explor Ltd. ....</td><td></td><td>$85,500</td></tr>
<tr><td></td><td>Shareholders' equity of Explor Ltd.</td><td></td><td></td></tr>
<tr><td></td><td>Capital stock ....</td><td>$100,000</td><td></td></tr>
<tr><td></td><td>Retained earnings, January 1 ....</td><td>90,000</td><td></td></tr>
<tr><td></td><td>Total ....</td><td>$190,000</td><td></td></tr>
<tr><td></td><td>A Company's ownership interest ....</td><td>45%</td><td>85,500</td></tr>
<tr><td></td><td>Purchase discrepancy ....</td><td></td><td>$ —</td></tr>
</table>

7 Consolidated shareholders' equity consists of the capital stock of A Company plus consolidated retained earnings.

The calculation of consolidated net income (page 456) yields the amount that A Company uses when it prepares the following Year 4 equity method journal entry:

<table>
<tr><td>Venturer's equity method journal entry Year 4</td><td>Investment in Explor Ltd. ....</td><td>34,218</td><td></td></tr>
<tr><td></td><td>Equity earnings from Explor Ltd. ....</td><td></td><td>34,218</td></tr>
<tr><td></td><td>To record 45% of the net income of Explor Ltd. less the</td><td></td><td></td></tr>
<tr><td></td><td>holdback of aftertax unrealized profit in inventory</td><td></td><td></td></tr>
<tr><td></td><td>($36,000 − $1,782 = $34,218).</td><td></td><td></td></tr>
</table>

SEGMENT REPORTING

The preparation of consolidated financial statements has been illustrated in the chapters preceding this one. This form of financial reporting treats a group of companies as a single economic entity by *aggregating* the components of separate financial statements. When all companies within the entity were in the same line of business conducted in a single geographic area, this form of reporting was considered to be adequate to satisfy used needs. However, with the development of *conglomerate businesses*, where the companies comprising the economic entity were in diverse lines of business, often conducted in more than one country, it was found that this single entity concept of reporting was inadequate. Economic prospects differ between countries, various lines of business often react in a different way to economic cycles, the components of earnings for different lines of business are often not similar, etc. For example, if the beverage line is not performing well, but real estate development is booming, consolidated financial statements of a company doing business in both areas will not necessarily disclose these facts. User needs might be more adequately met if there was some form of *disaggregation* of the financial data that was used to prepare the consolidated statements, and if this data was disclosed as a supplement to these financial statements. In 1979, *Handbook Section 1700* was issued, in which disaggregation was achieved by dividing an entity's activities into *industry segments*, *geographic segments*, and in addition by providing information about the amount of the company's *export sales*.

Section 1700 gives only general guidelines as to the identification of both industry and geographic segments. It suggests that profit centres may be a logical starting point in determining the products and services that might form an industry segment. The determination guidelines for geographic areas are even more vague than those provided for industry segments. This lack of direction leaves the *identification of segments* almost entirely to the *discretion of management*. Because of this, the segmented information provided will aid the user in assessing the performance of the company for the year, and will allow comparison with prior years, but it will not necessarily allow comparisons with other companies whose overall operations are similar, but who identify their segments in a different manner.

Section 1700 definitions

Paragraph 10 of the Section provides the following definitions:

1 *Industry segment* is an enterprise's distinguishable component which provides products or services or groups of related products or services, primarily to outside customers.

2 *Geographic segment* is a single operation or group of operations, which generate revenue, incur costs and have assets employed, and are located in a particular geographic area. *Domestic operations* are considered to be a *separate geographic segment*.

3 *Segment revenue* is revenue directly attributable to a segment, derived from sales to outside customers and from inter-segment sales or transfers of products and services. *Not included* are revenue earned at the head office or corporate level, income from investments accounted for by the equity method, interest and dividend income from assets not included in a segment's identifiable assets, extraordinary gains, and interest on advances to other segments unless the segment's operations are primarily financial in nature.

4 *Segment expense* is an expense directly attributable to a segment and those expenses that can be allocated on a reasonable basis to the segment for whose

benefit the expense was incurred. ***Not included*** are general corporate expenses loss on investments accounted for by the equity method, income taxes, extra ordinary losses, minority interest, and interest expense unless the segment's oper ations are primarily financial in nature.

5 ***Segment operating profit or loss*** is the difference between segment revenu and segment expense.

6 ***Identifiable assets*** are all tangible and intangible assets attributable to a seg ment, including the portion used jointly by two or more segments that can b allocated on a reasonable basis. ***Not included*** are advances to or investments it another segment except where the operations of the segment holding this type o asset are primarily financial in nature and such items are similar to those arisin from transactions with outside customers.

The Section requires the same accounting principles to be used for seg mented information as were used for the financial statements, and the reinstatement to a segment of any intercompany transactions eliminated ir the preparation of the financial statements, subject to the specific exclusions contained in the definitions.

Operations in different industries

To comply with the requirements of ***Section 1700***, accountants must carry out the following:

1 Specify the industry segments of the enterprise.
2 Compute the following for the specified segments: revenue, operating profit or loss, and identifiable assets.
3 Determine which of the specified segments are ***significant***, and thus possibly ***reportable***.
4 Test for adequacy and dominance.
5 Develop the required data for disclosure.

Determination of reportable industry segments

After management has identified the enterprise's industry segments, the reportable segments must be determined. The Section's requirements are as follows:

An industry segment that is considered to be significant to the enterprise should be identified as reportable. (1700.27)
The selection and determination of reportable industry segments should be such that they comprise a major portion of the enterprise's total operations. (1700.28)

A major portion of the enterprise's total operations would be achieved if at least 75% of the total operations (based on reported revenues excluding inter-segment sales and transfers) is contained in the industry segments identified. This 75% test is sometimes referred to as the ***adequacy test*** The section also contains a test for a ***dominant segment***. A segment would be considered dominant and not reportable, if the total of its revenue, operating profit and identifiable assets account for more than 90% of the combined total for all industry segments, and no other segment is identified as reportable.

A segment is **reportable** if it is **considered to be significant**. The Section recommends that a segment would be considered significant and therefore reportable if any one of the following three conditions is present:

(a) its revenue is 10 percent or more of the total revenue of all industry segments (including inter-segment sales and transfers);

(b) the absolute amount of its operating profit or loss is 10 percent or more of the greater, in absolute amount, of:
   (i) the total operating profit of all industry segments that earned an operating profit; and
   (ii) the total operating loss of all industry segments that incurred an operating loss;

(c) its identifiable assets are 10 percent or more of the total identifiable assets of all industry segments.   (1700.23)

To illustrate the determination of the significant industry segments of a business enterprise, assume that the four industry segments of Diverso, Inc., had the following revenue, operating profit or losses, and identifiable assets for the year ended December 31, Year 5:

Data for test for significant segments

	Segment A	B	C	D	Total
Revenue	$ 60,000	$ 80,000	$ 20,000	$ 50,000	$ 210,000
Operating profit (loss)	(20,000)	30,000	(10,000)	30,000	30,000
Identifiable assets	500,000	400,000	100,000	300,000	1,300,000

Segments A, B, and D of Diverso, Inc., meet the revenue test for significance because their revenue exceeds $21,000, which is 10% of total revenue for all four segments ($210,000 × 0.10 = $21,000). Segment C does not meet the revenue test for significance; its revenue of $20,000 is less than the $21,000 minimum. However, Segment C does meet the operating profit or loss test for significance, because the absolute amount of its operating loss — $10,000 — exceeds $6,000, which is 10% of total operating profit of Segment B and Segment D [($30,000 + $30,000) × 0.10 = $6,000]. The $60,000 total operating profit was used for the test because it exceeded the $30,000 absolute amount total of the combined operating losses of Segment A and Segment C ($20,000 + $10,000 = $30,000). Because all four industry segments meet either the revenue test or the operating profit or loss test for significance, the identifiable assets test is not used.

Disclosure of industry segments

Paragraph 33 requires the following disclosure:

A general description of the products and services from which each reportable industry segment derives its revenue should be provided.

Disclosure of the following data should be made for each reportable industry segment and, in aggregate, for the remainder of the enterprise's industry segments:

(a) segment revenue derived from sales to customers outside the enterprise;
(b) segment revenue derived from inter-segment sales or transfers and the basis of accounting therefor;
(c) segment operating profit or loss, the amount of depreciation, amortization and depletion expense, and any unusual items included in determining segment operating profit or loss; and
(d) total carrying amount of identifiable assets at the end of the fiscal year and the amount of capital expenditure for the period.

A reconciliation of the aggregate segment revenue, aggregate segment operating profit or loss and aggregate identifiable assets to the sales, net income and total assets reported in the financial statements of the enterprise should be provided.
(1700.33)

When an enterprise has a dominant industry segment, this fact should be disclosed together with a general description of the products and services from which revenue is derived.
(1700.34)

Operations in different geographic areas

The Section also requires the reporting of geographic segments considered to be significant. Adequacy or dominance tests are not used for geographic segments. A foreign geographic segment is significant if one of the two conditions is present:

(a) its revenue generated from sales to customers outside the enterprise is 10 percent of more of the total revenue reported in the income statement of the enterprise; or
(b) its identifiable assets are 10 percent or more of the total assets reported in the enterprise's balance sheet.
(1700.42)

The disclosure required for foreign geographic segments is similar to that of industry segments. The section's disclosure requirements are as follows:

The location of each reportable foreign geographic segment should be disclosed. Disclosure of the following data should be made for each reportable foreign geographic segment, in total for all other foreign geographic segments when they are in the aggregate identified as significant and for the domestic geographic segment:

(a) segment revenue derived from sales to customers outside the enterprise;
(b) segment revenue derived from sales or transfers between geographic segments and the basis of accounting therefor;
(c) segment operating profit or loss or, where appropriate, some other measure of profitability *(information as to after-tax profitability may be more appropriate when the tax structure applicable to the reportable foreign geographic segment is substantially different from that experienced by the enterprise's domestic operation);* and

(d) total carrying amount of identifiable assets at the end of the fiscal year.
A reconciliation of the aggregate segment revenue, aggregate measure of profitability and aggregate identifiable assets to the sales, net income and total assets reported in the financial statements of the enterprise should be provided. **(1700.44)**

Export sales

In addition to disclosing industry and geographic segments, an enterprise is required to disclose the sales to foreign countries made by its domestic operation, when these export sales account for more than 10% of total revenue.

An example of disclosure of segment information

The following illustration indicates how segmented information might be disclosed. While **Section 1700** suggests that the information should be presented in comparative form, only the current year's data is shown in the illustration. Many companies locate this information in the footnotes to their financial statements.

CONGLOM LTD.
Industry Segments — Current Year

	Food Products	Forest Products	Other	Eliminations	Consolidated
Sales — outside customers ...	$11,250	$25,000	$ 5,000		$ 41,250
— intersegment	1,000	800		$(1,800)	
Total revenue	$12,250	$25,800	$ 5,000	$(1,800)	$ 41,250
Operating profit	$ 2,400	$ 6,400	$ 380	$ (10)	$ 9,170
Interest expense					(700)
Income taxes					(2,800)
Investment income					1,000
General corporate expense ..					(1,400)
Minority interest					(200)
Net income					$ 5,070
Identifiable assets	$34,000	$53,000	$17,500	$ (60)	$ 104,440
Corporate assets					8,200
Investment in affiliates					900
Total assets					$ 113,540
Capital expenditure	90	$ 180	$ 300		
Depreciation	$ 1,300	$ 3,500	$ 670		

CONGLOM LTD.

Geographic Segments — Current Year

	Canada	U.S.A.	Other	Eliminations	Consolidated
Sales — outside customers . . .	$ 6,500	$30,750	$ 4,000		$ 41,250
— intersegment	3,000	5,000	1,500	$(9,500)	
Total revenue	$ 9,500	$35,750	$ 5,500	$(9,500)	$ 41,250
Operating profit	$ 1,970	$ 7,000	$ 210	$ (10)	$ 9,170
Interest expense					(700)
Income taxes					(2,800)
Investment income					1,000
General corporate expense . .					(1,400)
Minority interest					(200)
Net income					$ 5,070
Identifiable assets	$29,380	$63,120	$12,000	$ (60)	$ 104,440
Corporate assets					8,200
Investment in affiliates					900
Total assets					$ 113,540

Export sales Canadian operations include export sales of $4,300 to customers in the United States and Europe.

Reporting the disposal of a segment of a business enterprise

To this point, we have discussed accounting standards for financial reporting for segments of a business enterprise. We conclude our consideration of segment reporting with the reporting for effects of the disposal of a segment of a business enterprise.

In 1973, the Accounting Principles Board issued *APB Opinion No. 30*, "Reporting the Results of Operations . . ." The APB's conclusions included the following with respect to disposal of a segment of a business enterprise:[1]

> For purposes of this Opinion, the term *discontinued operations* refers to the operations of a segment of a business . . . that has been sold, abandoned, spun off, or otherwise disposed of or, although still operating, is the subject of a formal plan for disposal. . . . The Board concludes that the results of continuing operations should be reported separately from discontinued operations and that any gain or loss from disposal of a segment of a business . . . should be reported in conjunction with the related results of discontinued operations and

1 APB Opinion No. 30, "Reporting the Results of Operations — . . . ," AICPA (New York: 1973), pp. 558–559.

not as an extraordinary item. Accordingly, operations of a segment that has been or will be discontinued should be reported separately as a component of income before extraordinary items and the cumulative effect of accounting changes (if applicable) in the following manner:

Income from continuing operations before income taxes	$XXXX	
Provision for income taxes	XXX	
Income from continuing operations		$XXXX
Discontinued operations (Note ____):		
Income (loss) from operations of discontinued Division X (less applicable income taxes of $____)		XXXX
Loss on disposal of Division X, including provision of $____ for operating losses during phase-out period (less applicable income taxes of $____)	XXXX	XXXX
Net income		$XXXX

Amounts of income taxes applicable to the results of discontinued operations and the gain or loss from disposal of the segment should be disclosed on the face of the income statement or in related notes. Revenues applicable to the discontinued operations should be separately disclosed in the related notes.

The provisions of *APB Opinion No. 30* are discussed in the following sections.

Income from Continuing Operations   The purpose of the income from continuing operations amount is to provide a basis of comparison in the comparative income statements of a business enterprise that has discontinued a segment of its operations. In order for the income from continuing operations amounts to be comparable, the operating results of the discontinued segment of its operations *must be excluded from income from continuing operations for all accounting periods presented in comparative income statements*. For example, in comparative income statements for the three years ended December 31, Year 7, for Wexler Company, which disposed of one of its five divisions during Year 7, the income from continuing operations amounts for Years 5 and 6, as well as for Year 7, exclude the operating results of the discontinued division.

Income (Loss) from Discontinued Operations   The income or loss, net of applicable income taxes, of Wexler Company's discontinued operations (division) is included in its entirety in this section of Wexler's income statement for Years 5 and 6. For Year 7, the net-of-tax income or loss of the discontinued operations is for the period from January 1, Year 7, until the *measurement date*, defined as the date on which management of Wexler committed itself to a formal plan for disposal of the division. Assuming a measurement date of September 30, Year 7, Wexler's Year 7 income statement would include the income or loss of the discontinued operations, net of income taxes, for the nine months ended September 30, Year 7, under the caption "Income (loss) from operations of discontinued Division _____."

An example of the disclosure of discontinued operations taken from the annual report of an American company follows:

	Year ended Sept. 30,	
	Year 10	Year 9
Income from continuing operations	$ 94,024,000	$60,919,000
Discontinued operations (**Note X**):		
Income from operations (less applicable income taxes of $10,450,000 and $8,300,000, respectively)	12,294,000	9,526,000
Gain on sale (less applicable income taxes of $25,976,000)	46,424,000	
Net income	$152,742,000	$70,445,000

Note X: Discontinued Operations

On August 25, Year 10, the Company sold its Ogas Division, for $130,000,000 cash. The Ogas Division was engaged principally in the manufacture of equipment for drilling of oil and gas wells. As a result of this disposition, the Company recognized a gain on disposal of $46,424,000, net of related income taxes of $25,976,000.

The Year 10 results of operations of the discontinued Ogas Division have been segregated in the income statement to show separately the results of continuing operations. Similarly, Year 9 and prior income statements have been restated to show the same segregation. The Ogas Division results of operations are reported without allocation of general corporate expenses or interest expense. The net sales of the Ogas Division were $110,009,000 and $88,226,000 for the period ended August 24, Year 10 (the disposal date), and the year ended September 30, Year 9, respectively.

There is no Canadian pronouncement comparable to APB Opinion No. 30. *Section 1600 of the CICA Handbook* devotes one sentence to this topic as follows:

In the period of disposal it is desirable to report the results of continuing operations separately from the results of discontinued operations; this segregation would be made for both the current period and any prior periods which are presented for comparative purposes.

(**paragraph 72**)

This paragraph refers to the disposal of a subsidiary and its wording seems far from being mandatory. Also it would appear that disposals of segments which are not subsidiaries would not fall under the general guidelines suggested by the paragraph. However the concept of separate reporting for discontinued operations seems to be one that should be used, because this additional information would be useful in the evaluation of an enterprise's future prospects. Canadian companies whose shares trade on U.S. stock exchanges would be required to report this information. The only portion of APB Opinion No. 30 that is contrary to a Canadian pronouncement is the treatment of the gains or losses on the segment disposal. Under **Handbook Section 3480**, the gain or loss on the disposal of a significant business segment is an **extraordinary item**, whereas under **APB Opinion 30** it is to be reported before extraordinary items and therefore seems to be excluded from being such an item. In the opinion of the authors, Canadian companies should follow the American practice of separate reporting of the operating results of discontinued operations, and the Canadian practice of presenting the gains (losses) from disposals as extraordinary items.

INTERIM FINANCIAL REPORTS

Generally, financial statements are issued for the fiscal year of a business enterprise. However, many enterprises issue complete financial statements for interim accounting periods during the course of a fiscal year. For example, a closely held company with outstanding bank loans may be required to provide monthly or quarterly financial statements to the lending bank. However, interim financial statements usually are associated with the **quarterly reports** issued by publicly owned companies to their shareholders in order to satisfy the reporting requirements of regulatory bodies.

Problems in interim financial reports

The form, content, and accounting practices for interim financial reports were left to the discretion of business enterprises until 1971 when the CICA issued **Handbook Section 1750** "Interim Financial Reporting to Shareholders." In 1973, **APB Opinion No. 28**, covering this topic, was issued in the United States. Prior to this, there were unresolved problems regarding interim financial reports, including the following:

1 Enterprises employed a wider variety of accounting practices and estimating techniques for interim financial reports than they used in the annual financial statements examined by independent auditors. The enterprises' implicit view was that any misstatements in interim financial reports would be corrected by auditors' adjustments for the annual financial statements.

2 Seasonal fluctuations in revenue and irregular incurrence of costs and expenses during the course of a business enterprise's fiscal year limited the comparability of operating results for interim periods of the fiscal year. Furthermore, time constraints in the issuance of interim statements limited the available time to accumulate end-of-period data for inventories, payables, and related expenses.

3 Accountants held two divergent views on the theoretical issues underlying interim financial statements. These differing views are described below:

    a Under the **discrete approach** each interim period is treated as a distinct accounting period, with accounting principles applied essentially in the same manner as would be the case in an annual period.

    b Under the **integral approach** each interim period is treated as an integral part of the annual period, with accruals and deferrals based on expectations of what will happen in the full year.

The problems discussed in the preceding section led to a number of examples of published interim income statements with substantial quarterly earnings, and the income statements for the year showing a net loss.

Handbook Section 1750

Handbook Section 1750 provides minimum disclosure requirements and broad guidelines regarding the accounting practices that should be followed in interim periods. The section suggests that interim statements may show less detail than annual statements but should disclose:

(a) sales or gross revenues;
(b) investment income;
(c) depreciation, depletion and amortization for the period;
(d) interest expense;
(e) income tax expense;
(f) income (loss) before extraordinary items;
(g) extraordinary items (net of tax);
(h) net income (loss);
(i) basic and fully diluted earnings per share;
(j) significant changes in assets, liabilities and shareholders' equity, which could be in the form of a statement of changes in financial position.

Information with regard to changes in accounting principles, descriptions of the nature of extraordinary items, and events occurring subsequent to the statement should also be provided. With the exception of loss carry-forwards, extraordinary items should be recognized in the interim period in which they occur, and not prorated over the year's interim period.

A quarterly interim period is suggested and each interim report should contain information for the current year to date, with comparative figures for the corresponding period in the preceding year.

Section 1750 suggests a preference for the discrete approach, with the following statement contained in paragraph 13:

Interim financial reports should present information with respect to the results of operations for a specified period rather than a proration of expected results for an annual period.

Acknowledgement is made of the estimation difficulties involved in allocating and matching costs when the period involved is less than one year. The pronouncement on the accounting treatment for interim reports is contained in the following paragraph:

The preparation of financial data should be based on accounting principles and practices consistent with those used in the preparation of annual financial statements. Where necessary, appropriate estimates and assumptions should be made to match costs and revenues. Where, due either to the nature of the item or the short period involved, an estimate may be subject to substantial adjustment at the year end, disclosure of this fact should be made. **(1750.14)**

While the first sentence seems to imply the discrete approach, the second sentence contains concepts that would seem to be necessary under the integral approach. (In contrast, *APB Opinion No. 28* specifically adopts the integral approach.) The remainder of the section provides approaches that might be taken to solve some of the problems associated with interim period estimates.

Income taxes

A specific problem arises when a company is subject to a two-rate tax system. Should the lower rate apply only to the earlier interim periods or should it apply to all interim periods? The Section suggests that the lower rate should apply to all interim periods and that two acceptable methods can be used to achieve this:

1 Allocate income subject to the low rate evenly over interim periods,
2 Estimate the total income for the year, and calculate an effective rate of tax using the two rates. This calculated effective rate would be used for each interim period.

Losses in an interim period should show tax recoveries if the loss can be carried back to prior periods but a tax recovery due to loss carry-forward should not be recognized unless virtual certainty is present.

Unrecognized loss carry-forwards from prior years can be treated under either of the following methods:

1 recognize in the final interim period, or
2 prorate over all interim periods of the year if virtual certainty exists.

These previously unrecognized loss carry-forwards would be shown as extraordinary items on the interim statements.

Section 1750 also indicates that income tax allocation should be used in interim reports.

Inventories

The determination of interim inventory should be based on the same methods used for the year-end inventory, and if appropriate the retail or gross profit methods could be used. The Section indicates that declines in market or replacement values, and temporary depletions of lifo layers, should be taken into account when determining interim inventories. How these valuation problems should be handled is not mentioned. *APB Opinion No. 28* is much more specific regarding these two problems with interim inventories, and might serve as a guide for Canadian accountants. The Opinion provided the following guidelines with respect to determining cost of goods sold for interim financial reports:[2]

1 Enterprises that use the *lifo inventory method* and *temporarily* deplete base layer of inventories during an interim reporting period should include in cost of goods sold for the interim period the estimated *cost of replacing the depleted lifo base layer*.

   To illustrate, assume that Megan Company, which uses the lifo inventory method, temporarily depleted its base layer of inventories with a cost of $80,000 during the second quarter of the year ending December 31, Year 6. Replacement cost of the depleted base layer was $100,000 on June 30, Year 6. In addition to the usual debit to Cost of Goods Sold and credit to Inventories for the quarter ended

---

2 APB Opinion No. 28, "Interim Financial Reporting," AICPA (New York: 1973), pp. 524–525.

June 30, Year 6, which would include the $80,000 amount from the base layer, Megan prepares the following journal entry on June 30, Year 6:

Cost of goods sold ($100,000 − $80,000)	20,000	
Liability arising from depletion of base layer of lifo		
inventories		20,000

To record obligation to replenish temporarily depleted base layer of lifo inventories.

Assuming merchandise with a total cost of $172,000 was purchased by Megan on July 6, Year 6, the following journal entry is required:

Inventories ($172,000 − $20,000)	152,000	
Liability arising from depletion of base layer of lifo		
inventories	20,000	
Accounts Payable		172,000

To record purchase of merchandise and restoration of depleted base layer of lifo inventories.

2 Lower-of-cost-or-market write-downs of inventories should be provided for interim periods as for complete fiscal years, unless the interim date market declines in inventory are considered *temporary*, and not applicable at the end of the fiscal year. If an inventory market write-down in one interim period is offset by an inventory market price *increase* in a subsequent interim period, *a gain is recognized in the subsequent period to the extent of the loss recognized in preceding interim periods of the fiscal year*.

For example, assume that Reynolds Company, which uses lower-of-cost-or-market fifo accounting for its single merchandise item, had 10,000 units of merchandise with fifo cost of $50,000, or $5 a unit, in inventory at the beginning of Year 3. Assume further for simplicity that Reynolds made no purchases during Year 3. Quarterly sales and end-of-quarter replacement costs for inventory were as follows during Year 3:

Quarter	Quarterly sales (units)	End-of-quarter inventory replacement cost (per unit)
1	2,000	$6
2	1,500	4
3	2,000	7
4	1,200	3

If the market decline in the second quarter was not considered to be ***temporary***, Reynolds Company's cost of goods sold for the four quarters of Year 3 would be computed as follows:

Computation of quarterly cost of goods sold

Quarter	Computation for quarter	Cost of goods sold For quarter	Cumulative
1	2,000 × $5	$10,000	$10,000
2	(1,500 × $5) + (6,500 × $1)*	14,000	24,000
3	(2,000 × $4) − (4,500 × $1)†	3,500	27,500
4	(1,200 × $5) + (3,300 × $2)‡	12,600	40,100

*6,500 units remaining in inventory multiplied by $1 write-down to lower replacement cost.
†4,500 units remaining in inventory multiplied by $1 write-up to original cost.
‡3,300 units remaining in inventory multiplied by $2 write-down to lower replacement cost.

The $40,100 cumulative cost of goods sold for Reynolds Company for Year 3 may be verified as follows:

Verification of cumulative cost of goods sold

6,700 units sold during Year 3, at $5 fifo cost per unit	$33,500
Write-down of Year 3 ending inventory to replacement cost (3,300 units × $2)	6,600
Cost of goods sold for Year 3	$40,100

Alternative verification:

Cost of goods available for sale (10,000 × $5)	$50,000
Less: Ending inventory, at lower of cost or market (3,300 × $3)	9,900
Cost of goods sold for Year 3	$40,100

Depreciation

While an interim period's depreciation expense should be determined in the same manner as the expense for this annual period, estimation may have to be made for year-end balances in assets if the annual expense is based on this amount.

Annually-determined costs and revenues

Certain expenses and revenues can only be determined at the year end. Employee bonuses, and rental expense or revenue which are based on a full year's sales volume, are examples. ***Section 1750*** suggests that provisions for these items based on projected annual amounts should be made in interim reports.

Conclusions on interim financial reports

While ***Section 1750*** appears to favour the discrete approach to interim reporting, its guidelines with regard to cost estimations and allocations are so general that considerable latitude appears available in implementation. Because of this, there are probably no great differences between Canadian and American reporting practices even though *APB Opinion 28* has adopted the integral approach.

REVIEW QUESTIONS

1 Why has the joint venture form of organization gained in popularity in recent years?

2 In what way is the proportionate consolidation method different from the full consolidation method?

3 How does the accounting treatment of an unrealized intercompany asset profit differ between a parent-subsidiary affiliation and a venturer-joint venture affiliation?

4 Y Company has a 55% interest in Z Company. Does this mean that Z Company is a subsidiary of Y Company? Explain.

5 Describe the reporting requirements of *Handbook Section 3055* for an investment in a joint venture. (Assume that there are no intercompany profits to be considered.)

6 What is meant by joint control?

7 What unique reporting provision is contained in *Section 3055* of the *Handbook*?

8 Why did the development of conglomerates lead to the use of segment reporting?

9 Does segment reporting aid financial statement users in comparing the results of different companies? Explain.

10 Is the concept of segment reporting consistent with the theory of consolidated financial statements? Explain.

11 Outline the conditions which determine significance for both industry segments and geographic segments.

12 In what manner is a loss on disposal of a segment reported differently in the U.S.A. as compared to Canada? Explain.

13 The United States has chosen the integral approach to report interim results, while Canada appears to take the discrete approach. Does this mean that there are great differences in interim reporting between the two countries? Explain.

14 Explain the two methods for the computation of income tax provisions in interim reports when a company is subject to a two-rate tax system.

15 Differentiate between the discrete and integral approaches to interim reporting.

16 Explain the handling of income taxes on losses in interim reports.

17 How might the lower-of-cost-or-market accounting for inventories be applied in interim financial reports? Explain.

EXERCISES

Ex 11-1 R Company has a 52% interest in V Company, and uses the equity method to account for its investment. The following summarized balance sheets were prepared at the end of the current year:

	R Company	V Company
Current assets	$ 970,800	$100,000
Non-current assets	1,200,000	400,000
Investment in V Company	135,200	
Total	$2,306,000	$500,000
Current liabilities	$ 130,000	$ 60,000
Non-current liabilities	726,000	180,000
Capital stock	950,000	150,000
Retained earnings	500,000	110,000
Total	$2,306,000	$500,000

Prepare a consolidated balance sheet at the end of the current year assuming:
a V Company is a subsidiary **b** V Company is a joint venture

Ex 11-2 T Company, a joint venture, was formed at the beginning of the current year. S Company, a venturer, has a 30% interest in T Company. During the year the following intercompany transactions occurred:
(1) T Company paid $10,000 interest and $50,000 management fees to S Company.
(2) S Company paid $30,000 rent to T Company.
The following abbreviated income statements were prepared at the end of the current year:

	S Company	T Company
Revenues	$500,000	$180,000
Expenses	210,000	70,000
Net income	$290,000	$110,000

The revenues of both companies are derived entirely from the sale of goods and services.
Prepare a consolidated income statement for the current year.

Ex 11-3 L Company is 60% owned by M Company. At the end of the current year, L Company reported a net income of $70,000 and its year-end inventory contained an unrealized aftertax profit of $15,000.
Prepare M Company's equity method journal entries for the current year if
a L is a subsidiary **b** L is a joint venture

Ex 11-4 Assume the same facts as are given in Exercise 11-3 except that the $15,000 profit is contained in the inventory of M Company.
Prepare M Company's equity method journal entries for the current year if:
a L is a subsidiary **b** L is a joint venture

Ex 11-5 Crossley Company had net income of $600,000 for the year ended December 31, Year 8, after inclusion of the following special events that occurred during the year:
(1) The decision was made on January 2 to discontinue the cinder block manufacturing segment.
(2) The cinder block manufacturing segment was sold on July 1.
(3) Operating income from January 2 to June 30 for the cinder block manufacturing segment amounted to $90,000 before income taxes.
(4) Cinder block manufacturing equipment with a carrying amount of $250,000 was sold for $100,000.

Crossley was subject to income taxes at the rate of 40%.

a Compute Crossley's income from continuing operations for Year 8.

b Compute Crossley's total income taxes (expenses and allocated) for Year 8.

Ex 11-6 Canton Company allocates indirect expenses that benefit its three industry segments on the basis of net sales to unaffiliated customers. For the fiscal year ended April 30, Year 4, relevant segment data were as follows:

	Segment A	Segment B	Segment C
Revenue:			
Net sales to unaffiliated customers	$500,000	$300,000	$200,000
Intersegment transfers out	80,000	40,000	20,000
Costs and expenses:			
Direct expenses	400,000	100,000	200,000
Intersegment transfers in	30,000	60,000	50,000

Indirect expenses of Canton Company for the year ended April 30, Year 4, totaled $100,000.

Compute for each industry segment of Canton Company the following amounts for the year ended April 30, Year 4: revenue, operating expenses, operating profit or loss. Use a column for each industry segment, as shown above.

Ex 11-7 Data with respect to the foreign geographic area operations of Emmet Company for the year ended December 31, Year 3, follow:

	Latin America	Africa	Southeast Asia	Western Europe	Total
Net sales to outsiders . . .	$40,000	$20,000	$25,000	$ 5,000	$90,000
Interarea transfers out . . .	2,000	4,000	1,000	3,000	10,000
Interarea transfers in	4,000	3,000	2,000	1,000	10,000
Direct expenses	9,000	6,000	5,000	10,000	30,000
Indirect expenses					20,000

Foreign Geographic Areas

Emmet allocates indirect expenses to industry segments only.

Determine if each foreign geographic area of Emmet Company is significant for the year ended December 31, Year 3. Disregard identifiable assets of the foreign geographic areas.

Ex 11-8 On January 2, Year 6, Luigi Company paid property taxes of $40,000 on its plant assets for Year 6. In March, Year 6, Luigi made customary annual major repairs to plant assets in the amount of $120,000. The repairs will benefit the entire Year 6. In April, Year 6, Luigi incurred a $420,000 loss from a market decline of inventories that was considered to be permanent.

Show how the above items are reported in Luigi's quarterly income statements for Year 6.

Ex 11-9 Tovar Company's accounting records for the year ended August 31, Year 4, include the following data with respect to its Wallis Division. Sale of that division to Expansive Enterprises, Inc., for $300,000 took place on August 31, Year 4.

Wallis Division:

Net sales, year ended Aug. 31, Year 4 . . . . *$200,000*

Costs and expenses, year ended Aug. 31, Year 4 . . . . *150,000*

Carrying amount of net assets, Aug. 31, Year 4 . . . . *330,000*

Tovar's combined federal and provincial income tax rate is 60%. For the year ended August 31, Year 4, Tovar had $640,000 income from continuing operations before income taxes.

Prepare a partial income statement for Tovar Company for the year ended August 31, Year 4, to present the information given.

Ex 11-10 Lundy Company sells a single product, which it purchases from three different vendors. On May 1, Year 8, Lundy's inventory of the product consisted of 1,000 units priced at fifo cost of $7,500. Lundy's merchandise transactions for the year ended April 30, Year 9, were as follows:

Quarter	Units purchased	Cost per Unit purchased	Units sold	End-of-quarter replacement cost per unit
1	5,000	$8.00	4,500	$8.50
2	6,000	8.50	7,000	9.00
3	8,000	9.00	6,500	8.50*
4	6,000	8.50	5,500	9.50

*Decline not considered to be temporary.

Compute Lundy Company's cost of goods sold for each of the four quarters of the year ended April 30, Year 9. Show computations.

Ex 11-11 Companies O, P, Q and R each have a 25% interest in JV Inc. Company Q is affiliated with Company P. You are preparing the consolidated statements of Company P and JV Inc. The inventory of JV Inc. contains items purchased from Company P in which a $5,000 gross profit was recorded.

Assuming a 40% tax rate, calculate the amount of aftertax profit that should be eliminated in the consolidation process.

CASES

Case 11-1 The **CICA Handbook** requires the reporting of financial data for segments of a business enterprise.

Instructions
a What does financial reporting for segments of a business enterprise involve?
b Identify the reasons why financial data should be reported for segments of a business enterprise.
c Identify the possible disadvantages of reporting financial data for segments of a business enterprise.
d Identify the accounting difficulties inherent in segment reporting.

Case 11-2 Nanson Company, a publicly owned corporation listed on a major stock exchange, forecasted operations for the year ending December 31, Year 5, as shown at the top of page 476. Nanson has operated profitably for many years and has experienced a

NANSON COMPANY
Forecasted Income Statement
For Year Ending December 31, Year 5

Net sales (1,000,000 units)	$6,000,000
Cost of goods sold	3,600,000
Gross profit on sales	$2,400,000
Operating expenses	1,400,000
Operating income	$1,000,000
Nonoperating revenue and expenses	-0-
Income before income taxes	$1,000,000
Income taxes expense (current and deferred)	550,000
Net income	$ 450,000
Earnings per share of common stock	$4.50

seasonal pattern of sales volume and production similar to the following ones forecasted for Year 5:

Sales volume is expected to follow a quarterly pattern of 10%, 20%, 35%, 35%, respectively, because of the seasonality of the industry. Also, due to production and storage capacity limitations it is expected that production will follow a pattern of 20%, 25%, 30%, 25%, per quarter, respectively.

At the conclusion of the first quarter of Year 5, the controller of Nanson prepared and issued the following interim income statement:

NANSON COMPANY
Income Statement
For Quarter Ended March 31, Year 5

Net sales (100,000 units)	$ 600,000
Cost of goods sold	360,000
Gross profit on sales	$ 240,000
Operating expenses	275,000
Operating loss	$ (35,000)
Loss from warehouse explosion	(175,000)
Loss before income taxes	$(210,000)
Income taxes expense	-0-
Net loss	$(210,000)
Loss per share of common stock	$(2.10)

The following additional information is available for the first quarter just completed, but was not included in the information released by Nanson:

(1) Nanson uses a standard cost system in which standards are set at currently attainable levels on an annual basis. At the end of the first quarter, underapplied fixed factory overhead (volume variance) of $50,000 was treated as an asset. Production during the first quarter was 200,000 units, of which 100,000 were sold.

(2) The operating expenses were forecasted on a basis of $900,000 fixed expenses for the year plus $0.50 variable expenses per unit sold.

(3) The warehouse explosion loss met the conditions of an extraordinary loss. The warehouse had a carrying amount of $320,000; $145,000 was recovered from

insurance on the warehouse. No other gains or losses are anticipated this year from similar events or transactions, nor has Nanson had any similar losses in preceding years; thus, the full loss will be deductible as an ordinary loss for income tax purposes.

(4) The effective rate for federal and provincial taxes combined is expected to average 55% of income before income taxes for Year 5. There are no permanent differences between pre-tax accounting income and taxable income.

(5) Earnings per share were computed on the basis of 100,000 shares of common stock outstanding. Nanson has only one class of capital stock issued, no long-term debt outstanding, no stock option plan, and no warrants to acquire common stock outstanding.

Instructions

a Identify the weaknesses in form and content of Nanson Company's interim income statement, without reference to the additional information.

b For each of the five items of additional information, indicate the preferable treatment for interim reporting purposes and explain why that treatment is preferable.

Case 11-3 **a** In order to understand generally accepted accounting principles with respect to accounting for and reporting on segments of a business enterprise, as stated in *Handbook Section 1700*, it is necessary to be familiar with certain unique terminology.

Instructions With respect to segments of a business enterprise, explain the following terms:

(1) *Industry segment*
(2) *Segment revenue*
(3) *Segment expense*
(4) *Identifiable assets*

b A central issue in reporting on industry segments of a business enterprise is the determination of which segments are reportable.

Instructions

(1) What are the tests to determine whether or not an industry segment is reportable?

(2) What is the test to determine if enough industry segments have been separately reported on?

Case 11-4 In *Statement of Financial Accounting Concepts No. 1*, the Financial Accounting Standards Board states the following two objectives of financial reporting:

"Financial reporting should provide information to help present and potential investors, creditors and other users in assessing the amounts, timing, and uncertainty of prospective cash receipts from dividends or interest, and the proceeds from the sale, redemption, or maturity of securities or loans."

"Financial reporting should provide information about the economic resources of an enterprise, the claims to those resources (obligations of the enterprise to transfer resources to other entities and owners' equity), and the effects of transactions, events, and circumstances that change its resources and claims to those resources."

Instructions Listed below are two procedures that are sometimes used for financial reporting purposes in Canada. Do you believe that these procedures are consistent with the objectives that are stated above? Your answer should be brief and specific.

(1) The provision of segmented information by public companies.

(2) The provision of interim reports by public companies. (SMA adapted.)

PROBLEMS

11-1 Data with respect to the four industry segments of Wabash Company for the year ended November 30, Year 10, follow:

	Segment				
	Alpha	Beta	Gamma	Delta	Total
Net sales to outsiders	$40,000	$20,000	$25,000	$ 5,000	$90,000
Intersegment transfers out .	2,000	4,000	1,000	3,000	10,000
Intersegment transfers in . . .	4,000	3,000	2,000	1,000	10,000
Direct expenses	9,000	6,000	5,000	10,000	30,000
Indirect expenses					20,000

Wabash allocated indirect expenses that were of benefit to industry segments by the following reasonable method: Alpha — 40%; Beta — 30%; Gamma — 20%; Delta — 10%.

Instructions
a Prepare a working paper to compute the operating profit or loss for Wabash Company's four industry segments for the year ended November 30, Year 10.
b Prepare a working paper to determine if each industry segment of Wabash Company is **significant** for the year ended November 30, Year 10. Disregard segment identifiable assets.

11-2 On January 1, Year 1, Able Ltd., Baker Ltd., and Drexal Ltd., entered into a joint venture agreement to form the Frontier Exploration Company. Able contributed 30% of the assets to the venture and agreed that its share of the venture would be the same percentage. Presented below are the financial statements of Able Ltd. and Frontier Exploration Company as at December 31, Year 6.

	Balance Sheets	
	Able	Frontier
Current assets	$247,000	$ 40,000
Investment in Frontier	27,000	—
Other assets	530,000	70,000
Total	$804,000	$110,000
Current liabilities	$ 94,000	$ 20,000
Long-term debt	400,000	—
Capital stock	200,000	10,000
Retained earnings	110,000	80,000
Total	$804,000	$110,000

	Income statements	
Revenues	$900,000	$100,000
Income from Frontier	9,000	—
Total revenues	$909,000	$100,000
Cost of sales and expenses	812,000	70,000
Net income	$ 97,000	$ 30,000

Able conducts a significant portion of its activities through this investment format and is actively involved in the operations of Frontier. Its investment has been accounted for by the partial equity method (no adjustments have been made for intercompany transactions).

Able acts as the sole supplier for certain materials used by Frontier in its exploration activities. The December 31, Year 6 inventory of Frontier contains items purchased from Able on which Able recorded a gross profit of $10,000. At December 31, Year 6, Frontier owed Able $12,000 representing invoices not yet paid. Frontier's Year 6 intercompany purchases amounted to $70,000.

Instructions Prepare the necessary financial statements on a proportionate consolidated basis in accordance with *Section 3055* of the *CICA Handbook*. (Use a rate of 40% for income tax effects.)

11-3 Bixler Company, a diversified manufacturing enterprise, had four separate operating divisions engaged in the manufacture of products in each of the following industries: food products, health aids, textiles, and office equipment.

Financial data for the two years ended December 31, Year 8 and Year 7, are shown below:

	Net sales		Cost of goods sold		Operating expenses	
	Year 8	Year 7	Year 8	Year 7	Year 8	Year 7
Food products	$3,500,000	$3,000,000	$2,400,000	$1,800,000	$ 550,000	$ 275,000
Health aids	2,000,000	1,270,000	1,100,000	700,000	300,000	125,000
Textiles	1,580,000	1,400,000	500,000	900,000	200,000	150,000
Office equipment	920,000	1,330,000	800,000	1,000,000	650,000	750,000
Totals	$8,000,000	$7,000,000	$4,800,000	$4,400,000	$1,700,000	$1,300,000

On January 1, Year 8, Bixler adopted a plan to sell the assets and product line of the office equipment division at an anticipated gain. On September 1, Year 8, the division's assets and product line were sold for $2,100,000 cash, at a gain of $640,000 (exclusive of operations during the phase-out period).

Bixler's textiles division had six manufacturing plants that produced a variety of textile products. In April, Year 8, Bixler sold one of these plants and realized a gain of $130,000. After the sale, the operations at the plant that was sold were transferred to the remaining five textile plants that Bixler continued to operate.

In August, Year 8, the main warehouse of the food products division, located on the banks of the Colton River, was flooded when the river overflowed. The resulting uninsured damage of $420,000 is not included in the financial data given above. Historical records indicate that the Colton River normally overflows every four to five years, causing flood damage to adjacent property.

For the two years ended December 31, Year 8 and Year 7, Bixler earned interest revenue on investments of $70,000 and $40,000, respectively. For the two years ended December 31, Year 8 and Year 7, Bixler's net income was $960,000 and $670,000, respectively. Income taxes expense for each of the two years should be computed at a rate of 50%.

Instructions Prepare comparative income statements for Bixler Company for the two years ended December 31, Year 8 and Year 7. Footnotes and earnings per share disclosures are not required.

11-4 A Company and B Company formed Venture Ltd. on January 1, Year 3. Venture Ltd. is a joint venture according to *Section 3055* of the *CICA Handbook*. Both venturers contributed 50% of the capital, and profits and losses are shared on a 50-50 basis.

The following financial statements were prepared on December 31, Year 3:

| | Balance Sheets | |
	A Company Ltd.	Venture Ltd.
Current assets	$ 75,000	$ 6,000
Investment in Venture Ltd. — cost	10,000	
Fixed assets	190,000	72,000
Accumulated depreciation	(60,000)	(5,000)
Other assets	18,000	8,000
	$ 233,000	$ 81,000
Current liabilities	$ 33,000	$ 18,500
Long-term debt	45,000	40,000
Capital stock	85,000	20,000
Retained earnings January 1	30,000	
Net income for the year	40,000	2,500
	$ 233,000	$ 81,000

	Income Statements	
Sales	$ 150,000	$ 20,000
Cost of Sales	$ 90,000	$ 11,000
Expenses	20,000	6,500
Total	$ 110,000	$ 17,500
Net income	$ 40,000	$ 2,500

Additional information:
(1) During Year 3 Venture Ltd. made purchases totaling $4,000 from A Company. A
   Company recorded a gross profit of $1,200 on its sales to Venture Ltd.
(2) On December 31, Year 3, the inventories of Venture Ltd. contain 25% of the
   items purchased from A Company.
(3) Company A has used the cost method to account for its investment in Venture
   Ltd.
(4) A Company wished to prepare consolidated statements in accordance with
   Section 3055 of the **Handbook**.
(5) Use income tax allocation at a rate of 40%.

Instructions   Prepare A Company's consolidated financial statements on December 31, Year 3.

11-5   The balance sheets at the top of page 481 have been prepared as at December 31,
   Year 4.

Additional information
(1) M Company Ltd. acquired its 55% interest in Y Company Ltd. on July 1, Year 1
   for $352,000 when Y Company's retained earnings amounted to $50,000. On
   that date Y Company's inventory had a fair market value of $200,000 in excess
   of carrying value and Y Company's bonds payable had a fair market value
   $80,000 greater than carrying value. These bonds mature in 10 years. Any good-
   will is to be amortized over a five-year period.
(2) The December 31, Year 4 inventory of Y Company contains purchases from M
   Company amounting to $100,000. The gross profit on this merchandise was
   30%.
(3) Use income tax allocation at a rate of 40%.

	M Company Ltd.	Y Company Ltd.
Cash	$ 68,000	$ 30,000
Accounts receivable	80,000	170,000
Inventory	600,000	400,000
Plant & equipment	1,400,000	900,000
Investment in Y (Cost)	352,000	
Total	$2,500,000	$1,500,000
Current liabilities	$ 400,000	$ 150,000
Bonds payable	500,000	600,000
Capital stock	900,000	450,000
Retained earnings	700,000	300,000
Total	$2,500,000	$1,500,000

Instructions   Prepare a consolidated balance sheet under the following assumptions:
(a) Y Company is a subsidiary of M Company and the **CICA Handbook** recommendations for the consolidation of subsidiaries are followed.
(b) Y Company is a subsidiary of M Company and the entity concept is followed. (The entity concept is discussed in Chapter 5.)
(c) Y Company is a joint venture and will be consolidated in accordance with **Section 3055** of the **CICA Handbook**.

11-6   The Year 6 financial statements of Thompson Company are being prepared. The consolidated statements have been completed but the footnotes and additional disclosures are still under preparation. The following summarized consolidated income statement and information on total assets was taken from the Year 6 statements:

Revenues	
Sales	$ 75,600
Other	14,400
Total	$ 90,000
Cost of sales	$ 32,200
Depreciation expense	12,600
Other expense	11,200
Interest expense	9,800
Income taxes	14,000
Minority interest	3,200
Total	$ 83,000
Net income	$ 7,000
Total assets	$200,000

Information has been gathered for the preparation of segment reporting as shown at the top of page 482.

Additional information:
(1) Intersegment purchases amounted to $28,400 in Year 6.
(2) $800 of corporate expenses could not be allocated on a reasonable basis to the segments.

	Segments				
	A	**B**	**C**	**D**	**E**
Intersegment sales		$10,000		$18,400	
Outside sales	$23,800	14,000	$9,800	18,000	$10,000
Cost of sales	14,000	12,600	5,600	22,000	6,000
Depreciation expense	1,400	2,800	3,500	4,200	700
Other expense	2,700	2,500	1,400	2,400	1,400
Identifiable assets	25,200	26,600	8,400	30,800	9,800

(3) Corporate assets and investments in non-consolidated affiliates totaled $99,200.
(4) Other revenue consists of general corporate revenue and equity earnings from affiliates.

Instructions

a Prepare the necessary calculations to determine which segments are reportable Include tests for adequacy and dominance.

b Prepare suitable disclosure of segmented information for the Year 6 financial statements.

11-7 The Intercontinental Corporation Ltd. has its head office in Canada and conducts operations in Canada and in a number of countries throughout the world. Management has grouped the company's operations into geographic areas and assembled supporting data for the current year as follows:

	Sales to outside customers	Sales to geographic areas	Operating profit	Identifiable assets
Canada	$ 23,000	$19,000	$10,000	$ 54,000
South America	36,000	—	14,000	34,000
Europe	216,000	52,000	43,000	270,000
Great Britain	27,000	18,000	12,000	55,000
Africa	30,000	—	11,000	36,000
Total	$332,000	$89,000	$90,000	$449,000

The current year's consolidated financial statements yielded the following:

Revenues	$350,000
Net income before tax	$ 50,000
Income tax	22,000
Net income	$ 28,000
Total assets	$565,000

Additional information

(1) The consolidated income statement showed investment income of $18,000.
(2) General corporate expenses were $40,000, and assets not allocable to geographic areas amounted to $116,000.
(3) 15% of the Canadian operation's sales were to the U.S.A.

Instructions Determine which geographic segments are reportable and present the disclosure of this information as required by the *CICA Handbook*.

3 ACCOUNTING
FOR NONBUSINESS
ORGANIZATIONS

12 LOCAL GOVERNMENTAL UNITS: GENERAL FUND

The accounting and reporting practices of **nonbusiness organizations** have received considerable attention by Canada's professional accountants in recent years. The diagram that follows shows the breakdown of this broad area into three components that were the subject of research studies in the 1980s. This interest by Canadian accountants in the nonbusiness area developed soon after similar studies were undertaken in the United States. Among the factors that precipitated the U.S. action were the desperate financial condition of many large cities, and the scandals associated with the fund-raising activities of a few nonprofit organizations.

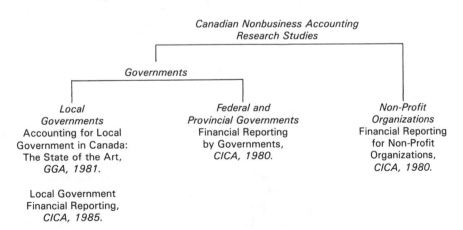

The development of accounting principles for nonbusiness organizations has historically been left to authorities other than professional accounting organizations. For example, because the *CICA Handbook* pronouncements apply specifically to profit-oriented organizations they have implicitly been viewed as not applicable in the nonbusiness area. Attempts have been made by other bodies to develop accounting principles. In the government area Statistics Canada has suggested the use of standard terminology and reporting practices, but the absence of authoritative support from the CICA has resulted in continued inconsistencies, and lack of uniformity in measurement and reporting practices, mainly because local governments are created by provincial legislatures and report as required by the various Acts of these bodies. A similar situation exists in the nonprofit area where associations such as the Canadian Hospital Association have produced accounting and reporting manuals which also have not received authoritative support. The results in the nonprofit area are similar to those in the government area.

The research study groups were asked to examine the accounting and reporting practices being used and to consider the need for a comprehensive body of accounting principles. It is not surprising that all four Canadian studies reported a wide divergence in accounting principles and reporting practices, and recommended actions that should be taken to bring greater uniformity in each area. The release of the study on federal and provincial government accounting led to the formation by CICA of the *Public Sector Accounting and Auditing Committee* in 1981. This committee will make recommendations to improve financial reporting, and accounting and auditing practices as they apply to the federal and provincial governments. It remains to be seen if the committee will extend its mandate to the local government area. The committee's success will depend on its ability to convince the federal and provincial governments to agree to its recommendations.

This chapter and Chapter 13 examine local government accounting. Accounting for nonprofit organizations is covered in Chapter 14. We begin by discussing the objectives of financial reporting for nonbusiness organizations and the nature of governmental units. We then examine a model for local governmental acccounting that has received authoritative support in the United States, that is essentially followed in Quebec, and that to some extent is followed by local governments in other Canadian provinces. Major differences in Canadian practice will be discussed.

OBJECTIVES OF FINANCIAL REPORTING FOR NONBUSINESS ORGANIZATIONS

As a result of conditions in the United States described at the beginning of this chapter, the FASB added financial reporting by nonbusiness organizations to the scope of its conceptual framework for financial accounting and reporting project, which is described in *Intermediate Accounting* of this series. In *Statement of Financial Accounting Concepts No. 4*, "Objectives of Financial Reporting by Nonbusiness Organizations," the FASB developed the following objectives:[1]

1 *Statement of Financial Accounting Concepts No. 4*, "Objectives of Financial Reporting by Nonbusiness Organizations," FASB (Stamford: 1980), pp. xiii–xiv.

1 Financial reporting by nonbusiness organizations should provide information that is useful to present and potential resource providers and other users in making rational decisions about the allocation of resources to those organizations.

2 Financial reporting should provide information to help present and potential resource providers and other users in assessing the services that a non-business organization provides and its ability to continue to provide those services.

3 Financial reporting should provide information that is useful to present and potential resource providers and other users in assessing how managers of a nonbusiness organization have discharged their stewardship responsibilities and about other aspects of their performance.

4 Financial reporting should provide information about the economic resources, obligations, and net resources of an organization, and the effects of transactions, events, and circumstances that change resources and interests in those resources.

5 Financial reporting should provide information about the performance of an organization during a period. Periodic measurement of the changes in the amount and nature of the net resources of a nonbusiness organization and information about the service efforts and accomplishments of an organization together represent the information most useful in assessing its performance.

6 Financial reporting should provide information about how an organization obtains and spends cash or other liquid resources, about its borrowing and repayment of borrowing, and about other factors that may affect an organization's liquidity.

7 Financial reporting should include explanations and interpretations to help users understand financial information provided.

The FASB stated that it was aware of no persuasive evidence that the seven objectives outlined in the foregoing section were inappropriate for general-purpose external financial reports of state and local governmental units. However, the FASB deferred a final decision on the matter, pending resolution of the question of how accounting standards for state and local governmental units should be established.

While each of the CICA research studies adopted its own set of objectives for financial reporting, they contain no major departures from the objectives stated by the FASB.

NATURE OF GOVERNMENTAL UNITS

Students beginning the study of accounting for governmental units temporarily must set aside many of the familiar accounting principles for business enterprises. Such fundamental concepts of accounting theory for business enterprises as the nature of the accounting entity, the primacy of the income statement, and the pervasiveness of the accrual basis of accounting have limited relevance in accounting for governmental units. Consequently, we begin our discussion with the features of governmental units that give rise to unique accounting concepts.

When thinking of governmental units of Canada, one tends to focus on the federal government, or on the governments of the 10 provinces. However, in addition to those major governmental units and the governments of the territories, there are approximately 5,000 local governments in Canada.[2]

Despite the wide range in size and scope of governance, all governmental units have a number of characteristics in common. Among these characteristics are the following:

1 *Organization to serve the citizenry.* A basic tenet of governmental philosophy in Canada is that governmental units exist to serve the citizens subject to their jurisdiction. Thus, the citizens as a whole establish governmental units through the constitutional process. In contrast, business enterprises are created by only a limited number of individuals.

2 *General absence of the profit motive.* With few exceptions, governmental units render services to the citizenry without the objective of profiting from those services. Business enterprises are motivated to earn profits.

3 *Taxation as the principal source of revenue.* The citizens subject to a governmental unit's jurisdiction provide resources to the governmental unit principally through taxation. Many of these taxes are paid on a self-assessment basis. There is no comparable revenue source for business enterprises.

4 *Impact of the legislative process.* Operations of governmental units are for the most part initiated by various legislative enactments, such as operating budgets, borrowing authorizations, and tax levies. Business enterprises are also affected by federal, provincial, and local laws and regulations, but not to such a direct extent.

5 *Stewardship for resources.* A primary responsibility of governmental units in financial reporting is to demonstrate adequate stewardship for resources provided by their citizenry. Business enterprises have a comparable responsibility to their owners, but not to the same extent as governmental units.

The five foregoing characteristics of governmental units are major determinants of accounting principles for such units.

ACCOUNTING PRINCIPLES FOR GOVERNMENTAL UNITS

For many years, accounting principles for governmental units have been established by the National Council on Governmental Accounting (NCGA), a 21-member organization composed primarily of local, state, and national finance officers, including two Canadian finance officers. Until 1979, the source of accounting principles for governmental units was a 1968 publication, **Governmental Accounting, Auditing, and Financial Reporting**. In 1979, the NCGA issued **Statement 1, Governmental Accounting and Financial Reporting Principles**, which included the following 12 principles of accounting for local governmental units.[3]

2 *Local Government Financial Reporting: A Research Study*, CICA (Toronto: 1985), foreword.

3 National Council on Governmental Accounting, *Governmental Accounting and Financial Reporting Principles*, Municipal Finance Officers Association of the United States and Canada (Chicago: 1979), pp. 2–4.

1 A governmental accounting system must make it possible both: (a) to present fairly and with full disclosure the financial position and results of financial operations of the funds and account groups of the governmental unit in conformity with generally accepted accounting principles; and (b) to determine and demonstrate compliance with finance-related legal and contractual provisions.

2 Governmental accounting systems should be organized and operated on a fund basis. A *fund* is defined as a fiscal and accounting entity with a self-balancing set of accounts recording cash and other financial resources, together with all related liabilities and residual equities or balances, and changes therein, which are segregated for the purpose of carrying on specific activities or attaining certain objectives in accordance with special regulations, restrictions, or limitations.

3 The following types of funds should be used by local governments:

Governmental Funds

(1) *The General Fund* — to account for all financial resources except those required to be accounted for in another fund.

(2) *Special Revenue Funds* — to account for the proceeds of specific revenue sources (other than special assessments, expendable trusts, or for major capital projects) that are legally restricted to expenditure for specified purposes.

(3) *Capital Projects Funds* — to account for financial resources to be used for the acquisition or construction of major capital facilities (other than those financed by proprietary funds, Special Assessment Funds, and Trust Funds).

(4) *Debt Service Funds* — to account for the accumulation of resources for, and the payment of, general long-term debt principal and interest.

(5) *Special Assessment Funds* — to account for the financing of public improvements or services deemed to benefit the properties against which special assessments are levied.

Proprietary Funds

(6) *Enterprise Funds* — to account for operations (a) that are financed and operated in a manner similar to private business enterprises — where the intent of the governing body is that the costs (expenses, including depreciation) of providing goods or services to the general public on a continuing basis be financed or recovered primarily through user charges; or (b) where the governing body has decided that periodic determination of revenues earned, expenses incurred, and/or net income is appropriate for capital maintenance, public policy, management control, accountability, or other purposes.

(7) *Internal Service Funds* — to account for the financing of goods or services provided by one department or agency to other

departments or agencies of the governmental unit, or to other governmental units, on a cost-reimbursement basis.

Fiduciary Funds

(8) *Trust and Agency Funds* — to account for assets held by a governmental unit in a trustee capacity or as an agent for individuals, private organizations, other governmental units, and/or other funds. These include (a) Expendable Trust Funds, (b) Nonexpendable Trust Funds, (c) Pension Trust Funds, and (d) Agency Funds.

Number of funds

4 Governmental units should establish and maintain those funds required by law and sound financial administration. Only the minimum number of funds consistent with legal and operating requirements should be established, however, since unnecessary funds result in inflexibility, undue complexity, and inefficient financial administration.

Accounting for fixed assets and long-term liabilities

5 A clear distinction should be made between (a) fund fixed assets and general fixed assets and (b) fund long-term liabilities and general long-term debt.

a Fixed assets related to specific proprietary funds or Trust Funds should be accounted for through those funds. All other fixed assets of a governmental unit should be accounted for through the General Fixed Assets Account Group.

b Long-term liabilities of proprietary funds, Special Assessment Funds, and Trust Funds should be accounted for through those funds. All other unmatured general long-term liabilities of the governmental unit should be accounted for through the General Long-Term Debt Account Group.

Valuation of fixed assets

6 Fixed assets should be accounted for at cost or, if the cost is not practicably determinable, at estimated cost. Donated fixed assets should be recorded at their estimated fair value at the time received.

Depreciation of fixed assets

7 a Depreciation of general fixed assets should not be recorded in the accounts of governmental funds. Depreciation of general fixed assets may be recorded in cost accounting systems or calculated for cost finding analyses; and accumulated depreciation may be recorded in the General Fixed Assets Account Group.

b Depreciation of fixed assets accounted for in a proprietary fund should be recorded in the accounts of that fund. Depreciation is also recognized in those Trust Funds where expenses, net income, and/or capital maintenance are measured.

Accrual basis in governmental accounting

8 The modified accrual or accrual basis of accounting, as appropriate, should be utilized in measuring financial position and operating results.

a *Governmental fund* revenues and expenditures should be recognized on the modified accrual basis. Revenues should be recognized in the accounting period in which they become available and measurable. Expenditures should be recognized in the accounting period in which the fund liability is incurred, if measurable, except for unmatured interest on general long-term debt and on special assessment indebtedness secured by interest-bearing special assessment levies, which should be recognized when due.

b *Proprietary fund* revenues and expenses should be recognized on the accrual basis. Revenues should be recognized in the accounting period in which they are earned and become measurable; expenses should be recognized in the period incurred, if measurable.

c *Fiduciary fund* revenues and expenses or expenditures (as appropriate) should be recognized on the basis consistent with the fund's accounting measurement objective. Nonexpendable Trust and Pension Trust Funds should be accounted for on the accrual basis; Expendable Trust Funds should be accounted for on the modified accrual basis. Agency Fund assets and liabilities should be accounted for on the modified accrual basis.

d *Transfers* should be recognized in the accounting period in which the interfund receivable and payable arise.

Budgeting, budgetary control, and budgetary reporting

9 a An annual budget(s) should be adopted by every governmental unit.

b The accounting system should provide the basis for appropriate budgetary control.

c Budgetary comparisons should be included in the appropriate financial statements and schedules for governmental funds for which an annual budget has been adopted.

Transfer, revenue, expenditure, and expense account classification

10 a Interfund transfers and proceeds of general long-term debt issues should be classified separately from fund revenues and expenditures or expenses.

b Governmental fund revenues should be classified by fund and source. Expenditures should be classified by fund, function (or program), organization unit, activity, character, and principal classes of objects.

c Proprietary fund revenues and expenses should be classified in essentially the same manner as those of similar business organizations, functions, or activities.

Common terminology and classification

11 A common terminology and classification should be used consistently throughout the budget, the accounts, and the financial reports of each fund.

Interim and annual financial reports

12 a Appropriate interim financial statements and reports of financial position, operating results, and other pertinent information should be prepared to facilitate management control of financial operations, legislative oversight, and, where necessary or desired, for external reporting purposes.

b A comprehensive annual financial report covering all funds and account groups of the governmental unit — including appropriate combined, combining, and individual fund statements; notes to the financial statements; schedules; narrative explanations; and statistical tables — should be prepared and published.

c General-purpose financial statements may be issued separately from the comprehensive annual financial report. Such statements should include the basic financial statements and notes to the financial statements that are essential to fair presentation of financial position and operating results (and changes in financial position of proprietary funds and similar trust funds).

Principles 2 and 3, and 8 to 11, are discussed in the following sections of this chapter. Chapter 13 covers principles 4 to 7 and 12, and funds other than the general fund identified in principle 3.

Funds: The accounting entities for governmental units (principles 2 and 3)

In accounting for business enterprises, *economic substance* of financial transactions is emphasized over their *legal form*. Thus, capital leases that are in substance installment acquisitions of personal property are accounted for as such in the financial statements of business enterprises. Similarly minority interest in a consolidated subsidiary, although theoretically a part of consolidated shareholders' equity, occasionally is reported as a liability under the "parent company theory" of consolidated financial statements and more often is shown between liabilities and shareholders' equity.

In contrast, accounting for governmental units emphasizes *legal form* over *economic substance*. This emphasis is necessitated by the characteristics of governmental units discussed in a preceding section of this chapter — especially the impact of the legislative process and the stewardship for resources. Emphasis on legal form for governmental units is manifested in several aspects of accounting for such units.

Accounting for business enterprises emphasizes the economic entity as an accounting unit. Thus, a partnership is considered to be an accounting entity separate from partners; and consolidated financial statements are issued for a group of affiliated — but legally separate — corporations that comprise a single economic entity under common control.

There is generally no single accounting entity for a specific governmental unit, such as a city or a municipality. Instead, the accounting entity for governmental units is the fund. As defined in principle 2, a *fund* is an accounting entity that includes *cash* and *other financial resources*, liabilities, and residual equities or balances. These elements are accounted for as a unit in accordance with laws or regulations established by the governmental unit involved.

Principle 3 identifies eight types of funds used in accounting for governmental units, grouped into three categories. The *governmental funds* account for financial resources of a governmental unit that are used in day-to-day operations. The ***proprietary funds*** carry out governmental unit activities that closely resemble the operations of a business enterprise. ***Fiduciary funds*** account for resources not ***owned*** by a governmental unit, but administered by the unit as a ***custodian*** or ***fiduciary***.

Every governmental unit has a general fund. As indicated by principle 4, any additional funds should be established as required by legislative action and the maintenance of adequate custodianship for financial resources of the governmental unit. Accounting for the general fund is discussed in subsequent sections of this chapter; accounting for other funds is explained in Chapter 13. At this point, we must emphasize that a governmental unit ***does not have a single accounting entity*** to account for its financial resources, obligations, revenues, and expenditures.

The modified accrual basis of accounting (principle 8)

Except for enterprise funds and internal service funds, which record sales of goods or services, governmental accounting does not emphasize the results of the governmental unit's operations for a fiscal year. Financial reporting for governments instead focuses on the stewardship provided for the governmental unit's assets. One consequence is that a ***modified accrual basis of accounting*** is appropriate for the five governmental funds and for expendable trust funds, as indicated by principle 8. The conventional accrual basis of accounting is used for the two proprietary funds, nonexpendable trust funds, and pension trust funds.

The National Council on Governmental Accounting has defined the modified accrual basis of accounting as follows:[4]

> ***Revenue Recognition*** Revenues and other governmental fund financial resource increments (e.g., bond issue proceeds) are recognized in the accounting period in which they become susceptible to accrual — that is, when they become both ***measurable*** and ***available*** to finance expenditures of the fiscal period. ***Available*** means collectible within the current period or soon enough thereafter to be used to pay liabilities of the current period. . . .
>
> ***Expenditure Recognition*** . . . the measurement focus of governmental fund accounting is upon ***expenditures*** — decreases in net financial resources — rather than expenses. Most expenditures and transfers out are measurable and should be recorded when the related liability is incurred. . . .
> . . . alternative expenditure recognition methods in governmental fund accounting, usually of a relatively minor nature, include: . . .
> (1) Inventory items (e.g., materials and supplies) may be considered expenditures either when purchased (purchases method) or when

4 Ibid., pp. 11–12.

used (consumption method), but significant amounts of inventory should be reported in the balance sheet.

(2) Expenditures for insurance and similar services extending over more than one accounting period need not be allocated between or among accounting periods, but may be accounted for as expenditures of the period of acquisition.

Revenues   Few revenues of the five governmental funds and expendable trust funds are susceptible to accrual. For example, there generally is no basis for the accrual of sales taxes, and taxes on gross business receipts. Similarly, fees for business licences, pet licences, and comparable permits generally are recorded when received in cash, because these fees are not billable in advance of the service or granting of a permit.

Perhaps the most commonly accrued revenue of a governmental unit is property taxes. These taxes customarily are billed by the governmental unit to the property owner and generally are payable in the fiscal year for which billed.

In summary, the cash basis of accounting is appropriate for many revenues of the five governmental funds (general, special revenue, capital projects, debt service, and special assessment) and expendable trust funds.

Expenditures   Because of the lack of emphasis on operating results, funds other than the two proprietary funds (enterprise and internal service) account for authorized *expenditures* of the government's resources, rather than accounting for *expenses* of operations. There is no attempt to match *cost expirations* against *realized revenues* in funds other than enterprise funds and internal service funds. As a result, depreciation is recorded only in enterprise funds and internal service funds, and, if appropriate, in certain trust funds. Similarly, there is no doubtful taxes expense in the general fund or in special revenue funds, because tax revenues susceptible to accrual are recorded in an amount *net* of the estimated uncollectible portion of the related receivables, as illustrated on page 500.

Recording the budget (principle 9)

Budgets are key elements of legislative control over governmental units. The executive branch of a governmental unit proposes the budgets, the legislative branch reviews, modifies, and enacts the budgets, and finally the executive branch carries out their provisions.

The two basic classifications of budgets for governmental units are the same as those for business enterprises — annual budgets and long-term or capital budgets. *Annual budgets* include the *estimated revenues* and *appropriations* for expenditures for a specific fiscal year of the governmental unit. Annual budgets are appropriate for the general fund and special revenue funds; they sometimes are used for debt service funds. An expendable trust fund also may have an annual budget, depending upon the terms of the *trust indenture*. *Capital budgets*, which are used to control the expenditures for construction projects or other plant asset acquisitions, may be appropriate for capital projects funds and special assessment funds. The annual or capital budgets often are recorded in all these funds, to aid in accounting for compliance with legislative authorizations.

The operations of the two proprietary funds (enterprise and internal service) are similar to those of business enterprises. Consequently, annual budgets are used by these funds as a managerial planning and control device *rather than as a legislative control tool*. Thus, annual budgets of enterprise funds and internal service funds generally *are not recorded in ledger accounts by these funds*.

Types of Annual Budgets   One or more of four types of annual budgets may be used by a governmental unit. A *traditional budget* emphasizes, by department, the *object* of each authorized expenditure. For example, under the legislative activity of the general government function, the traditional budget may include authorized expenditures for personal services, supplies, and capital outlays.

A *program budget* stresses measurement of total cost of a specific governmental unit *program*, regardless of how many departments of the governmental unit are involved in the program. Object of expenditure information is of secondary importance in a program budget.

In a *performance budget*, there is an attempt to relate the input of governmental resources to the output of governmental services. For example, the total estimated expenditures of the enforcement section of the taxation department might be compared to the aggregate collections of additional tax assessments budgeted for the fiscal year.

The fourth type of annual budget for a governmental unit is the *planning, programming, budgeting system (PPBS)*. This budgeting technique has been described as follows:[5]

> PPBS attempts to apply concepts of program and performance budgeting to the tasks of identifying the fundamental objectives of a government; selections are made from among alternative ways of attaining these objectives, on the basis of the full analysis of respective cost implications and expected benefit results of the alternatives.

Regardless of which types of annual budgets are used by a governmental unit, the final budget adopted by the governmental unit's legislative body will include *estimated revenues* for the fiscal year and the *appropriations* for expenditures authorized for that year. If the estimated revenues of the budget exceed appropriations (as required by law for many governmental units), there will be a *budgetary surplus*; if appropriations exceed estimated revenues in the budget, there will be a *budgetary deficit*.

Journal Entry for a General Fund Budget   To illustrate the recording of an annual budget in the accounting records of a general fund, assume that

---

5 *Audits of State and Local Governmental Units*, AICPA (New York: 1974), pp. 27–28.

the Town of Verdant Glen in June, Year 5, adopted the following condensed annual budget for its General Fund for the fiscal year ending June 30, Year 6

Estimated revenues:

General property taxes		$700,000
Other		100,000
Total estimated revenues		$800,000
Estimated other financing sources		50,000
Subtotal		$850,000
Less: Appropriations:		
General government	$420,000	
Other	340,000	
Total appropriations	$760,000	
Estimated other financing uses	60,000	820,000
Excess of estimated revenues and other financing sources over appropriations		
and other financing uses (budgetary surplus)		$ 30,000

The journal entry to record the annual budget on July 1, Year 5, is shown below.

Estimated Revenues	800,000	
Estimated Other Financing Sources	50,000	
Appropriations		760,000
Estimated Other Financing Uses		60,000
Budgetary Fund Balance		30,000

To record annual budget adopted for fiscal year ending June 30, Year 6.

An analysis of each of the accounts in the foregoing journal entry follows

1 The Estimated Revenues and Estimated Other Financing Sources accounts may be considered **pseudo asset** accounts because they reflect resources expected to be received by the General Fund during the fiscal year. These accounts are not actual assets, because they do not fit the accounting definition of an asset as a probable economic benefit obtained or controlled by a particular entity as a result of past transactions or events.[6] Thus, the two accounts in substance are **memorandum accounts**, useful for control purposes only, that will be closed after the issuance of financial statements for the General Fund for the fiscal year ending June 30, Year 6.

2 The Estimated Other Financing Sources account includes the budgeted amounts of such nonrevenues items as proceeds from the disposal of plant assets and transfers in from other funds. (See principle **10a**, page 491.)

6 *Statement of Financial Accounting Concepts No. 3*, "Elements of Financial Statements of Business Enterprises," FASB (Stamford: 1980), p. xi.

3 The Appropriations and Estimated Other Financing Uses accounts may be considered *pseudo liability* accounts because they reflect the legislative body's commitments to expend General Fund resources as authorized in the annual budget. These accounts are not genuine liabilities because they do not fit the definition of a liability as a probable future sacrifice of economic benefits arising from present obligations of a particular entity to transfer assets or provide services to other entities in the future as a result of past transactions or events.[7] The Appropriations and Estimated Other Financing Uses accounts are *memorandum accounts*, useful for control purposes only, that will be closed after issuance of year-end financial statements for the General Fund.

4 The Estimated Other Financing Uses account includes budgeted amounts of transfers out to other funds, which are not expenditures. (See principle *10a*, page 491.)

5 The Budgetary Fund Balance account, as its title implies, is an account that balances the debit and credit entries to accounts of a budget journal entry. Although similar to the owners' equity accounts of a business enterprise in this balancing feature, the Budgetary Fund Balance account does not purport to show an ownership interest in a general fund's assets. At the end of the fiscal year, the Budgetary Fund Balance account is closed by a journal entry that reverses the original entry for the budget.

The journal entry to record the Town of Verdant Glen General Fund's annual budget for the year ending June 30, Year 6, is accompanied by detailed entries to subsidiary ledgers for both estimated revenues and appropriations. The budget of the Town of Verdant Glen General Fund purposely was condensed; in practice, the general fund's estimated revenues and appropriations would be detained by source and function, respectively, into one or more of the following widely used subsidiary ledger categories (see principle *10b*, page 491):[8]

Estimated revenues:	Appropriations:
Taxes	General government
Licenses and permits	Public safety
Intergovernmental revenues	Public works
Charges for services	Health and welfare
Fines and forfeits	Culture — recreation
Miscellaneous	Conservation of natural resources
	Debt service
	Intergovernmental expenditures
	Miscellaneous

In summary, budgets of a governmental unit often are recorded in the accounting records of the five governmental funds. An expendable trust fund also may record a budget if required to do so by the trust indenture. The recording of the budget initiates the accounting cycle for each of the funds listed above. Recording the budget also facilitates the preparation of financial statements that compare budgeted and actual amounts of revenues and expenditures.

7 Ibid.
8 *Governmental Accounting, Auditing, and Financial Reporting*, Municipal Finance Officers Association of the United States and Canada (Chicago: 1980), pp. 84–97.

Encumbrances and Budgetary Control   Because of the need for the expenditures of governmental units to be in accordance with appropriations of governing legislative bodies, an *encumbrance* accounting technique is used for the general fund, special revenue funds, capital project funds, and special assessment funds. When a purchase order for goods or services is issued to a supplier by one of those funds, a journal entry similar to the following is made in the accounting records of the fund:

Journal entry for encumbrances	Encumbrances 18,413	
	Fund Balance Reserved for Encumbrances	18,41.
	To record encumbrance for purchase order No. 1685 issued to Wilson Company.	

When the supplier's invoice for the ordered merchandise or services is received by the governmental unit, it is recorded and the related encumbrance is reversed as illustrated below.

Journal entries for receipt of invoice and reversal of encumbrance	Expenditures 18,507	
	Vouchers Payable	18,50?
	To record invoice received from Wilson Company under purchase order No. 1685.	
	Fund Balance Reserved for Encumbrances 18,413	
	Encumbrances	18,413
	To reverse encumbrance for purchase order No. 1685 issued to Wilson Company.	

As indicated by the example above, the invoice amount may differ from the amount of the governmental unit's purchase order because of such items as shipping charges, sales taxes, and price changes.

The encumbrance technique is a memorandum method for assuring that total expenditures for a fiscal year do not exceed appropriations. Encumbrance journal entries *are not necessary for normal recurring expenditures such as salaries and wages, utilities, and rent*. The encumbrance technique used in accounting for governmental units has no counterpart in accounting for business enterprises.

ACCOUNTING FOR A GOVERNMENTAL UNIT'S GENERAL FUND

As indicated on page 489, a general fund is used to account for all transactions of a governmental unit not accounted for in one of the other seven types of funds. Thus, the general fund as an accounting entity serves the same *residual* purpose that the general journal provides as an accounting record. Although the general fund is residual, it usually accounts for the largest aggregate dollar amounts of the governmental unit's revenues and expenditures. Other descriptive terms used in Canada for this type of fund are, **general revenue fund**, **revenue fund** and **operating fund**.

In illustrating the accounting for a general fund, we expand the example of the Town of Verdant Glen used in the preceding section.

Illustration of accounting for a general fund

Assume that the balance sheet of the Town of Verdant Glen General Fund on June 30, Year 5 (**prior to the journal entry for the Fiscal Year 6 budget** illustrated on page 496), was as follows:

TOWN OF VERDANT GLEN GENERAL FUND
Balance Sheet
June 30, Year 5

Assets

Cash		$160,000
Inventory of supplies		40,000
Total assets		$200,000

Liabilities & Fund Balance

Vouchers payable		$ 80,000
Fund balance:		
Reserved for inventory of supplies	$40,000	
Unreserved	80,000	120,000
Total liabilities & fund balance		$200,000

The fund balance reserved for inventory of supplies is analogous to an appropriation of retained earnings in a business enterprise. It represents a reservation of the General Fund's fund balance, so that the $40,000 nonexpendable portion of the General Fund's total assets will not be appropriated for expenditures in the legislative body's adoption of the annual budget for the General Fund for the year ending June 30, Year 6.

Assume that, in addition to the budget illustrated on page 496, the Town of Verdant Glen General Fund had the following summarized transactions for the fiscal year ended June 30, Year 6:

1 Property taxes were billed in the amount of $720,000, of which $14,000 was of doubtful collectibility.

2 Property taxes collected in cash totaled $650,000; other revenues collected totaled $102,000.

3 Property taxes in the amount of $13,000 were uncollectible.

4 Purchase orders were issued to outside suppliers in the total amount of $360,000.

5 Expenditures for the year totaled $760,000, of which $90,000 applied to additions to inventory of supplies, and $350,000 applied to $355,000 of the purchase orders in the total amount of $360,000 issued during the year.

6 Billings for services and supplies from the Enterprise Fund and the Internal Service Fund totaled $30,000 and $20,000, respectively.

7 Cash payments on vouchers payable totaled $770,000. Cash payments to the Enterprise Fund and the Internal Service Fund were $25,000 and $14,000 respectively.

8 Transfers of cash to the Debt Service Fund for maturing principal and interest on general obligation serial bonds totaled $11,000.

9 A payment of $50,000 in lieu of property taxes was received from the Enterprise Fund.

10 Supplies with a cost of $80,000 were used during the year.

11 All uncollected property taxes on June 30, Year 6, were delinquent.

After the journal entry for the budget is recorded, as illustrated on page 496, the following journal entries, numbered to correspond to the transactions listed above, are entered in the accounting records of the Town of Verdant Glen General Fund during the year ended June 30, Year 6:

TOWN OF VERDANT GLEN GENERAL FUND
General Journal

1 Taxes Receivable — Current	720,000	
Allowance for Uncollectible Current Taxes		14,000
Revenues		706,000
To accrue property taxes billed and to provide for estimated		
uncollectible portion.		

As indicated earlier, the modified accrual basis of accounting for a general fund permits the accrual of property taxes, because they are **billed** to the property owners by the Town of Verdant Glen. The estimated uncollectible property taxes are **offset** against the total taxes billed; the net amount represents **estimated actual revenues** from property taxes for the year.

---

2 Cash	752,000	
Taxes Receivable — Current		650,000
Revenues		102,000
To record collections of property taxes and other revenues for the		
year.		

Under the modified accrual basis of accounting, revenues not susceptible to accrual are recorded on the cash basis. However, any taxes or other revenues collected in advance of the fiscal year to which they apply are credited to a liability account.

If a governmental unit's general fund has a cash shortage prior to collection of property taxes, it may issue short-term **tax anticipation notes** to borrow cash. Typically, tax anticipation notes are repaid from proceeds of the subsequent tax collections. Another alternative used is to offer **discounts** to property owners who prepay their taxes in advance of the final due date

3 Allowance for Uncollectible Current Taxes	13,000	
Taxes Receivable — Current		13,000
To write off receivables for property taxes that are uncollectible.		

The foregoing journal entry represents a shortcut approach. In an actual situation, uncollectible property taxes first would be transferred, together with estimated uncollectible amounts, to the Taxes Receivable — Delinquent account from the Taxes Receivable — Current account. Any amounts collected on these delinquent taxes would include revenues for interest and penalties required by law. Any uncollected delinquent taxes would be transferred, together with estimated uncollectible amounts, to the Tax Liens Receivable account. After the passage of an appropriate statutory period, the governmental unit might satisfy its tax lien by selling the property on which the taxes were levied.

4 Encumbrances	360,000	
Fund Balance Reserved for Encumbrances		360,000
To record purchase orders issued during the year.		

Encumbrance journal entries are designed to prevent the overexpending of an appropriated amount in the budget. The journal entry to the Encumbrances account is posted in detail to reduce the unexpended balances of each applicable appropriation in the subsidiary ledger for appropriations. The unexpended balance of each appropriation thus is reduced for the amount committed by the issuance of purchase orders.

5 a Expenditures	670,000	
Inventory of Supplies	90,000	
Vouchers Payable		760,000
To record expenditures for the year.		

The Expenditures account is debited with all expenditures, regardless of purpose, except for additions to the inventory of supplies. Principal and interest payments on debt, additions to the governmental unit's plant assets, payments for goods or services to be received in the future — all are debited to Expenditures rather than to asset or liability accounts. (Expenditures for debt principal and plant asset additions also are recorded *on a memorandum basis* in the general long-term debt and general fixed assets account groups, respectively, as explained in Chapter 13.)

The accounting for general fund expenditures described above emphasizes once again the importance of the annual budget in the accounting for a general fund. Expenditures are chargeable to amounts appropriated by the legislative body of the governmental unit. The detailed items making up the $670,000 total debit to the Expenditures account in the foregoing journal entry are posted to the appropriations subsidiary ledger as reductions of unexpended balances of each appropriation.

---

5 b *Fund Balance Reserved for Encumbrances* *355,000*
    Encumbrances *355,000*
    To reverse encumbrances applicable to vouchered expenditures
    totaling $350,000.

Recording actual expenditures of $350,000 (included in the $670,000 total in entry **5a** above) relevant to purchase orders totaling $355,000 makes this amount of the previously recorded encumbrances no longer necessary. Accordingly, $355,000 of encumbrances is reversed; the reversal is posted to the detailed appropriations subsidiary ledger as well as to the general ledger. Encumbrances of $5,000 remain outstanding.

---

6 *Other Financing Uses* *50,000*
      Payable to Enterprise Fund *30,000*
      Payable to Internal Service Fund *20,000*
    To record billings for services and supplies received from other
    funds.

Billings from other funds of the governmental unit are not vouchered for payment, as are billings from outside suppliers. Instead, billings from other funds are recorded in separate liability accounts. The related debit is to the Other Financing Uses account rather than to the Expenditures account.

---

7   *Vouchers Payable* *770,000*
    Payable to Enterprise Fund *25,000*
    Payable to Internal Service Fund *14,000*
      Cash *809,000*
    To record payment of liabilities during the year.

8   *Other Financing Uses* *11,000*
      Cash *11,000*
    To record transfer to Debt Service Fund for maturing principal
    and interest on general obligation serial bonds.

9   *Cash* *50,000*
      Other Financing Sources *50,000*
    To record payment in lieu of property taxes received from
    Enterprise Fund.

Amounts transferred in to the General Fund from other funds do not represent revenues. They are recorded in the Other Financing Sources account.

---

10 Expenditures	80,000	
Inventory of Supplies		80,000
To record cost of supplies used during the year.		
Unreserved Fund Balance	10,000	
Fund Balance Reserved for Inventory of Supplies		10,000
To increase inventory of supplies reserve to agree with balance		
of Inventory of Supplies account at end of year ($50,000 −		
$40,000 = $10,000).		

The immediately preceding journal entry represents a reservation of a portion of the Fund Balance account to prevent its being appropriated improperly to finance a deficit annual budget for the General Fund for the year ending June 30, Year 7. Only cash and other monetary assets of a general fund are available for appropriation to finance authorized expenditures of the succeeding fiscal year.

---

11 Taxes Receivable — Delinquent	57,000	
Allowance for Uncollectible Current Taxes	1,000	
Taxes Receivable — Current		57,000
Allowance for Uncollectible Delinquent Taxes		1,000
To transfer delinquent taxes and related estimated uncollectible		
amounts from the current classification.		

The foregoing journal entry clears the Taxes Receivable — Current account and the related contra account for uncollectible amounts so that they will be available for accrual of property taxes for the fiscal year ending June 30, Year 7.

Trial balance at end of fiscal year for a general fund

After all the foregoing journal entries (including the budget entry on page 496) have been posted to the general ledger of the Town of Verdant Glen General Fund, the trial balance on June 30, Year 6, is as illustrated at the top of page 504.

Financial statements for a general fund

The results of operations (that is, net income or net loss) are not significant for a general fund. Instead, two financial statements — a statement of revenues, expenditures, and changes in fund balance and a balance sheet — are appropriate. These two financial statements are shown on page 505 for the Town of Verdant Glen's General Fund for the year ended June 30, Year 6.

TOWN OF VERDANT GLEN GENERAL FUND
Trial Balance
June 30, Year 6

	Debit	Credit
Cash	$ 142,000	
Taxes receivable — delinquent	57,000	
Allowance for uncollectible delinquent taxes		$ 1,000
Inventory of supplies	50,000	
Vouchers payable		70,000
Payable to Enterprise Fund		5,000
Payable to Internal Service Fund		6,000
Fund balance reserved for encumbrances		5,000
Fund balance reserved for inventory of supplies		50,000
Unreserved fund balance		70,000
Budgetary fund balance		30,000
Estimated revenues	800,000	
Estimated other financing sources	50,000	
Appropriations		760,000
Estimated other financing uses		60,000
Revenues		808,000
Other financing sources		50,000
Expenditures	750,000	
Other financing uses	61,000	
Encumbrances	5,000	
Totals	$1,915,000	$1,915,000

The following aspects of the Town of Verdant Glen General Fund financial statements should be emphasized:

1 The statement of revenues, expenditures, and changes in fund balance compares budgeted with actual amounts. This comparison aids in the appraisal of the stewardship for the General Fund's resources and the compliance with legislative appropriations. (Expenditures in excess of appropriated amounts generally are not permitted unless a supplementary appropriation is made by the legislative body of the governmental unit.)

2 The amounts received from and paid to other funds of the Town of Verdant Glen are termed *operating transfers in* and *operating transfers out* respectively, to distinguish them from other types of financing sources and uses that might have been received or paid by the General Fund.

3 The assets of the General Fund include only monetary assets and inventory. Expenditures for prepayments other than supplies and for plant assets are not recorded as assets in the General Fund. (The differences in treatment are inconsistent.)

4 The unreserved fund balance in the balance sheet, $112,000, is a balancing amount to make the total of the reserved and unreserved fund balance equal to $167,000, the final amount in the statement of revenues, expenditures, and changes in fund balance. After the posting of the closing entries illustrated in the next section, the ending balance of the Unreserved Fund Balance ledger account is $112,000 (see page 507).

TOWN OF VERDANT GLEN GENERAL FUND
Statement of Revenues, Expenditures, and Changes in Fund Balance
For Year Ended June 30, Year 6

	Budget	Actual	Variance favourable (unfavourable)
Revenues:			
Taxes	$ 700,000	$ 706,000	$ 6,000
Other	100,000	102,000	2,000
Total revenues	$ 800,000	$ 808,000	$ 8,000
Expenditures:*			
General government	$ 420,000	$ 409,000	$ 11,000
Other	340,000	341,000	(1,000)
Total expenditures	$ 760,000	$ 750,000	$ 10,000
Excess of revenues over expenditures	$ 40,000	$ 58,000	$ 18,000
Other financing sources (uses):			
Operating transfers in	50,000	50,000	
Operating transfers out	(60,000)	(61,000)	(1,000)
Excess of revenues and other sources over			
expenditures and other uses	$ 30,000	$ 47,000	$ 17,000
Fund balance, beginning of year	120,000	120,000	
Fund balance, end of year	$ 150,000	$ 167,000	$ 17,000

* Breakdown of actual amounts between general government and other categories is assumed.

TOWN OF VERDANT GLEN GENERAL FUND
Balance Sheet
June 30, Year 6

Assets

Cash	$142,000
Taxes receivable, net of allowance for estimated uncollectible amounts, $1,000	56,000
Inventory of supplies	50,000
Total assets	$248,000

Liabilities & Fund Balance

Liabilities:		
Vouchers payable		$ 70,000
Payable to other funds		11,000
Total liabilities		$ 81,000
Fund balance:		
Reserved for encumbrances	$ 5,000	
Reserved for inventory of supplies	50,000	
Unreserved	112,000	167,000
Total liabilities & fund balance		$248,000

Closing entries for a general fund

After financial statements have been prepared for the Town of Verdant Glen General Fund, the budgetary and actual revenues, expenditures, and encumbrances accounts must be closed, to clear them for the next fiscal year's activities. The closing entries below are appropriate for the Town of Verdant Glen General Fund on June 30, Year 6. The journal entries do not close the Fund Balance Reserved for Encumbrances account. Thus, the reserve represents a restriction on the fund balance on June 30, Year 6, because the Town of Verdant Glen General Fund is committed in Fiscal Year 7 to make estimated expenditures of $5,000 attributable to budgetary appropriations carried over from Fiscal Year 6. If the Fund Balance Reserved for Encumbrances account had been closed, the Unreserved Fund Balance account would have been overstated by $5,000. The Unreserved Fund Balance account must represent the amount of the General Fund's assets that is available for appropriation for a ***deficit budget*** in Fiscal Year 7. When expenditures applicable to the $5,000 outstanding encumbrances on June 30, Year 6, are vouchered for payment in the succeeding fiscal year, the Fund Balance Reserved for Encumbrances account is debited for $5,000, the Vouchers Payable is credited for the amount to be paid, and the balancing debit or credit is entered in the Unreserved Fund Balance account.

Closing entries for general fund

Unreserved Fund Balance	5,000	
Encumbrances		5,000
To close Encumbrances account.		
Appropriations	760,000	
Estimated Other Financing Uses	60,000	
Budgetary Fund Balance	30,000	
Estimated Revenues		800,000
Estimated Other Financing Sources		50,000
To close budgetary accounts. (See page 496.)		
Revenues	808,000	
Other Financing Sources	50,000	
Expenditures		750,000
Other Financing Uses		61,000
Unreserved Fund Balance		47,000
To close revenues, expenditures, and other financing sources and uses.		

The budgetary accounts are closed at the end of the fiscal year because they are no longer required for control over revenues, expenditures, and other financing sources and uses. The amounts in the journal entry that closed the budgetary accounts were taken from the original journal entry to record the budget (page 496).

After the June 30, Year 6, closing entries for the Town of Verdant Glen General Fund are posted, the Unreserved Fund Balance ledger account appears as shown below.

Unreserved Fund Balance ledger account of general fund

Unreserved Fund Balance

Date	Explanation	Debit	Credit	Balance
6/30/5	Balance			80,000 cr
6/30/6	Increase in amount reserved for inventory of supplies (page 503)	10,000		70,000 cr
6/30/6	Close Encumbrances account (page 506)	5,000		65,000 cr
6/30/6	Close excess of revenues and other financing sources over expenditures and other financing uses (page 506)		47,000	112,000 cr

REVIEW QUESTIONS

1   What are *nonbusiness organizations*?

2   Does the CICA currently establish accounting principles for governmental units? Explain.

3   The four Canadian research study groups came to similar conclusions regarding accounting in the nonbusiness area. Briefly elaborate.

4   What does the Public Sector Accounting and Auditing Committee hope to accomplish?

5   What characteristics of governmental units have a significant influence on the accounting for governmental units? Explain.

6   What is a *fund* in accounting for governmental units?

7   What is the support for each of the following accounting principles for governmental units?
   a   The modified accrual basis of accounting
   b   The encumbrance accounting technique
   c   Recording the budget in the accounting records

8   Differentiate between a *program budget* and a *performance budget*.

9   The Estimated Revenues account of a governmental unit's general fund may be viewed as a *pseudo asset*, and the Appropriations account may be viewed as a *pseudo liability*. Why is this true?

10   What does the reference to a general fund as *residual* mean? Explain.

11   a   What are the basic financial statements for a governmental unit's general fund?
    b   What are the principal differences between the financial statements of a governmental unit's general fund and the financial statements of a business enterprise?

12   What revenues of a general fund usually are accrued? Explain.

13 Distinguish between the Expenditures ledger account of a governmental unit's general fund and the expense accounts of a business enterprise.

14 The accounting records for the City of Worthington General Fund include a ledger account titled Fund Balance Reserved for Inventory of Supplies. Explain the purpose of this account.

15 Explain the use of the Other Financing Sources and Other Financing Uses ledger accounts of a governmental unit's general fund.

16 What is the function of the Budgetary Fund Balance account of a general fund?

EXERCISES

Ex 12-1 Select the best answer for each of the following multiple-choice questions:

1 Repairs that have been made for a governmental unit, and for which an invoice has been received, should be recorded in the General Fund as an:
   a Appropriation
   b Encumbrance
   c Expenditure
   d Expense

2 Under the modified accrual basis of accounting, which of the following taxes usually is recorded in the accounting records of a governmental unit's general fund before it is collected?
   a Property
   b Income
   c Gross receipts
   d Gift
   e None of the foregoing

3 One of the differences between accounting for a governmental unit and accounting for a business enterprise is that a governmental unit should:
   a Not record depreciation expense in any of its funds
   b Always establish and maintain complete self-balancing accounts for each fund
   c Use only the cash basis of accounting
   d Use only the modified accrual basis of accounting

4 Which of the following general fund ledger accounts is closed at the end of the fiscal year?
   a Unreserved fund balance
   b Expenditures
   c Vouchers payable
   d Fund balance reserved for encumbrances
   e None of the foregoing

5 The offset for a general fund journal entry crediting the Allowance for Uncollectible Current Taxes ledger account is a debit to the:
   a Uncollectible Current Taxes Expense account
   b Unreserved Fund Balance account
   c Allowance for Uncollectible Delinquent Taxes account
   d Revenues account

6 The purpose of a governmental unit general fund's Fund Balance Reserved for Inventory of Supplies ledger account is to:

a Earmark resources for replacement of supplies

b Provide for outstanding purchase orders for supplies

c Prevent improper appropriation of the fund balance to finance a deficit budget

d Accomplish none of the above

7 The Town of Newbold General Fund issued purchase orders totaling $630,000 to vendors and suppliers. Which of the following journal entries (explanation omitted) is prepared to record this transaction?

a *Encumbrances*	*630,000*	
Fund Balance Reserved for Encumbrances		*630,000*
b *Expenditures*	*630,000*	
Vouchers Payable		*630,000*
c *Expenses*	*630,000*	
Accounts Payable		*630,000*
d *Fund Balance Reserved for Encumbrances*	*630,000*	
Encumbrances		*630,000*
e *None of the foregoing*		

Ex 12-2 On July 25, Year 3, office supplies estimated to cost $2,390 were ordered from a vendor for delivery to the office of the city manager of Gaskill. The City of Gaskill maintains a perpetual inventory system for such supplies. The supplies ordered July 25 were received on August 9, Year 3, accompanied by an invoice for $2,500.

Prepare journal entries to record the foregoing transactions in the City of Gaskill General Fund.

Ex 12-3 The after-closing trial balance of the Winston County General Fund included the following ledger account balances on June 30, Year 2:

Taxes receivable — delinquent	*$30,200 dr*
Allowance for uncollectible delinquent taxes	*1,300 cr*

The property taxes assessments for the year ending June 30, Year 3, totaled $640,000; 4% of Winston County's property tax assessments have been uncollectible in past fiscal years.

Prepare a journal entry for the property taxes of Winston County's General Fund on July 1, Year 2, the date on which the property taxes for the year ending June 30, Year 3, were billed to taxpayers.

Ex 12-4 The Glengarry School District General Fund had an inventory of supplies (and related reserve) of $60,200 on July 1, Year 8. For the year ended June 30, Year 9, supplies costing $170,900 were acquired; related purchase orders totaled $168,400. The physical inventory of unused supplies on June 30, Year 9, totaled $78,300.

Prepare journal entries for the foregoing facts for the year ended June 30, Year 9. Omit explanations.

Ex 12-5 Among the journal entries of Rainbow County General Fund for the year ended June 30, Year 7, were the following:

```
7/1/6   Accounts Receivable . . . . . . . . . . . . . . . . . . . . . . .   800,000
            Cash   . . . . . . . . . . . . . . . . . . . . . . . . . . . .              800,000
        To record nonreturnable transfer of cash to Internal
        Service Fund to provide working capital to establish
        that fund.

9/1/6   Equipment  . . . . . . . . . . . . . . . . . . . . . . . . . . .   120,000
            Vouchers Payable  . . . . . . . . . . . . . . . . . . . . .              120,000
        To record acquisition of equipment having a 10-year
        economic life and no residual value.
```

Prepare journal entries on June 30, Year 7, in the accounting records of Rainbow County General Fund to correct the records.

Ex 12-6 The Unreserved Fund Balance of the Town of Oldberry appeared as follows on June 30, Year 4:

Unreserved Fund Balance

Date	Explanation	Debit	Credit	Balance
6/30/3	Balance			62,400 cr
6/30/4	Decrease in amount reserved for inven-			
	tory of supplies		3,700	66,100 cr
6/30/4	Close Encumbrances account	6,200		59,900 cr
6/30/4	Close excess of revenues ($840,200)			
	over expenditures ($764,800)		75,400	135,300 cr

The Town of Oldberry did not have any other financing sources or uses during the year ended June 30, Year 4.

Reconstruct the journal entries indicated by the foregoing information.

Ex 12-7 At the top of page 511 is the statement of revenues, expenditures, and changes in fund balance for the Village of Mortimer General Fund for the year ended June 30, Year 8. The village did not have any other financing sources or uses for the year. Unfilled purchase orders on June 30, Year 8, totaled $11,400.

Prepare closing entries for the Village of Mortimer General Fund on June 30, Year 8.

Ex 12-8 On July 1, Year 9, the general ledger of the City of Winkle had the following fund balance accounts:

```
Reserved for inventory of supplies . . . . . . . . . . . . . . . . . . . . . . . . . . . . . . . . . . .   $ 80,600
Reserved for encumbrances  . . . . . . . . . . . . . . . . . . . . . . . . . . . . . . . . . . . . . . .      18,100
Unreserved  . . . . . . . . . . . . . . . . . . . . . . . . . . . . . . . . . . . . . . . . . . . . . . . . . .     214,700
```

The budget for the year ending June 30, Year 10, showed a budgetary surplus of $20,400. Revenues for the year ended June 30, Year 10, exceeded expenditures by $37,600. There were no other financing sources or uses for the year. The physical

VILLAGE OF MORTIMER GENERAL FUND

Statement of Revenues, Expenditures, and Changes in Fund Balance
For Year Ended June 30, Year 8

	Budget	Actual	Variance favourable (unfavourable)
Revenues:			
Taxes	$820,000	$814,200	$(5,800)
Other	160,000	162,500	2,500
Total revenues	$980,000	$976,700	$(3,300)
Expenditures:			
General government	$615,000	$618,800	$(3,800)
Other	275,000	277,400	(2,400)
Total expenditures	$890,000	$896,200	$(6,200)
Excess of revenues over expenditures	$ 90,000	$ 80,500	$(9,500)
Fund balance, beginning of year	280,400	280,400	
Fund balance, end of year	$370,400	$360,900	$(9,500)

inventory of supplies on June 30, Year 10, was $88,200, and outstanding encumbrances on June 30, Year 10, totaled $14,800.

Compute the balance of the Unreserved Fund Balance ledger account (after posting of closing entries) for the City of Winkle on June 30, Year 10.

CASES

Case 12-1 The inexperienced accountant of Corbin City prepared the following financial statements for the city's general fund:

CORBIN CITY GENERAL FUND

Income Statement
For Year Ended June 30, Year 9

Revenues:		
Taxes		$640,000
Other		180,000
Total revenues		$820,000
Expenses:		
General government	$600,000	
Depreciation	60,000	
Other	120,000	780,000
Net income		$ 40,000

CORBIN CITY GENERAL FUND

Statement of Changes in Fund Balance
For Year Ended June 30, Year 9

Fund balance, beginning of year	$4,850,000
Add: Net income	40,000
Fund balance, end of year	$4,890,000

CORBIN CITY GENERAL FUND

Balance Sheet
June 30, Year 9

Assets

Cash	$ 260,000
Property taxes receivable — delinquent	80,000
Inventory of supplies	110,000
Plant assets (net)	4,620,000
Total assets	$5,070,000

Liabilities, Reserves & Fund Balance

Vouchers payable	$ 160,000
Reserve for delinquent property taxes	20,000
Fund balance	4,890,000
Total liabilities, reserves & fund balance	$5,070,000

Instructions Identify the deficiencies of the foregoing financial statements of Corbin City General Fund. There are no arithmetic errors in the statements. Disregard notes to financial statements.

Case 12-2 Bertram Kent, an officer of a publicly owned corporation, has been elected to the city council of Independence City. Kent has asked you to explain the principal differences in the accounting and financial reporting of a city as compared with a business enterprise.

Instructions
a Describe the principal differences in the accounting and financial reporting of a city as compared with a business enterprise.
b The general funds of some governmental units do not reflect inventories of supplies in the accounting records or financial statements. Is this omission justifiable?
c Should depreciation be recorded in the general fund of a governmental unit? Explain.

PROBLEMS

12-1 The information at the top of page 513 was taken from the accounting records of the General Fund of the City of Lory after the records had been closed for the fiscal year ended June 30, Year 3. The budget for the fiscal year ended June 30, Year 3, included estimated revenues of $2,000,000 and appropriations of $1,940,000. There were no other financing sources or uses.

Instructions Prepare journal entries to record the budgeted and actual transactions of the City of Lory General Fund for the fiscal year ended June 30, Year 3. Also prepare closing entries. Do not differentiate between current and delinquent taxes receivable.

CITY OF LORY GENERAL FUND

	After-closing trial balance, June 30, Year 2	Transactions July 1, Year 2, to June 30, Year 3 Debit	Transactions July 1, Year 2, to June 30, Year 3 Credit	After-closing trial balance, June 30, Year 3
Debits				
Cash	$700,000	$1,820,000	$1,852,000	$668,000
Taxes receivable	40,000	1,870,000	1,828,000	82,000
Total debits	$740,000			$750,000
Credits				
Allowance for uncol-				
lectible taxes	$ 8,000	8,000	10,000	$ 10,000
Vouchers payable ...	132,000	1,852,000	1,840,000	120,000
Fund balance:				
Reserved for encum-				
brances		1,000,000	1,070,000	70,000
Unreserved	600,000	70,000	20,000	550,000
Total credits	$740,000	$6,620,000	$6,620,000	$750,000

12-2 At the start of your examination of the financial statements of the City of Riverdale, you discovered that the City's accountant failed to maintain separate funds. The trial balance (below) of the City of Riverdale General Fund for the year ended December 31, Year 11, was available.

CITY OF RIVERDALE GENERAL FUND
Trial Balance
December 31, Year 11

	Debit	Credit
Cash	$ 207,500	
Taxes receivable — current	148,500	
Allowance for uncollectible current taxes		$ 6,000
Revenues		992,500
Expenditures	760,000	
Donated land	190,000	
Construction in process — River Bridge	130,000	
River Bridge bonds payable		100,000
Contracts payable — River Bridge		30,000
Vouchers payable		7,500
Unreserved fund balance		300,000
Totals	$1,436,000	$1,436,000

Additional information
(1) The budget for Year 11, not recorded in the accounting records, was as follows: Estimated revenues, $815,000; appropriations, $775,000. There were no other financing sources or uses.

(2) Outstanding purchase orders on December 31, Year 11, for operating expenditures not recorded in the accounting records, totaled $2,500.

(3) Included in the Revenues account is a credit of $190,000 representing the current fair value of land donated by the province as a site for construction of the River Bridge.

(4) The taxes receivable became delinquent on December 31, Year 11.

Instructions   Prepare adjusting journal entries on December 31, Year 11, to correct the accounting records of the City of Riverdale General Fund. Adjusting entries for other funds and closing entries are not required.

12-3   The following financial activities affecting Canning County General Fund took place during the year ended June 30, Year 5:

(1) The following budget was adopted:

Estimated revenues:

Property taxes	$4,500,000
Licenses and permits	300,000
Fines	200,000
Total estimated revenues	$5,000,000

Appropriations:

General government	$1,500,000
Police services	1,200,000
Fire department services	900,000
Public works services	800,000
Acquisition of fire engines	400,000
Total appropriations	$4,800,000

There were no other financing sources or uses budgeted.

(2) Property tax bills totaling $4,650,000 were mailed. It was estimated that $150,000 of this amount will be uncollectible.

(3) Property taxes totaling $3,900,000 were collected. The $150,000 previously estimated to be uncollectible remained unchanged, and the balance not collected was reclassified as delinquent. It is estimated that delinquent taxes will be collected soon enough after June 30, Year 5, to make these taxes available to finance obligations incurred during the year ended June 30, Year 5. There was no balance of uncollected taxes on July 1, Year 4.

(4) Other cash collections were as follows:

Licences and permits	$270,000
Fines	200,000
Sale of public works equipment (original cost, $75,000)	15,000
Total other cash collections	$485,000

(5) No encumbrances were outstanding on June 30, Year 4. The following purchase orders were executed:

	Total amount	Outstanding, June 30, Year 5
General government	$1,050,000	$ 60,000
Police services	300,000	30,000
Fire department services	150,000	15,000
Public works services	250,000	10,000
Fire engines	400,000	
Totals	$2,150,000	$115,000

(6) The following vouchers were approved:

General government	$1,440,000
Police services	1,155,000
Fire department services	870,000
Public works services	700,000
Fire engines	400,000
Total vouchers approved	$4,565,000

(7) Vouchers totaling $4,600,000 were paid.

Instructions Prepare journal entries to record the foregoing financial activities in the Canning County General Fund for the year ended June 30, Year 5. Disregard interest accruals and closing entries.

12-4   The trial balance of Arden School District General Fund is presented below:

ARDEN SCHOOL DISTRICT GENERAL FUND
Trial Balance
December 31, Year 5

	Debit	Credit
Cash	$ 47,250	
Short-term investments	11,300	
Taxes receivable — delinquent	30,000	
Inventory of supplies	11,450	
Vouchers payable		$ 20,200
Payable to Internal Service Fund		950
Fund balance reserved for encumbrances		2,800
Fund balance reserved for inventory of supplies		11,450
Unreserved fund balance		59,400
Budgetary fund balance		7,000
Estimated revenues	1,007,000	
Appropriations		985,000
Estimated other financing uses		15,000
Revenues		1,008,200
Expenditures	990,200	
Other financing uses	10,000	
Encumbrances	2,800	
Totals	$2,110,000	$2,110,000

The balance of the Fund Balance Reserved for Inventory of Supplies ledger account on December 31, Year 4, was $9,500.

Instructions

a Prepare the following financial statements for Arden School District General Fund for the year ended December 31, Year 5:
  (1) Statement of revenues, expenditures, and changes in fund balance
  (2) Balance sheet
b Prepare closing entries for Arden School District General Fund on December 31, Year 5.

12-5 The following summary of transactions was taken from the accounting records of Melton School District General Fund before the accounting records had been closed for the year ended June 30, Year 5:

MELTON SCHOOL DISTRICT GENERAL FUND
Summary of Transactions
For Year Ended June 30, Year 5

	After-closing balances, June 30, Year 4	Before-closing balances, June 30, Year 5
Ledger accounts with debit balances:		
Cash	$400,000	$ 700,000
Taxes receivable	150,000	170,000
Estimated revenues		3,000,000
Expenditures		2,700,000
Other financing uses		142,000
Encumbrances		91,000
Totals	$550,000	$6,803,000
Ledger accounts with credit balances:		
Allowance for uncollectible taxes	$ 40,000	$ 70,000
Vouchers payable	80,000	408,000
Payable to other funds	210,000	142,000
Fund balance reserved for		
encumbrances	60,000	91,000
Unreserved fund balance	160,000	162,000
Revenues from taxes		2,800,000
Other revenues		130,000
Budgetary fund balance		20,000
Appropriations		2,810,000
Estimated other financing uses		170,000
Totals	$550,000	$6,803,000

Additional information

(1) The estimated taxes receivable for the year ended June 30, Year 5, were $2,870,000, and taxes collected during the year totaled $2,810,000.
(2) An analysis of the transactions in the Vouchers Payable ledger account for the year ended June 30, Year 5, follows:

	Debit (credit)
Current year expenditures (all subject to encumbrances)	$(2,700,000)
Expenditures applicable to June 30, Year 4, outstanding encumbrances	(58,000)
Vouchers for payments to other funds	(210,000)
Cash payments	2,640,000
Net change	$ (328,000)

(3) During Year 5 the General Fund was billed $142,000 for services furnished by other funds of Melton School District.

(4) On May 2, Year 5, purchase orders were issued for new textbooks at an estimated cost of $91,000. The books were to be delivered in August, Year 5.

Instructions

a Based on the foregoing data, reconstruct the original journal entries to record all transactions of Melton School District General Fund for the year ended June 30, Year 5, including the recording of the budget for the year. Disregard current and delinquent taxes receivable. (Hint: The $2,000 difference between the $60,000 fund balance reserved for encumbrances on June 30, Year 4, and the $58,000 amount vouchered for the related expenditures is credited to the Unreserved Fund Balance account.)

b Prepare closing entries on June 30, Year 5.

c Prepare an after-closing trial balance for Melton School District General Fund on June 30, Year 5.

12-6 Because the controller of the City of Romaine resigned, the assistant controller attempted to compute the cash required to be derived from property taxes for the General Fund for the year ending June 30, Year 7. The computation was made as of January 1, Year 6, to serve as a basis for establishing the property tax rate for the fiscal year ending June 30, Year 7. The mayor of Romaine has requested you to review the assistant controller's computations and obtain other necessary information to prepare for the City of Romaine General Fund a formal estimate of the cash required to be derived from property taxes for the fiscal year ending June 30, Year 7. Following are the computations prepared by the assistant controller:

City resources other than proposed property tax levy:	
Estimated General Fund cash balance, Jan. 1, Year 6	$ 352,000
Estimated cash receipts from property taxes, Jan. 1 to June 30, Year 6	2,222,000
Estimated cash revenues from investments, Jan. 1, Year 6, to June 30, Year 7	442,000
Estimated proceeds from issuance of general obligation bonds in August, Year 6	3,000,000
Total City resources	$6,016,000

General Fund requirements:	
Estimated expenditures, Jan. 1 to June 30, Year 6	$1,900,000
Proposed appropriations, July 1, Year 6, to June 30, Year 7	4,300,000
Total General Fund requirements	$6,200,000

Additional information

(1) The General Fund cash balance required for July 1, Year 7, is $175,000.

(2) Property tax collections are due in March and September of each year. You note that during February, Year 6, estimated expenditures will exceed available cash by $200,000. Pending collection of property taxes in March, Year 6, this deficiency will have to be met by the issuance of 30-day tax-anticipation notes of $200,000 at an estimated interest rate of 12% a year.

(3) The proposed general obligation bonds will be issued by the City of Romaine Enterprise Fund to finance the construction of a new water pumping station.

Instructions   Prepare a working paper as of January 1, Year 6, to compute the property tax levy requirement for the City of Romaine General Fund for the fiscal year ending June 30, Year 7.

12-7   The following data were taken from the accounting records of the Town of Tosca General Fund after the records had been closed for the fiscal year ended June 30, Year 3:

TOWN OF TOSCA GENERAL FUND
Data from Accounting Records
For Year Ended June 30, Year 3

	Balances July 1, Year 2	Fiscal Year 3 changes Debit	Fiscal Year 3 changes Credit	Balances June 30, Year 3
Assets				
Cash	$ 180,000	$ 955,000	$ 880,000	$ 255,000
Taxes receivable	20,000	809,000	781,000	48,000
Allowance for uncollectible				
taxes	(4,000)	6,000	9,000	(7,000)
Total assets	$ 196,000			$ 296,000
Liabilities & Fund Balance				
Vouchers payable	$ 44,000	880,000	889,000	$ 53,000
Payable to Internal Service				
Fund	2,000	7,000	10,000	5,000
Payable to Debt Service				
Fund	10,000	60,000	100,000	50,000
Fund balance reserved for				
encumbrances	40,000	40,000	47,000	47,000
Unreserved fund balance ..	100,000	47,000	88,000	141,000
Total liabilities & fund				
balance	$ 196,000	$2,804,000	$2,804,000	$ 296,000

Additional data

(1) The budget for Fiscal Year 3 provided for estimated revenues of $1,000,000 and appropriations of $965,000. There were no other financing sources or uses budgeted.

(2) Expenditures totaling $895,000, in addition to those chargeable against Fund Balance Reserved for Encumbrances ledger account, were made.

(3) The actual expenditure chargeable against the July 1, Year 2, Fund Balance Reserved for Encumbrances ledger account was $37,000.

Instructions Reconstruct the journal entries, including closing entries, for the Town of Tosca General Fund indicated by the foregoing data for the year ended June 30, Year 3. Do not attempt to differentiate between current and delinquent taxes receivable.

13

LOCAL GOVERNMENTAL UNITS: OTHER FUNDS AND ACCOUNT GROUPS

In this chapter we discuss and illustrate accounting for a governmental unit's funds other than the general fund, and for the general fixed assets and general long-term debt account groups. Also covered in this chapter are the form and content of annual reports of governmental units, an appraisal of accounting principles for governmental units, and a summary of the CICA research study's recommendations.

GOVERNMENTAL FUNDS

Accounting for the four governmental funds (special revenue funds, capital projects funds, debt service funds, special assessment funds) other than the general fund generally incorporates many of the accounting principles discussed in Chapter 12. For example, the modified accrual basis of accounting is appropriate for all governmental funds, and recording the budget (together with encumbrance accounting) is mandatory for special revenue funds and often useful for debt service funds, capital projects funds, and special assessment funds.

Accounting for special revenue funds

As indicated in principle 3 on page 489, special revenue funds are established by governmental units to account for the collections and expenditures associated with specialized revenue sources that are earmarked by law or regulation to finance specified governmental operations. Fees for rubbish collection and traffic violation fines are examples of governmental unit revenues that might be accounted for in separate special revenue funds.

Account titles, budgetary processes, and financial statements for special revenue funds are similar to those for general funds; therefore, they are not illustrated in this section.

Accounting for capital projects funds

Capital projects funds of a governmental unit record the receipt and payment of cash for the construction or acquisition of the governmental unit's plant assets, other than those financed by special assessment funds, proprietary funds, or trust funds. The resources for a capital projects fund usually are derived from proceeds of general obligation bonds, but the resources may also come from current tax revenues or from grants or shared revenues of other governmental units.

A capital budget, rather than an annual budget, is the **control device** appropriate for a capital projects fund. The capital budget should deal with both the authorized expenditures for the project and the bonds or other sources of revenues for the project.

Journal Entries for Capital Projects Funds   On July 1, Year 5, the Town of Verdant Glen authorized a $500,000, 20-year, 15% general obligation bond issue to finance an addition to the town hall. A capital budget was approved for the amount of the bonds, but it was not to be integrated in the accounting records of the capital projects fund authorized for the project. The journal entries on page 522 illustrate the issuance of the bonds and other activities of the Town of Verdant Glen Capital Projects Fund for the year ended June 30, Year 6. The following features of the journal entries should be noted:

1 The capital budget for the town hall addition is not entered in the accounting records of the Capital Projects Fund. The indenture for the 20-year, 15% general obligation bonds provides adequate control.

2 Neither the liability nor the discount applicable to the 20-year general obligation bonds is recorded in the Capital Projects Fund. The liability for the bonds is recorded at face amount in the general long-term debt account group (see page 542).

3 The proceeds of the general obligation bonds represent other financing sources to the Capital Projects Fund. The interest earned on the short-term investment in government treasury bills represents revenues to the Capital Projects Fund.

4 The encumbrances and expenditures accounting for the Capital Projects Fund is similar to that for the General Fund illustrated in Chapter 12. Also, closing entries for the two types of governmental funds are similar.

Expenditures for construction recorded in the Town of Verdant Glen Capital Projects Fund are accompanied in the General Fixed Assets Account Group by a journal entry at the end of the fiscal year with a debit to Construction in Progress and a credit to Investment in Fixed Assets from Capital Projects Fund. The accounting for the general fixed assets account group is illustrated in a subsequent section of this chapter.

At the end of each fiscal year prior to completion of a capital project, the Revenues, Other Financing Sources, Expenditures, and Encumbrances accounts of the Capital Projects Fund are closed to the Unreserved Fund

TOWN OF VERDANT GLEN CAPITAL PROJECTS FUND

General Journal

Cash	470,188	
Other Financing Sources		470,18
To record issuance of 20-year, 15% general obligation bonds due		
July 1, Year 25, interest payable Jan. 1 and July 1, to yield 16%,		
face amount $500,000.		
Investments	325,000	
Cash		325,00
To record acquisition of $350,000 face amount of government		
treasury bills, maturity 26 weeks.		
Encumbrances	482,000	
Fund Balance Reserved for Encumbrances		482,00
To record contracts with architect and construction contractor and		
issuance of purchase orders.		
Cash	350,000	
Investments		325,00
Revenues		25,00
To record receipt of cash for matured treasury bills.		
Expenditures	378,000	
Vouchers Payable		378,00
To record expenditures for the year.		
Fund Balance Reserved for Encumbrances	368,200	
Encumbrances		368,20
To reverse encumbrances applicable to vouchered expenditures.		
Vouchers Payable	327,500	
Cash		327,50
To record payment of vouchers during the year.		
Unreserved Fund Balance ($482,000 − $368,200)	113,800	
Encumbrances		113,80
To close Encumbrances account.		
Revenues	25,000	
Other Financing Sources	470,188	
Expenditures		378,00
Unreserved Fund Balance		117,18
To close revenues, expenditures, and other financing sources.		

Balance account. Upon completion of the project, the entire Capital Projects Fund is closed by a transfer of any unused cash to the Debt Service Fund or the General Fund, as appropriate; the Other Financing Sources account of the receiving fund would be credited. Any cash deficiency in the Capital Projects Fund probably would be made up by the General Fund; this financing would be credited to the Other Financing Sources account of the Capital Projects Fund and debited to the Other Financing Uses account of the General Fund.

Financial Statements for Capital Projects Fund A capital projects fund issues the same financial statements as a general fund — a statement of revenues, expenditures, and changes in fund balance, and a balance sheet.

TOWN OF VERDANT GLEN CAPITAL PROJECTS FUND

Statement of Revenues, Expenditures, and Changes in Fund Balance
For Year Ended June 30, Year 6

Revenues:	
Miscellaneous	*$ 25,000*
Expenditures: *	
Construction contracts	*$ 287,600*
Engineering and other	*90,400*
Total expenditures	*$ 378,000*
Excess (deficiency) of revenues over expenditures	*$(353,000)*
Other financing sources:	
Proceeds of general obligation bonds	*470,188*
Excess of revenues and other financing sources over expenditures	*$ 117,188*
Fund balance, beginning of year	*-0-*
Fund balance, end of year	*$ 117,188*

*Breakdown of expenditures is assumed.

TOWN OF VERDANT GLEN CAPITAL PROJECTS FUND

Balance Sheet
June 30, Year 6

Assets

Cash	*$167,688*

Liabilities & Fund Balance

Liabilities:		
Vouchers payable		*$ 50,500*
Fund balance:		
Reserved for encumbrances	*$113,800*	
Unreserved	*3,388*	*117,188*
Total liabilities & fund balance		*$167,688*

The financial statements for the year ended June 30, Year 6, appear on page 523.

To reiterate, the assets constructed with resources of the Capital Project Fund do not appear in that fund's balance sheet. Constructed plant assets appear in the governmental unit's **general fixed assets account group**. Furthermore, the general obligation bonds issued to finance the Capital Projects Fund are not a liability of that fund. Prior to the maturity date or dates of the bonds, the liability is carried in the **general long-term debt account group** (see page 541). On the date the bonds mature, the related liability is transferred to the debt service fund or to the general fund from the general long-term debt account group.

Accounting for debt service funds

Payments of principal and interest on long-term bonds of a governmental unit, other than special assessment bonds, revenue bonds, and general obligation bonds serviced by an enterprise fund, are accounted for either in the general fund or in debt service funds. *Special assessment bonds* are repaid from the proceeds of special assessment levies against specific properties receiving benefits from the special assessment improvement; accordingly, these bonds are accounted for in special assessment funds. *Revenue bonds* are payable from the earnings of a governmental unit enterprise and are accounted for in the appropriate enterprise fund. In some cases, *general obligation bonds*, which are backed by the full faith and credit of the issuing governmental unit, will be repaid from the resources of a governmental unit enterprise. These general obligation bonds are reported as liabilities of the appropriate enterprise fund.

We must stress that the liability for bonds payable from resources of the general fund or a debt service fund is not recorded in that fund until the debt matures. Prior to maturity date, the bond liability is carried in the general long-term debt account group.

The two customary types of general obligation bonds whose servicing is recorded in debt service funds are the following:

Serial bonds, with principal payable in annual installments over the term of the bond issue

Term bonds, with principal payable in total on a fixed maturity date, generally from proceeds of an accumulated sinking fund

Generally, legal requirements govern the establishment of debt service funds. In the absence of legal requirements or of a formal plan for accumulation of a sinking fund for repayment of a general obligation term bond, there is no need for a debt service fund to be created.

Journal Entries for Debt Service Fund   To illustrate the journal entries that are typical for a debt service fund, let us assume that the Town of Verdant Glen had only two general obligation bond issues outstanding during the year ended June 30, Year 6: A $100,000, 10% serial bond issue whose final annual installment of $10,000 was payable on January 1, Year 6, and a $500,000, 15% term bond issue due July 1, Year 25 (see page 521). The Town Council had authorized establishment of a debt service fund for the serial bonds. However, sinking fund accumulations on the term bonds were not required to begin until July 1, Year 8; therefore, a debt service fund for those bonds was unnecessary during the year ended June 30, Year 6.

Interest on both general obligation bond issues was payable each January 1 and July 1. Interest payments on the term bonds were recorded in the General Fund during the year ended June 30, Year 6, and were included in expenditures of that fund, as illustrated on page 502. Interest payments on the serial bonds were made from the Debt Service Fund to a fiscal agent, for remission to the bondholders.

TOWN OF VERDANT GLEN DEBT SERVICE FUND
General Journal

Cash	11,000	
Other Financing Sources		11,000
To record receipt of cash from General Fund for payment of serial		
bond principal ($10,000) and interest ($1,000) maturing on July 1,		
Year 5, and Jan. 1, Year 6.		
Cash with Fiscal Agent	11,000	
Cash		11,000
To record payment of cash to bank trust department acting as fiscal		
agent for payment of serial bond principal and interest.		
Expenditures	11,000	
Matured Bonds Payable		10,000
Matured Interest Payable		1,000
To record expenditures for interest due July 1, Year 5, and principal		
and interest due Jan. 1, Year 6.		
Matured Bonds Payable	10,000	
Matured Interest Payable	1,000	
Cash with Fiscal Agent		11,000
To record fiscal agent's payments of bond principal and interest.		
Expenditures	342	
Cash		342
To record payment of fiscal agent for services during year ended		
June 30, Year 6.		
Other Financing Sources	11,000	
Fund Balance Reserved for Debt Service	342	
Expenditures		11,342
To close fund on extinguishment of related serial bonds.		

The June 30, Year 5, balance sheet of the Town of Verdant Glen Debt Service Fund for the serial bonds was as follows:

TOWN OF VERDANT GLEN DEBT SERVICE FUND
Balance Sheet
June 30, Year 5

Assets

Cash $34

Liabilities & Fund Balance

Fund balance reserved for debt service $34

The journal entries for the Debt Service Fund for the year ended June 30 Year 6, are presented on page 525. Following are significant aspects of th illustrated journal entries for the Debt Service Fund:

1 There was no journal entry to record an annual budget. Generally, indentures fo general obligation bonds provide sufficient safeguards (such as restricting th fund balance of the debt service fund solely for the payment of debt and relate servicing costs), so that recording the budget in the Debt Service Fund is ur necessary. (Note, however, on page 502 of Chapter 12 that the General Fund' other financing use for payment of $11,000 to the Debt Service Fund had bee included in the General Fund's annual budget.)

2 Expenditures for principal and interest payments of the Debt Service Fund ar recorded only on the maturity dates of the obligations. Prior to the maturit dates, the liabilities are carried in the general long-term debt account group (se page 542). Because a debt service fund does not issue purchase orders, encum brance accounting is not required.

3 The closing entry extinguishes all remaining ledger account balances of the Deb Service Fund, because the final serial principal payment had been made.

The modified accrual basis of accounting is appropriate for a debt servic fund. Thus, any property taxes specifically earmarked for servicing of governmental unit's general obligation bonds may be accrued as revenues i the debt service fund. The accounting for such a tax accrual is the same a that for the general fund.

For a term bond, which requires the *accumulation of a sinking fund* the journal entries for a debt service fund include the investment of cash i interest-bearing securities and the collection of interest. Under the modi fied accrual basis of accounting, interest revenue accrued on sinking fund investments at the end of the governmental unit's fiscal year is recorded i the accounting records of the debt service fund.

Financial Statements for Debt Service Fund   We already have illustrated a balance sheet for a debt service fund above. There is no balance sheet fo the Town of Verdant Glen Debt Service Fund on June 30, Year 6, because the fund was completely closed. The statement of revenues, expenditures, and changes in fund balance for the Town of Verdant Glen Debt Service Fund is as follows for the year ended June 30, Year 6:

TOWN OF VERDANT GLEN DEBT SERVICE FUND
Statement of Revenues, Expenditures, and Changes in Fund Balance
For Year Ended June 30, Year 6

Expenditures:	
Principal retirement	$ 10,000
Interest and charges by fiscal agent	1,342
Total expenditures	$ 11,342
Excess (deficiency) of revenues over expenditures	$(11,342)
Other financing sources:	
Operating transfers in	11,000
Excess (deficiency) of revenues and other financing sources over	
expenditures	$ (342)
Fund balance, beginning of year	342
Fund balance, end of year	$ -0-

Accounting for special assessment funds

A special assessment fund accounts for the assets, liabilities, revenues, and expenditures attributable to special tax assessments, payable in installments, that are levied on property owners in the governmental unit's jurisdiction. These tax assessments finance construction projects primarily for the benefit of the assessed property owners.

Accounting for a special assessment fund is in many respects a composite of the accounting for a debt service fund and a capital projects fund. The accounting records of a special assessment fund include both the proceeds and the servicing of the *special assessment bonds* that are issued to finance the construction project prior to the collection of special assessments receivable.

Journal Entries for Special Assessment Fund   The town council of the Town of Verdant Glen enacted a special assessment for paving streets and installing sidewalks in a section of the town. The total assessment was $250,000, payable in five annual installments, beginning July 1, Year 5. Interest on unpaid balances at 16% a year was payable annually, beginning July 1, Year 6. To finance the cost of the construction project, the Town Council authorized the issuance of $200,000 face amount, 14%, four-year special assessment bonds, payable $50,000 a year plus interest payable annually, beginning July 1, Year 6. The Town Council approved contracts with a firm of contractors for the paving work.

Following are journal entries for the Town of Verdant Glen Special Assessment Fund for the year ended June 30, Year 6:

TOWN OF VERDANT GLEN SPECIAL ASSESSMENT FUND
General Journal

Special Assessments Receivable — Current	50,000	
Special Assessments Receivable — Deferred	200,000	
Revenues		50,000
Deferred Revenues		200,000
To record special assessment levied on property owners benefited by		
paving and sidewalk project.		
Cash	50,000	
Special Assessments Receivable — Current		50,000
To record receipt of current special assessment payments.		
Cash	196,183	
Discount on Bonds Payable	3,817	
Bonds Payable		200,000
To record issuance of $200,000 face amount of 14%, four-year		
special assessment bonds to yield 15%.		
Encumbrances	238,000	
Fund Balance Reserved for Encumbrances		238,000
To record contract with contractor and issuance of various purchase		
orders.		
Expenditures	126,000	
Vouchers Payable		126,000
To record expenditures for construction for the year.		
Fund Balance Reserved for Encumbrances	129,000	
Encumbrances		129,000
To reverse encumbrances applicable to vouchered expenditures.		
Vouchers Payable	109,600	
Cash		109,600
To record payment of vouchers during the year.		
Interest Receivable	32,000	
Revenues		32,000
To accrue interest on deferred special assessments on June 30,		
Year 6: $200,000 × 0.16 = $32,000.		
Expenditures	29,427	
Discount on Bonds Payable		1,427
Interest Payable		28,000
To accrue interest on special assessment bonds on June 30, Year 6:		
$200,000 × 0.14 = $28,000; and to provide for expenditures		
represented by effective interest on bonds:		
$196,183 × 0.15 = $29,427.		

(Continued

TOWN OF VERDANT GLEN SPECIAL ASSESSMENT FUND
General Journal (concluded)

Deferred Revenues	50,000	
Revenues		50,000
To transfer revenues represented by special assessment installment		
receivable in year ending June 30, Year 7, to current category.		
Special Assessments Receivable — Current	50,000	
Special Assessments Receivable — Deferred		50,000
To transfer special assessment installment receivable on July 1,		
Year 6, to current category.		
Unreserved Fund Balance ($238,000 − $129,000)	109,000	
Encumbrances		109,000
To close Encumbrances account.		
Revenues ($50,000 + $32,000 + $50,000)	132,000	
Unreserved Fund Balance	23,427	
Expenditures ($126,000 + $29,427)		155,427
To close revenues and expenditures.		

Significant features of the foregoing journal entries are as follows:

1 The capital budget for the paving and sidewalks project is not entered in the accounting records of the Special Assessment Fund. The Town Council's approval of the special assessment and the related bonds provides adequate control.

2 A **current** and **deferred** breakdown is provided for both the special assessments receivable and the related revenues. It is inappropriate to consider the total of the special assessments as revenues of the fiscal year in which the special assessment fund was established, because the collection of the related receivables is spread over a five-year period.

3 The special assessment bonds are repayable serially over a four-year period, from proceeds of the annual collections of special assessments and related interest receivable. Accordingly, the present value of the 14% bonds at the 15% yield rate is computed as illustrated below.

Principal and interest due July 1, Year 6:	
($50,000 + $28,000) × 0.869565*	$ 67,826
Principal and interest due July 1, Year 7:	
($50,000 + $21,000) × 0.756144*	53,686
Principal and interest due July 1, Year 8:	
($50,000 + $14,000) × 0.657516*	42,081
Principal and interest due July 1, Year 9:	
($50,000 + $7,000) × 0.571753*	32,590
Present value (proceeds) of special assessment bonds at 15% yield basis . .	$196,183

* From Table 2 of the Appendix in back of the book.

4 The encumbrances and expenditures accounting for the Special Assessment Fund is similar to that for the Capital Projects Fund illustrated on page 522. Also, closing entries are similar to those for the other governmental funds (General Fund, Special Assessment Fund, Capital Projects Fund, and Debt Service Fund illustrated in this chapter and in Chapter 12.

5 Both interest receivable and interest payable are accrued by the Special Assessment Fund at the end of the year, in accordance with the modified accrual basis of accounting. If differences between the two types of interest are not material, the accruals may be omitted.[1]

6 At the end of the fiscal year, the special assessments receivable that are to be collected in the following fiscal year, and the related revenue, are transferred from the ***deferred*** to the ***current*** classification. However, a comparable transfer is not required for the current portion of the special assessment bonds payable.

Trial Balance at End of Fiscal Year for Special Assessment Fund   Following is the trial balance of the Town of Verdant Glen Special Assessment Fund on June 30, Year 6, prior to the closing entry for revenues and expenditures:

TOWN OF VERDANT GLEN SPECIAL ASSESSMENT FUND
Trial Balance
June 30, Year 6

	Debit	Credit
Cash	$136,583	
Special assessments receivable — current	50,000	
Special assessments receivable — deferred	150,000	
Interest receivable	32,000	
Vouchers payable		$ 16,400
Interest payable		28,000
Deferred revenues		150,000
Bonds payable		200,000
Discount on bonds payable	2,390	
Fund balance reserved for encumbrances		109,000
Unreserved fund balance	109,000	
Revenues		132,000
Expenditures	155,427	
Totals	$635,400	$635,400

Financial Statements for Special Assessments Fund   The financial statements for a special assessments fund are the same as those for other governmental funds — a statement of revenues, expenditures, and changes

---

1 National Council on Governmental Accounting, *Governmental Accounting and Financial Reporting Principles*, Municipal Finance Officers Association of the United States and Canada (Chicago: 1979), p. 12.

in fund balance, and a balance sheet. For the Town of Verdant Glen Special Assessment Fund the financial statements for the year ended June 30, Year 6, are shown below.

TOWN OF VERDANT GLEN SPECIAL ASSESSMENT FUND
Statement of Revenues, Expenditures, and Changes in Fund Balance
For Year Ended June 30, Year 6

Revenues:	
Special assessments	$100,000
Interest	32,000
Total revenues	$132,000
Expenditures:	
Capital projects	$126,000
Debt service	29,427
Total expenditures	$155,427
Excess (deficiency) of revenues over expenditures	$ (23,427)
Fund balance, beginning of year	-0-
Fund balance (deficiency), end of year	$ (23,427)

TOWN OF VERDANT GLEN SPECIAL ASSESSMENT FUND

Balance Sheet
June 30, Year 6

Assets

Cash		$136,583
Receivables:		
Special assessments:		
Current	$ 50,000	
Deferred	150,000	200,000
Interest		32,000
Total assets		$368,583

Liabilities & Fund Balance

Liabilities:		
Vouchers payable		$ 16,400
Interest payable		28,000
Deferred revenues		150,000
Bonds payable	$200,000	
Less: Discount on bonds payable	2,390	197,610
Total liabilities:		$392,010
Fund balance (deficiency):		
Reserved for encumbrances	$ 109,000	
Reserved for debt service	(132,427)	(23,427)
Total liabilities & fund balance		$ 368,583

Because of the deferral of $150,000 of revenues in the foregoing balance sheet, there is a deficit of $132,427 in the Fund Balance Reserved for Debt Service ledger account on June 30, Year 6. This deficit will be eliminated in subsequent fiscal years as the deferred revenues are earned and expenditures for construction are completed.

In the foregoing illustration, we have assumed that all current special assessments receivable were collected. The accounting for delinquent special assessments parallels the accounting for delinquent property taxes receivable by a general fund, as described on pages 500 and 503.

PROPRIETARY FUNDS

Enterprise funds and internal service funds comprise the proprietary funds of a governmental unit. These funds are more similar to business enterprises than are the governmental funds or the trust and agency funds. Enterprise funds sell services to the citizens of the governmental unit, and sometimes to other funds of the governmental unit, for amounts designed to yield net income. Internal service funds, as their title indicates, sell goods or services to other funds of the governmental unit, but not to the public. Accordingly, earning significant amounts of net income is not an objective of an internal service fund.

Both enterprise funds and internal services funds use the accrual basis of accounting and issue financial statements similar to those for a business enterprise — a statement of revenues, expenses, and changes in retained earnings (which includes an amount labeled *net income*), a balance sheet, and a statement of changes in financial position. The balance sheets of both types of proprietary funds are classified into current and noncurrent sections. The plant assets of the two types of proprietary funds are recorded in their accounting records, and depreciation and amortization expenses are recorded by each proprietary fund.

Because of the many similarities in the accounting cycle and the financial statements of business enterprises and proprietary funds, we do not provide extended illustrations for proprietary funds in this section. Instead, we emphasize the unique features of proprietary funds, including differences from features of business enterprises.

Accounting for enterprise funds

Enterprise funds account for the operations of commercial-type activities of a governmental unit, such as utilities, airports, seaports, and recreational facilities. These commercial-type enterprises sell services to the public (and in some cases to other activities of the governmental unit) at a profit. Consequently, the accounting for enterprise funds is more akin to business enterprise accounting than the accounting for any other governmental unit fund. For example, the accrual basis of accounting is used for an enterprise fund, with short-term prepayments, depreciation expense, and doubtful accounts expense recorded in the fund's accounting records. The enterprise fund's accounting records also include the plant assets owned by the fund, as well as the liabilities for revenue bonds and any general obligation bonds payable by the fund. Encumbrance accounting is not used for enterprise funds, and their annual budgets generally are not recorded in the accounting records. Retained earnings of an enterprise fund may be debited with cash remittances to the general fund, similar to dividends declared and paid by a business enterprise.

However, there are a number of differences between accounting for an enterprise fund and accounting for a business enterprise. Among these differences are the following:

1 Enterprise funds are not subject to federal and provincial income taxes. However, an enterprise fund may be required to make payments in lieu of property or franchise taxes to the general fund. (See page 502 of Chapter 12.)

2 There is no capital stock in an enterprise fund's balance sheet. Instead, Contributions accounts set forth, in a *fund equity* section of the balance sheet, the assets contributed to the enterprise fund by the governmental unit, by customers of the enterprise fund, or by other public agencies.

3 An enterprise fund has many restricted assets, which are segregated from current assets in the balance sheet. Cash deposits made by customers of a utility enterprise fund, which are to assure the customers' payment for utility services, are restricted for cash or interest-bearing investments to offset the enterprise fund's liability for the customers' deposits. Cash received from proceeds of revenue bonds issued by the enterprise fund is restricted to payments for construction of plant assets financed by issuance of the bonds. Part of the cash generated by the enterprise fund's operations must be set aside and invested for payment of interest and principal of the revenue bonds issued by the enterprise fund.

4 Current liabilities payable from restricted assets are segregated from other current liabilities of an enterprise fund in a section that precedes long-term liabilities.

5 A number of retained earnings reserves appear in the accounting records of an enterprise fund. These reserves are equal to the cash and investments restricted to payment of revenue bond interest and principal.

Accounting for internal service funds

An internal service fund is established to sell goods and services to other funds of the governmental unit, but not to the public. This type of fund is created to assure uniformity and economies in the procurement of goods and services for the governmental unit as a whole, such as stationery supplies and the maintenance and repairs of motor vehicles.

The operations of internal service funds resemble those of a business enterprise, except that internal service funds are not profit-motivated. The revenues of internal service funds should be sufficient to cover all their operating costs and expenses, with perhaps a modest profit margin. In this way, the resources of internal service funds are "revolving"; the original contribution from the governmental unit to establish an internal service fund is expended for supplies, operating equipment, and employees' salaries or wages, and the amounts expended then are recouped through billings to other funds of the governmental unit.

Although an internal service fund should use an annual budget for managerial planning and control purposes, the budget need not be recorded in the accounting records of the fund. The accrual basis of accounting, including the perpetual inventory system and depreciation of plant assets, is required for an internal service fund. Encumbrance accounting is not required but may be useful in controlling nonrecurring purchase orders of an internal service fund.

Because internal service funds do not issue bonds and do not receive contributions or deposits from customers, the financial statements of internal service funds are nearly identical in form and content to those of business enterprises. However, similar to enterprise funds, internal service funds do not have owners' equity in their balance sheets. A Contribution from Government ledger account accompanies the Retained Earnings account in the *fund equity* section of the balance sheet for an internal service fund.

FIDUCIARY FUNDS

Expendable trust funds, nonexpendable trust funds, pension trust funds, and agency funds constitute the fiduciary funds of a governmental unit. The position of the governmental unit with respect to such funds is one of a *custodian* or a *trustee*, rather than an *owner*.

In explaining the accounting principles for local governmental units, the National Council on Governmental Accounting described accounting for trust funds as follows:[2]

> Each trust fund is classified for accounting measurement purposes as either a governmental fund or a proprietary fund. Expendable trust funds are accounted for in essentially the same manner as governmental funds. Nonexpendable trust funds and pension trust funds are accounted for in essentially the same manner as proprietary funds. Agency funds are purely custodial (assets equal liabilities) and thus do not involve measurement of results of operations.

Accounting for agency funds

Agency funds are of short duration. Typically, agency funds are used to account for sales taxes collected by a local government on behalf of the provincial government, and for payroll taxes and other deductions withheld from salaries and wages payable to employees of a governmental unit. The amounts withheld subsequently are paid to a federal or provincial collection unit. In addition, many Canadian cities and municipalities have school divisions which operate autonomously from the local government unit. The school boards levy property taxes which the city or municipality collects on their behalf. The collection and subsequent payment to the school divisions are further examples of the use of an agency fund.

2 Ibid., p. 6.

Agency funds do not have operations during a fiscal year; thus, the only financial statement for an agency fund is a balance sheet showing the cash or receivables of the fund and the amounts payable to other funds or governmental units or to outsiders.

Accounting for expendable and nonexpendable trust funds

Trust funds of a governmental unit are longer-lived than agency funds. An *expendable trust fund* is one whose principal and income both may be expended to achieve the objectives of the trust. A *nonexpendable trust fund* is one whose revenues are expended to carry out the objectives of the trust; the principal remains intact. For example, an *endowment* established by the grantor of a trust may specify that the revenues from the endowment are to be expended by the governmental unit for student scholarships, but the endowment principal is not to be expended. A nonexpendable trust fund requires two separate trust fund accounting entities — one for principal and one for revenues. Accounting for the two separate trust funds requires a careful distinction between transactions affecting the principal — such as changes in the investment portfolio — and transactions affecting revenues — such as cash dividends and interest on the investment portfolio. The *trust indenture*, which is the legal document establishing the trust, should specify distinctions between principal and revenues. If the trust indenture is silent with respect to such distinctions, the trust law of the governmental unit governs separation of principal trust fund and revenues trust fund transactions.

Because the governmental unit serves as a custodian for a trust fund, accounting for a trust fund should comply with the trust indenture under which the fund was established. Among the provisions that might affect the accounting for a trust fund are requirements that the annual budget for the trust fund be recorded in its accounting records and that depreciation be recorded for an endowment principal trust fund that includes depreciable assets.

To illustrate accounting for expendable and nonexpendable trust funds, assume that Karl and Mabel Root, residents of the Town of Verdant Glen, contributed marketable securities with a market value of $100,000 on July 1, Year 5, to a trust to be administered by the Town of Verdant Glen as trustee. Principal of the gift was to be maintained in an Endowment Principal Nonexpendable Trust Fund. Revenues from the marketable securities were to be used for scholarships for qualified students to attend Verdant Glen College; the revenues and expenditures for scholarships were to be accounted for in an Endowment Revenues Expendable Trust Fund. The Canada Trust Company was to receive an annual trustee's fee of $500 for administering the two trust funds on behalf of the Town of Verdant Glen.

Journal entries for the two trust funds for the year ended June 30, Year 6, are summarized on page 536.

Explanation of transactions	Account titles	Endowment Principal Nonexpendable Trust Fund	Endowment Revenues Expendable Trust Fund
Receipt of marketable securities in trust.	Investments	100,000	
	Revenues	100,000	
Accrual of revenues on marketable securities.	Interest Receivable . . .	5,000	
	Dividends Receivable . . .	8,000	
	Revenues	13,000	
Receipt of interest and dividends	Cash	13,000	
	Interest Receivable . . .	5,000	
	Dividends Receivable . . .	8,000	
Recognition of liability to Revenues Trust Fund for interest and dividends	Operating Transfers Out . . .	13,000	
	Payable to Revenues Trust Fund	13,000	
	Receivable from Principal Trust Fund		13,000
	Other Financing Sources		13,000
Transfer of cash from Principal Trust Fund to Revenues Trust Fund	Payable to Revenues Trust Fund . . .	13,000	
	Cash	13,000	
	Cash		13,000
	Receivable from Principal Trust Fund . . .		13,000
Payment of scholarships to students James Rich and Janet Wells	Expenditures		12,000
	Cash		12,000
Payment of trustee's fee	Expenditures		500
	Cash		500
Closing entries	Revenues	113,000	13,000
	Operating Transfers Out . . .	13,000	
	Fund Balance Reserved for Endowment	100,000	
	Other Financing Sources		13,000
	Expenditures		12,500
	Fund Balance Reserved for Scholarships . . .		500

Financial Statements of Nonexpendable Trust Fund   Because accounting for nonexpendable trust funds parallels accounting for proprietary funds, the financial statements for a nonexpendable trust fund are a statement of revenues, expenses, and changes in fund balance; a balance sheet; and a statement of changes in financial position. Financial statements of the Town of Verdant Glen Endowment Principal Nonexpendable Trust Fund are shown below for the year ended June 30, Year 6.

TOWN OF VERDANT GLEN ENDOWMENT PRINCIPAL NONEXPENDABLE TRUST FUND
Statement of Revenues, Expenses, and Changes in Fund Balance
For Year Ended June 30, Year 6

Operating revenues:	
Interest	$ 5,000
Dividends	8,000
Gifts	100,000
Total operating revenues	$113,000
Operating transfers out	13,000
Net income	$100,000
Fund balance, beginning of year	-0-
Fund balance, end of year	$100,000

TOWN OF VERDANT GLEN ENDOWMENT PRINCIPAL NONEXPENDABLE TRUST FUND
Balance Sheet
June 30, Year 6

Assets

Investments	$100,000

Liabilities & Fund Balance

Fund balance reserved for endowment	$100,000

TOWN OF VERDANT GLEN ENDOWMENT PRINCIPAL NONEXPENDABLE TRUST FUND

Statement of Changes in Financial Position
For Year Ended June 30, Year 6

Financial resources provided	
Operations — net income	$100,000
Financial resources applied	-0-
Increase in financial resources: working capital	$100,000

	Increase in working capital
Investments	$100,000

Financial Statements of Expendable Trust Fund   Accounting for expendable trust funds is comparable to accounting for governmental funds; therefore, financial statements for expendable trust funds are a statement of revenues, expenditures, and changes in fund balance, and a balance sheet. For the Town of Verdant Glen Endowment Revenues Expendable Trust Fund, financial statements for the year ended June 30, Year 6, are as follows:

TOWN OF VERDANT GLEN ENDOWMENT REVENUES
EXPENDABLE TRUST FUND
Statement of Revenues, Expenditures, and Changes in Fund Balance
For Year Ended June 30, Year 6

Revenues	$ -0-
Expenditures:	
Education	$ 12,000
Administration	500
Total expenditures	$ 12,500
Excess (deficiency) of revenues over expenditures	$(12,500)
Operating transfers in	13,000
Excess of revenues and other financing sources over expenditures	$ 500
Fund balance, beginning of year	-0-
Fund balance, end of year	$ 500

TOWN OF VERDANT GLEN ENDOWMENT REVENUES
EXPENDABLE TRUST FUND
Balance Sheet
June 30, Year 6

Assets

Cash	$500

Liabilities & Fund Balance

Fund balance reserved for scholarships	$500

There is no unreserved fund balance for either of the Town of Verdant Glen Trust Funds, because the trust indenture required the reservation of the entire fund balance of each fund to achieve the purpose of the trust.

Accounting for pension trust funds

Pension trust funds are perhaps the most complex of all the funds of a governmental unit, because they involve accounting for liabilities and fund balance reserves that are computed on the basis of actuarial assumptions. These actuarial assumptions include life expectancies of employees covered by the governmental unit's pension plans and rates of earnings on pension trust fund assets.

Pension trust funds are accounted for in essentially the same manner as proprietary funds, although pension trust funds do not have plant assets or depreciation expense. Thus, the accounting records of pension trust funds are maintained under the accrual basis of accounting and include all assets, liabilities, revenues, and expenses of the fund. The costs of administering some pension trust funds may be borne by the general fund of the governmental unit.

Because of the complexities of pension trust funds, illustrative journal entries for a pension trust fund are beyond the scope of this discussion. The financial statements below and on page 540 for the Town of Verdant Glen Employees' Retirement System Pension Trust Fund for the year ended June 30, Year 6, illustrate some of the accounting concepts involved.

TOWN OF VERDANT GLEN EMPLOYEES' RETIREMENT SYSTEM
PENSION TRUST FUND

Statement of Revenues, Expenses, and Changes in Fund Balance
For Year Ended June 30, Year 6

Operating revenues:	
Interest	$ 14,300
Contributions	82,400
Total operating revenues	$ 96,700
Operating expenses:	
Benefit payments	$ 23,400
Refunds	12,200
Total operating expenses	$ 35,600
Net income	$ 61,100
Fund balance, beginning of year	483,200
Fund balance, end of year	$544,300

TOWN OF VERDANT GLEN EMPLOYEES' RETIREMENT SYSTEM
PENSION TRUST FUND

Balance Sheet
June 30, Year 6

Assets

Cash		$ 12,300
Investments, at cost (market value $583,800)		552,100
Interest receivable		8,600
Total assets		$573,000

Liabilities & Fund Balance

Liabilities:		
Annuities payable		$ 28,700
Fund balance:		
Reserved for employees' retirement system	$727,800	
Unreserved (deficiency)	(183,500)	544,300
Total liabilities & fund balance		$573,000

**TOWN OF VERDANT GLEN EMPLOYEES' RETIREMENT SYSTEM
PENSION TRUST FUND**

Statement of Changes in Financial Position
For Year Ended June 30, Year 6

Financial resources provided

Operations — net income	$61,100
Sale or maturity of investments	22,800
Total financial resources provided	$83,900
Financial resources applied	
Acquisition of investments	68,200
Increase in financial resources: working capital	$15,700
Increase (decrease) in working capital	
Cash	$18,400
Interest receivable	4,200
Annuities payable	(6,900)
Increase in working capital	$15,700

Following is a discussion of important features of the financial statements for the Town of Verdant Glen Employees' Retirement System Pension Trust Fund:

1 Interest revenues and interest receivable of a pension trust fund include revenues such as dividends and rent, as well as interest itself, on the investments of the trust fund.
2 Contributions revenues represent amounts received from both the governmental unit and its employees under the **contributory pension plan** of the Town of Verdant Glen. (In a **noncontributory pension plan**, only the governmental unit would provide contributions to the pension trust fund.) From the point of view of the governmental unit, contributions to a pension trust fund are expenditures of the general fund.
3 Benefit payments are pension payments to retired employees of the Town of Verdant Glen. Refunds are amounts repaid to resigned employees or to estates of deceased employees for amounts contributed by them to the pension trust fund.
4 Annuities payable represent the unpaid current installments of pensions payable to retired employees.
5 The fund balance reserved for employees' retirement system is the total of several ledger accounts of the pension trust fund that are established to record the actuarially determined present values of the pensions ultimately to be paid to retired employees of the governmental unit.
6 The deficit in the unreserved fund balance in effect is the unfunded prior service cost of the pension trust fund. (**Prior service cost** of a pension plan is the estimated cost of employee services for years prior to the date of an actuarial valuation of the pension plan.)
7 In the statement of changes in financial position, working capital does not include the investments of the pension trust fund.

GENERAL FIXED ASSETS AND GENERAL LONG-TERM DEBT ACCOUNT GROUPS

Principle 5 of the accounting principles for local governmental units described in Chapter 12 (page 490) requires governmental units to use **account groups** to record plant assets and long-term debt of the governmental unit not recorded in a fund. A governmental unit's general fixed assets and general long-term debt account groups are not *funds;* they are **memorandum accounts**. Their purpose is to provide in one record the governmental unit's plant assets and long-term liabilities that are not recorded in one of the governmental unit's funds. Plant assets are recorded in enterprise, trust, and internal service funds; bond liabilities are recorded in debt service, enterprise, and special assessment funds.

Accounting for general fixed assets account groups

Assets in the general fixed assets group of accounts are recorded at their cost to the governmental unit or at their current fair value if donated to the governmental unit. The offsetting credit is to a memorandum account such as Investment in General Fixed Assets from (the source of the asset).

In accordance with principle 7 (page 490), depreciation may be recorded in the general fixed assets account group, with a debit to the appropriate Investment in General Fixed Assets account and a credit to an Accumulated Depreciation account. When a plant asset is sold or retired by the governmental unit, the carrying amount of the asset is removed from memorandum accounts in the general fixed assets account group; the sales proceeds are recorded as other financing sources in the general fund.

The journal entries below are typical of those for a governmental unit's general fixed assets account group. The first entry incorporates the assumption that equipment acquisitions were included in the expenditures of the Town of Verdant Glen General Fund for the year ended June 30, Year 6 (see page 501); the other two journal entries are made on June 30, Year 6, to

---

TOWN OF VERDANT GLEN GENERAL FIXED ASSETS ACCOUNT GROUP
General Journal

Machinery and Equipment	26,400	
Investment in General Fixed Assets from General Fund		
Revenues		26,400
To record acquisition of equipment by General Fund.		
Construction in Progress	378,000	
Investment in General Fixed Assets from Capital Projects		
Fund		378,000
To record construction work in progress on town hall		
addition.		
Construction in Progress	126,000	
Investment in General Fixed Assets from Special		
Assessment Fund		126,000
To record construction work in progress on street paving and		
sidewalk installation.		

---

record construction projects of the Town of Verdant Glen Capital Projects Fund (page 522) and Special Assessment Fund (page 528), respectively. The accounting records of the general fixed asset account group would provide the information for the preparation of the following statement:

TOWN OF VERDANT GLEN
Statement of General Fixed Assets
June 30, Year 6

Assets

Land	$ 200,000
Buildings	725,000
Improvements other than buildings	560,000
Machinery and equipment	720,000
Construction in progress	504,000
Total	$2,709,000

Investments in General Fixed Assets

General fund revenues	195,000
Capital projects funds	980,000
Special assessment funds	126,000
Federal and provincial grants	908,000
Donations	500,000
Total	$2,709,000

The total assets include the Year 6 acquisitions from the general fund, the capital projects fund, and the special assessment fund.

Accounting for general long-term debt account groups

General obligation bonds of a governmental unit, both serial and term, that are not recorded in an enterprise fund are recorded as memorandum credits in the general long-term debt account group. The offsetting memorandum debit entry is to an account such as Amount to Be Provided. When cash and other assets for the ultimate payment of a bond issue have been accumulated in a debt service fund, an Amount Available in Debt Service Fund account is debited and the Amount to Be Provided account is credited. When the bonds are paid by the debt service fund, the memorandum accounts are reversed in the general long-term debt account group in a closing entry at the end of the fiscal year.

The following journal entries for the Town of Verdant Glen General Long-Term Debt Account Group parallel the corresponding journal entries in the Debt Service Fund (page 525) and the Capital Projects Fund (page 522), respectively:

TOWN OF VERDANT GLEN GENERAL LONG-TERM DEBT ACCOUNT GROUP

General Journal

Amount Available in Debt Service Fund	10,000	
Amount to Be Provided		10,000

To record amount acquired by Debt Service Fund from General
Fund for retirement of principal of general obligation serial
bonds.

Amount to Be Provided	500,000	
Bonds Payable		500,000

To record issuance of general obligation term bonds for construction
of addition to town hall.

The following statement of general long-term debt would be prepared as at
June 30, Year 6:

TOWN OF VERDANT GLEN

Statement of General Long-Term Debt
June 30, Year 6

Amount Available and To Be Provided

Amount to be provided	$500,000

General Long-Term Debt

Term bonds:

15% general obligation bonds due	
July 1, Year 25	$500,000

The use of the two account groups is not common in Canada with the
exception of the province of Quebec. Some local governments use a ***capital
and loan fund*** which essentially is a combination of the two account
groups. The following illustrates this form of financial statement:

TOWN OF VERDANT GLEN

Capital and Loan Fund
Balance Sheet
June 30, Year 6

Capital Assets

Land	200,000
Buildings	725,000
Improvements other than buildings	560,000
Machinery and equipment	720,000
Construction in progress	504,000
Total	$2,709,000

**Long-Term Debt and
Investment in Capital Assets**

General long-term debt

  Term bonds — 15% general obligation

    bonds due July 1, Year 25 500,000

Investment in capital assets 2,209,000

Total $2,709,000

Purchases of assets from bond proceeds are recorded by a debit to assets and a credit to bonds payable. Fixed asset expenditures by the general fund would be recorded by a debit to assets and a credit to investment in assets. Retirement of bonds by an expenditure in the general fund or the debt service fund would be recorded by a debit to bonds payable and a credit to investment in assets.

The accounting treatment of fixed assets is one area where there is a substantial lack of uniformity in Canada. Some local governments do not capitalize fixed assets purchased by the general fund. Others show fixed assets at an amount equal to the amount of long-term debt. As the debt is retired, an equal amount of assets are removed from the statement. Another alternative used by some local governments is to combine the capital projects fund and the two account groups into a single capital and loan fund, but even in this case, some local governments only capitalize assets purchased from bond proceeds.

ANNUAL REPORTS OF GOVERNMENTAL UNITS

Principle *12b* of accounting for state and local governmental units (page 492 of Chapter 12) required governmental units to issue annual financial reports. The following general outline and minimum contents were specified:[3]

1 *Introductory Section*
(Table of contents, letter(s) of transmittal, and other material deemed appropriate by management)
2 *Financial Section*
  a *Auditor's Report*
  b *General-Purpose Financial Statements (Combined Statements — Overview)*
    (1) Combined Balance Sheet — All Fund Types and Account Groups

3 Ibid., pp. 19–20.

    (2) Combined Statement of Revenues, Expenditures, and Changes in Fund Balances — All Governmental Fund Types

    (3) Combined Statement of Revenues, Expenditures, and Changes in Fund Balances — General and Special Revenue Fund Types (and similar governmental fund types for which annual budgets have been legally adopted)

    (4) Combined Statement of Revenues, Expenses, and Changes in Retained Earnings (or Equity)—All Proprietary Fund Types

    (5) Combined Statement of Changes in Financial Position—All Proprietary Fund Types

    (6) Notes to the financial statements (Trust Fund operations may be reported in (2), (4), and (5) above, as appropriate, or separately.)

  c *Combining and Individual Fund and Account Group Statements and Schedules*

    (1) Combining Statements — By Fund Type — where a governmental unit has more than one fund of a given fund type

    (2) Individual fund and account group statements — where a governmental unit has only one fund of a given type and for account groups and/or where necessary to present prior year and budgetary comparisons

    (3) Schedules

        (a) Schedules necessary to demonstrate compliance with finance-related legal and contractual provisions

        (b) Schedules to present information spread throughout the statements that can be brought together and shown in greater detail (e.g., taxes receivable, including delinquent taxes; long-term debt; investments; and cash receipts, disbursements, and balances)

        (c) Schedules to present greater detail for information reported in the statements (e.g., additional revenue sources detail and object of expenditure data by departments).

    . . .

3 *Statistical Tables*

It is evident from the foregoing listing that financial reports of governmental units may be voluminous, and perhaps even overwhelming, in content. For example, the **combined financial statements** included in the financial section of the financial report do not show single combined amounts; the statements include columns for each of the eight fund types and two account groups, together with **memorandum only** total columns for both the current year and the prior year. Comparable multicolumn presentations constitute the **combining** statements and schedules. Thus, the principal financial statements included in the annual financial reports are far more complex than the **consolidated** financial statements of business enterprises making up a parent company-subsidiaries group. An example of a multicolumn financial statement appears on page 584.

Appraisal of accounting principles for governmental units

The preceding material on local government accounting principles and reporting practices has been based on the model outlined in *NCGA Statement 1*. With the exception of Quebec, local governments in Canada do not follow Statement 1 in its entirety. However, it is not simply the case of Quebec following the Statement 1 model and the remaining provinces following some single variation of the model. The 1981 *CGA* study indicated that there was a considerable lack of uniformity in the practices followed by local governments in the other nine provinces.[4] The study found many differences in terminology, in measurements, and in the types and descriptions of funds being used. This is particularly the case in the handling of fixed assets and on page 544 we illustrated some variations being used. The result is that many users experience difficulty in comprehending and comparing the statements issued by Canada's local governments.

CICA RESEARCH STUDY RECOMMENDATIONS

In 1985, *CICA* published the research study on *Local Government Financial Reporting (LGFR)*. Studies of this nature are issued to stimulate thought and debate on accounting matters but are not authoritative pronouncements requiring compliance as are the *CICA Handbook* pronouncements. The study group made reference to and summarized some of the problem areas mentioned in the 1981 CGA study and decided to build on its findings and to recommend solutions. Throughout the study, reference is made to the fact that local governments should issue general purpose financial statements for external users prepared in accordance with *generally accepted accounting principles for local government (GAAPLG)*. However, nowhere in the report are these principles specifically codified. Presumably, the *67 conclusions and recommendations* contained in the study could form the basis of specific Handbook sections should CICA decide to issue pronouncements on *GAAPLG*.[5] In the material that follows, we summarize some of the more important conclusions and recommendations and comment on how they compare with the requirements of Statement 1.

1 General purpose financial statements that avoid excessive complexity should be issued and should provide information on financial viability and condition, stewardship, inflow and outflow of resources and financial compliance with budgets.
2 The statements should provide an overview of the entity as a whole, and at the same time provide a distinction between operating revenues and expenditures, inflows from borrowings and transactions of a capital nature. This overview objective may be deterred by the very nature of fund accounting.

---

4 *Accounting for Local Government in Canada: The State of the Art*, A. Beedle, The Canadian Certified General Accountants Research Foundation (Vancouver: 1981).

5*Local Government Financial Reporting, A Research Study*, CICA (Toronto: 1985), pp. 81–93.

3 It is not essential that the statements demonstrate compliance with fiscal and legal requirements.

4 Reporting on the basis of funds should be left to the preferences of the preparers, and this type of information could be provided as supplements to the general purpose financial statements.

While *LGFR* does not specifically recommend against financial reporting by funds it seems to indicate that it would be *preferable not to use funds*. Leaving the decision to the preferences of the preparers may have been necessary because of the reporting requirements mandated by senior governments. *Statement 1* requires segregation of the financial statements into fund components due to its emphasis on satisfying legal requirements.

5 The accrual basis of accounting should be used for financial reporting and recognition should be given to inventories, prepayments and deferred items including revenues.

6 All fixed assets should be capitalized regardless of the method of financing and should be written off in the year that their useful life ends.

These recommendations do not at first seem significantly different from the requirements of Statement 1. The differences between the accrual basis and the modified accrual basis required for some funds by Statement 1, essentially apply only to interest on debt in the first and final years of a bond issue. However, *Statement 1* requires the accrual basis for some funds while *LGFR* recommends that it be used exclusively. The capitalization of fixed assets with no subsequent allocation as depreciation expense is consistent with Statement 1, except for proprietary funds which are operated similarly to business enterprises and report a net income or loss. It is in this area that *LGFR differs substantially from Statement 1*, especially when the next two recommendations are taken into account.

7 Consolidated financial statements of the local government entity and its component parts (particularly enterprises such as utilities) should comprise the general purpose financial statements, and should be prepared in accordance with *GAAPLG*. Interfund revenues and expenditures would be eliminated.

8 Consolidation is not appropriate if a subsidiary component does prepare its statements in accordance with *GAAPLG*. In this case, the investment would be reported by the modified equity method.

Under *Statement 1*, where fund accounting is the basis of reporting, proprietary funds report depreciation expense and net income while the government funds do not report depreciation and report revenues and expenditures. *LGFR* suggests that *all financial statements be prepared in accordance with GAAPLG*, which means that *depreciation is not recorded*. Consolidation of enterprises such as utilities could only occur if the utilities statements, which are prepared in accordance with *GAAP*, were restated in accordance with *GAAPLG*. If this did not occur, consolidation would not take place and the investment would be reported by the modified equity method. The recommendations seem to imply that separate statements of enterprises prepared in accordance with GAAP could form part of the supplementary information provided as part of the general purpose statements.

9 Encumbrances should not be included as expenditures and liabilities.

This is consistent with Statement 1. However, some local governments in Canada have shown these items as expenditures and liabilities.

10 Budget information should be communicated on a timely basis and should be prepared on a basis consistent with *GAAPLG*, so that the figures can be correlated with the financial statements. The information contained should include *preliminary policy guidelines, budget proposals* and a summary of the *final approved budget*.

Statement 1 requires budgetary comparisons in the annual report. *LGFR* does not mention this, but suggests that *budget information* should be released in some manner as the budgeting process evolves so that the timeliness requirement is satisfied. Because LGFR is only concerned with reporting externally, the recording of budgets as an internal control device could still be used.

If the recommendations of *LGFR* are eventually adopted by local governments in Canada, substantial changes from current practices will result. It remains to be seen if the users will find the financial statements easier to comprehend than those now being issued. Certainly consistent reporting practices will aid in comparisons. We again emphasize that *LGFR* is *not authoritative* and that each province mandates the accounting principles and reporting practices of the local governments within its jurisdiction.

REVIEW QUESTIONS

1 Describe the taxes or fees of governmental units that often are accounted for in special revenue funds.

2 How are proceeds of general obligation bonds issued to finance a construction project accounted for in a capital projects fund? Explain.

3 Is a separate debt service fund established for every issue of general obligation bonds of a governmental unit? Explain.

4 The following journal entry appeared in the Debt Service Fund of Charter County:

Cash with Fiscal Agent	83,000	
Cash		83,000

What is the probable explanation for this journal entry?

5 Why does a governmental unit's enterprise fund have a number of restricted assets in its balance sheet? Explain.

6 How is the Contribution from Government ledger account presented in the financial statements of a governmental unit's internal service fund? Explain.

7 Explain the nature of the *contributions revenues* appearing in the statement of revenues, expenses, and changes in fund balance of a governmental unit's pension trust fund.

8 Under what circumstances are general obligation bonds of a governmental unit recorded in the governmental unit's enterprise fund? Explain.

9 Discuss the similarities and differences between a governmental unit's capital projects fund and special assessment fund.

10 The accounting for a governmental unit's enterprise fund is in many respects similar to the accounting for a business enterprise, yet there are a number of differences between the two types of accounting. Identify at least three of the differences.

11 Accounting for nonexpendable trusts for which a governmental unit acts as custodian requires the establishment of two separate trust funds. Why is this true?

12 Explain the nature of a Capital and Loan fund used by some local governments in Canada.

13 Did the 1985 CICA research study recommend that local government financial statements be prepared in accordance with the current requirements of the *CICA Handbook*? Explain.

14 Briefly describe the areas in which there is a lack of uniformity in local government financial reporting in Canada.

EXERCISES

Ex 13-1 Select the best answer for each of the following multiple-choice questions:

1 The liability for a governmental unit's revenue bonds appears in:
a An enterprise fund
b A debt service fund
c The general long-term debt account group
d A special assessment fund

2 Which of the following funds does not use the encumbrance technique?
a General fund
b Capital projects fund
c Internal service fund
d None of the foregoing funds

3 Which of the following ledger accounts would be included in the general long-term debt account group?
a Amount to Be Provided
b Unreserved Fund Balance
c Fund Balance Reserved for Encumbrances
d Cash

4 Customers' meter deposits that cannot be spent for normal operating purposes are classified as restricted cash in the balance sheet of which fund?
a Internal service fund
b Trust fund
c Agency fund
d Enterprise fund

5 The general fixed assets account group is used for the plant assets of the:
a Special assessment fund
b Enterprise fund
c Trust fund
d Internal service fund

6 A city should record depreciation as an expense in its:
- **a** General fund and enterprise fund
- **b** Internal service fund and general fixed assets account group
- **c** Enterprise fund and internal service fund
- **d** Enterprise fund and capital projects fund

Ex 13-2 The ledger accounts listed below frequently appear in the accounting records of governmental units:

Account	Fund or account group
1 Bonds Payable	*a General fund*
2 Fund Balance Reserved for	*b Special revenue fund*
Encumbrances	*c Capital projects fund*
3 Contribution from Government	*d Special assessment fund*
4 Equipment	*e Debt service fund*
5 Appropriations	*f Internal service fund*
6 Estimated Revenues	*g Trust or agency fund*
7 Taxes Receivable — Current	*h Enterprise fund*
	i General fixed assets account group
	j General long-term debt account group

Select the appropriate identifying letter to indicate the governmental unit fund or account group in which those ledger accounts might properly appear. An account might appear in more than one fund or account group.

Ex 13-3 A citizen of Hays City donated ten acres of undeveloped land to the city for a future school site. The donor's cost of the land was $555,000. The current fair value of the land was $850,000 on the date of the gift.

Prepare a journal entry in the appropriate fund or account group to record the foregoing gift. Identify the fund or account group.

Ex 13-4 The Enterprise Fund of Orchard City billed the General Fund $16,400 for utility services on May 31, Year 5.

Prepare journal entries for the foregoing billing in the Orchard City General Fund and Enterprise Fund.

Ex 13-5 On July 1, property taxes totaling $480,000, of which 1½ % was estimated to be uncollectible, were levied by the County of Larchmont Special Revenue Fund. Property taxes collected by the Special Revenue Fund during July totaled $142,700.

Prepare journal entries in the County of Larchmont Special Revenue Fund for the foregoing transactions.

Ex 13-6 On July 1, Year 4, the City of Varro paid $860,000 from the General Fund for a central garage to service its vehicles, with $467,500 being applicable to the building, which has an economic life of 25 years, $232,600 to land, and $109,900 to machinery that has an economic life of 15 years. A $50,000 cash contribution was received by the garage from the General Fund on the same date.

Prepare the journal entry or entries to record the foregoing transactions in the appropriate fund established for the central garage. Identify the fund.

Ex 13-7 On June 30, Year 1, the Town of Warren issued $800,000 face amount of 16% special assessment bonds at 100 to finance in part a street improvement project estimated to cost $860,000. The project is to be paid by a $60,000 contribution from the Town of Warren General Fund and by an $800,000 special assessment against property owners (payable in five equal annual installments beginning July 1, Year 1).

Prepare the journal entry or entries to record the foregoing transactions in the appropriate fund established for the street improvement project. Identify the fund.

Ex 13-8 On July 1, Year 7, the County of Pinecrest issued $1,200,000 of 30-year, 16% general obligation term bonds of the same date at 100 to finance the construction of a public health centre.

Prepare the journal entry or entries to record the foregoing transaction in all funds or account groups affected. Identify the funds or account groups.

Ex 13-9 Agatha Morris, a citizen of Roark City, donated common stock valued at $220,000 to the city under a trust indenture dated July 1, Year 6. Under the terms of the indenture, the principal amount is to be kept intact; use of dividends revenues from the common stock is restricted to financing academic scholarships for college students. On December 14, Year 6, dividends of $42,000 were received on the common stock donated by Morris.

Prepare the journal entries to record the foregoing transactions in the appropriate funds. Identify the funds. Disregard entries for accrual of dividends. Omit explanations.

Ex 13-10 On April 30, Year 5, the fiscal agent for the Town of Wallen Debt Service Fund paid the final serial payment of $50,000 on the Town's 16% general obligation bonds, together with semiannual interest. The Debt Service Fund had provided sufficient cash to the fiscal agent a few days earlier.

Prepare a journal entry for the Town of Wallen Debt Service Fund to record the fiscal agent's payment of bond principal and interest on April 30, Year 5.

Ex 13-11 The Town of Morris uses a Capital and Loan fund. During Year 3, $100,000 in general obligation bonds were retired with a payment from the General Fund. Also during the year, equipment was purchased with general revenues at a cost of $12,000.

Prepare the journal entries to record the foregoing transactions in the Capital and Loan fund.

CASES

Case 13-1 The controller of the City of Darby has asked your advice on the accounting for an installment contract payable by the city. The contract covers the costs of installing automatic gates, coin receptacles, and ticket dispensers for the 20 city-owned parking lots in the downtown district. Installation of the self-parking equipment resulted in a decrease in the required number of parking attendants for the city-owned parking lots and a reduction in the salaries and related expenditures of the City of Darby General Fund.

The contract is payable monthly in amounts equal to 40% of the month's total parking revenue for the 20 lots. Because no legal or contractual provisions require the City of Darby to establish an enterprise fund for the parking lots, both parking revenue and parking-lot maintenance and repairs expenditures are recorded in the City of Darby General Fund. The parking-lot sites are carried at cost in the City of Darby General Fixed Assets Account Group.

The city controller describes the plans for accounting for payments on the contract as follows: Monthly payments under the contract are to be debited to the Expenditures account of the General Fund and to the Debt Service section of the expenditures subsidiary ledger. The payments also will be recorded in the General Fixed Assets

Account Group as additions to the Improvements Other than Buildings ledger account. A footnote to the General Fund balance sheet will disclose the unpaid balance of the installment contract at the end of each fiscal year. The unpaid balance of the contract will not be included in the General Long-Term Debt Account Group because the contract does not represent a liability for borrowing of cash, as do the bond and other long-term debt liabilities of the City of Darby.

Instructions   What is your advice to the controller of the City of Darby? Explain

Case 13-2   You have been requested to examine the financial statements of the funds and account groups of Ashburn City for the fiscal year ended June 30, Year 7. During the course of your examination you learn that on July 1, Year 6, the city issued at face amount $1,000,000 20-year, 16% general obligation serial bonds to finance additional power-generating facilities for the Ashburn City electric utility. Principal and interest on the bonds are repayable by the Ashburn City Electric Utility Enterprise Fund. However, for the first five years of the serial maturities of the bonds—July 1 Year 7, through July 1, Year 11—a special tax levy accounted for in the Ashburn City Special Revenue Fund is to contribute to the payment of 80% of the interest and principal of the general obligation bonds. At the end of the five-year period, it is anticipated that revenue from the electric utility's new power-generating facilities will create cash flow for the Ashburn City Electric Utility Enterprise Fund sufficient to pay all the serial maturities and interest of the general obligation bonds during the period July 1, Year 12, through July 1, Year 26.

You find that the accounting records of the Ashburn City Electric Utility Enterprise Fund include the following ledger account balances relative to the general obligation bonds on June 30, Year 7:

16% general obligation serial bonds payable ($50,000 due July 1, Year 7)	$1,000,000 cr
Interest payable (interest on the bonds is payable annually each July 1)	160,000 cr
Interest expense	160,000 dr

The statement of revenues, expenditures, and changes in fund balance for the year ended June 30, Year 7, prepared by the accountant for the Ashburn City Electric Utility Enterprise Fund shows a net loss of $40,000. You also learn that on July 1, Year 7, the Ashburn City Special Revenue Fund paid $168,000 ($210,000 × 0.80 = $168,000) and the Ashburn City Electric Utility Enterprise Fund paid the remaining $42,000 ($210,000 × 0.20 = $42,000) to the fiscal agent for the 16% general obligation serial bonds. The $210,000 was the total of the $50,000 principal and $160,000 interest due on the bonds July 1, Year 7. In the Enterprise Fund's journal entry to record payment of the bond principal and interest, the amount of $168,000 was credited to the Contribution from Government ledger account.

Instructions   Do you concur with the Ashburn City Electric Utility Enterprise Fund's accounting and reporting treatment for the 16% general obligation serial bonds? Discuss.

Case 13-3   Wallace and Brenda Stuart, residents of Colby City, have donated their historic mansion, "Greystone," in trust to Colby City to serve as a tourist attraction. For a nominal charge, tourists will be guided through Greystone to observe the paintings, sculptures, antiques, and other art objects collected by the Stuarts, as well as the mansion's unique architecture.

The trust indenture executed by the Stuarts provides that the admissions charges to Greystone (which was appraised at $5,000,000 on the date of the trust indenture) are to cover the operating expenditures associated with the tours, as well as maintenance and repairs costs for Greystone. Any excess of admissions revenues over the foregoing expenditures and costs is to be donated to Colby University for scholarships to art and architecture students.

Instructions Discuss the fund accounting issues, and related accounting matters such as depreciation, that should be considered by officials of Colby City with respect to the Stuart Trust.

Case 13-4 The City of Brendar, which is located in Canada, prepares its financial statements in a manner that is generally consistent with *NCGA Statement 1*. The controller of the city has just been informed of the release by CICA of the research study *"Local Government Financial Reporting" (LGFR)*. You have been appointed by the city to write a report that summarizes the major recommendations contained in this study and discusses how they would impact the way the city would have to report in the future should these recommendations be adopted by CICA.

Instructions Prepare an outline of the report that you will submit.

PROBLEMS

13-1 On July 1, Year 6, the Town of Logan began two construction projects: (1) an addition to the town hall accounted for in a capital projects fund, and (2) a curbing construction project accounted for in a special assessment fund. The special assessment totaled $400,000, payable by the assessed citizens in five annual installments beginning July 1, Year 6, together with interest at 16% a year on the unpaid assessments. Other details for the year ended June 30, Year 7, were as follows:

	Capital Projects Fund	Special Assessment Fund
Bonds issued July 1, Year 6, at face amount	$600,000 face amount, 14%, 20-year general obligation bonds, interest payable Jan. 1 and July 1	$320,000 face amount, 15%, 4-year special assessment bonds, interest payable July 1
Total encumbrances	$530,200	$384,600
Total expenditures	$380,600	$360,300
Encumbrances applicable to expenditures	$382,100	$354,700
Total cash paid on vouchers	$322,700	$347,600

Instructions Prepare journal entries, including year-end accruals but excluding closing entries, for **(a)** the Town of Logan Capital Projects Fund, and **(b)** the Town of Logan Special Assessment Fund.

13-2 In compliance with a newly enacted provincial law, Diggs County assumed the responsibility of collecting all property taxes levied within its boundaries as of July 1, Year 5. A composite property tax rate per $100 of net assessed valuation was developed for the fiscal year ending June 30, Year 6, and is presented below:

Diggs County General Fund	$ 6.00
Evans City General Fund	3.00
Hickman Township General Fund	1.00
Total	$10.00

All property taxes are due in quarterly installments. After collection, taxes ar
distributed to the governmental units represented in the composite rate.

In order to administer collection and distribution of such taxes, the County ha
established a Tax Agency Fund.

Additional Information

(1) In order to reimburse the County for estimated administrative expenses of oper
ating the Tax Agency Fund, the Tax Agency Fund is to deduct 2% from the ta
collections each quarter for Evans City and Hickman Township. The total amoun
deducted is to be remitted to the Diggs County General Fund.

(2) Current year tax levies to be collected by the Tax Agency Fund are as follows

	Gross levy	Estimated amount to be collected
Diggs County	$3,600,000	$3,500,000
Evans City	1,800,000	1,740,000
Hickman Township	600,000	560,000
Totals	$6,000,000	$5,800,000

(3) As of September 30, Year 5, the Tax Agency Fund had received $1,440,000 i
first-quarter payments. On October 1, Year 5, this fund made a distribution t
the three governmental units.

Instructions

For the period July 1, Year 5, through October 1, Year 5, prepare journal entrie
(explanations omitted) to record the transactions described above for the followin
funds:

Diggs County Tax Agency Fund
Diggs County General Fund
Evans City General Fund
Hickman Township General Fund

Your working paper should be organized as follows:

Account title	Diggs County Tax Agency Fund Dr(Cr)	Diggs County General Fund Dr(Cr)	Evans City General Fund Dr(Cr)	Hickman Township General Fund Dr(Cr)

13-3 The City of Ordway's fiscal year ends on June 30. During the fiscal year ende
June 30, Year 2, the City authorized the construction of a new library and the issu
ance of general obligation term bonds to finance the construction of the library. Th
authorization imposed the following restrictions:

(1) Construction cost was not to exceed $5,000,000
(2) Annual interest rate was not to exceed 15%

The City does not record project authorizations, but other appropriate accounts ar
maintained. The following transactions relating to the financing and constructing o
the library occurred during the fiscal year ended June 30, Year 3:

(1) On July 1, Year 2, the City issued $5,000,000 of 30 year, 14% general obliga
tion bonds for $5,100,000. The semiannual interest dates are December 31 an
June 30.
(2) On July 3, Year 2, the Library Capital Projects Fund invested $4,900,000 i
short-term notes. This investment was at face value, with no accrued interes
Interest on cash invested by the Library Capital Projects Fund must be trans

ferred to the Library Debt Service Fund. During the fiscal year ending June 30, Year 3, estimated interest to be earned is $140,000.

(3) On July 5, Year 2, the City signed a contract with Premier Construction Company to build the library for $4,980,000

(4) On January 15, Year 3, the Library Capital Projects Fund received $3,040,000, from the maturity of short-term notes acquired on July 3, Year 2. The cost of these notes was $3,000,000. The interest of $40,000 was transferred to the Library Debt Service Fund.

(5) On January 20, Year 3, Premier Construction Company billed the City $3,000,000 for work performed on the new library. The contract calls for 10% retention until final inspection and acceptance of the building. The Library Capital Projects Fund paid Premier $2,700,000.

(6) On June 30, Year 3, the Library Capital Projects Fund prepared closing entries.

Instructions

a Prepare journal entries to record the six preceding sets of facts in the City of Ordway Library Capital Projects Fund. Omit journal entry explanations. Use the following account titles:

Cash
Encumbrances
Expenditures
Fund Balance Reserved for Encumbrances
Interest Receivable
Investments
Other Financing Sources
Payable to Library Debt Service Fund
Unreserved Fund Balance
Vouchers Payable
Do not record journal entries in any other fund or account group.

b Prepare a balance sheet for the City of Ordway Library Capital Projects Fund on June 30, Year 3.

13-4 The Town of Northville was incorporated and began operations on July 1, Year 1. The following transactions occurred during the first fiscal year, July 1, Year 1, to June 30, Year 2:

(1) The Town Council adopted a budget for general operations during the fiscal year ending June 30, Year 2. Revenues were estimated at $400,000. Legal authorizations for budgeted expenditures were $394,000. There were no other financing sources or uses.

(2) Property taxes were levied in the amount of $390,000; it was estimated that 2% of this amount would be uncollectible. These taxes are available on the date of levy to finance current expenditures.

(3) During the year a resident of the town donated marketable securities valued at $50,000 to the town under a trust. The terms of the trust indenture stipulated that the principal amount is to be kept intact; use of revenues generated by the securities is restricted to financing college scholarships for needy students. Revenue earned and received on these marketable securities amounted to $5,500 through June 30, Year 2.

(4) A General Fund transfer of $55,000 was made to establish an Internal Service Fund to provide for a permanent investment in inventory of supplies.

(5) The Town Council decided to install lighting in the town park, and a special assessment project was authorized to install the lighting at a cost of $75,000. The assessments were levied for $72,000, with the town contributing $3,000 from the General Fund. All assessments were collected during the year, including the General Fund contribution.

(6) A contract for $75,000 was approved for the installation of the lighting. O
June 30, Year 2, the contract was completed but not approved. The contracto
was paid all but 5%, which was retained to ensure compliance with the term
of the contract. Encumbrances accounts are maintained.

(7) During the year, the Internal Service Fund purchased various supplies at a co
of $41,900.

(8) Cash collections recorded by the General Fund during the year were as follows:

Property taxes $386,000

Licenses and permits 7,000

(9) The Town Council decided to build a hall at an estimated cost of $500,000 t
replace space occupied in rented facilities. The town does not record projec
authorizations. It was decided that general obligation bonds bearing interest a
12% would be issued. On June 30, Year 2, the bonds were issued at their fac
amount of $500,000, payable June 30, Year 22. No contracts have been signed fo
this project and no expenditures have been made.

(10) A fire truck was acquired for $15,000, and the voucher was approved and pai
by the General Fund. This expenditure previously had been encumbered fo
$15,000.

Instructions Prepare journal entries to record each of the foregoing transaction
in the appropriate fund or account group. Omit explanations for the journal entrie
Do not prepare closing entries for any fund. Organize your working paper as follow

Transaction No.	Fund or account group	Account titles	Debit	Credit

Number each journal entry to correspond with the transactions described above
Use the funds (show fund symbol in working paper) and account titles below:

Capital Projects Fund (CPF)
   Cash
   Other Financing Sources

Endowment Principal Trust Fund (EPF)
   Cash
   Investments
   Operating Transfers Out
   Payable to Endowment Revenues Trust Fund
   Revenues

Endowment Revenues Trust Fund (ERF)
   Cash
   Other Financing Sources
   Receivable from Endowment Principal Trust Fund

General Fixed Assets Account Group (GFA)
   Improvements Other than Buildings
   Investment in General Fixed Assets
   Machinery and Equipment

General Fund (GF)
   Allowance for Uncollectible Current Taxes
   Appropriations
   Budgetary Fund Balance
   Cash
   Encumbrances
   Estimated Revenues

Expenditures
Fund Balance Reserved for Encumbrances
Payable to Special Assessment Fund
Revenues
Taxes Receivable — Current

General Long-Term Debt Account Group (GLTD)
Amount to Be Provided
Bonds Payable

Internal Service Fund (ISF)
Cash
Contribution from Government
Inventory of Supplies

Special Assessment Fund (SAF)
Cash
Encumbrances
Expenditures
Fund Balance Reserved for Encumbrances
Other Financing Sources
Receivable from General Fund
Revenues
Special Assessments Receivable — Current

13-5   The City of Cavendish operates a central garage in an Internal Service Fund to provide garage space and repairs for all city-owned and operated vehicles. The Internal Service Fund was established by a contribution of $200,000 from the General Fund on July 1, Year 1, at which time the building was acquired. The after-closing trial balance on June 30, Year 3, was as follows:

CITY OF CAVENDISH INTERNAL SERVICE FUND
After-Closing Trial Balance
June 30, Year 3

	Debit	Credit
Cash	$150,000	
Receivable from General Fund	20,000	
Inventory of material and supplies	80,000	
Land	60,000	
Building	200,000	
Accumulated depreciation of building		$ 10,000
Machinery and equipment	56,000	
Accumulated depreciation of machinery and equipment		12,000
Vouchers payable		38,000
Contribution from government		200,000
Unreserved retained earnings		306,000
Totals	$566,000	$566,000

The following information applies to the fiscal year ended June 30, Year 4:
(1) Material and supplies were purchased on account for $74,000.
(2) The perpetual inventory balance of material and supplies on June 30, Year 4, was $58,000, which agreed with the physical count on that date.
(3) Salaries and wages paid to employees totaled $230,000, including related fringe benefits.

(4) A billing was received from the Enterprise Fund for utility charges totaling $30,000, and was paid.

(5) Depreciation of the building was recorded in the amount of $5,000. Depreciation of the machinery and equipment amounted to $8,000.

(6) Billings to other funds for services rendered to them were as follows:

General Fund $262,000

Enterprise Fund 84,000

Special Revenue Fund 32,000

(7) Unpaid interfund receivable balances on June 30, Year 4, were as follows:

General Fund .... $ 6,000

Special Revenue Fund 16,000

(8) Vouchers payable on June 30, Year 4, were $14,000.

Instructions For the period July 1, Year 3, through June 30, Year 4, prepare journal entries to record all the transactions in the Internal Service Fund accounting records. Omit explanations for the entries. Use the following account titles, in addition to those included in the June 30, Year 3, after-closing trial balance:

Operating Expenses
Payable to Enterprise Fund
Receivable from Enterprise Fund
Receivable from Special Revenue Fund
Revenues

13-6 In a special election held on May 1, Year 3, the citizens of the City of Wilmore approved a $10,000,000 issue of 16% general obligation bonds maturing in Year 23. The proceeds of the bonds will be used to help finance the construction of a new civic centre. The total cost of the project was estimated at $15,000,000. The remaining $5,000,000 will be financed by an irrevocable provincial grant, which has been awarded. A capital projects fund was established to account for this project and was designated the Civic Centre Capital Projects Fund.

The following transactions occurred during the fiscal year beginning July 1, Year 3 and ending June 30, Year 4:

(1) On July 1, the General Fund loaned $500,000 to the Civic Centre Capital Projects Fund for defraying engineering and other costs.

(2) Preliminary engineering and planning costs of $320,000 were paid to Akron Company. There had been no encumbrance for this cost.

(3) On December 1, the bonds were issued at 101.

(4) On March 15, a contract for $12,000,000 was entered into with Carlson Construction Company for the major part of the project.

(5) Purchase orders were placed for material estimated to cost $55,000.

(6) On April 1, a partial payment of $2,500,000 was received from the provincial government.

(7) The material that was ordered previously was received at a cost of $51,000 and paid for.

(8) On June 15, a progress billing of $2,000,000 was received from Carlson Construction Company for work done on the project. In accordance with the contract, the city will withhold 6% of any billing until the project is completed.

(9) The General Fund was repaid the $500,000 previously loaned.

Instructions Prepare journal entries to record the transactions in the Civic Centre Capital Projects Fund for the period July 1, Year 3, through June 30, Year 4, and the closing entries on June 30, Year 4. Omit explanations for the journal entries. Use the following account titles in the journal entries:

Cash	Payable to General Fund
Encumbrances	Receivable from Provincial Government
Expenditures	Revenues
Fund Balance Reserved for	Unreserved Fund Balance
Encumbrances	Vouchers Payable
Other Financing Sources	

13-7 Your examination of the financial statements of the Town of Novis for the year ended June 30, Year 6, disclosed that the Town's inexperienced accountant was uninformed regarding governmental accounting and recorded all transactions in the General Fund. The following Town of Novis General Fund trial balance was prepared by the accountant:

TOWN OF NOVIS GENERAL FUND
Trial Balance
June 30, Year 6

	Debit	Credit
Cash	$ 12,900	
Accounts receivable	1,200	
Taxes receivable – current	8,000	
Vouchers payable		$ 15,000
Appropriations		350,000
Expenditures	332,000	
Estimated revenues	290,000	
Revenues		320,000
Town property	16,100	
Bonds payable	48,000	
Unreserved fund balance		23,200
Totals	$708,200	$708,200

Your audit disclosed the following:

(1) The accounts receivable balance was due from the Town's water utility for the sale of obsolete equipment on behalf of the General Fund. Accounts for the water utility operated by the Town are maintained in an enterprise fund.

(2) The total tax levy for the year was $270,000. The Town's tax collection experience in recent years indicates an average loss of 3% of the total tax levy for uncollectible taxes.

(3) On June 30, Year 6, the Town retired at face amount 12% general obligation serial bonds totaling $30,000. The bonds had been issued on July 1, Year 5, in the total amount of $150,000. Interest paid during the year also was recorded in the Bonds Payable account. There is no debt service fund for the serial bonds.

(4) On July 1, Year 5, to service various departments the Town Council authorized a supply room with an inventory not to exceed $10,000. During the year supplies totaling $12,300 were purchased and debited to Expenditures. The physical inventory taken on June 30, Year 6, disclosed that supplies totaling $8,400 had been used. No internal service fund was authorized by the Town Council.

(5) Expenditures for Year 6 included $2,600 applicable to purchase orders issued in the prior year. Outstanding purchase orders on June 30, Year 6, not entered in the accounting records, amounted to $4,100.

(6) The amount of $8,200, receivable from the province during Fiscal Year 6 for the Town's share of provincial gasoline taxes, had not been entered in the accounting records, because the province was late in remitting the $8,200.

(7) Equipment costing $7,500, which had been acquired by the General Fund, wა removed from service and sold for $900 during the year, and new equipmeꞑ costing $17,000 was acquired. These transactions were recorded in the Towꞑ Property ledger account. The Town does not record depreciation in the Generꜹ Fixed Assets Account Group.

Instructions

a Prepare adjusting and closing entries for the Town of Novis General Fund on Jurꞑ 30, Year 6.

b Prepare an after-closing trial balance for the Town of Novis General Fund for thꞇ year ended June 30, Year 6.

c Prepare adjusting entries for any other funds or account groups. (The Town accountant had recorded all the foregoing transactions in the General Fund, anꞑ had prepared no journal entries for other funds or account groups.)

13-8 You were engaged as independent auditor of the City of Engle for the year endꞇ June 30, Year 2. You found the following ledger accounts, among others, in thꞇ accounting records of the General Fund for the year ended June 30, Year 2:

Special Cash

Date	Explanation	Ref.	Debit	Credit	Balance
Year 1					
Aug. 1		CR 58	301,000		301,000 oꞇ
Sept. 1		CR 60	80,000		381,000 oꞇ
Dec. 1		CD 41		185,000	196,000 oꞇ
Year 2					
Feb. 1		CD 45		24,000	172,000 oꞇ
June 1		CR 64	52,667		224,667 oꞇ
June 30		CD 65		167,000	57,667 oꞇ

Construction in Progress — Main Street Sewer

Date	Explanation	Ref.	Debit	Credit	Balance
Year 1					
Dec. 1		CD 41	185,000		185,000 oꞇ
Year 2					
June 30		CD 65	167,000		352,000 dꞇ

Bonds Payable

Date	Explanation	Ref.	Debit	Credit	Balance
Year 1					
Aug. 1		CR 58		300,000	300,000 cꞇ
Year 2					
June 1		CR 64		50,000	350,000 cꞇ

Premium on Bonds Payable

Date	Explanation	Ref.	Debit	Credit	Balance
Year 1					
Aug. 1		CR 58		1,000	1,000 cꞇ

Assessments Revenues

Date	Explanation	Ref.	Debit	Credit	Balance
Year 1					
Sept. 1		CR 60		80,000	80,000 cr

Interest Expense

Date	Explanation	Ref.	Debit	Credit	Balance
Year 2					
Feb. 1		CD 45	24,000		24,000 dr
June 1		CR 64		2,667	21,333 dr

The ledger accounts resulted from the project described below:

The city council authorized the Main Street Sewer Project and a five-year, 16% bond issue of $350,000 dated August 1, Year 1, to permit deferral of assessment payments. According to the terms of the authorization, the property owners were to be assessed 80% of the estimated cost of construction; the balance was to be made available by the City of Engle General Fund on October 1, Year 1. On September 1, Year 1, the first of five equal annual assessment installments was collected from the property owners, and a contract for construction of the sewer was signed. The deferred assessments were to bear interest at 18% from September 1, Year 1. The project was expected to be completed by October 31, Year 2.

Instructions

a Prepare journal entries that should have been made in the City of Engle Special Assessment Fund for the year ended June 30, Year 2. Amortize the bond premium by the straight-line method. Do not prepare closing entries.

b Prepare journal entries on June 30, Year 2, for the City of Engle funds and account groups, other than the Special Assessment Fund, to record properly the results of transactions of the Main Street Sewer Project.

13-9 The following deficit budget was proposed for Year 3 for the Angelus School District General Fund:

ANGELUS SCHOOL DISTRICT GENERAL FUND
Budget
For Year Ending December 31, Year 3

Fund balance, Jan. 1, Year 3	$128,000
Revenues:	
Property taxes	112,000
Investment interest	4,000
Total	$244,000
Expenditures:	
Operating	$120,000
County treasurer's fees	1,120
Bond interest	50,000
Fund balance, Dec. 31, Year 3	72,880
Total	$244,000

A general obligation bond issue of the School District was proposed in Year 2. The proceeds were to be used for a new school. There are no other outstanding bond issues. Information about the bond issue follows:

Principal amount	$1,000,000	
Interest rate	15%	
Bonds dated	Jan. 1, Year 3	
Coupons mature	Jan. 1 and July 1, beginning July 1, Year 3	
Bonds mature serially at the rate of $100,000 a year, starting Jan. 1, Year 5.		

The School District uses a separate bank account for each fund. The General Fund trial balance on December 31, Year 2, follows:

ANGELUS SCHOOL DISTRICT GENERAL FUND
Trial Balance
December 31, Year 2

	Debit	Credit
Cash	$ 28,000	
Temporary investments — Government Treasury 12% bonds,		
interest payable on May 1 and Nov. 1	100,000	
Unreserved fund balance		$128,000
Totals	$128,000	$128,000

The county treasurer collects the property taxes and withholds a fee of 1% on all collections. The transactions for Year 3 were as follows:

Jan. 1   The proposed budget was adopted, the general obligation bond issue was authorized, and the property taxes were levied.

Feb. 28   Net property tax receipts from county treasurer, $49,500, were deposited.

Apr. 1   General obligation bonds were issued at 101 plus accrued interest. It was directed that the premium be used for payment of interest by the General Fund.

Apr. 2   The School District paid $147,000 for the new school site.

Apr. 3   A contract for $850,000 for the new school was approved.

May 1   Interest was received on temporary investments.

July 1   Interest was paid on bonds.

Aug. 31   Net property tax receipts from county treasurer, $59,400, were deposited.

Nov. 1   Payment on new school construction contract, $200,000, was made.

Nov. 1   Interest was received on temporary investments.

Dec. 31   Operating expenditures during the year were $115,000. (Disregard vouchering.)

Instructions   Prepare journal entries to record the foregoing Year 3 transactions in the following funds or account groups. (Closing entries are not required.)

a   General Fund

b   Capital Projects Fund

c   General Fixed Assets Account Group

d   General Long-Term Debt Account Group

Angelus School District does not use a Debt Service Fund.

13-10   The City of Rowland City Hall Capital Projects Fund was established on July 1, Year 2, to account for the construction of a new city hall. The building was to be constructed on a site owned by the City, and the building construction was financed by the issuance on July 1, Year 2, of $1,000,000 face amount of 14%, 10-year term bonds.

The only funds in which the transactions pertaining to the new city hall were recorded were the Capital Projects Fund and the General Fund. The Capital Projects Fund's trial balance on June 30, Year 3, follows:

CITY OF ROWLAND CITY HALL CAPITAL PROJECTS FUND
Trial Balance
June 30, Year 3

	Debit	Credit
Cash	$ 793,000	
Vouchers payable		$ 11,000
Fund balance reserved for encumbrances		723,000
Appropriations		1,015,000
Expenditures	240,500	
Encumbrances	715,500	
Totals	$1,749,000	$1,749,000

An analysis of the Fund Balance Reserved for Encumbrances ledger account follows:

	Debit (Credit)
Contract with General Construction Company	$(750,000)
Purchase orders placed for material and supplies	(55,000)
Receipt of and payment for material and supplies	14,500
Payment of General Construction Company invoice, less 10% retention	67,500
Balance of Fund Balance Reserved for Encumbrances account, June 30, Year 3	$(723,000)

An analysis of the Appropriations account follows:

	Debit (Credit)
Face amount of bonds	$(1,000,000)
Premium on bonds	(15,000)
Balance of Appropriations account, June 30, Year 3	$(1,015,000)

An analysis of the Expenditures account follows:

	Debit (Credit)
Progess billing invoice from General Construction Company (with which the City contracted for the construction of the new city hall for $750,000; other contracts will be let for heating, air conditioning, etc.) showing 10% of the work completed	$ 75,000
Charge from General Fund for clearing the building site	11,000
Payments to suppliers for building material and supplies	14,500
Payment of interest on bonds outstanding	140,000
Balance of Expenditures account, June 30, Year 3	$240,500

Instructions
a Prepare a working paper for the City of Rowland City Hall Capital Projects Fund on June 30, Year 3, showing:

(1) Preliminary trial balance.
(2) Adjustments. (Formal adjusting entries are not required; however, explai adjustments at bottom of working paper.)
(3) Adjusted trial balance.

b Prepare the required adjusting or closing entries on June 30, Year 3, for th following:
(1) Debt Service Fund
(2) General Fixed Assets Account Group
(3) General Long-Term Debt Account Group

14

ACCOUNTING FOR NONPROFIT ORGANIZATIONS

A ***nonprofit organization*** is a legal and accounting entity that is operated for the benefit of society as a whole, rather than for the benefit of an individual proprietor or a group of partners or shareholders. Thus, the concept of net income is not meaningful for a nonprofit organization. Instead, as the internal service fund described in Chapter 13, a nonprofit organization strives only to obtain revenue and support sufficient to cover its expenses.

Nonprofit organizations comprise a significant segment of the Canadian economy. Colleges and universities, voluntary health and welfare organizations such as United Way, hospitals, philanthropic foundations such as the Winnipeg Foundation, professional societies such as the CICA, and civic organizations such as Kiwanis are familiar examples of nonprofit organizations.

For many years, the accounting standards and practices that constitute generally accepted accounting principles were not considered to be entirely applicable to nonprofit organizations in the United States and Canada. The following quotation, which formerly appeared in various auditing publications of the AICPA, outlines the United States situation:[1]

> . . . the statements . . . of a not-for-profit organization . . . may reflect accounting practices differing in some respects from those followed by enterprises organized for profit. In some cases generally accepted accounting principles applicable to not-for-profit organizations have not been clearly defined. In those areas where the independent auditor believes generally accepted accounting principles have been clearly defined, he may state his opinion as to the conformity of the financial statements either with *generally accepted accounting principles* or

1 *Statement on Auditing Standards No. 1*, "Codification of Auditing Standards and Procedures," AICPA (New York: 1973), p. 136.

(less desirably) with *accounting practices* for not-for-profit organizations in the particular field, and in such circumstances he may refer to financial position and results of operations. In those areas where he believes generally accepted accounting principles have not been clearly defined, the provisions covering special reports as discussed under cash basis and modified accrual basis statements are applicable.

In the period 1972 to 1974, the unsettled state of accounting for nonprofit organizations was improved by the AICPA's issuance of three *Industry Audit Guides:* "Hospital Audit Guide," "Audits of Colleges and Universities," and "Audits of Voluntary Health and Welfare Organizations."[2] The status of an *Industry Audit Guide* is set forth in each Guide: the following language in the "Hospital Audit Guide" is typical:[3]

> This audit guide is published for the guidance of members of the Institute in examining and reporting on financial statements of hospitals. It represents the considered opinion of the Committee on Health Care Institutions and as such contains the best thought of the profession as to the best practices in this area of reporting. Members should be aware that they may be called upon to justify departures from the Committee's recommendations.

The accounting concepts included in an *Industry Audit Guide* have the *substantial authoritative support* required for all generally accepted accounting principles.

The three *Industry Audit Guides* above list only three types of nonprofit organizations. Thus, in 1978, the AICPA issued *Statement of Position 78-10*, "Accounting Principles and Reporting Practices for Certain Nonprofit Organizations," which applies to at least 18 types of nonprofit organizations, ranging from cemetery societies to zoological and botanical societies.[4]

The existence of four sources of authoritative support for generally accepted accounting principles for nonprofit organizations has led to some inconsistencies among the accounting standards for such organizations. In time, the FASB may resolve these inconsistencies as part of its work on accounting concepts for nonbusiness organizations, described in Chapter 12 (pages 485 to 487).

In Canada, a similar situation exists although there are some fundamental differences. The *CICA Handbook* pronouncements have been viewed as not applicable for nonprofit organizations. However, the Canadian accounting profession has not seen fit to issue industry audit guides or anything similar that would give authoritative support to specific practices. The situation is

---

2 "Audits of Colleges and Universities" was amended in 1974 by the AICPA in *Statement of Position 74-8,* "Financial Accounting and Reporting by Colleges and Universities." "Hospital Audit Guide" was amended in 1978 by the AICPA in *Statement of Position 78-1,* "Accounting by Hospitals for Certain Marketable Equity Securities."

3 "Hospital Audit Guide," AICPA (New York: 1972).

4 *Statement of Position 78-10,* "Accounting Principles and Reporting Practices for Certain Nonprofit Organizations," AICPA (New York: 1978), p. 8.

well summarized with the following quotation from the CICA research study "Financial Reporting for Non-Profit Organizations":[5]

> Financial reporting by non-profit organizations is hampered by the absence of generally accepted reporting standards, as evidenced by the lack of uniformity in the presentation of financial statements and in different disclosure practices and noticeable diversity in terminology and accounting policies. This situation has, at times, resulted in confusion and misunderstanding among the users of financial information provided by these organizations. Although reporting standards are recommended in some specialized studies in the non-profit area, the extent of implementation of these standards is not consistent even among similar organizations.

The specialized studies referred to include: the *Canadian Hospital Accounting Manual*, published by the Canadian Hospital Association; *Canadian Standards of Accounting and Financial Reporting for Voluntary Organizations*, a joint effort of CICA and various welfare and community funds agencies in Canada; and *Guide to Accounting Principles, Practices and Standards of Disclosure for Colleges and Universities of Ontario*, published by Ontario college and university finance officers.[6]

A major conclusion reached by the study group was that many of the *CICA Handbook* sections can be applied to nonprofit organizations, that some sections would require changes and rewording to make them applicable, and that some new sections dealing with nonprofit topics would have to be introduced, should the CICA concur with the study group's recommendation.[7] To date, such changes have not been made, and inconsistent reporting practices among nonprofit organizations continue.

Characteristics of nonprofit organizations

Nonprofit organizations are in certain respects hybrid because they have some characteristics comparable to those of governmental units and other characteristics similar to those of business enterprises.

Among the features of nonprofit organizations that resemble characteristics of governmental units are the following:

1 *Service to society.* Nonprofit organizations render services to society as a whole. The members of this society may range from a limited number of citizens of a community to almost the entire population of a city, province, or nation. Similar to the services rendered by governmental units, the services of nonprofit organizations are of benefit to the many rather than the few.

2 *No profit motivation.* Nonprofit organizations do not operate with the objective of earning a profit. Consequently, nonprofit organizations usually are exempt from federal and provincial income taxes. Governmental units, except for enterprise

---

5 *Financial Reporting for Non-profit Organizations: A Research Study*, Canadian Institute of Chartered Accountants (Toronto: 1980), p. 1.

6 Ibid., p. 136.

7 Ibid., pp. 125–134.

funds, have the same characteristics. (As pointed out in Chapter 13, enterprise funds sometimes are assessed an amount in lieu of property taxes by the legislative branch of the government.)

3 *Financing by the citizenry.* As with governmental units, most nonprofit organizations depend on the general population for a substantial portion of their support, because revenue from charges for their services is not intended to cover all their operating costs. Exceptions are professional societies and the philanthropic foundations established by wealthy individuals or families. Whereas the citizenry's contributions to government revenue are mostly ***involuntary*** taxes, their contributions to nonprofit organizations are ***voluntary*** donations.

4 *Stewardship for resources.* Because a substantial portion of the resources of a nonprofit organization are donated, the organization must account for the resources on a stewardship basis similar to that of governmental units. The stewardship requirement makes ***fund accounting*** appropriate for most nonprofit organizations as well as for governmental units.

5 *Importance of budget.* The four preceding characteristics of nonprofit organizations cause their ***annual budget*** to be as important as for governmental units. Nonprofit organizations may employ a ***traditional budget,*** a ***program budget***, a ***performance budget***, or a ***planning, programming, budgeting system***. These types of operating budgets are described in Chapter 12.

Among the characteristics of nonprofit organizations that resemble those of business enterprises are the following:

1 *Governance by board of directors.* As with a business corporation, a nonprofit corporation is governed by elected or appointed directors, trustees, or governors. In contrast, the legislative and executive branches of a governmental unit share the responsibilities of its governance.

2 *Measurement of cost expirations.* Governance by a board of directors means that a nonprofit organization does not answer to a lawmaking body as does a governmental unit. One consequence is that ***cost expirations***, or ***expenses***, rather than ***expenditures***, usually are reported in the ***statement of activity*** (explained on page 582) of a nonprofit organization. Allocation of expenses (including depreciation) and revenue to the appropriate accounting period thus is a common characteristic of nonprofit organizations and business enerprises.

3 *Use of accrual basis of accounting.* Nonprofit organizations should employ the same accrual basis of accounting used by business enterprises. The modified accrual basis of accounting used by some governmental unit funds is inappropriate for nonprofit organizations.[8]

ACCOUNTING FOR NONPROFIT ORGANIZATIONS

The accounting entity for most nonprofit organizations is the ***fund***, which is defined in Chapter 12 (page 489). Separate funds are often considered necessary to distinguish between assets that may be used as authorized by the board of directors and assets whose use is restricted by donors. Funds commonly used by nonprofit organizations include the following:

Unrestricted fund (sometimes called ***unrestricted current fund*** or ***current unrestricted fund***)

8 Ibid., p. 54.

Restricted fund (sometimes called *restricted current fund* or *current restricted fund*)

Endowment fund

Agency fund (sometimes called *custodian fund*)

Annuity and life income funds

Loan fund

Plant fund (sometimes called *land, building, and equipment fund*)

Revenue, support, and capital additions of nonprofit organizations

Nonprofit organizations obtain revenue from the sale of goods and services, and from sources such as membership dues and interest and dividends on investments. Typically, such revenue is inadequate to cover the expenses of the organizations; thus, they solicit support and capital additions from various donors. *Support* consists primarily of contributions from individuals, other nonprofit organizations, and governmental units to be used for current operations. *Capital additions* were defined by the AICPA as follows:[9]

> Capital additions include nonexpendable gifts, grants, and bequests restricted by donors to endowment, plant, or loan funds either permanently or for extended periods of time. Capital additions also include legally restricted investment income and gains or losses on investments held in such funds that must be added to the principal.

Unrestricted fund

In many respects, the ***unrestricted fund*** of a nonprofit organization is similar to the ***general fund*** of a governmental unit. The unrestricted fund includes all the assets of a nonprofit organization that are available for use as authorized by the board of directors and are not restricted for specific purposes. Thus, comparable to the general fund of a governmental unit, the unrestricted fund of a nonprofit organization is residual in nature.

Designated Fund Balance of Unrestricted Fund   The board of directors of a nonprofit organization may designate a portion of an unrestricted fund's assets for a specific purpose. The earmarked portion should be accounted for as a segregation of the unrestricted fund balance, rather than as a separate restricted fund. For example, if the board of directors of Civic Welfare, Inc., earmarks $25,000 of the unrestricted fund's assets for the acquisition of office equipment, the following journal entry is prepared for Civic Welfare, Inc., Unrestricted Fund:

<table>
<tr><td>**Journal entry for designation of portion of fund balance of unrestricted fund**</td><td>Undesignated Fund Balance ....</td><td>25,000</td><td></td></tr>
<tr><td></td><td>Designated Fund Balance — Office Equipment ....</td><td></td><td>25,000</td></tr>
<tr><td></td><td colspan="3">To record designation of portion of fund balance for acquisition of office equipment.</td></tr>
</table>

9 "Accounting Principles and Reporting Practices for Certain Nonprofit Organizations," p. 19.

The Designated Fund Balance — Office Equipment account is similar to a retained earnings appropriation account of a corporation and is reported in the balance sheet of Civic Welfare, Inc., as a portion of the fund balance of the Unrestricted Fund.

Revenue and Support of Unrestricted Fund   The revenue and support of the unrestricted fund of a nonprofit organization are derived from a number of sources. For example, a hospital derives unrestricted fund revenue and support from patient services, educational programs, research and other grants, unrestricted gifts, unrestricted income from endowment funds and miscellaneous sources such as donated material and services. A university's sources of unrestricted fund revenue and support include student tuition and fees; governmental grants and contracts; gifts and private grants; unrestricted income from endowment funds; and revenue from auxiliary activities such as student residences, food services, and intercollegiate athletics. The principal support sources of voluntary health and welfare organizations' unrestricted funds (and all other funds) are cash donations and pledges. Revenue may include membership dues, interest, dividends, and gains on the sale of investments.

Revenue for Services   A hospital's patient service revenue and a university's tuition and fees revenue are accrued at full rates, ***even though part or all of the revenue is to be waived or otherwise adjusted.*** Suppose, for example, that Community Hospital's patient service revenue records for June, Year 3, include the following amounts:

Patient service revenue components of a hospital

Gross patient service revenue (before recognition of contractual adjustments) ..	*$100,000*
Contractual adjustment allowed to Blue Cross	*16,000*

The journal entries at the top of page 571 are appropriate for the Community Hospital Unrestricted Fund on June 30, Year 3. The contractual adjustments recorded in the second journal entry on page 571 illustrate a unique feature of a hospital's operations. Many hospital receivables are collectible from a ***third-party payer***, rather than from the patient receiving services. Among third-party payers are the federal-provincial Medicare programs, Blue Cross, and private medical insurance carriers. The hospital's contractual agreements with third-party payers usually provide for payments by the third parties at less than full billing rates. Private wards are not covered under government programs, and are either paid for by the patients or by the patient's private insurance carrier.

In the statement of activity of Community Hospital for June, Year 3, the Contractual Adjustments, and Provision for Doubtful Accounts ledger accounts for the month are deducted from the Patient Service Revenue account to compute net patient service revenue for the month. The Allowances and Doubtful Accounts ledger account is offset against the Accounts Re-

Journal entries for patient
revenue of unrestricted
fund of a hospital

Accounts Receivable	100,000	
Patient Service Revenue		100,000

To record gross patient service revenue for month of June at full
rates.

Contractual Adjustments	16,000	
Allowances and Doubtful Accounts		16,000

To record contractual adjustments allowed to Blue Cross for June.

Provision for Doubtful Accounts	12,000	
Allowances and Doubtful Accounts		12,000

To provide for doubtful accounts for June.

ceivable account in the balance sheet, and the write-off of an account receivable is recorded in the customary fashion. For example, the uncollectible accounts receivable would be written off by Community Hospital by the following journal entry in the Unrestricted Fund on June 30, Year 3:

Journal entry to write off
uncollectible accounts
receivable of a hospital

Allowances and Doubtful Accounts	5,100	
Accounts Receivable		5,100

To write off uncollectible accounts receivable of patients as
follows:

J. R. English	$1,500
R. L. Knight	1,100
S. O. Newman	2,500
Total	$5,100

Donated Material and Services In addition to cash contributions, nonprofit organizations receive donations of material and services. For example, a hospital may receive free drugs, or a "thrift store" may receive articles of clothing. The donated material should be recorded in the Inventories account at its current fair value, with a credit to a support account in the unrestricted fund, as illustrated in the following journal entry for Community Hospital:

Inventories	5,000	
Other Operating Support		5,000

To record donated drugs at current fair value.

Donated services are recorded in the unrestricted fund as salaries expense, with an offset to a support account, if the services are rendered to the nonprofit organization in an employee-employer relationship. The value assigned to the services is the going salary rate for comparable salaried employees of the entity, less any meals or other living costs absorbed for the donor of the services by the nonprofit organization. The **CICA** study suggested the following requirements for recording donated materials and services in the accounting records of a nonprofit organization:[10]

(1)   The Study Group believes that donated services, materials and facilities (except for those discussed in paragraph 3) that have a material effect on the operations of a non-profit organization should be reported in the statement of operations as both current revenue and expenses in the period received. They should be disclosed at fair value at the date donated to the organization when the following conditions exist:

a. They are an essential service, material or facility that is normally purchased and would be paid for if not donated.

b. The organization controls the way they are used.

c. There is a measurable basis for arriving at a dollar value.

d. They are not intended solely for the benefit of the members of the organization.

(2)   Significant donated services, materials and facilities of a capital nature should be reported at fair value on the balance sheet as at the date received with a credit to the appropriate fund.

(3)   Services provided by a non-profit organization may depend directly on volunteer efforts and would not be available or would be considerably reduced if there were no volunteer participation. If these services would not be replaced by paid workers, it would not be appropriate to report a dollar amount for them in the general purpose financial statements. Nor should the value of volunteer efforts for fund raising drives, which can be difficult to measure in monetary terms, be included. The nature of volunteer services can, however, be described in an annual report accompanying the financial statements, as discussed in Chapter 4.

To illustrate the accounting for donated services that meet the foregoing criteria, assume that the services of volunteer nurses' aides were valued at $26,400 for the month of June, Year 3, by Community Hospital, and that the value of meals provided at no cost to the volunteers during the month was $2,100. The journal entry below is appropriate for Community Hospital on June 30, Year 3.

Journal entry for donated services	Salaries Expense 24,300	
	Other Operating Support	24,300
	To record donated services at current fair value of $26,400 less	
	$2,100 value of meals provided to donors. (Income tax effects	
	are disregarded.)	

10 *Financial Reporting for Non-profit Organizations*, p. 100.

Pledges   A *pledge* is a commitment by a prospective donor to contribute a specific amount of cash to a nonprofit organization on a future date or in installments. Because the pledge is in writing and signed by the *pledgor*, it resembles in form the *promissory note* used in business. However, pledges generally are not enforceable contracts.

Under the accrual basis of accounting, unrestricted pledges are recorded as receivables and support (in the accounting period specified by the pledgor) in the unrestricted fund of a nonprofit organization, with appropriate provision for doubtful accounts. If the accounting period specified by the donor occurs subsequent to the date of the pledge, the credit should be to a deferred revenue account. Recording of support from pledges in this fashion is required by "Hospital Audit Guide," "Audits of Voluntary Health and Welfare Organizations," and by *Statement of Position 78-10*.[11] However, the "Audits of Colleges and Universities" *Industry Audit Guide* makes the recording of pledges optional, as indicated below:[12]

> Pledges of gifts . . . should be disclosed in the notes unless they are reported in the financial statements. The notes to the financial statements should disclose the gross amounts by time periods over which the pledges are to be collected. . . .
>
> If the pledges are reported in the financial statements, they should be accounted for at their estimated net realizable value in the same manner as gifts received. . . .

The reason for the inconsistent treatment of pledges in the four accounting guides is not apparent. "Audits of Colleges and Universities" apparently sanctions use of notes to financial statements to correct an error in the application of accounting principles—the omission of receivables and support —in the financial statements themselves. The authors believe this to be an improper use of notes to financial statements. The CICA research study seemed to sanction this inconsistent treatment with the following statement:[13] "Nevertheless, when pledges are not legally enforceable, the cash basis can be used with disclosure of pledges receivable by a note to the financial statements."

To illustrate the accounting for pledges, assume that Civic Welfare Inc., a nonprofit organization, received pledges totalling $200,000 in a fund-raising drive. Based on past experience, 15% of the pledges are considered to be doubtful of collection. The journal entries at the top of page 574 are appropriate.

Contributions support is shown in the statement of activity net of the provision for doubtful pledges. Pledges receivable are presented in the balance sheet net of the allowance for doubtful pledges. The write-off of

11 "Hospital Audit Guide," p. 10; "Audits of Voluntary Health and Welfare Organizations." AICPA (New York: 1974), p. 14; "Accounting Principles and Reporting Practices for Certain Nonprofit Organizations," pp. 22–23.
12 "Audits of Colleges and Universities," AICPA (New York: 1973), p. 8.
13 *Financial Reporting for Non-profit Organizations*, p. 99.

Journal entries to record
receivable for pledges and
doubtful pledges

Pledges Receivable	200,000	
Contributions Support		200,000

To record receivable for pledges.

Provision for Doubtful Pledges	30,000	
Allowance for Doubtful Pledges		30,000

To record provision for doubtful pledges ($200,000 × 0.15 = $30,000).

uncollectible pledges is recorded by a debit to the Allowance for Doubtful Pledges account and a credit to the Pledges Receivable account.

Revenue from Pooled Investments   Many of the funds of nonprofit organizations have cash available for investments in securities and other money-market instruments. To provide greater efficiency and flexibility in investment programs, the investment resources of all funds of a nonprofit organization may be pooled for investment by a single portfolio manager. The pooling technique requires a careful allocation of investment revenue, including gains and losses, to each participating fund.

To illustrate the pooling of investments, assume that on January 2, Year 5, four funds of Civic Welfare, Inc., a nonprofit organization, pooled their individual investments as follows:

Pooling of investments by
nonprofit organization on
Jan. 2, Year 5

	Cost	Current fair value	Original equity, %
Unrestricted Fund	$ 20,000	$ 18,000	15
Restricted Fund	15,000	21,600	18
Plant Fund	10,000	20,400	17
Wilson Endowment Fund	55,000	60,000	50
Totals	$100,000	$120,000	100

The original equity percentages in the above tabulation are based on *current fair value*, not on *cost*. The current fair values of the pooled investments on January 2, Year 5, represent a common "measuring rod" not available in the cost amounts, which represent current fair values on various dates the investments were acquired.

Realized gains (or losses) and interest and dividend revenue of the pooled investments during Year 5 are allocated to the four funds in the ratio of the original equity percentages. For example, if $18,000 realized gains of the investment pool during Year 5 are reinvested, and if interest and dividend revenue of $9,000 is realized and distributed by the pool during Year 5, these amounts are allocated as shown at the top of page 575. Each of the funds participating in the investment pool debits Investments and credits Gains on Sale of Investments for its share of the $18,000. Each

Allocation of Year 5
revenue from pooled
investments to respective
funds

	Original equity, %	Realized gains	Interest and dividends revenue
Unrestricted Fund	15	$ 2,700	$1,350
Restricted Fund	18	3,240	1,620
Plant Fund	17	3,060	1,530
Wilson Endowment Fund	50	9,000	4,500
Totals	100	$18,000	$9,000

fund also debits Cash and credits Interest and Dividends Revenue or Fund Balance for its share of the $9,000 received from interest and dividends.

If another fund of Civic Welfare, Inc., entered the investment pool on December 31, Year 5, the original equity percentages would have to be revised, based on the December 31, Year 5, current fair values of the investment portfolio. For example, if the Harris Endowment Fund entered the Civic Welfare, Inc., investment pool (with a current fair value of $144,000) on December 31, Year 5, with investments having a cost of $32,000 and a current fair value of $36,000 on that date, the equity percentages would be revised as illustrated below:

Revision of fund equities
in pooled investments on
Dec. 31, Year 5

	Cost*	Current fair value†	Revised equity, %
Unrestricted Fund	$ 22,700	$ 21,600	12.0
Restricted Fund	18,240	25,920	14.4
Plant Fund	13,060	24,480	13.6
Wilson Endowment Fund	64,000	72,000	40.0
Subtotals	$118,000	$144,000	
Harris Endowment Fund	32,000	36,000	20.0
Totals	$150,000	$180,000	100.0

* Cost for four original pool member funds includes $18,000 realized gains of Year 5.
† Current fair value of original pooled investments totalling $144,000 on December 31, Year 5, allocated to original pool member funds based on original equity percentages computed on page 574.

Realized gains (or losses) and interest and dividend revenue for accounting periods subsequent to December 31, Year 5, are allocated in the revised equity percentages. The revised equity percentages are maintained until the membership of the investment pool changes again.

Expenses of Unrestricted Fund   The expenses of unrestricted funds are similar in many respects to those of a business enterprise — salaries and wages, supplies, maintenance, research, and the like. The question of whether depreciation should be recorded as an expense by a nonprofit organization has not been answered uniformly by the AICPA. The "Hospital Audit Guide,"

"Audits of Voluntary Health and Welfare Organizations," and **Statement of Position 78-10** specify that depreciation generally should be recorded as an expense of each accounting period.[14] However, "Audits of Colleges and Universities" takes a contrary position:[15]

> Current funds expenditures . . . comprise . . . all expenses incurred, determined in accordance with the generally accepted accrual method of accounting, except for the omission of depreciation. . . .
>
> Depreciation expense related to depreciable assets comprising the physical plant is reported neither in the statement of current funds revenues, expenditures, and other changes nor in the statement of changes in unrestricted current funds balance. The reason for this treatment is that these statements present expenditures and transfers of current funds rather than operating expenses in conformity with the reporting objectives of accounting for resources received and used rather than the determination of net income. Depreciation allowances, however, may be reported in the balance sheet and the provision for depreciation reported in the statement of changes in the balance of the investment-in-plant fund subsection of the plant funds group.

In the opinion of the authors, the activities of colleges and universities are not so different from those of other nonprofit organizations that the recognition of depreciation expense is inappropriate for colleges and universities.

However, **Statement of Position 78-10** does not require depreciation of assets that are **not exhaustible**, such as landmarks, cathedrals, historical treasures, and structures used primarily as houses of worship.[16]

The **CICA study group** also found the concept of depreciation accounting for nonprofit organizations a difficult one to come to grips with. They reported as follows:[17]

> As for the recording of depreciation and the related balance sheet valuation of fixed assets:
> (a) The majority of the members of the Study Group believe that depreciation need not always be recorded and:
> - Depreciation based on estimated useful life is significant where fixed assets are purchased (or related debt repaid) from operating funds, but is less significant, and could even be misleading, where fixed assets are purchased from special fund raising or grants.
> - Fixed asset acquisitions written off against current operations should be shown separately on the statement of operations after current activities.

14 "Hospital Audit Guide," p. 4; "Audits of Voluntary Health and Welfare Organizations," p. 12; "Accounting Principles and Reporting Practices for Certain Nonprofit Organizations," pp. 35–36.
15 "Audits of Colleges and Universities," pp. 26, 9–10.
16 "Accounting Principles and Reporting Practices for Certain Nonprofit Organizations," p. 36.
17 *Financial Reporting for Non-profit Organizations*, p. 95.

- Supplementary information on fixed assets, for example, estimated useful lives, should be presented when depreciation is not recorded on the basis of estimated useful life.
- As noted in Chapter 3, the statement of changes in financial position, which excludes depreciation, should also be provided.

(b) Some members of the Study Group believe that depreciation should always be recorded, as set out in Section 3060 of the *CICA Handbook*.

(c) One Study Group member believes that, in accordance with the cash flow basis of accounting, depreciation should never be recorded, as discussed in Chapter 15.

Assets and Liabilities of Unrestricted Fund   Most assets and liabilities of a nonprofit organization's unrestricted fund are similar to the current assets and liabilities of a business enterprise. Cash, investments, accounts receivable, receivables from other funds, inventories, and short-term prepayments are typical assets of an unrestricted fund.

"Audits of Colleges and Universities" and "Audits of Voluntary Health and Welfare Organizations" segregate plant assets into a separate fund. In contrast, "Hospital Audit Guide" takes the following position:[18]

Property, plant and equipment and related liabilities should be accounted for as a part of unrestricted funds, since segregation in a separate fund would imply the existence of restrictions on asset use.

In the opinion of the authors, segregation of plant assets in a separate fund is logical accounting practice for any nonprofit organization that uses fund accounting. Plant assets, with their extended economic life, should not be included in the same fund as liquid assets that are used in current operations of a nonprofit organization.

The liabilities of an unrestricted fund include payables, accruals, and deferred revenue comparable to those of a business enterprise, as well as amounts payable to other funds.

Restricted fund

Nonprofit organizations establish ***restricted funds*** to account for assets available for current use but expendable only as authorized by the donor of the assets. Thus, a restricted fund of a nonprofit organization resembles the special revenue fund of a government unit, because the assets of both types of funds may be expended only for specified purposes.

The AICPA's "Hospital Audit Guide" includes in the restricted funds category a broad spectrum of restricted resources:[19]

Funds for specific operating purposes
Funds for additions to property, plant, and equipment
Endowment funds

18 "Hospital Audit Guide," p. 4.
19 "Hospital Audit Guide," p. 9

In contrast, "Audits of Colleges and Universities" and "Audits of Voluntary Health and Welfare Organizations" limit the restricted fund category to resources for specific operating purposes.[20]

The assets of restricted funds are not derived from the operations of the nonprofit organization. Instead, the assets are obtained from (1) restricted gifts or grants from individuals or governmental units, (2) revenue from restricted fund investments, (3) gains on sales of investments of the restricted fund, and (4) restricted income from endowment funds. These assets are transferred to the unrestricted fund at the time the designated expenditure is made, with a credit to the Other Operating Support account if the expenditure is for current operating purposes, or to the Fund Balance account if the expenditure is for plant assets.

To illustrate, assume that on July 1, Year 4, Robert King donated $50,000 to Community Hospital, a nonprofit organization, for the acquisition of beds for a new wing of the hospital. On August 1, Year 4, Community Hospital paid $51,250 for the beds. These transactions are recorded by Community Hospital as shown below.

<table>
<tr><td>Journal entries for restricted donation</td><td colspan="3">In Robert King Restricted Fund:</td></tr>
<tr><td></td><td colspan="3">Year 4</td></tr>
<tr><td></td><td>July 1   Cash ....</td><td>50,000</td><td></td></tr>
<tr><td></td><td>   Fund Balance ....</td><td></td><td>50,000</td></tr>
<tr><td></td><td colspan="3">   To record receipt of gift from Robert King for acquisition of beds for new wing.</td></tr>
<tr><td></td><td>Aug. 1   Fund Balance ....</td><td>50,000</td><td></td></tr>
<tr><td></td><td>   Payable to Unrestricted Fund ....</td><td></td><td>50,000</td></tr>
<tr><td></td><td colspan="3">   To record obligation to Unrestricted Fund for cost of beds for new wing in accordance with Robert King's gift.</td></tr>
<tr><td></td><td colspan="3">In Unrestricted Fund:</td></tr>
<tr><td></td><td colspan="3">Year 4</td></tr>
<tr><td></td><td>Aug. 1   Plant Assets ....</td><td>51,250</td><td></td></tr>
<tr><td></td><td>   Cash ....</td><td></td><td>51,250</td></tr>
<tr><td></td><td colspan="3">   To record acquisition of beds for new wing.</td></tr>
<tr><td></td><td>   1   Receivable from Robert King Restricted Fund ....</td><td>50,000</td><td></td></tr>
<tr><td></td><td>   Fund Balance ....</td><td></td><td>50,000</td></tr>
<tr><td></td><td colspan="3">   To record receivable from Robert King Restricted Fund for beds acquired.</td></tr>
</table>

Endowment fund

An *endowment fund* of a nonprofit organization is comparable with a *nonexpendable trust fund* of a governmental unit, described in Chapter 13. A *pure endowment fund* is one for which the principal must be held

20 "Audits of Colleges and Universities," p. 16; "Audits of Voluntary Health and Welfare Organizations," p. 2.

indefinitely in revenue-producing investments. Only the revenue from the pure endowment fund's investments may be expended by the nonprofit organization. In contrast, the principal of a **term endowment fund** may be expended after the passage of a period of time or the occurrence of an event stipulated by the donor of the endowment principal. A **quasi-endowment fund** is established by the board of directors of a nonprofit organization, rather than by an outside donor. At the option of the board, the principal of a quasi-endowment fund later may be expended by the entity that established the fund.

The revenue of endowment funds is handled in accordance with the instructions of the donor or the board of directors. If there are no restrictions on the use of endowment fund income, it is transferred to the nonprofit organization's unrestricted fund. Otherwise, the endowment fund revenue is transferred to an appropriate restricted fund.

Agency fund

An **agency fund** of a nonprofit organization is identical to its counterpart in a governmental unit. An agency fund is used to account for assets held by a nonprofit organization as a custodian. The assets are disbursed only as instructed by their owner.

For example, a university may act as custodian of cash of a student organization. The university disburses the cash as directed by the appropriate officers of the student organization. The undistributed cash of the student organization is reported as a **liability** of the university's agency fund, rather than as a **fund balance**, because the university has no equity in the fund.

Annuity and life income funds

Annuity Fund Assets may be contributed to a nonprofit organization with the stipulation that the organization pay specified amounts periodically to designated recipients, for a specified time period. An **annuity fund** is established by the nonprofit organization to account for this arrangement. At the end of the specified time period for the periodic payments, the unexpended assets of the annuity fund are transferred to the unrestricted fund, or to a restricted fund or endowment fund specified by the donor.

The journal entries on page 580 illustrate the accounting for the Ruth Collins Annuity Fund of Ridgedale College, a nonprofit organization, for the fund's first fiscal year ending June 30, Year 2. Note on page 580 that, in the first journal entry on June 30, Year 2, the revenue and gains on the annuity fund's share of the investment pool are credited to the Annuity Payable ledger account. This is necessary because the actuarial computation of the annuity on the date of establishment of the annuity fund valued the annuity liability at its then present value.

Life Income Fund A **life income fund** is used to account for stipulated payments to a named beneficiary (or beneficiaries) during the beneficiary's

Year 1

July 1   Cash 50,000

                 Annuity Payable   35,000

                 Fund Balance   15,000

          To record receipt of cash from Andrea Collins for an annuity
          of $6,000 a year each June 30 to Ruth Collins for her lifetime.
          Liability is recorded at the actuarially determined present
          value of the annuity, based on life expectancy of Ruth Collins.

      1   Investments 45,000

                 Cash   45,000

          To record acquisition of interest in Ridgedale College's invest-
          ment pool.

Year 2

June 30   Cash 1,500

          Investments 2,000

                 Annuity Payable   3,500

          To record share of revenue and gains of Ridgedale College
          investment pool.

     30   Annuity Payable 6,000

                 Cash   6,000

          To record payment of current year's annuity to Ruth Collins.

     30   Fund Balance 1,000

                 Annuity Payable   1,000

          To record actuarial loss based on revised life expectancy
          actuarial valuation of Ruth Collins annuity.

---

lifetime. In a life income fund, only the *income* is paid to the beneficiary. Thus, payments to a life income fund's beneficiary vary from one accounting period to the next, but payments from an annuity fund are fixed in amount.

Loan fund

A *loan fund* may be established by any nonprofit organization, but loan funds most frequently are included in the accounting records of colleges and universities. Student loan funds usually are *revolving*; that is, as old loans are repaid, new loans are made from the receipts. Loans receivable are carried in the loan fund at estimated realizable value; provisions for doubtful loans are debited directly to the Fund Balance account, not to an expense account. Interest on loans is credited to the Fund Balance account, ordinarily on the cash basis of accounting.

Plant fund

We have already noted (page 576) the inconsistent accounting treatment for plant assets of hospitals as compared with colleges and universities and voluntary health and welfare organizations. There are also inconsistencies in the contents of the *plant funds* of the three types of nonprofit organizations, as follows:

1 A *plant replacement and expansion fund* is a subdivision of the *restricted fund* category of a hospital. In the hospital's plant replacement and expansion fund are recorded the cash, investments, and receivables earmarked by donors for expenditure for plant assets.[21]

2 The following excerpt describes the accounting for the plant fund of a voluntary health and welfare organization:[22]

> Land, building and equipment fund (often referred to as plant fund) is often used to accumulate the net investment in fixed assets and to account for the unexpended resources contributed specifically for the purpose of acquiring or replacing land, buildings, or equipment for use in the operations of the organization. Mortgages or other liabilities relating to these assets are also included in this fund. When additions to land, buildings, or equipment used in carrying out the organization's program and supporting services are acquired with unrestricted fund resources, the amount expended for such assets should be transferred from the unrestricted fund to the plant fund and should be accounted for as a direct addition to the plant fund balance. Gains or losses on the sale of fixed assets should be reflected as income items in the plant fund accounts. The proceeds from the sale of fixed assets should be transferred to the unrestricted fund; such transfers should be reflected as direct reductions and additions to the respective fund balances.

3 In contrast to the two preceding types of plant funds, "Audits of Colleges and Universities" provides for the following:[23]

> The plant funds group consists of (1) funds to be used for the acquisition of physical properties for institutional purposes but unexpended at the date of reporting; (2) funds set aside for the renewal and replacement of institutional properties; (3) funds set aside for debt service charges and for the retirement of indebtedness on institutional properties; and (4) funds expended for and thus invested in institutional properties.
>
> Some institutions combine the assets and liabilities of the four subfund groups for reporting purposes; however, separate fund balances should be maintained. Resources restricted by donors or outside agencies for additions to plant should be recorded directly in the particular fund subgroup, generally unexpended plant funds.

Thus, in the three AICPA *Industry Audit Guides* for nonprofit organizations, we find wide variations in the composition and accounting for plant funds. The differences in the plant funds of the three types of nonprofit organizations are not supported by any theoretical differences in their accounting objectives.

---

21 "Hospital Audit Guide," pp. 9, 41.

22 "Audits of Voluntary Health and Welfare Organizations," pp. 2–3.

23 "Audits of Colleges and Universities," p. 44.

Financial statements for nonprofit organizations

All nonprofit organizations issue a balance sheet incorporating all funds of the organization. The assets, liabilities, and fund balances for each fund are listed in horizontal or vertical sequence in the balance sheet. This type of balance sheet presentation emphasizes the unitary nature of the nonprofit organization, despite its use of separate funds for accountability purposes.

Because a nonprofit organization does not operate for gain, an income statement is inappropriate. Instead, a *statement of activity*, with a title such as "statement of revenue, expenses, support, and capital additions," is issued, with the final amount labeled "Excess of revenue and support over expenses" or a similar caption. Changes in fund balances may be summarized in a separate statement or may be annexed to the statement of activity.

The AICPA's "Hospital Audit Guide" recommends a statement of changes in financial position for the unrestricted fund.[24] However, "Audits of Voluntary Health and Welfare Organizations" and "Audits of Colleges and Universities" waive a statement of changes in financial position, because the information is available in the other financial statements.[25] *Statement of Position 78-10* requires nonprofit organizations that it covers to present a statement of changes in financial position.[26]

Many of the matters discussed in this chapter are illustrated in the financial statements and notes to financial statements of the American Accounting Association, a nonprofit organization, in the Appendix of this chapter beginning on page 584.

Summary of Major CICA Research Study Conclusions

We mentioned previously that with the exception for depreciation accounting the research study group concluded that the *CICA Handbook could be amended* in such a way that its provisions would be applicable to both profit and nonprofit organizations. It also suggested that *while fund accounting is often appropriate, it is not essential* and that information regarding restrictions on funds could be provided in footnotes to the financial statements.[27]

Its *recommendations regarding budget information* could result in substantial departures from current practice, and might receive opposition from the boards of directors of nonprofit organizations. The study group felt that budget information would be useful to financial statement users and that it would be desirable to include in an annual report:[28]

---

24 "Hospital Audit Guide," p. 38.
25 "Audits of Voluntary Health and Welfare Organizations," p. 33; "Audits of Colleges and Universities," p. 55.
26 Accounting Principles and Reporting Practices for Certain Nonprofit Organizations," p. 11.
27 *Financial Reporting for Non-profit Organizations*, Chapter 7.
28 Ibid., chapter 5.

1 the *current year's budget* as originally approved by the board;

2 the explanations of management of *significant variations* between budget and actual amounts; and

3 the *following year's approved budget*.

This proposal might receive opposition from some nonprofit organizations. Many budgeted revenues are "soft" numbers and are often difficult to achieve. This is especially true for cultural organizations in Canada. For example, symphony orchestras often receive as much as 50 per cent of their revenues from government grants (federal, provincial and civic) and from annual fund-raising activities. At the beginning of the fiscal year when the budget is approved, the amount of government grants is not known. Grant increases included in the budget are sometimes not achieved. On the other hand, a large proportion of the expenses are essentially fixed in nature. It is difficult to reduce the size of an orchestra, and guest artists and guest conductors are often signed to contracts years in advance. When planned revenues are not realized, deficits result which prove to be an embarrassment to the board. Many boards of directors may feel that the release of budget information with comparisons with actual results would adversely reflect on their management skills when many of the variances are perceived by them to be essentially uncontrollable.

The study group also introduced the concept of *condensed financial statements* for users who require minimal information from annual financial reports and who would prefer to see an overview rather than voluminous detail. Because this type of statement is not currently covered by the *CICA Handbook*, it was proposed that a new section be added to cover minimum disclosures that should be contained therein.[29] The study group concluded that the audit report should refer to accounting principles set out in the notes to the financial statements until such time as the *CICA Handbook* applies to nonprofit organizations.

Appraisal of accounting standards for nonprofit organizations

The accounting principles recommended by the AICPA for colleges and universities, hospitals, voluntary health and welfare organizations, and other nonprofit organizations collectively disclose many inconsistencies. More coordination in the efforts of the various committees that developed the separate sets of accounting principles probably would have eliminated most of these inconsistencies. It is to be hoped that the FASB soon will address the accounting for nonprofit organizations and, drawing on the objectives of financial reporting by nonbusiness organizations discussed in *Statement of Financial Accounting Concepts No. 4* (see pages 486 and 487), will develop uniform accounting standards for all nonprofit organizations. In Canada, the *Accounting Standards Committee* of CICA has commenced work on amending the Handbook so that it will apply to the nonprofit area.

---

29 Ibid., chapter 10.

APPENDIX: FINANCIAL STATEMENTS AND NOTES OF AMERICAN ACCOUNTING ASSOCIATION

REPORT OF INDEPENDENT CERTIFIED PUBLIC ACCOUNTANTS

To the Executive Committee,

American Accounting Association:

We have examined the balance sheet of AMERICAN ACCOUNTING ASSOCIATION as of August 31, 1981, and the related statements of support, revenue and expenses and changes in fund balances and changes in financial position for the year then ended. Our examination was made in accordance with generally accepted auditing standards and, accordingly, included such tests of the accounting records and such other auditing procedures as we considered necessary in the circumstances.

In our opinion, the financial statements referred to above present fairly the financial position of American Accounting Association as of August 31, 1981, and the results of its operations and the changes in its fund balances and changes in its financial position for the year then ended, in conformity with generally accepted accounting principles applied on a basis consistent with that of the preceding year.

Our examination was made for the purpose of forming an opinion on the basic financial statements taken as a whole. The statement of contributions earned for the year ended August 31, 1981, (Exhibit I) is presented for purposes of additional analysis and is not a required part of the basic financial statements. Such information has been subjected to the auditing procedures applied in the examination of the basic financial statements and, in our opinion, is fairly stated in all material respects in relation to the basic financial statements taken as a whole.

COOPERS & LYBRAND

Tampa, Florida
October 21, 1981

AMERICAN ACCOUNTING ASSOCIATION
BALANCE SHEET, August 31, 1981

	UNRESTRICTED		RESTRICTED			
	General Fund	Publications Fund	Sections Fund	Fellowship Fund	Educational Research Fund	Total All Funds
ASSETS						
Current assets:						
Cash, including invested cash of $11,525	$ 12,970	-	-	-	-	$ 12,970
Certificates of deposit	200,780	-	-	-	-	200,780
Marketable securities, at cost which approximates market (Note 1)	338,953	-	-	-	-	338,953
Current portion of pledges receivable (Note 1)	50,000	-	-	$ 5,000	$43,380	98,380
Accounts and interest receivable	31,877	$ 5,187	-	-	-	37,064
Publications inventory (Notes 1 and 3)	-	110,531	-	-	-	110,531
Prepaids and other assets	3,808	-	-	-	-	3,808
Due from (to) other funds	(90,628)	(21,071)	$56,254	28,878	26,567	-
Total current assets	547,760	94,647	56,254	33,878	69,947	802,486
Pledges receivable, less current portion (Note 1)	95,547	-	-	10,000	-	105,547
Property and equipment, at cost less accumulated depreciation of $28,872 (Notes 1 and 2)	160,148	-	-	-	-	160,148
	$803,455	$ 94,647	$56,254	$43,878	$69,947	$1,068,181
LIABILITIES AND FUND BALANCES						
Current liabilities:						
Accounts payable and accrued liabilities	$ 66,600	-	-	$11,800	-	$ 78,400
Accounts payable - research projects (Note 1)	45,174	-	-	-	$27,120	72,294
Current portion of deferred revenue (Note 1):						
Membership dues	71,277	-	-	-	-	71,277
Subscriptions	22,944	-	-	-	-	22,944
Current portion of deferred support (Note 1)	60,000	-	-	5,000	42,827	107,827
Total current liabilities	265,995	-	-	16,800	69,947	352,742
Deferred revenue, less current portion (Note 1):						
Membership dues	613	-	-	-	-	613
Subscriptions	1,395	-	-	-	-	1,395
Deferred support, less current portion (Note 1)	67,678	-	-	5,000	-	72,678
	69,686	-	-	5,000	-	74,686
Commitment (Note 4)						
Fund balances (Note 3)						
Unrestricted:						
Designated for fund purposes	-	$ 94,647	-	-	-	94,647
Undesignated, available for general purposes	455,774	-	-	-	-	455,774
Total unrestricted	455,774	94,647	-	-	-	550,421
Restricted	12,000	-	$56,254	22,078	-	90,332
Total fund balances	467,774	94,647	56,254	22,078	-	640,753
	$803,455	$ 94,647	$56,254	$43,878	$69,947	$1,068,181

See accompanying notes.

STATEMENT OF SUPPORT, REVENUE AND EXPENSES AND CHANGES IN FUND BALANCES
for the year ended August 31, 1981

	UNRESTRICTED		RESTRICTED			
	General Fund	Publications Fund	Sections Fund	Fellowship Fund	Educational Research Fund	Total All Funds
REVENUE AND SUPPORT (Note 1)						
Membership dues	$266,861	-	$55,068	-	-	$321,929
Subscriptions	69,911	-	-	-	-	69,911
Advertising	65,187	-	-	-	-	65,187
Publication sales	7,986	$67,611	2,353	-	-	77,950
Contributions (Exhibit I)	118,513	-	-	$26,410	$36,620	181,543
Interest and dividend income	63,438	-	-	-	-	63,438
Income from annual convention net of direct costs of $152,000	9,222	-	-	-	-	9,222
Other revenue, primarily programs and seminars	82,074	-	400	-	-	82,474
	683,192	67,611	57,821	26,410	36,620	871,654
EXPENSES (Note 1)						
Cost of publications:						
The Accounting Review and Committee Reports Supplement	175,569	-	-	-	-	175,569
Other	24,920	27,069	22,910	-	-	74,899
Programs and seminars	158,350	-	-	-	-	158,350
Research and education	28,413	-	-	-	36,620	65,033
Committees	39,005	-	-	-	-	39,005
Officers' meetings	32,493	-	-	-	-	32,493
Administration	189,232	-	24,496	-	-	213,728
Financial Accounting Foundation contribution	9,658	-	-	-	-	9,658
American Assembly of Collegiate Schools of Business contribution	5,000	-	-	-	-	5,000
Fellowship grants	-	-	-	24,500	-	24,500
Other expenses	16,840	-	-	-	-	16,840
	679,480	27,069	47,406	24,500	36,620	815,075
Excess of support and revenue over expenses	3,712	40,542	10,415	1,910	-	56,579
Fund balances, beginning of year	464,062	54,105	45,839	20,168	-	584,174
Fund balances, end of year	$467,774	$94,647	$56,254	$22,078	$ -	$640,753

See accompanying notes.

STATEMENT OF CHANGES IN FINANCIAL POSITION
for the year ended August 31, 1981

	UNRESTRICTED		RESTRICTED			
	General Fund	Publications Fund	Sections Fund	Fellowship Fund	Educational Research Fund	Total All Funds
SOURCES OF FUNDS						
From operations:						
Revenue and support in excess of expenses	$ 3,712	$40,542	$10,415	$ 1,910	-	$ 56,579
Add depreciation, which does not require funds	10,386	-	-	-	-	10,386
Funds provided from operations	14,098	40,542	10,415	1,910	-	66,965
Decrease (increase) in:						
Pledges receivable, current and long-term	(14,547)	-	-	-	$36,620	22,073
Marketable securities	42,732	-	-	-	-	42,732
Increase (decrease) in:						
Deferred revenue, current and long-term	2,705	-	-	-	-	2,705
Accounts payable - research projects	10,124	-	-	-	15,120	25,244
Interfund borrowings	(8,641)	18,476	(7,505)	12,790	(15,120)	-
Total sources of funds	46,471	59,018	2,910	14,700	36,620	159,719
USES OF FUNDS						
Increase (decrease) in:						
Inventory	-	56,426	-	-	-	56,426
Accounts and interest receivable	5,993	(350)	-	-	-	5,643
Prepaids and other assets	196	-	-	-	-	196
Decrease (increase) in:						
Accounts payable and accrued liabilities	(8,286)	2,942	2,910	9,700	-	7,266
Deferred support, current and long-term	(15,730)	-	-	5,000	36,620	25,890
Purchase of property and equipment	32,473	-	-	-	-	32,473
Total uses of funds	14,646	59,018	2,910	14,700	36,620	127,894
Net sources of funds	31,825	-	-	-	-	31,825
Cash and certificates of deposit, beginning of year	181,925	-	-	-	-	181,925
Cash and certificates of deposit, end of year	$213,750	$ -	$ -	$ -	$ -	$213,750

See accompanying notes.

NOTES TO FINANCIAL STATEMENTS AUGUST 31, 1981

1. SUMMARY OF SIGNIFICANT ACCOUNTING POLICIES:

Accounting Method –
The financial statements of American Accounting Association (the Association) are prepared in accordance with the Statement of Position entitled "Accounting Principles and Reporting Practices for Certain Nonprofit Organizations" prepared by the American Institute of Certified Public Accountants.

Pledges –
Pledges are recorded as receivables in the year made. Pledges for support of future periods are recorded as deferred amounts in the respective funds to which they apply. Support restricted by the donor for use in specified programs is recognized when the related program expenses are incurred.

Marketable Securities –
Marketable securities are recorded at cost.

Inventory –
Publications inventory is stated at the lower of cost (first-in, first-out) or market.

Depreciation –
Depreciation is provided using the straight-line method over the estimated useful lives of the assets. Depreciation expense of $10,386 is included in administrative expense.

Dues and Subscriptions –
General membership dues and subscriptions are recognized in the applicable membership and subscription period.

Publication Revenue –
Publication revenue is recognized when the related publications are issued.

Fellowship Grants –
Fellowship grants are expensed at the time the grant is approved by the Association.

Research Projects –
Research project expenses related to projects authorized by the Director of Research and Director of Education are accrued in the year the projects are authorized.

Income Taxes –
Pursuant to a determination letter received from the Internal Revenue Service, the Association is exempt from Federal income tax under Section 501(c)(3) of the Internal Revenue Code.

2. PROPERTY AND EQUIPMENT:

Property and equipment at August 31, 1981, consisted of the following:

Land	$ 29,748
Land improvements	13,246
Building	77,172
Furniture and equipment	40,062
Construction in progress	28,792
	189,020
Less accumulated depreciation	28,872
	$160,148

3. FUNDS:

The assets, liabilities and fund balances of the Association are reported in five self-balancing funds, as follows:

General Fund –
The General Fund is used to account for the operations of the Association, as well as those operations and activities not accounted for in other established funds. At August 31, 1981, $12,000 of the General Fund has been restricted for use in minority programs.

Publications Fund –
This fund was established to record the sale of publications of the Association other than *The Accounting Review* (which is provided to members in connection with payment of membership dues) and publications funded specifically by other funds.

Sections Fund –
This fund was established to account for the activities of the Association's special-interest membership groups, such as the auditing section, public sector section, etc.

Fellowship Fund –
This fund was established to record the operations of the fellowship program. Fellowships are awarded using funds generated by contributions to this fund.

Educational Research Fund –
This fund was established to record research projects which are directly funded by the related pledges received.

4. EMPLOYEE BENEFIT PLAN:

The Association has a contributory money purchase plan which covers substantially all employees. The Association's policy is to fund all related costs, which approximated $6,800 in 1981.

5. COMMITMENT:

In June 1981 the Association entered into a construction contract for expansion of its existing facilities. The remaining commitment at August 31, 1981, was approximately $63,000.

EXHIBIT I
STATEMENT OF CONTRIBUTIONS EARNED
FOR THE YEAR ENDED AUGUST 31, 1981

GENERAL FUND:

The Touche Ross Foundation	$ 82,444
Deloitte Haskins & Sells Foundation:	
1981 contribution	1,200
Recognition in 1981 of	
previously deferred support	31,369
Exxon Corporation	3,500
	$118,513

FELLOWSHIP FUND:

The Arthur Young Foundation	$ 5,000
Coopers & Lybrand Foundation	5,000
Ernst & Whinney Foundation	5,000
American Accounting Association	
members and others	4,910
The Touche Ross Foundation	3,000
Price Waterhouse Foundation	2,000
South-Western Publishing Company	1,000
International Business Machine Corporation	500
	$ 26,410

EDUCATIONAL RESEARCH FUND:

Coopers & Lybrand – recognition in	
1981 of previously deferred support	$ 36,620

REVIEW QUESTIONS

1 What is a ***nonprofit organization***?

2 List four types of nonprofit organizations in Canada.

3 What role do the AICPA's ***Industry Audit Guides*** play in the establishment of accounting principles for nonprofit organizations? Is the situation similar in Canada? Explain.

4 What are the three characteristics of nonprofit organizations that resemble those of governmental units?

5 What characteristics of nonprofit organizations resemble those of business enterprises?

6 What did the ***CICA*** study group conclude regarding generally accepted accounting principles for nonprofit organizations in Canada? Explain.

7 Define the following terms applicable to nonprofit organizations:
   a ***Designated Fund Balance***
   b ***Third-party payer***
   c ***Pledge***
   d ***Pooled investments***
   e ***Term endowment fund***

8 Differentiate between an ***annuity fund*** and a ***life income fund*** of a nonprofit organization.

9 There are several inconsistencies in the accounting principles for like items in the AICPA's ***Industry Audit Guides*** for nonprofit organizations. Identify three of these inconsistencies.

10 Hospitals and universities often "abate" or otherwise reduce their basic revenue charges to patients and students, respectively. How are these reductions reflected in the revenue accounting for the two types of nonprofit organizations? Explain.

11 a Should a nonprofit organization record donated material in its accounting records? Explain.
   b Should a nonprofit organization record donated services in its accounting records? Explain.

12 Identify the financial statements that are issued by a hospital.

13 How do ***support*** and ***capital additions*** differ from ***revenue*** of a nonprofit organization? Explain.

14 What did the CICA study group conclude regarding the recording of depreciation by nonprofit organizations?

15 What alternatives to the reporting of funds in financial statements of nonprofit organizations were suggested in the CICA research study?

16 Recommendations regarding budget information were contained in the CICA research study. Outline these recommendations and indicate why there may be opposition to them.

EXERCISES

Ex. 14-1   Select the best answer for each of the following multiple-choice questions:
1 The basis of accounting used by nonprofit organizations is the:

a Cash basis
b Modified accrual basis
c Accrual basis
d Modified cash basis

2 Interest is accounted for in a university's student loan fund on:
a The modified accrual basis of accounting
b The accrual basis of accounting
c The cash basis of accounting
d Some other basis of accounting

3 Which of the following receipts is recorded in a restricted fund in the accountin
records of a university?
a Tuition
b Student laboratory fees
c Housing fees
d None of the foregoing

4 Which of the following funds of a voluntary health and welfare organization doe
not have a counterpart fund in governmental accounting?
a Current unrestricted fund
b Land, building, and equipment fund
c Agency fund
d Endowment fund

5 A voluntary health and welfare organization received a pledge in Year 1 from
donor specifying that the amount pledged be used in Year 3. The donor paid th
pledge in cash in Year 2. The pledge should be accounted for as:
a A deferred credit in the balance sheet at the end of Year 1 and as support i
Year 2
b A deferred credit in the balance sheet at the end of Year 1 and Year 2 and a
support in Year 3
c Support in Year 1
d Support in Year 2 and no deferred credit in the balance sheet at the end o
Year 1

6 The Contractual Adjustments ledger account of a nonprofit hospital is a/an:
a Contra-asset account
b Expense account
c Contra-revenue account
d Loss account

Ex 14-2 In your examination of the financial statements of Cordova Hospital, a nonprofi
organization, for the year ended March 31, Year 6, you note the following journa
entry in the Unrestricted Fund:

Inventories 200
    Cash 200
To record purchase of medicine and drugs from manufacturer at nominal
cost. Current fair value of the items totals $6,400.

Prepare a journal entry to correct the accounting records of the Unrestricte
Fund of Cordova Hospital.

Ex 14-3 During the month of October, Year 4, volunteer teachers' aides rendered services a
no cost to Warner School, a nonprofit private elementary school. Salary rates fo
comparable employees of Warner School applied to the services gave a total value o

$3,400. Complimentary meals given to the volunteers at the Warner School cafeteria during October, Year 4, cost $180. The volunteer teachers' aides' services met the specifications for donated services in the CICA research study.

Prepare a journal entry in the Warner School Unrestricted Fund to record the services donated to Warner School during the month of October, Year 4. Disregard income taxes.

Ex 14-4   For the month of September, Year 6, Redwood Hospital's patient service revenue records included the following:

Contractual adjustment allowed for Medicare patients	18,500
Gross patient service revenue (before recognition of contractual adjust-	
ments)	225,000

Prepare the September 30, Year 6, journal entries to record the foregoing in the accounting records of Redwood Hospital.

Ex 14-5   On July 1, Year 5, three funds of Wilmington College pooled their individual investments, as follows:

	Cost	Current fair value
Restricted Fund	$ 80,000	$ 90,000
Quasi-Endowment Fund	120,000	126,000
Annuity Fund	150,000	144,000
Totals	$350,000	$360,000

During the year ended June 30, Year 6, the Wilmington College investment pool, managed by the Unrestricted Fund, reinvested realized gains of $10,000 and received dividends and interest totaling $18,000.

Prepare journal entries on June 30, Year 6, for each of the three Wilmington College funds to reflect the results of the investment pool's operations during Fiscal Year 6. Do not use Receivable from Unrestricted Fund ledger accounts.

Ex 14-6   In your examination of the financial statements of Local Health Centre, a nonprofit organization, you find the following journal entries in the Restricted Fund:

Receivable from Unrestricted Fund	10,000	
Fund Balance		10,000
To record board of directors' authorization of resources to be		
expended for clinic equipment.		
Clinic Equipment	9,500	
Accounts Payable		9,500
To record receipt of invoice for clinic equipment.		

No related journal entries had been made in any other fund.

Prepare adjusting journal entries on December 31, Year 1, for all affected funds of Local Health Centre.

Ex 14-7   The "Summary of Significant Accounting Policies" note to the financial statements prepared by the controller of Wabash Hospital for the year ended June 30, Year 3, includes the following sentence: "Pledges for contributions are recorded when the cash is received." Another note reads as follows:

Pledges: Unrestricted pledges receivable, received and collected during the year ended June 30, Year 3, were as follows:

Pledges receivable, July 1, Year 2 (10% doubtful)	$ 50,000
New pledges received during year ended June 30, Year 3	300,000
Pledges receivable, July 1, Year 2, determined to be uncollectible during year	(15,000)
Pledges collected in cash during year ended June 30, Year 3	(275,000)
Pledges receivable, June 30, Year 3 (12% doubtful)	$ 60,000

All pledges are due six months from the date of the pledge. Pledge support is recorded in the Unrestricted Fund.

Assume that you are engaged in the examination of the financial statements of Wabash Hospital for the year ended June 30, Year 3, and are satisfied with the propriety of the amounts recorded in the hospital's "Pledges" note. Prepare the necessary adjusting entry for the Unrestricted Fund of Wabash Hospital on June 30 Year 3.

CASES

Case 14-1 During the June 20, Year 10, meeting of the board of directors of Roakdale Nursing Home, a nonprofit organizaton, the following discussion transpired:

Chair. "We shall now hear the report from the controller."

Controller. "Our unrestricted contributions are at an all-time high. I projected an Unrestricted Fund excess of revenue over expenses of $100,000 for the year ending June 30."

Chair. "That's too large an amount for us to have a successful fund-raising drive next year. I'll entertain a motion that $80,000 of unrestricted contributions be transferred to the Restricted Fund."

Director Walker. "So moved."

Director Hastings. "Second."

Chair. "All those in favor say 'aye'."

All Directors. "Aye."

Chair. "The chair directs the controller to prepare the necessary journal entries for the Unrestricted Fund and the Restricted Fund."

Instructions Do you concur with the action taken by the board of directors of Roakdale Nursing Home? Explain.

Case 14-2 The controller of Lakeland Hospital, a nonprofit organization, proposes to present the Provision for Doubtful Accounts Receivable account as an expense in the statement of activity of Lakeland Hospital Unrestricted Fund. As the hospital's independent auditor you oppose this treatment. You point out that the AICPA's "Hospital Audit Guide" requires the provision for doubtful accounts to be offset against gross patient service revenue in the statement of activity of a hospital's unrestricted fund. The controller's rejoinder is that there are so many contradictions among the AICPA's *Industry Audit Guides* for nonprofit organizations that there should be some latitude for managers of nonprofit organizations to report operating results on the same basis as a business enterprise.

Instructions How would you respond to the controller of Lakeland Hospital? Support your reply by sound accounting theory for nonprofit organizations.

Case 14-3 The characteristics of voluntary health and welfare organizations differ in certain respects from the characteristics of governmental units. As an example, voluntary health and welfare organizations derive their support primarily from voluntary contributions, but governmental units derive their revenues from taxes and services.

Instructions
a Describe *fund accounting* and discuss whether its use is consistent with the concept that an accounting entity is an economic unit that has control over resources, accepts responsibilities for making and carrying out commitments, and conducts economic activity.
b Distinguish between the accrual basis of accounting and the modified accrual basis of accounting and indicate which method should be used for a voluntary health and welfare organization.
c Discuss how methods used to account for plant assets differ between voluntary health and welfare organizations and governmental units.

Case 14-4 The board of trustees of Toledo Day Care Centre, a nonprofit organization, has asked you, as independent auditor for the Centre, to attend a meeting of the board of trustees and participate in the discussion of a proposal to create one or more endowment funds. At the meeting, the board members ask you numerous questions regarding the operations and the accounting treatment of endowment funds. Among the questions posed by trustees were the following:

(1) Is only the revenue of an endowment fund expendable for current operations?
(2) Under what circumstances, if any, may endowment fund principal be expended at the discretion of the board?
(3) Must a separate set of accounting records be established for each endowment fund, or may all endowment fund operations be accounted for in the restricted fund?

Instructions Prepare a reply for each of the trustees' questions. Number your replies to correspond with the question numbers.

PROBLEMS

14-1 On July 1, Year 6, the four funds of Suburban Welfare Services, a nonprofit organization, formed an investment pool. On that date, cost and current fair value of the investment pool were as follows:

	Cost	Current fair value
Unrestricted Fund	$ 50,000	$ 59,400
Restricted Fund	20,000	16,200
Plant Fund	80,000	89,100
Arnold Life Income Fund	100,000	105,300
Totals	$250,000	$270,000

During the six months ended December 31, Year 6, the investment pool, managed by the Unrestricted Fund, reinvested realized gains totaling $15,000 and received dividends and interest totaling $25,000, which was distributed to the participating funds. On December 31, Year 6, the Restricted Fund withdrew from the pool and was awarded securities in the amount of its share of the pool's aggregate December 31, Year 6, current fair value of $300,000. On January 2, Year 7, the Edwards Endowment Fund entered the Suburban Welfare Services investment pool with investments having a cost of $70,000 and a current fair value of $78,000. During the six months ended June 30, Year 7, the investment pool reinvested realized gains totaling $40,000 and received dividends and interest totaling $60,000, which was distributed to the participating funds.

Instructions

a Prepare a working paper for the Suburban Welfare Services investment pool computing the following (round all percentages to two decimal places):

(1) Original equity percentages, July 1, Year.6

(2) Revised equity percentages, January 2, Year 7

b Prepare journal entries to record the operations of the Suburban Welfare Services investment pool in the accounting records of the Unrestricted Fund. Use Payable to Restricted Fund, Payable to Plant Fund, and Payable to Arnold Life Income Fund ledger accounts for amounts payable to other funds.

14-2 Among the transactions of the Unrestricted Fund of Harbour Hospital, a nonprofit organization, for the month of October, Year 8, were the following:

(1) Gross patient service revenue of $80,000 was billed to patients. Provision was made for contractual adjustments allowed to Blue Cross of $6,000; and doubtful accounts of $8,000.

(2) Donated services approximating $10,000 at going salary rates were received from volunteer nurses. Meals costing $200 were served to the volunteer nurses at no charge by the Harbour Hospital cafeteria.

(3) New pledges, due in three months, totaling $5,000 were received from various donors. Collections on pledges amounted to $3,500, and the provision for doubtful pledges for October, Year 8, was $800.

(4) Paid the $500 monthly annuity established for Arline E. Walters by a contribution by Walters to Harbour Hospital three years ago.

(5) Received and expended $3,000 from Charles Watson Restricted Fund for new surgical equipment, as authorized by the donor.

Instructions

a Prepare the journal entries for the October, Year 8, transactions of the Harbour Hospital Unrestricted Fund. Number each group of entries to correspond to the number of each transactions group.

b Prepare journal entries required for other funds of Harbour Hospital as indicated by the transactions of the Unrestricted Fund.

14-3 Presented on page 593 is the current funds balance sheet of McNill University at the end of the fiscal year ended June 30, Year 8:

The following transactions occurred during the fiscal year ended June 30, Year 9:

(1) On July 7, Year 8, a gift of $100,000 was received from an alumnus. The alumnus requested that one half of the gift be used for the acquisition of books for the university library and that the remainder be used for the establishment of a scholarship. The alumnus further requested that the revenue generated by the scholarship fund be used annually to award a scholarship to a qualified disadvantaged student, with the principal remaining intact. On July 20, Year 8 the board of trustees resolved that the cash of the newly established scholarship (endowment) fund would be invested in bank certificates of deposit. On July 21, Year 8, the certificates of deposit were acquired.

(2) Revenue from student tuition and fees applicable to the year ended June 30 Year 9, amounted to $1,900,000. Of this amount, $66,000 was collected in the prior year and $1,686,000 was collected during the year ended June 30, Year 9. In addition, on June 30, Year 9, the university had received cash of $158,000 representing tuition and fees for the session beginning July 1, Year 9.

(3) During the year ended June 30, Year 9, the university had collected $349,000 of the outstanding accounts receivable at the beginning of the year. The balance

MCNILL UNIVERSITY

Current Funds Balance Sheet
June 30, Year 8

Assets

Unrestricted Fund

Cash	$210,000	
Accounts receivable for student tuition and fees, less allowance for doubtful accounts, $9,000	341,000	
Provincial appropriation receivable	75,000	$626,000

Restricted Fund

Cash	$ 7,000	
Investments	60,000	67,000
Total		$693,000

Liabilities & Fund Balances

Unrestricted Fund

Accounts payable	$ 45,000	
Deferred revenue	66,000	
Fund balance	515,000	$626,000

Restricted Fund

Fund balance		67,000
Total		$693,000

was determined to be uncollectible and was written off against the allowance account. On June 30, Year 9, the allowance account was increased by $3,000.

(4) During the year interest charges of $6,000 were earned and collected on late student fee payments.

(5) During the year the provincial appropriation was received. An additional unrestricted appropriation of $50,000 was made by the province, but had not been paid to the university as of June 30, Year 9.

(6) Unrestricted cash gifts totaling $25,000 were received from alumni of the university.

(7) During the year restricted fund investments of $21,000 were sold for $26,000. Investment earnings amounting to $1,900 were received. (Credit Fund Balance.)

(8) During the year unrestricted operating expenses of $1,777,000 were recorded. On June 30, Year 9, $59,000 of these expenses remained unpaid.

(9) Restricted cash of $13,000 was spent for authorized purposes during the year. An equal amount was transferred from fund balance to revenue of the restricted fund.

(10) The accounts payable on June 30, Year 8, were paid during the year.

(11) During the year, $7,000 interest was earned and received on the certificate of deposit acquired in accordance with the board of trustees resolution discussed in item (1). (Credit Fund Balance.)

Instructions Prepare general journal entries to record the transactions for the year ended June 30, Year 9. Each journal entry should be numbered to correspond with the transaction described above. Omit explanations for the journal entries.

Your working paper should be organized as follows:

Transaction number	Accounts	Unrestricted Fund Dr(Cr)	Restricted Fund Dr(Cr)	Endowment Fund Dr(Cr)
(1)				

Use the following account titles in the journal entries:
Unrestricted Fund
    Accounts Payable
    Accounts Receivable for Student Tuition and Fees
    Allowance for Doubtful Accounts
    Cash
    Deferred Revenue
    Expenses
    Revenue
    Provincial Appropriation Receivable
Restricted Fund
    Cash
    Expenditures
    Fund Balance
    Investments
    Revenue
Endowment Fund
    Cash
    Fund Balance
    Investments

14-4   Presented below is the balance sheet of Resthaven Hospital on December 31, Year 6

RESTHAVEN HOSPITAL
Balance Sheet
December 31, Year 6
Unrestricted Fund
Assets

Current assets

Cash	$	20,000
Accounts receivable		37,000
Less: Allowances and doubtful accounts		(7,000)
Inventory of supplies		14,000
Total current assets	$	64,000

Plant assets

Land	$	370,000
Buildings		1,750,000
Less: Accumulated depreciation		(430,000)
Equipment		680,000
Less: Accumulated depreciation		(134,000)
Total plant assets		$2,236,000
Total assets		$2,300,000

Liabilities & Fund Balance

Current liabilities

Accounts payable	$	16,000
Accrued liabilities		6,000
Total current liabilities	$	22,000
Mortgage bonds payable		150,000
Total liabilities	$	172,000

Fund balance:

Investment in plant	$2,116,000
Undesignated	12,000
Total fund balance	$2,128,000
Total liabilities & fund balance	$2,300,000

Restricted Funds

Plant Replacement and Expansion Fund

Assets

Cash	$	53,800
Investments		71,200
Total assets	$	125,000

Fund Balance

Fund balance	$125,000

Endowment Fund

Assets

Cash	$	6,000
Investments		260,000
Total assets	$	266,000

Fund Balance

Fund balance	$266,000

During Year 7 the following transactions were completed:

(1) Gross debits to Accounts Receivable for hospital services were as follows:

Room and board	$	780,000
Other professional services		321,000
Total debits to Accounts Receivable	$	1,101,000

(2) Deductions from gross revenue were as follows:

Provision for doubtful accounts	$30,000
Contractual adjustments	15,000
Total deductions from gross revenue	$45,000

(3) The Unrestricted Fund paid $18,000 to retire mortgage bonds payable with an equivalent face amount.

(4) During the year the Unrestricted Fund received unrestricted gifts of $50,000 and revenue from Endowment Fund investments of $6,500. The Unrestricted Fund has been designated to receive the revenue on Endowment Fund investments.

(5) New equipment costing $26,000 was acquired. An x-ray machine that originally cost $24,000 and had a carrying amount of $2,400 was sold for $500.

(6) Vouchers totaling $1,191,000 were issued for the following items:

Administrative services expense	$ 120,000
Interest expense	95,000
General services expense	225,000
Nursing services expense	520,000
Other professional services expense	165,000
Inventory of supplies	60,000
Accrued liabilities, Dec. 31, Year 6	6,000
Total vouchers issued	$1,191,000

(7) Collections on accounts receivable totaled $985,000. Accounts receivable written off as uncollectible amounted to $11,000.

(8) Cash payments on accounts payable during the year were $825,000.

(9) Supplies of $37,000 were issued for nursing services.

(10) On December 31, Year 7, accrued interest earned on Plant Replacement and Expansion Fund investments was $800.

(11) Depreciation of buildings and equipment was as follows:

Buildings	$44,000
Equipment	73,000
Total depreciation	$117,000

(12) On December 31, Year 7, an accrual of $6,100 was made for interest on the mortgage bonds payable.

Instructions For the period January 1, Year 7, through December 31, Year 7 prepare journal entries (omit explanations) to record the transactions described above for the following funds of Resthaven Hospital:

Unrestricted Fund
Plant Replacement and Expansion Fund
Endowment Fund

Each journal entry should be numbered to correspond with the transactions described above.

Your working paper should be organized as follows:

Transaction number	Accounts	Unrestricted Fund Dr(Cr)	Plant Replacement and Expansion Fund Dr(Cr)	Endowment Fund Dr(Cr)
(1)				

In addition to the ledger acounts included in the December 31, Year 6, balance sheet of Resthaven Hospital, the following ledger accounts are pertinent:

Unrestricted Fund
    Administrative Services Expense
    Contractual Adjustments
    Depreciation Expense
    General Services Expense
    Interest Expense
    Loss on Disposal of Plant Assets
    Nursing Services Expense
    Other Professional Services Expense
    Patient Service Revenue
    Provision for Doubtful Accounts
    Unrestricted Gift Support ✓
    Unrestricted Revenue from Endowment Fund ✓

Plant Replacement and Expansion Fund
    Interest Receivable

14-5 A newly elected board of directors of Hospital of Sun Valley, a nonprofit organization, decided that effective January 1, Year 98:

(a) The existing ledger account balances are to be adjusted and three separate funds (Unrestricted Fund, James Dupar Endowment Fund, and Plant Replacement Fund) are to be established.

(b) The fund balance of the James Dupar Endowment Fund and an amount equal to the Accumulated Depreciation account of the Unrestricted Fund are to be invested in securities.

(c) The accounting records are to be maintained in accordance with the AICPA's "Hospital Audit Guide."

The board of directors engaged you to determine the appropriate ledger account balances for each of the funds. The trial balance of the ledger on January 1, Year 98, follows:

HOSPITAL OF SUN VALLEY
Trial Balance
January 1, Year 98

	Debit	Credit
Cash	$ 50,000	
Investment in Treasury bills	105,000	
Investment in common shares	417,000	
Interest receivable	4,000	
Accounts receivable	40,000	
Inventories	25,000	
Land	407,000	
Building	245,000	
Equipment	283,000	
Accumulated depreciation		$ 376,000
Accounts payable		70,000
Bank loan payable		150,000
James Dupar Endowment Fund		119,500
Surplus		860,500
Totals	$1,576,000	$1,576,000

Additional information

(1) Under the terms of the will of James Dupar, "the principal of the bequest is to be fully invested in trust forevermore in mortgages secured by productive real estate and/or in government securities . . . and the revenue therefrom is to be used to defray current expenses."

(2) The James Dupar Endowment Fund account balance consists of the following:

Cash received in Year 1 by bequest from James Dupar	$ 81,500
Net gains realized from Year 56 through Year 89 from the sale of real estate	
acquired in mortgage foreclosures	23,500
Revenue received from Year 90 through Year 97 from investment in	
Treasury bills	14,500
Balance, Jan. 1, Year 98	$119,500

(3) The Land account balance is composed of the following:

Year 20 appraisal of land at $10,000 and building at $5,000 received by	
donation at that time. (The building was demolished in Year 40)	$ 15,000
Appraisal increase based on insured value in land title policies issued	
in Year 57	380,000
Landscaping costs for trees planted	12,000
Balance, Jan. 1, Year 98	$407,000

(4) The Building account balance is composed of the following:

Cost of present hospital building completed in January, Year 57, when	
the hospital began operations	$300,000
Adjustment to record appraised value of building in Year 67	(100,000)
Cost of elevator installed in January, Year 83	45,000
Balance, Jan. 1, Year 98	$245,000

The economic lives of the hospital building and the elevator when new were 50 years and 20 years, respectively, with no residual value.

(5) The hospital's equipment was inventoried on January 1, Year 98. The total of the inventory agreed with the Equipment account balance in the ledger. The Accumulated Depreciation ledger account on January 1, Year 98, included $158,250 applicable to equipment, and that amount was approved by the board of directors as being accurate. All depreciation is computed on a straight-line basis, with no residual value.

(6) A bank loan was obtained to finance the cost of new operating room equipment acquired in Year 94. Interest on the loan was paid to December 31, Year 97.

Instructions   Prepare a working paper for Hospital of Sun Valley to present the adjustments necessary to restate the ledger account balances and to distribute the adjusted balances to establish the required fund accounts. Formal journal entries are not required; however, explain each adjustment (including supporting computations) at the bottom of the working paper. The following column headings are suggested:
   Unadjusted trial balance
   Adjustments
   Adjusted trial balance
   Unrestricted Fund
   James Dupar Endowment Fund
   Plant Replacement Fund

14-6 The accountant for Freida's Vocational School, a nonprofit organization, resigned on March 1, Year 8, after having prepared the following trial balance and analysis of cash on February 28, Year 8:

FREIDA'S VOCATIONAL SCHOOL
Trial Balance
February 28, Year 8

Debits

Cash for general current operations	$258,000
Cash for restricted current uses	30,900
Common stock donated by L.M. Nash	91,000
Bonds donated by O.P. Quinn	150,000
Land	22,000
Building	33,000
General current operating expenses	38,000
Faculty recruitment expenses	4,100
Total debits	$627,000

FREIDA'S VOCATIONAL SCHOOL
Trial Balance (concluded)
February 28, Year 8

Credits

Mortgage note payable	$ 30,000
Support from gifts for general operations	210,000
Support from gifts for restricted uses	196,000
Student fees	31,000
Surplus	160,000
Total credits	$627,000

FREIDA'S VOCATIONAL SCHOOL
Analysis of Cash
For Six Months Ended February 28, Year 8

Cash for general current operations:			
Balance, Sept. 1, Year 7		$ 80,000	
Add: Student fees	$ 31,000		
Gift of H.I. Johnson	210,000	241,000	
Subtotal		$321,000	
Less: General current operating			
expenses	$ 38,000		
Payment for land and building ...	25,000	63,000	$258,000
Cash for restricted current uses:			
Gift of H.I. Johnson for faculty recruitment		$ 35,000	
Less: Faculty recruitment expenses		4,100	30,900
Chequing account balance, Feb. 28, Year 8			$288,900

You were engaged to determine the appropriate ledger account balances for the school as of August 31, Year 8, the close of the school's first fiscal year. Your examination disclosed the following information:

(1) In September, Year 7, L.M. Nash donated 1,000 shares of Wilder, Inc., common stock with a current fair value of $91 a share on the date of donation. The terms of the gift provide that the stock and any dividend revenue are to be retained intact. On any date designated by the board of directors, the assets are to be liquidated and the proceeds used to assist the school's headmaster in acquiring a personal residence. The school will not retain any financial interest in the residence.

(2) O.P. Quinn donated 12% bonds in September, Year 7, with a face amount and current fair value of $150,000 on the date of donation. Annual payments of $12,500 are to be made to the donor during the donor's lifetime. On the donor's death the fund is to be used to construct a school cafeteria. The actuarial valuation of the O.P. Quinn annuity on August 31, Year 8, was $122,143.

(3) No transactions have been recorded in the school's accounting records since February 28, Year 8. An employee of the school prepared the following analysis of the chequing account for the period March 1 through August 31, Year 8:

Balance, Mar. 1, Year 8			$288,900
Less: General current operating expenses .	$14,000		
Acquisition of equipment	47,000	$61,000	
Less: Student fees		8,000	
Net expenses		53,000	
Payment for headmaster's residence	$91,200		
Less: Sale of 100 shares of Wilder,			
Inc., common stock	90,600	600	53,600
Subtotal		. . . . .	$235,300
Add: Interest on 12% bonds		$18,000	
Less: Payment to O.P. Quinn		12,500	5,500
Balance, Aug. 31, Year 8			$240,800

Instructions Prepare a working paper for Freida's Vocational School presenting the trial balance on February 28, Year 8, adjusting entries, transaction entries from March 1 through August 31, Year 8, and distributions to the proper funds. The following column headings are recommended:

Unadjusted trial balance, Feb. 28, Year 8
Adjustments and transactions — Debit
Adjustments and transactions — Credit
Adjusted trial balance, Aug. 31, Year 8
Unrestricted Current Fund
Restricted Current Fund
O.P. Quinn Annuity Fund
Plant Fund — Investment in Plant

Formal journal entries are not required; however, explain each adjustment and transaction (including supporting computations) at the bottom of the working paper. Disregard accrued interest on the mortgage note payable.

4

SPECIAL TOPICS IN FINANCIAL ACCOUNTING

15 INSTALLMENT SALES; CONSIGNMENTS

INSTALLMENT SALES

Although the concept of the installment sale first was developed in the field of real estate and for high-priced durable goods, it has spread through nearly every sector of the economy. Almost all single-family residences are sold on the installment plan, with monthly payments extending as long as 25 to 30 years. Installment sales also are used by dealers in home furnishings, automobiles, appliances, and farm equipment. For these products the installment payments usually are made monthly for periods of from 6 to 36 months.

For many business enterprises, installment sales have been a key factor in achieving large-scale operations. The automobile industry, for example, could not have developed to its present size without the use of installment sales. The large volume of output achieved by the automobile industry has made possible economies in tooling, production, and distribution that could not have been achieved on a small scale of operations. Credit losses often increase when sales are made on the installment plan, but this disadvantage generally is more than offset by the expanded sales volume.

Installment sales pose some difficult problems for accountants. The most basic of these problems is the matching of costs and revenue. Should the gross profit from an installment sale be recorded as realized in the accounting period the sale is made, or should it be spread over the term of the installment contract? What should be done with costs that occur in periods subsequent to the sale? How should defaults, trade-ins, and repossessions be recorded?

It should be clarified that these problems only exist if either of the following two conditions are present:

(1) a company is carrying its installment receivables; or
(2) a company has sold its installment receivables with recourse to a non affiliated finance company.

If a company sells an installment receivable with recourse to a finance company, and the company's customer fails to make all the contractual payments to the finance company required by the promissory note, it will be required to reimburse the finance company for the unpaid balance. If however, the promissory note was sold without recourse, no reimbursement would be required upon default by the customer. The discussions that follow focus on the situation where a company carries its installment receivables. However, if it sells its receivables with recourse, the issue of when profit should be recognized is still present. This issue also remains if the receivables are sold with recourse to an affiliated finance company, because of the single economic entity concept that exists in this situation.

Regardless of the accounting issues raised, we may assume that installment sales will continue to be a major force in our economy. Accountants, therefore, must examine the issues and develop the most effective techniques possible for measuring, controlling, and reporting installment sales. As we progress through this chapter, it will be apparent that installment sales are one of the many thorny problems confronting accountants as they search for a consistent body of accounting principles within the conceptual framework of accounting.

Characteristics of installment sales

An installment sale of real or personal property or services provides for a series of payments over a period of months or years. A down payment generally is required. Because the seller must wait a considerable period of time to collect the selling price, it is customary to provide for interest and carrying charges on the unpaid balance.

The risk of noncollection to the seller is increased greatly when sales are made on the installment plan. Customers generally are in weaker financial condition than those who buy on open account; furthermore, the credit rating of the customers and their ability to pay may change significantly during the period covered by an installment contract. To protect themselves against this greater risk of noncollection, sellers of real or personal property generally select a form of contract called a *security agreement* that enables them to repossess the property if the purchaser fails to make payments.

The sellers' right to protect their *security interest* (uncollected balance of a sales contract) and to repossess the asset sold varies by type of industry, the form of the contract, and the statutes relating to repossessions. For the service-type enterprise, repossession obviously is not available as a safeguard against the failure to collect. For sales of certain types of merchandise, the sellers' right to repossess may be more of a threat than a real assurance against loss. The asset sold may have been damaged or may have depreciated to a point that it is worth less than the balance due on the installment contract. A basic rule designed to minimize losses from the nonpayment of installment contracts is to require a sufficient down payment to cover the loss of value when an asset moves out of the "new" category. A corollary rule is that the cash payments by the purchaser should not be outstripped by the projected decline in value of the asset sold. For example, if a customer who purchases a used car on the installment plan finds after a year or so that the car is currently worth less than the balance owed on the contract, the customer's motivation to continue the payments may be reduced.

Competitive pressures in an industry often will not permit a business enterprise to adhere to rigid credit standards. Furthermore, repossession may be a difficult and expensive process. Reconditioning and repair may be necessary to make the repossessed merchandise salable, and the resale of such merchandise may be difficult. For these reasons, doubtful accounts expense is likely to be significantly higher on installment sales than on regular credit sales.

A related problem is the increased collection expense when payments are spread over an extended period. Accounting expenses also are increased when sales are made on the installment plan, and large amounts of working capital are tied up in installment contracts receivable. In recognition of these problems, many retailers sell installment contracts receivable to finance companies that specialize in credit and collection activities. If these contracts are sold with recourse and if default by the customer subsequently occurs, only a temporary solution to the company's cash flow problem is provided.

Realization of gross profit on installment sales

The determination of net income on installment sales is complicated by the fact that the amounts of revenue and related costs and expenses seldom are known in the accounting period when sales are made. Substantial expenses (as for collection, accounting, repairs, and repossession) may be incurred in subsequent accounting periods. In some situations, *the risk of noncollection may be so great as to raise doubt that any revenue or profit is realized at the time of sale.*

The first objective in the development of accounting policies for installment sales should be a reasonable matching of costs and revenue. However, in recognition of the diverse business conditions under which installment sales are made, accountants have available for use the following three approaches for the recognition of gross profit on installment sales: (1) the accrual basis of accounting, (2) the cost recovery method, and (3) the installment method of accounting.

Accrual Basis of Accounting   To recognize the entire gross profit as realized at the time of an installment sale is to say in effect that installment

sales are the same as regular sales on credit. The merchandise has bee
delivered to customers, and accounts receivable of definite amount hav
been acquired. The excess of the accounts receivable over the cost of me
chandise sold is *realized gross profit* in the traditional meaning of tł
term. The journal entry consists of a debit to Installment Contracts Receivabł
and a credit to Installment Sales. If the perpetual inventory system is used,
second journal entry is needed to transfer the cost of the merchandiŝ
from the Inventories account to the Cost of Installment Sales account. N
recognition is given to the seller's retention of title to the merchandiŝ
because the normal expectation is completion of the contract throug
collection of the receivable. Implicit in this recognition of gross profit at tł
time of sale is the assumption that most expenses relating to the sale will ł
recognized in the same accounting period.

The expenses relating to the sale include collection and doubtful a
counts expenses. Recognition of these expenses in the period of the sał
requires estimates of the customer's performance over the entire term c
the installment contract. Such estimates may be considerably more difficu
to make than the normal provision for doubtful accounts expense fror
regular sales. However, with careful analysis of experience in the industr
and in the particular business enterprise, reasonably satisfactory estimatĕ
can be made in most situations. The journal entries to record such expensĕ
consist of debits to expense accounts and credits to asset valuation accounł
such as Allowance for Doubtful Installment Contracts and Allowance fc
Collection Costs. The allowance accounts are debited in later periods a
uncollectible installment contracts become known and as collection cost
are incurred.

Cost Recovery Method   In some cases, installment contracts receivabł
may be collectible over a long period of time. In addition, the terms of sał
may not be definite, and the financial position of customers may ł
unpredictable, thus making it virtually impossible to find a reasonable basî
for estimating the degree of collectibility of the receivables. In such casĕ
either the installment method or the cost recovery method of accountin
may be used for installment sales. Under the *cost recovery method,* nŧ
profit is recognized until all costs of the merchandise sold have been re
covered. After all costs have been recovered, additional collections on thŧ
installment contracts receivable are recorded as revenue, and only curreń
collection costs are recognized as expenses. The cost recovery method o
accounting is rarely used; therefore, it is not illustrated in this chapter.

Installment Method of Accounting   The third approach to the meä
surement of income from installment sales is to recognize gross profit iⴖ
installments over the term of the contract as cash is collected. Emphasis i
shifted from the acquisition of receivables to the collection of the receivablĕ
as the basis for realization of gross profit; in other words, *a modified casł
basis of accounting is substituted for the accrual basis of accounŧ
ing.* This modified cash basis is known as the *installment method o
accounting.*

The installment method of accounting

Under the installment method of accounting, each cash collection on the contract is regarded as including both a return of cost and a realization of gross profit in the ratio that these two elements were included in the selling price.

For example, assume that a farm equipment dealer sells for $10,000 a machine that cost $7,000. The $3,000 excess of the sales price over cost is regarded as **deferred gross profit.** Because cost and gross profit constituted 70% and 30%, respectively, of the sales price, this 70:30 ratio is used to divide each collection under the contract between the recovery of cost and the realization of gross profit. If $1,000 is received as a down payment, $300 of the deferred gross profit is considered realized in the current accounting period. At the end of each period, the Deferred Gross Profit account will equal 30% of the installment contract receivable remaining uncollected. The Realized Gross Profit on Installment Sales account will show for each period an amount equal to 30% of the collections during that period. In this example, the question of interest and carrying charges is omitted; it is considered later in the chapter.

The method described is acceptable under current Canadian income tax law provided that certain conditions are met. For all items sold, other than land, the installments must be receivable more than two years from the date of sale. If the item sold was land, including buildings located thereon, the two year requirement does not apply. In the year of sale the entire gross profit is included in the calculation of taxable income, with a reserve for the gross profit not yet collected allowed as a deduction. The reserve deducted in one year becomes taxable income in the next year, and a further reserve for the gross profit not yet collected is allowed. However the reserve deductions can only take place for a maximum period of three years from the date of sale. This means that the entire gross profit must be included in taxable income within three years from the date of sale even though the installments will be received over a longer period.

The opportunity to postpone the recognition of taxable income has been responsible for the popularity of the installment method for income tax purposes. Although the income tax advantages are readily apparent, the theoretical support for the installment method of accounting is less impressive.

Many years ago a committee of the American Accounting Association (AAA) stated:[1]

> There is no sound accounting reason for the use of the installment method for financial statement purposes in the case of closed transactions in which collection is dependent upon lapse of time and the probabilities of realization are properly evaluated. In the opinion of the Committee, such income has accrued and should be recognized in the financial statements, . . .

1 Accounting and Reporting Standards for Corporate Financial Statements and Preceding Statements and Supplements, AAA (Sarasota: 1957), p. 33.

Accounting Research Study No. 3 stated that revenue should b
recognized in the accounting period in which the major economic activit
necessary for the production and disposition of goods is performed, an
rejected the use of the installment method of accounting.[2]

> Collectibility of receivables is not necessarily less predictable because
> collections are scheduled in installments. The postponement of recog-
> nition of revenues until they can be measured by actual cash receipt is
> not in accordance with the concept of an accrual accounting. Any
> uncertainty as to collectibility should be expressed by a separately
> calculated and separately disclosed estimate of uncollectibles rather
> than by a postponement of the recognition of revenue.

Subsequently, *APB Opinion No. 10* virtually removed the installme
method of accounting from the body of generally accepted accountin
principles because it reaffirmed the general concept that income is realize
when a sale is made, unless the circumstances are such that the collection
the selling price is not reasonably assured. *APB Opinion No. 10* stated:[3]

> Revenues should ordinarily be accounted for at the time a transaction
> is completed, with appropriate provision for uncollectible accounts.
> Accordingly, . . . in the absence of the circumstances referred to above,
> the installment method of recognizing revenue is not acceptable.

The "circumstances" in which use of the installment method of accoun
ing is permitted are: (1) Collection of installment receivables is not reasonab
assured, (2) receivables are collectible over an extended period of time, an
(3) there is no reasonable basis for estimating the degree of collectibility.
such situations, either the installment method or the cost recovery metho
of accounting may be used. No Canadian pronouncements on this subjec
have been issued by the CICA.

Because the installment method of accounting still may be used for financi
accounting in some cases, and because *its concepts are widely used fo
income tax purposes,* we shall illustrate its use in the following page
first for a single sale of land and then for retail sales of merchandise.

Single sale of land on the installment plan

The owner of land that has appreciated in value often is willing to sell on
on the installment plan so that the gain can be spread over several years f
income tax purposes.

Let us assume that on December 31, Year 1, Clara Kane, who maintair
accounting records on a calendar-year basis, sold for $100,000 a parc
of land acquired for $52,000. Commission and other expenses of sa
in the amount of $8,000 were charged to Kane in the escrow state
ment. Because Kane was not a dealer in real estate, these expenses ar
considered as additional costs of the land rather than expenses of th

2 Robert T. Sprouse and Maurice Moonitz, *Accounting Research Study No. 3,* "A Tentative Set of Broa
Accounting Principles for Business Enterprises," AICPA (New York: 1962), p. 48.

3 *APB Opinion No. 10,* "Omnibus Opinion — 1966," AICPA (New York: 1966), p. 149.

year in which the sale took place. Thus, the gain on the sale of the land is $40,000 ($100,000 − $52,000 − $8,000 = $40,000), and all collections of cash from the purchaser are regarded as consisting of 60% cost recovery and 40% realization of gain (profit).

CLARA KANE

Journal Entries to Record Sale of Land on Installment Plan
For Year 1 and Year 2

Year 1

Dec. 31   Cash (net of $8,000 paid for commission and and other ex-
         penses of sale) 17,000
        Notes Receivable 75,000
             Land 52,000
             Deferred Gain on Installment Sale of Land 40,000
        To record sale of land on installment plan; notes receivable are
        due at the rate of $7,500 every six months, plus 10% annual
        interest on the unpaid principal balance of notes. Commission
        and other expenses of sale of $8,000 were deducted in com-
        putation of net cash received and deferred gain.

     31   Deferred Gain on Installment Sale of Land 10,000
           Realized Gain on Installment Sale of Land 10,000
        To record realized gain, computed at 40% of cash collected as
        down payment in Year 1 ($25,000 × 0.40 = $10,000).

Year 2

June 30   Cash 11,250
           Interest Revenue 3,750
           Notes Receivable 7,500
        To record collection of semiannual principal installment on
        note receivable ($7,500), plus interest for six months
        ($75,000 × 0.10 × 6/12 = $3,750).

Year 2

Dec. 31   Cash 10,875
           Interest Revenue 3,375
           Notes Receivable 7,500
        To record collection of semiannual principal installment on
        notes receivable ($7,500), plus interest for six months on un-
        paid balance ($75,000 − $7,500) × 0.10 × 6/12 =
        $3,375).

     31   Deferred Gain on Installment Sale of Land 6,000
           Realized Gain on Installment Sale of Land 6,000
        To record realized gain computed at 40% of amount collected
        on notes receivable in Year 2 ($15,000 × 0.40 = $6,000).

The contract of sale called for a down payment of $25,000 and promissory notes, with principal payments every six months for five years in the amount of $7,500 plus interest at the annual rate of 10% on the unpaid principal balance of the notes. A portion ($8,000) of the down payment was applied in the escrow statement to pay the commission and other expenses of sale. The journal entries presented on page 609 record the sale of the land on December 31, Year 1, the collections on the notes in Year 2, and the realization of a portion of the deferred gain in Years 1 and 2. Because this was a sale by a nondealer in real estate, there was no need to use an Installment Sale account, and the deferred gain on sale of land was recorded at the time of sale.

Journal entries for the remaining four years would follow the same pattern illustrated for Year 2, assuming that the purchaser makes all payments as required by contract.

This example brings out the contrast between the timing of gross profit on ordinary sales and on sales accounted for by the installment method of accounting. If the land sold by Clara Kane had been recorded as an ordinary sale, a gross profit of $40,000 would have been reported in Year 1; use of the installment method of accounting resulted in the recognition of only $10,000 gross profit in Year 1, and $6,000 ($15,000 × 0.40 = $6,000) in each of the next five years. If a sale on the installment plan results in a loss, *the entire loss must be recognized in the year of sale.*

Retail sale of merchandise on the installment plan

In the preceding example we dealt with a single sale of land on the installment plan by a nondealer. Now we shall consider a large volume of installment sales of merchandise by a retailing enterprise that uses the installment method of accounting because the collectibility of the installment contracts receivable cannot be reasonably estimated.

A first requirement is to keep separate all sales made on the installment plan as distinguished from regular sales. The accounting records for installment receivables usually are maintained by contract rather than by customer; if a customer makes several purchases on the installment plan, it is convenient to account for each contract separately. However, it is not necessary to compute the rate of gross profit on each sale or to apply a different profit rate to collections on each contract. The average rate of gross profit on all installment sales during a year generally is computed and applied to all cash collections (net of interest and carrying charges) on installment contracts receivable originating in that year.

Illustration of Accounting for Installment Sales of Merchandise   To illustrate the accounting for installment sales of merchandise, assume that Oak Desk Company sells merchandise on the installment plan, as well as on regular terms (cash or 30-day open accounts), and uses the perpetual inventory system. For an installment sale, the customer's account is debited for the full amount of the selling price, including interest and carrying charges, and is credited for the amount of the down payment. The Installment Contract Receivable account thus provides a complete record of the transaction. Uncollectible installment contracts expense is recognized at the time the accounts receivable are **known to be uncollectible.** Assume that on January 1, Year 5, Oak Desk's general ledger included the following ledger account balances:

Account balances, Jan. 1, Year 5

Installment contracts receivable — Year 3	$20,000 dr
Installment contracts receivable — Year 4	85,000 dr
Deferred interest and carrying charges on installment sales	17,500 cr
Deferred gross profit — Year 3 installment sales	4,500 cr
Deferred gross profit — Year 4 installment sales	19,460 cr

The gross profit rate on installment sales (excluding interest and carrying charges) was 25% in Year 3 and 28% in Year 4. During Year 5, the following transactions were completed by Oak Desk Company:

(1) Installment sales, cost of installment sales, and deferred gross profit for Year 5 are listed below:

Installment sales and cost of installment sales for Year 5

Installment sales (excluding $30,000 deferred interest and carrying charges)	$200,000
Cost of installment sales	138,000
Deferred gross profit — Year 5 installment sales ($200,000 − $138,000) . . .	62,000
Rate of gross profit on installment sales ($62,000 ÷ $200,000)	31%

(2) Cash collections on installment contracts receivable during Year 5 are summarized below:

Cash collections on installment contracts receivable during Year 5

	Selling price	Interest and carrying charges	Total cash collected
Installment contracts receivable — Year 5	$ 80,000	$10,000	$ 90,000
Installment contracts receivable — Year 4	44,500	12,500	57,000
Installment contracts receivable — Year 3	17,000	1,850	18,850
Totals	$141,500	$24,350	$165,850

(3) Customers who purchased merchandise in Year 3 were unable to pay the balance of their contracts, $1,150. The contracts consisted of $1,000 sales price and $150 of interest and carrying charges, and included $250 ($1,000 × 0.25 = $250) of deferred gross profit. The current fair (net realizable) value of the merchandise repossessed was $650.

Recording Transactions   The journal entries to record the transaction
for Oak Desk Company relating to installment sales for Year 5 are:

(1) Installment Contracts Receivable — Year 5   230,000
    Cost of Installment Sales   138,000
        Installment Sales   200,00
        Deferred Interest and Carrying Charges on Installment
           Sales   30,00
        Inventories   138,00
    To record installment sales and cost of installment sales for
    Year 5.

(2) Cash   165,850
        Installment Contracts Receivable — Year 5   90,00
        Installment Contracts Receivable — Year 4   57,00
        Installment Contracts Receivable — Year 3   18,85
    To record collections on installment contracts during Year 5.

(3) Inventories (repossessed merchandise)   650
    Deferred Gross Profit — Year 3 Installment Sales   250
    Deferred Interest and Carrying Charges on Installment Sales . . .   150
    Uncollectible Installment Contracts Expense   100
        Installment Contracts Receivable — Year 3   1,15
    To record default on Year 3 installment contracts and re-
    possession of merchandise.

Adjusting Entries   The adjusting journal entries for Oak Desk Company
on December 31, Year 5, are as shown at the top of page 613.

The Realized Gross Profit on Installment Sales and the Revenue from
Interest and Carrying Charges accounts are closed to the Income Summary
account at the end of Year 5. The accounts relating to installment sales
appear in Oak Desk Company's general ledger at the end of Year 5 as
follows:

Ledger accounts	Balances
Installment contracts receivable — Year 4 ($85,000 − $57,000)	$ 28,000
Installment contracts receivable — Year 5 ($230,000 − $90,000)	140,000
Deferred interest and carrying charges on installment sales ($17,500 +	
$30,000 − $150 − $24,350)	23,000
Deferred gross profit — Year 4 installment sales ($19,460 − $12,460)	7,000
Deferred gross profit — Year 5 installment sales ($62,000 − $24,800)	37,200

These amounts may be arranged as illustrated on page 613 to prove the
accuracy of the deferred gross profit on installment contracts receivable at
the end of Year 5.

Installment Sales	200,000	
Cost of Installment Sales		138,000
Deferred Gross Profit — Year 5 Installment Sales		62,000
To record deferred gross profit on Year 5 installment sales.		

Deferred Gross Profit — Year 5 Installment Sales	24,800	
Deferred Gross Profit — Year 4 Installment Sales	12,460	
Deferred Gross Profit — Year 3 Installment Sales	4,250	
Realized Gross Profit on Installment Sales		41,510
To record realized gross profit on installment sales, as computed		
below:		

Year 5: $80,000 × 0.31	$24,800
Year 4: $44,500 × 0.28	12,460
Year 3: $17,000 × 0.25	4,250
Total realized gross profit	$41,510

Deferred Interest and Carrying Charges on Installment Sales	24,350	
Revenue from Interest and Carrying Charges		24,350
To record revenue from interest and carrying charges for Year 5		
(see page 611 for computations).		

OAK DESK COMPANY
Proof of Deferred Gross Profit
December 31, Year 5

	Installment contracts receivable	Deferred interest and carrying charges	Net installment contracts receivable	Gross profit percentage	Deferred gross profit
Year 4					
contracts	$ 28,000	$ 3,000	$ 25,000	28%	$ 7,000
Year 5					
contracts	140,000	20,000	120,000	31	37,200
Totals	$168,000	$23,000	$145,000		$44,200

Alternative computation of gross profit percentage

Instead of segregating the collections applicable to the selling price and to the interest and carrying charges, a retailing enterprise may determine the gross profit percentage by inclusion of the interest and carrying charges in the selling price. The resulting *larger gross profit percentage* then is applied to the total amount of cash collected in each accounting period to determine the realized gross profit. Application of this method to the Year 5 installment sales of Oak Desk Company is illustrated below:

The 40% gross profit percentage thus determined is applied to the tot
cash collections on installment contracts receivable in each year to con
pute the realized gross profit on installment sales. Under this approac
the realized gross profit on installment sales for Year 5 is $36,0C
($90,000 × 0.40 = $36,000.[4]

The use of the installment method of accounting requires installmer
contracts receivable and cash collections to be segregated by year of origi
In addition, the gross profit rate must be computed separately for each yea
However, a single controlling account for installment contracts receivab
may be used if the accounting records are computerized or if the installmer
contracts receivable are analyzed at the end of each year to ascertai
uncollected balances by year of origin.

The journal entry on page 612 to record the default on installment contrac
originating in Year 3 and the repossession of merchandise by Oak Des
Company is explained in the following section.

Defaults and repossessions

If a customer defaults on an installment contract for services and no furthe
collection can be made, we have an example of default without the possibi
ity of repossession. A similar situation exists for certain merchandise tha
has no significant resale value. The journal entry required in such cases is t
write off the uncollectible installment contract receivable, cancel the deferre
gross profit related to the receivable, and debit Uncollectible Installmer
Contracts Expense for the difference. In other words, the uncollectibl
installment contracts expense is equal to the **unrecovered cost** included i
the balance of the installment contract receivable.

However, in most cases a default by a customer leads to repossession c
merchandise. The uncollectible installment contracts expense is reduced b
the current fair value of the merchandise repossessed, and it is possible fc
the repossession to result in a gain.

The principal difficulty in accounting for defaults followed by repossessio
is the estimate of the **current fair value** of the merchandise at the time c
repossession. In the determination of a current fair value of repossesse
merchandise, the objective is to choose an amount that will allow for an
reconditioning costs and provide a normal gross profit on resale. An
reconditioning costs incurred are added to the Inventories account, provide
this does not become unreasonable in relation to the expected selling price

---

4 This procedure could be used for income tax purposes by dealers in personal property who compu
taxable income on the installment basis.

For financial accounting purposes, the carrying amount of the repossessed merchandise should not exceed its **net realizable value.**

The journal entry on page 612 to record the defaults and repossessions by Oak Desk Company accomplishes the following: (1) It eliminates the defaulted installment contracts receivable of $1,150, (2) it cancels the deferred gross profit of $250 ($1,000 × 0.25 = $250) and the deferred interest and carrying charges of $150 applicable to the defaulted installment contracts receivable, (3) it recognizes an asset equal to the $650 current fair value of the repossessed merchandise, and (4) it recognizes uncollectible installment contracts expense of $100, the difference between the unrecovered cost in the defaulted installment contracts receivable ($750) and the current fair value of the repossessed merchandise ($650). When the installment method of accounting is used, no loss or expense is recognized with respect to the deferred gross profit and interest and carrying charges contained in the defaulted installment contract receivable, because these amounts had not been recognized previously as realized revenue.

Other accounting issues relating to installment sales

Special accounting issues arise in connection with (1) the acceptance of used property as a trade-in, (2) the computation of interest on installment contracts receivable, (3) the use of the installment method of accounting solely for income tax purposes, and (4) retail land sales. These issues are discussed in the following sections.

Trade-ins   A familiar example of the use of trade-ins is the acceptance by a dealer of a used car as partial payment for a new car. An accounting problem exists only if the dealer grants an **overallowance** on the used car taken in trade. An overallowance is the excess of the trade-in allowance over the current fair value of the used car in terms of the dealer's ability to resell it at a price that will recover all direct costs and result in a normal gross profit. A rough approximation of the current fair value of the used car to the dealer may be the currently quoted wholesale price for used cars of the particular make and model.

An overallowance on trade-ins is significant because it represents a reduction in the stated selling price of the new merchandise. **The stated selling price must be reduced by the amount of the overallowance** to compute the net selling price. The gross profit on the sale of the new merchandise is the difference between the net selling price and cost.

As an illustration, assume that merchandise with a cost of $2,400 is sold on the installment plan for $3,300. Used merchandise is accepted as a trade-in at a "value" of $1,100, but the dealer expects to spend $50 in reconditioning the used merchandise before reselling it for only $1,000. Assume that the customary gross profit percentage on used merchandise of this type is 15%, an amount that will cover the selling and overhead costs, and also provide a normal gross profit on the resale. The current fair value of the trade-in and the amount of the overallowance are computed as follows:

Trade-in allowance give to customer			$1,1(
Deduct current fair value of trade-in:			
Estimated resale value of merchandise traded in	$1,000		
Less: Reconditioning cost expected to be incurred	$ 50		
Gross profit ($1,000 × 0.15)	150	200	
Current fair value of merchandise traded in			8(
Overallowance on trade-in			$ 3(

Assuming that a perpetual inventory system is used, the journal entry t
record the installment sale and the trade-in appears below.

Inventories (trade-ins)	800	
Installment Contracts Receivable ($3,300 − $1,100)	2,200	
Cost of Installment Sales	2,400	
Installment Sales ($3,300 − $300)		3,0(
Inventories (new)		2,4(
To record sale of merchandise for $3,000, consisting of gross sales price		
of $3,300 minus a $300 overallowance on the trade-in.		

Cost of the new article was $2,400; therefore, the deferred gross profit o
the installment sale of $3,000 amounts to $600. The gross profit percentag
is 20% ($600 ÷ $3,000 = 0.20). This percentage will be applied in th
computation of realized gross profit on the basis of cash collections. Th
current fair value of the merchandise accepted as a trade-in, $800,
considered equivalent to a cash collection for this purpose.

Interest on Installment Contracts Receivable   Installment contrac
usually provide for interest and carrying charges to be paid concurrentl
with each installment payment. Such *deferred payment charges*, regar
less of the label placed on them, represent a cost of borrowing to th
purchaser and may be referred to collectively as "interest." Only the po:
tion of the payment that is applied to reduce the principal of the contracts
considered in the measurement of realized gross profit under the installmer
method of accounting.

The arrangement for adding interest to installment contracts may follo
one of the following plans:

1 Equal periodic payments, with a portion of each payment representing interest o
the principal balance, and the remainder of the payment representing a reductio
of principal

2 Interest computed on each individual installment payment of principal from th
beginning date of the contract to the date each payment of principal is received

3 Interest computed each month on the outstanding principal balance during th
month

4 Interest computed throughout the entire contract period on the original amount of the sale minus any down payment

The first plan probably is the most widely used. Contracts with customers generally state how payments are to be allocated between principal and interest. Regardless of the plan used by dealers to add interest to installment contracts, interest revenue for financial accounting is computed periodically by applying the **effective interest rate** to the outstanding principal balance of the installment contracts receivable.

Installment Method for Income Tax Purposes Only The installment method of accounting is widely used for income tax purposes because it postpones the payment of income taxes. For example, assume that Markowski Company, a retailing enterprise, uses the accrual basis of accounting for financial accounting purposes. The pre-tax accounting income for Year 10 is $200,000, as indicated by the following condensed partial income statement (revenue from interest and carrying charges is ignored in this example):

MARKOWSKI COMPANY
Condensed Partial Income Statement (accrual basis of accounting)
For Year 10

Sales	$800,000
Cost of goods sold	500,000
Gross profit on sales	$300,000
Operating expenses	100,000
Income before income taxes	$200,000

Assume that the deferred gross profit on installment sales was $55,000 at the beginning of Year 10 and $105,000 at the end of Year 10, and that Markowski Company uses the installment method of accounting for income tax purposes. The taxable income for Year 10 is determined as follows:

Taxable income for Year 10

Pre-tax accounting income for Year 10 (accrual basis of accounting)		$200,000
Less: Deferred gross profit on installment sales, end of		
Year 10	$105,000	
Add: Deferred gross profit on installment sales, beginning of		
Year 10	55,000	(50,000)
Taxable income for Year 10 (installment method of accounting)		$150,000

Income taxes for Year 10 would be recorded as follows, assuming that the income tax rate for Markowski Company is 45% of taxable income:

Income Taxes Expense   90,000
      income Taxes Payable . . . .   67,5(
      Deferred Income Tax Liability . . . .   22,5(
To record income taxes for Year 10, determined as follows:
  Income taxes expense: $200,000 × 0.45 = $90,000.
  Income taxes payable: $150,000 × 0.45 = $67,500.
  Deferred income tax liability: $50,000 × 0.45 = $22,500.

The deferred income tax liability is classified as a current liability in th
balance sheet because the installment contracts receivable to which th
deferred taxes relate are classified as current assets. For a complete discussic
of the problem of income tax allocation, refer to the **Intermediat
Accounting** text of this series.

Accounting for Retail Land Sales   In 1973, the AICPA published a
Industry Accounting Guide, "Accounting for Retail Land Sales," th
called for the use of the accrual basis of accounting for land developmer
projects in which collections on installment contracts receivable are reaso
ably assured and **all four** of the following conditions are present:[5]

1 The land clearly will be useful for residential or recreational purposes at the er
of the normal payment period.
2 The project's improvements have progressed beyond preliminary stages, ar
there is evidence that the project will be completed according to plan.
3 The installment contracts receivable are not subject to subordination to ne
loans on the land (except for home construction purposes).
4 Collection experience for the project indicates that collectibility of the installmer
contracts receivable is reasonably predictable and that 90% of the contracts i
force six months **after sales are recorded** will be collected in full.

Unless all four of these conditions for the use of the accrual basis c
accounting are met for the entire project, the installment method of ac
counting should be used for all sales of land. If all four conditions subse
quently are satisfied, a change to the accrual basis of accounting should b
adopted for the entire project and accounted for as a **change in accoun,
ing estimate.**

The **Industry Accounting Guide** suggested that the procedures to b
applied under the installment method of accounting for retail land sale
should include the following:[6]

1 The entire contract price applicable to the installment sale, without reduction fc
cancellations or discounts, is reported as revenue in the income statement of th
year the sale is recorded.

---

5 *An AICPA Industry Accounting Guide*, "Accounting for Retail Land Sales," AICPA (New York: 197:
pp. 7–8.
6 Ibid., pp. 15–16.

2 Cost of sales (including provision for future improvement costs) and nondeferable operating expenses (except to the extent deferred in 3 below) are charged to income of the current accounting period.

3 Gross profit, less selling costs directly associated with the project, is deferred and recognized in income as payments of principal are received on the installment contracts receivable.

4 Interest at the stated contract rate is recorded as revenue when received, and the unamortized deferred profit is *deducted from related installment contracts receivable* in the balance sheet.

5 Disclosure is made of the portion of sales and contracts receivable applicable to the installment method of accounting.

There have been no Canadian guidelines issued with respect to retail land sales.

Presentation of installment sales data in financial statements

The presentation of accounts relating to installment sales in the financial statements raises some interesting theoretical issues, regardless of whether the accrual basis of accounting or the installment method of accounting is used.

Income Statement   A partial income statement for Year 5 for Oak Desk Company, which uses the installment method of accounting, is presented below. This statement is based on the installment sales information illustrated on pages 610 to 614, plus additional assumed data for regular sales.

OAK DESK COMPANY
Partial Income Statement
For Year Ended December 31, Year 5

	Installment sales	Regular sales	Combined
Sales	$200,000	$300,000	$500,000
Cost of goods sold	138,000	222,000	360,000
Gross profit on sales	$ 62,000	$ 78,000	$140,000
Less: Deferred gross profit on Year 5 installment sales	37,200		37,200
Realized gross profit on Year 5 sales	$ 24,800	$ 78,000	$102,800
Add: Realized gross profit on prior years' installment sales (see page 613)			16,710
Total realized gross profit			$119,510

If the accrual basis of accounting were used for all sales, a gross profit of $140,000 would be reported in Year 5. The three-column form illustrated above, although useful for internal purposes, generally would not be used to report the results of operations to outsiders. In a multiple-step income statement, revenue from interest and carrying charges on installment contracts is reported as Other Revenue.

Balance Sheet Installment contracts receivable, net of deferred interest and carrying charges, are classified as current assets, although the collection period often extends more than a year beyond the balance sheet date. This rule is applicable whether the accrual basis of accounting or the installment method of accounting is used. The definition of current assets specifically includes installment contracts and notes receivable if they conform generally to normal trade practices and terms in the industry. This classification is supported by the concept that current assets include all resources expected to be realized in cash, sold, or consumed during the normal operating cycle of the business enterprise.

The listing of installment contracts receivable in the current asset section of the balance sheet is more informative when the amounts maturing each year are disclosed. Such disclosure by a large publicly owned corporation is illustrated below.

<table>
<tr><td>Balance sheet presentation
of installment contracts
receivable</td><td>Current assets:</td><td></td></tr>
<tr><td></td><td>Installment contracts receivable **(Note 1)** . . . .</td><td>$998,200,000</td></tr>
<tr><td></td><td>Less: Provision for doubtful contracts . . . .</td><td>(9,700,000</td></tr>
<tr><td></td><td>Unearned interest and carrying charges . . . .</td><td>(20,100,000</td></tr>
<tr><td></td><td>Net installment contracts receivable . . . .</td><td>$968,400,000</td></tr>
</table>

Note 1: Installment contracts receivable arise from sales of residential houses to customers for time payments over periods of 12 to 18 years. Of the gross amount of $998,200,000, an amount of $905,580,000 is due after one year. Installment contracts receivable are included in current assets because they are within the operating cycle of the residential home construction industry. Installment payments estimated to be receivable within each of the next five years are $92,620,000, $89,880,000, $93,100,000, $88,900,000, and $79,700,000, respectively, and $554,000,000 after five years.

The classification of deferred gross profit on installment sales in the balance sheet *when the installment method of accounting is used for financial accounting* has long troubled accountants. A common practice for many years was to classify the deferred gross profit in the liabilities section of the balance sheet. Critics of this treatment pointed out that no obligation to an outsider existed and that the liability classification was improper.

The existence of a deferred gross profit account indicates that the profit element in installment contracts receivable has not been realized. Acceptance of this view suggests that the installment contracts receivable will be overstated unless the deferred gross profit is deducted from installment contracts receivable. This classification as an asset valuation account is theoretically preferable and was recommended in the **AICPA Industry Accounting Guide,** "Accounting for Retail Land Sales."[7]

In view of these conflicting approaches, it has been suggested that the deferred gross profit be subdivided into three parts: (1) an allowance for collection costs and doubtful contracts that would be deducted from installment contracts receivable, (2) a liability representing future income taxes on the gross profit not yet realized, and (3) a residual income element. The residual income element would be classified by some accountants as a separate item in the stockholders' equity section and by others in an undefined section between liabilities and stockholders' equity. Such a detailed classification of deferred gross profit in the balance sheet seldom is encountered in the business world.

The lack of agreement as to the classification of deferred gross profit in the balance sheet is evidence of the inherent contradiction between the installment method of accounting and the accrual basis of accounting. Because the chief reason for the use of the installment method of accounting is the income tax advantage it affords, a satisfactory solution in most cases is to recognize gross profit on installment sales on the accrual basis of accounting for financial accounting purposes and to defer recognition of gross profit for income tax purposes until installment contracts receivable are collected.

CONSIGNMENTS

The meaning of consignments

The term **consignment** means a transfer of possession of merchandise from the owner to another person who acts as the sales agent of the owner. Title to the merchandise remains with the owner, who is called a **consignor;** the sales agent who has possession of the merchandise is called a **consignee**.

From a legal viewpoint, a consignment represents a **bailment**.[8] The relationship between the consignor and the consignee is that of **principal** and **agent,** and the law of agency controls the determination of the obligations and rights of the two parties.

Consignees are responsible to consignors for the merchandise placed in their custody until it is sold or returned. Because consignees do not acquire title to the merchandise, they neither include it in inventories nor record an account payable or other liability. The only obligation of consignees is to give reasonable care to the consigned merchandise and to account for it to consignors. When the merchandise is sold by a consignee, the resulting account receivable is the property of the consignor. At this point the consignor records a sale.

The shipment of merchandise on consignment may be referred to by the consignor as a **consignment out,** and by the consignee as a **consignment in**.

---

7 Ibid., p. 16.

8 A *bailment* is a contract for the delivery or transfer of possession of money or personal property for a particular purpose, such as for safekeeping, repairs, or sale.

Distinguishing between a consignment and a sale

Although both a sale and a consignment involve the shipment of merchandise, a clear distinction between the two is necessary for the proper measurement of income. Because title does not pass when merchandise is shipped on consignment, the consignor continues to carry the consigned merchandise as part of inventories. No profit should be recognized at the time of the consignment shipment because there is no change in ownership of merchandise. If the consignee's business should fail, the consignor would not be in the position of a creditor; instead, the consignor is the rightful owner of any unsold consigned merchandise.

Why should a producer or wholesaler prefer to consign merchandise rather than to make outright sales? One possible reason is that the consignor may be able to persuade dealers to stock the items on a consignment basis whereas they would not be willing to purchase the merchandise outright. Second, the consignor avoids the risk inherent in selling on credit to dealers of questionable financial strength.

From the viewpoint of a consignee, the acquisition of merchandise on consignment rather than by purchase requires less capital investment and avoids the risk of loss if the merchandise cannot be sold.

Rights and duties of the consignee

When merchandise is shipped on consignment, a formal written contract is needed on such points as credit terms to be granted to customers by the consignee, expenses of the consignee to be reimbursed by the consignor, commission allowed to the consignee, frequency of reporting and payment by the consignee, and handling and care of the consigned merchandise. In addition to any explicit contractual provisions, the general rights and duties of the consignee may be summarized as follows:

Rights of Consignee

1 To receive **compensation** for merchandise sold for the account of consignor.

2 To receive **reimbursement** for expenditures (such as freight and insurance) made in connection with the consignment.

3 To sell consigned merchandise on **credit** if the consignor has not forbidden credit sales.

4 To make the usual **warranties** as to the quality of the consigned merchandise and to bind the consignor to honour such warranties.

Duties of Consignee

1 To give **care and protection** reasonable in relation to the nature of the consigned merchandise.

2 To keep the consigned merchandise **separate from owned inventories** or be able to identify the consigned merchandise. Similarly, the consignee must **identify** and **segregate the consignment receivables** from other receivables.

3 To use care **in extending credit** on the sale of consigned merchandise and to be diligent in **setting prices** on consigned merchandise and in collecting consignment receivables.

4 To **render complete reports** of sale of consigned merchandise and to make appropriate and timely payments to the consignor.

In granting credit, as in caring for the consigned merchandise, the consignee is obliged to act prudently and to protect the property rights of the consignor. Because the receivables from the sale of consigned merchandise are the property of the consignor, the consignor bears any credit losses, providing the consignee has exercised due care in granting credit and making collections. However, the consignee may guarantee the collection of receivables; under this type of consignment contract, the consignee is said to be a ***del credere agent***.

The consignee also must follow any special instructions by the consignor as to care of the merchandise. If the consignee acts prudently in providing appropriate care and protection, the consignee is not liable for any damage to the merchandise that may occur.

The account sales

The report rendered by the consignee is called an ***account sales;*** it includes the quantity of merchandise received and sold, expenses incurred, advances made, and amounts owned or remitted. Payments may be made as portions of the shipment are sold or may not be required until the consigned merchandise either has been sold or has been returned to the consignor.

Assume that Sherri Company ships on consignment to Robert Thorell 10 television sets to be sold at $400 each. The consignee is to be reimbursed for freight costs of $135 and is to receive a commission of 20% of the stipulated selling price. After selling all the consigned merchandise, Thorell sends the consignor an account sales similar to the one below, accompanied by a cheque for the amount due:

Account sales

ROBERT THORELL
Toronto, Ontario
Account Sales

August 31 , 19___

Sales for account and risk of:

Sherri Company

Winnipeg, Manitoba

Sales: 10 TV sets @ $400		$4,000
Charges:		
Freight costs	$135	
Commission ($4,000 × 0.20)	800	935
Balance (remittance to consignor)		$3,065
Consigned TV sets on hand		none

---

Accounting for consignees

The receipt of the consignment shipment of 10 television sets by Rober Thorell may be recorded in any of several ways. The objective is to create memorandum record of the consigned merchandise; no purchase has bee made and no liability exists. The receipt of the consignment could be recorde by a **memorandum notation** in the general journal, by an entry in separate ledger of consignment shipments, or by a memorandum entry in general ledger account entitled Consignment In — Sherri Company. In thi illustration, the latter method is used, and the ledger account appears a follows:

Consignee receives merchandise on consignment

	Consignment in — Sherri Company				
Date	Explanation	Debit	Credit	Balance
	Received 10 sets to be sold for $400 each at a commission of 20% of selling price			

The journal entries for the consignee to record the payment of freigh costs on the shipment and the sale of the television sets are as follows:

Consignee records freight costs and sale of consigned TV sets

Consignment in — Sherri Company 135
    Cash 13
To record payment of freight costs on shipment from consignor.

Cash 4,000
        Consignment In — Sherry Company 4,00
To record sale of 10 TV sets at $400 each.

The journal entry to record the 20% commission charged by the consignee consists of a debit to the Consignment In account and a credit to a revenue account, as follows:

Commission revenue recorded by consignee

Consignment In — Sherri Company 800
        Commission Revenue — Consignment Sales .... 80(
To record commission of 20% earned on TV sets sold.

The payment by the consignee of the full amount owed is recorded by a debit to the Consignment In account and results in closing that account. The journal entry is below.

To record payment to consignor

Consignment In — Sherri Company 3,065
    Cash .... 3,06!
To record payment in full to consignor.

After the posting of this journal entry, the ledger account for the consignment appears as follows in the consignee's accounting records:

Summary of Consignment in account

Consignment In — Sherri Company

Date	Explanation	Debit	Credit	Balance
	Received 10 TV sets to be sold for $400 each at a commission of 20% of selling price			
	Freight costs	135		135 dr
	Sales: 10 sets @ $400 each		4,000	3,865 cr
	Commission: $4,000 × 0.20	800		3,065 cr
	Payment to consignor	3,065		-0-

Several variations from the pattern of journal entries illustrated might be mentioned. If the policy of Robert Thorell is to debit inbound freight costs on both consignment shipments and purchases of merchandise to a Freight In account, the portion applicable to the Sherri Company consignment should be reclassified at a later date by a debit to Consignment In — Sherri Company and a credit to Freight In. If a cash advance is made by the consignee to the consignor, it is recorded as a debit to the Consignment In account, and the final payment is reduced by the amount of advance. If merchandise is received on consignment from several consignors, a Consignments In controlling account may be used, and a supporting account for each consignment set up in a subsidiary consignments ledger.

If the consignee, Robert Thorell, does not determine profits from consignment sales separately from regular sales, the sale of the consigned merchandise is credited to the regular Sales account. Concurrently, a journal entry is made debiting Cost of Goods Sold (or Purchases) and crediting the Consignment In account for the amount payable to the consignor for each unit sold (sales price minus the commission). Costs chargeable to the consignor are recorded by debits to the Consignment In account and credits to Cash or expense accounts, if the costs previously were recorded in expense accounts. No journal entry is made for commission revenue, because the profit element is measured by the difference between the amount credited to Sales and the amount debited to Cost of Goods Sold (or Purchases). The Consignment In account is closed by a debit for the payment made to the consignor in settlement. This method may be less desirable, because information relating to gross profits on consignment sales as compared with regular sales may be needed by the consignee as a basis for business decisions.

At the end of the accounting period when financial statements are prepared, some Consignment In accounts in the subsidiary consignments ledger may have debit balances and others credit balances. A debit balance will exist in a Consignment In account if the total of expenditures, commission, and advances to the consignor is larger than the proceeds of sales of that particular lot of consigned merchandise. A credit balance will exist if the proceeds of sales are in excess of the expenditures, commission, and advances to the consignor. The total of the Consignment In accounts with debit balances is included among the current assets in the balance sheet; the total of the Consignment In accounts with credit balances is classified as a current liability. Any commission earned but not recorded is entered in the accounting records before financial statements are prepared. The balance of the Consignments In controlling account represents the difference between the subsidiary accounts with debit balances and those with credit balances.

Accounting for consignors

When the consignor ships merchandise to consignees, it is essential to have a record of the location of this portion of inventories. Therefore, the consignor may establish in the general ledger a Consignment Out account for every consignee (or every shipment on consignment). If consignment shipments are numerous, the consignor may prefer to use a controlling account for subsidiary consignment-out accounts. If the inventory records are computerized, special coding may be used to identify inventories in the hands of consignees. The Consignment Out account should not be intermingled with accounts receivable, because it represents a special category of inventories rather than receivables.

Separate determination of gross profit

First, let us distinguish between a separate determination of **net income** on consignment sales and a separate determination of **gross profits** on consignment sales. Another possibility to consider is a separate determination of consignment sales revenue apart from regular sales revenue.

Although it may be useful to develop detailed information on the profitability of selling through consignees as compared with selling through regular channels, the accumulation of such information must be influenced by several practical considerations. First, the determination of a separate net income from consignment sales seldom is feasible, because this would require allocations of many operating expenses on a rather arbitrary basis. The work required would be extensive, and the resulting data would be no better than the arbitrary expense allocations. In general, the determination of **net income** from consignment sales cannot be justified.

The determination of gross profits from consignment sales as distinguished from gross profits on regular sales is much simpler, because it is based on the identification of **direct costs** associated with consignment sales. However, the compilation of these direct costs may be an expensive process, especially if the gross profit is computed by individual consignments or consignees. A separate determination of gross profits on consignments becomes more desirable if consignment transactions are substantial in relation to regular sales.

A separation of consignment sales revenue from regular sales revenue usually is a minimum step to develop information needed by management if consignment sales are an important part of total sales volume. However, no separation of consignment sales from regular sales may be justified if only an occasional sale is made through consignees.

Accounting for consignor illustrated

The choice of accounting methods by the consignor depends on whether (1) consignment gross profits are determined separately from gross profits on regular sales, or (2) sales on consignment are combined with regular sales without any effort to measure gross profits separately for the two categories of sales.

The journal entries required under these alternative methods of accounting for consignment shipments now will be illustrated, first under the assumption that gross profits on consignment sales are determined separately, and second under the assumption that consignment sales are combined with regular sales without a separate determination of gross profits. The assumed transactions for these illustrations already have been described from the consignee's viewpoint but now are restated to include the data relating to the consignor. In all remaining illustrations, we assume that the consignor uses the perpetual inventory system.

Sherri Company shipped on consignment to Robert Thorell 10 television sets that cost $250 each. The selling price was set at $400 each. The cost of packing was $30; all costs incurred in the packing department were debited by Sherri to the Packing Expense account. Freight costs of $135 by an independent truck line to deliver the shipment to Robert Thorell were paid by the consignee. All 10 sets were sold by the consignee for $400 each. After deducting the commission of 20% and the freight costs of $135, Robert Thorell sent Sherri Company a cheque for $3,065, along with the account sales illustrated on page 623.

The journal entries for the consignor, assuming that gross profits on consignment sales are determined separately, and gross profits on consignment sales are not determined separately, are summarized on page 628 for the completed consignment.

If the consigned merchandise is sold on credit, the consignee may send the consignor an account sales but no cheque. In this case the consignor's debit would be to Accounts Receivable rather than to the Cash account. When sales are reported by the consignee and gross profits are not determined separately by the consignor, the account credited is Sales rather than Consignment Sales, because there is no intent to separate regular sales from consignment sales. Similarly, the commission paid to consignees is combined with other commission expense, and freight costs applicable to sales on consignment are recorded in the Freight Expense account.

Accounting for partial sale of consigned merchandise

In the preceding example, we have assumed that the consignor received an account sales showing that all the merchandise shipped on consignment had been sold by the consignee. The account sales was accompanied by remittance in full, and the consignor's journal entries were designed to record the gross profit from the completed consignment.

Let us now change our conditions by assuming that only four of the ten TV sets consigned by Sherri Company to Robert Thorell had been sold by

SHERRI COMPANY (Consignor)

Journal Entries, Ledger Account, and Income Statement Presentation for a Completed Consignment

Explanations	Gross profits determined separately		Gross profits not determined separately	

(1) Shipment of merchandise costing $2,500 on consignment; consigned merchandise is transferred to a separate inventories account. Consignor uses the perpetual inventory system.	Consignment Out – Robert Thorell 2,500
	  Inventories ....
		2,500	Consignment Out – Robert Thorell 2,500
			  Inventories ....
				2,500

(2) Packing expense of $30 allocated to consigned merchandise; this expense previously was recorded in the Packing Expense account.	Consignment Out – Robert Thorell .... 30 Packing Expense	30	No journal entry required; total packing expense is reported among operating expenses.	

(3) Consignment sales of $4,000 reported by consignee and payment of $3,065 received. Charges by consignee: freight costs, $135; commission, $800.	Cash 3,065
	Consignment Out – Robert Thorell 135
	Commission Expense 800
	  Consignment Sales ...
		4,000	Cash 3,065
			Freight Expense 135
			Commission Expense 800
			  Sales ....
				4,000

(4) Cost of consignment sales recorded, $2,665 ($2,500 + $30 + $135 = $2,665).	Cost of Consignment Sales .. 2,665
	  Consignment Out – Robert Thorell ....
		2,665	Cost of Goods Sold 2,500
			  Consignment Out – Robert Thorell ....
				2,500

(5) Summary of Consignment Out account:	Consignment Out – Robert Thorell
	 2,500 2,665
	   30
	  135
	 2,665 2,665
			Consignment Out – Robert Thorell
			 2,500 2,500	

(6) Presentation in the income statement:	Consignment sales $4,000
	Less: Cost of consignment
	  sales $2,665
	  Commission 800 3,465
	Gross profit on consignment
	  sales ...... $ 535
			Included in total sales $4,000
			Included in cost of all merchandise
			  sold 2,500
			Included in total packing expense ... 30
			Included in total freight expense 135
			Included in total commission
			  expense 800	

the end of the accounting period. To prepare financial statements, the consignor must determine the amount of gross profit realized on the four units sold and the inventory value of the six unsold units. The account sales received by Sherri Company at the end of the current period includes the following information:

ROBERT THORELL

Account Sales to Sherri Company

Sales: 4 TV sets at $400		$1,600
Charges: Freight costs	$135	
Commission ($1,600 × 0.20)	320	455
Total payable to consignor		$1,145
Cheque enclosed		500
Balance payable to consignor		$ 645
Consigned merchandise on hand		6 TV sets

The journal entries for the consignor to account for this uncompleted consignment are presented on page 630.

In the illustration of a partial consignment sale, we have employed the familiar accounting principle of carrying forward as part of inventories a pro rata portion of the costs incurred to place the inventories in a location and condition necessary for sale. The commission charged by the consignee for the units sold is an operating expense of the current accounting period.

Return of unsold merchandise by consignee

We have stressed that the costs of packing and shipping merchandise to a consignee, whether paid directly by the consignor or by the consignee, properly are included in inventories. However, if the consignee for any reason returns merchandise to the consignor, the packing and freight costs incurred on the original outbound shipment should be recorded as an expense of the current accounting period. The *place utility* originally created by these costs is lost when the merchandise is returned. Any costs incurred by the consignor on the return shipment also should be recorded as an expense, along with any repair costs necessary to place the merchandise in salable condition.

Finally, a clear distinction should be made between freight costs on consignment shipments and outbound freight costs on regular sales. The freight costs on consignment shipments create an increment in value of the merchandise that is still the property of the consignor. This increment, together with the cost of purchasing or producing the merchandise, is to be offset against revenue in future accounting periods when the consigned merchandise is sold. Outbound freight costs on regular sales are recorded as expenses of the period that such sales are made.

SHERRI COMPANY (Consignor)

Journal Entries, Ledger Account, and Balance Sheet Presentation for a Partial Sale of Consigned Merchandise

Explanations	Gross profits determined separately	Gross profits not determined separately

(1) Shipment of merchandise costing $2,500 on consignment; consigned merchandise is transferred to a separate Inventories account. Consignor uses the perpetual inventory system.	Consignment Out – Robert
	  Thorell 2,500
	    Inventories 2,500
		Consignment Out – Robert
		  Thorell 2,500
		    Inventories 2,500

(2) Packing expense of $30 allocated to consigned merchandise; this expense previously was recorded in the Packing Expense account.	Consignment Out – Robert
	  Thorell 30
	    Packing Expense 30
		No journal entry required; total packing expense is reported among operating expenses.

(3) Consignment sales of $1,600 reported by consignee and payment of $500 received. Charges by consignee: freight costs, $135; commission, $320.	Cash 500
	Accounts Receivable 645
	Consignment Out – Robert
	  Thorell 135
	Commission Expense – Consignment Sales 320
	    Consignment Sales 1,600
		Cash 500
		Accounts Receivable 645
		Freight Expense 135
		Commission Expense 320
		    Sales 1,600

(4) Cost of consignment sales recorded:
($250 + $3 + $13.50) × 4 = $1,066;
$250 × 4 = $1,000
	Cost of Consignment Sales .. 1,066
	  Consignment Out –
	  Robert Thorell 1,066
		Cost of Goods Sold 1,000
		  Consignment Out – Robert
		  Thorell 1,000

(5) Direct costs relating to unsold merchandise in hands of consignee deferred when profits are not determined separately:
Packing costs ($3 × 6) $18
Freight costs ($13.50 × 6) 81
  Total $99
	No journal entry required.	Consignment Out – Robert
		  Thorell 99
		    Packing Exense 18
		    Freight Expense 81

(6) Summary of Consignment Out account:

Consignment Out – Robert Thorell			
2,500		1,066	
30	Balance		
135		1,599	
2,665		2,665	
Balance	1,599		

Consignment Out – Robert Thorell			
2,500		1,000	
99	Balance		
2,599		1,599	
Balance	1,599		

(7) Presentation in the balance sheet:

Current assets:
Inventories on consignment ... $1,599

Current assets:
Inventories on consignment ... $1,599

Advances from consignees

Although cash advances from a consignee sometimes are credited to the Consignment Out account, a better practice is to credit a liability account, Advances from Consignees. The Consignment Out account then will continue to show the carrying amount of the merchandise on consignment, rather than being shown net of a liability to the consignee.

Nature of the Consignment Out account

When accounting students encounter for the first time a ledger account such as Consignment Out, they may gain a clear understanding of its function more quickly by considering where it belongs in the five basic types of accounts: assets, liabilities, owners' equity, revenue, and expenses. Classification of the Consignment Out account in this structure will depend on the methods employed by a business enterprise in accounting for consignments.

Whether or not an enterprise uses a system of determining gross profits on consignment sales separately from regular sales, the Consignment Out account belongs in the asset category. The account is debited for the cost of merchandise shipped to a consignee; when the consignee reports sale of all or a portion of the merchandise, the cost is transferred from Consignment Out to Cost of Consignment Sales. To be even more specific, Consignment Out is a current asset, one of the inventories group to be listed on the balance sheet as Inventories on Consignment, or perhaps combined with other inventories if the amount is not material. As stated earlier, the costs of packing and transporting consigned merchandise constitute costs of inventories, and these costs are recorded as debits to the Consignment Out account.

Another concept of the Consignment Out account is summarized briefly as follows: The Consignment Out account may be debited for the cost of merchandise shipped to the consignee and credited for the sales proceeds remitted by the consignee. This generally will result in a credit balance in the Consignment Out account when the entire shipment has been sold. This credit balance represents the profit earned by the consignor and is closed by a debit to Consignment Out and a credit to an account such as Profit on Consignment Sales. No separate accounts are used for Consignment Sales and Cost of Consignment Sales, and the income statement does not show the amount of sales made through consignees. Under this system, the Consignment Out account does not fit in any of the five basic classes of accounts. It is a mixture of asset elements and revenue and must be closed or reduced to its asset element (cost of unsold consigned merchandise) before financial statements are prepared at the end of an accounting period.

The methods we have illustrated in accounting for consignments are widely used, but many variations from these methods are possible.

REVIEW QUESTIONS

1 What are the most important characteristics that distinguish an installment sale from an ordinary sale on 30-day credit terms?

2 In a discussion of the theoretical support for the installment method of accounting, a student stated: "If a business enterprise is going to sell personal property over a period as long as 36 months, no one can predict how difficult or costly collections may be. To recognize the gross profit as realized at the time of sale would violate well-established accounting concepts such as *conservatism* and *reliability*." What opposing arguments can you offer?

3 What position did *APB Opinion No. 10* establish for the use of the installment method of accounting for financial accounting purposes?

4 On November 10, Year 3, Ann Haggard agreed to sell for $150,000 a tract of land acquired five years ago for $60,000. The purchaser offered to pay $44,000 down and the balance in 20 semiannual installments plus interest at 15% on the unpaid principal balance. Haggard agreed to these terms, and the sale was completed.

Assuming that Haggard (who is not a dealer in real estate) computes net income on a calendar-year basis and elects to use the installment method of accounting for income tax purposes, how much gross profit did she realize in Year 3 for income tax purposes?

5 The following journal entry appears in the accounting records of a land developer who uses the installment method of accounting:

Inventories (repossessed land)	2,000	
Deferred Gross Profit on Installment Sales — Year 10	1,505	
Uncollectible Installment Contracts Expense	795	
Installment Contracts Receivable		4,300

Compute the rate of gross profit on the original sale. What was the probable source of the $2,000 debit to the Inventories account?

6 How should the *current fair value* of merchandise traded in be determined? What accounting treatment would you recommend for any *overallowance* granted to customers on merchandise accepted as a trade-in?

7 What conditions generally must be present before the accrual basis of accounting may be used to account for retail sales of land on the installment plan?

8 Discuss the balance sheet classification of deferred gross profit on the installment sales of land. Include former practice and theoretical considerations in your answer.

9 How does a *consignment* of merchandise differ from a *sale* of merchandise?

10 Majors Corporation sells merchandise for cash and on 30-day credit terms; it also makes sales through consignees. Explain how the two methods of marketing differ with respect to the time when profit is realized. What relationship, if any, exists between the realization of profit and the receipt of cash by Majors Corporation?

11 Give reasons why the use of consignments may be advantageous for the consignor and for the consignee.

12 On December 31, HP Motors received a report from one of its consignees that 40 motors of a consignment of 100 had been sold. No cheque was enclosed, but the report indicated that payment would be made later. HP Motors maintains its accounting records on a calendar-year basis and uses the perpetual inventory system. It determines profits on consignment sales separately from profits on regular sales. What accounting action, if any, should be taken by HP Motors on December 31 with respect to the consignee's report?

13 A manufacturer of outboard motors accumulates production costs on job cost sheets. On March 20, Lot No. K-37, consisting of 100 identical motors, was completed at a cost of $14,000. Twenty-five motors were shipped on consignment to a dealer in Ontario, and another 25 were sent to a consignee in Alberta. The remaining 50 motors were in the manufacturer's stockroom on March 31, the end of the fiscal year. Neither consignee submitted an account sales for March. Explain the quantity and valuation of motors in the manufacturer's balance sheet on March 31.

14 Identify each of the following ledger accounts by indicating whether it belongs in the general ledger of consignors or consignees; whether it normally has a debit balance or a credit balance; and how the account would be classified in the financial statements.
  a Cost of Consignment Sales
  b Consignment Out
  c Consignment Sales
  d Consignment In

15 What difference, if any, do you see between outbound freight costs on regular sales and outbound freight costs on consignment shipments?

16 Cal Marine, Inc., makes a number of shipments on consignment, although most of its merchandise is sold on 30-day credit terms. Consignment shipments are recorded on sales invoices that are posted as debits to Accounts Receivable and credits to Sales. Cal Marine has not been audited by independent public accountants, but at the suggestion of the company's bank you are retained to audit the financial statements for the current year.
  Would you take exception to Cal Marine's method of accounting for consignments? Explain. What adjusting journal entries, if any, are required at year-end?

EXERCISES

Ex 15-1 Select the best answer for each of the following multiple-choice questions:
  1 Dalton Company sold machinery to Ford Company on January 1, Year 1. The cash selling price would have been $379,100, but the sale was made on an installment contract that required annual payments of $100,000, including interest at 10%, over five years. The first payment was due on December 31, Year 1. What amount of interest revenue should be included in Dalton's income statement for the year ended December 31, Year 3 (the third year of the contract)?
  a $24,180
  b $24,871
  c $37,910
  d $50,000
  e Some other amount

  2 An automobile dealer lists a new model costing $5,000 at $8,000. A customer trades in an old model for an allowance of $2,000; the balance of $6,000 plus interest is payable $310 a month for 24 months. The dealer expects to sell the old model for $1,800 after reconditioning it at a cost of $300. Normal gross profit on used automobiles is 10%. In the journal entry to record the sale of the new model, the accountant for the dealer should:
  a Debit the Inventories (trade-ins) account for $2,000
  b Credit the Inventories (new) account for $4,320
  c Credit the Installment Sales account for $7,320
  d Debit the Loss on Trade-Ins account for $680

3 Which of the following is not a factor in the determination of current fair value of merchandise repossessed under a defaulted installment sales contract?
a Deferred gross profit on contract on date of default
b Necessary reconditioning costs for the merchandise
c Normal gross profit on resale of the merchandise
d Expected selling price (after reconditioning) of the merchandise

4 Joanie Reberry received a consignment of 100 toys from Dan Company on October 7, Year 5. Dan instructed Reberry to sell the toys for $100 each, which represented a gross profit rate of 20% to Dan. Reberry paid freight costs of $240 on the shipment on October 7, Year 5. Reberry should debit the Consignment In- Dan Company account on October 7, Year 5, in the amount of:
a $240   b $10,000   c $8,000   d $8,240   e Some other amount

5 The inventories of Benson Company on September 30, Year 1, included the following items:

	Amount
Merchandise on consignment (owned by Benson), at selling price (including markup of 40% on cost)	$7,000
Merchandise purchased, in transit (shipped by supplier FOB shipping point)	6,000
Merchandise held on consignment by Benson	4,000
Merchandise out on approval (selling price $2,500, cost $2,000)	2,500

Based on the above information, Benson's inventories on September 30, Year 1 should be reduced by:
a $6,500   b $7,300   c $8,500   d $13,500   e Some other amount

Ex 15-2   On September 30, Year 1, Urban Land Company sold for $50,000 a tract of land that had a cost of $30,000. Urban Land received a down payment of $8,000, the balance to be received at the rate of $3,000 every three months, starting December 31, Year 1. In addition, the purchaser agreed to pay interest at the rate of 2% a quarter on the unpaid principal. Because collection of the installments was highly uncertain, Urban Land elected to report the gain under the installment method of accounting, both for financial accounting and for income tax purposes.
    Prepare journal entries to record the (a) sale of the land, (b) receipt of the first installment on December 31, and (c) gain realized in Year 1 under the installment method of accounting. Ignore expenses of sale.

Ex 15-3   Early in Year 1, Vargo Company sold a parcel of land with a carrying amount of $40,000 for $100,000. The purchaser paid $10,000 down and agreed to pay the balance plus interest in three equal annual installments starting on December 31, Year 1.
    Assuming that collections are made as agreed, prepare a working paper showing the gross profit that Vargo would recognize each year under (a) the accrual basis of accounting, (b) the installment method of accounting, and (c) the cost recovery method of accounting. Ignore expenses of sale.

Ex 15-4   Gross profits for Sunset Home Products, Inc., were 35%, 33%, and 30% of sales price for Year 1, Year 2, and Year 3, respectively. The account balances at the top of page 635 are available at the end of Year 3. The installment contracts receivable and the deferred gross profit include interest and carrying charges.
    Prepare a journal entry at the end of Year 3 to record the realized gross profit on installment sales.

	Sales	Installment contracts receivable	Deferred gross profit (before adjustment)
Year 1		$ 6,000	$ 7,230
Year 2		61,500	60,750
Year 3		195,000	120,150

Ex 15-5   In Year 5, merchandise was sold on an installment contract by Fong for $1,600 at a gross profit of 25% on cost. In Year 5, a total of $600 was collected on this contract; in Year 6, no collections were made on this contract, and the merchandise was repossessed. The current fair value of the merchandise was $680; however, Fong's accountant recorded the repossession as follows:

Allowance for Doubtful Installment Contracts Receivable   1,000
    Installment Contracts Receivable — Year 5   1,000
To write off balance of defaulted installment contract receivable.

Prepare a journal entry to correct the accounting records, assuming that the ledger accounts are still open for Year 6 and that Fong uses an allowance for doubtful installment contracts receivable. Ignore interest and carrying charges, and assume that Fong records installment sales on the accrual basis of accounting.

Ex 15-6   Chasen Motors sold a new car for a list price of $6,600. Cash of $300 was received on the sale, together with a used car accepted at a trade-in allowance of $1,500. The balance of $4,800 was due in 24 monthly installments. Cost of the new car was $5,100. Chasen Motors anticipated reconditioning cost on the trade-in of $200 and a resale price of $1,300. Used cars normally are sold at a gross profit of 25% of selling price.

Prepare journal entries to record (**a**) the sale of the new car, (**b**) reconditioning costs of $200 on the car acquired as a trade-in, and (**c**) the sale of the used car for cash at a "sacrifice" price of $1,250. Ignore interest and carrying charges.

Ex 15-7   Coronado Corporation sells merchandise on three-year installment sales contracts. On February 28, Year 5, the end of Coronado's first fiscal year, the pre-tax results of operations are summarized below:

Sales $1,000,000
Cost of goods sold   700,000
Operating expenses   80,000

The balance of the Installment Contracts Receivable account on February 28, Year 5, was $600,000. No allowance for doubtful contracts receivable was required.

Prepare a journal entry to record federal and provincial income taxes on February 28, Year 5, assuming that Coronado accounts for sales on the accrual basis of accounting for financial accounting and on the installment basis of accounting for income taxes. Assume a combined federal and provincial income tax rate of 45%.

Ex 15-8   For financial accounting, Holland Company uses the accrual basis of accounting for installment sales; for income taxes, it uses the installment method of accounting. Holland has no other differences between pre-tax accounting income and taxable income. For the fiscal year ended November 30, Year 2, Holland's pre-tax accounting income was $500,000; its combined federal and provincial income tax rates totaled 60%. The income tax accounting records show total deferred gross profit on installment sales on November 30, Year 1, of $80,000 and on November 30, Year 2, of $120,000.

Prepare the journal entry or entries to record Holland's income taxes expense for the year ended November 30, Year 2.

Ex 15-9 The Consignment Out account in the accounting records of Rogers Company for Year 1 appears below:

Consignment Out — Bend Sales Company

Date	Explanation	Debit	Credit	Balance
	Shipped 20 units	3,200		3,200 dr
	Freight costs paid by consignor	260		3,460 dr
	Unpacking costs incurred by consignee	100		3,560 dr
	Commission on sale of 12 units	360		3,920 dr
	Selling price of 12 units		3,600	320 dr

Rogers debited the Consignment Out account for all costs relating to the consignment and credited the account for the full selling price of units sold. Cash of $3,140 was received from the consignee.

a Prepare a journal entry in the accounting records of the consignor to correct the Consignments Out account at the end of Year 1, assuming that consignment profits are determined separately. (Show computations.)

b Prepare the journal entries that would appear in the accounting records of the consignee, assuming that consignment profits are determined separately. The consignee sold the units for cash and made remittance in full to the consignor at the end of Year 1.

Ex 15-10 Dan Thomas consigns radios to retailers, debiting Accounts Receivable for the retail sales price of the radios consigned and crediting Sales. All costs relating to consigned radios are debited to expenses of the current accounting period. Net remittances from consignees are credited to Accounts Receivable.

In December, 500 radios costing $60 a unit and retailing for $100 a unit were consigned to Sunset Shop. Freight costs of $1,100 were debited to Freight Expense by the consignor. On December 31, Sunset Shop remitted $35,550 to Dan Thomas, in full settlement to date; Accounts Receivable was credited for this amount. The consignee deducted a commission of $10 on each radio sold and $450 for delivering the radios sold.

a Compute the number of radios sold by Sunset Shop, the consignee.

b Prepare a single correcting journal entry required in the accounting records of the consignor on December 31, assuming that the accounting records are still open, that the perpetual inventory system is used, and that profits on consignments are determined separately by use of separate revenue and expense accounts. Allocate costs between radios sold and radios on hand.

Ex 15-11 Information relating to regular sales and consignment sales of Jewelry Products for the year ended June 30, Year 6, follows:

	Regular sales	Consignment sales	Total
Sales	$120,000	$30,000	$150,000
Cost of goods sold	84,000	26,000	110,000
Operating expenses	?	1,760	16,910

Income taxes expense is 20% of pre-tax accounting income.

You ascertain that merchandise costing $6,500 is in the possession of consignees and is included in cost of consignment merchandise sold. Operating expenses of $15,150 (more than half of which are fixed) are to be allocated to regular sales and to consignment sales on the basis of volume. The $1,760 of operating expenses relating to consignment sales includes a commission of 5% and $260 of costs incurred by consignees relating to the entire shipment costing $26,000.

Prepare an income statement showing the net income on regular sales, consignment sales, and total sales in separate columns. Advise management of Jewelry Products whether it should continue to sell on a consignment basis.

CASES

Case 15-1 Janice Denson and Tyrone Awan, professional accountants, are attempting to develop the management advisory services segment of their practice. One of the firm's income tax clients, Zorro Corporation, affords an opportunity for work along this line. Zorro, a manufacturer of machinery, in the past has sold its products through wholesalers and also directly to some large retail outlets.

During a telephone conversation on income tax matters between the president of Zorro and Janice Denson, the president posed the following question: "We are considering making sales of our products on a consignment basis as well as through our present outlets; would it be feasible to establish an accounting system that would show separately the net income we earned on consignment sales? I don't have time to discuss it now, but write me a memo and let me have your reactions."

Instructions   Prepare a memo that Janice Denson might write to the president of Zorro Corporation, making any assumptions you consider necessary and summarizing the issues involved and the alternatives available.

Case 15-2 Sound Delight sells stereo equipment and maintains its accounting records on a calendar-year basis. On October 1, Year 1, Sound Delight sold a stereo set to Hermine Pak. Cost of the set was $800, and the selling price was $1,200. A down payment of $300 was received along with a contract calling for the payment of $50 on the first day of each month for the next 18 months. No interest or carrying charge was added to the contract. Hermine Pak paid the monthly installments promptly on November 1 and December 1, Year 1. She also made seven payments in Year 2 but then defaulted on the contract. Sound Delight repossessed the set on November 1, Year 2.

Instructions
a State three different amounts that might be reported as realized income from this transaction for Year 1, and indicate the circumstances under which each of the three amounts might be acceptable.
b Without regard to income tax considerations, which of the three amounts do you believe has the strongest support from a theoretical standpoint? Which has the weakest support? Explain.
c If the stereo set repossessed on November 1, Year 2, has a wholesale value of $200 and a retail value of $300, prepare a journal entry to record the repossession under the installment method of accounting. Explain fully the reasoning applicable to the journal entry. Assume that an allowance for doubtful installment contracts is not used.

Case 15-3 Teakwood Sales Company sells furniture on the installment plan. For its income tax returns, it reports gross profit from sales under the installment method of accounting. For financial accounting, it considers the entire gross profit to be earned in the year of sale.

Instructions

a Discuss the relative merits of the two methods of reporting gross profit.

b Explain the installment method of accounting used for income tax purposes.

c Discuss the effects of the concurrent use of these two bases of accounting by Teakwood Sales Company on its annual net income. What recommendation would you make to the company to produce an income statement in accordance with generally accepted accounting principles?

Case 15-4 Hungry Bear sells franchises to independent operators. The contract with the franchisee includes the following provisions:

(1) The franchisee is charged an initial fee of $30,000. Of this amount $5,000 is payable when the contract is signed, and a $5,000 noninterest-bearing promissory note is payable at the end of each of the five subsequent years.

(2) All the initial franchise fee collected by the franchisor is to be refunded and the remaining obligation cancelled if, for any reason, the franchisee fails to open the franchise.

(3) In return for the initial franchise fee, the franchisor agrees to (1) assist the franchisee in selecting the location for the business, (2) negotiate the lease for the land, (3) obtain financing and assist with building design, (4) supervise construction, (5) establish accounting and income tax records, and (6) provide advice over a five-year period relating to such matters as employee and management training, quality control, and product promotion.

(4) In addition to the initial franchise fee, the franchisee is required to pay to Hungry Bear a monthly fee of 2% of sales for menu planning, recipe innovations, and the privilege of purchasing ingredients from Hungry Bear at or below prevailing market prices.

Management of Hungry Bear estimates that the value of the services rendered to the franchisee at the time the contract is signed amounts to at least $5,000. All franchisees to date have opened their locations at the scheduled time, and none has defaulted on any of the notes receivable.

The credit ratings of all franchisees would entitle them to borrow at the current interest rate of 10%. The present value of an ordinary annuity of five annual rents of $5,000 each discounted at 10% is $18,954.

Instructions

a Discuss the alternative methods that Hungry Bear might use to account for the initial franchise fee; evaluate each method by applying generally accepted accounting principles to this situation; and prepare illustrative journal entries for each method. Assume that a Discount on Notes Receivable account is used.

b Given the nature of the contract with franchisees, when should revenue be recognized by Hungry Bear? Discuss the question of revenue realization for both the initial franchise fee and the additional monthly fee of 2% of sales, and prepare illustrative journal entries for both types of revenue.

c Assume that Hungry Bear sells some franchises for $40,000, which includes $10,000 for the rental of equipment for its economic life of ten years, that $15,000 of the fee is payable immediately and the balance on noninterest-bearing promissory notes at $5,000 a year; that no portion of the $10,000 rental payment is refundable in case the franchisee goes out of business; and that title to the equipment remains with the franchisor. What would be the preferable method of accounting for the rental portion of the initial franchise fee? Explain.

PROBLEMS

15-1 Thompson Technologies, Inc., sells computers. On January 2, Year 5, Thompson entered into an installment sale contract with Andersen Company for a seven-year period expiring December 31, Year 11. Equal annual payments under the installment contract are $1,000,000 and are due on January 2. The first payment was made on January 2, Year 5.

Additional information is as follows:
(1) The cash selling price of the computer was $5,355,000. ($1,000,000 × 5.355 present value of annuity due of 7 rents of 1 at 10% = $5,355,000.)
(2) The cost of the computer was $4,284,000.
(3) Interest relating to the installment period amounted to $1,645,000, based on a stated (and appropriate) interest rate of 10%. For income tax purposes, Thompson uses the accrual basis of accounting for recording interest revenue.
(4) Circumstances are such that the collection of the installment contract receivable is reasonably assured.
(5) The installment sale qualified for the installment method of accounting for income tax purposes.
(6) The income tax rate for Thompson is 45%.

Instructions
a Compute the pre-tax accounting income (loss) that Thompson should record for financial accounting as a result of this transaction for the year ended December 31, Year 5. Compute interest revenue for a full year and show supporting computations.
b Compute the amount of deferred income taxes, if any, that Thompson should record for financial accounting as a result of this transaction for the year ended December 31, Year 5. Show supporting computations.
c Prepare a journal entry to record income taxes expense on December 31, Year 5, as a result of this transaction. Ignore any expenses other than cost of goods sold.

15-2 Mojave Company accounts for its retail sales of recreational land under the installment method of accounting because the collection of contracts **is not reasonably assured**. The balances in the accounts for installment contracts receivable at the beginning and end of Year 10 were:

	January 1, Year 10	December 31, Year 10
Installment contracts receivable — Year 8 (sales and cost of goods sold for Year 8 were $600,000 and $480,000, respectively)	$420,000	$320,000
Installment contracts receivable — Year 9 (sales and cost of goods sold for Year 9 were $675,000 and $526,500, respectively)	595,000	470,000
Installment contracts receivable — Year 10 (sales and cost of goods sold for Year 10 were $920,000 and $690,000, respectively)		800,000

The company opened for business early in Year 8 and sells the land on 60-month contracts.

An allowance for doubtful contracts is not used. Interest and carrying charges are included in the selling price and in the computation of the yearly gross profit rates.

Upon default in payment by customers in Year 10, the company repossessed land that had a current fair value on the date of repossession of $3,800; in recording the repossession, the company debited Inventories and credited Installment Contracts Receivable — Year 8 for $3,800. The sale of the land had been made in Year 8 for $10,000, and $4,000 had been collected prior to the default.

Instructions

a Prepare a journal entry to record the total realized gross profit for the year ended December 31, Year 10.

b Prepare any correcting journal entries required as a result of the incorrect treatment of the repossession of land in Year 10.

15-3 Mod, Inc., a new department store, plans to use the installment method of recognizing gross profit on installment sales for income tax purposes. Under this method, the expected 40% gross profit on sales will be recognized only as cash payments are received; this serves to postpone until future accounting periods taxable income equal to 40% of the year-end balance in installment contracts receivable. Because collection of the full sales price *is reasonably assured*, for financial accounting Mod recognizes the entire gross profit at the time sales are made. The following information has been developed as a part of the company's income-planning activities.

	Year 1	Year 2	Year 3	Year 4	Year 5
Expected installment sales	$1,000,000	$1,500,000	$1,800,000	$2,000,000	$2,000,000
Expected installment contracts					
receivable balances at year-end	200,000	400,000	500,000	550,000	525,000
Gross profit to be recognized:					
In accounting records	400,000	600,000	720,000	800,000	800,000
In income tax returns	320,000	520,000	680,000	?	?

Instructions

a Compute the two missing items in the summary above.

b Compute the balances that should appear in the Deferred Income Tax Liability account at the end of each of the five years, assuming an income tax rate of 45%. State how these balances should be classified in the balance sheet (remember the defined relationship between current assets and the operating cycle).

c Assume that Mod's projections show income before income taxes of $220,000 in Year 1 and $350,000 in Year 5. Prepare partial income statements for these two years (as if the projected events had actually occurred), showing in the statement or accompanying notes the provisions for current and deferred income taxes.

d Assume that, at the beginning of Year 6, Mod decided to stop selling on the installment plan, and that by the end of the year all installment contracts receivable had been collected. If income before income taxes for Year 6 is assumed to be $400,000, prepare a journal entry to record Mod's income taxes for Year 6.

15-4 Newport Sales Company started operations in Year 1. It sells merchandise on the installment plan and on regular 30-day open accounts. Activities for Year 1 are summarized below:

Regular sales	$360,000
Installment sales, including $90,000 deferred interest and carrying	
charges	690,000
Cost of regular sales	203,000
Cost of installment sales	360,000
Operating expenses	177,000
Collections on regular sales	310,000
Collections on installment sales, including $30,000 interest and carrying	
charges, all of which were earned in Year 1	255,000

Newport Sales uses the perpetual inventory system and does not include interest and carrying charges in the computation of gross profit on installment sales. Income taxes are levied at 45% of taxable income.

Instructions
a Prepare journal entries to record all transactions and adjustments for Year 1, using only the information given in the problem. Assume that the accrual basis of accounting is used for financial accounting and the installment method is used for income tax purposes. Accrued interest and carrying charges at the end of Year 1 may be ignored. Closing entries are not required.
b Prepare journal entries to record all transactions for Year 1 (including the establishment of deferred gross profit and adjusting entries), using only the information given in the problem. Assume that the installment method of accounting is used both for financial accounting and for income tax purposes. Closing entries are not required.

15-5 Art Company derives a major part of its revenue from sales made by consignees throughout Canada. The company determines profits on consignment sales by the use of separate sales, cost of goods sold, and expense accounts. Under the perpetual inventory system designed by the company's accountant, all costs relating to consigned merchandise initially are recorded in the Inventory on Consignment account. During the last quarter of Year 1, the following transactions were completed with Peter Jason, a new consignee in Windsor:

Oct. 2   Consigned 25 lathes costing $12,000, and paid $500 shipping costs.
Nov. 28   Sent a mechanic to Windsor to install safety devices on 10 lathes that had not yet been sold. The costs of this alteration were: parts from inventories, $60; cash expenditures, $40.
Dec. 31   Received an account sales as follows:

Sales: 20 lathes @ $950		$19,000
Charges: Commission (15% of $19,000)	$2,850	
Advertising	95	
Delivery and installation costs on 20		
lathes sold	140	3,085
Balance (cheque no. 1269 enclosed)		$15,915

Instructions
a Prepare a working paper for Art Company showing the allocation of costs and expenses to lathes sold by Jason and to the consignment inventories at the end of Year 1.
b Prepare journal entries for Art Company to record the transactions with Jason, including a journal entry to record the cost of consignment sales on December 31, Year 1.

15-6 Ken Cable sells tables for Rosewood, Inc., on a consignment basis. The ledger account at the top of page 642 for Ken Cable summarizes consignment activities for the month of May.

The cost of the tables for Rosewood, Inc., was $1,440 each. The accounting policies of Rosewood provide for a separate determination of profits on consigned tables as distinguished from profits on direct sales. Rosewood uses the perpetual inventory system and also maintains a separate Consignment Out account for each consignee. All costs applicable to a consignment of tables are debited to the Consignment Out account. When sales are reported by a consignee, the gross sales

Consignment In — Rosewood, Inc.

Date	Explanation	Debit	Credit	Balance
May 4	Memorandum entry: Received 10 tables			
4	Freight and insurance paid	370		370 dr
31	Delivery costs of 6 tables sold	240		610 dr
31	Sale of 6 tables		14,544	13,934 cr
31	Commission revenue realized	2,180		11,754 cr
31	Storage charges for 4 unsold tables	72		11,682 cr
31	Remittance to consignor	4,682		7,000 cr

price is credited to Consignment Sales. The Consignment Out account then is credited for the cost of the units sold, and this amount is transferred (debited) to a Cost of Consignment Sales account.

Instructions

a Prepare all journal entries required in the accounting records of the consignor Rosewood, Inc., during the month of May. The tables were shipped to Ken Cable on May 1.

b Construct the Consignment Out ledger account for Rosewood, Inc., relating to the transactions with Ken Cable, showing all journal entries during the month of May.

c How should the month-end balances in the Consignment Out and Consignment In accounts appear in the financial statements of the consignor (Rosewood, Inc., and the consignee (Ken Cable), respectively, on May 31?

15-7 Valleyview Corporation sold a parcel of undeveloped land on December 31, Year 1 for "a consideration of $318,611." The land had a carrying amount of $179,997 in the accounting records of Valleyview. The consideration received consisted of the following:

Cash down payment, Dec. 31, Year 1	$ 51,310
Three promissory notes of $100,000 each with payments starting Dec. 31, Year 2, including interest at an annual rate of 6% (present value of an ordinary annuity of three rents of 1 at 6% = 2.673012)	267,301
Total consideration received	$318,611

You conclude that 10% is a more reasonable rate of interest and that the current fair value of the three promissory notes should be computed as follows:

Annual payments due on three notes	$100,000
Present value of ordinary annuity of three rents of $1 discounted at 10%	2.486852
Current fair value of notes	$248,685

The notes were recorded by Valleyview Corporation at current fair value on a 10%-yield basis without the use of a Discount on Notes Receivable account. The gain realized each year on this transaction should be recorded net of a 25% income tax rate applicable to capital gains.

Instructions

a Assuming that the installment method of accounting is used for this transaction, both for financial accounting and for income tax purposes, prepare journal entries to record all transactions through Year 4. Round all computations to nearest dollar.

b Assuming that the installment method of accounting is used to report the gain for income tax purposes and that the accrual basis is used for financial accounting, prepare journal entries to record all transactions from December 31, Year 1, through December 31, Year 4.

15-8 On January 2, Year 5, Homeowners, Inc., entered into a contract with a manufacturer to purchase air conditioners and to sell the units on the installment plan with collections over 30 months, with no separately identified interest or carrying charge.

For income tax purposes, Homeowners elected to report income from its sales of air conditioners under the installment method of accounting.

Purchases and sales of new units were as follows:

| | Units purchased | | Units sold | |
	Quantity	Price (each)	Quantity	Price (each)
Year 5	4,800	$100	4,000	$150
Year 6	7,200	90	8,000	140
Year 7	3,200	105	2,800	143

Cash receipts on installment contracts receivable were as follows:

| | Cash receipts | | |
	Year 5	Year 6	Year 7
Year 5 sales	$120,000	$240,000	$240,000
Year 6 sales		280,000	460,000
Year 7 sales			100,000

In Year 7, 160 units from the Year 6 sales were repossessed and sold for $90 each on the installment plan. At the time of repossession, $4,800 had been collected from the original purchasers, and the units had a current fair value of $10,080.

Operating expenses for Year 7 were $200,000. No charge has been made against current revenue for the applicable insurance expense under a three-year policy expiring June 30, Year 8, costing $9,600, and for an advance payment of $40,000 on a new contract to purchase air conditioners beginning January 2, Year 8.

Instructions Assuming that the weighted-average method is used for determining the cost of inventories, including repossessed air conditioners, prepare working papers to compute the following:

a (1) The cost of goods sold on the installment plan for each year

  (2) The weighted-average unit cost of goods sold on the installment plan for each year

b The gross profit percentages for each year

c The gain or loss on repossessions in Year 7

d The taxable income from installment sales for Year 7

15-9 Lei Corporation sells a limited number of its products through consignees. In the spring of Year 1, Lei arranged to sell outboard motors through a consignee, Ernie's. The motors were to be sold by the consignee at a price of $300 each, and the consignee was allowed a 15% commission on gross selling price. The consignee agreed to guarantee the accounts receivable and to remit all collections less the commission on consignment accounts receivable collected. The consignee also was allowed to deduct certain reimbursable costs; these costs were chargeable to the consignor as incurred. Both the consignor and the consignee maintain perpetual inventory records.

Transactions relating to the consignment during the first six months of year were as follows:

Consignor's (Lei Corporation's) transactions:

Apr. 10	Shipped 90 motors to consignee; cost of each motor, $180.
	Total packing costs paid for shipment, $360
June 30	Received account sales from consignee and cheque for $12,765.

Consignee's (Ernie's) transactions:

Apr. 15	Received 90 motors and paid freight charges, $450.
May 1–June 23	Sold 60 motors and collected $15,600.
June 2	Paid $45 for minor repairs on six motors sold.
June 30	Mailed account sales to consignor with a cheque for $12,765.

Instructions

a Prepare all journal entries in the accounting records of Lei Corporation and in the accounting records of Ernie's, assuming that both enterprises report profits on consignment sales separately. Closing journal entries are not required.

b Prepare all journal entries in the accounting records of Lei Corporation and in the accounting records of Ernie's, assuming that consignment sales are combined with regular sales. Closing journal entries are not required.

c Would the balance of the Consignment In account maintained by Ernie's be the same amount on June 30 under the differing assumptions in *a* and *b* above? What is the balance in the Consignment In account, and how is it reported in the balance sheet of Ernie's on June 30?

15-10 Hilo Sales Corporation began operations on January 2, Year 1. All sales of new merchandise are made on installment contracts. Because of the risks of noncollection Hilo Sales recognizes profit from the sale of new merchandise under the installment method of accounting and employs the periodic inventory system. The following information was taken from the accounting records of Hilo Sales on December 31 for the years indicated:

	Year 2	Year 1
Installment contracts receivable:		
Year 1 sales	$ 17,300	$ 40,000
Year 2 sales	56,000	
Cash sales of trade-ins	20,500	
Installment sales	310,000	221,000
Purchases	176,700	170,180
Inventories of new merchandise, Jan. 1	42,000	
Operating expenses	59,296	53,700
Uncollectible installment contracts expense	9,900	

Your audit for the year ended December 31, Year 2, disclosed the following:

(1) The inventories of new and repossessed merchandise on hand on December 31 Year 2, were $35,882 and $4,650, respectively.

(2) When a customer defaults on a contract, the repossessed merchandise is recorded at its approximate wholesale market value in a separate inventory account.

Differences between the unpaid balance on the contract and the wholesale value are debited to the Uncollectible Installment Contracts Expense account. Repossessed merchandise is sold on the installment plan.

(3) The wholesale value of repossessed merchandise is determined as follows:
    (a) Merchandise repossessed during year of sale is valued at 40% of original selling price.
    (b) Merchandise repossessed subsequent to the year of sale is valued at 20% of original selling price.

(4) There were no defaulted installment contracts during Year 1. An analysis of installment contracts defaulted and written off during Year 2 follows:

	Original selling price	Unpaid contract balance
Year 1 contracts	$19,500	$10,500
Year 2 contracts	11,000	8,200

(5) On January 1, Year 2, Hilo Sales began granting allowances on merchandise traded in as part payment on new sales. During Year 2, Hilo Sales granted trade-in allowances of $22,600. The wholesale market value of traded-in merchandise was $15,800. All merchandise traded in during the year was sold for cash.

(6) Hilo Sales uses the installment method of accounting for merchandise sold on the installment plan, both for financial accounting and for income tax purposes. The income tax rate is 20%.

Instructions

a Compute the amounts of deferred gross profit on installment sales on December 31, Year 1 and Year 2. Include a supporting computation of the gross profit percentage on installment sales for each year.

b Compute the adjustment (if any) that you would recommend for the Uncollectible Installment Contracts Expense account on December 31, Year 2.

c Prepare an income statement (showing cash sales, installment sales, and total sales) for the year ended December 31, Year 2. A total of 20,000 shares of a single class of capital stock is outstanding. The following supporting exhibits should be prepared:
    (1) Unrealized gross profit on Year 2 installment sales
    (2) Realized gross profit on Year 1 installment sales
    (3) Realized gross profit on sales of traded-in merchandise

16 ACCOUNTING FOR INTERNATIONAL OPERATIONS

Many Canadian companies carry on business in foreign countries. For some foreign business involvement is limited to importing and/or exporting transactions. Others, however, are more heavily involved with foreign operations and are called *multinational enterprises* because they carry on business in more than one nation through a network of branches, divisions, influenced investees, joint ventures, and subsidiaries. Multinational enterprises obtain raw material and capital in countries where such resources are plentiful. Multinational enterprises manufacture their products in nations where wages and other operating costs are lowest, and they sell their products in countries that provide the most profitable markets. There are a number of large enterprises headquartered in Canada, that either are multinationals, or are involved in significant export/import operations. Among these companies are MacMillan Bloedel Limited, Massey-Ferguson Ltd., Inter-City Gas Corporation, Inco Limited, and Loblaw Companies Limited.

In this chapter, we discuss the three principal accounting and reporting issues of enterprises with international operations — uniformity in international accounting standards, accounting for transactions involving foreign currencies, and the translation of the financial statements of foreign subsidiaries, investees, or branches.

UNIFORMITY IN INTERNATIONAL ACCOUNTING STANDARDS

The variety of accounting standards and practices among the nations of the world has been a substantial problem for multinational enterprises. Recently, however, significant efforts have been made to achieve uniformity in international accounting and auditing standards. The following summary describes these efforts:[1]

> The rapid growth in international activities by enterprises has led to a need and demand for international standards of financial accounting and reporting. A variety of private sector and governmental standard-setting organizations has developed to satisfy these needs and demands.

Five major international standard-setting organizations have emerged as leaders in this endeavour. The five organizations are as follows:

The International Accounting Standards Committee (IASC)   IASC is a private voluntary organization formed in 1973 by leading accounting professional bodies from various countries. IASC concentrates on issuing financial accounting standards on specific problems which are similar in format to those issued by the Financial Accounting Standards Board. To date, IASC has issued thirteen Statements of International Accounting Standards and has issued six other Exposure Drafts. The Statements cover topics such as inventories, consolidated financial statements, depreciation accounting, research and development and income taxes. The Exposure Drafts include accounting for foreign currency translation, segments, pensions, changing prices, property, plant and equipment, and leases. IASC has no authority, but must rely on its member organizations (such as the CICA in Canada) who have pledged to use their best efforts to have the international standards adopted by the respective national authoritative standard-setting bodies.

The International Federation of Accountants (IFAC)   IFAC is a private voluntary organization comprised of 75 professional accounting organizations from 57 countries. IFAC concerns itself with auditing and other professional matters, such as ethics and education, that would lead to the development and enhancement of a coordinated worldwide accounting profession. IFAC has seven standing committees; the auditing practices committee has issued three International Audit Guidelines and four other Exposure Drafts. IFAC has no authority other than that which is self-imposed by the member organizations.

The European Economic Community (EEC)   The EEC, also known as the Common Market, is a supra-government organization. Its authority is governmental, but is restricted to the ten member countries: France, West Germany, Italy, the United Kingdom, Belgium, Denmark, Greece, Ireland, Luxembourg and the Netherlands. EEC directives are addressed to and are binding on the Member States who must bring the Directives into national laws within specified periods. Eight Directives impinging on accounting reports and related matters have been issued to date. The most important of these is the Fourth Directive which deals with corporate powers, mergers, stock exchanges and listing requirements, and protection of employees in the event of employer insolvency. Six proposed Directives have also been issued, the most important of which is the amended proposed Seventh Directive dealing with consolidated statements. Other proposed Directives deal with corporate management, auditor qualifications, interim statements and employee information and consultation.

The United Nations Commission on Transnational Corporations   This Commission is an arm of the United Nations (UN). As such, it is a quasi-governmental organization with worldwide participation. The Commission reports to the UN Economic and Social Council; its accounting standard setting work is assigned to a

---

1 Deloitte Haskins & Sells, *The Week in Review* (Feb. 20, 1981), pp. 3–4.

"Working Group of Experts" which has 34 members from UN countries. The Working Group of Experts has broad objectives for (a) the development of a comprehensive information system designed to determine the effects of transnational corporation on home and host countries, to contribute to national goals and worldwide economic growth, and to aid the negotiating capacity of host countries, and (b) development of a code of conduct for transnational corporations. Only two reports have been issued by the UN pertaining to accounting and related matters. One essential presented extended lists of minimum requirements for the disclosure of accounting and financial information, the other dealt with minimum information to be made available by corporations designed to improve understanding of the structure, activities, and policies of the corporation as a whole. Six background papers have also been prepared. The work of the UN Commission is strongly influenced by a perceived desire (a) to aid Member countries, especially those from the developing countries, in coping with transnational corporations, (b) to help the Member countries in their economic development, and (c) to assist and protect employees of transnational corporations.

The Organization for Economic Cooperation and Development (OECD) The OECD is an intergovernmental organization of 24 countries formed in 1960; includes most of Western Europe and the Commonwealth countries, Japan, and the United States. The OECD is an outgrowth of the Organization for European Economic Cooperation established in 1948 under the Marshall Plan. In 1975, OECD formed committee on International Investment and Multinational Enterprises; the Committee will offer Guidelines that establish standards for the activities of multinational enterprises including Guidelines on disclosure of information, competition, financing taxation, and employment and industrial relations. Guidelines are voluntary and not legally enforceable, but the governments of the Member countries have agreed to recommend the observance of the Guidelines. Like the UN, the objectives of OECD are broader than financial reporting: they include economic growth and social progress objectives, regulation of entry of foreign enterprises and furtherance of world trade.

Of the five organizations described in the foregoing paragraphs, the IASC with its membership of professional accounting organizations of more than 40 countries, is the most active in the setting of accounting standards However, because it lacks authority to prescribe accounting standards, as the Accounting Standards Committee does in Canada, the accounting standards developed by the IASC are not certain of being used by all member countries of the IASC. For example, ***Handbook Section 1501*** indicates that the Accounting Standards Committee will review IASC standards to see if the Handbook should be revised. Until revisions are made, existing Canadian standards will prevail, and the degree of conformity with IASC standards should be disclosed.

ACCOUNTING FOR TRANSACTIONS INVOLVING FOREIGN CURRENCIES

In most countries, a foreign country's currency is treated as though it were *commodity*, or a *money-market instrument*, and the price paid is called the *exchange rate*. In Canada, for example, foreign currencies are bought and sold by the international banking departments of commercial banks These foreign currency transactions are entered into on behalf of the bank multinational enterprise customers, and for the bank's own account.

The buying and selling of foreign currencies as though they were commodities result in variations in the *exchange rate* between the currencies of two countries. For example, a daily newspaper quoted the selected exchange rates shown below.

The first rates quoted for each country's currency are *selling spot rates* charged by the bank for current sales of the foreign currency. The bank's

FOREIGN EXCHANGE

Country	Canadian dollar equivalent	Currency per Canadian dollar
Australia (Dollar)	0.9669	1.0342
Austria (Schilling)	0.0694	14.4092
Belgium (Franc)	0.0241	41.4938
Britain (Pound)	1.8861	0.5302
1 Month Forward	1.8818	0.5314
2 Months Forward	1.8787	0.5323
3 Months Forward	1.8763	0.5330
6 Months Forward	1.8721	0.5342
12 Months Forward	1.8666	0.5357
Chile (Peso)	0.0077	129.8701
Cyprus (Pound)	2.3586	0.4240
Denmark (Krone)	0.1347	7.4239
Egypt (Pound)	1.0774	0.9282
France (Franc)	0.1594	6.2735
Germany (Deutsche Mark)	0.4875	2.0513
1 Month Forward	0.4887	2.0462
3 Months Forward	0.4930	2.0284
Hong Kong (Dollar)	0.1745	5.7307
India (Rupee)	0.1142	8.7566
Italy (Lira)	0.00073	1369.8630
Japan (Yen)	0.00572	174.8252
Lebanon (Pound)	0.0798	12.5313
Mexico (Peso)	0.00408	245.0980
Netherlands (Guilder)	0.4337	2.3057
Norway (Krone)	0.1652	6.0532
Pakistan (Rupee)	0.8618	1.1604
Sweden (Krona)	0.1637	6.1087
Taiwan (Dollar)	0.0335	29.8507
Venezuela (Bolivar)	0.0966	10.3519
United States (Dollar)	1.3574	0.7367
1 Month Forward	1.3586	0.7361
2 Months Forward	1.3597	0.7354
3 Months Forward	1.3609	0.7348
6 Months Forward	1.3649	0.7326
12 Months Forward	1.3698	0.7300

buying spot rate for the currency typically is less than the selling sp
rate; the *agio* (or *spread*) between the selling and buying spot rat
represents gross profit to a trader in foreign currency.

In our discussions of rates in subsequent sections of this chapter we w
generally refer only to a single spot rate. If a company is purchasing forei
currency the spot rate used will be the bank's selling rate. Conversely, if tl
company is selling foreign currency the spot rate used will be the bank
buying rate.

The "1 month forward" and comparable exchange rates in the illustratic
on page 649 are *forward rates*, which apply to foreign currency transa
tions to be consummated at a future date. Forward rates apply to *forwar
exchange contracts*, which are discussed in a subsequent section of th
chapter.

To illustrate the application of exchange rates, assume that a Canadi₤
multinational enterprise required £10,000 (10,000 British pounds). At tl
selling exchange rate, the Canadian multinational enterprise would p₤
$18,861 (£10,000 × $1.8861 = $18,861) for the 10,000 British pounds

Factors influencing fluctuations in exchange rates include a nation's b₤
ance of payments surplus or deficit, differing global rates of inflation, mone
market variations (such as interest rates) in individual countries, capit
investment levels, and monetary actions of central banks of various nation

Handbook Section 1650

In July 1983, the CICA issued *Handbook Section 1650*, "Foreign Currenc
Translation," in which it established uniform accounting standards for m₤
ters involving foreign currencies. In the following sections, we discuss tl
accounting standards established by the CICA for foreign currency transa
tions such as purchases and sales of merchandise and forward exchan₤
contracts.

Transactions involving foreign currencies

A multinational enterprise headquartered in Canada engages in sale
purchases, and loans with independent foreign enterprises as well as wit
its branches, divisions, influenced investees, or subsidiaries in other countrie
If the transactions with independent foreign enterprises are consummated i
terms of the Canadian dollar, no accounting problems arise for the Canadi₤
multinational enterprise. The sale, purchase, or loan transaction is recorde
in dollars in the accounting records of the Canadian enterprise; the ind₤
pendent foreign enterprise must obtain the dollars necessary to comple₤
the transaction through the foreign exchange department of its bank.

Often, however, the transactions described above are negotiated an₤
settled in terms of the foreign enterprise's *local currency units* (LCU). I
such circumstances, the Canadian enterprise must account for the transa₤
tion denominated in foreign currency in terms of Canadian dollars. Th
accounting for *foreign currency transactions* is accomplished by appl₤
ing the appropriate exchange rate between the foreign currency and th
Canadian dollar.

When hedging is not involved, **Section 1650** requires the recording of foreign currency transactions in Canadian dollars using the **spot rate** in effect on **the date of the transactions**. Any foreign currency receivables or payables, not settled by a subsequent balance sheet date, are to be reported at the equivalent amount of Canadian dollars which is obtained by translating the receivable or payable at the current rate on the date of the balance sheet.

> "At each balance sheet date, monetary items denominated in a foreign currency should be adjusted to reflect the exchange rate in effect at the balance sheet date." **(1650.16)**

Adjusting the receivables or payables as at the date of the balance sheet will result in **gains or losses** if there has been a **change** in the exchange rate.

Section 1650 adopted the two-transaction perspective (to be illustrated later), and requires that gains or losses be taken into the **current year's income**, except in situations where the monetary items have a fixed life and will be collected or paid more than one year beyond the date of the balance sheet. In this case the gains and losses are **deferred and amortized** over the current and future years. The handling of gains and losses on current monetary items will be illustrated first, followed by an illustration showing the deferral and amortization of gains or losses on noncurrent monetary items.

Current Monetary Items   To illustrate, assume that on April 18, Year 6, Worldwide Corporation Ltd. purchased merchandise from a West German supplier at a cost of 100,000 deutsche marks (DM). The April 18, Year 6, spot rate was DM1 = $0.45. Because Worldwide was a customer of good credit standing, the West German supplier made the sale on 30-day open account.

Assuming that Worldwide uses the perpetual inventory system, it records the April 18, Year 6, purchase as follows:

Journal entry for purchase of merchandise from West German supplier

Inventories	*45,000*	
Accounts Payable		*45,000*

To record purchase on 30-day open account from West German
supplier for DM 100,000, translated at spot rate of DM1 = $0.45
(DM 100,000 × $0.45 = $45,000).

The spot rate used in the journal entry was the selling rate, because it was the rate at which the liability to the West German supplier could have been settled on April 18, Year 6.

Transaction gains and losses

During the period that the account payable to the West German supplier remains unpaid, the spot rate for deutsche marks may change. If the spot

rate *decreases*, Worldwide will realize a *transaction gain*; if the sp
rate *increases*, Worldwide will incur a *transaction loss*. Transactic
gains and losses on current items are included in the determination of n
income for the accounting period in which the spot rate changes.

To illustrate, assume that on April 30, Year 6, the spot rate for deutsch
marks was DM1 = $0.446, and Worldwide prepares financial statemen
monthly. The accountant for Worldwide records the following journal ent:
with respect to the account payable to the West German supplier:

Journal entry to record transaction gain on date financial statements are prepared

Accounts Payable		400
Transaction Gains and Losses		4(

To record transaction gain applicable to April 18, Year 6, purchase from
West German supplier, as follows:

Liability recorded on Apr. 18, Year 6	$45,000	
Less: Liability translated at Apr. 30, Year 6, spot rate		
DM1 = $0.446 (DM 100,000 × $0.446 = $44,600)	44,600	
Transaction gain	$ 400	

Assume further that the spot rate on May 18, Year 6, was DM1 = $0.4
The May 18, Year 6, journal entry for Worldwide's payment of the liabili
to the West German supplier is given below.

Journal entry for payment of liability to West German supplier

Accounts Payable	44,600	
Transaction Gains and Losses		6(
Cash		44,0(

To record payment for DM 100,000 draft to settle liability to West
German supplier, and recognition of transaction gain (DM 100,000 ×
$0.44 = $44,000).

Two-Transaction Perspective and One-Transaction Perspective Th
journal entries above and on page 651 reflect the *two-transaction pei*
spective for viewing a foreign trade transaction. Under this concept, whic
was sanctioned by *Section 1650*, Worldwide's dealings with the We
German supplier essentially were *two separate transactions*. One tran
action was the purchase of the merchandise; the second transaction was th
acquisition of the foreign currency required to pay the liability for th
merchandise purchased. Supporters of the two-transaction perspective a
gue that an importer's or exporter's assumption of a risk of fluctuations i
the exchange rate for a foreign currency is a financial decision, not a me
chandising decision.

Advocates of an opposing viewpoint, the *one-transaction perspectiv*
maintain that Worldwide's total transaction gains of $1,000 ($400

$600 = \$1,000$) on its purchase from the West German supplier should be applied to reduce the cost of the merchandise purchased. Under this approach, Worldwide would not prepare a journal entry on April 30, Year 6, but would prepare the following journal entry on May 18, Year 6 (assuming that all the merchandise purchased on April 18 had been sold by May 18):

Journal entry under
one-transaction
perspective

Accounts Payable	45,000	
Cost of Goods Sold		1,000
Cash		44,000

Payment for DM 100,000 (DM 100,000 × $0.44 = $44,000) to settle liability to West German supplier, and allocation of resultant transaction gain to cost of goods sold.

In effect, supporters of the one-transaction perspective for foreign trade activities consider the original amount recorded for a foreign merchandise purchase as an **estimate**, subject to adjustment when the exact cash outlay required for the purchase is known. Thus, the one-transaction proponents emphasize the **cash-payment** aspect of the transaction, rather than the **bargained-price** aspect of the transaction.

The authors concur with the two-transaction perspective for foreign trade activities and for loans receivable and payable denominated in a foreign currency. The separability of the merchandising and financial aspects of a foreign trade transaction is an undeniable fact. In delaying payment of a foreign trade purchase transaction, an importer has made a decision to assume the risk of exchange rate fluctuations. This risk assumption is measured by the transaction gain or loss recorded at the time of payment for the purchase of merchandise (or on the dates of intervening financial statements). In a later section we will describe how this risk can be minimized through the use of forward exchange contracts.

Transaction gains and losses from noncurrent monetary items

As mentioned previously, Section 1650 requires that any **gains or losses** resulting from the translation of **noncurrent monetary items** denominated in a foreign currency be **deferred and amortized** in a rational and systematic manner over the remaining life of the monetary item. Because any change that occurred in exchange rates was an economic event that took place during the accounting period, the current period's income statement has to bear a portion of the amortization, and therefore the remaining life is measured from the **beginning of the period**.

Let us suppose that a Canadian company borrowed DM 20,000,000 from a German financial institution on January 1, Year 1. The loan carries an interest rate of 10% payable each December 31 and is to be repaid in four years.

The spot rates for deutsche marks over the life of the loan were as follow

Jan. 1, Year 1	$0.445
Dec. 31, Year 1	0.439
Dec. 31, Year 2	0.442
Dec. 31, Year 3	0.441
Dec. 31, Year 4	0.446

The Canadian company's Year 1 journal entries to record the transactior
would be as follows:

Jan. 1	Cash	8,900,000	
	Loan Payable		8,900,0C
	To record borrowing of DM 20,000,000		
	translated at a spot rate DM 1 = $0.445		
	(DM 20,000,000 × $0.445 = $8,900,000)		
Dec. 31	Interest expense	878,000	
	Cash		878,0C
	To record interest payment of DM 2,000,000		
	translated at Dec. 31, Year 1 spot rate		
	(DM 2,000,000 × $0.439 = $878,000)		
	Loan payable	120,000	
	Deferred transaction gains and losses		120,0C
	To calculate translation gain as follows:		
	Liability recorded Jan. 1	$8,900,000	
	Less: Liability translated at Dec. 31 spot rate:		
	DM 20,000,000 × $0.439	8,780,000	
	Transaction gain	$ 120,000	
	Deferred transaction gains and losses	30,000	
	Transaction gains and losses		30,0C
	To amortize Dec. 31, Year 1, transaction gain to		
	Year 1 income ($120,000 ÷ 4 years = $30,000)		

The journal entries for Years 2 to 4 are not illustrated. On Dec. 31 of eacl
year the interest paid would be recorded at the spot rate on that date. The
liability of DM 20,000,000 would appear on each balance sheet translated a
the year-end spot rates. Any additional gains or losses would be deferre
and amortized in a manner similar to the Year 1 illustration. The chart at th
top of page 655 indicates how this deferral and amortization process woul
affect the net incomes for each year of the loan's life.

The deferral and amortization of exchange gains and losses was not adopte
by either the United States or Britain. Both of these countries record th
liability in the same manner as Canada does, but report each year's gains o
losses in income for that year. Canada relies on foreign capital markets mor

	Spot rate	Gain (loss) on DM 20,000,000	Year 1	Year 2	Year 3	Year 4
				Amortization		
Jan. 1/1	$0.445					
Dec. 31/1	0.439	$ 120,000	$30,000	$ 30,000	$ 30,000	$ 30,000
Dec. 31/2	0.442	(60,000)		(20,000)	(20,000)	(20,000)
Dec. 31/3	0.441	20,000			10,000	10,000
Dec. 31/4	0.446	(100,000)				(100,000)
Total		$ (20,000)	$30,000	$ 10,000	$ 20,000	$ (80,000)

extensively than do the U.S. and Britain. The Canadian treatment attempts to diffuse the impact of large changes in exchange rates on a particular year's net income.

Forward exchange contracts

Forward exchange contracts are another type of transaction involving foreign currencies. A *forward exchange contract* is an agreement to exchange currencies of different countries on a specified date at the forward rate in effect when the contract was made. As indicated by the exchange rates illustrated on page 649, forward rates may be larger or smaller than spot rates for a foreign currency, depending on the foreign currency dealer's expectations regarding fluctuations in exchange rates for the currency. Forward exchange contracts may be used to hedge actual foreign currency positions and expected foreign currency positions, or for purely speculative purposes.

When a foreign currency transaction is to be consummated in the future, a contract entered into today can establish the price of that future transaction. When this occurs the *future transaction* is said to be *hedged*. For example, suppose that on June 1, a Canadian company has a receivable from a German customer for DM 10,000 which is to be collected in 90 days. If the spot rate on June 1 is DM 1 = $0.445 this receivable has a value in Canadian dollars of $4,450. During the 90-day period, the receivable is exposed to changes in the spot rate. If the spot rate is DM 1 = $0.430 on the date of collection, the amount received will be $4,300 and the company will have incurred an exchange loss of $150 during the 90-day period. The risk of incurring a loss can be removed on June 1 if the company enters a contract to sell (deliver) DM 10,000 in 90 days. If the 90-day forward rate is DM 1 = $0.439 on June 1, and the company contracts to sell DM 10,000, the amount to be received in 90 days has been established at $4,390. The $60 difference ($4,450 − $4,390 = $60) is the cost of entering the contract and is *amortized over the contract's life*.

It should be noted that if the actual spot rate on the date of collection was DM 1 = $0.441, instead of the DM 1 = $0.430 that we used in the example, the company would have been better off if it had not hedged the receivable because it would have collected $4,410 instead of the contracted amount of $4,390. By hedging the receivable on June 1, the company was *insulated from subsequent changes* in exchange rates in any direction (but it was not insulated from the economic loss of $20 indicated in the above example, where the rate rose contrary to expectations).

In a similar manner, if a Canadian company has a payable to a German supplier of DM 25,000 due in 30 days, it can determine today the exact amount of Canadian dollars it will have to pay by entering *a forward exchange contract to purchase* DM 25,000 in 30 days.

Premiums and discounts on forward exchange contracts

Premiums or discounts exist on forward exchange contracts when, on a particular date, forward rates are different than spot rates. When the forward rate is less than the spot rate the forward contract can be entered into at a *discount*. When the forward rate is higher than the spot rate, the forward contract has a *premium*. The effect that each will have on a company's income depends on whether the forward contract is for the purchase or sale of foreign currency. When the contract is for *the purchase of currency, discount* will be accounted for as *revenue*, whereas a *premium* will be accounted for as an *expense*. When the contract is for the *sale of currency* the converse is the case. A *discount* will be accounted for as an *expense*, while a *premium* will be accounted for as *revenue*. In certain situations the discounts or premiums will be accounted for as adjustments to the Canadian dollar price associated with a foreign currency transaction.

When the forward exchange contract is *hedging an existing monetary position*, the premiums or discounts are *amortized* to income over the *life of the contract*, and thus accounted for as revenues or expenses. We will illustrate this in the examples that follow. Accounting for premiums or discounts as adjustments to the price of a foreign currency transaction will be discussed subsequently.

Hedging an account receivable

On June 1, Year 2, when the spot rate was DM 1 = $0.445, Ontario Mfg. Co. Ltd. sold merchandise to a West German customer for DM 10,000. Payment is to be received in 90 days. The transaction was recorded with the following entry:

<table>
<tr><td>Journal entry for sale of merchandise</td><td>Accounts Receivable . . . .</td><td>4,450</td><td></td></tr>
<tr><td></td><td>   Sales . . . .</td><td></td><td>4,450</td></tr>
<tr><td></td><td colspan="3">To record sale for DM 10,000 translated at spot rate of
DM 1 = $0.445.</td></tr>
</table>

The company hedged the receivable by entering into a forward exchange contract to deliver DM 10,000 to its bank in 90 days at the forward rate of DM 1 = $0.439 and recorded this event with the following entry:

Journal entry for acquisition of forward exchange
contract to deliver foreign
currency

Forward Exchange Contract Receivable

    (DM 10,000 × $0.439 forward rate)   4,390

Discount on Forward Exchange Contract   60

    Forward Exchange Contract (DM 10,000 × $0.445 spot rate)   4,450

To record the amount to be received in dollars in 90 days, and the con-

tract to deliver DM 10,000

The forward exchange contract receivable is recorded at the amount that the company will receive when it delivers DM 10,000 to the bank in 90 days. This receivable is denominated in Canadian dollars and **will not be affected** by subsequent **changes in the spot rate**. The forward exchange contract is an obligation to deliver DM 10,000 recorded at the spot rate, and is the same amount as the receivable from the West German customer. Both the contract and customer receivable will change with subsequent changes in the spot rate, but **the gains or losses on one will be offset with equal losses or gains on the other**. It should be noted that the **customer account receivable** is hedged by the forward exchange contract which is an **account payable to the bank**.

The spot rate was unchanged on June 30, Year 2 requiring only the following entry to amortize the discount for the preparation of monthly statements:

Journal entry to amortize
discount on forward
exchange contract

Forward Contract Expense   20

    Discount on Forward Exchange Contract   20

To amortize one-third of the discount for the month of June.

On July 31, Year 2, the spot rate was DM 1 = $0.441 and the following entries were made:

Journal entries to record
gain on forward exchange
contract, and to amortize
discount, and to record
offsetting loss on account
receivable

Forward Exchange Contract [DM 10,000 × ($0.445 − $0.441)]   40

Forward Contract Expense   20

    Transaction Gains and Losses   40

    Discount on Forward Exchange Contract   20

To recognize transaction gain on forward exchange contract resulting from decrease of spot rate from $0.445 to $0.441, and to amortize the discount on contract for July.

Transaction Gains and Losses   40

    Accounts Receivable [DM 10,000 × ($0.445 − $0.441)]   40

To recognize transaction loss on the receivable from West German customer resulting from decrease of spot rate from $0.445 to $0.441

Assuming a $0.430 spot rate on August 29, Year 2, the maturity date of the forward exchange contract, and the date of collection of DM 10,000 from the West German customer, the following entries would be made:

Forward Exchange Contract [DM 10,000 × ($0.441 − $0.430)] 110
Forward Contract Expense 20
   Transaction Gains and Losses 11
   Discount on Forward Exchange Contract 2
To recognize transaction gain on forward exchange contract resulting from decrease of spot rate from $0.441 to $0.430, and to amortize the remaining discount on contract.
Transaction Gains and Losses 110
   Accounts Receivable [DM 10,000 × ($0.441 − $0.430)] 110
To recognize transaction loss on receivable from West German customer resulting from decrease of spot rate from $0.441 to $0.430.
Cash — DM 10,000 4,300
   Accounts Receivable 4,300
To record receipt of DM 10,000 from customer.
Forward Exchange Contract 4,300
   Cash — DM 10,000 4,300
To record delivery of DM 10,000 to the bank.
Cash 4,390
   Forward Exchange Contract Receivable 4,390
To record receipt of $4,390 from bank on delivery of DM 10,000.

Hedging an account payable

On Sept. 1, Year 5 Alberta Importers Ltd. purchased merchandise from a West German supplier for DM 20,000, with payment to be made on Sept. 30. The spot rate on Sept. 1 was DM 1 = $0.451. The company immediately entered into a forward exchange contract to purchase DM 20,000 in 30 days at a forward rate of DM 1 = $0.459. These transactions were recorded as follows:

Inventory 9,020
   Accounts Payable 9,020
To record purchase of inventory for DM 20,000 translated at spot rate of DM 1 = $0.451.

Forward Exchange Contract (DM 20,000 × $0.451 spot rate) 9,020
Premium on Forward Exchange Contract 160
   Forward Exchange Contract Payable
      (DM 20,000 × $0.459 forward rate) 9,180
To record contract to receive DM 10,000 and the amount to be paid in dollars in 30 days.

The forward *exchange contract payable* is recorded at the Canadian dollar amount that the company has agreed to pay the bank for the purchase of DM 20,000, and *will not be affected* by changes in the spot rate. Both the account payable and the offsetting forward exchange contract will change with changes in the spot rate, but any gains or losses on one will be offset by losses or gains on the other. The *customer account payable* is hedged by the forward exchange contract which is an *account receivable from the bank*.

On Sept. 30, Year 5 the spot rate was 1 DM = $0.460. The following entries would be made to adjust the forward contract and the account payable to the current spot rate and to amortize the premium on the contract.

<table>
<tr><td>**Journal entries to record offsetting gains and losses on forward exchange contract and accounts payable, and to amortize premium**</td><td>Forward Exchange Contract [DM 20,000 × ($0.460 − $0.451)] . . . .</td><td>180</td><td></td></tr>
</table>

Journal entries to record offsetting gains and losses on forward exchange contract and accounts payable, and to amortize premium

Forward Exchange Contract [DM 20,000 × ($0.460 − $0.451)]	180	
Forward Contract Expense	160	
Transaction Gains and Losses		180
Premium on Forward Exchange Contract		160
To recognize transaction gain on forward exchange contract resulting from increase of spot rate from $0.451 to $0.460, and to amortize the premium on contract.		
Transaction Gains and Losses	180	
Accounts Payable [DM 20,000 × ($0.460 − $0.451)]		180
To recognize transaction loss on payable to West German supplier resulting from increase of spot rate from $0.451 to $0.460.		

The payable to the West German supplier is now due for payment. Alberta Importers Ltd. pays $9,180 to the bank and receives DM 20,000 which it sends to its West German supplier. The following entries record the two transactions:

Journal entries to record purchase of foreign currency and delivery of same to creditor

Forward Exchange Contract Payable	9,180	
Cash		9,180
To record payment to bank		
Cash — DM 20,000	9,200	
Forward Exchange Contract		9,200
To record receipt of DM 20,000 from bank.		
Account payable	9,200	
Cash — DM 20,000		9,200
To record payment of DM 20,000 to West German supplier.		

Our illustrations of forward exchange contracts have followed an accounting method that records the contract on its inception date. This method is useful to illustrate the premium or discount and the hedge that has taken place. Some accountants would advocate that *no entries be recorded at the time of entering a forward exchange contract* because the obligations of both parties have not been fulfilled on this date, and therefore *no asset or liability exists*. Executory contracts are not normally recorded in accounting. We will not illustrate this *alternative method*. It is sufficient to note that under either method the net income would be identical.

Hedging prior to a foreign currency transaction

In our prior discussion of premiums and discounts on forward exchange contracts, we mentioned that, in certain situations, these items would be considered as *adjustments to the price of a foreign currency transaction*. Section 1650, paragraphs 51 and 52, outlines the situations where this would be the case. Many companies, anticipating the future purchase or sale of goods or services, *hedge these events before the actual transaction takes place*. The paragraphs suggest that when this has occurred *the hedge has established the Canadian dollar price* for these goods or services purchased or sold. Any costs associated with the hedge are included in the dollar price of items purchased or sold. The example that follows will illustrate this concept, as it applies to the cost of inventory purchased.

Assume that Alberta Importers Ltd. on May 1, Year 6, issued a purchase order to a West German supplier at a total price of DM 175,000. Delivery and payment were scheduled for June 30, Year 6.

To hedge against fluctuations in the exchange rate for deutsche marks, Alberta Importers acquired on May 1, Year 6, a forward exchange contract to purchase DM 175,000 on June 30, Year 6. Selected exchange rates for deutsche marks from May 1 to June 30, Year 6, were as follows:

Exchange rates for deutsche marks		May 1	May 31	June 3
Spot rate		0.462	0.458	0.466
Forward rates:				
30-day contracts		0.477	0.472	0.487
60-day contracts		0.493	0.488	0.498
90-day contracts		0.519	0.502	0.520

Alberta Importers' journal entries for acquisition of the forward exchange contract, receipt of the merchandise from the West German supplier, payment of the forward exchange contract, and payment of the supplier's invoice, are presented on page 661.

The result of the journal entries is that the merchandise purchased by Alberta Importers from the West German supplier is valued at the total cost including contract premiums, of the transaction with the supplier. These costs are summarized at the bottom of page 661.

ALBERTA IMPORTERS LTD.
General Journal

Year 6

May 1   Forward Exchange Contract (DM 175,000 × $0.462 spot rate)   80,850

Premium on Forward Exchange Contract Payable   5,425

     Forward Exchange Contract Payable (DM 175,000 × $0.493 forward rate)   86,275

To record acquisition of DM 175,000 forward exchange contract for 60 days, at

forward rate of DM1 = $0.493.

31   Deferred Transaction Gains and Losses [DM 175,000 × ($0.462 − $0.458)]   700

     Forward Exchange Contract   700

To defer transaction loss resulting from decrease of spot exchange rate for

deutsche marks to DM 1 = $0.458 from DM 1 = $0.462.

June 30   Forward Exchange Contract

[DM 175,000 × ($0.466 − $0.458)]   1,400

     Deferred Transaction Gains and Losses   1,400

To defer transaction gain resulting from increase of spot exchange rate for

deutsche marks to DM 1 = $0.466 from DM 1 = $0.458.

30   Inventories ($81,550 − $700 + $5,425)   86,275

Deferred Transaction Gains and Losses ($1,400 − $700)   700

     Premium on Forward Exchange Contract Payable   5,425

     Accounts Payable (DM 175,000 × $0.466)   81,550

To record purchase of merchandise from West German supplier for DM 175,000,

translated at spot rate of DM 1 = $0.466, and to increase cost of

merchandise for premium on forward exchange contract, less deferred net

transaction gain on contract.

June 30   Forward exchange contract payable   86,275

     Cash   86,275

To record payment to bank.

Cash — DM 175,000   81,550

     Forward exchange contract   81,550

To record receipt from bank of DM 175,000.

Accounts payable   81,550

     Cash — DM 175,000   81,550

To record settlement of liability to West German supplier.

Total cost of merchandise purchased from West German supplier

Invoice cost of merchandise (DM 175,000 × $0.466 spot rate on date

received) . . . . $ 81,550

Premium on forward exchange contract for deutsche marks   5,425

Net deferred transaction gain on forward exchange contract . . . .   (700)

     Total cost of merchandise $86,275

The illustrated accounting is appropriate because the forward exchange contract enabled Alberta Importers to predetermine its total cost of the merchandise purchased from the West German supplier at $86,275, the total cash outlay for the forward exchange contract.

Forward Exchange Contract for Speculation   There is no separate accounting treatment for the discount or premium on a forward exchange contract acquired for speculation in the foreign currency involved. The speculation forward exchange contract is similar to a short-term investment in a marketable bond that will not be held to maturity; thus, the accounting for discount or premium is similar for these two investments.

The transaction gain or loss on a speculation forward exchange contract is computed by multiplying the foreign currency amount of the contract by the difference between (1) the forward rate available for the remaining term of the contract and (2) the contracted forward rate or the forward rate last used to compute a transaction gain or loss. Transaction gains and losses on speculation forward exchange contracts are included in the computation of net income for the period in which the forward rate changes.

To illustrate, assume the following exchange rates for deutsche marks from May 1 to June 30, Year 6:

<table>
<tr><td>Exchange rates for
deutsche marks</td><td></td><td>May 1</td><td>May 31</td><td>June 30</td></tr>
<tr><td></td><td>Spot rate: ....</td><td>$0.454</td><td>$0.449</td><td>$0.455</td></tr>
<tr><td></td><td>Forward rates:</td><td></td><td></td><td></td></tr>
<tr><td></td><td>30-day contracts ....</td><td>0.477</td><td>0.472</td><td>0.487</td></tr>
<tr><td></td><td>60-day contracts ....</td><td>0.493</td><td>0.488</td><td>0.495</td></tr>
<tr><td></td><td>90-day contracts ....</td><td>0.519</td><td>0.502</td><td>0.520</td></tr>
</table>

On May 1, Year 6, Speco, Inc., acquired a 60-day forward exchange contract to purchase DM 200,000, in anticipation of an increase in the spot rates for deutsche marks during the 60-day period.

The journal entries of Speco, Inc., for the forward exchange contract, assuming that Speco prepares monthly financial statements, are presented on page 663.

The increase in the spot rates for deutsche marks that Speco, Inc., had anticipated did not occur; thus, Speco incurred a total transaction loss of $7,600 ($4,200 + $3,400 = $7,600) on the forward exchange contract for speculation.

TRANSLATION OF FINANCIAL STATEMENTS OF FOREIGN OPERATIONS

When a Canadian enterprise prepares consolidated or combined financial statements that include the assets, liabilities, and operations of foreign subsidiaries or branches, the Canadian enterprise must *translate* the amounts

SPECO, INC.

General Journal

Year 6			
May 1	Forward Exchange Contract /R		
	(DM 200,000 × $0.493)	98,600	
	Forward Exchange Contract Payable		98,600
	To record acquisition of DM 200,000 forward exchange contract for 60 days, at forward rate of DM 1 = $0.493.		
31	Transaction Gains and Losses		
	[DM 200,000 × ($0.493 − $0.472)]	4,200	
	Forward Exchange Contract /R		4,200
	To recognize transaction loss on forward exchange contract resulting from difference between contracted forward rate (DM 1 = $0.493) and forward rate for remaining 30-day term of contract (DM 1 = $0.472).		
June 30	Investment in Deutsche Marks	94,400	
	Forward Exchange Contract Payable	98,600	
	Forward Exchange Contract ($98,600 − $4,200)		94,400
	Cash		98,600
	To record payment of DM 200,000 forward exchange contract, and receipt of deutsche marks.		
30	Cash (DM 200,000 × $0.455)	91,000	
	Transaction Gains and Losses [DM 200,000 × ($0.472		
	− $0.455)]	3,400	
	Investment in Deutsche Marks		94,400
	To record sale of DM 200,000 at buying spot rate of DM 1 = $0.455, and resultant transaction loss.		

in the financial statements of the foreign entities from the entities' *foreign currency* to Canadian dollars. Similar treatment must be given to the assets and income statement amounts associated with foreign subsidiaries that are not consolidated, and with other foreign investees for which the Canadian enterprise uses the equity method of accounting.

Alternative methods for translating foreign entities' financial statements prior to Section 1650

If the exchange rate for the currency of a foreign subsidiary or branch remained constant instead of fluctuating, translation of the foreign entity's financial statements to Canadian dollars would be simple. All financial statement amounts would be translated to Canadian dollars at the constant exchange rate. However, exchange rates fluctuate frequently. Thus, accountants charged with translating amounts in a foreign entity's financial statements to Canadian dollars face a problem similar to that involving inventory valuation during a period of price fluctuations. Which exchange rate or rates should be used to translate the foreign entity's financial statements? A number of answers were proposed for this question prior to the issuance of **Handbook Section 1650**, because Canadian accounting standards required only the disclosure of the method of translation and the accounting for any exchange gains and losses. As a result several methods of translation were used by Canadian companies. The several methods for foreign currency translation may be grouped into three basic classes: **current noncurrent, monetary/nonmonetary,** and **current rate**. (A fourth method, the **temporal method**, essentially is the same as the monetary nonmonetary method.) The three classes differ principally in translation techniques for balance sheet accounts.

Current/Noncurrent Method   In the **current/noncurrent method** of translation, current assets and current liabilities are translated at the exchange rate in effect on the balance sheet date of the foreign entity (the **current rate**). All other assets and liabilities, and the elements of owners' equity, are translated at the **historical rates** in effect at the time the assets, liabilities and equities first were recorded in the foreign entity's accounting records. In the income statement, depreciation and amortization are translated at historical rates applicable to the related assets, while all other revenue and expenses are translated at an **average** exchange rate for the accounting period.

The current/noncurrent method of translating foreign investees' financial statements was popular for many years. This method supposedly best reflected the **liquidity** aspects of the foreign entity's financial position by showing the current Canadian dollar equivalents of its working capital components. Today, the current/noncurrent method has few supporters. The principal theoretical objection to the current/noncurrent method is that, with respect to inventories, it represents a departure from historical cost. Inventories are translated at the **current rate**, rather than at **historical rates** in effect when the inventories were acquired, when the current/noncurrent method of translating foreign currency accounts is followed.

Monetary/Nonmonetary Method   The **monetary/nonmonetary method** of translating foreign currencies focuses on the characteristics of assets and liabilities of the foreign entity, rather than on their balance sheet classifications. This method is founded on the same monetary/nonmonetary aspects of assets and liabilities that are employed in historical-cost/constant-dollar accounting, described in **Intermediate Accounting** of this series. **Monetary assets and liabilities** — those representing claims or obligations expressed in a fixed monetary amount — are translated at the current exchange rate. All other assets, liabilities, and owners' equity accounts are translated at appropriate historical rates. In the income statement, average exchange rates are applied to all revenue and expenses except depreciation, amortization, and cost of goods sold, which are translated at appropriate historical rates.

Supporters of the monetary/nonmonetary method emphasized its retention of the historical-cost principle in the foreign entity's financial statements. Because the foreign entity's financial statements are consolidated or combined with those of the Canadian enterprise, consistent accounting principles are applied in the consolidated or combined financial statements.

The **temporal method** differs from the monetary/nonmonetary method only in its treatment of nonmonetary items carried at current values. Examples are inventories and investments carried at market values. These items would be translated at the **current exchange rate** rather than historical rates. Because most companies carry their nonmonetary items at historical cost, the two translation methods are essentially the same. Under the temporal method the translated statements yield basically the **same results** that would have occurred had the Canadian enterprise entered into the identical transactions on its own, rather than through its foreign subsidiary or branch as was the actual situation.

Current Rate Method   Critics of the monetary/nonmonetary method point out that this method emphasizes the **parent company** aspects of a foreign entity's financial position and operating results. By reflecting the foreign entity's changes in assets and liabilities, and operating results, as though they were made by the parent company, the monetary/nonmonetary method misstates the actual financial position and operating relationships of the foreign entity.

Critics of the monetary/nonmonetary method of foreign currency translation generally have supported the **current rate method**. Under the current rate method, all balance sheet accounts other than owners' equity accounts are translated at the current exchange rate. Owners' equity accounts are translated at historical rates. All revenue and expenses are translated at the current rate on the respective transaction dates, if practical. Otherwise, an average exchange rate is used for all revenue and expenses.

Standards for translation established by Section 1650

Section 1650 adopted the current rate method for **self-sustaining** foreign operations and the temporal method for **integrated** foreign operations. (An exception was made in situations where a self-sustaining operation operates in a highly inflationary environment. In this case the temporal method would be used.) Whether a foreign operation would be considered to be self-sustaining or integrated would depend on a number of factors such as its cash flows, sales prices, markets for products, source of labour, material costs, and financing, and the scope of intercompany transactions.

Judgment is to be used to determine the effect of these factors on its Canadian parent or head office. Basically a **self-sustaining foreign operation** is operationally and financially independent of the Canadian enterprise, while an **integrated foreign operation** is operationally and financially interdependent with the Canadian enterprise. If a foreign operation is **self-sustaining**, the sales prices of its products, its sales market, labour and material costs, and sources of financing would be to a large extent local (ie. located in, or influenced by conditions in, the foreign country where it is situated), and there would be few intercompany transactions. If a foreign operation is *integrated* the opposite would be true and the Canadian parent would be directly affected by the cash flows of its foreign operation.

Exchange rates for translation process

The chart that follows illustrates the rates to be used for self-sustaining foreign operations (the current rate method) and for integrated foreign operations (the temporal method). Current rates are the exchange rates on the date of the balance sheet. Historical rates are the exchange rates in effect when an item was acquired. Averages are suggested for revenues and expenses because of the impracticality of recording actual rates on the date such items occurred. Therefore **average rates are surrogates** for historical rates. Dividends would be translated at the rate in effect on the date of declaration.

	Exchange rates	
Financial statement items	*Self-sustaining*	*Integrated*
Monetary	current	current
Non-monetary — at cost	current	historical
Non-monetary — at current values	current	current
Capital stock	historical	historical
Dividends	historical	historical
Revenues	average	average
Depreciation and amortization	average	historical
Cost of sales	average	—
Opening inventory		historical
Purchases		average
Ending inventory		historical

Treatment of exchange gains and losses

In either situation, self-sustaining or integrated, the translation process will yield exchange **gains** or **losses** when exchange rates have **changed**. If the foreign operation is **self-sustaining**, the exposure to exchange rate change is limited to the entity's net assets and therefore the parent company's net investment. Any gains or losses are **deferred** and reported as a **separate component of shareholders' equity**. These exchange gains/losses will be reported in this manner until the parent company's interest is reduced by a disposal, or by its foreign affiliate declaring dividends in excess of net income, in which case an appropriate portion of the deferred items accumulated would be included in the determination of net income in the year that such change takes place.

If the foreign operation is **integrated**, the translation process treats the foreign transactions as if they had been transacted by the parent company.

Gains or losses on *current monetary items* are reported in the *current year's net income*. Gains or losses on *noncurrent monetary items* with a fixed life are *deferred and amortized* to income over the fixed life.

Illustration of translation of a foreign entity's financial statements

On December 31, Year 1, Montreal Corp. Ltd. acquired 100% of the outstanding common shares of a corporation in Venezuela at a cost of 2,000,000 bolivars (B). The spot rate on this date was B1 = $0.128. The acquisition was recorded by Montreal Corp. Ltd. with the following journal entry (in Canadian dollars):

Investment in Venezuelan Subsidiary	256,000	
Cash		256,000

To record acquisition of 100% of outstanding common shares at a cost of B 2,000,000 translated at the spot rate of B1 = $0.128

The balance sheet of the Venezuelan subsidiary on this date in bolivars and translated to Canadian dollars was as follows:

VENEZUELAN SUBSIDIARY
Translation of Balance Sheet to Canadian Dollars
December 31, Year 1

	Venezuelan bolivars	Exchange rate	Canadian dollars
Cash	40,000	0.128	$ 5,120
Accounts receivable	360,000	0.128	46,080
Inventories	1,200,000	0.128	153,600
Plant and Equipment (net)	900,000	0.128	115,200
	2,500,000		$320,000
Current liabilities	50,000	0.128	$ 6,400
Bonds payable	450,000	0.128	57,600
Common stock	1,500,000	0.128	192,000
Retained earnings	500,000	0.128	64,000
	2,500,000		$320,000

In this example we are assuming that, on acquisition date, the carrying values of the subsidiary's net assets were equal to fair values and that there was no goodwill. The bonds payable mature in 10 years and require interest payments each December 31. If a consolidated balance sheet was prepared on December 31 Year 1, the parents' investment account and the shareholders' equity accounts of the subsidiary would be eliminated, the assets and liabilities of the two companies would be added together, and the share holders' equity would be that of the parent company. Because this was a "**purchase type**" business combination, the exchange rate on the date of acquisition is used to translate all accounts of the subsidiary and become the historical rate for use in subsequent years, where appropriate.

On December 31, Year 2, the Venezuelan subsidiary forwarded the following financial statements to its Canadian parent company:

VENEZUELAN SUBSIDIARY
Financial Statements
For Year Ended December 31, Year 2
(in bolivars)

Income Statement

Sales	B 9,000,000
Cost of goods sold	B 7,000,000
Depreciation expense	100,000
Bond interest expense	45,000
Other expense	1,555,000
Total	B 8,700,000
Net income	B 300,000

Statement of Retained Earnings

Balance, beginning of year	B 500,000
Net income	300,000
Subtotal	B 800,000
Dividends (declared December 31)	100,000
Balance, end of year	B 700,000

Balance Sheet

Cash	B 100,000
Accounts receivable	400,000
Inventory	1,600,000
Plant and equipment (net)	800,000
	B 2,900,000
Current liabilities	B 250,000
Bonds payable	450,000
Common stock	1,500,000
Retained earnings	700,000
	B 2,900,000

The translation process will be illustrated under the following two assumptions:

1 the subsidiary is self-sustaining, and
2 the subsidiary is integrated.

The exchange rates for the year were as follows:

December 31, Year 1	B1 =	$0.128
December 31, Year 2	B1 =	$0.104
Average for Year 2	B1 =	$0.115
Date inventory was purchased	B1 =	$0.110
Date dividends declared	B1 =	$0.104

Self-sustaining foreign operation

If the Venezuelan subsidiary is considered to be self-sustaining the translation of its Year 2 financial statements would be as illustrated below. The

VENEZUELAN SUBSIDIARY
Translation of Financial Statements to Canadian Dollars
Year Ended December 31, Year 2

	Bolivars	Exchange rates	Dollars
Income Statement			
Sales	9,000,000	$0.115	$1,035,000
Cost of goods sold	7,000,000	0.115	$ 805,000
Depreciation expense	100,000	0.115	11,500
Bond interest expense	45,000	0.115	5,175
Other expense	1,555,000	0.115	178,825
Total expense	8,700,000		$1,000,500
Net income	300,000		34,500
Statement of Retained Earnings			
Balance, beginning of year	500,000	0.128	$ 64,000
Net income	300,000		34,500
Subtotal	800,000		$ 98,500
Dividends	100,000	0.104	10,400
Balance, end of year	700,000		$ 88,100
Balance Sheet			
Cash	100,000	0.104	$ 10,400
Accounts receivable	400,000	0.104	41,600
Inventory	1,600,000	0.104	166,400
Plant and equipment (net)	800,000	0.104	83,200
	2,900,000		$ 301,600
Current liabilities	250,000	0.104	26,000
Bonds payable	450,000	0.104	46,800
Common stock	1,500,000	0.128	192,000
Retained earnings	700,000		88,100
Cumulative translation adjustment			(51,300)
	2,900,000		$ 301,600

following features of the translation process should be emphasized:

1 All assets and liabilities are translated at the current rate.
2 The common stock account and the beginning retained earnings are translated at the historical rate on the date that Montreal Corp Ltd. acquired its investment in the Venezuelan subsidiary. Dividends are translated at the historical rate on the date of declaration.
3 The average rate for Year 2 is used to translate all revenue and expenses in the income statement.
4 A balancing amount labeled as *cumulative translation adjustment* is used to reconcile total liabilities and shareholders equity with total assets in the translated balance sheet. Cumulative translation adjustments are included in the shareholders' equity of the translated balance sheet.
5 While the cumulative translation adjustment is a balancing amount, an independent calculation is illustrated below.

Independent calculation of cumulative translation adjustment			
Net assets Dec. 31, Year 1	B	2,000,000 × $0.128 =	$256,000
Change in net assets during Year 2:			
Net income	B	300,000 × $0.115 =	34,500
Dividends	B	(100,000) × $0.104 =	(10,400)
Calculated net assets			$280,100
Actual net assets	B	2,200,000 × $0.104	228,800
Cumulative loss			$ 51,300

Consolidated financial statements   The translated financial statements of the Venezuelan subsidiary are used for the preparation of the consolidated financial statements and the following equity method journal entries made by the parent company:

MONTREAL CORP. LTD
General Journal
December, 31, Year 2

Investment in Venezuelan Subsidiary	34,500	
Investment Income		34,500
To record 100% of net income of subsidiary.		
Dividends Receivable	10,400	
Investment in Venezuelan Subsidiary		10,400
To record dividends receivable from subsidiary.		
Cumulative Translation Adjustment	51,300	
Investment in Venezuelan Subsidiary		51,300
To record 100% of the change in the cumulative translation adjustment for the year.		

In the consolidation process, the balance in the investment account ($256,000 + $34,500 − $10,400 − $51,300 = $228,800) is eliminated against the shareholders' equity of the subsidiary ($192,000 + $88,100 −

$51,300 = $228,800$). The **consolidated shareholders' equity** is that of the parent and **includes the cumulative translation adjustment** shown as a separate item.

If the subsidiary is less than 100% owned, the equity method journal entries would reflect the parents' share of the changes in the subsidiary's net asets during the year. Minority interest in the consolidated financial statements is based on the translated statements of the subsidiary.

VENEZUELAN SUBSIDIARY

Translation of Financial Statements to Canadian Dollars

Year Ended December 31, Year 2

	Bolivars	Exchange rates	Dollars
Income Statement			
Sales	9,000,000	$0.115	$1,035,000
Cost of goods sold	7,000,000	Calculated	$ 828,600
Depreciation expense	100,000	0.128	12,800
Bond interest expense	45,000	0.104	4,680
Other expense	1,555,000	0.115	178,825
Total expense	8,700,000		$1,024,905
Net income — before translation loss (**Note 1**)	300,000		$ 10,095
Statement of Retained Earnings			
Balance, beginning of year	500,000	0.128	$ 64,000
Net income (**Note 1**)	300,000		10,095
Subtotal	800,000		$ 74,095
Dividends	100,000	0.104	10,400
Balance, end of year (**Note 1**)	700,000		$ 63,695
Balance Sheet			
Cash	100,000	0.104	$ 10,400
Accounts receivable	400,000	0.104	41,600
Inventory	1,600,000	0.110	176,000
Plant and Equipment (net)	800,000	0.128	102,400
	2,900,000		$ 330,400
Current liabilities	250,000	0.104	$ 26,000
Bonds payable	450,000	0.104	46,800
Common stock	1,500,000	0.128	192,000
Retained earnings (**Note 1**)	700,000		63,695
Subtotal			$ 328,495
Balancing translation adjustment (**Note 1**)			1,905
	2,900,000		$ 330,400

Note 1   The translation adjustment is a preliminary balancing amount. The final disposition of this amount is shown on pages 672 and 673. The net income and retained earnings are not the final translated amounts.

Integrated foreign operation

If the Venezuelan subsidiary is considered to be an integrated foreign operation, the translation of its Year 2 financial statements would be as shown on page 671.

In the review of the exchange rates used in the translation process, the following should be noted:

1 Monetary items are translated at the current rate; nonmonetary items at the appropriate historical rate.
2 Common stock and beginning of year retained earnings are translated at the appropriate historical rate; dividends at the historical rate on date of declaration
3 Revenue and expenses, with the exception of depreciation, cost of goods sold and bond interest, are translated at the average rates for the year. Bond interest was paid on December 31, and thus translated at the exchange rate on that date

---

ANALYSIS OF TRANSLATION ADJUSTMENT

Calculation of Year 2 noncurrent monetary position translation gain, and amortization	**Noncurrent Monetary Position**					
	Bonds payable Dec. 31, Year 1	B	450,000	× $0.128	$	57,600
	Bonds payable Dec. 31, Year 2		450,000	× 0.104		46,800
	Gain on bonds				$	10,800
	Amortized to Year 2 net income					
	($10,800 ÷ 10 years)					1,080
	Deferred gain Dec. 31, Year 2				$	9,720
Calculation of Year 2 current monetary position translation loss, less Year 2 amortization of gain on noncurrent monetary position	**Current Monetary Position**					
	Balance Dec. 31, Year 1:					
	Cash	B	40,000			
	Accounts receivable		360,000			
		B	400,000			
	Current liabilities		50,000			
	Net monetary position	B	350,000	× $0.128	$	44,800
	Changes during Year 2					
	Sales	B	9,000,000	× 0.115	$1,035,000	
	Purchases		(7,400,000)	× 0.115	(851,000	
	Bond interest expense		(45,000)	× 0.104	(4,680	
	Other expense		(1,555,000)	× 0.115	(178,825	
	Dividends		(100,000)	× 0.104	(10,400	
	Net changes	B	(100,000)		$(9,905	
	Calculated net monetary position Dec. 31, Year 2				$	34,895
	Actual net monetary position Dec. 31, Year 2	B	250,000	× 0.104		26,000
	Loss during Year 2				$	8,895
	Bond gain amortized Year 2				(	1,080
	Net translation loss Year 2				$	7,815

Depreciation and amortization are translated at the historical rates used to translate the assets to which they relate.

4 The translation of cost of goods sold requires a separate calculation as follows:

Beginning inventory	1,200,000 × 0.128 =	$153,600
Purchases	7,400,000 × 0.115 =	851,000
Subtotal	8,600,000	$1,004,600
Ending inventory	1,600,000 × 0.110 =	176,000
Cost of goods sold	7,000,000	$828,600

Purchases in Bolivars were calculated as a balancing amount. The inventories are translated at historical rates. Purchases are translated at the average rate for the year.

5 The balance sheet item labeled ***translation adjustment*** is the amount needed to balance total assets with total liabilities and shareholders' equity, and is a result of the change in exchange rates during the year. Gains or losses on bonds payable are deferred and amortized over the fixed life of this item, including the current year. Gains or losses on current monetary items are reflected on the current year's income statement. An analysis of the effect of exchange rate changes on both types of monetary items shown on page 672 yields the ***disposition*** of the ***translation adjustment*** as follows:

Deferred foreign exchange gain to be shown in liability section of Year 2 balance sheet	$9,720
Foreign exchange loss — to be shown on Year 2 income statement	7,815
Translation adjustment	$1,905

Consolidated statements   After the allocation of the translation adjustment to the subsidiary's income statement and balance sheet, the translated statements are used for the consolidation process and the following equity method journal entries of the parent company:

MONTREAL CORP. LTD.
General Journal
December 31, Year 2

Investment in Venezuelan Subsidiary	$ 2,280	
Investment Income		$ 2,280
To record 100% of the net income of the subsidiary ($10,095 − $7,815 = $2,280)		
Dividends Receivable	$10,400	
Investment in Venezuelan Subsidiary		$10,400
To record dividends receivable from subsidiary.		

After the journal entries have been entered the consolidation proces
proceeds in the same manner as described previously. The deferred exchang
gain which will appear on the translated balance sheet of the subsidiary :
carried forward to the consolidated balance sheet like any other subsidiar
liability. The foreign exchange loss which will appear on the subsidiary'
income statement is carried forward to the consolidated income statemen
In the case of less than 100% owned subsidiaries, the equity method journa
entries would reflect the parent's ownership percentage. Minority interes
in the consolidated financial statements is based on the translated assets
liabilities, and net income of the subsidiary.

REVIEW QUESTIONS

1 What is a *multinational* enterprise?

2 Identify four of the organizations that support the development of internationa
accounting standards.

3 Differentiate between the *International Federation of Accountants* an
the *International Accounting Standards Committee*.

4 Define the following terms associated with foreign currencies:
   a *Exchange rate*
   b *Forward rate*
   c *Selling rate*
   d *Spot rate*

5 A newspaper listed quoted prices for the Japanese yen (¥) as follows:

   Buying rate: ¥1 = $0.0039
   Selling rate: ¥1 = $0.0043

   How many Canadian dollars does a Canadian company have to exchange fo
   ¥50,000 at the above rates to settle an account payable in that amount to
   Japanese supplier? Explain.

6 On March 27, Year 3, a Canadian company purchased merchandise on 30-da
   credit terms from a Philippines exporter at an invoice cost of ₱80,000. (₱ is th
   symbol for the Philippines peso.) What Canadian dollar amount does the Canadia
   company credit to Accounts Payable if the March 27, Year 3, exchange rates fo
   Philippine pesos are as follows:

   Buying rate: ₱1 = $0.11
   Selling rate: ₱1 = $0.12

7 How does a Canadian multinational enterprise *hedge* against the risk o
   fluctuations in exchange rates for foreign currencies? Explain.

8 Explain the *one-transaction perspective* regarding the nature of a transac
   tion gain or loss.

9 What arguments are advanced in support of the *two-transaction perspective*
   for transaction gains and losses? Explain.

10 Should transaction gains or losses be recorded in the accounting records prio
   to collection of a receivable or payment of a liability in foreign currency
   Explain.

11 What is a *forward exchange contract*?

12 In what way is the temporal method of translating foreign currency financial statements different from the monetary/nonmonetary method?

13 A Canadian company enters a forward contract with its bank to purchase 750,000 deutsche marks (DM) for delivery in four months at the forward rate of 1DM = $.37, and records a liability of $277,500. During the four-month period, both the spot rate and forward rates for deutsche marks fluctuate. Explain how the company's liability to the bank is affected by subsequent exchange rate movements.

14 Will all transaction gains and losses that occurred during a period be shown in the income statement for the period? Explain.

15 Is the accounting treatment of exchange gains and losses on noncurrent monetary items denominated in foreign currencies consistent between Canada, Britain, and the United States? Explain.

16 What are premiums and discounts on forward exchange contracts? What effect will each have on a company's net income? Explain.

17 Explain how the accounting for the premium on a forward exchange contract that is entered into as a hedge of an existing foreign currency payable will differ from one that is entered into to hedge an expected foreign currency payable.

18 Differentiate between the translation method used for a self-sustaining foreign operation and that used for an integrated foreign operation.

19 Is there any difference in the accounting treatment of translation gains and losses between a self-sustaining foreign operation and an integrated foreign operation? Explain.

EXERCISES

Ex 16-1 Select the best answer for each of the following multiple-choice questions:
1 Canadian Company purchased 5,000 toys from Central America Exporters, S.A., at 12.5 pesos each, when the selling exchange was $0.08 a peso. What amount should Canadian Company record as the total dollar cost for the merchandise purchased?
   a $400
   b $625
   c $5,000
   d $6,250
   e Some other amount

2 According to *Handbook Section 1650*, "Foreign Currency Translation," all elements of financial statements of a self-sustaining foreign operation should be translated to Canadian dollars by the:
   a Monetary/nonmonetary method
   b Current rate method
   c Temporal method
   d Current/noncurrent method

3 The discount or premium on a forward contract that hedges an existing current monetary position is:

a Included with the gain or loss on the contract
b Accounted for separately from the gain or loss on the contract
c Included with translation adjustments
d Not accounted for separately

4 A gain that is a consequence of translation of a self-sustaining foreign currenc financial statement should be:

a Included in net income of the accounting period in which it occurs
b Deferred and amortized over a period not to exceed 40 years
c Deferred until a subsequent accounting period when a loss occurs and offse against that loss
d Included as a separate item in the equity section of the balance sheet

5 Gains and losses resulting from the translation of the current monetary position c an integrated foreign operation should be included as:
a A part of equity in the balance sheet
b An extraordinary item in the income statement for the accounting period i which the rate changes
c An ordinary item in the income statement for losses but deferred for gains
d An ordinary item in the income statement for the accounting period in whic the rate changes

6 According to the **CICA Handbook**, the translation of an integrated foreign sub sidiary's accounting records should be accomplished by the:
a Monetary/nonmonetary method
b Current rate method
c Current/noncurrent method
d Temporal method

Ex 16-2 On March 31, Year 5, Kingston Company acquired a 30-day forward exchang contract for 100,000 local currency units (LCU) of a foreign country. The contrac was acquired to hedge a LCU foreign currency payable. On April 30, Year 5, Kingsto paid cash to settle the contract and obtain the LCU 100,000, which were remitted t its creditor. Kingston prepares adjusting entries and financial statements only at th end of its fiscal year, April 30. Relevant exchange rates for one unit of the loca currency were as follows:

	March 31, Year 5	April 30, Year 5
Spot rates:		
Buying	$0.18	$0.19
Selling	0.20	0.22
Forward rates:		
30-day contracts	0.25	0.28

Prepare journal entries for Kingston Company on March 31, Year 5, and April 30 Year 5.

Ex 16-3 On November 5, Year 9, Transnational Company sold merchandise costing $500 t an Indian customer for 10,000 rupees (Rs). On December 5, Year 9, Transnationa received from the Indian customer a draft for Rs 10,000, which it exchanged fo Canadian dollars. Transnational closes its accounting records monthly and uses th perpetual inventory system. Selected spot exchange rates for the rupee were a follows:

	Nov. 5	Nov. 30	Dec. 5
Buying spot rate	$0.09	$0.10	$0.11
Selling spot rate	0.12	0.13	0.14

Prepare journal entries related to the transaction with the Indian customer in the accounting records of Transnational Company.

Ex 16-4 A wholly owned foreign subsidiary of Multiverse Company had selected expense accounts stated in local currency units (LCUs) for the fiscal year ended November 30, Year 10, as follows:

Doubtful accounts expense	LCU 60,000
Patent amortization expense (patent acquired Dec. 1, Year 7)	40,000
Rent expense	100,000

The foreign subsidiary is an integrated foreign operation. The exchange rates for LCUs for various dates or periods were as follows:

December 1, Year 7	$0.25
November 30, Year 10	0.20
Average for fiscal year ended Nov. 30, Year 10	0.22

Compute the total dollar amount to be included in the income statement of Multiverse Company's foreign subsidiary for the fiscal year ended November 30, Year 10, for the foregoing expense accounts.

Ex 16-5 The accountant for Transglobal Company is a proponent of the one-transaction perspective of accounting for foreign trade transactions. On November 19, Year 1, Transglobal's accountant prepared the following journal entry:

Accounts Payable	60,000	
Cost of Goods Sold ($3,000 × 33⅓%)	1,000	
Inventories ($3,000 × 66⅔%)	2,000	
Cash		63,000

To record payment for F315,000 draft (F315,000 × $0.20 = $63,000) to settle liability to French supplier, and allocation of resultant transaction loss to cost of goods sold and to inventories.

Prepare a journal entry on November 19, Year 1, to correct the foregoing journal entry.

Ex 16-6 The foreign subsidiary of Paloma Company, a Canadian enterprise, has plant assets on December 31, Year 5, with a cost of 3,600,000 local currency units (LCU). Of this amount, plant assets with a cost of LCU 2,400,000 were acquired in Year 3, when the exchange rate was LCU 1 = $0.625; and plant assets with a cost of LCU 1,200,000 were acquired in Year 4, when the exchange rate was LCU 1 = $0.556. The exchange rate on December 31, Year 5, was LCU 1 = $0.500, and the weighted-average exchange rate for Year 5 was LCU 1 = $0.521. The foreign subsidiary depreciates plant assets by the straight-line method over a 10-year economic life with no residual value. The subsidiary is an integrated foreign operation.

Compute for Year 5 the depreciation expense for Paloma Company's foreign subsidiary, in Canadian dollars, for the translated income statement.

Ex 16-7 Assume the same facts as those given in exercise 16-6 except that the subsidiary is a self-sustaining foreign operation.

Compute for Year 5 the depreciation expense in Canadian dollars.

Ex 16-8 On August 6, Year 7, Concordia Company, a Canadian enterprise that uses the perpetual inventory system, purchased from a Belgian supplier on 30-day open account goods costing 80,000 Belgian francs. On that date, various exchange rates for Belgian francs (BF) were as follows:

Spot rates:
Buying: BF1 = $0.025
Selling: BF1 = $0.029
30-day forward rate: BF1 = $0.031

Also on August 6, Year 7, Concordia acquired a 30-day forward exchange contract for BF 80,000, to hedge the BF commitment.

Prepare journal entries to record the August 6, Year 7, transactions of Concordia Company, as well as the related transactions on September 5, Year 7, on which date the selling spot rate was BF 1 = $0.029. Concordia does not close its accounting records monthly or prepare monthly financial statements.

Ex 16-9 On June 30, Year 6, Iberia Company, a Canadian multinational enterprise, sold merchandise costing $75,000 to a Portuguese customer, receiving in exchange a 60-day, 12% note for 7,500,000 escudos (Esc). The buying rate for escudos on June 30, Year 6, was Esc 1 = $0.014. On August 29, Year 6, Iberia received from the Portuguese customer a draft for Esc 7,650,000, which Iberia converted on that date to Canadian dollars at the buying rate for escudos of Esc 1 = $0.016.

Prepare journal entries for Iberia Company to record the June 30, Year 6, sale, under the perpetual inventory system, and the August 29, Year 6, conversion of the Portuguese customer's Esc 7,650,000 draft to Canadian dollars.

Ex 16-10 Winnipeg Utilities Ltd. borrowed $50,000,000 in U.S. funds on January 1, Year 1, at an annual interest rate of 12%. The loan is due on December 31, Year 4. The Canadian exchange rates for U.S. dollars over the life of the loan were as follows:

Jan. 1, Year 1	$1.359
Dec. 31, Year 1	$1.368
Dec. 31, Year 2	$1.360
Dec. 31, Year 3	$1.352
Dec. 31, Year 4	$1.355

Instructions
a Prepare journal entries for Winnipeg Utilities Ltd. for Year 1.
b Calculate the transaction gains or losses that would be reported in the net income of the company each year over the life of the loan.
c Compute the balance of the deferred gain or loss that would appear on the balance sheet at the end of each year.

Ex 16-11   On January 1, Year 5, Glenville Company Ltd. purchased, in U.S. funds, $1,000,000 of the bonds of the Boston Corporation. The bonds were trading at par on this date, pay interest at 9% each December 31, and mature on December 31, Year 7. The following Canadian exchange rates for U.S. dollars were quoted during years 5 to 7:

Jan. 1, Year 5	$1.372
Dec. 31, Year 5	$1.321
Dec. 31, Year 6	$1.325
Dec. 31, Year 7	$1.375

Instructions

a Prepare the journal entries for Glenville Company Ltd. for the three-year period.

b Compute the deferred gain or loss that would appear on the balance sheet at the end of each year.

c Compute the carrying amount of the investment at the end of each year.

CASES

Case 16-1   In order to incorporate the financial accounting data of foreign operations in the financial statements of the reporting entity and to achieve the objectives of currency translation for foreign operations, the **CICA Handbook** has classified foreign operations into two categories: integrated foreign operation and self-sustaining foreign operation.

Instructions

a Explain how currency translation objectives for foreign operations would be achieved by classifying foreign operations into the above two categories, and indicate what factors should be taken into consideration for distinguishing integrated foreign operations from self-sustaining foreign operations.

b State how exchange gains or losses arising out of translation of foreign currency financial statements of a self-sustaining foreign operation are reported.   [SMA]

Case 16-2   During January, Year 12, Perisphere Corporation, a Canadian company, established a subsidiary, Sillah Company, in a foreign country. Perisphere owns 90% of Sillah's outstanding common stock; the remaining 10% is owned by citizens of the foreign country.

Instructions

a What criteria should Perisphere use to determine whether to prepare consolidated financial statements with Sillah for the year ended December 31, Year 12? Explain.

b What criteria should Perisphere use to determine the method used to translate the financial statements of Sillah? Explain.

Case 16-3   The management of a Canadian manufacturing company is considering expansion into foreign countries. While it is felt that the company's unique products will be well accepted, there is some concern regarding the effect that exchange rate changes will have on earnings. Sales and earnings have shown a steady growth in the past and management feels that foreign expansion is necessary to sustain this growth. Two alternatives are being considered. One involves establishing foreign sales offices with orders filled from the company's Canadian plants. Sales, billings and collections would be in local currency units.

The second alternative would see the formation of wholly-owned foreign subsidiaries that would manufacture and distribute the company's products. Sources of financing needed for the purchase of plant and equipment have not yet been decided upon. All transactions will be recorded in local currency units.

You have been hired by the company to prepare a report for management that will discuss the financial reporting implications for both alternatives being considered

Instructions Prepare an outline of all the factors that you will discuss in your report.   [SMA adapted]

PROBLEMS

16-1 On March 1, Year 2, Transcontinent Company, a Canadian enterprise, established branch in Mideastia, a foreign country. Transcontinent sent cash and merchandise (billed at cost) to the Mideastia Branch only on March 1, Year 2, and the branch made sales and incurred rent and other operating expenses in Mideastia during the month of March, Year 2. Transcontinent maintained accounts in its general ledger for the branch's plant assets. Mideastia Branch's operations are an integral component of Transcontinent's operations. The branch maintained its accounting records in local currency units (LCU).

The general ledger trial balance of the Mideastia Branch on March 31, Year 2, is as follows:

TRANSCONTINENT COMPANY

Mideastia Branch Trial Balance
March 31, Year 2

	Debit	Credit
Cash	LCU 2,000	
Accounts receivable	58,000	
Allowance for doubtful accounts		LCU 1,000
Inventories	126,000	
Home office		220,000
Sales		184,000
Cost of goods sold	160,000	
Operating expenses	59,000	
Totals	LCU 405,000	LCU 405,000

Appropriate exchange rates for Mideastia Branch's local currency units were as follows:

Mar. 1, Year 2	$0.60
Mar. 31, Year 2	0.64
Average for March, Year 2	0.62

Instructions Prepare a working paper to translate the trial balance of Mideastia Branch of Transcontinent Company to Canadian dollars.

16-2 On August 1, Year 3, Concord Importers, a Canadian company that prepares financial statements monthly, acquired a 60-day forward exchange contract for £50,000 Exchange rates for the British pound (£) on various dates in Year 3 were as follows

	Aug. 1	Aug. 31	Sept. 30
Spot rates:			
Buying	$1.80	$1.82	$1.83
Selling	1.90	1.91	1.92
Forward rates:			
30-day contracts	1.92	1.94	1.94
60-day contracts	1.94	1.96	1.97
90-day contracts	1.97	1.99	1.98

Instructions Prepare journal entries (omit explanations) for Concord's forward exchange contract during its 60-day term under the following assumptions:
a The contract was acquired for speculation.
b The contract was acquired as a hedge of a payable due Sept. 30, Year 3.
c The contract was firm and was designated as a hedge of a £50,000 purchase order issued by Concord on August 1, Year 3, to a British supplier to be delivered and paid for on September 30, Year 3.

16-3 On December 1, Year 5, Videon Company of Canada formed a foreign subsidiary, which issued all of its currently outstanding common stock on that date. Selected items from the subsidiary's trial balances, all of which are shown in local currency units (LCU), are as follows:

	Nov. 30, Year 7		Nov. 30, Year 6	
Accounts receivable (net of allowance for doubt-				
ful accounts of LCU 2,200 on Nov. 30, Year 7,				
and LCU 2,000 on Nov. 30, Year 6)	LCU	40,000	LCU	35,000
Inventories, at cost		80,000		75,000
Plant assets (net of accumulated depreciation of				
LCU 31,000 on Nov. 30, Year 7, and LCU				
14,000 on Nov. 30, Year 6)		163,000		150,000
Long-term debt		100,000		120,000
Common stock, authorized 10,000 shares, LCU				
10 par, issued and outstanding 5,000 shares				
on Nov. 30, Year 7, and Nov. 30, Year 6		50,000		50,000

Additional information
(1) Exchange rates were as follows:

Dec. 1, Year 5–June 30, Year 6	2 LCU to $1
July 1, Year 6–Sept. 30, Year 6	1.8 LCU to $1
Oct. 1, Year 6–May 31, Year 7	1.7 LCU to $1
June 1, Year 7–Nov. 30, Year 7	1.5 LCU to $1
Average monthly rate for fiscal year ended Nov. 30, Year 6	1.9 LCU to $1
Average monthly rate for fiscal year ended Nov. 30, Year 7	1.6 LCU to $1

(2) An analysis of the accounts receivable (net) balance follows:

	Year ended Nov. 30,	
	Year 7	Year 6
Accounts receivable:		
Balances, beginning of year	LCU 37,000	
Sales (LCU 36,000 a month in Year 7 and LCU		
31,000 a month in Year 6)	432,000	LCU 372,000
Collections	(423,600)	(334,000)
Write-offs (April, Year 7, and November,		
Year 6)	(3,200)	(1,000)
Balances, end of year	LCU 42,200	LCU 37,000
Allowance for doubtful accounts:		
Balances, beginning of year	LCU 2,000	
Provision for doubtful accounts	3,400	LCU 3,000
Write-offs (April, Year 7, and November,		
Year 6)	(3,200)	(1,000)
Balances, end of year	LCU 2,200	LCU 2,000

(3) An analysis of inventories, for which the first-in, first out (fifo) inventory method is used, follows:

	Year ended November 30,	
	Year 7	Year 6
Inventories, beginning of year	LCU 75,000	
Purchases (May, Year 7, and May, Year 6)	335,000	LCU 375,000
Goods available for sale	410,000	375,000
Inventories, end of year	80,000	75,000
Cost of goods sold	LCU 330,000	LCU 300,000

(4) On December 1, Year 5, Videon's foreign subsidiary acquired land for LCU 24,000 and depreciable plant assets for LCU 140,000. On June 4, Year 7, additional depreciable plant assets were acquired for LCU 30,000. Plant assets are being depreciated by the straight-line method over a 10-year economic life with no residual value. A full year's depreciation is taken in the year of acquisition of plant assets.

(5) On December 15, Year 5, 14% serial bonds with a face amount of LCU 120,000 were issued. These bonds mature serially each year through December 15, Year 11, and interest is paid semiannually on June 15 and December 15. The first principal payment was made on December 15, Year 6.

(6) The subsidiary is an integrated foreign operation.

Instructions Prepare a working paper to translate the foregoing items to Canadian dollars, on November 30, Year 7, and November 30, Year 6, respectively. Show supporting computations. Round all exchange rates to the nearest cent.

16-4 Imex Company, an Alberta enterprise with an April 30 fiscal year, had the transactions (on page 683), among others, during March and April, Year 8.

Instructions
a Prepare journal entries for Imex Company to record the transactions in Canadian dollars, under the perpetual inventory system.

Date	Explanation of transactions	Exchange rates		
		Spot		Forward
		Buying	Selling	
Year 8				
Mar. 6	Received merchandise purchased from Brazilian supplier on 30-day open account, cost 100,000 cruzeiros (Cr$). Acquired firm 30-day forward exchange contract for Cr$100,000 as effective hedge.	$0.006	$0.007	$0.008
18	Received merchandise purchased from Danish supplier on 30-day open account, cost 75,000 kroner (DKr).	0.12	0.13	0.14
25	Sold merchandise to Swiss customer on 30-day open account for 50,000 francs (Sfr). Cost of goods sold $15,000.	0.52	0.53	0.54
Apr. 4	Received merchandise purchased from Spanish supplier on 30-day open account for 150,000 pesetas (Ptas).	0.008	0.009	0.010
5	Liquidated Cr$100,000 forward exchange contract, and paid Brazilian supplier for Mar. 6 purchase.	0.006	0.007	0.009
17	Acquired draft for DKr75,000 for payment to Danish supplier for Mar. 18 purchase.	0.13	0.14	0.15
24	Received draft for Sfr50,000 from Swiss customer for sale of Mar. 25. Exchanged draft for Canadian dollar credit to bank chequing account.	0.53	0.54	0.55
30	Obtained exchange rates quotation for Spanish pesetas.	0.009	0.01	0.011

b Prepare an adjusting journal entry for Imex Company on April 30, Year 8. Imex does not prepare monthly financial statements.

16-5 On August 1, Year 8, Westpac Corporation Limited established a sales branch in Singapore. The transactions of Westpac's home office with the Singapore branch, and the branch's own transactions, during August, Year 8, are described below. Following each transaction is the appropriate spot exchange rate for Singapore dollars (S$).

(1) Cash of $50,000 sent to branch (S$1 = $0.45)
(2) Merchandise with a cost of $75,000 shipped to branch at a billed price of $100,000 (S$1 = $0.45)
(3) Rent of leased premises for August paid by branch, S$1,000 (S$1 = $0.45)
(4) Store and office equipment acquired by branch for S$5,000, to be carried in home office accounting records (S$1 = $0.45)
(5) Sales by branch on credit, S$25,000 (S$1 = $0.46). Cost of goods sold, S$15,000
(6) Collections of accounts receivable by branch, S$20,000 (S$1 = $0.455)
(7) Payment of operating expenses by branch, S$5,000 (S$1 = $0.47)
(8) Cash remitted to home office by branch, S$10,000 (S$1 = $0.44)

(9) Operating expenses incurred by home office charged to branch, $2,0(
(S$1 = $0.445)
(10) Uncollectible account receivable written off by branch, S$1,000 (S$1 = $0.44

Instructions Prepare journal entries for the home office of Westpac Corporatic
in Canadian dollars, and for the Singapore branch in Singapore dollars, to record th
foregoing transactions. Both home office and branch use the perpetual inventor
system and the direct write-off method of accounting for uncollectible account
Round all amounts to the nearest dollar. Omit journal entry explanations.

16-6   Portero Corporation, a Canadian enterprise, combined with Sudamerica Compan
on January 2, Year 3, by the acquisition at carrying amount of all of Sudamerica
outstanding common stock. Sudamerica is located in Nicaduras, whose monetai
unit is the peso ($N). Sudamerica's accounting records were continued withou
change. A trial balance, in Nicaduran pesos, on January 2, Year 3, follows:

SUDAMERICA COMPANY

Trial Balance (Nicaduran pesos)
January 2, Year 3

	Debit	Credit
Cash	$N 3,000	
Accounts	5,000	
Inventories	32,000	
Plant assets	204,000	
Accumulated depreciation		$N 42,000
Accounts payable		81,400
Common stock		50,000
Retained earnings		70,600
Totals	$N 244,000	$N 244,000

Sudamerica's trial balance, in Nicaduran pesos, on December 31, Year 4, is show
at the top of page 685.

Additional information
(1) Sudamerica Company is a self-sustaining foreign operation.
(2) Depreciation is computed by the straight-line method over a 10-year econom:
life with no residual value for all depreciable assets. Machinery costing $N20,0(
was acquired by Sudamerica on December 31, Year 3, and no depreciation w:
recorded for this machinery in Year 3. There have been no other depreciabl
assets acquired since January 2, Year 3, and no assets are fully depreciated.
(3) Certain assets that were in the Plant Assets account on January 2, Year 3, wei
sold on December 31, Year 4. For Year 4, a full year's depreciation was recorde
before the assets were removed from the accounting records. Informatio
regarding the sale follows:

Cost of assets	$N 14,000
Accumulated depreciation	4,900
Carrying amount	$N 9,100
Proceeds of sale	14,100
Gain on sale of plant assets	$N 5,000

SUDAMERICA COMPANY

Trial Balance (Nicaduran pesos)
December 31, Year 4

	Debit	Credit
Cash	$N 25,000	
Accounts receivable	53,000	
Allowance for doubtful accounts		$N 500
Inventories	110,000	
Plant assets	210,000	
Accumulated depreciation		79,900
Notes payable		60,000
Accounts payable		22,000
Income taxes payable		40,000
Common stock		50,000
Retained earnings		100,600
Sales		370,000
Cost of goods sold	207,600	
Depreciation expense	22,400	
Other operating expenses	60,000	
Income taxes expense	40,000	
Gain on sale of plant assets		5,000
Totals	$N 728,000	$N 728,000

(4) No journal entries have been made in the Retained Earnings account of Sudamerica since its acquisition other than the net income for Year 3. The Retained Earnings account balance on December 31, Year 3, was translated to $190,000.

(5) The exchange rates for the Nicaduran peso follow:

Jan. 2, Year 3	$2.00
Year 3 average	2.10
Dec. 31, Year 3	2.20
Year 4 average	2.30
Dec. 31, Year 4	2.40

(6) The accumulated translation adjustments totaled $22,000 (credit) on December 31, Year 3.

Instructions Prepare a working paper to translate the trial balance of Sudamerica Company for the year ended December 31, Year 4, from Nicaduran pesos to dollars. The working paper should show the financial statement amounts in pesos, the exchange rates, and the amounts in dollars.

16-7 Prairie Manufacturing Ltd., a Canadian company, acquired a controlling interest in Weinholdt Corp., a West German company, during Year 1. On the date of acquisition the exchange rate was DM1 = $0.40. On December 31, Year 6, the following financial statements, in marks, were forwarded to the Canadian parent company:

WEINHOLDT CORP.

Financial Statements
December 31, Year 6

In Marks

Balance Sheet

Cash		105,000
Accounts receivable	178,500	
Allowance for doubtful accounts	10,500	168,000
Inventories at cost		357,000
Land		420,000
Buildings	1,470,000	
Accumulated depreciation	420,000	1,050,000
Equipment	483,000	
Accumulated depreciation	168,000	315,000
		2,415,000
Accounts payable		210,000
Miscellaneous current payables		105,000
Bonds payable		600,000
Capital stock		850,000
Retained earnings		650,000
		2,415,000

Retained Earnings Statement

Balance, January 1	420,000
Net Income	630,000
	1,050,000
Dividends	400,000
Balance, December 31	650,000

Income Statement

Sales	3,150,000
Cost of goods sold	1,680,000
Depreciation — building	105,000
Depreciation — equipment	63,000
Other expense	672,000
Total	2,520,000
Net income	630,000

Additional information

(1) Relevant exchange rates for the mark were

December 31, Year 6	$0.5
December 31, Year 5	0.4
Average for Year 6	0.4

(2) The land and buildings were held on the date the subsidiary was acquired, ar
there have been no additions or disposals since that date.

(3) On December 31, Year 5, equipment costing 126,000 marks was purchased. Depreciation totaling 21,000 marks was recorded on this equipment in Year 6. The remaining equipment was held on the date the subsidiary was acquired, and no other changes have taken place since that date.

(4) The December 31, Year 6 inventory was acquired during the last quarter of Year 6 when the average exchange rate was $0.49.

(5) On December 31, Year 5, the inventory was 525,000 marks, and was acquired when the average exchange rate was $0.44.

(6) The bonds were issued on December 31, Year 5, and mature on December 31, Year 10.

(7) There have been no changes in capital stock since Year 1.

(8) On December 31, Year 5 the retained earnings translated to $134,400.

(9) Other operating expenses (excluding doubtful account expense of 4,500 marks) were incurred equally throughout Year 6.

(10) Dividends were declared and paid on December 31, Year 6.

(11) Weinholdt Corp. is an integrated foreign operation.

Instructions   Prepare financial statements for Weinholdt Corp. in Canadian dollars.

16-8   The Carakus Corp. is a Canadian company with both domestic and foreign subsidiaries. The 100% owned foreign subsidiary was originally acquired for $85,000 and is located in downtown Sao Paulo, Brazil. As of January 1, Year 3, the translated Canadian dollar retained earnings of Carakus Corp. Brazil Inc. amounted to $100,000 and the net current liabilities at this date were $226,000 (Cz 2,260,000). The income statement, balance sheet, and supplemental information concerning the Brazilian operation for the year ended December 31, Year 3 are as follows:

CARAKUS CORP. — BRAZIL INC.
Statement of Income and Retained Earnings
For the Year Ended December 31, Year 3
(in Cruzieros)

Revenues		Cz 8,000,000
Cost of goods sold	Cz 4,000,000*	
Depreciation	500,000	
Amortization (of goodwill)	10,000	
Interest	390,000	
Income taxes	1,000,000	5,900,000
Net income		Cz 2,100,000
Retained earnings — opening balance		1,000,000
		Cz 3,100,000
Less: Dividends		(1,100,000
Retained earnings — closing balance		Cz 2,000,000

* Beginning inventory	Cz 1,000,000
Cost of production	4,000,000
	Cz 5,000,000
Ending inventory	1,000,000
Cost of goods sold	Cz 4,000,000

Balance Sheet
As At December 31, Year 3
(in Cruzieros)

Cash	Cz 500,000
Accounts receivable	750,000
Inventory	1,000,000
Fixed assets (net):	
Land	100,000
Equipment	2,000,000
Buildings	1,000,000
Goodwill	500,000
Total assets	Cz 5,850,000
Current liabilities	Cz 2,000,000
Long-term debt (due in 4 years)	1,000,000
Share capital	850,000
Retained earnings	2,000,000
Total liabilities and shareholders' equity	Cz 5,850,000

Exchange Rate Information:

The following table lists the major assets and liabilities and specifies the exchange rates in effect at the date they were acquired or assumed:

Cash, accounts receivable,	
current liabilities	1 Cz = $.05 (the current exchange rate as at December 31, Year 3)
Ending inventory	1 Cz = $.08
Fixed assets	1 Cz = $.10
Goodwill	1 Cz = $.10
Long-term debt (issued on	
January 1, Year 3)	1 Cz = $.10
Share capital	1 Cz = $.10

The following table lists the exchange rate in effect at the date the following revenues or expenses were incurred:

Revenues, cost of production	1 Cz = $.08 (average rate for Year 3)
Beginning inventory	1 Cz = $.10
Interest, income taxes,	
dividend	1 Cz = $.08 (average rate for Year 3)

The exchange rate in effect on December 31, Year 2 was $.10.

Instructions

a i) The *CICA Handbook* recommendations on foreign currency translation adopt a situational approach to foreign currency translation. Briefly describe the two major methods of translation which the *CICA Handbook* recommends and indicate when they would be appropriate.

    ii) For *each* of the two translation methods, identify which of Carakus Corp. Brazil Inc. assets and liabilities are translated at the year-end rate.

b Assuming the subsidiary is an integrated foreign operation, calculate, in detail, the exchange gain or loss for Year 3 and translate the income statement of Carakus Corp.–Brazil Inc. for the year ending December 31, Year 3.

c Assuming a self-sustaining foreign operation, calculate, in detail, the equity adjustment from translation (i.e., exchange gain or loss) for Year 3, and translate the income statement of Carakus Corp.–Brazil Inc. for the year ending December 31, Year 3.

[SMA adapted]

16-9 Sentex Limited of Montreal, Quebec, has an 80%-owned subsidiary, Cellular Company Inc., which operates in Erewhon, a small country located in Central America. Cellular was formed by Sentex and Erewhon Development Inc. (located in Erewhon) on January 1, Year 4. Advantages to Sentex of locating in Erewhon are: easy access to raw materials, low operating costs, government incentives, and the fact that the plastics market of Erewhon is not well developed. All management, including the Chief Operating Officer, Mr. V. Globe, has been appointed by Sentex. Top management of Cellular is paid directly by Sentex.

Cellular makes plastic coatings from petrochemical feedstock purchased from Mexico. The process is automated but still uses significant amounts of native Erewhonese labour. The government of Erewhon has determined that this type of development is good for the country, and has underwritten 22,000 cuzos (local currency of Erewhon) of staff training expenses in Year 4 by reducing the taxes payable by Cellular. This employment assistance is not expected to continue in the future.

Approximately 75% of total sales by Cellular is made to Sentex which uses the plastic coatings in its Montreal operations. These coatings are generally of a heavy grade and require special set-up by Cellular. The Sentex orders are handled directly by Mr. Globe and his assistant, Mr. A. Oppong, and the price is set on the basis of variable costs of manufacture, plus freight and a 30% markup, less applicable export tax incentives. The export tax incentive received by Cellular has been about 1,000 cuzos per order. Plastic coatings are also sold to both commercial and wholesale outlets in Erewhon, with commercial users constituting 20% of the total sales revenue of Cellular.

Cellular has agreed with the Erewhon government not to pay any dividends out of profits for two years. After that, it is anticipated that the majority of profits will be remitted by Cellular to Sentex and its other major stockholder, Erewhon Development Inc.

The opening balance sheet of Cellular Company Inc. at January 1, Year 4, was as follows:

(in cuzos)

Cash	30,000	Long-term debt	180,000
Fixed assets	350,000	Common Stock	200,000
	380,000		380,000

All debt financing was provided by Sentex. The debt was incurred on January 1, Year 4, in cuzos, and is secured by the assets of Cellular.

Additional Information:

(1) Raw material and labour costs were incurred uniformly throughout the year.
(2) Sales were made uniformly throughout the year.
(3) The fixed assets were acquired on January 1, Year 4, and are depreciated using the sum-of-the-years'-digits method over four years.
(4) The note receivable is a 90-day non-interest-bearing note received from a customer in exchange for merchandise sold in October.
(5) Land was purchased on December 31, Year 4, for 10,000 cuzos.

(6) Cost of sales and inventory include depreciation of 98,000 cuzos and 22,000 cuzos respectively. See Cost of Goods Sold schedule below.

The following exchange rates were in effect for Year 4:

Rate at January 1, Year 4	1 cuzo = $2.00 Canadian
Average rate for Year 4	1 cuzo = $1.82 Canadian
Rate at December 31, Year 4	1 cuzo = $1.65 Canadian

CELLULAR COMPANY INC.
Income Statement
For the Year Ended December 31, Year 4
(in cuzos)

Sales			600,000
Cost of goods sold*			400,000
Gross margin			200,000
Selling and administrative expenses		70,000	
Interest		20,000	90,000
Net income before taxes			110,000
Local taxes		33,000	
Less allowance for:			
Export incentive	6,500		
Training costs	22,000	28,500	4,500
Net Income after taxes			105,500

*Cost of Goods Sold Schedule (in cuzos)

Material purchases	300,000
Labour	70,000
Depreciation	120,000
Total	490,000
Less Inventory at Dec. 31, Year 4 . . .	(90,000)
Cost of goods sold	400,000

CELLULAR COMPANY INC.
Balance Sheet
December 31, Year 4
(in cuzos)

Assets
Current assets

Cash	25,000
Notes receivable	100,000
Accounts receivable	65,000
Inventories (at cost)	90,000
	280,000
Fixed assets (at cost less accumulated depreciation of 120,000)	230,000
Land (for future development)	10,000
	520,000

Liabilities

Current liabilities

Accounts payable	30,000
Taxes payable	4,500
	34,500

Long-term liabilities

10% Bonds payable due January 1, Year 11	180,000
	214,500

Equities

Common stock	200,000
Retained earnings	105,500
	305,500
	520,000

Required:

Sentex is in the process of preparing consolidated financial statements for the year ended December 31, Year 4.

a Which method of translation should Sentex use, according to Canadian generally accepted accounting principles? Justify your selection, using the information from the question.

b Translate into Canadian dollars at December 31, Year 4, according to Canadian generally accepted accounting principles, the following balance sheet accounts of Cellular Company Inc.

(i) 10% Bonds payable

(ii) Fixed assets (net)

c Calculate the translation gain/loss on the accounts of Cellular Company Inc. and show its disposition, according to Canadian generally accepted accounting principles. [SMA adapted]

5

ACCOUNTING FOR FIDUCIARIES

17 RECEIVERSHIP AND BANKRUPTCY: LIQUIDATION AND REORGANIZATION

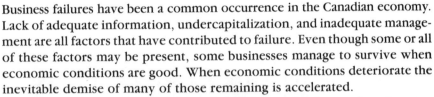

Business failures have been a common occurrence in the Canadian economy. Lack of adequate information, undercapitalization, and inadequate management are all factors that have contributed to failure. Even though some or all of these factors may be present, some businesses manage to survive when economic conditions are good. When economic conditions deteriorate the inevitable demise of many of those remaining is accelerated.

The economic recession of the early 1980s brought about a sharp increase in business failures. The decline in economic activity coupled with record high interest rates left many businesses in serious financial condition. Profits dropped drastically, and severe cash shortages followed. The resultant inability to pay debts as they came due led to the receivership or bankruptcy of an increasing number of businesses. The annual Statistical Summary issued by the Office of the Superintendent of Bankruptcy, Ottawa, Canada, yielded the following information regarding business bankruptcies over a six-year period:

Year	Number of Business Bankruptcies
1978	5546
1979	5694
1980	6595
1981	8055
1982	10765
1983	10260

The full picture of the magnitude of business failure during this period is not presented in these statistics due to the fact that they only reflect bankruptcies and do not include businesses that went into receivership. In this chapter, we discuss the various legal and accounting issues associated with receivership and bankruptcy.

SECURED AND UNSECURED CREDITORS

In conjunction with the going concern concept, the liabilities of a business are classified as either current or long-term. When a business is in financial difficulty and the going concern concept is questionable, it is more informative and useful to view the creditors of a business as either secured or unsecured.

A *secured creditor* is one who holds a mortgage, charge or lien against the property of a debtor as security for a debt due from the debtor. The secured category can be further classified into fully secured and partially secured. An *unsecured creditor* is one who holds a debt due from a debtor against which no property of the debtor has been pledged. The Bankruptcy Act provides a further classification of the unsecured category by describing certain types of claims as having a priority requiring payment in full before the remaining unsecured creditors are paid. The further classifications of secured and unsecured creditors will be discussed later in this chapter. (See page 703.) It should be noted that the classification of secured and unsecured is not dependent on the current or long-term classification. Both current and long-term liabilities are either secured or unsecured.

THE DIFFERENCE BETWEEN RECEIVERSHIP AND BANKRUPTCY

Confusion exists because the terms receivership and bankruptcy are often used incorrectly to represent similar conditions when in fact the terms are descriptions of two different conditions. A *condition of receivership* exists when, because of a violation of the terms of a debt covenant, a secured creditor has appointed an agent (the receiver-manager) to seize the debtor's property pledged against the debt. While the result of this action is often the complete liquidation of the debtor's business, the business itself is not legally bankrupt. Confusion is increased by the terms "official receiver," "interim receiver," and "receiving order" used in the Bankruptcy Act.

Bankruptcy is a legal state in which, under the jurisdiction of the court, the assets of a debtor have been seized by a licensed trustee in bankruptcy for the protection and benefit of the unsecured creditors. This legal state may be the result of actions taken by the unsecured creditors (involuntary bankruptcy) or actions taken by the debtor (voluntary bankruptcy). In most cases the eventual result is also the complete liquidation of the business.

RECEIVERSHIP

In many situations the assets of a business have been pledged as security against its debts. Many bank loans are secured by a general assignment of accounts receivable and/or the assignment of inventory under Section 178 of the **Bank Act**. Land, buildings and equipment are often pledged as security to the mortgage and debenture liabilities of a business. When a default of the loan requirements occurs the secured creditor appoints a **receiver-manager** to seize the pledged assets. (Technically speaking, the person appointed by the bank to seize receivables or inventory is called an agent, and a receiver-manager is the person who seizes the assets secured by a debenture, which in most cases involves all of a firm's assets.) It is the duty of the receiver-manager to sell the assets at the highest price possible on behalf of his client, the secured creditor. If the proceeds from the sale exceed the secured creditor's claim, the amount of the excess reverts to the debtor. If the proceeds from the sale are not sufficient to discharge the liability, the deficiency becomes an unsecured claim. Any payment on this deficiency may only be possible if the business is forced into bankruptcy.

Often the person appointed as receiver-manager is a licensed trustee in bankruptcy, although this is not a necessary condition for his appointment. In some instances the receiver-manager operates the business for a period of time in order to maximize the amount received from the sale of the pledged assets. A factory is operated in order to transform any raw material and work in process inventories into finished products which might command higher prices than if the inventories were sold in their incomplete condition. The receiver-manager may attempt to sell the business as a going concern, rather than sell the individual assets on a piecemeal basis, especially if the business appears to be viable and an infusion of capital, either debt or equity, is all that appears necessary to turn the operation around. In all of the situations that have been described the owners will probably lose the business and receive little if any payment on their equity.

BANKRUPTCY

A federal statute, the Bankruptcy Act was first passed in 1919, and has been amended from time to time, with the last significant change taking place in 1966. Attempts at further amendments by the parliament of Canada have not been successful. The purpose of the Act is to control the distribution of the assets of a financially troubled business to its creditors so that all creditors of a particular class receive equal treatment. While all creditors come under the Act's jurisdiction, most of the remedies available to secured creditors by nature of their security agreement are not affected. As a result the Act's provisions and remedies exist primarily for the **benefit of the unsecured creditors** of a business.

Administration

The Bankruptcy Act falls within the portfolio of the Minister of Consumer and Corporate Affairs. The senior civil servant located in Ottawa, responsible for administering the Act, is called the **Superintendent of Bankruptcy**. The Superintendent is also responsible for the licensing of persons who act as trustees in bankruptcy.

Each province in Canada is designated as a bankruptcy district and necessary can be further divided into two or more bankruptcy division Each division is administered by a civil servant called the **Official Receiver** When bankruptcy proceedings are initiated against a business, the Official Receiver becomes involved, and among other things examines the bankrupt under oath, fixes the amount of the bond posted by the trustee in bankruptcy, and chairs the first meeting of creditors.

The Act provides the senior court of each province with jurisdiction i bankruptcy proceedings. All bankruptcy matters are heard either by th **Bankruptcy Judge** or the **Registrar**, both of whom are appointed b court. The Registrar handles all matters not requiring judicial interpretation

The actual administration of the estate of the bankrupt is handled by **licensed trustee in bankruptcy** who is often a professional accountant in private practice. Upon receiving his appointment by the court, the trustee

(1) takes possession of the assets and accounting records of the bankrupt
(2) prepares an inventory of the assets,
(3) takes all necessary precautions to protect the assets including the insuring of all insurable assets,
(4) notifies all creditors by registered mail as to the date of the first meeting of creditors, and
(5) verifies the bankrupt's statement of affairs.

The first meeting of creditors is held to examine the bankrupt's statement of affairs, to confirm the appointment of the trustee or to appoint a subst tute, and to elect **inspectors** to assist the trustee in the administration c the estate. Creditors must file a proof of claim with the trustee in order t participate at meetings and share in the proceeds from the sale of the debtor' assets. Under the direction of the inspectors the trustee sells the unpledge assets of the estate and distributes the proceeds to the unsecured creditor in accordance with the provisions of the Act. Assets that have been pledge to secured creditors are not normally realized by the trustee in bankruptcy although the secured creditors may allow the trustee to realize the pledge assets if they so choose.

It is not uncommon to have a business go into receivership upon th action of a secured creditor, and later be declared bankrupt upon actions o unsecured creditors. Further complications occur when the receiver-manage and the trustee in bankruptcy are different persons. A situation such as thi requires cooperation between the two trustees and may involve cour intervention to resolve any conflicts.

Insolvency and bankruptcy

The Act describes "insolvent persons" and "bankrupt persons". **Person** include individuals, partnerships, unincorporated associations, corporation and cooperative societies. Not included are banks, insurance companies trust and loan companies and railway companies. Bankruptcy provision for these companies are covered under their incorporation statutes. The main focus of our discussion is the bankruptcy of incorporated businesses, although most of the provisions would also apply to individuals.

An **insolvent person** is one

(1) who is not bankrupt but carries on business in Canada and has liabilities exceeding one thousand dollars, and
(2) who is unable to meet, or has ceased paying his obligations as they come due, or
(3) whose assets, measured at fair market value, are less than the amount of his debts.

A **bankrupt person** is one who, in accordance with the provisions of the Act:

(1) has made an assignment of his assets for the benefit of his creditors, or,
(2) against whom a receiving order has been made.

Bankruptcy is a legal state while insolvency is not. A person can be insolvent without being bankrupt but cannot be bankrupt without being insolvent.

Voluntary and involuntary bankruptcy

A person may **declare bankruptcy voluntarily** (as a result of his own actions) or may be **declared bankrupt involuntarily** (as a result of the actions of his creditors). Voluntary bankruptcy occurs when a person makes an assignment of his assets for the benefit of his creditors. The assignment is made to the Official Receiver accompanied by a statement of affairs and a listing of creditors. A trustee is appointed and the administration of the bankrupt's estate commences. There is one other voluntary action that a person may institute that could result in bankruptcy. This action is called **a proposal** and will be discussed in a later section of this chapter (see page 700).

A person may involuntarily be declared bankrupt as a result of an action taken by his creditors. The Act provides that one or more creditors with claims totaling at least one thousand dollars may file a petition with the court for the **granting of a receiving order against a debtor**. The petitioning creditor(s) must show that the debtor has committed an ''act of bankruptcy'' within the preceding six months.

The following is a partial outline of actions that constitute ''acts of bankruptcy'' under the Act:

(1) A debtor gives notice to any of his creditors that he has suspended or is about to suspend payments of his debts.
(2) A debtor exhibits to any meeting of his creditors a statement of assets and liabilities that shows he is insolvent.
(3) A debtor makes a fraudulent conveyance, gift or transfer of his property or any part thereof.
(4) A debtor ceases to meet his liabilities as they become due.

It should be obvious from this partial listing that it is not too difficult for a creditor to show that an ''act of bankruptcy'' has been committed. Once the court agrees and grants the receiving order the debtor is bankrupt.

From the foregoing it would appear that it is fairly easy for an unsecured creditor to avail himself of the protection and remedies provided under the Act. However, it is not quite as easy as it seems. The petition for a receiving order must include the name of a licensed trustee who is willing to act. The trustee's remuneration comes only from the proceeds received from the sale of the non-pledged assets of the debtor. If all or a majority of the assets are pledged against claims of secured creditors the trustee will not be able to collect a fee for his services and therefore will not be willing to act. Before allowing a petitioning unsecured creditor to include his name in the petition, the trustee will require that creditor to guarantee the payment of his fees. In some cases a trustee's fee could exceed $10,000, and therefore this guarantee of fee requirement may be too risky for a small creditor to assume.

Proposals

Occasionally a debtor will call a meeting of his creditors, outline his financial difficulties, and suggest remedies to alleviate the situation. This process is called a *proposal*. The remedies might include some of the following:

(1) postponement of payment of principal or interest,
(2) reduction in the rate of interest,
(3) forgiveness of debt,
(4) acceptance of the payment of a percentage of the claims as full payment,
(5) conversion of debt to equity.

The purpose of such a proposal is to convince the creditors that the business is viable and worth saving, and that a larger payment will eventually be forthcoming as a result of the suggested remedies than would be the case under a forced liquidation.

Proposals can be made *either outside or within* the provisions of the Bankruptcy Act. There is a danger involved when a proposal is made outside of the Act. The creditors have become aware of the extent of the debtor's financial difficulty, and any one creditor armed with this knowledge can commence receivership or bankruptcy proceedings.

A proposal made under the Act immediately stops all actions by unsecured creditors against the debtor. A licensed trustee is appointed to investigate and report to the creditors on the merits of the proposal. During this period the trustee does not take possession of the debtor's assets. The Act requires that the proposal must insure the payment in full of unsecured claims having priority. In order for the proposal to be accepted, a majority of creditors representing three quarters in value of claims must agree to its provisions and the court must also be in agreement. The risk involved in this situation is that rejection by the creditors or the court results in bankruptcy.

It is also possible for a *bankrupt* to *submit a proposal* to his creditors. In this situation the trustee has control and title to the debtor's assets due to his bankruptcy. If the proposal is accepted by the creditors the bankruptcy is annulled; if rejected the liquidation under bankruptcy proceeds.

Interim receivership

During the period between the presentation of a proposal made under the Act and its acceptance or rejection by the creditors, the debtor's assets are not held under the jurisdiction of the court. This is also true during the period between the application for and granting of a receiving order. In both situations the period may be a week or greater. In order to protect the interests of the creditors during these time periods, the Act allows the appointment of an *interim receiver* to take place, upon the application of a creditor to the court. If the application is granted, a trustee is appointed as an interim receiver to supervise the operation of the debtor's business. The trustee does not acquire title to the debtor's assets, but rather oversees the cash flows that occur during the period. Thus, the debtor's business comes under the control of the court which prevents any *fraudulent disposals* of assets. The granting of a receiving order or the acceptance or rejection of the proposal would end the period of interim receivership. Note that the term "receivership" used in this context describes the result of actions taken by unsecured creditors, while the normal use of the term "receivership" is to describe the result of action taken by secured creditors.

Unsecured liabilities with priority

During the liquidation of a bankrupt estate, the non-pledged assets are sold and the proceeds therefrom, together with the excess of the proceeds from the sale of pledged assets over the amount of their secured claims, become available for payment to the unsecured creditors. However Section 107 of the Act describes certain unsecured claims as having a priority for payment in full before the remaining unsecured creditors receive payment. This is like saying all unsecured creditors will be treated equally, but some will be treated more equally than others. The content of the items listed in Section 107 can be summarized as follows:

1 Funeral expenses of a deceased bankrupt. Obviously this is not applicable to incorporated businesses.
2 Fees and expenses of the trustee, and legal expenses incurred in the administration of the estate.
3 The levy of the Superintendent of Bankruptcy. The Act provides that 2% of the amount available to pay unsecured creditors is to be deducted to help defray the government's costs of administering the Act.
4 Wages owed to employees for a period not exceeding three months prior to bankruptcy, provided that the total amount owing to one person does not exceed five hundred dollars. Any amount owing that exceeds five hundred dollars but is within the three-month period, or any amount owing for a period exceeding three months, is unsecured without priority.
5 Municipal taxes.
6 All other claims of the Crown.

After the unsecured claims with priority have been paid in full, the remaining cash is paid ratably to the remaining unsecured creditors, subject of course to the deduction for the Superintendent's levy.

Creditor preferences, disposal of assets, and customer deposits

Bankruptcy law exists basically to insure that an insolvent person's creditors of a particular class receive equal treatment. The Act allows the trustee to examine all transactions entered into by a bankrupt person for varying time periods prior to the date of bankruptcy in order to ascertain whether any creditors have received *preferential treatment*, or whether the bankrupt's property has been disposed of for *inadequate consideration*; and if necessary have the transactions *set aside* by the court. For example, if a debtor had paid one unsecured creditor in full just prior to being declared bankrupt without treating the remaining unsecured creditors in a similar manner the transaction could be set aside. If this happened the creditor that received payment would have to return it to the estate of the bankrupt. In a like manner, the sale of assets by a debtor at less than fair value prior to becoming bankrupt, could result in a court order reversing the transaction.

The treatment of *deposits* made by customers to a business that subsequently goes bankrupt has long been a contentious issue with consumer groups lobbying for changes in the Act. Newspaper reports outline the dilemmas that individuals find themselves in after making large deposits with furniture stores or automobile dealers only to learn that the store or dealership has gone bankrupt the very next day. They are understandably dismayed when they realize that they rank as ordinary unsecured creditors without priority, and will probably receive very little of their deposits back. This problem could have been avoided if the monies had been deposited into a legal trust account by the now bankrupt company. However a legal trust is not established simply by making an accounting entry in the books of the company. It must be a trust established in accordance with some statute, and in most situations this has not been done. It is of little consolation to know that the bankrupt might be charged under the Act for accepting deposits knowing that he was insolvent.

Discharge from bankruptcy

Bankrupt individuals can receive a discharge from their bankruptcy by the court. This means that they are free from this legal state and can have a fresh start without the burden of debt. Incorporated companies can only receive a discharge if all their creditors are paid in full. This effectively means that bankrupt corporations cannot be discharged.

Role of trustee in bankruptcy liquidation

The trustee's role in liquidation proceedings is concerned with the proper reporting of the financial condition of the debtor and adequate accounting and reporting for the trustee for the debtor's estate.

Financial condition of debtor enterprise: Statement of affairs

A business enterprise that enters liquidation proceedings is a *quitting concern,* not a *going concern.* Consequently, a balance sheet, which reports the financial position of a going concern, is inappropriate for an enterprise in liquidation.

The financial statement designed for a business enterprise entering liquidation is the **statement of affairs.** The purpose of the statement of affairs is to present the assets and liabilities of the debtor enterprise from a **liquidation viewpoint,** because liquidation is the outcome of the bankruptcy proceedings. Thus, assets in the statement of affairs are valued at estimated **current fair values**; carrying amounts of the assets are presented on a memorandum basis. In addition, assets and liabilities in the statement of affairs are classified according to the rankings and priorities set forth in the Bankruptcy Act; the current/noncurrent classification used in a balance sheet for a going concern is not appropriate for the statement of affairs. It should be noted that the accounting statement of affairs does not use the same format as the statement with the same name required by the Act. However the information contained is basically the same, and the accounting statement is easier to comprehend.

Classifications Used in the Statement of Affairs   The classifications used in the statement of affairs can be described as follows:

1 *Assets Pledged with Fully Secured Liabilities.* These include all pledged assets with an expected net realizable value that is equal to or exceeds the amount of the liability that each secures.

2 *Assets Pledged with Partially Secured Liabilities.* All other pledged assets with an expected net realizable value that is less than the amount of the liability that each secures.

3 *Free Assets.* Assets that have not been pledged as security to any liability.

4 *Unsecured Liabilities with Priority.* Unsecured claims which in accordance with section 107 of the Bankruptcy Act must be fully satisfied before any monies are paid to the remaining unsecured claims.

5 *Fully Secured Liabilities.* Liabilities that are secured by the pledge of specific assets the net realizable value of which is expected to be equal to or exceed the amount of the claim.

6 *Partially Secured Liabilities.* Liabilities that are secured by the pledge of specific assets the net realizable value of which is expected to be less than the amount of the claim.

7 *Unsecured Liabilities without Priority.* All liabilities that are not secured by the pledge of specific assets, except those that have priority for payment under section 107 of the Act.

8 *Shareholders' Equity.* The total of all shareholders' equity accounts.

Illustration of Statement of Affairs   The balance sheet of Sanders Company on June 30, Year 4, the date the company filed a voluntary bankruptcy assignment, is shown on page 704.

Other information available from notes to financial statements and from estimates of current fair values of assets follows:

1 Notes receivable with a face amount plus accrued interest totaling $19,300, and a current fair value of $13,300, collateralize the notes payable to National Bank.

2 Finished goods are expected to be sold at a markup of 33⅓% over cost, with disposal costs estimated at 20% of selling prices. Estimated cost to complete

SANDERS COMPANY
Balance Sheet
June 30, Year 4

Assets

Current assets:

Cash		$ 2,700
Notes receivable and accrued interest, less allowance		
for doubtful notes, $6,000		13,300
Accounts receivable, less allowance for doubtful		
accounts, $23,240		16,110
Inventories, at fifo cost:		
Finished goods		12,000
Goods in process		35,100
Material		19,600
Factory supplies		6,450
Short-term prepayments		950
Total current assets		$106,210
Plant assets, at cost:		
Land	$ 20,000	
Buildings (net)	41,250	
Machinery (net)	48,800	
Tools (net)	14,700	
Total plant assets		124,750
Total assets		$230,960

Liabilities & Shareholders' Equity

Current liabilties:

Notes payable:		
National Bank, including accrued interest		$ 15,300
Suppliers, including accrued interest		51,250
Accounts payable		52,000
Salaries and wages payable		8,850
Property taxes payable		2,900
Accrued interest on first mortgage bonds payable		1,800
Payroll and income taxes withheld and accrued		1,750
Total current liabilities		$133,850
First mortgage bonds payable		90,000
Total liabilities		$223,850
Shareholders' equity:		
Common stock, no par value, 750 shares authorized		
and issued	$ 75,000	
Deficit	(67,890)	7,110
Total liabilities & shareholders' equity		$230,960

goods in process is $15,400, of which $3,700 would be cost of material and factory supplies used. The estimated selling price of goods in process when completed is $40,000, with disposal costs estimated at 20% of selling prices. Estimated current fair values for material and factory supplies not required to complete goods in process are $8,000 and $1,000, respectively. All short-term prepayments are expected to be consumed in the course of liquidation.

3 Land and buildings, which collateralize the first mortgage bonds payable, have a current fair value of $95,000. Machinery with a carrying amount of $18,200 and current fair value of $10,000 collateralizes notes payable to suppliers in the amount of $12,000, including accrued interest. The current fair value of the remaining machinery is $9,000, net of disposal costs of $1,000, and the current fair value of tools after the amounts used in completing the goods in process inventory is $3,255.

4 Salaries and wages payable are debts having priority under the Bankruptcy Act.

The statement of affairs for Sanders Company on June 30, Year 4, is shown on pages 706 and 707.

The following points should be stressed in the review of the June 30, Year 4, statement of affairs for Sanders:

1 The "Carrying amount" columns in the statement of affairs serve as a tie-in to the balance sheet of Sanders on June 30, Year 4, as well as a basis for determination of expected losses or gains on realization of assets.

2 The classifications facilitate the computation of estimated amounts available for unsecured creditors — those with priority and those without priority.

3 A *contra*, or *offset*, technique is used where the *legal right of setoff* exists. For example, amounts due to fully secured creditors are deducted from the estimated current fair value of the assets serving as collateral; and unsecured liabilities with priority are deducted from estimated amounts available to unsecured creditors from the proceeds of asset realization.

4 An estimated settlement per dollar of unsecured liabilities without priority can be computed by dividing the estimated amount available for unsecured, nonpriority creditors by the total unsecured liabilities, thus:

$$\frac{\$62,865}{\$95,250} = 66 \text{ cents on the dollar}$$

The foregoing computation provides an estimate of the aggregate cash that will be available to unsecured, nonpriority creditors in a liquidation proceeding.

5 The levy of the Superintendent of Bankruptcy has not been included on the statement of affairs. The effect of the levy would be a 2% reduction in the amount available for unsecured creditors, resulting in an estimated deficiency of 36¢ on the dollar and an estimated settlement of 64¢.

Some accountants recommend the preparation of a **statement of estimated deficiency to unsecured creditors** as an adjunct to the statement of affairs. This supplementary financial statement appears unnecessary, because the information it contains is included entirely in the "Estimated amount available" column of the statement of affairs. If the balance sheet prepared on the same date as a statement of affairs includes adequate allowances for doubtful accounts and for estimated liabilities, the statement of affairs will be adequate for comprehensive analysis of the financial condition of a "quitting concern."

Carrying amount	Assets	Current fair value	Estimated amount available	Loss or (gain) on realization
	Assets pledged with fully secured liabilities:			
$20,000	Land ....⎫	$95,000		$(33,750)
41,250	Building ....⎭			
	Less: Fully secured liabilities			
	(contra)	91,800	$ 3,200	
	Assets pledged with partially secured liabilities:			
13,300	Notes and interest receivable (deducted contra)	$13,300		
18,200	Machinery (deducted contra)	$10,000		8,200
	Free assets:			
2,700	Cash	$ 2,700	2,700	
16,110	Accounts receivable	16,110	16,110	
	Inventories:			
12,000	Finished goods	12,800	12,800	(800)
35,100	Goods in process	20,300*	20,300*	14,800
19,600	Material	8,000	8,000	11,600
6,450	Factory supplies	1,000	1,000	5,450
950	Short-term prepayments	-0-	-0-	950
30,600	Machinery	9,000	9,000	21,600
14,700	Tools	3,255	3,255	11,445
	Total estimated amount available		$76,365	$ 39,495
	Less: Unsecured liabilities with priority (contra) ...		13,500	
	Estimated amount available for unsecured, nonpriority creditors (66¢ on the dollar)		$62,865	
	Estimated deficiency to unsecured, nonpriority creditors (34¢ on the dollar)		32,385	
$230,960			$95,250	

* Estimated selling price	$40,000
Less: Estimated "out-of-pocket" completion costs ($15,400 − $3,700)	(11,700)
Estimated disposal costs ($40,000 × 0.20)	(8,000)
Net realizable value	$20,300

Accounting and reporting for trustee

Traditionally, the accounting records and reports for trustees have been extremely detailed and elaborate. However, the provisions of the Bank-ruptcy Act are general; therefore, simple accounting records and reports should be adequate. The authors recommend the following with respect to the accounting records for a liquidating debtor:

SANDERS COMPANY
Statement of Affairs (concluded)
June 30, Year 4

Carrying amount	Liabilities & shareholders' equity		Amount unsecured
	Unsecured liabilities with priority:		
$ 8,850	Salaries and wages payable	$ 8,850	
2,900	Property taxes payable	2,900	
1,750	Payroll and income taxes withheld and accrued . .	1,750	
	Total (deducted contra)	$13,500	
	Fully secured liabilities:		
90,000	First mortgage bonds payable	$90,000	
1,800	Accrued interest on first mortgage bonds		
	payable	1,800	
	Total (deducted contra)	$91,800	
	Partially secured liabilities:		
15,300	Notes and accrued interest payable to National		
	Bank	$15,300	
	Less: Net realizable value of notes receivable		
	pledged as collateral (contra)	13,300	$ 2,000
12,000	Notes and accrued interest payable to suppliers .	$12,000	
	Less: Estimated realizable value of machinery		
	pledged as collateral (contra)	10,000	2,000
	Unsecured liabilities without priority:		
39,250	Notes payable to suppliers		39,250
52,000	Accounts payable		52,000
7,110	Shareholders' equity		
$230,960			$95,250

1 The accounting records of the debtor should be used during the period that a trustee carries on the operations of the debtor's business.

2 An **accountability** technique should be used once the trustee begins realization of the debtor's assets. In the accountability method of accounting the assets and liabilities for which the trustee is responsible are recorded in the accounting records of the trustee at their statement of affairs valuations, with a balancing debit to a memorandum-type balancing account with a title such as Estate Deficit. The amount of the debit is equal to the estimated deficiency to unsecured creditors in the statement of affairs. Appropriate cash receipts and cash payments journal entries are made for the trustee's realization of assets and payment of liabilities. No "gain" or "loss" account is necessary because the business enterprise in liquidation does not require an income statement. Differences between cash amounts realized and carrying amounts of the related assets or liabilities are debited or credited directly to the Estate Deficit account.

3 The Act requires the trustee to report to the court the receipts and disbursements made since the date of bankruptcy. In addition to this legal requirement, a statement of realization and liquidation would be useful to present to interim meetings of creditors and inspectors.

Illustration of Accountability Technique Assume that Arline Wells, the trustee in the voluntary bankruptcy proceedings for Sanders Company (see pages 703 to 705), took custody of the assets of Sanders on June 30, Year 4. The accountant for the trustee prepared the following journal entry on June 30, Year 4:

SANDERS COMPANY, IN BANKRUPTCY
Arline Wells, Trustee
General Journal
June 30, Year 4

Cash	2,700	
Notes and Interest Receivable	13,300	
Accounts Receivable	16,110	
Finished Goods Inventory	12,800	
Goods in Process Inventory	20,300	
Material Inventory	8,000	
Factory Supplies	1,000	
Land and Buildings	95,000	
Machinery ($10,000 + $9,000)	19,000	
Tools	3,255	
Estate Deficit	32,385 (1)	
Notes and Interest Payable		66,550
Accounts Payable		52,000
Salaries and Wages Payable		8,850
Property Taxes Payable		2,900
Payroll and Income Taxes Withheld and Accrued		1,750
Accrued Interest on First Mortgage Bonds Payable		1,800
First Mortgage Bonds Payable		90,000

To record current fair values of assets and liabilities of Sanders
Company, in voluntary bankruptcy proceedings.

(1) Equal to estimated deficiency to unsecured, nonpriority creditors in statement of affairs on page 706.

When the trustee realizes assets of Sanders, the required journal entry is a debit to Cash, a credit to the appropriate asset account, and a debit or credit to the Estate Deficit account for a loss or gain on realization, respectively. Expenses of administering the estate also are debited to the Estate Deficit account.

Statement of Realization and Liquidation A form of realization and liquidation statement that should be useful to the bankruptcy court and creditors is illustrated on page 709. This financial statement is based on the assumed activities of the trustee for the estate of Sanders Company during the month of July, Year 4, including operating the business long enough to complete the goods in process inventory.

An accompanying statement of cash receipts and cash payments for the month ended July 31, Year 4, would show the sources of the $39,654 total

SANDERS COMPANY, IN BANKRUPTCY

Arline Wells, Trustee
Statement of Realization and Liquidation
For Month Ended July 31, Year 4

Estate deficit, June 30, Year 4 . . . . $32,385

Assets realized:

	Current fair value, June 30, Year 4	Realization proceeds	Loss or (gain)	
Accounts receivable	$14,620	$12,807	$ 1,813	
Finished goods inventory	12,800	11,772	1,028	
Goods in process inventory . . .	14,820	15,075	(255)	
Totals	$42,240	$39,654		2,586

Liabilities with priority liquidated at carrying amounts:

Salaries and wages payable . . . . $ 8,850

Property taxes payable 2,900

Payroll and income taxes withheld and accrued 1,750

Total liabilities with priority liquidated $13,500

Estate administration expenses paid 1,867

Estate deficit, July 31, Year 4 . . . . $36,838

realization proceeds, and the dates, cheque numbers, payees, and amounts of the $13,500 paid for liabilities with priority and the $1,867 paid for estate administration expenses. Supporting exhibits would summarize assets not yet realized and liabilities not yet liquidated.

Liquidation involves realization of the assets of the debtor's estate. In many cases, an insolvent business enterprise may be restored to a sound financial footing if it can defer payment of its debts. A section of the Bankruptcy Act, dealing with proposals, enables a business enterprise to continue operations under court protection from creditor lawsuits, while the proposal is being considered.

BANKRUPTCY REORGANIZATION (PROPOSAL)

As discussed previously, a company in financial difficulty can seek a remedy by making a proposal to its creditors. Typically a proposal involves the reduction of the amounts payable to some creditors, other creditors' acceptance of equity securities of the debtor for their claims and a restructuring of the par or stated value of the common stock of the debtor. If the proposal is accepted by a majority of the creditors and the court, the plan is binding on the enterprise, and on all creditors and owners of the enterprise. The accounting term for such a plan is a *reorganization*.

Accounting for a reorganization

The accounting for a reorganization typically requires journal entries for write-downs of assets; reductions of par or stated value of capital stock (with recognition of resultant contributed surplus in excess of par or stated value); extensions of due dates of notes payable; exchanges of debt securities for equity securities; and the elimination of a deficit. The journal entries for a bankruptcy reorganization thus resemble the entries to record a *quasi-reorganization*, as illustrated in *Intermediate Accounting* of this series. In essence, the only difference for accounting purposes between a bankruptcy reorganization and a quasi-reorganization is the authority for the journal entries. Bankruptcy reorganization journal entries result from the acceptance of a proposal by the court; journal entries for a quasi-reorganization are authorized by action of shareholders.

It is important for an accountant to be thoroughly familiar with the plan of reorganization, in order to account properly for its implementation. The accountant must be careful to avoid charging post-reorganization operations with losses that arose before the reorganization.

To illustrate the accounting for a reorganization, assume that Sanders Company (see pages 703 to 705) filed a petition for reorganization, rather than for liquidation, on June 30, Year 4. The plan of reorganization, which was approved by shareholders and all unsecured creditors and confirmed by the court, included the following:

1 Deposit $21,000 with trustee, as soon as cash becomes available, to cover liabilities with priority and costs of reorganization proceedings.
2 Amend articles of incorporation to provide for 20,000 shares of authorized no par value stock with a stated value of $10 per share. The new common stock to be exchanged on a two-for-one basis for each of the 750 no par value common shares now outstanding. In addition, each existing common shareholder agrees to subscribe to a new issue of common stock at $10 per share on a three-for-one basis for each of the 750 no par value shares now outstanding.
3 Extend due date of unsecured notes payable to suppliers totaling $15,250 for four years, until May 31, Year 9. Decrease the interest rate on the notes from 14% to 11%, the current fair rate of interest.
4 Exchange 2,400 shares of new no par common stock (at a stated value of $10 a share) for unsecured notes payable to suppliers totaling $24,000.
5 Pay vendors 70 cents per dollar of accounts payable owed.

The journal entries on page 711, numbered to correspond with the provisions of the reorganization plan outlined above, were recorded by Sanders Company as cash became available from the collection of receivables, the sale of inventory, and the subscription to the new share issue.

After the plan of reorganization has been carried out, the following journal entry is appropriate for eliminating the $67,890 accumulated deficit of Sanders Company on June 30, Year 4:

Journal entry to eliminate deficit	Contributed Surplus	59,290	
	Gain from Discharge of Indebtedness in Bankruptcy	15,600	
	Costs of Bankruptcy Proceedings		7,000
	Retained Earnings		67,890
	To eliminate deficit on June 30, Year 4, and close bankruptcy gain and costs to Contributed Surplus.		

SANDERS COMPANY
General Journal

(1) Cash with Trustee	21,000	
Cash		21,000
To record deposit of cash with trustee under terms of bankruptcy reorganization.		
Salaries and Wages Payable	8,850	
Property Taxes Payable	2,900	
Payroll and Income Taxes Withheld and Accrued	1,750	
Cash with Trustee		13,500
To record trustee's payment of liabilities with priority.		
Costs of Bankruptcy Proceedings	7,000	
Cash with Trustee		7,000
To record trustee's payment of costs of bankruptcy proceedings.		
(2) Common Stock (old)	75,000	
Common Stock (new)		15,000
Contributed Surplus		60,000
To record issuance of 1,500 shares of no par common stock with a stated value of $10 in exchange for 750 shares of no par common stock.		
Cash	22,500	
Common stock (new)		22,500
To record issuance of 2,250 shares of no par common stock at $10 per share to existing shareholders.		
(3) 14% Notes Payable to Suppliers, due May 31, Year 5	15,250	
11% Notes Payable to Suppliers, due May 31, Year 9		15,250
To record extension of due dates of notes payable to suppliers and decrease of interest rate from 14% to 11%.		
(4) Notes Payable to Suppliers	24,000	
Common Stock (new)		24,000
To record exchange of 2,400 shares of no par common stock for $24,000 face amount of notes payable, at a stated value of $10 a share.		
(5) Accounts Payable	52,000	
Cash		36,400
Gain from Discharge of Indebtedness in Bankruptcy		15,600
To record payment of $0.70 per dollar of accounts payable to vendors.		

The effect of the foregoing journal entries is to show a "clean slate" for Sanders Company as a result of the bankruptcy reorganization and the write-off of the accumulated deficit existing on the date of the petition for reorganization. The extension of due dates of some liabilities, conversion of other liabilities to common stock, and liquidation of accounts payable at less than their face amount, should enable Sanders to resume operations as a going concern. For a reasonable number of years subsequent to the reorganization, Sanders should "date" the retained earnings in its balance sheets to disclose that the earnings were accumulated after the reorganization. The elaborate and often complex issues involved in a reorganization must be disclosed in a note to the financial statements for the period in which the plan of reorganization was carried out. The shareholder's equity section of the Sanders Company balance sheet after the above journal entries would appear as follows:

Shareholders' equity:
　Common stock, no par with a stated value of $10, authorized
　　20,000 shares, issued 6,150 shares $61,50
Contributed surplus   71
　　　Total $62,21

REVIEW QUESTIONS

1　Identify the various classes of creditors whose claims are dealt with in bankruptcy liquidations.

2　Describe the process of *liquidation* under the Bankruptcy Act.

3　Differentiate between *voluntary* and *involuntary bankruptcy*.

4　What is a *statement of affairs*?

5　Describe the unsecured debts having priority over other unsecured debts under the provisions of the Bankruptcy Act.

6　Who can file an *involuntary petition* for bankruptcy liquidation? What is this petition called?

7　Describe the priority of claims for wages and salaries under the Bankruptcy Act.

8　Describe the authority of a bankruptcy trustee with respect to a *preference*.

9　What are the effects of a *discharge* in bankruptcy? Explain.

10　What use is made of the accounting financial statement known as a *statement of affairs*? Explain.

11　The annual statistical summary issued by the Superintendent of Bankruptcy is an accurate portrayal of business failure in a given year. Do you agree with this statement? Explain.

12　Differentiate between *secured* and *unsecured* creditors.

13　Is there any difference between *receivership* and *bankruptcy*? Explain.

14　Explain the following terms: *official receiver, receivership, receiving order, interim receiver*, and *receiver-manager*.

15　Describe three ways in which a business organization could be declared bankrupt.

16 Distinguish between an *insolvent* person and a *bankrupt* person.

17 All unsecured creditors are treated equally under the Bankruptcy Act. Do you agree with this statement? Explain.

18 Deposits made by customers of a bankrupt business are given special treatment under the Bankruptcy Act. Do you agree? Explain.

19 A business is being liquidated under the provisions of the Bankruptcy Act. Its balance sheet shows a deferred tax liability of $200,000 due to the excess of capital cost allowance over book depreciation. How will this liability be reported on the statement of affairs? Explain.

20 Describe the *accountability* method of accounting used by a trustee in a bankruptcy liquidation.

21 Must all classes of creditors accept a reorganization plan before the plan may be confirmed by the bankruptcy court? Explain.

EXERCISES

Ex 17-1   Select the best answer for each of the following multiple-choice questions:

1 In the journal entry to open the accounting records of a trustee in a bankruptcy liquidation, the debit to the Estate Deficit ledger account is in the statement of affairs amount of the:
   a Estimated deficiency to unsecured, nonpriority creditors
   b Total estimated amount available
   c Estimated amount available for unsecured, nonpriority creditors
   d Shareholders' equity of the debtor corporation

2 In journal entries for a bankruptcy reorganization, the difference between the carrying amount of a liability of the debtor and the amount accepted by the creditor in full settlement of the liability is credited to:
   a Retained earnings (deficit)
   b Contributed surplus
   c Cash with trustee
   d Some other ledger account

3 The bankruptcy trustee for Insolvent Company sold assets having a carrying amount of $10,000 for $8,500 cash. The journal entry (explanation omitted) to record the sale is:

a Cash	8,500	
Loss on Realization of Assets	1,500	
Assets		10,000
b Cash	8,500	
Estate Administration Expenses	1,500	
Assets		10,000
c Cash	8,500	
Cost of Goods Sold	10,000	
Sales		8,500
Assets		10,000
d Cash	8,500	
Estate Deficit	1,500	
Assets		10,000

4 In the **accounting** statement of affairs, assets pledged for partially secur
liabilities are:
  a Deducted from the related liabilities in the liabilities and shareholders' equi
  section
  b Included in the "estimated amount available" column of the assets section
  c Reduced by the related liabilities in the assets section
  d Included only in the "carrying amount" column of the assets section

5 If a secured creditor's claim exceeds the current fair value of the collateral o.
debtor in bankruptcy liquidation, the secured creditor will be paid the to
amount realized from the sale of the collateral and will:
  a Not have any claim for the balance
  b Become an unsecured creditor for the balance
  c Retain a secured creditor status for the balance
  d Be paid the balance only after all unsecured creditors without priority a
  paid.

6 Insolvus Company is in serious financial difficulty and is unable to meet curre
unsecured obligations of $25,000 to some 15 creditors who are demandi
immediate payment. Insolvus owes Payless Company $5,000, and Payless h
decided to file a petition for a receiving order against Insolvus. Which of t
following is necessary in order for Payless to file?
  a Payless must be joined by at least two other creditors
  b Insolvus must have committed an act of bankruptcy within six months of t
  filing
  c Payless must allege and subsequently establish that the liabilities of Insolv
  exceed the current fair value of its assets
  d Payless must be a secured creditor

Ex 17-2 Edward Ross, the trustee in bankruptcy for Winslow Company, set up accounti
records based on the April 30, Year 5, statement of affairs for Winslow. The trust
completed the following transactions early in May, Year 5:

May 2 Sold for $10,000 cash the finished goods inventory with a statement
       affairs valuation of $10,500.
    3 Paid wages with a statement of affairs valuation of $8,000.
    4 Collected $6,000 on accounts receivable with a statement of affairs val
       ation of $6,200. The balance was considered to be uncollectible.
    7 Paid trustee fee for one week, $500.

Prepare journal entries in the accounting records of Edward Ross, trustee
bankruptcy for Winslow Company, for the transactions described above. Om
explanations.

Ex 17-3 Among the provisions of the reorganization of Hayward Company under the Ban
ruptcy Act were the following:

(1) Issued 1,000 shares of $5 par common stock in exchange for 1,000 shares
    $100 par common stock outstanding.
(2) Issued 600 shares of $5 par common stock for notes payable to suppliers wit
    unpaid principal of $2,500 and accrued interest of $500.
(3) Paid $8,000 to vendors in full settlement of claims of $10,000.

Prepare journal entries (omit explanations) for the foregoing provisions, all c
which were completed on January 20, Year 7.

Ex 17-4 In auditing the financial statements of Delbert Company for the six months ende
December 31, Year 10, you find items **a** through **e** on page 715 had been debited c

credited to the Retained Earnings account during the six months immediately following a bankruptcy reorganization, which was finalized and made effective July 1, Year 10:

a Debit of $25,000 arising from an additional income tax assessment applicable to Year 9.

b Credit of $48,000 resulting from gain on sale of equipment that was no longer used in the business. This equipment had been written down by a $50,000 increase in the Accumulated Depreciation account on July 1, Year 10.

c Debit of $15,000 resulting from the loss on plant assets destroyed in a fire on November 2, Year 10.

d Debit of $32,000 representing cash dividends declared on preferred stock.

e Credit of $60,400, the net income for the six-month period ended December 31, Year 10.

For each of these items, state whether you believe it to be correctly debited or credited to the Retained Earnings account. Give a brief reason for your conclusion.

Ex 17-5 The statement of affairs for Wicks Corporation shows that approximately $0.78 on the dollar probably will be paid to unsecured creditors without priority before deducting the superintendent's levy. The corporation owes Stark Company $23,000 on a promissory note, plus accrued interest of $940. Inventories with a current fair value of $19,200 collateralize the note payable.

Compute the amount that Stark should receive from Wicks after the deduction of the superintendent's levy, assuming that actual payments to unsecured creditors without priority consist of 78% of total claims. Round all amounts to the nearest dollar.

Ex 17-6 Compute the amount that will be paid to each class of creditors, using the following data taken from the statement of affairs for Kent Corporation (ignore the effect of the Superintendent's levy):

Assets pledged with fully secured liabilities (current fair value, $75,000)	$ 90,000
Assets pledged with partially secured liabilities (current fair value, $52,000)	74,000
Free assets (current fair value, $40,000)	70,000
Unsecured liabilities with priority	7,000
Fully secured liabilities	30,000
Partially secured liabilities	60,000
Unsecured liabilities without priority	112,000

Ex 17-7 The following information for Progress Book Company was obtained by an accountant retained by the company's creditors:

a Furniture and fixtures: Carrying amount, $70,000; current fair value, $60,500; pledged on a note payable of $42,000 on which unpaid interest of $800 has accrued.

b Book manuscripts owned: Carrying amount, $15,000; current fair value, $7,200; pledged on a note payable of $9,000; interest on the note is paid to date.

c Books in process of production: Accumulated cost (direct material, direct labor, and factory overhead), $37,500; estimated sales value on completion, $60,000; additional out-of-pocket costs of $14,200 will be required to complete the books in process.

Prepare the headings for the asset side of a statement of affairs and illustrate how each of the three items described should be shown in the statement.

Ex 17-8 Easypay Furniture Ltd. was declared bankrupt on February 7, Year 5. Two concern individuals have approached you to advise them how their claims against the compan will be handled, in accordance with the Bankruptcy Act.

Janet Rothman ordered a dining room suite from Easypay on February 5, Year She paid the company $1,000 as a deposit and was promised delivery of the furnitu by February 28, Year 5.

Bill Williams is a salesman of Easypay and has not yet received his salary an commissions for the month of January Year 5.

Instructions What would you say to Bill and Janet?

Ex 17-9 Jason James, appointed trustee of Brown's Bootery Ltd. has prepared a statement affairs. This statement shows that the estimated realizable value of uncommitte assets is $65,000 while the total of unsecured claims amounts to $93,125. Th following five creditors have approached you for advice. They have not yet receive the statement of affairs and, knowing that you have received a copy, they wish yo to determine the amount that each may expect to realize.

(1) Judy Bart holds a note for $1,100 on which $70 of interest has accrued. The no is not secured.

(2) Bill Wright is owed one month's wages totaling $1,400.

(3) Linda Gamble holds a note for $3,300 secured by $4,500 of receivables. Th statement of affairs indicates that 60% of the receivables are collectible.

(4) The Village of Pense is owed $4,000 for property taxes.

(5) Scott Landger holds a $1,600 note on which $30 of interest has accrued. Proper with a book value of $1,000 and an estimated market value of $1,700 is show on the statement to be pledged as collateral to this note.

Determine the amount each of the claimants may expect to realize. (Show calc lations.)

CASES

Case 17-1 You have been asked to conduct a training program explaining the preparation of statement of affairs (financial statement) for the staff of Bixby & Canfield, CAs.

Instructions Explain how each of the following is presented in a statement o affairs (financial statement) for a corporation in bankruptcy liquidation proceedings a Assets pledged for partially secured liabilities
b Unsecured liabilities with priority
c Shareholder's equity

Case 17-2 Paul Martin has been appointed trustee of Zeman Company, a corporation involve in liquidation under the Bankruptcy Act. He asks you for advice on what accountin records he should maintain and what financial statements he should prepare in h role of trustee.

Instructions Give Paul Martin the advice he requested, in the form of a letter.

Case 17-3 Your client has approached you for advice. His customer, Insolvo Company, owe him a substantial amount. All collection attempts have been fruitless. He has hear of the terms receivership and bankruptcy, but is unsure whether either would provide a remedy for him.

Instructions Draft a letter to your client in which you explain the difference between the two terms and outline the requirements necessary and the processes that would be followed under each.

Case 17-4 Dame Oil Company is in serious financial difficulty due to a deterioration in its cash flow. Its management feels that the company is viable and will be able to reverse the situation in the future. However, it is felt that the company's creditors may soon take action and management wishes to take steps to forestall such actions.

Instructions Write a letter to management explaining how a proposal might alleviate the situation, the remedies that might be included, and the risks involved.

Case 17-5 The following notice, which appeared in a recent edition of a local newspaper, has been presented to you by one of your clients:

> IN THE MATTER OF THE BANKRUPTCY OF RICHAR CUSHION PRODUCTS LTD. A PRIVATE ONTARIO CORPORATION HAVING ITS HEAD OFFICE AND PRINCIPAL PLACE OF BUSINESS IN THE MUNICIPALITY OF METROPOLITAN TORONTO IN THE PROVINCE OF ONTARIO.
>
> NOTICE IS HEREBY GIVEN that the above noted filed an assignment on the 9th day of October, Year 4, and that the first meeting of creditors will be held on Monday, the 29th day of October, Year 4 at the hour of 2:00 o'clock in the afternoon at the office of The Official Receiver, 25 St. Clair Avenue, E., 7th flr., Toronto, Ontario.
>
> Dated at North York, Ontario, this 11th day of October, Year 4.
>
> INNIS & CO. INC.
TRUSTEE

Per: Roger Jones, C.A.

Your client informs you that Richar Cushion Products Ltd. has been his company's customer for years. He believes that his account receivable from Richar has a current balance of approximately $10,000. He wants to know what this notice is all about, what will happen at the meeting mentioned in this notice, and what he can expect to happen in the future. He particularly wants to know whether his receivable is in jeopardy, and if it is, why?

Instructions Outline your response to your client.

Case 17-6 An acquaintance, who once took a course in Introductory Financial Accounting and who is able to read and interpret conventional accounting statements, approaches you as follows:

"I thought I could read financial statements, but yesterday I came across one that I cannot comprehend. It had strange headings and classifications and a title that I have never heard of. I copied down the terms that I have not seen before in financial statements but I forgot to write down the name of the statement and I don't remember what it was called. Here is the list. Please tell me what all this is about."

He presents you with a piece of paper upon which the following is written:

Fully secured creditors, appraised value, free assets, estimated deficiency, book value, liabilities with priority, assets pledged with fully secured creditors, estimated amount available, assets pledged with partially secured creditors, unsecured creditors, total deducted contra, loss or (gain), partially secured creditors.

Instructions Tell your acquaintance what this is all about. (Remember that h knows something about accounting and also remember to include all the terms tha he has listed in your answer.)

PROBLEMS

17-1 The following information is available on October 31, Year 5, for Dodge Company which is having difficulty paying its liabilities as they become due:

	Carrying Amount
Cash	$ 4,000
Accounts receivable (net): Current fair value equal to carrying	
amount	46,000
Inventories: Net realizable value, $18,000; pledged on $21,000	
of notes payable	39,000
Plant assets: Current fair value, $67,400; pledged on mortgage note	
payable	134,000
Accumulated depreciation	27,000
Supplies: Current fair value, $1,500	2,000
Wages payable, all earned during October, Year 5	5,800
Property taxes payable	1,200
Accounts payable	60,000
Notes payable, $21,000 secured by inventories	40,000
Mortgage note payable, including accrued interest of $400	50,400
Common stock, $5 par	$100,000
Deficit	59,400

Instructions
a Prepare a statement of affairs.
b Prepare a working paper to compute the estimated percentage of claims eac group of creditors should expect to receive if Dodge Company becomes bankrup (ignore the effect of the Superintendent's levy).

17-2 Robaire Corporation was in financial difficulty because of declining sales and poo cost controls. Its shareholders and principal creditors had asked for an estimate o the financial results of the sale of the assets, the payment of liabilities, and the liquidation of the corporation. Thus, the accountant for Robaire prepared the state ment of affairs that appears on page 719.

ROBAIRE CORPORATION
Statement of Affairs
December 31, Year 3

Carrying amount	Assets	Current fair value	Estimated amount available	Loss or (gain) on realization
	Assets pledged for fully secured liabilities:			
$ 4,000	Land	$20,000		$(16,000)
25,000	Buildings	30,000		(5,000)
	Total	$50,000		
	Less: Fully secured liabilities (contra)	42,500	$ 7,500	
	Assets pledged for partially secured liabilities:			
10,000	Accounts receivable (deducted contra)	$10,000		
	Free assets:			
700	Cash	$ 700	700	
10,450	Accounts receivable	10,450	10,450	
40,000	Inventories $19,350			
	Less: Cost to complete 400	18,950	18,950	21,050
9,100	Factory supplies	-0-	-0-	9,100
5,750	Public Service Company bonds	900	900	4,850
38,000	Machinery and equipment	18,000	18,000	20,000
	Total estimated amount available		$56,500	$34,000
	Less: Unsecured liabilities with priority (contra)		5,500	
	Estimated amount available for unsecured, non-priority creditors		$51,000	
	Estimated deficiency to unsecured, nonpriority creditors		10,000	
$143,000			$61,000	

Carrying amount	Liabilities & shareholders' equity			Amount unsecured
	Unsecured liabilities with priority:			
$ 1,500	Wages payable		$ 1,500	
800	Payroll and income taxes withheld and accrued		800	
	Estimated liquidation cost payable		3,200	
	Total (deducted contra)		$ 5,500	
	Fully secured liabilities:			
42,000	Mortgage note payable		$42,000	
500	Accrued interest payable		500	
	Total (deducted contra)		$42,500	
	Partially secured liabilities:			
25,000	Notes payable to bank		$25,000	
	Less: Assigned accounts receivable		10,000	$15,000
	Unsecured liabilities without priority:			
20,000	Notes payable to suppliers			20,000
26,000	Accounts payable			26,000
27,200	Shareholders' equity			
$143,000				$61,000

On January 2, Year 4, a receiving order against Robaire Corporation was granted by the court. Charles Stern was appointed as trustee by the bankruptcy court to take custody of the assets, make payments to creditors, and implement an orderly liquidation. The trustee completed the following transactions:

Jan. 2   Recorded the assets and liabilities of Robaire Corporation in a separate set of accounting records. The assets were recorded at current fair value and all liabilities were recorded at the estimated amounts payable to the various groups of creditors.

Jan. 7   Sold the land and buildings at an auction for $52,000 cash and paid $42,550 to the mortgagee. The payment included interest of $50 that accrued in January.

Jan. 10   Made cash payments as follows:

Wages payable	$ 1,500
Payroll and income taxes withheld and accrued	800
Completion of inventories	400
Liquidation costs	600

Jan. 31   Cash receipts from Jan. 8 to Jan. 31 were as follows:

Collection of accounts receivable at carrying amount, including $10,000 of assigned accounts	17,500
Sale of inventories	18,000
Sale of Public Service Company bonds	920

Jan. 31   Additional cash payments were:

Liquidation costs	1,250
Note payable to bank (from proceeds of collection of assigned accounts receivable)	10,000
Dividend of $0.50 on the dollar to unsecured creditors	30,500

Instructions
a Prepare journal entries for the foregoing transactions in the accounting records of the trustee for Robaire Corporation.
b Prepare a statement of realization and liquidation for the month of January, Year 4. Use the form illustrated on page 709.
c Prepare a trial balance for the trustee on January 31, Year 4.

17-3 Javits Corporation advises you that it is facing bankruptcy proceedings. As the company's independent auditor, you are aware of its financial condition.
The unaudited balance sheet of Javits on July 10, Year 10, is presented on page 721

Additional Information

(1) Cash includes a $500 travel advance that has been spent.

(2) Accounts receivable of $40,000 have been pledged as collateral for notes payable to banks in the amount of $30,000. Credit balances of $5,000 are netted in the accounts receivable total. All accounts are expected to be collected except those for which an allowance has been established.

(3) Short-term investments consist of government bonds costing $10,000 and 500 shares of Owens Company common stock. The current fair value of the bonds is $10,000; the current fair value of the stock is $18 a share. The bonds have accrued interest receivable of $200. The short-term investments are pledged as collateral for a $20,000 note payable to bank.

JAVITS CORPORATION
Balance Sheet
July 10, Year 10

Assets

Cash	$ 12,000
Short-term investments, at cost	20,000
Accounts receivable, less allowance for doubtful accounts	90,000
Finished goods inventory	60,000
Material inventory	40,000
Short-term prepayments	5,000
Land	13,000
Buildings (net)	90,000
Machinery (net)	120,000
Goodwill	20,000
Total assets	$470,000

Liabilities & Shareholders' Equity

Notes payable to banks	$135,000
Accounts payable	94,200
Wages payable	15,000
Mortgage notes payable	130,000
Common stock	100,000
Retained earnings (deficit)	(4,200)
Total liabilities & shareholders' equity	$470,000

(4) Estimated realizable value of finished goods is $50,000 and of material is $30,000. For additional out-of-pocket costs of $10,000 the material would realize $59,900 as finished goods.

(5) Short-term prepayments will be consumed during the liquidation period.

(6) The current fair value of plant assets is as follows: Land, $25,000; buildings, $110,000; machinery, $65,000.

(7) Accounts payable include $15,000 withheld payroll and income taxes and $6,000 payable to creditors who had been reassured by the president of Javits that they would be paid. There are unrecorded employer's payroll taxes in the amount of $500.

(8) Wages payable are not subject to any limitations under the Bankruptcy Act.

(9) Mortgage notes payable consist of $100,000 secured by land and buildings, and a $30,000 installment contract secured by machinery. Total unrecorded accrued interest for these liabilities amounts to $2,400.

(10) Probable judgement on a pending damage suit is estimated at $50,000.

(11) Costs to be incurred in connection with the liquidation are estimated at $10,000.

(12) You have not submitted an invoice for $5,000 for the April 30, Year 10, annual audit of Javits, and you estimate a $1,000 fee for liquidation work.

Instructions

a Prepare correcting journal entries for Javits Corporation on July 10, Year 10.

b Prepare a statement of affairs for Javits Corporation on July 10, Year 10. Amounts in the statement should reflect the journal entries in **a** (ignore the effect of the Superintendent's levy).

17-4 The trial balance of Laurel Company on June 30, Year 6, is shown below:

LAUREL COMPANY
Trial Balance
June 30, Year 6

	Debit	Credit
Cash	$14,135	
Notes receivable	29,000	
Accrued interest on notes receivable	615	
Accounts receivable	19,500	
Common stock subscriptions receivable	5,000	
Allowance for doubtful accounts		$ 800
Inventories	48,000	
Land	10,000	
Building	50,000	
Accumulated depreciation of building		15,000
Machinery and equipment	33,000	
Accumulated depreciation of machinery and equipment		19,000
Furniture and fixtures	21,000	
Accumulated depreciation of furniture and fixtures		9,500
Goodwill	8,000	
Organization costs	1,600	
Note payable to City Bank		18,000
Notes payable to Municipal Trust Company		6,000
Notes payable to vendors		24,000
Accrued interest on notes payable		1,280
Accounts payable		80,520
Wages payable		1,400
Payroll and income taxes withheld and accrued		430
Mortgage bonds payable		32,000
Accrued interest payable on mortgage bonds		1,820
Common stock		65,000
Common stock subscribed		5,000
Retained earnings — deficit	39,900	
Totals	$279,750	$279,750

Additional information

(1) Notes receivable of $25,000 were pledged to collateralize the $18,000 note payable to City Bank. Interest of $500 was accrued on the pledged notes and $600 was accrued on the $18,000 note payable to the bank. All the pledged notes were collectible. Of the remaining notes receivable, a $1,000 noninterest-bearing note was uncollectible. The note had been received for an unconditional cash loan.

(2) Accounts receivable include $7,000 from Boren Company, which currently is being liquidated. Creditors expect to realize $0.40 on the dollar. The allowance for doubtful accounts is adequate to cover any other uncollectible accounts. A total of $3,200 of the remaining collectible accounts receivable was pledged as collateral for the notes payable to Municipal Trust Company of $6,000 with accrued interest of $180 on June 30, Year 6.

(3) The subscriptions receivable from shareholders for no-par common stock are due July 31, Year 6, and are considered fully collectible.

(4) Inventories are valued at cost and are expected to realize 25% of cost on a forced liquidation sale after the write-off of $10,000 of obsolete stock.

(5) Land and buildings, which are appraised at 110% of their carrying amount, are mortgaged as collateral for the bonds. Interest of $1,820 was accrued on the bonds on June 30, Year 6. The company expects to realize 20% of the cost of its machinery and equipment, and 50% of the cost of its furniture and fixtures after incurring refinishing costs of $800.

(6) Estimated costs of liquidation are $4,500. Depreciation and accruals have been adjusted to June 30, Year 6.

Instructions Prepare a statement of affairs for Laurel Company on June 30, Year 6. (Ignore the Superintendent's levy.)

17-5 A trustee was appointed for Denis Corporation, on May 1, at which time the following trial balance was prepared from the general ledger:

Trial Balance
May 1

Cash	$ 66,000	
Notes receivable	114,000	
Accounts receivable	438,000	
Inventory of merchandise	291,000	
Investments — cost	60,000	
Plant and equipment	1,040,000	
Accumulated depreciation		$ 170,000
Notes payable		210,000
Accounts payable		960,000
Capital stock		300,000
Retained earnings		369,000
Totals	$2,009,000	$2,009,000

Additional information
(1) Accrued expenses, not recorded as of this date, amount to $20,100, of which $6,600 is for property taxes and $7,200 is for wages for the past month. (Not more than $500 is owed to any one employee.)
(2) The investments have a market value of $65,000 and have been pledged as collateral on a note for $60,000.
(3) Accounts receivable of $180,000 have been assigned as security for the remainder of the notes payable.
(4) It is estimated that 95% of the notes receivable, 80% of the assigned accounts receivable, and 75% of the remaining accounts receivable will be collected. A

quick sale of the inventory will realize $180,000 and of the plant $330,000. The corporation also owns a patent not recorded on the books which is expected to realize $10,000.

Instructions Prepare the statement of affairs that the trustee would present to the first meeting of the creditors (ignore the effect of the Superintendent's levy).

17-6 Bilbo Corporation, which is in bankruptcy reorganization, had $105,000 of dividends in arrears on its 7% cumulative preferred stock on March 31, Year 20. While retained earnings were adequate to permit the payment of accumulated dividends, Bilbo's management did not wish to weaken its working capital position. They also realized that a portion of the plant assets was no longer used by Bilbo. Therefore, management proposed the following plan of reorganization, which was accepted by shareholders and confirmed by the bankruptcy court, to be effective on April 1, Year 20:

(1) The preferred stock was to be exchanged for $300,000 face amount and current fair value of 15%, 10-year bonds. Dividends in arrears were to be settled by the issuance of $120,000 of $10 par, 15%, noncumulative preferred stock having a current fair value equal to par.

(2) Common stock was to be assigned a stated value of $50 a share.

(3) Goodwill was to be written off; plant assets were to be written down, based on appraisal and estimates of current fair value, by a total of $103,200, consisting of $85,400 increase in the Accumulated Depreciation account and $17,800 decrease in plant assets; other current assets were to be written down by $10,460 to reduce accounts receivable and inventories to net realizable values.

The condensed balance sheet on March 31, Year 20, is presented below.

BILBO CORPORATION
Balance Sheet
March 31, Year 20

Assets

Cash		$ 30,000
Other current assets		252,890
Plant assets	$1,458,250	
Less: Accumulated depreciation	512,000	946,250
Goodwill		50,000
Total assets		$1,279,140

Liabilities & Shareholders' Equity

Current liabilities	$ 132,170
7% cumulative preferred stock, $100 par ($105,000 dividends in arrears)	300,000
Common stock, no-par, 9,000 shares issued and outstanding	648,430
Contributed surplus: preferred stock	22,470
Retained earnings	176,070
Total liabilities & shareholders' equity	$1,279,140

Instructions
a Prepare journal entries to give effect to the plan of reorganization on April 1, Year 20.

b Prepare a balance sheet on April 30, Year 20, assuming that net income for April was $15,000. The operations resulted in $11,970 increase in cash, $18,700 increase in other current assets, $7,050 increase in current liabilities, and $8,620 increase in the Accumulated Depreciation account.

17-7 Tara Manufacturing Inc. is unable to discharge its obligations as they become due. Management has submitted the following proposal to its creditors:
(1) Pay unsecured creditors 75 cents in full settlement of their respective claims.
(2) Of the 75 cents, 15 cents would be payable in cash immediately with the balance payable in quarterly installments.
(3) Additional cash required for the initial payment to be obtained through the sale of the company's investments.
(4) Present shareholders to invest additional capital in the company in order to provide more working funds.
As trustee, you have called a meeting of the creditors to consider the proposal.
  The following is a current condensed balance sheet of Tara Manufacturing Inc.

Assets

Cash	$ 20,000
Accounts receivable	160,000
Inventories — at cost	60,000
Prepaid insurance	1,050
Investments	65,000
Fixed assets (net)	230,000
Goodwill	40,000
	$576,050

Liabilities & Shareholders' Equity

Bank loan (secured by receivables)	$ 80,000
Accounts payable	306,000
Income taxes	1,000
Accrued wages and salaries	5,000
Mortgage (secured by fixed assets)	60,000
Capital stock	140,000
Deficit	(15,950)
	$ 576,050

Additional information
(1) Accounts receivable will realize 55 cents on the dollar.
(2) Inventories can be sold for 60% of their cost, with the exception of special parts included in inventory at $1,800 which will realize only $300 as scrap.
(3) 30% of the prepaid insurance is recoverable.
(4) Investments can be sold for $59,165.
(5) Fixed assets can be sold for $168,000.
(6) Cost of liquidation at present would be $10,000.

Instructions Prepare the report that you would submit to the creditors' meeting.

17-8 Tapp Corporation is being reorganized because one of the three shareholders, Adam Wright, cannot get along with the other two, Ben Yates and Carla Zorb. At the end of Year 7, Yates and Zorb agree to reorganize the corporation into a partnership.

The information relative to the reorganization plan, confirmed by the court, follows:

(1) The balance sheet of Tapp Corporation on December 31, Year 7, is shown below.

TAPP CORPORATION
Balance Sheet
December 31, Year 7

Assets

Current assets:

Cash		$105,000
Accounts receivable, net of $22,000 allowance for doubtful accounts		135,000
Inventories		225,000
Short-term prepayments		4,500
Total current assets		$469,500
Building, at current fair value	$125,000	
Less: Accumulated depreciation	27,500	97,500
Investment in land		20,000
Other assets		10,000
Total assets		$597,000

Liabilities & Shareholders' Equity

Current liabilities:

Note payable to Adam Wright, a shareholder		$ 30,000
Accounts payable		110,000
Accrued liabilities		32,000
Total current liabilities		$172,000

Shareholders' equity:

Preferred stock, $100 par (liquidation value $110); authorized, 1,000 shares; in treasury, 400 shares; outstanding, 600 shares		$100,000
Common stock, no par; stated value $1; authorized, 200,000 shares; issued and outstanding, 100,000 shares	100,000	
Contributed surplus from common stock	150,000	
Total contributed capital	$350,000	
Unrealized appreciation from revaluation of building	50,000	
Retained earnings	72,250	
Subtotal	$472,250	
Less: Treasury stock, 400 shares of preferred stock, at cost	47,250	425,000
Total liabilities & shareholders' equity		$597,000

(2) The capital stock records of Tapp on December 31, Year 7, indicate that the three shareholders have retained their respective interests since the corporation was organized five years ago as follows:

Shareholder	Total invested	Preferred		Common	
		Shares	Amount	Shares	Amount
Ben Yates	$115,000	300	$30,000	35,000	$ 85,000
Carla Zorb	105,000	100	10,000	40,000	95,000
Adam Wright	90,000	200	20,000	25,000	70,000
Totals	$310,000	600	$60,000	100,000	$250,000

(3) In accordance with the reorganization plan, Tapp will acquire Wright's preferred and common stock, and thereafter Tapp will be liquidated by an appropriate disposition of its net assets.

(4) In order to finance the acquisition of Wright's stock, the building was appraised as a basis for an $80,000 mortgage loan arranged by Tapp with an insurance company. The appraisal was made on December 31, Year 7, and was recorded as follows:

	Current fair value per appraisal	Cost	Unrealized appreciation
Building	$125,000	$70,000	$55,000
Less: Accumulated depreciation	27,500	22,500	5,000
Totals	$ 97,500	$47,500	$50,000

(5) Wright's stock is to be acquired for cash of $110 a share for the preferred stock and $3 a share for the common stock. The stock acquired from Wright is to be retired.

(6) After the acquisition of Wright's stock, disposition of the net assets of Tapp in complete liquidation is to be made as follows:

(a) The note payable to Wright is to be paid in cash.

(b) The treasury stock is to be cancelled, and the preferred stock owned by Yates and Zorb is to be retired at $110 a share.

(c) The investment in land is to be transferred to Zorb at its current fair value of $36,000.

(d) The remaining assets are to be acquired and the liabilities (including the $80,000 mortgage loan) are to be assumed by a partnership organized by Yates and Zorb. Yates is to withdraw cash from the partnership as necessary to equalize his capital account with that of Zorb.

Instructions Prepare a working paper giving effect to the reorganization of Tapp Corporation into a partnership on December 31, Year 7, in accordance with the agreement among the three shareholders. Use the following columnar headings in the working paper:

Accounts	Tapp Corporation balance sheet, Dec. 31, Year 7		Transactions to implement reorganization		Yates & Zorb Partnership balance sheet, Dec. 31, Year 7	

18

ACCOUNTING FOR ESTATES AND TRUSTS

Estates and trusts are accounting entities as well as taxable entities. The individuals or corporations that manage the assets of estates and trusts are *fiduciaries*; they exercise stewardship for those assets in accordance with the provisions of a will, a trust document, or provincial laws.

In this chapter we deal first with certain aspects of estates, including wills, and then discuss and illustrate the accounting for estates; the last section covers the legal and accounting aspects of trusts.

LEGAL AND ACCOUNTING ASPECTS OF ESTATES

Provincial laws regulate the administration and distribution of estates. Many variations exist among provincial laws in this area, and therefore the discussions of the legal requirements and terminology that follow should be viewed as applicable in a general sense. A person administering an estate should seek legal advice concerning specific provincial law before proceeding.

Wills

A will is a document through which a person directs the distribution of his assets after his death. The person making the will is called the *testator*, and after death is called the *decedent*. All property of the decedent that exists on the date of death forms what is known as the *decedent's estate*. Upon death the decedent's estate is distributed as directed by the will, or if no valid will exists — a condition known as *intestacy* — in accordance with provincial law. In both cases the distribution of the estate comes under the jurisdiction of the provincial *surrogate* courts. If there was a valid will, the will's provisions will generally be followed, unless such provisions are contrary to provincial statutes. For example, some provinces have *Dower*

Acts which specify that the spouse of a decedent is entitled to a certain portion of the real property of the estate. If the will specified a lower portion, the provisions of the act would be followed by the court.

The persons named in the will to receive the testator's property are called **beneficiaries**, and the gifts of property are called **bequests**. A **devise** is the name given for a bequest of real property, and the beneficiary is called a **devisee**. A **legacy** is the name given to a bequest of personal property and the beneficiary is called a **legatee**.

At the time of drawing up the will, the testator names a personal representative to carry out the provisions of the will. This personal representative is called the **executor**. If the decedent dies **intestate** (without having a valid will) the court appoints a representative called the **administrator** to distribute the estate in accordance with provincial law. The court would also appoint an administrator if the executor was unable or not willing to act, but in this case the estate would be distributed in accordance with the provisions of the will.

Most provincial laws require that a will shall be in writing, signed by the testator, or in the testator's name by some other person in the testator's presence, and by the testator's direction, and signed by at least two witnesses. A few provinces allow a **holograph will** which must be entirely in the handwriting of the testator and signed by him, but does not need to be witnessed.

Probate of wills

The **probate** of a will is the action by the surrogate court that validates the will. During the process the will is presented in court accompanied by an inventory of the estate assets valued at fair market on the date of death, and in some provinces supported with evidence that the executor has notified all creditors of the decedent to file their claims. Usually the placing of newspaper advertisements is required in this regard. At this time it is determined whether or not the will presented is the last will made by the decedent prior to death. If the will is accepted, a document called **letters probate** is issued by the court. While not all provincial laws require the probate of a will it is usually desirable that this action be taken by the executor. Letters probate, accompanied by a certified copy of the will, gives the executor the legal authority to transfer title to real property and securities, and such title transfers are often difficult to achieve without this document. There are costs involved in the probate process. While it is not a requirement, a lawyer is usually used by the executor for the court appearance, resulting in legal costs. In addition, the court assesses probate fees. Both the legal costs and the probate costs are a function of the fair market value of the estate assets.

Taxation implications

Prior to 1972, Canada's federal and provincial governments levied estate and succession duty taxes. The amount of tax was dependent on the fair value of the estate assets and the relationship of the beneficiaries to the decedent. In 1972 this form of taxation, often called **death taxes**, was abolished in all jurisdictions in Canada with the exception of the Province of Quebec. Quebec finally followed suit in 1985. Other countries — for example, the United States — still levy estate taxes and therefore, a decedent's assets located outside Canada may be subject to this form of taxation.

In addition to the possibility of death taxes, the executor must also be aware of the **income tax implications** that arise on the date of death. An income tax return must be filed for the decedent for the period January 1 to the date of death. All income, as defined by the Income Tax Act, earned during that period is subject to tax, and there are capital gains tax implications involved with the deemed disposal of the decedent's assets on the date of death. Special provisions exist for the deduction of personal exemptions and the exemption of certain property from capital gains tax.

Income earned by the estate assets after death is also subject to tax. If the income-producing assets are distributed to beneficiaries within the taxation year, and if the beneficiaries declare the income earned by these assets since the date of death in their personal tax returns, the estate itself is not subject to further tax. If, however, there is a long delay in the distribution of the estate assets, or income beneficiaries are established by the will, thus creating a **trust**, the estate or trust is subject to tax on the income earned and an estate tax return is required. The calculations of, and laws pertaining to, succession duty and income tax are beyond the scope of this book.

Classification of legacies

A **specific legacy** is a gift of a particular item of personal property of the decedent. Examples are jewellery, furniture, bonds, shares and clothing.

A **general legacy** is a gift of a sum of money, or a gift of a non-identifiable portion of property, such as "$1,500 of my Province of Manitoba bonds."

A **residual legacy** is the gift of all estate property remaining after all specific and general legacies, and all devises of real property, have been distributed and all debts of the decedent and administration costs have been settled.

A residual legatee will receive nothing until all debts, devises and other legacies have been paid. If the personal property is insufficient to pay all legacies, general legacies are proportionally reduced — called **abatement** — until specific legacies are paid in full.

Legacies and devises may be granted in trust, which requires the establishment of a **testamentary trust** — one provided for by a will. Trusts are discussed in a subsequent section of this chapter.

Duties of the executor/administrator

The executor/administrator as a fiduciary, must observe standards of care in administering an estate that prudent persons would observe in dealing with property of others. His duties would include the following:

1 Read the will, noting beneficiaries and all provisions.
2 Take control of all assets of the estate and prepare an inventory thereof.

3 Determine all debts of the decedent on date of death. This would include determining the decedent's income tax liability as of the date of death.

4 Where necessary apply for probate of the will.

5 Maintain records of estate assets and liabilities distinguished between estate principal and estate income.

6 Pay all legitimate debts of the decedent. If the estate is bankrupt the provisions of the Bankruptcy Act with regard to the payment of claims would apply.

7 Invest estate assets as required by the provisions of the will or in accordance with legal requirements (which generally specify investing in securities with a minimum of risk involved).

8 Distribute devises and legacies in accordance with the directions of the will if not contrary to provincial law.

9 Obtain a discharge for fiduciary responsibilities. In small estates this is accomplished by obtaining written approval by beneficiaries. In larger estates this may require a *passing of accounts* before the court.

Normally, in relatively simple estates, this process takes approximately six months. However, in more complicated estates, especially where the will establishes a trust and the executor is named as trustee, the process could take many years. Executor's fees are awarded by the surrogate court.

Passing of accounts

Passing of accounts is the formal discharge from fiduciary responsibilities for an estate, and involves *an accounting* by the executor/administrator for:

1 the property of the estate on date of probate,

2 all transactions which have been undertaken since the date of probate including any dispositions of estate property, and

3 the property still on hand.

Each provincial surrogate court establishes rules determining the form and content of the accounts to be presented. Often this form of accounting is difficult to follow by persons other than lawyers and court officials. Because of this, and because each province's rules are not necessarily similar, we will illustrate a general form of reporting which is easier to understand, and which contains most of the information required by the various courts. This general form of reporting is called the "*Charge and Discharge*" statement and is illustrated on page 738.

Accounting for principal and income

The chief accounting problem for an estate is the allocation of revenue and expense to principal and income. This type of allocation is particularly important where a will provides that income of a testamentary trust is paid to an *income beneficiary*, and that trust principal is paid to a different principal beneficiary or *remainderman*. A proper accounting for principal and income by the executor/administrator is essential before the estate is closed.

If the will specifies the distinction between principal and income, the provisions of the will would apply. If the will is silent, the executor/administrator would be guided by provincial statutes, or in some cases by common law.

The **general rule of allocation** is that revenue earned (on an accrual basis) to the date of death is principal, while revenue earned after death is income. This would apply to interest earned by securities and deposits, as well as rents. In the case of dividends the date of declaration is the date usually used. If dividends were declared prior to death they are principal, if they were declared after death they are income. Losses and gains on the sale of principal assets are charged or credited to principal. The following provisions regarding principal and income would probably apply in most Canadian provinces:

1 **Income** is defined as the return in money or property derived from the use of principal, including rent, interest, cash dividends, or any other revenue received during administration of an estate.

2 **Principal** is defined as property set aside by its owner to be held in trust for eventual delivery to a remainderman. Principal includes proceeds of insurance on principal assets, stock and liquidating dividends, and allowances for depreciation. Any accrued rent or other revenue on the date of death of the testator is included in the principal of the estate.

3 Premium or discount on investments in bonds included in principal is not amortized. All proceeds from sale or redemption of bonds are principal.

4 Income is charged with a reasonable provision for depreciation, computed in accordance with generally accepted accounting principles, on all depreciable assets except assets used by a beneficiary, such as a residence or a personal automobile. Income also is charged with expenses of administering and preserving income-producing assets. Such expenses include property taxes, ordinary repairs, and property insurance premiums.

5 Principal is charged with expenditures incurred in preparing principal property for sale or rent, cost of investing and reinvesting principal assets, major repairs to principal assets, and income taxes on receipts or gains allocable to principal.

6 Court costs, attorney's fees, trustees' fees, and accountants' fees for periodic reporting to the probate court are apportioned between principal and income.

Where doubt exists about a particular item, the executor/administrator would be wise to seek legal advice.

Illustration of accounting for an estate

Now that we have reviewed certain legal issues involved in estates, we shall illustrate the accounting for estates, including the charge and discharge statement rendered by the personal representative at the closing of the estate. Estate accounting is carried out in accordance with the **accountability** technique illustrated in Chapter 17. The accounting records of the personal representative include only those items for which the representative is accountable, under the equation Assets = Accountability.

Our illustration is based on the following information for the estate of Jessica Davis:

1 Jessica Davis, a single woman, died March 18, Year 3, after a brief illness which required her to be hospitalized. Her will, approved for probate on March 25, Year 3, contained the following bequests:
   a $10,000 in cash to each of three household employees: Alice Martin, cook; Angelo Bari, housekeeper; Nolan Ames, gardener and maintenance man. Legatees must waive claims for unpaid wages on date of death.
   b 200 shares of Preston Company common stock to Nancy Grimes, a niece.

c Paintings, other art objects, clothing, jewelry, and personal effects to Frances Davis Grimes, sister of Jessica Davis.

d Residence, furniture, and furnishings to Wallace Davis, brother of Jessica Davis.

e $5,000 cash to Universal Charities, a nonprofit organization.

f Residue of estate in trust (First Trust Co., Trustee) to Nancy Grimes; income to be paid to her at the end of each calendar quarter until her twenty-first birthday on October 1, Year 8, at which time the principal also is paid to Nancy Grimes.

2 Paul Hasting, the executor of her estate, published the required newspaper notice to creditors and received the following claims from creditors:

<table>
<tr><td>**List of claims against estate of Jessica Davis**</td><td>Funeral expenses (Watts Mortuary) . . . .</td><td>$ 810</td></tr>
<tr><td></td><td>Hospital bills (Suburban Hospital) . . . .</td><td>1,928</td></tr>
<tr><td></td><td>Doctor's fees (Charles Carson, M.D.) . . . .</td><td>426</td></tr>
<tr><td></td><td>Morningside Department Store . . . .</td><td>214</td></tr>
<tr><td></td><td>Various residence bills . . . .</td><td>87</td></tr>
<tr><td></td><td>Total claims against estate of Jessica Davis . . . .</td><td>$3,465</td></tr>
</table>

3 Hasting prepared a final federal and provincial income tax return for Jessica Davis for the period January 1 to March 18, Year 3. The return showed income tax due in the amount of $457.

4 Hasting prepared an inventory of assets owned by Jessica Davis on March 18, Year 3. It appears below.

5 Subsequent to preparing the inventory below, Hasting discovered a certificate for 600 shares of Campbell Company common stock with a market value of $18,000.

<table>
<tr><td>**List of assets included in estate of Jessica Davis**</td><td align="center">**Description of assets**</td><td align="center">**Current fair value, Mar. 18, Year 3**</td></tr>
<tr><td></td><td>Bank chequing account . . . .</td><td>$ 2,157</td></tr>
<tr><td></td><td>Bank savings account (including accrued interest) . . . .</td><td>43,217</td></tr>
<tr><td></td><td>Savings and loan association 2-year certificate of deposit maturing</td><td></td></tr>
<tr><td></td><td>June 30, Year 3 (including accrued interest) . . . .</td><td>26,475</td></tr>
<tr><td></td><td>Accrued salary earned for period Mar. 1 to Mar. 8, Year 3 . . . .</td><td>214</td></tr>
<tr><td></td><td>Claim against medical insurance carrier . . . .</td><td>1,526</td></tr>
<tr><td></td><td>Canada Pension Plan benefits receivable . . . .</td><td>2,080</td></tr>
<tr><td></td><td>Proceeds of life insurance policy (payable to estate) . . . .</td><td>25,000</td></tr>
<tr><td></td><td>Marketable securities:</td><td></td></tr>
<tr><td></td><td>Common stock of Preston Company, 200 shares . . . .</td><td>8,000</td></tr>
<tr><td></td><td>Common stock of Arthur Corporation, 100 shares . . . .</td><td>6,500</td></tr>
<tr><td></td><td>Residence . . . .</td><td>40,800*</td></tr>
<tr><td></td><td>Furniture and furnishings . . . .</td><td>2,517</td></tr>
<tr><td></td><td>Paintings and other art objects . . . .</td><td>16,522</td></tr>
<tr><td></td><td>Clothing, jewelry, personal effects . . . .</td><td>625</td></tr>
<tr><td></td><td>Automobile . . . .</td><td>2,187</td></tr>
<tr><td></td><td>Total current fair value of estate assets . . . .</td><td>$177,820</td></tr>
</table>

* Subject to unpaid mortgage note of $15,500 due $500 monthly on the last day of the month, plus interest at 10% a year on the unpaid balance.

6 Hasting administered the estate, charging a fee of $2,500, and closed the estate by filing the required legal documents and a charge and discharge statement.

The journal entries on pages 735 to 737 are entered in the accounting records for the Estate of Jessica Davis, Deceased. (Dates for journal entries are assumed.) Comments relating to specific journal entries that require particular emphasis follow.

Mar. 18 Journal Entry   This entry records the executor's inventory of estate assets, including accrued interest and accrued salary on the date of death. The mortgage note payable applicable to the residence is recorded as a liability for accountability purposes. Claims of creditors *are not* recorded as liabilities because the accounting records for an estate are not designed to record all aspects of the estate's financial position. Accounting records for an estate reflect only the executor's accountability for assets and any claims against the assets.

Mar. 31 Journal Entries   A separate ledger account, Income Cash, is used to record cash receipts attributable to income. In accordance with provisions of the will of Jessica Davis, the income of $55 attributable to the income beneficiary, Nancy Grimes, is distributed to her at the end of the calendar quarter.

Apr. 2 Journal Entry   No depreciation was recorded on the automobile prior to its sale, because it was not a revenue-producing asset for the estate.

Apr. 16 Journal Entry   The Liabilities Paid account represents a reduction of the executor's accountability for estate assets; it is neither an asset account nor an expense account.

Apr. 24 Journal Entry   Dividends received on marketable securities required segregation in the accounting records, because the securities are allocable to separate legatees, as follows:

Preston Company common stock, $1,000: Allocable to general legacy to Nancy Grimes

Arthur Corporation and Campbell Company common stocks, $1,500: Allocable to residuary legacy to Nancy Grimes

Although Nancy Grimes is the recipient of both legacies, the residuary legacy ultimately will be placed in a testamentary trust for the legatee.

May 1 Journal Entry   The entire fee of the executor was charged to estate principal because the time spent by Paul Hasting on income assets was nominal. The allocation of fees is more appropriate for a trust than for an estate of relatively short duration.

May 3 Journal Entry   No adjusting entries are required for interest on the certificate of deposit or any declared but unpaid dividends on the marketable securities. An accrual-basis cutoff for an estate is appropriate only at the time the executor prepares the inventory of estate assets in order to

Year 3

Mar. 18 | Principal Cash (bank chequing account) . . . . | 2,157 |
Savings Account	43,217
Certificate of Deposit	26,475
Accrued Salary Receivable	214
Medical Insurance Claim Receivable	1,526
C.P.P. Benefits Receivable	2,080
Life Insurance Claim Receivable	25,000
Marketable Securities	14,500
Residence	40,800
Furniture and Furnishings	2,517
Paintings and Other Art Objects	16,522
Clothing, Jewelry, Personal Effects	625
Automobile	2,187
Mortgage Note Payable		15,500
Accrued Interest Payable	
($15,500 × 0.10 × 18/360)		78
Estate Principal Balance ($177,820 − $15,578) . . .		162,242

To record inventory of assets owned by decedent Jessica
Davis on date of death, net of lien against residence.

25 | Marketable Securities . . . . | 18,000 |
| Assets Discovered . . . . | | 18,000 |

To record assets discovered subsequent to filing of original
inventory of assets.

31 | Principal Cash . . . . | 70,511 |
Income Cash	55
Savings Account		43,217
Accrued Salary Receivable		214
C.P.P. Benefits Receivable		2,080
Life Insurance Claim Receivable		25,000
Interest Revenue		55

To record realization of various assets, including $55 interest
received on savings account for period Mar. 18–31, Year 3.

| Distributions to Income Beneficiaries . . . . | 55 |
| Income Cash . . . . | | 55 |

To distribute income cash payable to income beneficiary
Nancy Grimes, as required by the will.

Apr. 2 | Principal Cash . . . . | 2,050 |
| Loss on Disposal of Principal Assets . . . . | 137 |
| Automobile . . . . | | 2,187 |

To record sale of automobile at a loss.

(Continued)

4	Legacies Distributed		5,000	
	Principal Cash			5,000
	To record distribution of general legacy to Universal			
	Charities.			
16	Liabilities Paid		3,922	
	Principal Cash			3,922
	To record following liabilities paid:			
	Funeral expenses (Watts Mortuary)	$ 810		
	Hospital bills (Suburban Hospital)	1,928		
	Doctor's fees (Charles Carson, M.D.)	426		
	Final income tax	457		
	Morningside Department Store	214		
	Various residence bills	87		
	Total	$3,922		
19	Principal Cash		1,526	
	Medical Insurance Claim Receivable			1,526
	To record collection of medical insurance claim.			
24	Income Cash		1,500	
	Principal Cash		1,000	
	Payable to Legatee			1,000
	Dividend Revenue			1,500
	To record receipt of quarterly cash dividends on			
	common stock, as follows:			
	Preston Company (payable to Nancy Grimes)	$1,000		
	Arthur Corporation	300		
	Campbell Company	1,200		
	Total	$2,500		
27	Legacies Distributed		30,000	
	Principal Cash			30,000
	To record payment of cash to general legatees, as follows:			
	$10,000 devises payable to Alice Martin,			
	Angelo Bari, Nolan Ames: $10,000 × 3. . .	$30,000		

(Continued)

facilitate the distinction between estate principal and estate income. If the will provides that the accrual basis of accounting must be used, the executor must comply.

In the preceding illustration, federal and provincial income taxes on the estate were disregarded. In addition, it was assumed that devisee Wallace Davis immediately occupied the decedent's residence, so that depreciation on the residence was not required as it would be if rent revenue were

PAUL HASTING, EXECUTOR

Of the Will of Jessica Davis, Deceased

General Journal (continued)

Apr. 30	Mortgage Note Payable	15,500	
	Accrued Interest Payable	78	
	Legacies and Devises Distributed	52,886	
	Payable to Legatee	1,000	
	Marketable Securities		8,000
	Residence		40,800
	Furniture and Furnishings		2,517
	Paintings and Other Art Objects		16,522
	Clothing, Jewelry, Personal Effects		625
	Principal Cash		1,000

To transfer to legatee Nancy Grimes cash for dividend
received on Preston Company common stock, and to record
distribution of devises as follows:

General legacy to Nancy Grimes:		
200 shares of Preston Company common		
stock	$8,000	
Specific legacy to Frances Davis Grimes:		
Paintings, other art objects, clothing,		
jewelry, personal effects	17,147	
Specific devise and legacy to Wallace Davis:		
Residence, net of mortgage note payable,		
with furniture and furnishings	27,739	
Total	$52,886	

May 1	Administrative Expenses	2,500	
	Principal Cash		2,500
	To record payment of executor's fee.		
3	Legacies Distributed (residual)	85,797	
	Distributions to Income Beneficiaries	1,500	
	Principal Cash (balance of account)		34,822
	Income Cash		1,500
	Certificate of Deposit		26,475
	Marketable Securities		24,500
	To record distribution of residuary legacy (principal and		
	income) to First Trust Co., trustee for Nancy Grimes,		
	legatee.		

realized from a lease. A further assumption was that devisee Wallace Davis
paid the March 31 and April 30, Year 3, instalments on the mortgage note
secured by the residence.

Trial Balance of Estate Accounts   Following is a trial balance of the
ledger accounts of the Estate of Jessica Davis on May 3, Year 3:

PAUL HASTING, EXECUTOR

Of the Will of Jessica Davis, Deceased

Trial Balance
May 3, Year 3

	Debit	Credit
Principal		
Estate principal balance		$162,242
Assets discovered		18,000
Loss on disposal of principal assets	$ 137	
Liabilities paid	3,922	
Legacies and Devises distributed	173,683	
Administrative expenses	2,500	
Totals	$180,242	$180,242
Income		
Interest revenue		$ 55
Dividend revenue		1,500
Distributions to income beneficiaries	$ 1,555	
Totals	$ 1,555	$ 1,555

Charge and Discharge Statement

The executor's charge and discharge statement and supporting exhibits for the Estate of Jessica Davis are presented

PAUL HASTING, EXECUTOR

Of the Will of Jessica Davis, Deceased

Charge and Discharge Statement
For Period March 18 through May 3, Year 3

First, as to Principal

I charge myself as follows:

Inventory of estate assets, Mar. 18, Year 3 (Exhibit 1)	$162,242	
Assets discovered (Exhibit 2)	18,000	$180,242

I credit myself as follows:

Loss on disposal of principal assets (Exhibit 3)	$ 137	
Liabilities paid (Exhibit 4)	3,922	
Legacies and Devises distributed (Exhibit 5)	173,683	
Administrative expenses (Exhibit 6)	2,500	180,242
Balance, May 3, Year 3		$ -0-

Second, as to Income

I charge myself as follows:

Interest revenue (bank savings account)	$ 55	
Dividend revenue (Exhibit 7)	1,500	$ 1,555

I credit myself as follows:

Distributions of income (Exhibit 8)		1,555
Balance, May 3, Year 3		$ -0-

on page 738, below, and on page 740. The items in the statement were taken from the trial balance at the top of page 738.

PAUL HASTING, EXECUTOR

Of the Will of Jessica Davis, Deceased
Exhibits Supporting Charge and Discharge Statement
For Period March 18 through September 18, Year 3

Exhibit 1 — Inventory of estate assets, Mar. 18, Year 3:

Bank chequing account		$ 2,157
Bank savings account (including accrued interest)		43,217
Savings and loan association 2-year certificate of deposit maturing June 30,		
Year 3 (including accrued interest)		26,475
Accrued salary earned for period Mar. 1 to 8, Year 3		214
Claim against medical insurance carrier		1,526
Canada Pension Plan benefits receivable		2,080
Proceeds of life insurance policy (payable to estate)		25,000
Marketable securities:		
Common stock of Preston Company, 200 shares		8,000
Common stock of Arthur Corporation, 100 shares		6,500
Residence	$40,800	
Less: Balance of mortgage note payable, including accrued		
interest of $78	15,578	25,222
Furniture and furnishings		2,517
Paintings and other art objects		16,522
Clothing, jewelry, personal effects		625
Automobile		2,187
Total inventory of estate assets		$162,242

Exhibit 2 — Assets discovered:

On Mar. 25, Year 3, a certificate for 600 shares of Campbell Company
common stock was discovered among the decedent's personal effects.
All other securities were located in the decedent's safe deposit box
(valued at market value on date of Jessica Davis's death) .... $ 18,000

Exhibit 3 — Loss on disposal of principal assets:

Sale of automobile, Apr. 3, Year 3:

Carrying amount		$ 2,187
Less: Cash proceeds		2,050
Loss on disposal of principal assets		$ 137

Exhibit 4 — Liabilities paid:

Watts Mortuary		$ 810
Suburban Hospital		1,928
Charles Carson, M.D.		426
Final income tax		457
Morningside Department Store		214
Various residence bills		87
Total liabilities paid		$ 3,922

(Continued)

PAUL HASTING, EXECUTOR

Of the Will of Jessica Davis, Deceased
Exhibits Supporting Charge and Discharge Statement (concluded)
For Period March 18 through September 18, Year 3

Exhibit 5 — Legacies and Devises distributed:

General legacy to Universal Charities: Cash		$ 5,00(
General legacy to Alice Martin: Cash		10,00(
General legacy to Angelo Bari: Cash		10,00(
General legacy to Nolan Ames: Cash		10,00(
General legacy to Nancy Grimes: 200 shares of Preston Company common		
stock		8,00(
Specific legacy to Frances Davis Grimes: Paintings, other art objects,		
clothing, jewelry, personal effects		17,14
Specific devise and legacy to Wallace Davis: Residence, net of mortgage		
note payable, with furniture and furnishings		27,73.
Residuary legacy to Nancy Grimes: Cash, certificate of deposit, 100 shares		
of Arthur Corporation common stock, and 600 shares of Campbell		
Company common stock		85,79
Total legacies and devises distributed		$173,68(

Exhibit 6 — Administrative expenses:

Fee of executor (charged entirely to principal because income		
administration activities were nominal)		$ 2,50(

Exhibit 7 — Dividend revenue:

Arthur Corporation common stock		$ 30
Campbell Company common stock		1,20(
Total dividend revenue		$ 1,50(

Exhibit 8 — Distributions of income:

Mar. 31, Year 3: To residuary legatee Nancy Grimes		$ 5.
May 3, Year 3: To First Trust Co., trustee for Nancy Grimes		1,50(
Total distributions of income		$ 1,55

The charge and discharge statement shows the executor's ***accountabil ity***, not the financial position or cash transactions of the estate. The state ment discloses the charges to the executor for estate principal and estate income assets for which the executor is accountable, and the credits to the executor for the dispositions made of estate assets.

Closing Entry for Estate Once the executor's closing statement and charge and discharge statement have been accepted by the court, the ac countant for the estate may prepare an appropriate closing entry. The closing entry for the Estate of Jessica Davis on May 3, Year 3, appears at the top of page 741.

The example of estate accounting in this chapter was simplified in term of details and time required for the liquidation of the estate. In practice many estates take many months and sometimes years to settle. For many estates, preparation of the estate income tax return is a complex task

Estate Principal Balance	*162,242*	
Assets Discovered	*18,000*	
Interest Revenue	*55*	
Dividend Revenue	*1,500*	
Loss on Disposal of Principal Assets		*137*
Liabilities Paid		*3,922*
Legacies and Devises Distributed		*173,683*
Administrative Expenses		*2,500*
Distributions to Income Beneficiaries		*1,555*

To close estate of Jessica Davis in accordance with court authorization.

Furthermore, the estate of an intestate decedent involves complicated legal issues. The accountant involved in accounting for an estate must be familiar with provisions of the decedent's will and with appropriate provincial probate laws and principal and income laws, and should work closely with the attorney and executor (or administrator) for the estate.

LEGAL AND ACCOUNTING ASPECTS OF TRUSTS

A trust created by a will, as illustrated in the preceding sections of this chapter, is termed a ***testamentary trust***. A trust created by the act of a living person is known as an ***inter vivos*** or ***living trust***. The parties to a trust are (1) the ***settlor*** (also known as the ***donor*** or ***trustor***)—the individual creating the trust, (2) the ***trustee*** — the fiduciary individual or corporation holding legal title to the trust property and carrying out the provisions of the ***trust document*** for a fee, and (3) the ***beneficiary*** — the party for whose benefit the trust was established. As we have noted previously, the income from trust property may be distributed to an ***income beneficiary***, but the principal of a trust ultimately goes to a ***principal beneficiary*** or ***remainderman***.

The rules for allocations between principal and income (see page 732) are applicable to trusts as well as to estates.

Illustration of accounting for a trust

The journal entries in the accounting records of a trust usually differ from those of an estate because of the longer life of a trust. Whereas the personal representative for an estate attempts to complete the administration of the estate as expeditiously as possible, the trustee for a trust must comply with the provisions of the trust document during the stated term of the trust. Accordingly, the trustee's activities include investment of trust assets and maintenance of accounting records for both trust principal and trust income.

To illustrate the accounting issues for a trust, we shall return to the testamentary trust created by the will of Jessica Davis (see page 732). The

NANCY GRIMES TRUST

First Trust Co., Trustee
General Journal

Year 3				
May 3	Principal Cash	34,822	
	Income Cash	1,500	
	Certificate of Deposit	26,475	
	Marketable Securities	24,500	
	Trust Principal Balance		85,797
	Trust Income Balance		1,500
	To record receipt of principal and income assets in trust		
	from Paul Hasting, executor of estate of Jessica Davis.		
May 6	Marketable Securities	19,900	
	Accrued Interest Receivable	180	
	Principal Cash		20,080
	To record acquisition of following securities:		
	$15,000 face amount of 12% bonds of		
	Warren Company, due Mar. 31, Year 23 $15,000		
	Accrued interest 180		
	$5,000 face amount of commercial paper		
	of Modern Finance Company, due July 5,		
	Year 3, acquired at 12% discount 4,900		
	Total cash paid $20,080		
June 30	Principal Cash	26,475	
	Income Cash	612	
	Certificate of Deposit		26,475
	Interest Revenue		612
	To record proceeds of matured certificate of deposit and		
	interest since Mar. 18, Year 3.		
30	Administrative Expenses	250	
	Expenses Chargeable to Income	250	
	Principal Cash		250
	Income Cash		250
	To record payment of trustee fee for period May 3–		
	June 30, Year 3, chargeable equally to principal and		
	to income.		
30	Marketable Securities	25,000	
	Principal Cash		25,000
	To record acquisition of 14% Treasury notes due		
	June 30, Year 8, at face amount.		
30	Distributions to Income Beneficiary	1,862	
	Income cash		1,862
	To record regular quarterly distribution to income		
	beneficiary Nancy Grimes.		

trust was created by the residuary legacy to Nancy Grimes, which required the trustee to pay income from the trust to Grimes at the end of each calendar quarter until her twenty-first birthday (October 1, Year 8), at which time the trust principal would be paid to Grimes. Thus, Grimes is both the income beneficiary and the principal beneficiary.

The journal entries on page 742 illustrate the activities of First Trust Co., trustee for Nancy Grimes, during the calendar quarter ended June 30, Year 3. The journal entries for the Nancy Grimes Trust are *cash-basis* entries; there is no need to accrue interest or dividends on trust investments because financial position or income statements normally are not prepared for a trust.

The May 3, Year 3, opening journal entry for the trust is the counterpart of the journal entry for the Estate of Jessica Davis on the same date (see page 737).

Trial Balance of Trust Accounts   The trial balance of the Nancy Grimes Trust on June 30, Year 3, appears below.

NANCY GRIMES TRUST
First Trust Co., Trustee
Trial Balance
June 30, Year 3

	Debit	Credit
Principal		
Principal cash	$15,967	
Marketable securities	69,400	
Accrued interest receivable	180	
Trust principal balance		85,797
Administrative expenses	250	
Totals	$85,797	$85,797
Income		
Trust income balance		$ 1,500
Interest revenue		612
Expenses chargeable to income	$ 250	
Distributions to income beneficiary	1,862	
Totals	$ 2,112	$ 2,112

Charge and Discharge Statement for Trust   A charge and discharge statement for the trustee of the Nancy Grimes Trust would resemble the charge and discharge statement for an estate illustrated on pages 738 to 740. The major difference would be an exhibit for the details of the $85,547 ($85,797 − $250 = $85,547) trust principal balance on June 30, Year 3.

Periodic Closing Entry for Trust   A closing entry should be made for a trust at the end of each period for which a charge and discharge statement is prepared to clear the nominal accounts for the next reporting period. The closing entry for the Nancy Grimes Trust on June 30, Year 3, is as illustrated below.

Periodic closing entry for a trust

Trust Principal Balance	250	
Trust Income Balance	1,500	
Interest Revenue	612	
Administrative Expenses		250
Expenses Chargeable to Income		250
Distributions to Income Beneficiary		1,862
To close nominal accounts of trust.		

At the time specified in the trust document for transfer of the trust principal to the principal beneficiary, a journal entry would be made to debit the Distributions to Principal Beneficiary account and credit the various trust principal asset accounts. A closing entry for the termination of the trust would then be required, in the form of the comparable estate journal entry illustrated on page 741.

REVIEW QUESTIONS

1 Are estate laws uniform throughout Canada?

2 Define the following terms:
   a *Estate*
   b *Intestacy*
   c *Testator*
   d *Executor*
   e *Administrator*
   f *Letters probate*
   g *Legacy*
   h *Devise*
   i *Remainderman*
   j *Inter vivos trust*
   k *Settlor*

3 What is the purpose of the *probate* of a will?

4 What types of taxes can be levied against an estate?

5 Why must there be a sharp distinction between *principal* and *income* in the administration of an estate?

6 Do the provisions of a will always have to be followed? Explain.

7 What type of bequest is each of the following? Explain.
   a The beach house at 1411 Ocean Avenue, Vancouver, B.C.
   b $25,000 cash
   c $60,000 face amount of Canadian Treasury bonds
   d 1,000 shares of Rogers Corporation common stock represented by certificate No. G-1472
   e All my remaining property

8 Is the accrual basis of accounting ever used for an estate or a trust? Explain.

9 What is involved in the passing of accounts?

10 Describe the use of the Assets Discovered ledger account in accounting for an estate.

11 Compare a personal representative's **charge and discharge statement** with the financial statements issued by a business enterprise.

12 Discuss the similarities and differences in the journal entries for estates and for trusts.

13 List the duties of the personal representative of a testator.

EXERCISES

Ex 18-1   Select the best answer for each of the following multiple-choice questions:

1 Assets in the inventory of property of a decedent must be valued at:
   a Carrying amount to the decedent
   b Current fair value
   c Historical cost to the decedent
   d Amounts established by the surrogate court

2 First Bank and Trust Company is the trustee of the Collins Trust. A significant portion of the trust principal has been invested in high-rated bonds. Some of the bonds have been acquired at face amount, some at a discount, and others at a premium. Which of the following is a proper allocation of the various items to income?
   a The income beneficiary is entitled to the entire interest without dilution for the premium paid, but is not entitled to the proceeds attributable to the discount on collection
   b The income beneficiary is entitled to the entire interest without dilution and to the proceeds attributable to the discount
   c The income beneficiary is entitled to only the interest less the amount of the premium amortized over the term of the bond
   d The income beneficiary is entitled to the full interest and to an allocable share of the gain resulting from the discount

3 Carl Raymond's will named Norman Reid as the executor of Raymond's estate. In respect to Reid's serving as executor, which of the following is correct?
   a He serves without compensation unless the will provides otherwise
   b He may acquire the estate's assets the same as any other person dealing at arm's length
   c Raymond must have obtained Reid's consent in writing to serve as executor of the estate
   d On appointment by the surrogate court, Reid serves as the personal representative of the estate.

4 Martha Mather's will created a trust, and designated her husband as the income beneficiary and her children as the remaindermen. She is dead. Which of the following does not apply to the trust?
   a It is a testamentary trust
   b The husband has the right to appoint the ultimate beneficiaries
   c The children have a vested interest in the trust
   d The trustee owes a fiduciary duty to both the husband and the children

Ex 18-2 Marjorie Singer is trustee of a testamentary trust established in the will of Car Cohen. The trust principal consists of stocks, bonds, and a building subject to mortgage note. The will provides that trust income is to be paid to the survivin husband, Luka Cohen, during his lifetime, that the trust will terminate upon h death, and that the principal then is to be distributed to the Soledad School for Girl Indicate whether each of the following statements is true or false:

a A cash dividend received on one of the trust securities may not be used withou compensating Luka Cohen.

b A 5% stock dividend on Z Co. stock should be distributed to Luka Cohen.

c The cost of insurance on the office building should be deducted from the incom paid to Luka Cohen.

d Monthly principal payments to amortize the mortgage note are deducted fro income.

e Proceeds from fire insurance on the office building would be a part of the tru principal.

f The cost of exercising stock warrants is chargeable to trust income.

g The Soledad School for Girls is the residuary beneficiary of the trust establishe under Carla Cohen's will.

h If Luka Cohen and the Soledad School for Girls agree to terminate the trust an divide the trust assets, the trustee would have to comply with their wishes.

Ex 18-3 Indicate whether each of the following items would be charged to trust principal c to trust income of a testamentary trust:

a Depreciation of building

b Legal fees for managing trust assets

c Special assessment tax levied on real property for street improvements

d Interest on mortgage note payable

e Loss on disposal of trust investments

f Major repairs to property prior to disposal of the property

Ex 18-4 Indicate how each of the following cash payments should be allocated or classifie in the charge and discharge statement for an estate:

a Executor's fees

b Fire insurance premiums

c Special assessments that add permanent value to real property

d Monthly family allowances to beneficiaries

e Expenses of probating the will of a decedent

f Legal fees for defending claims against the estate

g Funeral and terminal-illness expenses

Ex 18-5 Selected transactions completed by the executor of the estate of Charles Fellne who died on October 15, Year 10, are listed below:

Oct. 20 Inventory of estate assets (at current fair value) was filed with the court a follows:

Cash	$ 56,700
Real property	148,000
Jenson Company common stock	60,000
9% bonds of Guam Corporation ($40,000 face amount)	40,000
Accrued interest on bonds of Guam Corporation	600
Personal and household effects	23,500

Oct. 29 A certificate for 150 shares of IBM Corporation common stock valued a $9,000 was found in the coat pocket of an old suit belonging to the de cedent.

Nov. 10 A dividend of $520 was received on the Jenson Company common stock. The stock was willed as a specific legacy to Rollo Fellner, son of Charles Fellner.

Nov. 15 Liabilities of Charles Fellner in the amount of $30,000 were paid.

Nov. 22 Administrative expenses of $3,240 were paid. All expenses are chargeable to principal.

Nov. 29 The bonds of Guam Corporation were sold at 98, plus accrued interest of $1,050.

Nov. 30 The Jenson Company common stock and the cash dividend of $520 received on November 10 were transferred to Rollo Fellner.

Prepare journal entries to record the transactions listed above in the accounting records of the executor for the estate of Charles Fellner.

Ex 18-6 Helen Long, executor for the estate of Harvey Hill, who died on August 10, Year 2, prepared the following trial balance on February 10, Year 3:

	Debit	Credit
Principal cash	$ 26,000	
Income cash	490	
Estate principal balance		$117,000
Assets discovered		1,800
Gain on disposal of principal assets		1,200
Administrative expenses	3,000	
Liabilities paid	24,500	
Legacies and devises distributed	66,500	
Interest revenue		3,590
Distributions to income beneficiaries	2,000	
Expenses chargeable to income	1,100	
Totals	$123,590	$123,590

Prepare a charge and discharge statement for the period August 10, Year 2, through February 10, Year 3. Do not prepare supporting exhibits.

Ex 18-7 Pursuant to the will of Gabriela Bonita, the balance of her estate after probate is to be transferred to a testamentary trust. The following trial balance was prepared from the ledger accounts of the estate on June 30, Year 5:

	Debit	Credit
Principal cash	$115,000	
Income cash	6,750	
Marketable securities	105,000	
Estate principal balance		$265,000
Assets discovered		13,000
Gain on disposal of principal assets		12,000
Administrative expenses	5,400	
Liabilities paid	16,000	
Legacies and devises distributed	48,600	
Interest revenue		4,000
Dividend revenue		4,500
Expenses chargeable to income	1,750	
Totals	$298,500	$298,500

a Prepare a journal entry to close the accounting records of the estate.

b Prepare a journal entry to open the accounting records of the trust.

Ex 18-8 The inexperienced accountant for Lillian Crane, executor of the will of Marion Wilson, deceased, prepared the following journal entries, among others:

Apr. 25	Marketable Securities	10,400	
	Estate Principal Balance		10,400
	To record supplemental inventory for property discovered subsequent to filing of original inventory.		

Apr. 30	Distribution Expense	800	
	Income Cash		800
	To record distribution of income cash to income beneficiary, as required by the will.		

May 27	Accounts Payable	7,400	
	Principal Cash		7,400
	To record following liabilities paid:		

Funeral expenses	$2,500	
Hospital bills	3,800	
Doctor's fees	1,100	
Total	$7,400	

Prepare journal entries for Lillian Crane, executor of the will of Marion Wilson, deceased, on May 31, to correct the foregoing journal entries. Do not reverse the foregoing entries.

CASES

Case 18-1 The estate of Paul Easley included the following items on the date of death, April 16, Year 2 (all assets are a part of the residuary legacy):

(1) Sunrise Company 12% bonds due June 16, Year 12; face amount $100,000, current fair value on April 16, Year 2 (excluding accrued interest), $103,500, interest payable June 16 and December 16 of each year.

(2) Polanco Corporation common stock, 5,000 shares, dividend of $1 a share declared April 1, payable May 1 to shareholders of record April 14.

(3) Polanco Corporation 8%, $100 par, cumulative preferred stock, 1,000 shares (Dividends are paid semiannually January 1 to July 1, and there are no dividends in arrears.)

Instructions

a The executor of the estate asks you for advice as to which items constitute income and which constitute principal of the estate.

b Suppose that dividends were in arrears on the Polanco Corporation 8%, $100 par cumulative preferred stock; would your answer to **a** be any different? If so, explain in what way.

Case 18-2 James Imahiro transferred a manufacturing enterprise and 10,000 shares of M Company common stock to Fidelity Trust Company to be held in trust for the benefit of his son, Robert, for life, with the remainder to go to Robert's son, Edward. Fidelity Trust Company insured the enterprise with Boston Insurance Company under two policies. One policy was a standard fire insurance policy covering the buildings and equipment. The other policy covered any loss of income during periods when the enterprise was inoperable as a result of fire or other catastrophe. The buildings and equipment subsequently were destroyed by fire, and Boston Insurance Company paid claims under both policies to Fidelity Trust Company.

Shortly after the 10,000 shares of MP Company common stock had been transferred to Fidelity Trust Company, MP Company declared a dividend of 10 shares of Monte Oil Corporation common stock for each 100 shares of MP Company common stock held. The Monte Oil common stock had been acquired as an investment by MP Company.

During the same year, MP Company directors split the common stock two-for-one. After the distribution of the new shares, Fidelity Trust Company sold 10,000 shares of MP Company common stock.

Instructions How should Fidelity Trust Company handle the events that have been described above as to distribution between the income beneficiary and the remainderman? State reasons for making the distribution in the manner that you recommend.

Case 18-3 In analyzing the accounting records of Stanley Koyanagi, executor of the estate of Edward Dunn, who died January 16, Year 7, you review the will and other documents, which reveal that (1) Dunn's son had been specifically bequeathed the decedent's only rental property and 12% bonds of Padre Corporation, $50,000 face amount due March 1, Year 21; (2) Dunn's daughter was the beneficiary of a life insurance policy (face amount $100,000) on which the decedent had paid the premiums; and (3) Dunn's widow had been left the remainder of the estate in trust.

Your examination also reveals the following transactions occurring from the time of Dunn's death to March 1, Year 7:

(1) Jan. 20 $3,105 was received from the redemption of $3,000 face amount of Camm Corporation 13% bonds that matured on January 15, Year 7.

(2) Jan. 20 $500 was received from Pittson Corporation as a cash dividend of $1 a share on common stock, declared December 1, Year 6, payable January 15, Year 7, to shareholders of record January 2, Year 7.

(3) Jan. 20 $5,040 was paid to Witter & Company, brokers, for the acquisition of five Seaboard, Inc., 14% bonds due June 30, Year 18.

(4) Jan. 21   30 shares of common stock were received from Ragusa Company, constituting a 2% stock dividend declared December 14, Year 6, distributable January 20, Year 7, to shareholders of record January 15, Year 7.

(5) Feb. 1 $200 quarterly interest was paid by the executor on a promissory note payable due January 31, Year 8.

(6) Feb. 1   Dunn's physician was paid $2,500 for services rendered during Dunn's last illness.

(7) Feb. 2 $600 was collected from East Corporation as a cash dividend of $0.25 a share on common stock, declared January 18, Year 7, payable January 30, Year 7, to shareholders of record January 27, Year 7.

(8) Feb. 3 $575 rent revenue for February was received and deposited in the bank.

(9) Feb. 10 $890 was paid for property taxes covering the period from February 1 to July 31, Year 7.

(10) Mar. 1 $1,802 was paid to Revenue Canada as the remaining income ta[x]
owed by the decedent for Year 6 taxable income.

Instructions   Indicate whether each transaction should be:
Allocated between principal and income
Allocated between principal and beneficiaries
Attributed solely to income
Attributed solely to principal
Attributed solely to beneficiaries

Give reasons supporting your conclusions as to how each transaction should b[e]
handled.

Case 18-4   Thompson Logan died on September 1, Year 1. Logan's will established a trus[t]
providing that the income, after costs of administration, be paid to his widow
Begonia during her lifetime.

During the first year of the trust, the trustee received the following:

(1) Dividend revenue:

Cash dividends declared on Aug. 5, Year 1, payable to shareholders of
    record Aug. 30 . . . . $ 9,200
Cash dividends declared at various times from Sept. 2, Year 1, to July
    31, Year 2 27,500
Stock dividend declared on Dec. 1, Year 1, and received Dec. 28, Year 2,
    a total of 75 shares of Anatolia Company common stock. The market
    value of the stock on date of declaration of the dividend was $40 a
    share.

(2) Interest revenue:

Semiannual interest on municipal bonds paid on Dec. 1, Year 1 . . . . $ 4,000
Semiannual interest on municipal bonds paid on June 1, Year 2 (bonds were
    acquired by trustee) 5,500
Semiannual interest on corporate bonds paid on Feb. 28 and Aug. 31,
    Year 2 (for the two periods) 21,200

(3) Marketable securities with an inventory valuation of $45,000 were sold fo[r]
$49,280.

The trustee's expenses and fees paid in accordance with the provisions of the trust
document totalled $4,444.

Instructions
a Prepare an income statement for the year ended August 31, Year 2, to show the
amount to which Begonia Logan is entitled in accordance with the terms of the
trust document.
b For those items not considered income, explain why they are excluded.

PROBLEMS

18-1   Lisa Popov died on June 5, Year 10. Mike Flinn was named executor of the estate in
the will prepared by Popov's attorney. On December 31, Year 10, the accountant for
the executor prepared the following trial balance:

MIKE FLINN, EXECUTOR

Of the Will of Lisa Popov, Deceased

Trial Balance
December 31, Year 10

	Debit	Credit
Principal cash	$ 40,000	
Income cash	3,000	
Investments in bonds	168,300	
Investments in common shares	124,300	
Household effects	9,500	
Gains on disposal of principal assets		$ 2,200
Assets discovered		16,800
Liabilities paid	26,200	
Administrative expenses	9,000	
Legacies and devises distributed	10,000	
Estate principal balance		368,300
Dividend revenue		4,200
Interest revenue		8,500
Expenses chargeable to income	720	
Distributions to income beneficiaries	8,980	
Totals	$400,000	$400,000

Instructions The amount in the Estate Principal Balance account represents the inventory of estate assets on June 5, Year 10. Prepare a charge and discharge statement for the estate of Lisa Popov. Supporting exhibits are not required for any items except the listing of assets comprising the estate principal balance on December 31, Year 10.

18-2 Angel Moreno died on March 1, Year 8, leaving a valid will in which he named Andrew Kallman as executor and trustee of his assets pending final distribution to Peter Kell, a nephew. The will instructed the executor to transfer Moreno's personal effects and automobile to the nephew, to pay estate taxes, outstanding liabilities, and administrative expenses of the estate, and to transfer the remaining estate assets to a trust for the benefit of the nephew. Income from the estate and the trust is to be paid to the nephew, who will receive the principal (corpus) upon graduation from business school.

The inventory of estate assets on March 1, Year 8, consisted of the following:

Cash	$ 24,400
Certificate of deposit at Federal Savings and Loan Association; includes	
accrued interest of $1,100	101,100
Personal effects	13,200
Automobile	2,800
Investments in common shares	77,000

The following transactions were completed by the executor through December 10, Year 8:

(1) Discovered a savings account of $6,290 in the name of Angel Moreno. (Debit Principal Cash.)

(2) Paid administrative expenses for the estate, $5,200. All expenses are chargeable to principal.

(3) Sold common stock with a carrying amount of $20,000 for $26,020, net of commissions.

(4) Transferred personal effects and automobile to Peter Kell.

(5) Received income as follows (there were no expenses chargeable to income): Interest, $5,200 (includes accrued interest on certificate of deposit on March 1, Year 8); dividends, $1,400.

(6) Distributed the income of the estate to Peter Kell.

(7) Paid liabilities of decedent, $8,050.

(8) Paid estate taxes, $32,000. (Debit the account Estate Taxes Paid.)

(9) Closed the accounting records of the estate and transferred assets to the Peter Kell Trust.

Instructions

a Prepare journal entries to record the transactions and to close the accounting records of the estate.

b Prepare a charge and discharge statement immediately after the transfer of estate assets to the Peter Kell Trust. Do not prepare any supporting exhibits.

c Prepare a journal entry to establish the accounting records for the testamentary trust, the Peter Kell Trust.

18-3 John Lee died in Year 1, and under the terms of the will the beneficiaries were listed as follows:

(1) Alice Lee, widow of John Lee, was left a general legacy of $100,000 payable immediately, and in addition a life interest in 50% of the residuary estate.

(2) Betty Lee, daughter, was left 25% of the residuary estate. One-half of this was left outright, and the other half was to remain in trust.

(3) Carol Lee, daughter, was left a life interest in 15% of the residuary estate.

(4) David Lee, son, was left a 10% interest in the residuary estate, to be paid outright.

John Lee's will specified that the executor had the power to defer sale of any estate assets and to hold such assets in trust until, in the opinion of the executor, conditions were favourable, and to make intermediate distributions of principal from the funds so realized to the beneficiaries. The income from the estate (or trust) was to be distributed annually in the proportion of the beneficiaries' interests.

On December 31, Year 3, the following advances on principal were made:

Betty Lee $400,000

David Lee 250,000

The general legacy to Alice Lee had not been paid as of December 31, Year 3.

The trustee rendered the first accounting to the surrogate court on December 31, Year 3, on which date all income, after payment of all expenses applicable to income, was paid to the beneficiaries.

The surrogate court's decree on the accounting of December 31, Year 3, specified that (1) in considering the distribution of future income, all intermediate payments of principal should be treated as advances to the beneficiaries; and (2) in order to make a fair and equitable division of income, interest at 15% a year was to be charged or credited to the beneficiaries subsequent to Year 3.

The income for Year 4 amounted to $715,500 after all expenses applicable to income had been paid. No other distributions of principal were made.

Instructions Prepare a journal entry to record the payments to income beneficiaries on December 31, Year 4. Support the journal entry with an exhibit showing how the amounts payable to the beneficiaries were determined.

18-4 Duke Hester died December 31, Year 1, and left all property in trust to his daughter, Sally. Income was to be paid to her as she needed it, and at her death the trust principal was to go to Hester's nephew, Neal Hester. Any income (including accrued interest) not paid to Sally by the time of her death would be paid to her estate. Duke Hester appointed Donald Chu trustee at a fee of $3,100 a year. All expenses of settling the estate were paid and accounted for by the executor before the trustee assumed responsibility for the trust.

Sally Hester died on October 1, Year 5, and left all her property in trust to her cousin, Lori Miller. Donald Chu, who also was appointed executor and trustee of Sally Hester's estate, agreed not to charge additional fees for these services. All income subsequent to October 1, Year 5, was to be paid to Lori Miller as soon as the income was received by the trustee. The estate of Sally Hester consisted solely of her unexpended income from the Duke Hester Trust. Principal cash of the Duke Hester Trust was invested immediately at 8% interest, payable quarterly.

From October 1, Year 5, to December 31, Year 6, Neal Hester received "advances" from the income of his uncle's trust. On December 31, Year 6, the remainder of the trust was turned over to Neal Hester.

The property received by Donald Chu under the will of Duke Hester on January 1, Year 2, consisted of the following:

(1) 20,000 shares of Armco Corporation common stock with a current market value of $25 a share.

(2) $150,000 bonds of Armco Corporation, paying interest on June 30 and December 31 at 9% a year. The bonds had a current market value equal to their face amount.

In the five years ended December 31, Year 6, the trustee received the following dividends on the Armco Corporation common stock: February 1, Year 2, Year 3, and Year 4, $25,000 a year; February 1, Year 5, and Year 6, $30,000 a year. The trustee made the following payments:

Trustee's fees and expenses: $3,100 a year

To beneficiaries:

Sally Hester, income beneficiary of the Duke Hester Trust, from Dec. 31, Year 1, to Oct. 1, Year 5:

Year 2	*$18,625*
Year 3	*17,500*
Year 4	*19,375*
Year 5	*28,500*

Neal Hester, principal beneficiary of the Duke Hester Trust, from Oct. 1, Year 5, to Dec. 31, Year 6:

Year 5	*$ 8,500*
Year 6	*23,000*

Lori Miller, beneficiary of the Sally Hester Trust, from Oct. 1, Year 5, to Dec. 31, Year 6:

Year 5 and Year 6, all trust income as determined on cash basis of accounting.

The trustee of the Duke Hester Trust kept the remaining cash in a chequing account, where it earned no interest for the beneficiaries.

Instructions

a Prepare a statement for the Duke Hester Trust from December 31, Year 1, to October 1, Year 5, showing the undistributed income comprising the Sally Hester Trust. Assume that interest on the Armco Corporation bonds was accrued by the trustee from July 1 to October 1, Year 5.

b Compute the amount to be distributed to Neal Hester on December 31, Year 6.

c Compute the income received by Lori Miller from the Sally Hester Trust in Year 5 and in Year 6.

18-5 Sarah Manfred died in an accident on May 31, Year 1. The will provided that all liabilities and expenses were to be paid and that the property was to be distributed as follows:

(1) Personal residence to George Manfred, widower of Sarah Manfred.

(2) Govt. of Canada 12% bonds and Permian Company common stock — to be placed in trust. All income to go to George Manfred during his lifetime.

(3) Sonar Corporation 9% bonds — bequeathed to Eleanor Manfred, daughter of Sarah Manfred.

(4) Cash — a bequest of $15,000 to Matthew Manfred, son of Sarah Manfred.

(5) Residue of estate — to be divided equally between the two children of Sarah Manfred, Eleanor and Matthew.

The will further provided that during the administration period George Manfred was to be paid $500 a month from estate income. Estate and inheritance taxes were to be borne by the residue of the estate. Matthew Manfred was named as executor and trustee.

The following inventory of the decedent's property was prepared:

Personal residence	$195,000
Jewelry — diamond ring	14,600
First National Bank — chequing account; balance May 31, Year 1	143,000
$100,000 Govt. of Canada 12% bonds, due Year 20, interest payable Mar. 1 and Sept. 1 (includes accrued interest of $3,000)	103,000
$10,000 Sonar Corporation 9% bonds, due Year 10, interest payable May 31 and Nov. 30	9,900
Permian Company common stock, 800 shares	64,000
Dividends receivable on Permian Company common stock	800
XY Company common stock, 700 shares	70,000

The executor opened an estate chequing account and transferred the decedent's chequing account balance to it. Other deposits in the estate chequing account through July 1, Year 2, were as follows:

Interest received on $100,000 Govt. of Canada 12% bonds:	
Sept. 1, Year 1	$ 6,000
Mar. 1, Year 2	6,000
Dividends received on Permian Company common stock:	
June 15, Year 1, declared May 7, Year 1, payable to holders of record May 27, Year 1	800
Sept. 15, Year 1	800
Dec. 15, Year 1	1,200
Mar. 15, Year 2	1,500
June 15, Year 2	1,500
Net proceeds of June 19, Year 1, sale of 700 shares of XY Company common stock	68,810

Payments were made from the estate's chequing account through July 1, Year 2, for items shown at the top of page 755.

The executor, Matthew Manfred, waived his fee. However, he desired to receive his mother's diamond ring in lieu of the $15,000 cash legacy. All parties agreed to this in writing, and the court's approval was secured. All legacies other than the assets to be held in trust and the residue of the estate were delivered on July 1, Year 1.

Liabilities of decedent paid (including funeral expenses)	$12,000
Additional prior years' federal and provincial income taxes, plus interest, to	
May 31, Year 1	1,810
Year 1 income taxes of Sarah Manfred for the period Jan. 1, Year 1,	
through May 31, Year 1.	9,100
Federal and provincial fiduciary income taxes, fiscal years ending June 30,	
Year 2	2,400
Estate and inheritance taxes	73,000
Monthly payments to George Manfred, 13 payments of $500	6,500
Attorney's and accountant's fees (allocated entirely to principal)	25,000

Instructions

a Prepare a charge and discharge statement as to principal and income, with supporting exhibits, to accompany the attorney's formal court accounting on behalf of the executor of the Estate of Sarah Manfred for the period from May 31, Year 1, through July 1, Year 2. In accordance with the will, the executor accrued the interest and dividends on the estate investments to July 1, Year 2.

b Prepare a summary showing the allocation of principal and income assets on July 1, Year 2, between the trust for the benefit of George Manfred and the residual estate to be divided between Eleanor Manfred and Matthew Manfred.

18-6 The will of Nikola Toma directed that the executor, Scott Hodgkins, liquidate the entire estate within two years of the date of death and pay the net proceeds and income to United Way. Nikola Toma, a bachelor, died on February 1, Year 10, after a brief illness.

An inventory of the decedent's property was prepared, and the current fair value of all items was determined. The preliminary inventory, before the computation of any appropriate income accruals on inventory items, follows:

	Current *fair value*
Royal Bank chequing account	$ 8,500
$60,000 face amount Sun City bonds, interest rate 12%, payable Jan. 1	
and July, maturity date July 1, Year 14	59,000
2,000 shares Rex Corporation common stock	220,000
Term life insurance: beneficiary, Estate of Nikola Toma	20,000
Residence ($86,500) and furniture ($8,000)	94,500

During Year 10, the following transactions occurred:

(1) The interest on the Sun City bonds was collected. The bonds were sold on July 1, for $59,000, and the proceeds and interest accrued on February 1, Year 10 ($600), were paid to United Way.

(2) Rex Corporation paid cash dividends of $1 a share on March 1 and December 1, and distributed a 10% stock dividend on July 1. All dividends were declared 45 days before each payment date and were payable to holders of record as of 40 days before each payment date. In September, 1,000 shares of Rex Corporation common stock were sold at $105 a share, and the proceeds were paid to United Way.

(3) Because of a depressed real estate market, the personal residence was rented furnished at $300 a month commencing April 1, Year 10. The rent was paid monthly, in advance. Property taxes of $1,200 for the calendar Year 10 were paid. The house and furnishings had estimated economic lives of 40 years and 8 years, respectively. The part-time gardener was paid four months' wages totalling $500 on April 30 for services performed, and then was released.

(4) The Royal Bank chequing account was closed, and the balance of $8,500 wa̟ transferred to a bank chequing account for the estate.

(5) The proceeds of the term life insurance were received on March 1 and deposite in the bank chequing account for the estate.

(6) The following cash payments were made:
   (a) Funeral expenses and expenses of last illness, $3,500.
   (b) Balance due on Year 9 income taxes of decedent, $700.
   (c) Attorney's and accountant's fees, $15,000, of which $1,000 was allocate to income.

(7) On December 31, the balance of the undistributed income, except for $250, wa̟ paid to United Way. The balance of the cash on hand derived from the principa of the estate also was paid to United Way on December 31. On December 31, th̟ executor resigned and waived all fees.

Instructions   Prepare a charge and discharge statement, together with supportin̟ exhibits, for the executor of the Estate of Nikola Toma for the period Februar 1–December 31, Year 10. Disregard depreciation.

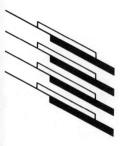

COMPOUND INTEREST TABLES

Table 1 Future Amount of 1 at Compound Interest Due in *n* Periods: $a_{\overline{n}|i} = (1 + i)^n$

n \ i	½%	1%	1½%	2%	2½%	3%
1	1.005000	1.010000	1.015000	1.020000	1.025000	1.030000
2	1.010025	1.020100	1.030225	1.040400	1.050625	1.060900
3	1.015075	1.030301	1.045678	1.061208	1.076891	1.092727
4	1.020151	1.040604	1.061364	1.082432	1.103813	1.125509
5	1.025251	1.051010	1.077284	1.104081	1.131408	1.159274
6	1.030378	1.061520	1.093443	1.126162	1.159693	1.194052
7	1.035529	1.072135	1.109845	1.148686	1.188686	1.229874
8	1.040707	1.082857	1.126493	1.171659	1.218403	1.266770
9	1.045911	1.093685	1.143390	1.195093	1.248863	1.304773
10	1.051140	1.104622	1.160541	1.218994	1.280085	1.343916
11	1.056396	1.115668	1.177949	1.243374	1.312087	1.384234
12	1.061678	1.126825	1.195618	1.268242	1.344889	1.425761
13	1.066986	1.138093	1.213552	1.293607	1.378511	1.468534
14	1.072321	1.149474	1.231756	1.319479	1.412974	1.512590
15	1.077683	1.160969	1.250232	1.345868	1.448298	1.557967
16	1.083071	1.172579	1.268986	1.372786	1.484506	1.604706
17	1.088487	1.184304	1.288020	1.400241	1.521618	1.652848
18	1.093929	1.196147	1.307341	1.428246	1.559659	1.702433
19	1.099399	1.208109	1.326951	1.456811	1.598650	1.753506
20	1.104896	1.220190	1.346855	1.485947	1.638616	1.806111
21	1.110420	1.232392	1.367058	1.515666	1.679582	1.860295
22	1.115972	1.244716	1.387564	1.545980	1.721571	1.916103
23	1.121552	1.257163	1.408377	1.576899	1.764611	1.973587
24	1.127160	1.269735	1.429503	1.608437	1.808726	2.032794
25	1.132796	1.282432	1.450945	1.640606	1.853944	2.093778
26	1.138460	1.295256	1.472710	1.673418	1.900293	2.156591
27	1.144152	1.308209	1.494800	1.706886	1.947800	2.221289
28	1.149873	1.321291	1.517222	1.741024	1.996495	2.287928
29	1.155622	1.334504	1.539981	1.775845	2.046407	2.356566
30	1.161400	1.347849	1.563080	1.811362	2.097568	2.427262
31	1.167207	1.361327	1.586526	1.847589	2.150007	2.500080
32	1.173043	1.374941	1.610324	1.884541	2.203757	2.575083
33	1.178908	1.388690	1.634479	1.922231	2.258851	2.652335
34	1.184803	1.402577	1.658996	1.960676	2.315322	2.731905
35	1.190727	1.416603	1.683881	1.999890	2.373205	2.813862
36	1.196681	1.430769	1.709140	2.039887	2.432535	2.898278
37	1.202664	1.445076	1.734777	2.080685	2.493349	2.985227
38	1.208677	1.459527	1.760798	2.122299	2.555682	3.074783
39	1.214721	1.474123	1.787210	2.164745	2.619574	3.167027
40	1.220794	1.488864	1.814018	2.208040	2.685064	3.262038
41	1.226898	1.503752	1.841229	2.252200	2.752190	3.359899
42	1.233033	1.518790	1.868847	2.297244	2.820995	3.460696
43	1.239198	1.533978	1.896880	2.343189	2.891520	3.564517
44	1.245394	1.549318	1.925333	2.390053	2.963808	3.671452
45	1.251621	1.564811	1.954213	2.437854	3.037903	3.781596
46	1.257879	1.580459	1.983526	2.486611	3.113851	3.895044
47	1.264168	1.596263	2.013279	2.536344	3.191697	4.011895
48	1.270489	1.612226	2.043478	2.587070	3.271490	4.132252
49	1.276842	1.628348	2.074130	2.638812	3.353277	4.256219
50	1.283226	1.644632	2.105242	2.691588	3.437109	4.383906

Table 1   Future Amount of 1 (*continued*)

n \ i	3½%	4%	4½%	5%	5½%	6%
1	1.035000	1.040000	1.045000	1.050000	1.055000	1.060000
2	1.071225	1.081600	1.092025	1.102500	1.113025	1.123600
3	1.108718	1.124864	1.141166	1.157625	1.174241	1.191016
4	1.147523	1.169859	1.192519	1.215506	1.238825	1.262477
5	1.187686	1.216653	1.246182	1.276282	1.306960	1.338226
6	1.229255	1.265319	1.302260	1.340096	1.378843	1.418519
7	1.272279	1.315932	1.360862	1.407100	1.454679	1.503630
8	1.316809	1.368569	1.422101	1.477455	1.534687	1.593848
9	1.362897	1.423312	1.486095	1.551328	1.619094	1.689479
10	1.410599	1.480244	1.552969	1.628895	1.708144	1.790848
11	1.459970	1.539454	1.622853	1.710339	1.802092	1.898299
12	1.511069	1.601032	1.695881	1.795856	1.901207	2.012196
13	1.563956	1.665074	1.772196	1.885649	2.005774	2.132928
14	1.618695	1.731676	1.851945	1.979932	2.116091	2.260904
15	1.675349	1.800944	1.935282	2.078928	2.232476	2.396558
16	1.733986	1.872981	2.022370	2.182875	2.355263	2.540352
17	1.794676	1.947901	2.113377	2.292018	2.484802	2.692773
18	1.857489	2.025817	2.208479	2.406619	2.621466	2.854339
19	1.922501	2.106849	2.307860	2.526950	2.765647	3.025600
20	1.989789	2.191123	2.411714	2.653298	2.917757	3.207135
21	2.059431	2.278768	2.520241	2.785963	3.078234	3.399564
22	2.131512	2.369919	2.633652	2.925261	3.247537	3.603537
23	2.206114	2.464716	2.752166	3.071524	3.426152	3.819750
24	2.283328	2.563304	2.876014	3.225100	3.614590	4.048935
25	2.363245	2.665836	3.005434	3.386355	3.813392	4.291871
26	2.445959	2.772470	3.140679	3.555673	4.023129	4.549383
27	2.531567	2.883369	3.282010	3.733456	4.244401	4.822346
28	2.620172	2.998703	3.429700	3.920129	4.477843	5.111687
29	2.711878	3.118651	3.584036	4.116136	4.724124	5.418388
30	2.806794	3.243398	3.745318	4.321942	4.983951	5.743491
31	2.905031	3.373133	3.913857	4.538039	5.258069	6.088101
32	3.006708	3.508059	4.089981	4.764941	5.547262	6.453387
33	3.111942	3.648381	4.274030	5.003189	5.852362	6.840590
34	3.220860	3.794316	4.466362	5.253348	6.174242	7.251025
35	3.333590	3.946089	4.667348	5.516015	6.513825	7.686087
36	3.450266	4.103933	4.877378	5.791816	6.872085	8.147252
37	3.571025	4.268090	5.096860	6.081407	7.250050	8.636087
38	3.696011	4.438813	5.326219	6.385477	7.648803	9.154252
39	3.825372	4.616366	5.565899	6.704751	8.069487	9.703507
40	3.959260	4.801021	5.816365	7.039989	8.513309	10.285718
41	4.097834	4.993061	6.078101	7.391988	8.981541	10.902861
42	4.241258	5.192784	6.351615	7.761588	9.475526	11.557033
43	4.389702	5.400495	6.637438	8.149667	9.996679	12.250455
44	4.543342	5.616515	6.936123	8.557150	10.546497	12.985482
45	4.702359	5.841176	7.248248	8.985008	11.126554	13.764611
46	4.866941	6.074823	7.574420	9.434258	11.738515	14.590487
47	5.037284	6.317816	7.915268	9.905971	12.384133	15.465917
48	5.213589	6.570528	8.271456	10.401270	13.065260	16.393872
49	5.396065	6.833349	8.643671	10.921333	13.783849	17.377504
50	5.584927	7.106683	9.032636	11.467400	14.541961	18.420154

Table 1 Future Amount of 1 (*continued*)

n \ i	7%	8%	9%	10%	12%	15%
1	1.070000	1.080000	1.090000	1.100000	1.120000	1.150000
2	1.144900	1.166400	1.188100	1.210000	1.254400	1.322500
3	1.225043	1.259712	1.295029	1.331000	1.404928	1.520875
4	1.310796	1.360489	1.411582	1.464100	1.573519	1.749006
5	1.402552	1.469328	1.538624	1.610510	1.762342	2.011357
6	1.500730	1.586874	1.677100	1.771561	1.973823	2.313061
7	1.605781	1.713824	1.828039	1.948717	2.210681	2.660020
8	1.718186	1.850930	1.992563	2.143589	2.475963	3.059023
9	1.838459	1.999005	2.171893	2.357948	2.773079	3.517876
10	1.967151	2.158925	2.367364	2.593742	3.105848	4.045558
11	2.104852	2.331639	2.580426	2.853117	3.478550	4.652391
12	2.252192	2.518170	2.812665	3.138428	3.895976	5.350250
13	2.409845	2.719624	3.065805	3.452271	4.363493	6.152788
14	2.578534	2.937194	3.341727	3.797498	4.887112	7.075706
15	2.759032	3.172169	3.642482	4.177248	5.473566	8.137062
16	2.952164	3.425943	3.970306	4.594973	6.130394	9.357621
17	3.158815	3.700018	4.327633	5.054470	6.866041	10.761264
18	3.379932	3.996019	4.717120	5.559917	7.689966	12.375454
19	3.616528	4.315701	5.141661	6.115909	8.612762	14.231772
20	3.869684	4.660957	5.604411	6.727500	9.646293	16.366537
21	4.140562	5.033834	6.108808	7.400250	10.803848	18.821518
22	4.430402	5.436540	6.658600	8.140275	12.100310	21.644746
23	4.740530	5.871464	7.257874	8.954302	13.552347	24.891458
24	5.072367	6.341181	7.911083	9.849733	15.178629	28.625176
25	5.427433	6.848475	8.623081	10.834706	17.000064	32.918953
26	5.807353	7.396353	9.399158	11.918177	19.040072	37.856796
27	6.213868	7.988061	10.245082	13.109994	21.324881	43.535315
28	6.648838	8.627106	11.167140	14.420994	23.883866	50.065612
29	7.114257	9.317275	12.172182	15.863093	26.749930	57.575454
30	7.612255	10.062657	13.267678	17.449402	29.959922	66.211772
31	8.145113	10.867669	14.461770	19.194342	33.555113	76.143538
32	8.715271	11.737083	15.763329	21.113777	37.581726	87.565068
33	9.325340	12.676050	17.182028	23.225154	42.091533	100.699829
34	9.978114	13.690134	18.728411	25.547670	47.142517	115.804803
35	10.676581	14.785344	20.413968	28.102437	52.799620	133.175523
36	11.423942	15.968172	22.251225	30.912681	59.135574	153.151852
37	12.223618	17.245626	24.253835	34.003949	66.231843	176.124630
38	13.079271	18.625276	26.436680	37.404343	74.179664	202.543324
39	13.994820	20.115298	28.815982	41.144778	83.081224	232.924823
40	14.974458	21.724521	31.409420	45.259256	93.050970	267.863546
41	16.022670	23.462483	34.236268	49.785181	104.217087	308.043078
42	17.144257	25.339482	37.317532	54.763699	116.723137	354.249540
43	18.344355	27.366640	40.676110	60.240069	130.729914	407.386971
44	19.628460	29.555972	44.336960	66.264076	146.417503	468.495017
45	21.002452	31.920449	48.327286	72.890484	163.987604	538.769269
46	22.472623	34.474085	52.676742	80.179532	183.666116	619.584659
47	24.045707	37.232012	57.417649	88.197485	205.706050	712.522358
48	25.728907	40.210573	62.585237	97.017234	230.390776	819.400712
49	27.529930	43.427419	68.217908	106.718957	258.037669	942.310819
50	29.457025	46.901613	74.357520	117.390853	289.002190	1083.657442

Table 2 Present Value of 1 at Compound Interest Due in n Periods: $p_{\overline{n}|i} = \dfrac{1}{(1 + i)^n}$

n \ i	$\frac{1}{2}$%	1%	$1\frac{1}{2}$%	2%	$2\frac{1}{2}$%	3%
1	0.995025	0.990099	0.985222	0.980392	0.975610	0.970874
2	0.990075	0.980296	0.970662	0.961169	0.951814	0.942596
3	0.985149	0.970590	0.956317	0.942322	0.928599	0.915142
4	0.980248	0.960980	0.942184	0.923845	0.905951	0.888487
5	0.975371	0.951466	0.928260	0.905731	0.883854	0.862609
6	0.970518	0.942045	0.914542	0.887971	0.862297	0.837484
7	0.965690	0.932718	0.901027	0.870560	0.841265	0.813092
8	0.960885	0.923483	0.887711	0.853490	0.820747	0.789409
9	0.956105	0.914340	0.874592	0.836755	0.800728	0.766417
10	0.951348	0.905287	0.861667	0.820348	0.781198	0.744094
11	0.946615	0.896324	0.848933	0.804263	0.762145	0.722421
12	0.941905	0.887449	0.836387	0.788493	0.743556	0.701380
13	0.937219	0.878663	0.824027	0.773033	0.725420	0.680951
14	0.932556	0.869963	0.811849	0.757875	0.707727	0.661118
15	0.927917	0.861349	0.799852	0.743015	0.690466	0.641862
16	0.923300	0.852821	0.788031	0.728446	0.673625	0.623167
17	0.918707	0.844377	0.776385	0.714163	0.657195	0.605016
18	0.914136	0.836017	0.764912	0.700159	0.641166	0.587395
19	0.909588	0.827740	0.753607	0.686431	0.625528	0.570286
20	0.905063	0.819544	0.742470	0.672971	0.610271	0.553676
21	0.900560	0.811430	0.731498	0.659776	0.595386	0.537549
22	0.896080	0.803396	0.720688	0.646839	0.580865	0.521893
23	0.891622	0.795442	0.710037	0.634156	0.566697	0.506692
24	0.887186	0.787566	0.699544	0.621721	0.552875	0.491934
25	0.882772	0.779768	0.689206	0.609531	0.539391	0.477606
26	0.878380	0.772048	0.679021	0.597579	0.526235	0.463695
27	0.874010	0.764404	0.668986	0.585862	0.513400	0.450189
28	0.869662	0.756836	0.659099	0.574375	0.500878	0.437077
29	0.865335	0.749342	0.649359	0.563112	0.488661	0.424346
30	0.861030	0.741923	0.639762	0.552071	0.476743	0.411987
31	0.856746	0.734577	0.630308	0.541246	0.465115	0.399987
32	0.852484	0.727304	0.620993	0.530633	0.453771	0.388337
33	0.848242	0.720103	0.611816	0.520229	0.442703	0.377026
34	0.844022	0.712973	0.602774	0.510028	0.431905	0.366045
35	0.839823	0.705914	0.593866	0.500028	0.421371	0.355383
36	0.835645	0.698925	0.585090	0.490223	0.411094	0.345032
37	0.831487	0.692005	0.576443	0.480611	0.401067	0.334983
38	0.827351	0.685153	0.567924	0.471187	0.391285	0.325226
39	0.823235	0.678370	0.559531	0.461948	0.381741	0.315754
40	0.819139	0.671653	0.551262	0.452890	0.372431	0.306557
41	0.815064	0.665003	0.543116	0.444010	0.363347	0.297628
42	0.811009	0.658419	0.535089	0.435304	0.354485	0.288959
43	0.806974	0.651900	0.527182	0.426769	0.345839	0.280543
44	0.802959	0.645445	0.519391	0.418401	0.337404	0.272372
45	0.798964	0.639055	0.511715	0.410197	0.329174	0.264439
46	0.794989	0.632728	0.504153	0.402154	0.321146	0.256737
47	0.791034	0.626463	0.496702	0.394268	0.313313	0.249259
48	0.787098	0.620260	0.489362	0.386538	0.305671	0.241999
49	0.783183	0.614119	0.482130	0.378958	0.298216	0.234950
50	0.779286	0.608039	0.475005	0.371528	0.290942	0.228107

Table 2 Present Value of 1 at Compound Interest Due in n Periods: $p_{\overline{n}|i} = \dfrac{1}{(1 + i)^n}$

n	$\frac{1}{2}$%	1%	$1\frac{1}{2}$%	2%	$2\frac{1}{2}$%	3%
1	0.995025	0.990099	0.985222	0.980392	0.975610	0.970874
2	0.990075	0.980296	0.970662	0.961169	0.951814	0.942596
3	0.985149	0.970590	0.956317	0.942322	0.928599	0.915142
4	0.980248	0.960980	0.942184	0.923845	0.905951	0.888487
5	0.975371	0.951466	0.928260	0.905731	0.883854	0.862609
6	0.970518	0.942045	0.914542	0.887971	0.862297	0.837484
7	0.965690	0.932718	0.901027	0.870560	0.841265	0.813092
8	0.960885	0.923483	0.887711	0.853490	0.820747	0.789409
9	0.956105	0.914340	0.874592	0.836755	0.800728	0.766417
10	0.951348	0.905287	0.861667	0.820348	0.781198	0.744094
11	0.946615	0.896324	0.848933	0.804263	0.762145	0.722421
12	0.941905	0.887449	0.836387	0.788493	0.743556	0.701380
13	0.937219	0.878663	0.824027	0.773033	0.725420	0.680951
14	0.932556	0.869963	0.811849	0.757875	0.707727	0.661118
15	0.927917	0.861349	0.799852	0.743015	0.690466	0.641862
16	0.923300	0.852821	0.788031	0.728446	0.673625	0.623167
17	0.918707	0.844377	0.776385	0.714163	0.657195	0.605016
18	0.914136	0.836017	0.764912	0.700159	0.641166	0.587395
19	0.909588	0.827740	0.753607	0.686431	0.625528	0.570286
20	0.905063	0.819544	0.742470	0.672971	0.610271	0.553676
21	0.900560	0.811430	0.731498	0.659776	0.595386	0.537549
22	0.896080	0.803396	0.720688	0.646839	0.580865	0.521893
23	0.891622	0.795442	0.710037	0.634156	0.566697	0.506692
24	0.887186	0.787566	0.699544	0.621721	0.552875	0.491934
25	0.882772	0.779768	0.689206	0.609531	0.539391	0.477606
26	0.878380	0.772048	0.679021	0.597579	0.526235	0.463695
27	0.874010	0.764404	0.668986	0.585862	0.513400	0.450189
28	0.869662	0.756836	0.659099	0.574375	0.500878	0.437077
29	0.865335	0.749342	0.649359	0.563112	0.488661	0.424346
30	0.861030	0.741923	0.639762	0.552071	0.476743	0.411987
31	0.856746	0.734577	0.630308	0.541246	0.465115	0.399987
32	0.852484	0.727304	0.620993	0.530633	0.453771	0.388337
33	0.848242	0.720103	0.611816	0.520229	0.442703	0.377026
34	0.844022	0.712973	0.602774	0.510028	0.431905	0.366045
35	0.839823	0.705914	0.593866	0.500028	0.421371	0.355383
36	0.835645	0.698925	0.585090	0.490223	0.411094	0.345032
37	0.831487	0.692005	0.576443	0.480611	0.401067	0.334983
38	0.827351	0.685153	0.567924	0.471187	0.391285	0.325226
39	0.823235	0.678370	0.559531	0.461948	0.381741	0.315754
40	0.819139	0.671653	0.551262	0.452890	0.372431	0.306557
41	0.815064	0.665003	0.543116	0.444010	0.363347	0.297628
42	0.811009	0.658419	0.535089	0.435304	0.354485	0.288959
43	0.806974	0.651900	0.527182	0.426769	0.345839	0.280543
44	0.802959	0.645445	0.519391	0.418401	0.337404	0.272372
45	0.798964	0.639055	0.511715	0.410197	0.329174	0.264439
46	0.794989	0.632728	0.504153	0.402154	0.321146	0.256737
47	0.791034	0.626463	0.496702	0.394268	0.313313	0.249259
48	0.787098	0.620260	0.489362	0.386538	0.305671	0.241999
49	0.783183	0.614119	0.482130	0.378958	0.298216	0.234950
50	0.779286	0.608039	0.475005	0.371528	0.290942	0.228107

Table 2   Present Value of 1 (*continued*)

n	7%	8%	9%	10%	12%	15%
1	0.934580	0.925926	0.917431	0.909091	0.892857	0.869565
2	0.873439	0.857339	0.841680	0.826446	0.797194	0.756144
3	0.816298	0.793832	0.772183	0.751315	0.711780	0.657516
4	0.762895	0.735030	0.708425	0.683013	0.635518	0.571753
5	0.712986	0.680583	0.649931	0.620921	0.567427	0.497177
6	0.666342	0.630170	0.596267	0.564474	0.506631	0.432328
7	0.622750	0.583490	0.547034	0.513158	0.452349	0.375937
8	0.582009	0.540269	0.501866	0.466507	0.403883	0.326902
9	0.543934	0.500249	0.460428	0.424098	0.360610	0.284262
10	0.508349	0.463193	0.422411	0.385543	0.321973	0.247185
11	0.475093	0.428883	0.387533	0.350494	0.287476	0.214943
12	0.444012	0.397114	0.355535	0.318631	0.256675	0.186907
13	0.414964	0.367698	0.326179	0.289664	0.229174	0.162528
14	0.387817	0.340461	0.299246	0.263331	0.204620	0.141329
15	0.362446	0.315242	0.274538	0.239392	0.182696	0.122894
16	0.338735	0.291890	0.251870	0.217629	0.163122	0.106865
17	0.316574	0.270269	0.231073	0.197845	0.145644	0.092926
18	0.295864	0.250249	0.211994	0.179859	0.130040	0.080805
19	0.276508	0.231712	0.194490	0.163508	0.116107	0.070265
20	0.258419	0.214548	0.178431	0.148644	0.103667	0.061100
21	0.241513	0.198656	0.163698	0.135131	0.092560	0.053131
22	0.225713	0.183941	0.150182	0.122846	0.082643	0.046201
23	0.210947	0.170315	0.137781	0.111678	0.073788	0.040174
24	0.197147	0.157699	0.126405	0.101526	0.065882	0.034934
25	0.184249	0.146018	0.115968	0.092296	0.058823	0.030378
26	0.172195	0.135202	0.106393	0.083905	0.052521	0.026415
27	0.160930	0.125187	0.097608	0.076278	0.046894	0.022970
28	0.150402	0.115914	0.089548	0.069343	0.041869	0.019974
29	0.140563	0.107328	0.082155	0.063039	0.037383	0.017369
30	0.131367	0.099377	0.075371	0.057309	0.033378	0.015103
31	0.122773	0.092016	0.069148	0.052099	0.029802	0.013133
32	0.114741	0.085200	0.063438	0.047362	0.026609	0.011420
33	0.107235	0.078889	0.058200	0.043057	0.023758	0.009931
34	0.100219	0.073045	0.053395	0.039143	0.021212	0.008635
35	0.093663	0.067635	0.048986	0.035584	0.018940	0.007509
36	0.087535	0.062625	0.044941	0.032349	0.016910	0.006529
37	0.081809	0.057986	0.041231	0.029408	0.015098	0.005678
38	0.076457	0.053690	0.037826	0.026735	0.013481	0.004937
39	0.071455	0.049713	0.034703	0.024304	0.012036	0.004293
40	0.066780	0.046031	0.031838	0.022095	0.010747	0.003733
41	0.062412	0.042621	0.029209	0.020086	0.009595	0.003246
42	0.058329	0.039464	0.026797	0.018260	0.008567	0.002823
43	0.054513	0.036541	0.024584	0.016600	0.007649	0.002455
44	0.050946	0.033834	0.022555	0.015091	0.006830	0.002134
45	0.047613	0.031328	0.020692	0.013719	0.006098	0.001856
46	0.044499	0.029007	0.018984	0.012472	0.005445	0.001614
47	0.041587	0.026859	0.017416	0.011338	0.004861	0.001403
48	0.038867	0.024869	0.015978	0.010307	0.004340	0.001220
49	0.036324	0.023027	0.014659	0.009370	0.003875	0.001061
50	0.033948	0.021321	0.013449	0.008519	0.003460	0.000923

Table 3 Future Amount of Ordinary Annuity of 1 per Period: $A_{\overline{n}|i} = \dfrac{(1 + i)^n - 1}{i}$

n	½%	1%	1½%	2%	2½%	3%
1	1.000000	1.000000	1.000000	1.000000	1.000000	1.000000
2	2.005000	2.010000	2.015000	2.020000	2.025000	2.030000
3	3.015025	3.030100	3.045225	3.060400	3.075625	3.090900
4	4.030100	4.060401	4.090903	4.121608	4.152516	4.183627
5	5.050251	5.101005	5.152267	5.204040	5.256329	5.309136
6	6.075502	6.152015	6.229551	6.308121	6.387737	6.468410
7	7.105879	7.213535	7.322994	7.434283	7.547430	7.662462
8	8.141409	8.285671	8.432839	8.582969	8.736116	8.892336
9	9.182116	9.368527	9.559332	9.754628	9.954519	10.159106
10	10.228026	10.462213	10.702722	10.949721	11.203382	11.463879
11	11.279167	11.566835	11.863262	12.168715	12.483466	12.807796
12	12.335562	12.682503	13.041211	13.412090	13.795553	14.192030
13	13.397240	13.809328	14.236830	14.680332	15.140442	15.617790
14	14.464226	14.947421	15.450382	15.973938	16.518953	17.086324
15	15.536548	16.096896	16.682138	17.293417	17.931927	18.598914
16	16.614230	17.257864	17.932370	18.639285	19.380225	20.156881
17	17.697301	18.430443	19.201355	20.012071	20.864730	21.761588
18	18.785788	19.614748	20.489376	21.412312	22.386349	23.414435
19	19.879717	20.810895	21.796716	22.840559	23.946007	25.116868
20	20.979115	22.019004	23.123667	24.297370	25.544658	26.870374
21	22.084011	23.239194	24.470522	25.783317	27.183274	28.676486
22	23.194431	24.471586	25.837580	27.298984	28.862856	30.536780
23	24.310403	25.716302	27.225144	28.844963	30.584427	32.452884
24	25.431955	26.973465	28.633521	30.421862	32.349038	34.426470
25	26.559115	28.243200	30.063024	32.030300	34.157764	36.459264
26	27.691911	29.525632	31.513969	33.670906	36.011708	38.553042
27	28.830370	30.820888	32.986679	35.344324	37.912001	40.709634
28	29.974522	32.129097	34.481479	37.051210	39.859801	42.930923
29	31.124395	33.450388	35.998701	38.792235	41.856296	45.218850
30	32.280017	34.784892	37.538681	40.568079	43.902703	47.575416
31	33.441417	36.132740	39.101762	42.379441	46.000271	50.002678
32	34.608624	37.494068	40.688288	44.227030	48.150278	52.502759
33	35.781667	38.869009	42.298612	46.111570	50.354034	55.077841
34	36.960575	40.257699	43.933092	48.033802	52.612885	57.730177
35	38.145378	41.660276	45.592088	49.994478	54.928207	60.462082
36	39.336105	43.076878	47.275969	51.994367	57.301413	63.275944
37	40.532785	44.507647	48.985109	54.034255	59.733948	66.174223
38	41.735449	45.952724	50.719885	56.114940	62.227297	69.159449
39	42.944127	47.412251	52.480684	58.237238	64.782979	72.234233
40	44.158847	48.886373	54.267894	60.401983	67.402554	75.401260
41	45.379642	50.375237	56.081912	62.610023	70.087617	78.663298
42	46.606540	51.878989	57.923141	64.862223	72.839808	82.023196
43	47.839572	53.397779	59.791988	67.159468	75.660803	85.483892
44	49.078770	54.931757	61.688868	69.502657	78.552323	89.048409
45	50.324164	56.481075	63.614201	71.892710	81.516131	92.719861
46	51.575785	58.045885	65.568414	74.330564	84.554034	96.501457
47	52.833664	59.626344	67.551940	76.817176	87.667885	100.396501
48	54.097832	61.222608	69.565219	79.353519	90.859582	104.408396
49	55.368321	62.834834	71.608698	81.940590	94.131072	108.540648
50	56.645163	64.463182	73.682828	84.579401	97.484349	112.796867

Table 3 Future Amount of Ordinary Annuity of 1 (*continued*)

n \ i	3½%	4%	4½%	5%	5½%	6%
1	1.000000	1.000000	1.000000	1.000000	1.000000	1.000000
2	2.035000	2.040000	2.045000	2.050000	2.055000	2.060000
3	3.106225	3.121600	3.137025	3.152500	3.168025	3.183600
4	4.214943	4.246464	4.278191	4.310125	4.342266	4.374616
5	5.362466	5.416323	5.470710	5.525631	5.581091	5.637093
6	6.550152	6.632975	6.716892	6.801913	6.888051	6.975319
7	7.779408	7.898294	8.019152	8.142008	8.266894	8.393838
8	9.051687	9.214226	9.380014	9.549109	9.721573	9.897468
9	10.368496	10 582795	10.802114	11.026564	11.256260	11.491316
10	11.731393	12.006107	12.288209	12.577893	12.875354	13.180795
11	13.141992	13.486351	13.841179	14.206787	14.583498	14.971643
12	14.601962	15.025805	15.464032	15.917127	16.385591	16.869941
13	16.113030	16.626838	17.159913	17.712983	18.286798	18.882138
14	17.676986	18.291911	18.932109	19.598632	20.292572	21.015066
15	19.295681	20.023588	20.784054	21.578564	22.408664	23.275970
16	20.971030	21.824531	22.719337	23.657492	24.641140	25.672528
17	22.705016	23.697512	24.741707	25.840366	26.996403	28.212880
18	24.499691	25.645413	26.855084	28.132385	29.481205	30.905653
19	26.357181	27.671229	29.063562	30.539004	32.102671	33.759992
20	28.279682	29.778079	31.371423	33.065954	34.868318	36.785591
21	30.269471	31.969202	33.783137	35.719252	37.786076	39.992727
22	32.328902	34.247970	36.303378	38.505214	40.864310	43.392290
23	34.460414	36.617889	38.937030	41.430475	44.111847	46.995828
24	36.666528	39.082604	41.689196	44.501999	47.537998	50.815577
25	38.949857	41.645908	44.565210	47.727099	51.152588	54.864512
26	41.313102	44.311745	47.570645	51.113454	54.965981	59.156383
27	43.759060	47.084214	50.711324	54.669126	58.989109	63.705766
28	46.290627	49.967583	53.993333	58.402583	63.233510	68.528112
29	48.910799	52.966286	57.423033	62.322712	67.711354	73.629798
30	51.622677	56.084938	61.007070	66.438848	72.435478	79.058186
31	54.429471	59.328335	64.752388	70.760790	77.419429	84.801677
32	57.334502	62.701469	68.666245	75.298829	82.677498	90.889778
33	60.341210	66.209527	72.756226	80.063771	88.224760	97.343165
34	63.453152	69.857909	77.030256	85.066959	94.077122	104.183755
35	66.674013	73.652225	81.496618	90.320307	100.251364	111.434780
36	70.007603	77.598314	86.163966	95.836323	106.765189	119.120867
37	73.457869	81.702246	91.041344	101.628139	113.637274	127.268119
38	77.028895	85.970336	96.138205	107.709546	120.887324	135.904206
39	80.724906	90.409150	101.464424	114.095023	128.536127	145.058458
40	84.550278	95.025516	107.030323	120.799774	136.605614	154.761966
41	88.509537	99.826536	112.846688	127.839763	145.118923	165.047684
42	92.607371	104.819598	118.924789	135.231751	154.100464	175.950545
43	96.848629	110.012382	125.276404	142.993339	163.575989	187.507577
44	101.238331	115.412877	131.913842	151.143006	173.572669	199.758032
45	105.781673	121.029392	138.849965	159.700156	184.119165	212.743514
46	110.484031	126.870568	146.098214	168.685164	195.245719	226.508125
47	115.350973	132.945390	153.672633	178.119422	206.984234	241.098612
48	120.388257	139.263206	161.587902	188.025393	219.368367	256.564529
49	125.601846	145.833734	169.859357	198.426663	232.433627	272.958401
50	130.997910	152.667084	178.503028	209.347996	246.217476	290.335905

Table 3 Future Amount of Ordinary Annuity of 1 (*continued*)

n \ i	7%	8%	9%	10%	12%	15%
1	1.000000	1.000000	1.000000	1.000000	1.000000	1.000000
2	2.070000	2.080000	2.090000	2.100000	2.120000	2.150000
3	3.214900	3.246400	3.278100	3.310000	3.374400	3.472500
4	4.439943	4.506112	4.573129	4.641000	4.779328	4.993375
5	5.750740	5.866601	5.984711	6.105100	6.352847	6.742381
6	7.153291	7.335929	7.523335	7.715610	8.115189	8.753738
7	8.654021	8.922803	9.200435	9.487171	10.089012	11.066799
8	10.259803	10.636628	11.028474	11.435888	12.299693	13.726819
9	11.977989	12.487558	13.021036	13.579477	14.775656	16.785842
10	13.816448	14.486562	15.192930	15.937425	17.548735	20.303718
11	15.783599	16.645487	17.560293	18.531167	20.654583	24.349276
12	17.888451	18.977126	20.140720	21.384284	24.133133	29.001667
13	20.140643	21.495297	22.953385	24.522712	28.029109	34.351917
14	22.550488	24.214920	26.019189	27.974983	32.392602	40.504705
15	25.129022	27.152114	29.360916	31.772482	37.279715	47.580411
16	27.888054	30.324283	33.003399	35.949730	42.753280	55.717472
17	30.840217	33.750226	36.973705	40.544703	48.883674	65.075093
18	33.999033	37.450244	41.301338	45.599173	55.749715	75.836357
19	37.378965	41.446263	46.018458	51.159090	63.439681	88.211811
20	40.995492	45.761964	51.160120	57.274999	72.052442	102.443583
21	44.865177	50.422921	56.764530	64.002499	81.698736	118.810120
22	49.005739	55.456755	62.873338	71.402749	92.502584	137.631638
23	53.436141	60.893296	69.531939	79.543024	104.602894	159.276384
24	58.176671	66.764759	76.789813	88.497327	118.155241	184.167841
25	63.249038	73.105940	84.700896	98.347059	133.333870	212.793017
26	68.676470	79.954415	93.323977	109.181765	150.333934	245.711970
27	74.483823	87.350768	102.723135	121.099942	169.374007	283.568766
28	80.697691	95.338830	112.968217	134.209936	190.698887	327.104080
29	87.346529	103.965936	124.135356	148.630930	214.582754	377.169693
30	94.460786	113.283211	136.307539	164.494023	241.332684	434.745146
31	102.073041	123.345868	149.575217	181.943425	271.292606	500.956918
32	110.218154	134.213537	164.036987	201.137767	304.847719	577.100456
33	118.933425	145.950620	179.800315	222.251544	342.429446	644.665525
34	128.258765	158.626670	196.982344	245.476699	384.520979	765.365353
35	138.236878	172.316804	215.710755	271.024368	431.663496	881.170156
36	148.913460	187.102148	236.124723	299.126805	484.463116	1014.345680
37	160.337402	203.070320	258.375948	330.039486	543.598690	1167.497532
38	172.561020	220.315945	282.629783	364.043434	609.830533	1343.622161
39	185.640292	238.941221	309.066463	401.447778	684.010197	1546.165485
40	199.635112	259.056519	337.882445	442.592556	767.091420	1779.090308
41	214.609570	280.781040	369.291865	487.851811	860.142391	2046.953854
42	230.632240	304.243523	403.528133	537.636992	964.359478	2354.996933
43	247.776497	329.583005	440.845665	592.400692	1081.082615	2709.246473
44	266.120851	356.949646	481.521775	652.640761	1211.812529	3116.633443
45	285.749311	386.505617	525.858734	718.904837	1358.230032	3585.128460
46	306.751763	418.426067	574.186021	791.795321	1522.217636	4123.897729
47	329.224386	452.900152	626.862762	871.974853	1705.883752	4743.482388
48	353.270093	490.132164	684.280411	960.172338	1911.589803	5466.004746
49	378.999000	530.342737	746.865648	1057.189572	2141.980579	6275.405458
50	406.528929	573.770156	815.083556	1163.908529	2400.018249	7217.716277

Table 4   Present Value of Ordinary Annuity of 1 per Period: $P_{\overline{n}|i} = \dfrac{1 - \dfrac{1}{(1+i)^n}}{i}$

n	½%	1%	1½%	2%	2½%	3%
1	0.995025	0.990099	0.985222	0.980392	0.975610	0.970874
2	1.985099	1.970395	1.955883	1.941561	1.927424	1.913470
3	2.970248	2.940985	2.912200	2.883883	2.856024	2.828611
4	3.950496	3.901966	3.854385	3.807729	3.761974	3.717098
5	4.925866	4.853431	4.782645	4.713460	4.645829	4.579707
6	5.896384	5.795476	5.697187	5.601431	5.508125	5.417191
7	6.862074	6.728195	6.598214	6.471991	6.349391	6.230283
8	7.822959	7.651678	7.485925	7.325481	7.170137	7.019692
9	8.779064	8.566018	8.360517	8.162237	7.970866	7.786109
10	9.730412	9.471305	9.222185	8.982585	8.752064	8.530203
11	10.677027	10.367628	10.071118	9.786848	9.514209	9.252624
12	11.618932	11.255077	10.907505	10.575341	10.257765	9.954004
13	12.556151	12.133740	11.731532	11.348374	10.983185	10.634955
14	13.488708	13.003703	12.543382	12.106249	11.690912	11.296073
15	14.416625	13.865053	13.343233	12.849264	12.381378	11.937935
16	15.339925	14.717874	14.131264	13.577709	13.055003	12.561102
17	16.258632	15.562251	14.907649	14.291872	13.712198	13.166118
18	17.172768	16.398269	15.672561	14.992031	14.353364	13.753513
19	18.082356	17.226009	16.426168	15.678462	14.978891	14.323799
20	18.987419	18.045553	17.168639	16.351433	15.589162	14.877475
21	19.887979	18.856983	17.900137	17.011209	16.184549	15.415024
22	20.784059	19.660379	18.620824	17.658048	16.765413	15.936917
23	21.675681	20.455821	19.330861	18.292204	17.332110	16.443608
24	22.562866	21.243387	20.030405	18.913926	17.884986	16.935542
25	23.445638	22.023156	20.719611	19.523456	18.424376	17.413148
26	24.324018	22.795204	21.398632	20.121036	18.950611	17.876842
27	25.198028	23.559608	22.067617	20.706898	19.464011	18.327031
28	26.067689	24.316443	22.726717	21.281272	19.964889	18.764108
29	26.933024	25.065785	23.376076	21.844385	20.453550	19.188455
30	27.794054	25.807708	24.015838	22.396456	20.930293	19.600441
31	28.650800	26.542285	24.646146	22.937702	21.395407	20.000428
32	29.503284	27.269589	25.267139	23.468335	21.849178	20.388766
33	30.351526	27.989693	25.878954	23.988564	22.291881	20.765792
34	31.195548	28.702666	26.481728	24.498592	22.723786	21.131837
35	32.035371	29.408580	27.075595	24.998619	23.145157	21.487220
36	32.871016	30.107505	27.660684	25.488842	23.556251	21.832253
37	33.702504	30.799510	28.237127	25.969453	23.957318	22.167235
38	34.529854	31.484663	28.805052	26.440641	24.348603	22.492462
39	35.353089	32.163033	29.364583	26.902589	24.730344	22.808215
40	36.172228	32.834686	29.915845	27.355479	25.102775	23.114772
41	36.987291	33.499689	30.458961	27.799489	25.466122	23.412400
42	37.798300	34.158108	30.994050	28.234794	25.820607	23.701359
43	38.605274	34.810008	31.521232	28.661562	26.166446	23.981902
44	39.408232	35.455454	32.040622	29.079963	26.503849	24.254274
45	40.207196	36.094508	32.552337	29.490160	26.833024	24.518713
46	41.002185	36.727236	33.056490	29.892314	27.154170	24.775449
47	41.793219	37.353699	33.553192	30.286582	27.467483	25.024708
48	42.580318	37.973959	34.042554	30.673120	27.773154	25.266707
49	43.363500	38.588079	34.524683	31.052078	28.071369	25.501657
50	44.142786	39.196118	34.999688	31.423606	28.362312	25.729764

Table 4   Present Value of Ordinary Annuity of 1 (*continued*)

n \ i	3½%	4%	4½%	5%	5½%	6%
1	0.966184	0.961538	0.956938	0.952381	0.947867	0.943396
2	1.899694	1.886095	1.872668	1.859410	1.846320	1.833393
3	2.801637	2.775091	2.748964	2.723248	2.697933	2.673012
4	3.673079	3.629895	3.587526	3.545951	3.505150	3.465106
5	4.515052	4.451822	4.389977	4.329477	4.270284	4.212364
6	5.328553	5.242137	5.157872	5.075692	4.995530	4.917324
7	6.114544	6.002055	5.892701	5.786373	5.682967	5.582381
8	6.873956	6.732745	6.595886	6.463213	6.334566	6.209794
9	7.607687	7.435332	7.268791	7.107822	6.952195	6.801692
10	8.316605	8.110896	7.912718	7.721735	7.537626	7.360087
11	9.001551	8.760477	8.528917	8.306414	8.092536	7.886875
12	9.663334	9.385074	9.118581	8.863252	8.618518	8.383844
13	10.302738	9.985648	9.682852	9.393573	9.117079	8.852683
14	10.920520	10.563123	10.222825	9.898641	9.589648	9.294984
15	11.517411	11.118387	10.739546	10.379658	10.037581	9.712249
16	12.094117	11.652296	11.234015	10.837770	10.462162	10.105895
17	12.651321	12.165669	11.707191	11.274066	10.864609	10.477260
18	13.189682	12.659297	12.159992	11.689587	11.246074	10.827603
19	13.709837	13.133939	12.593294	12.085321	11.607654	11.158116
20	14.212403	13.590326	13.007936	12.462210	11.950382	11.469921
21	14.697974	14.029160	13.404724	12.821153	12.275244	11.764077
22	15.167125	14.451115	13.784425	13.163003	12.583170	12.041582
23	15.620410	14.856842	14.147775	13.488574	12.875042	12.303379
24	16.058368	15.246963	14.495478	13.798642	13.151699	12.550358
25	16.481515	15.622080	14.828209	14.093945	13.413933	12.783356
26	16.890352	15.982769	15.146611	14.375185	13.662495	13.003166
27	17.285365	16.329586	15.451303	14.643034	13.898100	13.210534
28	17.667019	16.663063	15.742874	14.898127	14.121422	13.406164
29	18.035767	16.983715	16.021889	15.141074	14.333101	13.590721
30	18.392045	17.292033	16.288889	15.372451	14.533745	13.764831
31	18.736276	17.588494	16.544391	15.592811	14.723929	13.929086
32	19.068865	17.873552	16.788891	15.802677	14.904198	14.084043
33	19.390208	18.147646	17.022862	16.002549	15.075069	14.230230
34	19.700684	18.411198	17.246758	16.192904	15.237033	14.368141
35	20.000661	18.664613	17.461012	16.374194	15.390552	14.498246
36	20.290494	18.908282	17.666041	16.546852	15.536068	14.620987
37	20.570525	19.142579	17.862240	16.711287	15.673999	14.736780
38	20.841087	19.367864	18.049990	16.867893	15.804738	14.846019
39	21.102500	19.584485	18.229656	17.017041	15.928662	14.949075
40	21.355072	19.792774	18.401584	17.159086	16.046125	15.046297
41	21.599104	19.993052	18.566109	17.294368	16.157464	15.138016
42	21.834883	20.185627	18.723550	17.423208	16.262999	15.224543
43	22.062689	20.370795	18.874210	17.545912	16.363032	15.306173
44	22.282791	20.548841	19.018383	17.662773	16.457851	15.383182
45	22.495450	20.720040	19.156347	17.774070	16.547726	15.455832
46	22.700918	20.884654	19.288371	17.880067	16.632915	15.524370
47	22.899438	21.042936	19.414709	17.981016	16.713664	15.589028
48	23.091244	21.195131	19.535607	18.077158	16.790203	15.650027
49	23.276565	21.341472	19.651298	18.168722	16.862751	15.707572
50	23.455618	21.482185	19.762008	18.255925	16.931518	15.761861

Table 4 Present Value of Ordinary Annuity of 1 (*continued*)

n \ i	7%	8%	9%	10%	12%	15%
1	0.934579	0.925926	0.917431	0.909091	0.892857	0.869565
2	1.808018	1.783265	1.759111	1.735537	1.690051	1.625709
3	2.624316	2.577097	2.531295	2.486852	2.401831	2.283225
4	3.387211	3.312127	3.239720	3.169865	3.037349	2.854978
5	4.100197	3.992710	3.889651	3.790787	3.604776	3.352155
6	4.766540	4.622880	4.485919	4.355261	4.111407	3.784483
7	5.389289	5.206370	5.032953	4.868419	4.563757	4.160420
8	5.971299	5.746639	5.534819	5.334926	4.967640	4.487322
9	6.515232	6.246888	5.995247	5.759024	5.328250	4.771584
10	7.023582	6.710081	6.417658	6.144567	5.650223	5.018769
11	7.498674	7.138964	6.805191	6.495061	5.937699	5.233712
12	7.942686	7.536078	7.160725	6.813692	6.194374	5.420619
13	8.357651	7.903776	7.486904	7.103356	6.423548	5.583147
14	8.745468	8.244237	7.786150	7.366687	6.628168	5.724476
15	9.107914	8.559479	8.060688	7.606080	6.810864	5.847370
16	9.446649	8.851369	8.312558	7.823709	6.973986	5.954235
17	9.763223	9.121638	8.543631	8.021553	7.119630	6.047161
18	10.059087	9.371887	8.755625	8.201412	7.249670	6.127966
19	10.335595	9.603599	8.950115	8.364920	7.365777	6.198231
20	10.594014	9.818147	9.128546	8.513564	7.469444	6.259331
21	10.835527	10.016803	9.292244	8.648694	7.562003	6.312462
22	11.061241	10.200744	9.442425	8.771540	7.644646	6.358663
23	11.272187	10.371059	9.580207	8.883218	7.718434	6.398837
24	11.469334	10.528758	9.706612	8.984744	7.784316	6.433771
25	11.653583	10.674776	9.822580	9.077040	7.843139	6.464149
26	11.825779	10.809978	9.928972	9.160945	7.895660	6.490564
27	11.986709	10.935165	10.026580	9.237223	7.942554	6.513534
28	12.137111	11.051078	10.116128	9.306567	7.984423	6.533508
29	12.277674	11.158406	10.198283	9.369606	8.021806	6.550877
30	12.409041	11.257783	10.273654	9.426914	8.055184	6.565980
31	12.531814	11.349799	10.342802	9.479013	8.084986	6.579113
32	12.646555	11.434999	10.406240	9.526376	8.111594	6.590533
33	12.753790	11.513888	10.464441	9.569432	8.135352	6.600463
34	12.854009	11.586934	10.517835	9.608575	8.156564	6.609099
35	12.947672	11.654568	10.566821	9.644159	8.175504	6.616607
36	13.035208	11.717193	10.611763	9.676508	8.192414	6.623137
37	13.117017	11.775179	10.652993	9.705917	8.207513	6.628815
38	13.193473	11.828869	10.690820	9.732651	8.220993	6.633752
39	13.264928	11.878582	10.725523	9.756956	8.233030	6.638045
40	13.331709	11.924613	10.757360	9.779051	8.243777	6.641778
41	13.394120	11.967235	10.786569	9.799137	8.253372	6.645025
42	13.452449	12.006699	10.813366	9.817397	8.261939	6.647848
43	13.506962	12.043240	10.837950	9.833998	8.269589	6.650302
44	13.557908	12.077074	10.860505	9.849089	8.276418	6.652437
45	13.605522	12.108402	10.881197	9.862808	8.282516	6.654293
46	13.650020	12.137409	10.900181	9.875280	8.287961	6.655907
47	13.691608	12.164267	10.917597	9.886618	8.292822	6.657310
48	13.730474	12.189136	10.933575	9.896926	8.297163	6.658531
49	13.766799	12.212163	10.948234	9.906296	8.301038	6.659592
50	13.800746	12.233485	10.961683	9.914814	8.304498	6.660515

INDEX